Ju... ystems

... pectives

Uruguay

Juvenile Justice Systems
International Perspectives

second edition

edited by John A. Winterdyk

Canadian Scholars' Press Inc.   Toronto   2002

Juvenile Justice Systems: International Perspectives, second edition
Edited by John A. Winterdyk

First published in 2002 by
Canadian Scholars' Press Inc.
180 Bloor Street West, Suite 1202
Toronto, Ontario
M5S 2V6

www.cspi.org

CSPI gratefully acknowledges the financial support of the Government of Canada through the Book Publishing Industry Development Program for our publishing activities.

National Library of Canada Cataloguing in Publication Data

Main entry under title:

Juvenile justice systems : international perspectives / John A. Winterdyk, editor. — 2e ed.

Includes bibliographical references.
ISBN 1-55130-202-0

1. Juvenile justice, Administration of. 2. Juvenile delinquency.
I. Winterdyk, John

HV9069.J797 2002   364.36   C2002-900700-3

Cover design: George Kirkpatrick
Page design and layout: Brad Horning

02   03   04   05   06   07   7   6   5   4   3   2   1

Printed and bound in Canada by AGMV Marquis Imprimeur Inc.

Table of Contents

Acknowledgments

I would like to first acknowledge my parents who, in their philanthropic lifestyle, exposed me to many different cultures at a very early age. I quickly developed a love for travel and a curiosity for learning about other cultures, languages, and ways of life. I have since carried this passion over into my academic career. Since joining Mount Royal College in 1988 (the year Calgary hosted the Winter Olympics), I have conducted accredited criminology study tours to various European countries on a biannual basis. In response to rising costs and supportive feedback from students and colleagues, the inception of this book was spawned and the first edition was published in 1997.

In order to produce an in-depth and comprehensive textbook with a truly global perspective, for this edition the volume has been expanded from eleven contributions to nineteen. Again, for the new countries (Austria, Belgium, China, India, Namibia, Scotland, South Africa, and South Korea, and some new box inserts offering mini-country profiles – only one former contributing country was unable to participate in this edition), I have sought out leading experts from the respective countries. To all the contributors I am indebted for their support and commitment to this project. Without their efforts, this collection of original contributions would not be possible. All the contributors, in spite of language barriers, distances, and their other commitments, were all exceptionally accommodating. To work in such company and under such a supportive environment is both heartwarming and exciting. I am deeply grateful to Canadian Scholars' Press for initially embracing this project and having the foresight to produce this second edition. I would like to acknowledge Ruth

Bradley-St-Cyr, the former managing editor of Canadian Scholars' Press, for her encouragement and diligence in bringing this project to print form, and to Jack Wayne, the publisher, for seeing the merit in producing this text. A heart-felt thanks to Betsy Struthers, who was parachuted in at the last minute to help shepherd the manuscript through its final edits.

To my partner, Rosemary Buck, I am blessed by her enduring support and wonderful insights. She is a true pillar of strength and an inestimable companion.

Thank you to my colleagues, especially Sandie McBrien, who again read several chapters for me, and to students who gave of their time and patience and feedback. To Emmett Hogan, our chairperson, who graciously allowed me to hunker down to work on this project and other undertakings. Once again, thanks to Brenda Laing, our administrative assistant and dear friend, who continues to do those "little extra things" to ensure I could complete this book.

Juvenile Justice Systems

International Perspectives

Introduction

A national crisis is seldom merely national anymore.—Oyen, 1992:2.

At the Eighth (United Nations, 1990) and Ninth United Nations (UN) National Congress on the Prevention of Crime and the Treatment of Offenders (*CJ International*, 1995), crime and managing criminal justice were recognized as a growing problem worldwide. Be it drugs, violence, hate crime, gang activity, organized crime, or youth crime, there are few places in the world that are not currently dealing with one or more of these issues.

At the Ninth UN Congress it was also reported that youth crime is increasing around the world—especially in countries experiencing transition (see Table 1). It was also noted that the average age of onset of criminal behavior was dropping. The fact "that by the year 2000 more than 50% of the world population will be under the age of 15" serves to further "highlight the seriousness of the problem of juvenile delinquency and youth crime" (United Nations, 1995a: 17).

In addition to the pragmatic concerns that accompany the presence of youth crime, it is also important to note and examine the wide range in which young offenders are brought before their respective justice systems and dealt with. Some countries still use the death penalty (e.g., see endnote 2), many still exercise corporal punishment (e.g., Bolivia, Honduras, Sudan, Zimbabwe, and Singapore)[1]; while others have no separate legislation for young offenders (e.g., Kenya, Norway and Sweden) (Prince, 1997).

Table 1: Juvenile Delinquency: Country Profiles*

Country Maximum Age	Minimum[1]—	Conditions/Justice Model[2]
Egypt	? -18...	Juvenile Law No. 31 (1974). Youth are segregated by age: 12 & under, 12-15, & 15-18. Under 15 required to attend school & over receive vocational skills. Judge aided in deliberation by 2 (appointed) experts—one must be female. / **Corporatism**
Singapore	?-12...	Islamic law set the minimum age of criminal responsibility at puberty. **Welfare-Justice Model** (see Box 2)
Cuba	6-16...	The Castro regime in 1959 introduced a progressive **Welfare** based model for "children with conduct problems." (see Box 7)
United States	7-15+..	The upper limit can range up to Age 20 in some States; for most it is 17/**Crime Control** (see Ch. 10)
India	7-16...	for boys and 18 for girls./**Welfare-Justice** (see Box 5)
Cayman Islands	8-17...	8-14 classified as young persons, 14-17 classified as juveniles/**Welfare**
Philippines	9-15...	youth offenders, 15-18 suspended sentences. 18-20 criminally responsible but entitled to leniency/**Welfare-Justice Model**
Australia	10-16/17..	two jurisdictions have lower minimum age/ **Welfare** (see Ch. 2)
Canada	12-18...	/**Modified Justice** (see Ch. 6)
England	12-18...	/**Corporatist** (see Ch. 4)
The Netherlands	12-18...	/**Modified Justice** (see Ch. 3)
France	13-18...	Problem youth are addressed under the Ordinance No. 45-174 of Feb. 2, 1945. Modified 1958 and 1970. Specially trained 'children's judges/magistrates and social services for educational help used. Compared to most western European countries rate of increase among the lowest (2% from 1992 thru 1993./ **Welfare** (social defense system) Lorenz, (1996).
Israel	13-16...	for boys and 18 for girls. In 1977 boys max. age also raised to 18. Juvenile Offenders Section(JSO), 1959. The ethical code of JSO personnel goes beyond the limits established by the Youth Act stressing protection./**Corporatist**
Poland	13-17...	responsibility based on mental and moral ability. 16-17 yr. olds' can be held criminally responsible/**Justice**
New Zealand	14-17...	Criminal responsibility begins at age ten but unless 'mens rea' can be proven, till age 14 they are not convicted. Exception to the rule is murder or manslaughter/**Welfare** (see Box 6)

Germany	14-17...	18-20 may be transferred to juvenile Court/ **Justice** (see Ch. 9)
Hungary	14-18...	no separate juvenile legislation/**Crime Control** (see Ch. 11)
China	14-25...	partially responsible officially till 18. Law requires limited punishment. Between 1977 and 1991 steady increase and proportionate amount are young offenders./**Participatory**
Italy	14-18...	/**Legalistic** (see Ch. 7)
Japan	14-20...	/**Participatory** (see Ch. 1)
Norway	14-18...	In 1990 the minimum age was raised to 15. 18 yr. olds are the most frequently represented, recidivism rate continue to climb—41% among young offenders/**Welfare-Modified Justice**
Russia	14-18...	/**Justice Model** (see Ch. 8)
Austria	14-19...	Juvenile Justice Act 1988, amended 1993/ **Modified Justice Model**. Between 1981-91 youth rates dropped—1799 to 763.
Sweden	15-20...	Known as "Juvenile criminals". Youth between ages 15-17 given special consideration./**Justice Model**(see Box 3)
Finland	15-21...	Have three important age limits: 15, 18, & 21. Under 15 not liable. Under the Penal Code, those under 18 recommended lighter sentences—"child", under 21 "juvenile". 1991 proposal to lower limit to 14—response to increase in youth crime./**Justice Model**
Switzerland	15-18...	7-15 are considered children, 15-18 are considered adolescent, & 18-25 are young adults— treated less severely.
Argentina	16-18...	their legal system for juveniles was described as being similar to that of Italy (Devoto, 1996). Youth regulated under the Penal Regulations for Youth Law 22.778, 1980. Very little work on youth crime. Only one study in 1994. Robbery and theft most common crimes and approx. 68% of crimes committed in "groups"/**Legalistic**
Scotland	- 16...	or 18 if already under supervision./**Welfare** (see Box 4)
Hong Kong	16-20...	juveniles (7-15)/**Corporatist Model** (see Ch. 5).

* Information for this Table has been obtained primarily through contacting foreign embassies and/or relevant juvenile departments.

1 A 1985 United Nations report noted that some countries do not recognize a minimum age of criminal responsibility. Hence for some countries no age is given. The Napoleonic Code in 1804 in France was among the first codes to prescribe limited responsibility to youth under the age of 16.

   Five countries still practice capital punishment of juvenile offenders— Bangladesh, Barbados, Iran, Pakistan, and the United States (Souryal, 1992).

2 Models are only provided for countries in which sufficient information was available to attempt a description of their juvenile justice practices.

We live in a world of perpetual social unrest and instability, and such conditions can create opportunity for crime and delinquency to thrive. Thus a very practical issue that most countries must face is how to manage youth crime. But since the question of what is in the best interest of young persons has historically haunted every nation, we must be realistic when looking for quick or simple solutions.

RATIONAL FOR COMPARATIVE STUDIES

There is no reason to believe there exists an easy and straightforward entry in comparative research (Oyen, 1992:1).

While the vast majority of criminological and sociological literature on crime has been based on a unilinear model—"focused within countries and without pretense to being general"—this has begun to change in recent years (Teune, 1992, p. 35). The interest in comparative research would seem closely aligned to macro global changes as well as advances in technology. For example, as a result of the Great Depression many researchers turned their focus inwards, while in the aftermath of World War II it became necessary to do comparative research as a necessary part of decentralizing world order (see Nelken, 1994; Teune, 1992). The process, as Marsh (1967) observed, emerged rather slowly, especially with respect to the phenomena of crime. But in recent years there has been a dramatic shift.

At the Seventh UN Congress on the Prevention of Crime and the Treatment of Offenders, held in Beijing, China, from 14 to 18 May 1984, the United Nations endorsed the "Standard Minimum Rules for the Administration of Juvenile Justice." These standards are commonly referred to as "the **Beijing Rules**" (see Box 1) and are perhaps the most important guidelines for improving the quality of juvenile justice around the world. However, given the diverse cultural, economic, political, and social factors involved, it is questionable whether such ideas can be universally embraced.

The Beijing Rules have subsequently been incorporated into the *Implementation Handbook for the Convention on the Rights of the Child* in 1998 which was prepared by UNICEF. Three specific Articles (i.e., 37, 39, and 40) deal with the treatment of young persons, rehabilitation and reintegration strategies, as well as the administration of juvenile justice. For example, Article 37 provides the child with the right to be protected from:
- torture or other cruel, inhuman or degrading treatment or punishment;
- capital punishment;
- life imprisonment without possibility of release; and
- unlawful or arbitrary deprivation of liberty (Juvenile Justice: Information Portfolio, 2000).

Box 1: Highlights of "the Beijing Rules" (1984)

<u>Fundamental perspectives</u>: 1.1 To further the well-being of the juvenile and her or his family; 1.2 To develop conditions that will ensure a meaningful life in the community for the juvenile; 1.4 Administration of juvenile justice should represent an integral part of the natural development process of each country.

<u>Age of responsibility</u>: 4.1 The beginning age shall not be fixed at too low an age level, bearing in mind the facts of emotional, mental, and intellectual maturity.

<u>Aim of juvenile justice</u>: 5.1 Emphasize the well-being of the juvenile and ensure that any reaction to juvenile offenders shall always be in proportion to the circumstance of both the offender and the offence.

<u>Scope of discretion</u>: 6.2 Efforts shall be made to ensure sufficient accountability at all stages and levels in the exercise of any such discretion.

<u>Protection of privacy</u>: 8.1 Right to privacy shall be respected at all stages in order to avoid harm being caused by undue publicity or by the process of labelling. 8.2 No information that may lead to the identification of a juvenile offender shall be published (UN, 1986).

In Article 40 the Committee acknowledges the rules and guidelines relating to juvenile justice as defined by the UN. For example, Article 40 also recognizes the legal rights of children. Article 40 recommends that all countries should:

- establish a minimum age of criminal responsibility;
- not take any action against a young person unless there are provisions within the law;
- presume a youth is innocent until proven guilty;
- not compel a youth to give testimony or to confess;
- ensure that all persons have access to legal counsel; and
- provide a variety of alternative dispositions to incarceration and/or institutional care (Juvenile Justice..., 2000).

As can be seen in Table 1 and Figure 1, the level of attention different systems and societies pay to the "age of responsibility" reflects major practical and theoretical differences between systems and countries. Also in Table 1, it can be seen how countries vary in their definition of what legally constitutes a *juvenile* or *young offender*. The variations reflect different cultural, historical, political, and social differences than can make comparisons challenging.

Not only are there variations between countries but even within countries. In Canada, for example, the current *Young Offenders Act* defines the minimum age of responsibility as 12 and the upper limit at 18 (see Box 2). However, because the provinces are responsible for administering the Act, there is considerable variation between the provinces in their sentencing and transfer to adult court practices and their respective interpretation of the Act. As we will see in Chapter 3, the government is considering replacing the current Act with new legislation (i.e., *Youth Criminal Justice Act*).[2] If successful, it will represent the third time in seven years that the government has attempted to introduce a new law to replace the much-criticized *Young Offenders Act*.

Box 2: Juvenile Justice in Singapore

The republic of Singapore is a city/nation with a population of around 3 million. Although Singapore's legal system is adversarial in nature and modeled after the British judicial system, the existing Malay customary law and Muslim law sets the age of accountability at puberty – which is legally defined as being between 14 to16 years of age. The Children and Young Persons Act of 1949 created the Juvenile Court. The courts recognize differences in children and their differing maturation periods and do not allow the public to attend any proceedings. Following a **welfare** type model of juvenile justice, male offenders are sent to approval schools while female delinquents are sent to approval homes. In spite of its harsh penal code, juvenile crime increased 30 percent from 1988 to 1993 (Wiechman, 1994). In the aftermath of the highly publicized case involving the caning of the American Michael Fay in 1996, Western media has been quite critical of their justice process. (Fay received a caning for defacing an automobile with water-soluble paint.) For an interesting account of these ideas, simply type in Fay's name into any search engine and you will get a list of sites that offer varying comments on (youth) justice in Singapore.

By contrast, countries like Norway and Sweden (Box 3) have no special act regarding juvenile delinquency. However, the General Civil Penal Code (section 46) of Norway states that criminal responsibility begins at age 15 and section 55 makes special provisions for the sentencing of young offenders (Askim and Berg, 1996). Their neighbour to the east, Sweden, has no direct equivalent in their language for the English concept of "juvenile delinquent." Rather, they speak of juvenile criminality that does not include status offences (i.e., acts declared by statute to be an offence but only when committed by a juvenile). In Sweden juvenile criminal responsibility begins at age 15 and the upper limit is 20 (Sarnecki, 1996). However, like Norway, Sweden has special provisions for young criminals between the ages of 15 and 17. By contrast, in Denmark, there are no special courts for minors. Therefore, for cases where a child shows a likelihood of becoming delinquent or needs help, the youth is, again, likely to be referred to a social worker. Only for serious offences such as murder or assault are juvenile offenders directed through the legal system.

Box 3: Juvenile Justice in Sweden

In Sweden the responsibility for handling young people is shared by the social authorities and the judicial system. *In the Swedish language there is no equivalent concept for "juvenile delinquent."* Instead they speak of juvenile criminality. This system does not formally recognize status offenses. Such behaviors are dealt with through **social welfare** measures. All juvenile crime falls under the Swedish Penal Code of 1990. By law juveniles receive special consideration when found committing a crime. Social authorities, rather than the police, handle youth under the age of 15. Criminal responsibility begins at age 15. Over 80% of all juvenile crimes are not prosecuted but dealt with informally, such as by cautioning. However, its use varies considerably throughout the country (Granath, 2000). Nearly 50% are resolved through the use of day fines (approx. Can. $30) without a trial procedure being used. Fewer than 10% of delinquent youth are placed on probation. The Swedish model is more treatment-oriented than most Western countries. But, in recent years, the model has been subjected to substantial criticism, as youth crime in Sweden has been on the increase and there does not appear to be any empirical support for the treatment-oriented programs (Sarnecki, 1996).

In 1998 the Swedish government gave the National Council for Crime Prevention the responsibility for introducing a pilot project of mediation for young offenders. The initial evaluation results (qualitative and quantitative) were released in March 2000. Between 1998 and 2000 there were 16 mediation projects involving some 170 *mediations* that for evaluation purposes were divided into two groups – those representing businesses and those representing individual victims. Although approved by the government, the projects developed without clear standards and regulations, making specific comparisons difficult. For example, the police run some projects while others are run by voluntary organizations. However, the initial results indicate the majority of the offenders found the mediation process fair, but that the offenders were more positive when mediation involved private citizens rather than business owners. It was also observed that the mediation was more effective for more serious crimes than for petty type offences (Mediation – the revelations of young offenders, 1999). Data provided by the National Council for Crime Prevention also reveals that female criminality was not only increasing (as in most parts of the world) but also that it is still a neglected area of research in Sweden (see Box 3 Figure). It is also interesting to observe that between 1980 and 1998 the number of convictions dropped from a high of around 24,000 in 1982 to a low of nearly 16,000 in 1998. This is likely due to the introduction of mediation. Between 1980 and 1998, assaults and shoplifting have shown the most dramatic increase among the conventional crime categories (Granath, 2000).

Box 3 Figure: Proportions (in percent) of the total number of convictions for juvenile delinquency for boys and girls. 1980-98.

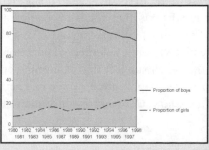

Another qualm to conducting comparisons stems from the fact that, just because most countries have legally prescribed lower and upper limits of criminal responsibility for youth, there are, in many instances, situational factors that enable exceptions to the law. For example, Reichel (1994) found that in China and Romania, while 16 is the preferred lower limit it can be dropped to 14 if the offence is very serious (China – see Chapter 4) or if the youth is capable of understanding right from wrong (Romania). Even within Europe, Walgrave and Mehlbye (1998:4) point out how, although the nine countries they present share some common approaches (i.e., a **welfare-justice model**) when dealing with young offenders, each country's system is slightly different, and that "a satisfactory solution has not been found anywhere." For example, Denmark and Scotland have specialized courts for minors, but their respective authority and organization differ. Similarly, in this text, we will see how in a number of the countries represented (e.g., Canada and the United States) the limits of criminal responsibility may also involve transfer conditions to the adult system.

Aside from these categorical differences, six different juvenile justice models can be defined to describe the handling of juveniles. The models are based on research by Corrado (1992) and Reichel (1994), and on consideration given to the work of Walgrave and Mehlbye (1998). The models, summarized in Figure 1, provide a set of criteria by which the different justice models/systems can be compared. The variation in these models can serve as visible indicators of how different nations view the same phenomena (i.e., juvenile delinquency) and form different perspectives. Yet, as Reichel (1994) notes, the models are not mutually exclusive. In fact, the reader will find that the distinctions between certain countries, despite their allocation in the book, are not as dissimilar as might be implied. Furthermore, because such countries as the United States and Canada allow a degree of state or provincial autonomy in administering their respective juvenile justice systems, one can identify different justice models within individual countries. This had been especially evident in Australia (see Box 4). A number of countries covered in this text use one model (primarily a welfare model) for youth under the age of 16 and another, more punitive approach for those over 16 years of age (e.g., Belgium, Canada, Netherlands, England and Wales).

Between the release of the first edition and the present edition, there have been but a few additional texts that focus on comparative juvenile justice issues (see suggested readings). While they all take a different approach to examining criminal justice systems, a number of common themes run throughout the books. First, they each suggest that examining crime trends and reactions to crime may provide insight into how one can better address the crime situation in one's own country. Comparative information, after all, provides a

Box 4: Juvenile Justice in Australia[3]

Australia is unique in that it is an island as well as a continent with some 19 million inhabitants spread out over 7,682,292 sq. km. Their government is based on the British Westminster system and is a Commonwealth parliamentary system. Although their juvenile justice system can be described as a **welfare model**, some question the extent to which **social control** and/or **due process** play major roles in the administration of juvenile justice. This discrepancy lies in the fact that each state and territory is responsible for administering and legislating its own youth justice. As in North America, Australia's Aboriginal youth are disproportionately represented (see Carcach, 1998). However, compared to its North American counterparts, youth crime is not as extensive. Starting in the early 1990s, a number of regions began to introduce the Family Group Conferencing (i.e., restorative justice) first established in New Zealand (Atkinson, 1997).

practical window of opportunity to gain new insights and adopt, adapt, and develop new responses. For example, why is it that juvenile crime rates not only differ between northern and southern European countries but the importance of socio-demographic factors, in some instances, also varies between these countries (see Junger-Tas, 1994a; Walgrave and Mehlbye, 1998)?

A second theme is that cross-cultural comparisons allow for the comparison of (current) criminological theories and/or philosophies and criminal justice practices. For example, researchers at the Research Centre for Criminology and Youth Criminology of the State University of Groningen (Holland) embrace a sociological model to explain and respond to youth crime. The primary model being tested entails four major concepts: delinquency, feeling of societal injustice, personal bonds, and societal position as an explanatory model of youth crime (see Ferwerda, 1992; Ploeg, 1991). Ferwerda (1992:236) notes a proactive "interdisciplinary approach involving school, police, justice authorities, parents and assistance organizations" for preventing delinquency is usually advocated. By contrast, other parts of Europe, such as France (see Box 5), prefer to focus on the guilt or innocence of a particular youth, rather than to conduct a philosophical or scientific examination of youth crime generally. French judges are well informed about their cases and effectively apply their inquisitorial model to constructively assess the circumstances surrounding the youths' behavior (Hackler, 1994). And as we will see in a number of the contributions, different countries use very different approaches when dealing with juvenile delinquents. While this book focuses on how different countries react against juveniles who offend, it should be noted that some wonder whether the juvenile justice system will be abolished (see Junger-Tas, 1994b). While not an immediate reality, some of the countries presented in this text have adopted models of juvenile justice that increasingly approximate their adult models of justice. The United States has perhaps been the most vocal in this regard (see Feld, 1993; Hirschi and Gottfredson, 1991).

Box 5: Juvenile Justice in France

France, like most Western European countries, seems to share a contradiction when trying to administer juvenile justice. The French attempt to find a balance between punishing youth who have committed a crime and treating and rehabilitating them so they can become productive members of society (Furbish, 1999). Although their concerns appear similar to those of a number of other countries covered in this text, the French approach to penal law was influenced by Roman law, which recognized that minors must be treated differently ("excuse minorité") than adults for similar offences. Juvenile courts were established in 1912, and separate juvenile law was first established in 1945 with revisions in 1953 and then again in 1970. Age of responsibility is 13 to 18 years of age with exceptions for youths between the ages of 16 to 21. Below the age of 16 the **welfare** approach is emphasized, while for those youth over 16 a **crime control** approach is more common. Juvenile Court emphasizes three areas of responsibility: criminal behavior, educational help, and supervisory power. Punishment ideally is accompanied with a (re)educative approach. France, along with Belgium (see Ch. 2) and the Netherlands (see Ch. 13), has been actively developing restorative justice initiatives since the late 1980s. Former President Mitterand was instrumental in implementing a nation-wide social crime prevention initiative that encourages coordination between youth services, youth social workers, and local authorities.

For policy-makers the choice between empirical information, philosophical ideals, and even moralistic principles can result in a delicate balance between morality and social science. And until the emergence of comparative studies, ethnocentric practices limited juvenile justice (and criminal justice, in general) from breaking traditional modes of operations. Such limited perspectives can, and have, left their mark on society. For example, countries like Canada and the United States, which tend to be provincial in their approach, have until recently been plagued by increasing rates in youth crime. Their "get-tough" mentality has been both unimaginative and counter-productive in addressing crime (see Chapters 3 and 18).[4] Similar views have been expressed by Walgrave and Mehlbye (1998). They suggest that, in spite of the desire of most European countries to embrace a welfare model, an attitude of "moral panic" has prompted more punitive reactions than rehabilitative approaches. Fortunately, however, some politicians and criminologists in Canada, the United States, and elsewhere around the world have begun to break ground in this arena. In particular, initiatives by the United Nations Crime Prevention and Criminal Justice Program and the activities of UNICRI (United Nations Interregional Crime and Justice Research Institute) have provided guidelines and recommendations for standardizing juvenile justice systems.

Increasingly, provincial thinking has given way to openness to the use of alternative measures and to testing different ideas under different conditions. In the early 1990s in Calgary, for example, the police used the Los Angeles Police Department's (LAPD) model and definition of youth gangs to better address a growing youth gang problem in the city. Calgary's CRASH (Community Response Against Street Hoodlums) program for youth gangs was based on a LAPD program for dealing with gangs. (The program was terminated in 1993 due to organizational concerns and was not replaced in spite of the continued presence of youth gangs). In the early 1990s, Australia adapted the New Zealand **family group conference model** as well as elements of the "boot camp" programs currently popular in the United States. And as we will see, other countries have even more recently begun to introduce variations of the family group conference model (i.e., restorative justice, transformative justice, and family group conferencing).

As the world gets smaller, it becomes more imperative that we seek universal laws. Marvin Wolfgang (1991:v) illustrates this need in the foreword to a German book on crime and crime control:

> ...the gap, between what empirical criminology in Germany has produced and what English and American scholars know, has been unfortunate.... This collection is probably the most sophisticated, theoretically and empirically, that has appeared during the past quarter century in Germany.

The United Nations Crime Prevention and Justice Branch in Vienna, Austria, has expressed the idea that different social and political views can be brought into alignment. Under Rule 5.1 of the Standard Minimum Rules for the Administration of Juvenile Justice (see Box 1), the UN advocates the use of the **welfare model**. The UN takes the position that the well-being of young offenders should always come first. They cite South and Western Australia (see Box 4) and Scotland (see Chapter 15) as contemporary examples of the welfare model in action. Each country has adopted a welfare approach (e.g., education, cautioning, community-based supervision, and restorative-based programs) to dealing with young offenders. However, since none of these countries has a specialized juvenile penal law, an offending youth is dealt with through a regular criminal court. So, while some countries do use a model approach, there is considerable diversity in how they balance the principles of welfare with criminal responsibility.

A third theme found in comparative criminal justice text books, as noted earlier, is that comparisons allow us to understand and appreciate the significance of different cultural, economic, moral, political, and social values. India, for example, which did not pass its first national *Children's Act* until 1986, set

Figure 1: Cortinuum of Juvenile Justice Models

	Participatory	Welfare	Corporatism	Modified Justice	Justice	Crime Control
General Features	Informality Minimal formal intervention Resocialization	Informality Generic referrals Individualized sentencing Indeterminate sentences	Administrative decision-making Offending Diversion from court / custody programs	Due Process informality Criminal offences Bifurcation: soft offenders diverted, hard offenders punished	Due Process Criminal offences Least restrictive alternative / sanctions / educational concerns	Due process/ discretion Offending/ status offences Punishment / retribution Determinate sentences
Key Personnel	Educators	Childcare experts	Juvenile justice specialists	Lawyers/childcare experts	Lawyers	Lawyers/criminal justice actors
Key Agency	Community agencies / citizens School and community agencies	Social work	Interagency structure	Law/social work	Law	Law
Tasks	Help and education team	Diagnosis	Systems intervention	Diagnosis/ punishment	Punishment	Incarceration/ punishment
Understanding of Client Behavior	People basically good	Pathology/ environmentally determined	Unsocialized	Diminished individual responsibility	Individual responsibility	Responsibility/ accountability

Purpose of Intervention	Re-education	Provide treatment (*Parens Patriae*)	Retrain	Sanction behavior/ provide treatment	Sanction behavior	Protection of society/retribution deterrence
Objectives	Intervention ....through education	Respond to individual needs/ rehabilitation	Implementation of Policy	Respect individual rights/respond to "special" needs	Respect individual rights/punish	Order maintenance
Countries	Japan	Austria* The Netherlands India*, S. Korea* Italy*, Scotland Belgium*	England/Wales* Hong Kong	Canada South Africa	Germany* Russia, China* Namibia*	USA Hungary

* In the text, the author(s) sometimes indicate that there has been a shift in how their juvenile justice system has changed. Therefore, the designations are intended to reflect general characteristics of the respective country's juvenile justice system. For example, in recent years an increasing number of countries have taken steps to embrace the UN and other international standards which share many of the characteristics of the welfare model. See Table 1 for more details.

uniform age limits for criminal culpability at 16 for boys and 18 for girls (Hartjen, 1991; also see Chapter 9). Hartjen notes that while criminal conduct among Indian youth is not a serious national problem, the trend is changing as Western influences invade the Indian economy and culture. Similarly, since Romania and Bulgaria's (see Box 6) accelerated transition to a free market economy, the countries have begun to experience an increasing problem with juvenile delinquents. In Romania, for example, the increase in youth crime has been attributed to the "removal of old structures, without rapid replacement by newer, more efficient structures" (Nistoreanu, 1992:4). Ogburn (1952) refers to this concept as *culture lag*. He argued that crime increases because the non-material culture does not evolve as rapidly as the material culture. On the other hand, in response to their rapid economic growth, the Japanese government introduced major crime prevention measures for an escalating delinquency problem during the early 1960s in order to counterbalance the temporary material and non-material gap. One of the unexpected benefits was a drop in the number of rape offences (Yokoyama, 1995; also see Chapter 11).

Finally, in New Zealand married (or formally married) persons aged 14 and over but under 17 are subject to the formal process of trial and conviction for all offences. In New Zealand it would appear that if you feel you are old enough to be married then you are old enough to bear full responsibility (Mclellan, 1996). This is a concept that does appear to be widely embraced (see Box 7).

By examining countries that use different juvenile justice models as well as countries that are undergoing major social or political change, we move into a position of being better able to understand how and why different models may work in some countries and not others. As well, such comparisons may help to illuminate what kinds of factors appear universal in their effect.

Box 6: Juvenile Justice in Bulgaria

Bulgaria is a small country surrounded by Romania to the north, the former Yugoslavia to the west, Greece and Turkey to the south, and nestled against the Black Sea in the east. In accordance with Bulgaria's Constitution, established in 1991, the parliamentary republic operates under Roman civil and criminal law. Not unlike many Western countries, all court proceedings are open to the public unless the proceeding is deemed unfair to the youth or a possible threat to national security. The National Investigative Service works directly with the police and review police evidence before making recommendations to the prosecutor's office. Once a youth has been formally arrested they are referred to the Local Commission for Combating Juvenile Delinquency. This group consists of a panel of individuals from the community, appointed annually (Allen and Carper, 1999). Their juvenile justice model could be described as being a modified **welfare/justice model.**

Hackler (1994:343), for example, argues, "Canada, perhaps less than the United States, has developed an inferior criminal justice system." He suggests that this is largely due to the self-righteous attitudes that many countries have about their legal systems. Hackler (1994) also point out that, unlike France, Canadian youth court judges have no mandatory specialized training; that the system is out of touch with societal needs; and that Canada's "get tough on young criminals" policy not only lacks imagination but serves to avoid "facing issues that might make a difference" (p. 346). And while it may be that decision-makers and legislatures try to make informed decisions, it seems apparent that such perceptions can be both limiting and naive. Hackler refers to the differences between the Swiss legal model and the common-law-based model of England to illustrate the strengths and weaknesses of each. In Switzerland "the guilty were more likely to be convicted and the innocent never brought to trial," while the slower, drawn-out process in common-law in countries like England and Canada "favored guilty persons with resources" (p. 344).

Box 7: Juvenile Justice in New Zealand

In 1989 New Zealand introduced new legislation for the handling of juveniles: *The Children, Young Persons and Their Families Act*. Under the Act, criminal responsibility begins at age 10 but under section 22 of the Crimes Act (1961), youth between ages 10-14 cannot be convicted unless *mens rea* has been proven. However, under the 1989 Act, youth between ages 10 to 13 can be prosecuted for murder and manslaughter. Initial preliminary hearings take place in Youth Court, but should the case go to trial then the process involves a jury trial in the High Court. Youths aged 14 to 17 can be charged with criminal offences—summary (less serious) ones are handled in Youth Court. The New Zealand model can best be described as a **Welfare Model** (Saxon, 1996). As in Australia, Canada, and the United States, the indigenous people of New Zealand, the Maori, are over-represented in the criminal justice system and suffer from many of the same ailments—social oppression, high unemployment, and limited access to quality education. A recent admission of injustice and a 133-year-old land claim settlement may bear promise for the Maori (Louisan, 1996).

A fourth theme is that cross-cultural comparisons put different crime phenomena and societal reactions into perspective (see Box 8). For example, while North Americans are preoccupied with punishing young offenders, Europeans and several other countries covered in this book are more open to a wide variety of alternatives (see Figure 1). Boers and Sesser (1991), for example, found that Germans see restitution as a more constructive form of conflict resolution than fines or imprisonment. An understanding of their respective social, cultural, and political history helps to put trends and practices into perspective. In Germany the deterrence principle had been somewhat suspect given the negative experiences during the Nazi regime. However, Schumann and Kaulitzki (1991:18) argue that "positive" general deterrence (e.g., perceived certainty of being caught) with juveniles has gained acceptance as a leading principle to legitimize penal law (see Chapter 6 for further discussion).

Box 8: Juvenile Justice in Cuba

According to a UNICEF report (n.d.), Cuba's experience with juvenile offenders is more evolved than that of most Latin American and Caribbean countries. Cuba emphasizes education as a preventative measure. From 1953 to 1988, the percent of youth between 6 and 14 years of age who were enrolled at school rose from 55.6% to 98.5%. Prior to the Cuban revolution in 1959 problem youth received minimal treatment. Instead, many were used as a cheap labour source. The Castro regime did away with corporal punishment and inhumane treatment of youth and replaced it with resocialization programs through special school and social integration programs. The legal principles were formally drawn up in Decree 64, dated September 30, 1982.

The decree is directed to youth "with conduct problems" from ages 6 through 16. The causes of their anti-social behavior are seen to be multi-faceted and multi-variable in nature with an emphasis on home life, living conditions, and mental capacity (p. 60). Anti-social youth are categorized into one of three classifications based on the gravity of their problem and on their conduct. In addition to re-education through schooling, treatment also involves family programs and social and other popular organizations. The UNICEF report states that the problem of anti-social youth is very low with only 0.4% of youth between ages 6-16 being so classified. Petty theft and robbery are the most prevalent crimes, although blackmarketeering is also a problem. Conceptually, Decree 64 could be described as promoting a **welfare model** of juvenile justice; however, given limited resources and qualified staff, its implementation and actualization is an area of concern (see Box 10 for a description of other Caribbean countries).

Understanding social and political differences and history may also help to identify means by which to initiate constructive change (see, for example, Yokoyama's excellent article on prostitution in Japan, 1995). Fortunately, thanks in large part to some of the macro global changes and better methodologies, there is a growing acceptance of comparative research. It is an acceptance that would seem long overdue.

GAINING POPULARITY

The growing awareness of the importance of comparative criminal justice studies is further supported by the growing number of schools which offer courses on comparative criminal justice. Today several universities offer comparative criminology/criminal justice courses and international comparative excursions for undergraduate and graduate students. The OICJ (Office of International Criminal Justice), located in Chicago, Illinois, has an extensive international program, and it produces three publications in the area of international criminal justice. The Max Plank Institute in Freiburg, Germany, specializes in foreign and international penal law. There are a number of similar institutes around the world. The Department of Criminology and Criminal Justice at St. Thomas University in New Brunswick, Canada, also has the Centre for Research on Youth-at-Risk. It focuses on issues pertaining to young offenders and youth-at-risk. I have merely identified three centers with which I am familiar. Finally, Freda Adler (1996), in her 1995 presidential address to the American Society of Criminology, and David Farrington (1999), in his presidential address, both stressed the importance of comparative criminology and the need to develop a macro-level model of the relationship between social change and crime.

Since the early 1980s we have also witnessed a growing number of books (see suggested readings), articles, and international conferences. The advances in electronic data processing and telecommunications technologies have further facilitated the interest in, and the ease of, doing comparative research. Speaking at the Ninth UN Congress, Coldren (1995:7) noted that the "possibilities for international co-operation and technical assistance have never been more obtainable." Unfortunately one area that has received comparatively little attention in this regard has been juvenile justice and juvenile delinquency. A number of years ago, however, Malcolm Klein (1984) compiled such a reader after participating in an international symposium on delinquency at the University of Wuppertal in Germany (see suggested readings). Since then, however, there has been a dearth of similar collections. Two recent exceptions are projects originating in Europe. Josine Junger-Tas and her colleagues (1994) have been involved in a longitudinal and comprehensive self-report study on youth crime in 13 different countries—mostly European. Since the study is ongoing, the authors cautiously offer only some key findings. These include (p. 379):

- Rates of delinquency among the participating countries are similar.
- The use of drugs is more prevalent in the United States and Western Europe than Southern Europe.
- The lower the educational level, the more violent behavior is reported.
- Parental supervision appears to be a strong predictor of delinquent behavior.
- "Ever" prevalence rates are generally quite high, which may mean that some delinquent behavior forms part of the growing-up process of Western children.

The other project involves the edited work of Lode Walgrave and Jill Mehlbye which, similarly to this text, collected ten contributions from different European countries. Each chapter addresses their respective juvenile crime and juvenile justice systems. The book focuses on three main themes: the problems of dealing with juvenile crime; the systems of intervention, and prevention strategies in the respective countries (see Suggested Readings below).

Therefore, it seems timely that another edition be prepared which can offer a cross-sectional view of juvenile justice from around the world.

A TRULY INTERNATIONAL PHENOMENA

All human beings are born free and equal in dignity and rights. – Universal Declaration of Human Rights, 1948.

Delinquency, or youth crime, is perhaps of greater concern in the West than elsewhere (Reichel, 1994). But, as reflected in Table 1, few societies appear to have escaped this growing phenomenon (see Box 9). As we will see, the rates and patterns of delinquency can vary dramatically from one country to another as well as over time.

By comparing procedural and statistical similarities and differences between the countries and juvenile justice models, readers will hopefully be able to draw some conclusions that will further help them to understand the strengths and weaknesses of each system. They may also identify possible responses which may not be practiced in their respective countries. For example, as mentioned earlier, in Canada none of the legal actors in the juvenile justice system receive any special training in the handling of young offenders. While this fact may reflect the nature of juvenile justice administration it is not in keeping with the Beijing Rule 1.2 (see Box 1).

Other questions or concerns that might be explored include: How do different countries define the concept of "juvenile delinquency," and what do they consider to be the causes of delinquency? How do they respond to youth crime? What are their respective concerns? What measures are being undertaken or being considered? What kind of current or future actions are being taken to ensure that the Beijing Rules, designed to protect youth from exploitation, are being addressed? Can these issues be realistically compared?

This text makes no direct attempt to answer any of the comparative issues directly. Rather, comparisons are left to the reader. Part of the challenge is for readers to remain objective in their approach and guard against social and/or cultural biases when drawing conclusions.

Box 9: Juvenile Justice in Tanzania

The United Republic of Tanzania became an independent sovereign African state on 9 December, 1961. It has a population of approximately 28 million and covers a land mass of 945,087 sq. km. Although a signatory to the UN Convention on the Rights of the Child, at the time of preparing this section, the country had not legally defined the term "juvenile delinquency." The Ministry for Community Development of Women's Affairs and Children has been established to oversee the safeguards and welfare of children and to promote their development. Yet, when a youth is found guilty of an offence, he or she may be flogged at the court premises, as opposed to in a prison (Masanche, 1998). When a young person is apprehended for an offence one or more of the following legislations may be used to deal with the youth: the *Children and Young Persons Ordinance,* the *Corporal Punishment Act* and the *Minimum Sentence Act.* At this point it is not feasible to describe the model of justice being applied but it appears that legislators are trying to embrace a **welfare** approach.

Given the problems of access to adequate education and employment, Judge Joseph Masanche (1998:15) notes how the country is "trying to grapple with this growing problem." As of 1996, with the assistance of the Canadian High Commissioner to Tanzania, the country established a special Juvenile Court to deal with young offenders. However, the country does not have a process for dealing with juvenile offences. Although official crime data is limited, Masanche observes that delinquency among young males and females tends to parallel many of the Western nations. As Masanche reveals in his paper, juvenile justice in Tanzania requires considerable attention in light of its growing presence. Judges and practitioners are sensitive to the problem and are striving to treat juvenile offenders in more humane ways.

PROBLEMS WITH COMPARATIVE STUDIES

Until recently, a number of researchers believed that comparative studies have generally resulted in fragmented knowledge since the comparisons tend to use "temporal and/or spatial logic" (Teune, 1992:38). Newman (1977) identified several other key obstacles, some of which include:

- **Language barriers**: An obvious limitation if you do not have access to an interpreter.
- **Definition barriers**: Known offenses vary from country to country. For example, in the United States the *Uniform Crime Reports* provide compilations of known offenses for eight categories of crime, called Index offenses (Part 1). Yet in England and Wales *Criminal Statistics* include 64 known crimes that are further divided into eight major categories. As for Canada, *Crime and Traffic Enforcement Statistics* lists 25 known offenses that are divided into several subcategories. The UN reports that some countries do not even have formal legislation for juvenile offenders.

- **Reporting and recording practices**: In Canada, for example, official reporting agencies utilize different reporting and recording practices than are employed in different countries. This is sometimes due to political agendas, or financial and/or manpower available. In Greece, officials keep separate statistics on convicted, recorded, and suspected young criminals. In Oman there is only data available on male juvenile offenders (UN, 1990).

- **Administrative variations**: There are numerous factors such as law enforcement, the judicial system, corrections or public support that can affect how justice is administered, as illustrated by the different contributions in this book.

Yet, in spite of these apparent hurdles, the academic and technological study of criminology has become increasingly international and comparative. In recognizing the hurdles, non-equivalent concepts, and array of other possible unknown intervening factors, it is possible, if not necessary, to engage in objective analysis that may provide new insights into a complex problem. As mentioned in the previous section, this book, through its varied collection of contributions and standardized format (see below), represents an effort to allow the reader to engage in comparative analysis.

CRITICAL LESSONS

When there is crime in society there is no justice. (Plato)

In recognizing the limitations identified above, our technological and theoretical advances can now enable us to engage in comparative research. As already noted, the doors have been opened and the growing volume of literature in the area would suggest that the movement is gaining credibility and is indeed necessary (see Beirne and Hill (1991) for a comprehensive annotated bibliography on comparative criminology). In fact, one of the major "requests" made of the Commission on the Prevention of Crime at the Ninth UN Congress (UN, 1995b) was that it not only acknowledge resolutions being explored by member states but also engage in "comparing national crime and criminal justice databases." This process has been facilitated as the methodological techniques for conducting comparative research have evolved from basic description (see Nelken, 1994; Stewart, 1982) to functional analysis that transcends national boundaries (see Hackler, 1984; 1994). This volume presents a conceptual framework for a constructive functional comparative analysis.

Rather than attempt to impose a strict set of criteria to be covered, each author was asked to provide an overview of their juvenile justice system with the following key points in mind:
- social and legal definition of delinquency;
- nature and status of delinquency;
- the model of juvenile justice, as presented in Figure 1, which best describes the country's administrative policies, and how it works in the local context;
- role of law enforcement, juvenile courts, corrections, and the broader community in administering juvenile justice;
- general philosophy and practice of juvenile justice;
- current theoretical 'bias' used to explain and justify responding to young offenders;
- current issues, legally and socially, confronting young offenders; and
- any Internet links that would allow the reader to follow-up on key issues discussed and/or keep current with any developing issues presented throughout the chapter.

The format will enable the reader to accomplish several tasks. First, countries can be examined on an individual basis. Second, two or more countries can be compared based on a variety of criteria ranging from descriptive information to comparing juvenile justice models. And thirdly, a transnational approach can be adopted in which all countries are examined in light of the larger international phenomena of delinquency. As Kohn (1989) has noted, each approach may produce different practical and theoretical outcomes.

Since this book is intended to serve a wide international audience, the contributors were asked not to make any direct comparisons to any specific country(ies) other than those they might feel comfortable discussing. In this way readers are free to compare and contrast, as they deem relevant. The editor has made any direct reference to other chapters in this collection. The major factors listed in Figure 1 may be used to formulate comparisons, or one can compare countries based on their different juvenile justice models, whether their laws are based on civil or common law principles, or whether they comply with the Standard Minimum Rules for the Administration of Juvenile Justice as defined by the UN (see Box 1). Finally, readers in countries not profiled in this book can even examine and compare specific issues that may be unique to their country.

In an attempt to facilitate comparisons, the countries were divided according to their general model of juvenile justice (see Figure 1). However, as noted earlier, the classifications in some instances may appear arbitrary as new legislation or current practices do not necessarily enable strict classification.

LIMITATIONS OF THIS BOOK

While I attempted to solicit a respectable list of international contributors, it is apparent that there is no detailed representation from Islamic countries or South America and only limited coverage from Asian or the Caribbean countries (see Box 10). This void is in part due to the difficulty in locating contributors in these areas as well as the fact that many of their juvenile justice systems are not seen to be very progressive and/or the information is quite limited. However I did attempt, through contacting their Canadian embassies/high commissions, to contact the relevant juvenile justice administrative departments, and source various other comparative/international criminal justice sources. An eclectic and incomplete summary is presented in Table 1.

Since the intent of this book was to offer a cross-section of original contributions from countries whose juvenile justice systems represent one of the six models identified (see Figure 1), it is considered less critical to have equal global representation. However, as can be seen from the countries represented, there is a strong international flavor, and Table 1, along with the various box inserts, provides additional international coverage. Finally, in a reader of this nature, the extent to which ambitious goals can be realized is necessarily finite. There is a limit to the range and diversity that can be included while still remaining within the publisher's guidelines.

ORGANIZATION AND STRENGTHS OF THIS BOOK

As noted above, there are a variety of ways in which this book could have been produced. In developing the concept I felt that, rather than attempt to offer a one-sided interpretation, or solicit North American experts who would likely be more comfortable writing in English, I should solicit original contributions from sources who are recognized experts on the subject in their respective countries. The list was compiled in two ways. Most of the contributors were solicited on others' recommendations, while several more were identified after I read some of their published works. Each country is discussed in terms of the extent to which its juvenile justice system corresponds to one (or more) of the six juvenile justice models described in Figure 1.

Any significant grammatical difficulties I have tried to correct without detracting from the contributors' style of writing or perspective. In inviting contributors to submit an original article, I asked only that they each address, as well as possible, the list of common subject areas identified above. Hence, each chapter is somewhat similar in its layout and format. And rather than having to deal with possibly limited contextual comparative interpretations,

Box 10: Juvenile Justice in Barbados and Jamaica

The Caribbean Association of Criminology is a relatively new special interest group within the American Society of Criminology, and its February 2001 conference, "Crime and Criminal Justice," was only its second annual meeting. Therefore, it comes as no surprise that in spite of its proximity to the United States, comparatively little is known about juvenile justice in this region (see Box 8 for a profile on Cuba).

Barbados is the most easterly of the Caribbean islands, with a population of just over one-quarter million inhabitants. Their parliamentary system and criminal justice system is modeled closely after that of the British, who ruled over the island until 1966, when it gained independence within the Commonwealth. With the passing of the *Juvenile Offenders Act* in 1932, separate legislation for adjudicating young offenders was introduced. The act resembles a **corporatist model.** The act authorized the establishment of the juvenile court and juvenile probation. Juveniles are legally defined as seven to 16 years. As the usual first contact for young offenders, police cautioning is a formalized procedure, but it seems somewhat ineffectual since many of those who end up in court are "graduates" from diversion initiatives. Joseph (2000) reports that juvenile crime increased marginally through the early 90s. The island has two industrial schools in which youth can be detained from between three to five years. Under the act prevention programs are favoured over detention. The main programs include: the Juvenile Liaison Scheme, which involves police trying to identify youth at risk of being involved in delinquency; a School Attendance Officer Program, and a School Liaison Program. In her account of the juvenile justice system in Barbados, Joseph (2000) considers the lower age limit to be too harsh. She also argues that the act also inappropriately enforces status offences, that there is a general lack of cooperation between vested agencies, and that there is "little research and evaluation of the juvenile justice system and its programs" (p. 124).

The Juvenile Justice System in **Jamaica** is in a state of transition.[5] As a former British Colony, Jamaica possessed a rudimentary approach to dealing with juvenile offenders until independence in 1962. The common law of the United Kingdom fixed the age of criminal responsibility at seven years of age. Juveniles between the age of seven and 14 were treated as adults and were subject to the same penalties and punishment as an adult.

It was not until 1951 that separate treatment was provided by legislation for dealing with juveniles. In addition to special courts to hear juvenile cases there was the Juvenile Authority, responsible for administrative matters and for approving reformatory schools for the housing and rehabilitation of juveniles.

The modern or post-independence period has been marked by a more holistic approach to dealing with juveniles. Although the existing legislation had not yet been repealed, this period marked a number of administrative changes which emphasized the need for rehabilitation and special treatment for young offenders. The role of NGOs has also supported in great measure the advances made by the state.

Jamaica is a signatory to all major international treaties which impact on children and, as such, has embarked on a comprehensive legislative and administrative review in this regard. The new legislation, which was approved in 2001, provides a special regime which enhances the treatment of juveniles from arrest through the court process to their eventual sentence, which reflects a more enlightened approach in keeping with international norms.

readers can utilize their own criteria in conducting comparative analysis. In this way it is hoped that the book will have a wider international appeal. Again, by not drawing direct comparisons to any one country or any one model of juvenile justice, it is hoped that the book will tend to generate discussion rather than simply answer questions. Readers (and instructors) are encouraged to use the material to draw comparisons as best suits their respective interests. To this end I hope that the contributions are both general enough to provide a good overview and specific enough to allow for a deeper level of analysis where appropriate. Naturally, any limitations in this regard are the sole fault of the editor, as I defined the chapter format and pedagogy for the contributors.

Finally, should you have any comments or suggestions for a possible third edition, I would appreciate hearing from you. I can be reached in a number of ways:

John Winterdyk
Department of Justice Studies
Mount Royal College
Calgary, AB., CANADA T3E 6K6
Tel.: (403) 240-6992
Fax: (403) 240-6201
E-mail: jwinterdyk@mtroyal.ab.ca

In the meantime, thank you for selecting this book, and I hope you find it as informative and useful to read as I found it interesting and challenging to produce.

HELPFUL WEBSITES

www.akf.dk/eng98/juvenile.htm Here you will find an excellent summary of Lode Walgrave and Jill Mehlbye's 1998 edited text *Confronting Youth in Europe – Juvenile Crime and Juvenile Justice.*

www.iuscrim.mpg.de/ The official site for the Max Plank Institute in Germany. Includes some links to international work on juvenile justice.

www.unicef.org/ The official site for Juvenile Justice Portfolio. Includes the UN Convention on the Rights of the Child prepared for UNICEF as well as information on the Beijing Rules and more.

www.un.org/search/ The search site for United Nations publications. By typing in juvenile justice, juvenile crime, or related topics you will be presented with a wide range of documents.

www.oicj.org OICJ. The official website for *Crime and Justice International.* Their publications regularly include articles on juvenile justice systems around the world.

http://eurochild.gla.ac.uk Dedicated to the protection of children's rights. Includes documents from the Council of Europe's Program for Children as well as numerous other informative links.

KEY WORDS AND CONCEPTS

Welfare-Justice Model	Welfare-Modified Justice
Welfare	Justice Model
Crime Control	Modified Justice Model
Modified Justice	Corporatist Model
Corporatist	Beijing Rules
Justice	Social Welfare
Participatory	Family Group Conference Model
Legalistic	Welfare Model

NOTES

1   In 1998 the Convention on the Rights of the Child (prepared by UNICEF) reported that Nepal allows mentally ill children to be put in jail and chained while a host of other countries engage of other practices that contravene Article 37 of the Convention (see Chapter 3 for further discussion).

2   On February 5, 2001, the Liberal government re-introduced the youth justice bill. Although considered to be the same as Bill C-3, the new bill includes more than 180 changes (see Chapter 3 for further details).

3   A Chapter contribution appears in the first edition of this book. However, due to unfortunate circumstances, it was not possible to locate an alternate contributor for this edition. The information in this Box is based, in-part, on the material from the first edition as well as extensive Internet searches.

4   In Canada, for example, there has been a steady decline in the youth crime rate since the early 1990s. This has been primarily attributed to the declining representation of young persons in the population and less to do with any policy changes. See Chapter 3 for further discussion.

5   The text for the overview was provided by Keith Sobian (December, 2000).

REFERENCES

Adler, F. (1996). 1995 presidential address: Our American Society of Criminology, the world, and the state of the art. *Criminology*, 34 (1), 1-9.

Allen, J.M., & Carper, G.T. (1999, November). Juvenile justice systems in comparative context. *Crime and Justice International*, 7-8, 24-25.

Askim, B., & Berg, J. (1996, July 1). (Personal communication). The Royal Ministry of Justice and Police. Oslo, Norway.

Beirne, P., & Hill, J. (1991). *Comparative criminology: An annotated bibliography*. New York: Greenwood Press.

Boers, K., & Sesser, K. (1991). Do people really want punishment? In K. Sessar and H.-J. Kerner (Eds.), *Developments in crime and crime control research* (Ch. 7). New York: Springer-Verlag.

Coldren, J.D. (1995). Change at the speed of light: Doing justice in the information age. *CJ International*, 11 (4), 7-12.

Corrado, R. (1992). Introduction. In R.R. Corrado, N. Bala, R. Linden, and M. LeBlanc (Eds.), *Juvenile justice in Canada*. Toronto: Butterworths.

CJ International. (1995). United Nations: Crime congress targets terrorist crimes, firearms regulations, and transnational crime. 11 (4), 1, 4-6.

Devoto, G.E. (1996, March 6). (Personal communication). Second Secretary, Embassy of Argentina, Ottawa.

Dijksterhuis, F.P.H., & Nijboer, J.A. (1986). *LBO—Onderwijs en delinquentie.* The Hague: CIP-Gevens Koninklijke Bibliotheek.

Farrington, D. (1999, November). Presidential address to the American Society of Criminology annual conference. Toronto.

Ferwerda, H. (1992). *Watjes en ratjes.* Grongingen: Wolters-Noordhoff B.V.

Granath, S. (2000, Nov.). (Personnal coummication). Research officer with the National Council for Crime Prevention. Stockholm.

Hackler, J.C. (1984). Implications of variability in juvenile justice. In M.W. Klein (Ed.), *Western systems of juvenile justice.* Beverly Hills, CA: Sage.

Hackler, J.C. (1994). *Crime and Canadian public policy.* Scarborough, ON: Prentice-Hall.

Hartjen, C.A. (1991). Delinquency in India. *CJ International,* 7 (1): 5-6, 10.

International criminal justice: Issues in a global perspective (Ch. 9). Needham Heights, MA: Allyn and Bacon.

Joseph, J. (2000). Juvenile justice and delinquency prevention in Barbados. In D. Rounds (Ed.).

Junger-Tas, J. (1994a). Delinquency in thirteen western countries: Some preliminary conclusions. In J. Junger-Tas, G.-J. Terlouw, and M.W. Klein (Eds.), *Delinquent behavior among young people in the western world* (pp. 370-380). New York: Kugler.

Junger-Tas, J. (1994b). Will the juvenile justice system survive? *European Journal on Criminal Policy and Research,* 2, 76-91.

Junger-Tas, J., Terlouw, G-J., & Klein, M.W. (Eds.). (1994). *Delinquent behavior among young people in the western world.* New York: Kugler.

Klein, M. (Ed.). (1984). *Western systems of juvenile justice.* Beverly Hills, CA: Sage.

Kohn, M. L. (1989). *Cross-national research in sociology.* Newbury Park, CA: Sage.

Lorenz, O. (1996, January 10). (Personal communication). Information Officer, French Embassy, Ottawa.

Louisan, S. (1996, June 15). 133-year-old Maori injustice admitted. *Calgary Herald,* J12.

Marsh, R.M. (1967). *Comparative sociology: A codification of cross-societal analysis.* New York: Harcourt Brace and World.

Masanche, Hon. Mr. Justice J. (1998, August). Juvenile delinquency and juvenile justice: The experience of Tanzania. Paper presented at the 12th International Congress on Criminology. Seoul, Korea.

Mclellan, A. (1996, January 24). (Personal communication). Department of Social Welfare, Government of New Zealand. Wellington.

Mediation – the revelations of young offenders. (1999). Stockholm, Sweden: National Council for Crime Prevention. (#14). Available at: www.bra.org

Nelken, D. (Ed.). (1994). *The futures of criminology* (Ch. 10). London: Sage.

Newman, G.R. (1977). Problems of method in comparative criminology. *International Journal of Comparative and Applied Criminal Justice,* 1 (1), 17-31.

Nistoreanu, G. (1992). Juvenile delinquency: Realities and prospects. (Stefan Nimara, Trans.). *CJ International,* 2 (3), 4.

Ogburn, W.F. (1952). *Social change* (2nd ed.). New York: Viking Press.

Oyen, E. (1992). Comparative research as a sociological strategy. In E. Oyen (Ed.), *Comparative Methodology* (Ch. 1). Newbury Park, CA: Sage.

Ploeg, G.J. (1991). *Maatschappelijke positie en criminaliteit.* Grongingen: Wolters-Noordhoff B.V.

Prince, C.J. (1997, October 22). Justice lags for world's juveniles. *The Christian Science Monitor International*, pp. 1-3.

Reichel, P.L. (1994). *Comparative criminal justice systems* (Ch. 9). Englewood Cliffs, NJ: Prentice-Hall.

Sarnecki, J. (1996). Juvenile criminality in Sweden. In J.Winterdyk (Ed.), *Issues and perspectives on young offenders in Canada* (appendix, pp. 301-311). Toronto: Harcourt-Brace.

Saxon, T. (1996, January 31). (Personal communication). Children and Young Persons Service: National Office. Wellington, New Zealand.

Schumann, K.F., & Kaulitzki, R. (1991). Limits of general deterrence: The case of juvenile delinquency. In K. Sessar and Hans-Jurgen Kerner (Eds.), *Developments in crime and crime control research* (Ch. 1). New York: Springer-Verlag.

Scottish Police (n.d.). [Brochure]. Compliments of the Falkirk Police Department.

Sobian, K. (2000, December 16). (Personal communication). University of the West Indies, Mona Campus. Kingston, Jamaica.

Souryal, S.S. (1996). Juvenile delinquency in the cross-cultural context: The Egyptian experience. In C.B. Fields and R.H. Moore, Jr. (Eds.), *Comparative criminal justice* (Ch. 31). Prospect Heights, Ill: Waveland.

Stewart, V.L. (1982). *Justice and troubled children around the world* (Vol. 1-5). New York: New York University Press.

Teune, H. (1992). Comparing countries: Lessons learned. In E. Oyen (Ed.), *Comparative methodology* (Ch. 3). Newbury Park, CA: Sage.

UNICEF (n.d.). Care for children with conduct problems in Cuba. Information Series Regional Programme No. 7.

United Nations (1986). *United Nations standard minimum rules for the administration of juvenile justice.* New York: U.N. Department of Information.

United Nations (1990). *Prevention of delinquency, juvenile justice and the protection of the young: Policy approaches and directions* (A/CONF.144/16). Vienna: U.N. Crime Prevention and Criminal Justice Branch.

United Nations (1995a). *Ninth United Nations congress on the prevention of crime and the treatment of offenders* (A/CONF.167/7 24 January 1995). Vienna, Austria. UN Crime Prevention and Criminal Justice Branch.

United Nations (1995b). *Ninth United Nations congress on the prevention of crime and the treatment of offenders* (A/CONF.169/Rev.1). Vienna: UN Crime Prevention and Criminal Justice Branch.

Walgrave, L., & Mehlbye, J. (Eds.). *Confronting youth in Europe: Juvenile crime and juvenile justice.* Copenhagen: Institute of Local Government Studies.

Wiechman, D. (1994, September/October). Caning and corporal punishment: Viewpoint. *CJ International*, 13-19.

Wolfgang, M. (1991). Foreword. In K. Sessar and Hans-Jurgen Kerner (Eds.), *Developments in crime and crime control research.* New York: Springer-Verlag.

Wolfgang, M. (1996, May). Delinquency in China: Study of a birth cohort. *National Institute of Justice.* Rockville, MD: U.S. Dept. of Justice.

Yokoyama, M. (1995). Analysis of prostitution in Japan. *International Journal of Comparative and Applied Criminal Justice*, 19 (1), 47-60.

SUGGESTED READINGS

CJ Europe and *CJ International*: Two criminal justice newsletters published bimonthly by the Office of International Criminal Justice (OICJ) out of the University of Illinois at Chicago. These publications provide a broad range of information on current events and issues in Europe and internationally. In addition to providing general coverage of criminal justice events, the newsletters regularly include comparative or detailed information on various aspects of criminal justice. Furthermore, the newsletters serve as an excellent source for listing other publications dealing with comparative issues.

There are a host of other international/comparative journals that occasionally include articles on comparative juvenile justice. Some of these include: *Criminal Justice: The International Journal of Policy and Practice; International Journal of Comparative Criminology* (available online); and *International Review of Criminal Policy*.

Bala, N., Hornick, J.P., Snyder, H.N., and Paetsch, J. (Eds.). (2002). *Juvenile Justice Systems: An International Comparison of Problems and Solutions*. Toronto: Thompson Educational Publishing. This collection of ten chapters focuses on eight predominantly English-speaking jurisdictions. The countries represented include Australia, Canada, England, New Zealand, Northern Ireland, Republic of Ireland, Scotland, and the United States. The editors followed a comparable format to the current text, but their book is admittedly somewhat narrower in its scope of coverage.

Fairchild, E., and Dammer, H. (2001). *Comparative criminal justice systems*. 2nd ed. Belmont, CA: Wadsworth. Although not a comparative text on juvenile justice, it serves as an excellent text on the value and need for comparative research. Fairchild provides a comprehensive overview of six model nations (England, France, Germany, the former Soviet Union, Japan, and Saudi Arabia). Fairchild systematically covers each element of the criminal justice system, from the development of criminal justice systems to modern dilemmas of the criminal law as well as future developments in the field.

Fields, C.B., & Moore, Jr., R.H. (1996). *Comparative criminal justice*. Prospect Heights, IL: Waveland. The authors have collected 33 diverse articles (both original and previously published) in an attempt to offer a wide range of comparative views across five major subject areas. Primarily American scholars rather than local contributors have written the article(s) for the country being addressed. The sections range from a comparative view of "crime and criminality" to "corrections and punishment," with the final section entailing five articles on comparative juvenile justice. Two of the articles examine various aspects within Japan, while the other chapters cover Finland, Egypt, and Australia. Although an ambitious effort, this section lacks any standardization making it somewhat difficult to draw comparative analysis.

Heiner, R. (Ed.). (1996). *Criminology: A cross-cultural perspective*. St. Paul, MN: West. While this book does not focus on comparative juvenile justice, it does offer a fine review of comparative criminal justice issues. The book consists of a collection of 27 published articles that are divided into four major subject areas. Heiner begins each contribution with a brief article summary, highlighting their significance as they might pertain to American criminologists. Part I consists of ten articles dealing with the subject of crime from different perspectives. Part II includes five articles that address policing issues in several different countries ranging from Canada to Germany. Part III contains six contributions on "Conceptions of Justice and Societal Responses." The articles cover topics ranging from Maori criminal justice to the legal system in Iran and the capital punishment controversy in the United States. The final part includes six articles covering correctional system issues. A summary of this book can be found on the Internet.

Junger-Tas, J., Terlouw, G-J., & Klein, M.W. (Eds.). (1994). *Delinquent behavior among young people in the western world*. New York: Kugler. Part of an ongoing international self-report delinquency study involving twelve countries (mostly European), this report offers a comprehensive account of delinquency trends and socio-economic as well as demographic characteristics of young offenders. Even though the results are preliminary, the volume of information is worth examining, and the tentative observations, drawn strongly, suggest that not only are delinquency rates similar between countries but that juveniles in the Western world share many similar characteristics.

Klein, M.W. (Ed.). (1984). *Western systems of juvenile justice*. Beverly Hills, CA: Sage. This book might well mark the first concerted effort to provide a comparative review of juvenile justice systems. While other authors have compiled descriptive accounts of different countries, the contributions in Klein's book begin with a diagram depicting the structure of their national system. This allows for easy comparisons between countries. In addition, each chapter covers seven common categories (e.g., age, status offences, discretion, other systems, diversion, demographic bias, and trends). This further enables comparisons on common categories and the opportunity to examine differences. The final contribution from the Canadian criminologist James Hackler was solicited "as an illustration of the third stage of development, a conceptual analysis based upon comparative descriptions" (p. 14). For a retrospective look at juvenile justice, this is an excellent source.

Reichel, P.L. (2002). *Comparative criminal justice systems*. 3rd ed. Englewood Cliffs, NJ: Prentice-Hall. A well-written and organized book. In addition to its ten chapters covering everything from "Taking an International Perspective" to "Legal Traditions," policing, courts, corrections, delinquency, and a "case study" of Japan, the author includes an appendix which is an "Almanac [of] Information for Countries Referenced." Each chapter begins with a list of the key topics to be covered, key terms, and a list of the countries referenced. Chapter 9, "International Perspective on Juvenile Justice," provides an excellent overview of four of the models covered in this book. They include the welfare, legalistic, corporatist, and participatory juvenile justice models.

Terrill, R.J. (1997). *World criminal justice systems: A survey* (3rd ed.). Cincinnati, OH: Anderson. The fact that this book is in its third edition speaks to the need for comparative work. Drawing on five different types of legal systems, Terrill discusses the various aspects of their criminal justice systems including the juvenile justice system of each legal system/country. In his introduction, Terrill notes that comparisons are made to the United States throughout the book. This rather voluminous and ambitious textbook provides a fine general legalistic survey of the respective juvenile systems covered.

United Nations Standard Minimum Rules for the Administration of Juvenile Justice. (1986). New York: Department of Public Information. In addition to providing a list of the minimum rules the publication provides commentary for each section, offering the rational for setting the standards. The recommendations cover everything from "general principles" to "institutional treatment" and "research, planning, policy formulation and evaluation." Since the rules were adopted by the member states in 1984 in Beijing, subsequent U.N. Congress meetings on the Prevention of Crime and Treatment of Offenders have updated the progress of member states' adoption of these rules. As some of the information can be accessed through the Internet, it should become more commonly referenced by anyone interested in learning more about international efforts.

Walgrave, L., & Mehlbye, J. (Eds.). (1998). *Confronting youth in Europe: Juvenile crime and juvenile justice.* Denmark: Institute of Local Government Studies (AKF). This book is an excellent collection of contributions from nine European countries (Belgium, France, Italy, Germany, The Netherlands, England and Wales, Scotland, Ireland, and Denmark). The book covers three main themes: "The problem of juvenile crime demonstrated by rates and types of delinquency; the systems of intervention to juvenile crime; and prevention strategies" (p. 1). In addition to providing a historical overview of the evolution of juvenile justice in Europe, the book presents an interesting examination of how the countries represented have struggled to follow the welfare/justice model. Numerous summary tables are provided to facilitate comparisons across the major themes.

Chapter 1

Juvenile Justice System: An Austrian Perspective

Mag. Maximilian Edelbacher
Federal Police of Austria, Vienna
Judge Dr. Claudia Fenz
Juvenile Court of Austria, Vienna

FACTS ON AUSTRIA

Austria is situated in south-central Europe, covering a part of the eastern Alps and the Danube region. And although it is land-locked, it borders on the Mediterranean area. The country has a wide variety of landscapes ranging from the Eastern Alps to the Pannonon Lowlands, Vienna Basin and the Granite and Gneiss Highlands. **Population**: According to the latest population statistics (1997), Austria has a population of 8.07 million. This represented an increase of some 274,000 since 1991. In 1997, 3.9 million (48.5%) of the population were male, 4.1 million (51.5%) female. For those born in 1997 average life expectancy for men was 73.9, for women 80.2. Austria's population is 98% German-speaking. Members of six ethnic groups officially recognized in Austria are found in five of the Austrian provinces. Recognition under the Ethnic Group Act of 1976 can only be granted to what are called indigenous ("autochthonous") ethnic groups, which term is defined as comprising those who have lived in Austria for at least three generations and who are Austrian citizens. **Political and security structure**: Austria is a Democratic Republic. Our citizens can choose among several parties to vote for—at present our National Assembly consists of the four biggest parties. The Austrian executive is a federal institution. Our secretary of the interior is the head of the Department of the Interior. We differentiate between the federal police, who are located in the 14 largest cities, and the so-called federal Gendarmerie, which operates in the rural areas. Out of the 8 million inhabitants, 5.2 million live in the countryside. **The Economy**: Austria—a member of the European Union since the beginning of 1995—has now achieved full integration with its chief foreign markets. The chief industries are mechanical and steel engineering, chemistry and foodstuffs, beverages and tobacco. In the latter industry, the manufacture of engines and transmissions is the most important area, with an export share of more than 90%. The average unemployment rate stood at 7.1% according to national criteria and 4.4% according to EU criteria which, compared to international figures, is still low. **Education**: An analysis of the population by educational attainment shows that nearly 60% of the population has achieved com-

pulsory education in 1997. In 1869 the
Imperial Education Law unified the entire
system of compulsory education and increased the duration of compulsory education from six to eight years. The most
important education authority was Otto
Glöckel. He felt that all children should
have the opportunity to enjoy the best
possible education irrespective of sex or
social background[1] (*Austria Facts and Figures*, 2000).

*It is crucial...that the problems of juvenile delinquents should be solved
exclusively or even primarily by means of criminal law*—Udo Jesionek, 2000.

HISTORICAL OVERVIEW OF THE JUVENILE JUSTICE SYSTEM

In Austria special legislation in the field of juvenile justice has a long and
distinguished tradition. As early as 1852 special provisions for juveniles were
introduced to the Penal Code. The age of criminal responsibility was fixed at
the age of 10. Juveniles between the age of 10 and 14 who had committed a
minor offence were handed over to their parents for further "treatment." "Non-
violent education" obviously was not an issue at that time. Major offences
were punished by detention lasting from one to six months. From the age of 14
upward juveniles were treated like adults. Until the age of 20 neither the death
penalty nor a life sentence could be imposed. Instead, the sentences imposed
ranged from 10 to 20 years. It was **Franz Klein** who in 1907 first tried to establish an independent juvenile justice system. Owing to this famous politician's
special interest in that field, a multitude of provisions improving the position
of juveniles in criminal proceedings were introduced between 1905 and 1908.
Their legal representatives were given certain rights—appointment of a defence counsel became mandatory for grave offence; pre-trial detention was
only possible under certain limited conditions etc. The political troubles of
this period, which eventually led to World War I, prevented the draft that Klein
presented in 1907 from passing Parliament. Immediately after the end of World
War I, however, special courts for juveniles were established. There specialized judges applied adult criminal law to juveniles.

In 1923 neighboring Germany introduced a juvenile justice act. Following
this example, Austria adopted its first juvenile justice act
(Jugendgerichtsgesetz) on 18 July 1928. This law was the first to contain special provisions for juveniles both in the fields of statutory and procedural law.
As a guiding principle the legislator stated that legal punishment was only one
method among several others, and by no means the only or even the best to
deal with juvenile delinquency. Judges were instructed to substitute legal punishment by other educational means wherever possible (i.e., **welfare model**).
After having virtually been suspended during the period leading up to World
War II, the act was reintroduced in 1949 and amended in 1961.

In the following 27 years between then and 1988—the year that saw the current juvenile justice act pass Parliament—a great deal of work has been invested in this area, mainly by the practitioners of law who worked in the field. Much of this effort has gone into drafting a new juvenile justice act. And since this development is unique—at least in the history of Austrian legislation—the description here will be detailed.

The spirit behind it can only be called revolutionary, the way chosen was uncommon—to put it mildly. The guiding idea was that, besides the traditional tracks of criminal law based on treatment or punishment, a third one should be opened up based on the principles of reparation, reconciliation, mediation, and restorative justice as both the means and end of penal law. It could be described as a **modifed justice model** (W. Bogensberger, personal communication, January 1996).

For various reasons the first bill dedicated to these principles did not pass Parliament at the beginning of the 1980s. The frustration caused by this lack of progress gradually led to a unique experiment. In 1984, a group of highly motivated juvenile judges, public prosecutors and probation officers in three Austrian provinces took matters into their own hands. They started to apply the aforementioned principles in their work.

Fortunately there was one provision in the "old juvenile justice act" that was broad enough to allow experiments within its boundaries. The limits were stretched rather shamelessly—but it worked, allowing the participants in this exciting endeavor to test their ideas in practice and to develop concepts in the field of extra-judicial compensation. Surprisingly enough, this experiment, which challenged more than one principle of Austrian criminal law hitherto deemed immovable, did not cause much opposition in the beginning. The reason was probably that at the time most of the conservative judges—apt to oppose any new approach—simply did not catch on to the importance and impact of what was going on. When they finally did, things had developed far enough to be irreversible.

The advocates of this development were lucky in one respect: It was the right thing at the right time. The years before 1988 had seen a decrease in the number of juvenile offenders. No spectacular crime committed by a juvenile made the headlines. The political events that led to the opening of the borders towards Eastern Europe—the end of the Iron Curtain which was to bring with it many real and many imagined security problems—were yet to come.

Another important factor that contributed to the ultimate success of the experiment was that it was done professionally from the start. Right from the beginning, the Vienna Institute of Sociology of Law and Deviance was commissioned to evaluate the available data. This provided the participants with findings and in-depth information to give to the media when they went public. The press was friendly from the very beginning, which was certainly one of the reasons why the general public welcomed the new practices.

Once the experiment had proved itself a public success, politicians no longer hesitated to endorse it—and on 20 October 1988, the new *Juvenile Justice Act* passed Parliament. The following years saw an overwhelming acceptance of the new provisions both by the general public and the practitioners of law.

That is why in 1992 another experiment was initiated in the field of adult penal law. In some provinces of Austria the project "**Extra-judicial Compensation** in Adult Criminal Cases" was started by selected courts on nearly all (court) levels. Once more, a provision of the Penal Code was used to experiment within its limits. The experiences of this model project, and the know-how acquired by the judges and public prosecutors working in the juvenile justice system, led to the incorporation of "diversion" into the Penal Code for adults in 1999.

THE AUSTRIAN JUSTICE SYSTEM: THE CURRENT LEGISLATION AS IT PERTAINS TO YOUNG OFFENDERS

The Guiding Principles of Austrian Procedural Law

Due to their importance the following principles have been incorporated in the Constitution.

Principle of the independence of judicature:
Right of having criminal proceedings conducted by the "legal judge":

The two principles are closely related. Only complete independence of the courts from the influence of the state administration guarantees the protection of the citizen from the state's power. Judges are independent. That is, only the law binds them. Instructions, or any direct or indirect attempt to exert influence by anyone (e.g., the president of the court, the minister of justice), are illegal. To guarantee this position, judges are appointed for life and cannot in the normal course of things be removed from their court or transferred to another court without their consent. To complete this concept of judicial independence, a case cannot be taken away from the judge under whose jurisdiction it comes pursuant to the rules of procedure.[2]

Principle of accusation:

In most European countries, criminal proceedings were formerly governed by the principle of inquisition (i.e., the functions of judge, defence counsel and prosecutor were exercised by the same person). In Austria this principle had governed criminal proceedings until 1873 when, following the ideas of the French Revolution, these roles were assigned to different persons. While in the Anglo-American law system the public prosecutor and the defendant act as parties, and the court decides only on the strength of the evidence provided by the two of them, in continental Europe a different form of procedure developed. Here criminal proceedings can only be initiated and continued upon a request made by a prosecutor. The preliminary investigation is conducted by a judge and not by a party. Most European countries have abolished the concept of the "investigating judge."

Principle of oral proceedings and principle of direct proceedings:
These two principles are closely connected. The law demands that the ruling court examine all relevant evidence. Witnesses have to testify at the trial, court experts must give their opinions in court. The reading of depositions made previously (e.g., before the police or during the preliminary investigation before the investigating judge) in the course of the trial is the exception to the rule and therefore only allowed under certain restricted preconditions.

Principle of the public trial:
The issue of the publicity of the trial as an alternative to a "judicature *in camera*" was raised during the French Revolution and the Revolution of 1848. Today, it is an expression of an "open" judicature that allows control by the general public and the media during the trial. Exceptions can be made if they pertain to the protection of people or their reputation. TV and radio transmission, taking photographs or video filming during the court sessions is forbidden.

Principle of participation of the people in the legal decision:
In Austria lay judges play an important role in trials where major offences are concerned. One professional judge tries minor cases. When the court is dealing with a graver offence, two lay judges and two professional judges decide upon guilt and penalty together. In the case of the most severe crimes a body of eight lay judges (the jury) decides the verdict. The eight lay judges and three professional judges fix the sentence together. Unlike the American system, Austrian law does not demand unanimity. A (simple) majority of votes suffices. The votes of the professional judges and the lay judges carry the same weight. In the case of a draw, the milder sentence prevails. When the professional judges feel (unanimously) that the jury has erred, they can suspend the verdict. Then the case has to be tried again, and by a different jury. Appealing the verdict is only possible under certain very restricted precondi-

tions. Rarely is the verdict of the jury set aside by the second instance (the Supreme Court). The Austrian system with its extreme emphasis on lay participation is unique in continental Europe.

Further principles governing court proceedings in criminal cases can be found in the Austrian Code of Criminal Procedure.

Principle of prosecution by the state:

In principle, prosecution is a right of the state. The authorities have the duty to prosecute if there is reasonable evidence that an offence has been committed. This duty to prosecute is called the **principle of legality**. The question of whether the trial is appropriate or economical can never be an issue. In this uncompromising form, Austrian justice is unique among Europe's legal systems.

Principle of the "material truth":

The court has to take all the necessary evidence and consider all the circumstances of the case *ex officio* independently of any motions of the public prosecutor or the defendant.

Principle of free evaluation of the evidence:

Only evidence that has been obtained under circumstances in violation of the Declaration of Human Rights is not admitted in the trial. The Austrian Penal Code knows no binding rules on the evaluation of evidence. In the end the judge renders a verdict. Of course the judge has to give the reasons for that decision and the judgment has to be based upon the evidence taken in the course of the trial. Only complete certainty, or at least a "probability that borders on certainty," carries a guilty verdict. In case of doubt the defendant has to be acquitted (*in dubio pro reo*).

The Main Stages of Criminal Proceedings in Austria
Investigation on police level:

The police begin an investigation as soon as an offence comes to their knowledge. In very grave cases, or in cases where either a search warrant or an arrest warrant are required, the police act under the guidance of the public prosecutor or the investigating judge. In practice, however, in the majority of all cases, in the beginning the police act more or less on their own. Usually the public prosecutor only learns about the case when the police report is transferred to him or her. This is not the kind of procedure the authors of the Code of Criminal Procedure had in mind when they drafted the provisions for the pre-trial investigation. What they had intended was pre-trial proceedings governed by the public prosecutor (and in special cases by the investigating judge) from the very beginning. In practice, however, it turned out different. Since the protection of basic human rights proves difficult in proceedings that are exclusively conducted by the police, this part of the Code of Criminal Procedure is about to be amended soon.

Arrest Procedure:

Arrest by the police can occur in two ways:

1. When the suspect is apprehended in, or immediately after, the act, or when s/he is apprehended due to "imminent danger." No reasons in writing are required. However, the police officer must inform the arrested person of the general reasons for the arrest.
2. When executing an arrest warrant issued by the judge applied for by the public prosecutor. An arrest warrant has to be in writing. In practice, the majority of police arrests are based on police powers. Before transferring an arrested person to remand, the police have to contact the public prosecutor. If the public prosecutor considers it likely that s/he will request a detention order s/he will order the police to transfer the defendant to the court jail.

The sources of law governing pre-trial detention are:

1. the Constitutional Law of 1988 on the Protection of Personal Freedom (Federal Law Journal 1988/684);
2. the Code of Criminal Procedure (Federal Law Journal,1993/526); and
3. the Special Law on Appeal to the Supreme Court for Violation of the Fundamental Right to Personal Freedom (Federal Law Journal, 1992/864).

Investigation at Court Level:

When the public prosecutor receives the police report, s/he has to decide if it contains all the necessary information to proceed on. If this is the case he can either drop the case or file charges. If the prosecutor decides to prosecute, the file is transferred to the judge who will preside over the trial. However, if the public prosecutor feels more information on the case is required, the file can be transferred to the investigating judge, who collects additional evidence before proceeding. The investigating judge is excluded from judgement in the trial.

If a person has been detained they must then appear before the investigating judge within 48 hours. There are a series of legal safeguards protecting the suspect from inadvertently being detained. The maximum time in pre-trial detention until the beginning of the trial is six months. Under exceptional circumstances, which hardly ever occur in practice, the time limit is one year; for the gravest crimes, two years.

An arrested or detained person has a constitutional right to immediately inform a family member or a friend, as well as a defence lawyer, of the fact that s/he has been arrested or jailed. A person detained also has the legal right to be assisted by counsel, who can be chosen and paid by the detainee or be appointed by the court (legal aid scheme).

Preliminary investigations are not open to the general public.

The Trial:

In the proceedings sections we described the principles that characterize the trial process as well as the legal criteria that must be followed when trying a case. In the following section we will review the range of sanctions and available dispositions. In Figure 1.1 below, we present a graphic overview of a criminal investigation. The graph applies to both young offenders and adult offenders.

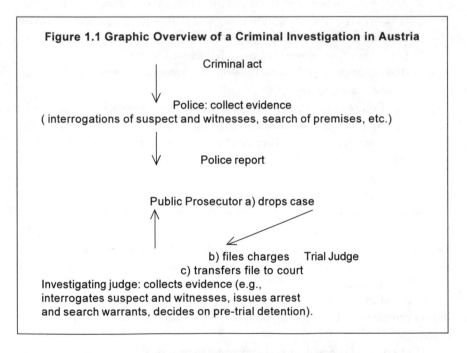

Figure 1.1 Graphic Overview of a Criminal Investigation in Austria

Criminal act

Police: collect evidence
(interrogations of suspect and witnesses, search of premises, etc.)

Police report

Public Prosecutor a) drops case

b) files charges   Trial Judge
c) transfers file to court
Investigating judge: collects evidence (e.g.,
interrogates suspect and witnesses, issues arrest
and search warrants, decides on pre-trial detention).

In the next section, we will provide a brief overview of the Austrian Criminal Code since some of its major elements also pertain to how juvenile offenders are dealt with. Then, later in the chapter, we will examine more closely the role of the family court in relation to juvenile delinquents.

THE CRIMINAL CODE

Sanctions and Dispositions

The Austrian criminal law acknowledges the traditional modes of punishment: imprisonment and fines, either with probation (when the penalty imposed does not exceed two years), not with probation, or partly with probation (when the penalty does not exceed two—or, under certain circumstances, three—years).

The range of sanctions is clearly defined by the Criminal Code. Murder, for instance, carries a sentence from ten to 20 years, or life. However, in the case of petty offence there is no minimum sentence.[3]

Commitment to an institution is possible in three cases:

1. if a person cannot be held responsible for their crime because they are found to be mentally ill;
2. if there is a risk that they might commit the same type of offence again; and
3. if the person can be held responsible but is seriously disturbed, an additional custodial sentence can be imposed that has to be served even after the person has been pronounced sane.[4]

Diversion

Diversion in Austria refers to a wide range of penalties that dispense with formal court proceedings or formal sanctions. If there are no formal sanctions that are deemed appropriate, it is referred to as **non-intervening diversion**. However, if some sort of conditions are required (e.g., compensation or reparation for the harm and damage done) the technical term is **intervening diversion**.

Preconditions:

The public prosecutor can drop a case provided the main facts are clear and it does not take a formal conviction to prevent the criminal from re-offending. If so, the offender must agree to:

- a court-ordered payment,
- some type of community service,
- extra-judicial compensation, and/or
- probation.

A **court-ordered payment** to the state is to be paid within 14 days and must not exceed a certain amount. If payment of the whole sum is especially hard on the defendant, a respite up to six months can be granted. If possible and necessary, the public prosecutor can additionally require the reparation of damages within a time span of up to six months.

Unpaid **community services** have to be performed within six months. The public prosecutor can require reparation of damages additionally. The maximum duration is eight hours a day, 40 hours a week or 240 hours in total.

Charges can be dropped if the offender takes responsibility for his criminal act and is willing to prove this fact by **compensating** for, or repairing, the harm and damage done. If possible, the victim is invited to participate in the proceedings provided he is willing to do so. The public prosecutor can ask a mediator (e.g., social worker) to assist the parties involved.

Two advantages of this diversion measure should be specifically stressed: first, the possibility of reacting quickly; and second, the way it strengthens the position of the victim. In most extra-judicial procedures the offender does not come into contact with judges and lawyers. However, social workers leave no doubt that they are acting on behalf of the judicial system and that they are dealing with the consequences of a crime for which the offender has to take responsibility.

Regarding the second aspect, extra-judicial compensation allows for an informal setting where victims can express their fears and frustration caused by the offence. There are few victims who wish to waive their right to a personal confrontation with the offender. This may, in part, be mediated by the fact that the victim usually receives financial compensation faster this way, without any further legal hassle.

Probation

The public prosecutor can drop charges on condition that the suspect does not commit any offence within up to two years. Additionally they can give certain orders and/or provide for a probation officer. When the probation period has expired the prosecutor has to drop charges unconditionally. However, formal court proceedings have to be re-opened if one or more of the following events occur:

1. upon request by the suspect at any time,
2. if the court-ordered payment was not made in time, or was incomplete,
3. if community service was not performed,
4. if court orders were not obeyed,
5. if the probation officer was avoided, and
6. if the suspect has re-offended.

Conditional Release (parole)

Convicts who have served half of the sentence imposed and not less then three months can be released if they are not likely to re-offend. Those who have served two-thirds of their prison term have to be released providing there are no special reasons to assume that they might re-offend.

DESCRIPTION OF PRAGMATIC FACTORS

Police Power and Youth Repression—Special Unit to Fight Juvenile Crime

Police power is based on two pillars. On the one hand, police conduct is determined by the Penal Code, on the other hand, they are bound by the *Security Police Act*. While crime control has always been a key objective of police work, the increasing crime rates of the 1990s prompted police to take more overt steps to control and repress crime. In 1991 the federal police in Vienna established the first **Special Unit** to combat juvenile crime.

In the beginning of the 1990s, structured criminal groups of juveniles were acting very violently in Vienna. The Special Unit was very successful. Today nearly all structured criminal youth groups are under control of the police. The Special Unit of the police is responsible for:

- investigating criminal and political crimes,
- fighting crime by organized criminal juveniles,
- preventing violence by soccer groups,
- investigating skinheads and hooligans,
- investigating illegal graffiti,
- educating police officers about occultism, and
- collecting data on extremistic groups.

In the last three years a lot of crimes have been dealt with as a result of the activities of the Special Unit. Table 1.1 shows the following figures:

Table 1.1: Crimes Dealt with by the Special Unit			
Year	**1997**	**1998**	**1999**
Injuries	55	25	25
Robberies	14	15	10
Damage/Graffiti	6	77	248
Neo-Nazi-Activities	—	4	7
Drug-dealing	14	13	8

Community Crime Prevention

The Security Police Act:

On the first of May 1993 the *Security Police Act,* which serves as the legal basis of all powers and duties of the police toward the citizens, took effect. This act created a new relationship between the police and the citizens, balancing the power and duties between citizens and the police. This act also forms the basis for crime prevention. Crime prevention is primarily carried out by the Criminal Advisory Service, criminal counseling being a part of crime prevention (Security Police Act, 1993).

New Concept and Nature of Crime Prevention in Austria:
Crime prevention is the prevention of offences punishable by the court. There is a strong interaction between clearing up (repression) and prevention. The police consider themselves authorized to carry out preventive measures not only because of their legal mandate but also because of their special potential of experience and knowledge (Jedelsky, 1999).

Under the new Act, prevention is the task of all police employees. To further support the crime prevention initiatives Austria has established trained experts who deal exclusively with crime prevention. Comprehensive experience, competence, and technical knowledge can only be obtained by intensively dealing with the topic of prevention. To keep up with the knowledge and the developments at security fairs alone, it is necessary to gather far-ranging information on everything on display, which takes time and requires specialization.

The Criminal Advisory Service—The Vienna Model:
The **Criminal Advisory Service** of the Vienna Police, the central authority for all prevention work, consists of four groups (Jedelsky, 1999). The problem of crime prevention and community policing in Austria was based on the hierarchic structure of the federal Austrian police and Gendarmerie. Therefore, a new strategy had to be created. The idea was that "The police come to the people," and not that "The people have to go to the police."

Table 1.2 The Criminal Advisory Service

Office of The Criminal Advisory Service

Group for prevention of property offences	Group for prevention of violence against children, youths and family	Group for prevention of sexual offences	Group for prevention of addiction

The central department, consisting of police, lawyers, criminal investigation officers, security guard officers and other employees, can be referred to as the "prevention team of the Viennese police force" (see Box 1.1). Apart from that, additional officers perform preventive tasks in other central departments and at the district police stations. The Office of the Criminal Advisory Service regularly organizes training courses and information lectures for these officers. All officers of the federal police headquarters in Vienna are also trained in matters of the Criminal Advisory Service in the course of their basic training.

Box 1.1 Measures of the Crime Prevention Programs

Property offence like burglary, pickpocketing, fraud and robbery are the most common criminal offences. The increase in the past 10 years shows that everybody is at risk. The concentrated prevention work that has been carried out in Vienna since 1992 to combat burglaries has led to a decline in property offences. Prevention can start by teaching adequate behavior and organizational measures on the one hand, and by using mechanical, electronical or technical security devices on the other. A study conducted in 1991 and repeated in 1997 by the University of Graz shows that almost 70% of burglars are deterred by alarm systems, 50% are deterred by dogs, but only 20% by police patrols.

"Blackmail at school, robbery on the way to school, drugs in the schoolyard"— these are newspaper headlines. While believed to be somewhat distorted, the risk exists. Gangs of youth and soccer hooligans represent other facets of juvenile delinquency.

A group of the Criminal Advisory Service deals with the prevention of violence against children and youths and the prevention of domestic violence. The first and foremost task is to detect problems in good time in certain neighborhoods, parks, recreation grounds and other meeting places; knowledge of these scenes is required. The second task is to inform other institutions early so that they can become active as well.

Apart from that, there are attempts at sensitization by initiation of, or participation in, problem-related events, to provide information and to create an awareness of the problem. This prevention group organizes soccer and streetball games and anti-violence training courses, sets up contact between hostile groups deliberately, takes care of groups of fans or individual persons and presents meaningful alternatives. By explaining the legal situation—often the youths are not aware of the significance of a "robbery" — an awareness of problems may be achieved.

It is also the task of this group to address and discuss the problem of violence against women and children. In this area cooperation with other institutions is particularly important and the Criminal Advisory Service considers itself a coordination and contact body for giving advice to individual people and organizing social or medical help.

Methods of mere deterrence have proved a failure, just like detailed information on negative effects. As young people tend to take risks more readily, stressing these risks may produce exactly the opposite effect due to curiosity, experimental behavior and thirst for adventure. Experience from Germany shows that young people have accepted professional preventive work in the field of narcotic drugs.

Within the framework of the Criminal Advisory Service this group holds individual consultations, organizes exhibitions, workshops, anti-drug discos and lectures to pupils, parents and teachers.

JUVENILE CRIME TRENDS

People are more and more prepared to use violence. Teachers in their respective schools notice that the number of young people who are ready to use violence is on the increase (see Table 1.3). Violence is thus becoming a serious threat. Within families, violence is used against women and children, whereas in the street or public transport, vandalism and damage to property can be encountered more and more often. However, the increase in violence among juvenile delinquents as such is not worrying us so much at the moment. One reason for this might be that the unemployment rate among juveniles is quite low in comparison to other countries. However, it is impossible to anticipate the appearance of youth gangs. As a consequence there are often violent fights and arguments between local and foreign gangs. What's more, **xenophobia** is a serious problem these days. The danger of extremism was best illustrated by recent letter-bomb attacks that concerned Austria a lot.

Table 1.3 Juvenile Crime Statistics: 1990-1999

Juvenile Criminals – Percentages	1990	1991	1992	1993	1994
Punishable acts against life	7.3	7.8	7.7	8.0	8.3
— of which are criminal offences	6.1	8.6	8.2	8.0	6.9
— of which are misdemeanors	7.3	7.8	7.7	8.0	8.3
Punishable acts against property	16.7	16.8	17.0	17.0	18.2
— of which are criminal offences	21.5	23.1	23.5	23.3	25.7
— of which are misdemeanors	15.7	15.6	15.6	15.6	16.4
Sexual offences	11.2	8.1	8.7	8.9	9.4
— of which are criminal offences	12.7	9.8	8.5	10.0	10.5
— of which are misdemeanors	9.4	6.3	8.9	7.4	8.0
Total punishable acts prosecuted by courts	10.8	11.1	11.5	11.7	12.4
— of which are criminal offences	18.4	19.5	19.7	19.5	21.0
— of which are misdemeanors	10.2	10.4	10.7	10.9	11.4
Juvenile Criminals—Percentage	**1995**	**1996**	**1997**	**1998**	**1999**
Punishable acts against life	8.0	8.1	8.7	9.2	9.5
— of which are criminal offences	6.1	9.0	9.6	9.3	10.6
— of which are misdemeanors	8.0	8.1	8.7	9.2	9.5
Punishable acts against property	19.7	19.8	19.2	20.6	21.6
— of which are criminal offences	25.7	25.6	23.9	25.3	24.9
— of which are misdemeanors	18.4	18.4	18.1	19.6	20.9
Sexual offences	7.9	10.9	10.2	9.6	10.9
— of which are criminal offences	9.3	13.0	12.5	11.2	11.2
— of which are misdemeanors	6.2	8.5	7.2	7.8	10.5
Total punishable acts	12.8	13.7	13.6	14.4	15.3
— of which are criminal offences	21.2	21.8	20.4	21.4	22.1
— of which are misdemeanors	11.9	12.8	12.9	13.6	14.6
Fields of Juvenile Criminals—Percentage	**1990**	**1991**	**1992**	**1993**	**1994**
Murder § 75 Penal Code	6.0	5.1	5.4	2.2	5.6
Physical injury § 83, § 84 PC	9.4	10.2	11.0	11.7	12.2
Negligent bodily injury § 88 PC	6.2	6.4	5.8	5.6	5.6
Damage to property § 125 PC	20.8	21.3	21.9	20.9	24.7
— of which are criminal offences § 126 PC	33.7	35.8	41.1	37.7	41.1

Theft § 127 PC	19.8	20.1	20.5	21.1	21.3
— of which are criminal offences					
§ 128 PC	10.4	11.3	9.9	11.1	10.9
Burglary § 129 PC	26.4	29.3	29.0	29.0	32.4
Robbery § 142, § 143 PC	24.2	28.0	29.7	29.9	37.3
Fraud § 146–148 PC	2.8	3.0	2.7	2.9	2.6
Rape, sexual compulsion					
§ 201, § 202 PC	11.5	8.2	8.8	10.5	9.6
Rape, sexual compulsion					
of juveniles § 206, § 207 PC	21.1	17.5	12.2	15.9	16.3
Juvenile Criminals—Percentage	**1995**	**1996**	**1997**	**1998**	**1999**
Murder § 75 PC	3.6	8.1	6.3	4.8	4.8
Physical injury § 83, § 84 PC	12.2	12.8	13.1	13.8	14.4
Negligent bodily injury § 88 PC	5.3	5.2	5.8	5.9	5.9
Damage of property § 125 PC	26.3	26.2	25.5	27.6	29.0
— of which are criminal offences					
§ 126 PC	46.7	47.1	41.0	40.8	44.0
Theft § 127 PC	24.4	25.0	24.1	26.1	27.6
— of which are criminal offences					
§ 128 PC	8.5	11.0	11.8	9.5	11.2
Burglary § 129 PC	35.3	4.2	33.3	34.6	34.6
Robbery § 142, § 143 PC	32.4	34.7	34.0	41.7	32.5
Fraud § 146–148 PC	2.7	3.1	3.0	3.6	4.7
Rape, sexual compulsion § 201, § 202 PC	8.3	11.6	12.6	10.9	10.3
Rape sexual compulsion					
of juveniles § 206, § 207 PC	12.6	17.5	16.7	14.8	13.5

Source: *Bendesministerium for inners...* 1990-1999.

Actual Criminal Crime Trends of Juveniles

From Table 1.3 it can be said that the police and Gendarmerie in Austria are confronted with violence problems of juveniles attending soccer games, drug dealing and drug abusing, drug-related crime like robberies, burglaries, thefts and sometimes gang fights. Gang fights are not a real threat but sometimes there are some fights between "right-wing" and "left-wing" gangs. Graffiti are not really a problem in Austria.

HOW THE JUVENILE JUSTICE SYSTEM RESPONDS TO YOUNG OFFENDERS

In Austria, unlike in many other European countries, criminal courts and family courts hardly ever co-operate in the course of criminal proceedings concerning a juvenile. The scopes of their functions do not overlap.

The criminal court deals with juveniles who have reached the age of criminal responsibility, investigates the crime and imposes one of the sanctions described below. It may inform the social welfare authorities or the family court if the judge feels that the crime has its roots in neglect by the family or guardian of their parental responsibilities. After that it is up to the family court judge or the social welfare authorities to decide what kind of measures to take. The criminal court has absolutely no say in the proceedings after it provides its information, and cannot commit a juvenile delinquent to foster parents.

On the other hand, the family court or social welfare agencies never impose a penalty or sanction on a juvenile offender, even when the criminal court informs them that the offender has been convicted of a criminal act. However, the fact that a crime has been committed can be a reason for the social welfare authorities to check on the family background of the juvenile criminal. If the authorities find it wanting they can take action to improve the situation of the young person. This has nothing to do with the criminal proceedings or their outcome. Even if the juvenile is acquitted, actions under the *Social Welfare Act* might prove necessary.

The *Juvenile Justice Act* of 1988

As a general rule, the provisions of statutory and procedural law for adults found in the procedural code and the criminal code apply also to juveniles. The *Juvenile Justice Act* contains the noticeable and important exceptions to be described as well as special provisions for juveniles in both areas. The new act can be described as "procedural decriminalization" with the aim of pushing back or restricting the use of criminal sentences and sanctions.

Special Provisions:

The act applies to juvenile offenders, defined as persons between the age of 14 and 19 (18 before 1988) who have committed an offence. Children under the age of 14 cannot be held responsible, not even for the most severe crimes. If the crime is a result of neglect on the part of their parents, welfare officials and court magistrates of the family courts can take action under the *Youth Welfare Act*. The measures, however, are chiefly limited to placing the child with foster parents or in a social welfare institution. However, unlike in Germany (see Chapter 6), Austria does not have the in-between category of young adults (i.e., 18 to 19 year olds). They are now classified as juveniles under the new act (Jedelsky, 1999).

There are no lock-up institutions (so-called "reform schools") in Austria. It is consequently quite common for minors to run away from an institution after being placed there against their will—in fact, there is nothing that can be done to prevent it (see Box 1.2)!

Special Juvenile Courts

The *Juvenile Justice Act* has established special juvenile courts in three major Austrian cities: The Vienna juvenile court deals with all kinds of crimes,

---

Box 1.2: "Beyond help and punishment"

The following example may serve to illustrate the problem. There was a minor in Vienna who had more than 40 registered contacts with the police by the time he had turned 14. Two of them were for attempted murder—in one case, he cut the throat of a drunk to see how long it would take him to bleed to death. Mental institutions would not take him. In fact, they pronounced him sane. In any case he would not have fit into any of the existing mental institutions. All the police could do was take his name, notify the father and send him home. He never stayed in any institution. After he had turned 14, he spent most of the eight years that remained before he died of AIDS in jail.

It is a very small group of really dangerous minors that has fired the discussion about re-installing closed institutions in Austria.

Luckily no serious crime by a minor made the headlines in the last few years. So the lower age limit remains undisputed—at least so far.

---

while the juvenile courts in the provincial cities of Linz and Graz only deal with offences that come under the jurisdiction of the district court (i.e., minor offences). In the other court circuits, special divisions for juveniles in the criminal courts for adults have been established. All judges working in these fields are expected either to possess or to acquire special knowledge in the fields of psychology and social welfare. The same goes for the lay judges who are taken from a list of teachers, social workers and the like provided by the Ministry of Education every year for use of the courts. If a lay judge who does not meet these criteria takes part in a trial the sentence can be nullified on these grounds.

Criminal records:

As with adults, all sentences imposed on juveniles are registered with official criminal records. But whereas the registration of an adult offender is available to third parties when the sentence exceeds three months, in the case of a juvenile the limit is six months.

Publicity of court sessions:

Unlike virtually all other European countries, in Austria sessions in juvenile court are open to the public. It is, however, comparatively easy to exclude the public; for instance, if this is deemed "in the interest" of the juvenile.

Legal representation:

The appointment of a defence counsel is mandatory in all but minor cases. In petty cases, it is only mandatory if the offender is in custody. Even if this is not the case, legal counsel can still be appointed if the judge considers it necessary.

If the legal representatives of the juvenile do not turn up at the trial despite their having been invited properly, the counsel of defence acts as legal representative of the juvenile for the duration of the court session. He can launch an appeal on behalf of the legal representatives but is not allowed to waive their right to appeal.

The juvenile's parents or legal guardians have the right to be present during all court proceedings. They have more or less the same rights as the juvenile. They have to be notified of virtually all court decisions and have the right to appeal them even against the will of the juvenile. The young offender on the other hand does not need their legal representative's permission to either launch or withdraw an appeal.

Provisions concerning custody pending trial (pre-trial detention):
Depending on the crime, no juvenile can be detained for more than six months. However, although it seldom occurs, in very difficult and serious cases this time limit can be extended up to one year. In this case a written decision that gives the reasons in detail is necessary.

Once the trial has begun there is no longer any time limit. Juveniles are detained before trial in seperate sections of adult prisons. In Vienna, pre-trial detention facilities for young male offenders have been established within the building of the juvenile court.

Trusted adult:
A young offender who is detained by the police, or in custody of the court, has the right to have an adult s/he trusts present while being interrogated. The authorities have the duty to inform offenders of this right. That person may be a parent, a teacher, a social welfare official or a probation officer.

Trial in absentia:
Juvenile cannot be sentenced in their absence. They can be excluded from the court session temporarily if they disturb the proceedings (e.g., by unruly behavior), if the discussion of some special matter in their presence might exert a bad influence on them, or if a witness refuses to testify in their presence for fear of retribution.

Juvenile Court Assistance Service (Jugendgerichtshilfe):
A juvenile's personal situation, in particular the family background, has to be taken into consideration before the court makes a decision. For example, at the Vienna Juvenile Court, six psychologists, teachers and social workers employed by the Ministry of Justice act as the Juvenile Court Assistance Ser-

vice. They file a report on each juvenile defendant. This report is based upon interviews with the parents, the juvenile's teachers, doctors, and other relevant individuals. After discussing the opportunity with the suspect, they may recommend imposing certain instructions or orders on the juvenile. This helps to ensure that no decisions come as a surprise to the defendant in court. Here the Juvenile Court Assistance Service acts as a kind of clearing agency. Up to now, all attempts to establish Juvenile Court Assistance Services in other parts of the country have failed for reasons of cost.

Deviations from the Criminal Code

Minimum -maximum penalties:

In cases where the penalty for a crime committed by an adult is 10 to 20 years or life, the minimum penalty for a juvenile under the age of 16 who has committed the same crime is one year to 10 years. Over the age of 16 the minimum sentence is one year, the maximum 15 years (e.g., murder, robbery that causes the death of the victim).

In cases where the law states that the penalty for an adult ranges from 10 to 20 years, the minimum sentence for a juvenile is six months, the maximum 10 years (e.g., robbery, rape that causes the death of the victim).

In all other cases the maximum penalties provided by the law for any given crime must be cut in half (e.g., robbery carries a minimum penalty of one year and a maximum penalty of 10 years for adults, so for a juvenile the maximum penalty is five years and the minimum penalty six months). The minimum penalty is one day.

Suspended and partly suspended sentences:

The option to grant probation, whether alone or as part of a sentence, is not limited by the length of the penalty.

Exemption from punishment:

The Austrian law has chosen to set the level for the age of criminal responsibility at the age of 14. It is, however, a well-known fact that physical and mental development varies individually. This is why juveniles who for certain reasons are not mature enough to understand the harm they have done cannot be punished. Simiarly, a person under the age of 16 who has committed a minor offence and is not likely to re-offend will also not normally be punished.

The scale of sanctions for juveniles:

Juvenile delinquency is very often a passing phenomenon in the personal development of a young person. Often this phase will pass without any intervention by the state at all. Even though the state has to react to antisocial behavior, this reaction should be moderate. The ensuing disadvantages to the defendant must neither outnumber nor outweigh the advantages to society. Balance is needed in this area. If 'soft' intervention can achieve the same goal then it should obviously be given preference.

In addition to the traditional modes of punishment, the *Juvenile Justice Act* provides for a variety of measures at the lower end of the sanction scale, thus allowing the judge or public prosecutor to start off with "soft intervention" and progressively resort to more severe measures if the criminal activity persists—and very often it does not. Until recently there has been a general consensus that the imprisonment of a juvenile should be avoided as long as possible. It is a fact that prisons are not constructive environments for reforming juvenile delinquents.

Non-intervening diversion:

The public prosecutor is not allowed to bring a case against a juvenile suspected of only a minor offence (i.e., maximum penalty five years); however, sometimes informal penalties may be imposed if they are deemed necessary to prevent the juvenile from re-offending (see "Diversion," above).

If cautioning is considered necessary, the family court can be notified. This is one of the few cases where criminal and family court co-operate in the course of criminal proceedings against a juvenile. It must be kept in mind that this measure is not a formal sanction.

This non-intervening measure is not recorded in a registry but only in the family court file.

Intervening Diversion:

Further to the earlier discussion on intervening diversion, the public prosecutor has to take one of the diversion meassures described above when a juvenile is suspected of a petty offence, provided there are no special reasons to assume that it takes formal proceedings to prevent others from committing similar criminal acts (general crime prevention). The investigating judge and the trial judge can drop the case under the same preconditions, with the noticeable exception that the judge can do this in all cases of juvenile delinquency, no matter what the maximum penalty is.

Community service must not exceed 120 hours and the consent of the parents to the participation of the juvenile in an extrajudicial compensation process is not required.

In the Vienna Juvenile Court more than 80% of the caseload is settled by means of diversion. Since the introduction of diversionary measures the sentencing rate has dropped steadily from the early 1980s through to the mid-1990s.

Verdict of Guilty

Instead of imposing a small penalty, the judge can dispense with any penalty at all if it may be assumed that a verdict of guilty alone will suffice to prevent the defendant from re-offending. This verdict of guilty is registered as an official criminal record. This sanction has virtually become obsolete today. It is still interesting in the historical context, though, as it was this very provision that was used as a tool during the experimental period preceding the introduction of diversion into the *Juvenile Justice Act*.

Verdict of guilty—Penalty reserved:

The dictum containing the penalty can be reserved for a probation period of one to three years if it may be assumed that the verdict of guilty in combination with the pending dictum of a penalty will suffice to prevent the defendant from re-offending. If the juvenile re-offends during the probation period, or refuses to co-operate with the probation officer assigned to him, the case is re-opened and a penalty imposed.

Prison sentences and fines, either on probation or not on probation, or partly on probation, can be applied, with the deviations as given above. Meanwhile, the minimum sentence that has to be served before conditional release is possible is one month. General prevention is not an issue.

Deviations from the *Prison Act*

If the young offender is not deemed particulary dangerous, the execution of any custodial sentence can be postponed for an unlimited period to allow the youth to finish vocational training. If they successfully finish it without committing any more crimes the sentence can be commuted to probation. This provision has proved extremely useful and successful. Courts make generous use of it.

Juvenile convicts should be imprisoned in separate correctional facilities or at least in special sections, separated from the adult convicts. Austria has only one separate prison for male juvenile convicts; it is located in Gerasdorf, in the province of Lower Austria. There all sentences exceeding six months are served. Under certain conditions this prison also takes older convicts up to the age of 22. Once a convict has started to serve his or her term s/he can stay there until over the age of 22.[5]

There is no separate jail for delinquent girls serving long prison terms since there are very few of them. They are held in a special section of the central correctional facility for women in Schwarzau, Lower Austria. In 2000 there were about ten females in such facilities. Short prison terms (not exceeding six months) are served in the local jails.

Issues Confronting Young Offenders Today
Migration:

In recent years, massive immigration of foreigners (especially young people from the former Yugoslavia) and the obvious increase in crime caused by these foreigners has had a negative influence on the native Austrian population's sense of security. In fact, foreigners are responsible for committing approximately 30% of all reported offences. The reason is obvious: many people of the neighboring Eastern countries would like to profit from the supposed wealth of the West. As a consequence, there is a lot of legal and illegal immigration into Austria. This, however, creates a feeling of fear among the Austrian population, caused by the differences in the immigrants' social behavior and the resulting consequences in living, working, health, school, and social matters. As a result, various forms of radicalism are often encountered (Edelbacher, et al., 1996).

The Fear of Crime, Youth Delinquency, Drugs and Organized Crime

Some experts suggest that an increase in delinquency is related to increased freedom, democracy and the availability of welfare services. These experts believe that the abuse of privileges goes hand-in-hand with times of social transformation, in which old structures have ceased to work and new ones have not been sufficiently developed. They are also of the opinion that welfare and abundance of material goods provoke more crime, in the same way as democracy and freedom offer more chances to satisfy individual needs— legally as well as illegally. These ideas correspond to the criteria defined by the theory of **anomie.** Essentially, the theory states that crime and delinquency is closely linked to social disorder, the lack of norms, poor performance of the law and divergences between social aims and available means.

Based on the evidence, it appears that people are more and more prepared to use violence. Teachers notice that the number of young people who are ready to use violence is on the increase. The use of violence is thus becoming a serious threat in Austria. Fortunately this threat is not of major concern among young people. One reason for this might be that the unemployment rate among juveniles is quite low in comparison to other countries.

Out of all punishable offences the share attributed to organized crime is estimated at 20% to 25%. It seems a given that this share is going to increase considerably over time. Illegal human trafficking, drug trafficking, car trafficking, arms trafficking, the extortion of protection rackets, fraudulent manipulation of trade and taxes as well as international fraud, computer criminality and the illegal transfer of technology are the most "popular" offences of organized criminality. Alongside the crimes mentioned above, organized gangs of burglars as well as pickpockets and confidence tricksters have already been working in Vienna for decades. The so-called Russian Mafia frightens Austrians tremendously, especially as five big gangs have already established their subsidiaries in Vienna.

At present, Vienna and Austria are mainly seen as "recreation areas" and the main activities are centered around financial investment and money laundering. As a consequence, Austria decided to take legal measures against money laundering in 1994. While a serious concern, it does not appear to involve many young persons, but the opportunity for exploitation is quite apparent.

The Changes of Moral Concepts within our Society

Austria was liberated in 1945 after it had been occupied by Nazi Germany between 1938 and 1945. In 1955 we succeeded in signing a treaty with the former occupying powers of France, Britain, the U.S.S.R. and the U.S.A. Since then Austria has become the tenth wealthiest country in the world and achieved high economic growth, which accordingly also places us among the best countries to live in Europe. What's more, the rate of unemployment is relatively low and the majority of Austrians are materialistically well off (Edelbacher et al., 1996).

When referring to the topic "Society and Criminality," Mag. Michael Sika, the general director of public security matters, characterized the development of the change in values by calling his speech "We All Are Sinking into Moral Squalor." He feels that Austrian citizens are unwilling to live in accordance with the rules of society. People tend to give only token acknowledgement to the rules. In fact, he considers "ruthlessness" to be a central theme in today's society. The solution, according to Sika, lies in the family and schooling. But since the support structure is weak, it should come as no surprise that schools do not have the resources to deal with the issues alone.

As in many other Western countries, every third marriage ends in divorce in Austria (in Vienna every second). Stress and selfishness are ruining the Austrian family fabric and predispose children to delinquent tendencies. In times of increasing demands, the question arises of how a democratic society responds to the challenges of the population explosion, ecological damage, the running out of natural resources, the increase of "needs" due to the consumerist attitude of the society and increase of criminality that thus results. As a consequence, the change of values within our society also offers new challenges for the executive.

SUMMARY

The history of Austria's *Juvenile Justice Act* is a success story. Diversion, which the act introduced to Austria, has now found its place in the Criminal Code. Since 1 January 2000, diversion measures can also be applied to adult offenders. Sceptics who had predicted the breakdown of Austria's legal system if diversion should be introduced have been proved wrong. One can still walk the streets of Vienna comparatively safely. And while sharing characteristics of the modified justice model, the new act also embraces many elements of the welfare model. For example, the concept that the state should withdraw from conflicts that can be solved in a viable way by the persons involved has been readily accepted. This is not to say, of course, that the state should withdraw completely. The very delicate balance between public interest and the interests of the defendant should always be kept in mind. Yet it can be said that we have broken our long-standing tradition by moving from positive penal law to more informal and humane standards by which to address the problem of delinquency.

New challenges in store for Austria's judges:
At the time of preparing this chapter, the upper age limit of 19 was the object of a heated debate between conservative politicans on the one side and virtually all experts in the fields of juvenile law, youth psychology, and psychiatry on the other. Politicians argue that lowering the full age in civil law from 19 to 18 must accordingly entail the lowering of the upper age limit in juvenile penal law. Experts suggested that politicians should at least take the opportunity to introduce a provision allowing for the juvenile judge to decide whether s/he chooses to apply adult or juvenile law to young adults (i.e., offenders past the age of 18).

At first, politicians completely rejected this concept of "young adults" even though similar concepts exist in many other European countries. More recently a compromise has been reached that will change juvenile justice in Austria considerably. A draft containing new provisions in the field of juvenile justice is expected to pass parliament in the near future. According to this draft the provisions of the *Juvenile Justice Act* of 1988 as described above only apply to juveniles between the ages of 14 and 18. In the future, "young adults" (i.e., people between the ages of 18 and 21) will also come under the jurisdiction of the juvenile criminal courts. However, only some of the provisions of the *Juvenile Justice Act* will apply, and it is not yet known which provisions these will be. The act is supposed to come into force by July 1, 2001. Evaluation will have to wait till all the provisions are known. The stormy discussion preceding this recent development showed a certain tendency to turn away from principles that have guided juvenile law during the last decade. "Law and order" has lately become a very popular phrase in political speeches.

Finally, another controversial issue is the recent discussion about the correction system. The Ministry of Justice has decided to take a major part of the money the minister of finance wants saved under the national austerity program out of the correctional system. Since most of the costs in this field are fixed, staff must be reduced. As a consequence, vocational training facilities in prisons have to be closed. Recreational activities are reduced as well as the number of jobs for psychologists and social workers.

Since prisoners do not have a lobby, this new development needs to be closely and critically observed by all practitioners in the field. Following these developments in the field of juvenile justice, the next years will certainly be a most interesting and exciting experience.

Claudia Fenz obtained her doctorate of law from the University of Vienna in 1980. In 1984 she was appointed as a judge at a district court in Vienna and then in 1985 was appointed judge in juvenile court. In 1991 she was elected president of the Juvenile Justice Association of Austria and has held the position since then. In addition to her judgeship duties, Dr. Fenz has lectured and consulted extensively on juvenile justice and legal topics as they relate to Austria.

Maximillian Edelbacher obtained his law degree at the University of Vienna in 1968. In 1972 he became the legal expert for the Federal Police in Vienna. While working for the police's Major Crime Bureau, he developed an expertise in dealing with burglary, fraud, forgery, and prostitution offences. Between 1986-1988 he served as head of homicide. In addition, he teaches at several local academic and professional institutions. Since 1998, he has been the vice-president of the International Police Executive Symposiums and editor for the International Journal Police Practice. From 2001 till 2003 he is President of the International Chapter of the ACJS. He has also served as a consultant on police issues for the Council of Europe, the United Nations and several eastern European countries, and his list of publications has addressed such topics as insurance fraud, organized crime in Europe, and police-related issues.

HELPFUL WEBSITES

www.imnrw.de/jk/jk0.htm Jugendkriminalität in NRW (youth crime in NRW)
home.germany.net/101-267900/K_Diplomarbeit.htm Jugendkriminalität (youth-crime-related information)
www.derjugendrichter.de/forum/messages/3.htmlJugendkriminalität (youth-crime-related information)

www.cdu.de/politik-a-z/recht/kap55.htm Jugendkriminalität (youth-crime-related
   information)
www.ph-weingarten.de/Homepage Kinder- und Jugendkriminalität (crime of children
   and juveniles)
www.nrw.jugendschutz.de/publikat/gewalt.htm AJS Jugendkriminalität (AJS youth
   crime)

KEY TERMS AND CONCEPTS

Special Unit	modified justice model
Franz Klein	principle of legality
non-intervening diversion	intervening diversion
extra-judicial compensation	Criminal Advisory Service
welfare model	xenophobia
court-ordered payment	compensating
community services	anomie

STUDY QUESTIONS

1. How does the new *Juvenile Justice Act* compare with your country's legislation for
   young offenders and how does Austria's act comply with the international standards
   and guidelines?
2. How would you describe and characterize the procedural guidelines for handling
   and processing juveniles in Austria?
3. Austria has initiated a number of changes that reflect a shift in the model of justice.
   What model does Austria appear to be embracing? Comment on your impressions
   of the merits of these changes.
4. How do the juvenile issues confronting Austria compare to those in other countries?

NOTES

1 In 1962 the education system was completely reorganized in a comprehensive
   education law. Compulsory education was extended from eight to nine years and
   teacher training at pedagogic academies was reformed. Since 1993, handicapped
   primary school pupils can be integrated into regular primary school classes; since
   1997 also into secondary school classes.
2 A set of rules distributing the workload among all the judges of a certain court,
   fixed by a body of judges of the court every January for one year.
3 Capital punishment has been abolished.
4 These options are not open to the court in the case of petty offence.
5 The number of inmates in Gerasdorf, who come from all parts of the country, has
   been about 100 for the last few years.

REFERENCES

Austria facts and figures. (2000). Vienna: The Federal Press Service.
Bundesministerium für Inneres: Kriminalstatistik der jahre 1975, 1990—1999, Federal
   Ministry of the Interior: Police criminal statistics of the years 1975, 1990—1999.
   Vienna.
Edelbacher, M., et al. (1996, Nov/Dec.). Unpublished paper presented at the European
   chapter at the Yokohama conference. Yokohama, Japan.

Jedelsky, P. (1999, May). Kriminalpolizeiliches Vorbeugungsprogramm der Wiener Polizei, September 1995 und Mai 1999—Criminal Advisory Center Program, Vienna.

Jesionek, U. (2000). President of the juvenile court, Professor at the University of Linz, Upper Austria. Excerpt from a lecture at the Vienna Institute of Criminology.

Security Police Act (Sicherheitspolizeigesetz). (1993, May 1). Vienna.

Chapter 2

Juvenile Justice in Belgium

Lode Walgrave
Faculty of Law, Catholic University, Leuven

FACTS ON BELGIUM

Area: Belgium is a small country with an area of 30,514 sq. km., located in between the Netherlands, Germany and France. Its capital city, Brussels, also hosts the European Commission and the European Parliament, and can therefore also be considered as the capital city of Europe. **Population**: With about ten million inhabitants, Belgium is very densely populated. Of this total, 53% live in Flanders (the Dutch-speaking part of Belgium), 30% in Wallonia (the French-speaking part) and 17% in Brussels (the bilingual capital region). About 10% of the population are not Belgians; of these, about 60% are citizens of other E.U. countries. The most important non-European population is concentrated in the big cities, and consists of Moroccans (about 130,000) and Turks (about 75,000). Belgium has high welfare and education standards. Three quarters of the Belgian population consider themselves to be Catholic. **Youth in Belgium**: About 2,300,000 (or 23%) inhabitants of Belgium are younger than 18. This is not only the age of majority, but also the end of compulsory school attendance. About half of the population continues to study after the age of 18. **Climate**: You better take your umbrella wherever you go. **Economy**: Belgium is a highly industrialized country. Flanders, located in the north of the country, is one of the richest regions in Europe. Compared to five years ago, the unemployment rate is relatively low now (11.2% in July 2000). The rate is much higher in Wallonia (16.9%) than in Flanders (9.2%). **Politics and Government**: Though three major lines divide political life in Belgium (labour/capital; Catholic/non-Catholic; Flemish/French-speaking), the so-called "common sense" and Belgian skill at compromise-making, have resulted in a complicated politico-administrative system. Belgium is divided into three "regions" (Flanders, Brussels, and Wallonia) with autonomous jurisdiction, especially with regard to economics and labor, and into three 'communities' (Flanders, including the Dutch-speaking population in Brussels; the French community in Belgium, including the French-speaking population in Brussels; a smaller German community), whose jurisdiction mainly includes welfare, education and culture.

Juveniles are responsible actors; sanctions for juvenile offenders must be constructive for the victim; they must be guaranteed all legal safeguards; and a strict distinction must be drawn between offering support and using formal interventions. – Key principles; referred to as a "constructive sanctioning system for youth"; extracted from the November 1994 *Youth Protection Act.*[1]

A BRIEF HISTORICAL REVIEW[2]

From the end of the nineteenth century, the history of the Belgian juvenile justice system runs very parallel to the histories of the systems in the other Western European countries. It resulted nevertheless in a system that may be considered as the most deliberately welfare-oriented of all.

From Philanthropy to Legal Protection of Children

When Belgium became independent in 1830, the country was mainly populated with poor farmers and a middle class in the smaller towns. Only in the larger industrial centers, such as Ghent or Liège, and around the international harbor of Antwerp, could one find a beginning of proletarianism, but here lived also the upper-middle class which controlled and expanded the capitalistic economic system. There were few complaints of crime. In 1843-1844, for example, the police of Brussels reported three nocturnal burglaries and 300 petty thefts. The new Belgian state adopted the French penal law system, which made it possible to apply security measures (instead of penalties) to juveniles younger than 16 years old if *discernement* was considered to be missing.

Soon after its independence, however, Belgium had to reckon with serious economic problems (especially through the decline of the textile industry) and an agricultural crisis, followed by typhus and cholera epidemics which severely touched the rural areas between 1845 and 1849. As a result there was an increase in the number of vagrant groups, who begged and stole, among which were many children. It caused unrest in the middle classes. Begging and crime were tackled and treated more severely. More and more people were confined to *dépôts de mendicité*, workhouses or prisons. The roaming and begging children began to be treated seperately. From 1844 onwards, special penitentiaries and other closed facilities were created for children, which provided training in agriculture or sailing for the merchant navy.

Around the 1860s came a turning point. The economy had passed the worst of the crisis and it started to expand. The industrial revolution gave rise to two separate worlds, the *belle époque* of the bourgeoisie, and the miserable living conditions of the proletariat in urban areas. The latter were a fruitful soil for the rise of socialism.

Concern for the poor, and in particular for their children, grew among the ruling classes. It had three bases: a religious one, a philanthropic one, and a concern for keeping "the masses" under control by making them dependent on charity.

The philanthropic movement created three main fields of institutionalization. First, child labor laws of 1889, 1892 and 1914 gradually regulated the presence of children in the economic labor market, finally prohibiting child labor till the age of 14. Second, an offer of increased basic schooling was made by the Catholic Church and by other philanthropists, which resulted in the law of 1914 on compulsory education. School attendance became mandatory up to the age of 14. Third, philanthropists gradually grew concerned about morally abandoned children and children in the justice system. From the 1880s on, several committees and commissions were founded. In 1889 the minister of justice introduced a bill on child protection, which however was not passed. In an increasing number of judicial districts, judges and lawyers established, often together with (mostly female) philanthropists, "committees for the defence of children in the justice system." At the beginning of the twentieth century, time seemed to be ripe for an official regulation of the treatment of children by the justice system. The establishment of the first youth court in Chicago (1899) was echoed in Belgium, as an experiment with such a children's court was conducted in Leuven from 1908 onwards.

Finally, the Belgian *Children's Protection Act* was passed on 15 May 1912. It was the outcome of a judicial and philanthropic movement that had long pleaded for the exclusion of children from the procedures of common penal law. At about the same time neighboring countries passed comparable laws, subjecting children to special (penal) procedures. However, of all countries, Belgium had the strongest educative tendency. A specialised children's judge would handle all cases of delinquency, misconduct, vagrancy and school absenteeism committed by minors under the age of 16. The children's judge could enforce only measures for the protection of minors, and had to take account of the "dangerous situations" in which the children lived. Punishment *senso strictu* was excluded.

The court was supported by *comités de patronage* (supervision committees), consisting mostly of middle class women, for writing social reports and for supervising and helping families at risk. Members of these committees were trained in schools for social work. These committees were organized by the Ministry of Justice, within the Department of Child Protection, from 1920 onwards.

Already in 1913, two residential clinical observation centers became operative in Mol and in St. Hubert, in order to inform the judges about the personality and social environment of the juveniles, and help to orient the implementation of the measures 'in the best interest of the child."

From the Protection of Children to the Protection of Youth

Quite soon, however, problems arose for the implementation of the law. "Restrictivists" complained about a growing interventionism on vague legal grounds, whereas "maximalists" were of the opinion that the *Children's Protection Act* was too restrictive and excluded preventive judicial intervention (Walgrave, 1993).

The latter tendency was much stronger. After the First World War, the Belgian socio-economic system became more and more a collective bargaining economy, providing social peace for employers, and increasingly decent standards of living and a system of social benefits for the workers. Belgium developed gradually into a welfare state. In such a climate, socio-clinical sciences flourished and supplied new arguments for further expansion of intervention with juveniles and "families at risk" (see Box 2.1).

Box 2.1: Defining delinquency in Belgium

"The field of juvenile delinquency is no longer reserved for penalists only, but now is subjected to control by pedagogues, medical doctors, psychologists and social workers also. Would not the statement *nulla poena, nullum crimen sine lege* lose its meaning in a system that obviously is not repressive, but educative and protective?"[3] (Aimée Racine, 1937. Aimée Racine was the director of the Research Centre on Juvenile Delinquency, funded directly and entirely by the Ministry of Justice).

Interventions with juveniles and their families increased. Between 1939 and 1959, the number of children referred to the justice system doubled to more than 31,000. However, the use of individualized treatment blurred the concept of delinquency. Delinquency was now an illness, requiring preventive care. After the Second World War, the need for reform was seriously tackled.

After several ministerial commissions and three bills, a new *Youth Protection Act* was finally passed on 8 April 1965. The exclusively protective option was further extended and additional organizations were founded in order to work in a more preventive manner. The law included two sections, a section on social protection and a section on judicial protection. The "committees for the protection of youth," founded in each ***arrondissement***,[4] offered voluntary aid and assistance to "endangered" minors (up to 21) and to their families. In principle, the committee could also be charged with the execution of youth court orders, but this practice was gradually applied less often. The youth court, also set up in each *arrondissement*, could:

1. deal with a number of civil measures (for example, adoption or permission to marry);
2. impose measures on parents who are judged to be neglecting their parental duties; and
3. impose measures on minors who were considered to be "endangered" (up to the age of 21), or who have committed delinquent acts (up to the age of 18).

This chapter only deals with the latter. Under the age of 18, no punishments are pronounced, nor are any other repressive sanctions administered. There are a few exceptions, though, and they will be expounded upon.

The youth court was given its own social services and the authority to refer to residential and ambulant psycho-medical centers for observation. Responsibility for executing these measures was assigned to the court's social services and to private institutions, most of which are part of the Catholic welfare "pillar." Moreover, minors could also be placed in state facilities for observation and re-education, with a more closed and disciplined character.

Criticism and Political Pressure to Change the System

Quite soon the solely rehabilitative character of the law was criticized. The implementation of an individualistic concept of prevention in the judicial context appeared to result, in fact, in a judicial control system that became uncontrollable itself: in juvenile court, elementary legal rights, such as legality, due process or proportionality were hardly safeguarded. Moreover, the children's rights movement complained that the purely protective viewpoint considered youngsters only as objects of education and did not acknowledge them sufficiently as active subjects. Finally, the instrumental effectiveness of the re-educative measures appeared to be highly questionable, if not nonexistent.

These discussions remained on a relatively academic level, until the political changes of the Belgian state gave them a more pragmatic turn. The state reform law of 1980 passed on the jurisdiction over youth protection to the Belgian communities, as it was considered a "personal matter" (i.e., relevant to education, welfare, or culture).[5] An exception was made for the matters of civil law, penal law, and judicial law.

The communities interpreted their new authorities in a maximalist way, but that was disputed by the central government. A long period of intense tug-of-war followed, complicated by a new law of August 1988 on the reform of the institutions (extending still more the jurisdiction of the communities), by the condemnation of the Belgian state by the European Court of Human Rights for specific procedures in the juvenile courts (the Bouamar judgement of February 29, 1988), and by the lowering of the age of majority from 21 to 18 (in 1990).

The Current Situation

In this section, I will briefly outline Belgium's approach to the prevention and management of juvenile delinquency in Belgium.

The "hard core" of the social response to juvenile delinquency remains in the control of a specialized court, nested within the judicial structure of the federal government. This is dictated by the "Belgian Law of February 2, 1994, on the Adaptation of the Law of 1965 on Youth Protection," which is still purely protection-oriented. But this law has been presented as being transitional, pending a more fundamental reform, which has still not been accomplished.

The three Belgian communities possess authority for prevention and assistance with regard to all behaviors and situations that can be considered detrimental to the positive development of children and juveniles. Each of the communities has developed its own system. The two larger communities administered their systems through the coordination of the Flemish Decrees on the Special Support for Youth, published 4 April 1990, and the Decree of the French Community on Youth Assistance of 4 March 1991. Even when no offence has been committed, these systems can make referrals to youth courts when youngsters and/or their families refuse voluntary cooperation, and assistance is considered to be indispensable in the interest of the child. On the other hand, these systems also tend to integrate with the broader network of voluntary welfare agencies for children, young people and their families.

Moreover, these systems also take initiatives of "general prevention" (i.e., actions that aim at structural and/or [sub-]collective levels), in order to prevent behavior and/or situations that could be detrimental to the positive development of youth.

Judicial Interventions against Juvenile Offenders[6]

The judicial response to juvenile delinquency is governed by the Law of 2 February 1994 on the adaptation of the *Youth Protection Act* of 8 April 1965 (YPA). This law maintains the basic principles of the YPA, but puts in some adaptations in order to bring Belgian legislation in line with international rules, especially concerning due process, and with the new decrees of the Belgian communities concerning youth assistance. Pending a more fundamental reform, the Belgian youth courts still deal with juvenile crime in a purely "protective" way, meaning that no punishments can be imposed, but only measures with a view to the rehabilitation of the young offender. Youth courts in fact are competent in the following matters:

1.   youthful offending;

2. civil matters regarding minority; for example, in adoption, execution of parental authority, making independent decisions, authorization to marry, etc.;
3. measures against parents, such as dispossession of parental authority or control over the use of family allowances; and
4. matters of coercive assistance, referred by the community agencies, because parents and/or the juveniles do not accept voluntary assistance, and assistance is nevertheless considered to be indispensable in the interest of the minor.

In this chapter we focus on the delinquency matters mentioned under point 1, though it is often difficult to distinguish them from the assistance matters mentioned under point 4. Indeed, because of the purely welfare orientation of the law, many of the procedural rules and several measures apply to both categories, and even the judicial procedures may cause confusion between the delinquency and the welfare matters.

The age of penal majority in Belgium is 18. Juveniles under the age of 18 do not appear before a criminal court, but before the youth court.

Basic judicial organisms are the public prosecutor (with a specialized youth division), the youth court (with a single specialized judge) and the youth chamber in the Court of Appeal. The youth court judge has disposition over a section of the social service, provided by the communities.

The Police and the Public Prosecutor

Belgium is in the process of a fundamental police reform. Until now, there were three main police structures, the judicial police, the state police (*Gendarmerie*) and the municipal police. The reform will fuse these structures into one single differentiated police force, in principle, from 1 January 2001 on. Whereas the three earlier police structures mostly had specialized youth brigades, one can expect that the new force will also provide specialized youth sections in one form or another.

As in most countries with a **legalistic judicial system**, Belgian legal procedure obliges the police to report every complaint concerning offences, misconduct or so-called "situations of danger" to the public prosecutor. In practice, however, this is not workable. The police never refer a great part of the reporting or even established facts to the public prosecutor because they regard this stage as informal. Quite often the police deliver warnings or mediate informally. With a few specific exceptions, no information about these practices exists, as in principle they are illegal. At the time being, a few local experiments are running to allow the police some margin of discretion, still under the supervision of the public prosecutor's office.

Every public prosecutor's office has a specialized youth division. All matters wherein youngsters are involved are handled there. In smaller *arrondissements*, the specialization is limited and the prosecutor of youths deals with other cases as well.

Matters of Intervention

The reason for the police to report to the public prosecutor (and for the prosecutor to seek a judgement from the juvenile court) is regulated in articles 36 and 91§11 of the YPA. Before the 1994 reform, it respectively dealt with: (1) complaints made by parents/tutors because of misconduct or intractability of the minor (art. 36.1); (2) minors whose health, safety or morality is endangered (art. 36.2); (3) vagrancy or runaways (art. 36.3); (4) minors prosecuted because of acts defined as offences (juvenile delinquency in the narrow sense of the word) (art. 36.4); (5) school absenteeism (art. 36.5); (6) moral protection of the youth (art. 95§11), concerning attendance of movies and discotheques. It should be noticed that the law specifies "acts defined as offences," and not "offences," to make clear that juveniles do not commit offences because they cannot be punished. They do commit acts that are defined as offences in penal law, which only applies to adults. For practical reasons, we shall later on nevertheless use the word "offence," even when we deal with "acts defined as offences" committed by juveniles.

When the amendments of February 1994 became effective, matters requiring intervention were reduced so that only those found in Art. 36. 4 (acts defined as offences) now come directly to the public prosecutor. All the other matters, considered as problems of welfare or as "protective" issues, only come to the prosecutor through the decrees of the communities (see next section). However, when the "physical or psychological integrity of the minor is severely threatened" and urgent measures are considered necessary, the judicial system may take immediate provisional measures. We shall come back to this in the next section.

Investigative Phase

When a minor has been referred for an act defined as an offence, the territoriality principle in the Belgian YPA attributes jurisdictional competency according to the place where the juvenile is living, not where s/he has committed the offence. Therefore, the public prosecutor will refer all juveniles who are living outside their *arrondissement* to the other territorially competent public prosecutor's office. Moreover, all traffic offences committed by juveniles of 16 years and older are dealt with by the normal adults' jurisdiction.

In all other cases, the public prosecutor can start the criminal investigation with regard to the facts. For the enquiry on the "personality and the social circumstances" of the offender, however, the public prosecutor refers to the youth court judge.

In an increasing number of *arrondissements*, the Public Prosecutor also refers certain dossiers to private services for trying a voluntary process of victim-offender mediation or restitution reflective of our **welfare** approach. The outcome can have an impact on the furtherance of the procedure.

During the investigative phase, the youth court can, on the request of the public prosecutor, take "provisional measures." The following provisional measures are possible:

1. The juvenile can be placed under supervision, while remaining in his/her original environment. The supervision order can be combined with certain conditions, such as attending school regularly, avoiding certain places at certain times, or taking specific courses or training programs. The implementation of the measure is done under the supervision of a consultant of the social service of the youth court (in the Flemish community) or of the *directeur de l'aide à la jeunesse* (in the French community of Belgium) (see next section);

2. The juvenile can be placed in a private family, in a foster home or in a private institution with an open regime authorized for the guardianship and education of children and youths from youth protection. The authorization is arranged by the communities (see next section);

3. The juvenile can be placed in a public facility for supervised observation and education. There are a few, managed by the communities. Because these facilities are more closed and impose a more disciplined regime, several conditions and modalities are added. First, it may only be imposed on juveniles who misbehave persistently, or display dangerous behavior, or when such placement is needed for the criminal investigation. Second, the maximum period is three months, but it can be extended once for another three months. Further extensions are possible, but then for a maximum of one month each. Third, the placement in a public facility can be combined with a strict prohibition on leaving the premises. Fourth, the court can, for a maximum of thirty days, also forbid free communication with a delimited list of persons indicated by name, except his lawyer; and

4. As a more exceptional measure, the juvenile can also provisionally be placed in a house of custody, but only when another facility cannot be found to carry out the provisional measures discussed in points 2 and 3 above, and for a maximum of 15 days, which cannot be extended nor repeated in the course of a procedure.[7] Moreover, this measure is ap-

plicable only to juveniles at least 14 years old who committed an act that is severely punishable under penal law.

It should be noticed that the youth court judge must hear juveniles 12 or older personally before any of these provisional measures can be imposed. Moreover, legal assistance is assured, since it is carried over from the investigative phase. A lawyer will be appointed officially if the juvenile himself did not appoint one. Appeal is possible against the provisional measures.

In principle, the investigation phase must be finished after six months. This also includes the social and personality enquiry, the results of which must be communicated by the youth court judge to the public prosecutor. The public prosecutor then has two months to decide whether to refer the case to youth court for trial, so as to ensure that definite steps are taken to intervene, or to dismiss without prosecution. The public prosecutor also can decide that the offending is to be considered primarily as a welfare problem and, using his/her discretion, refer the case to the agencies of the communities (see next section).

THE YOUTH COURT

The Formal Judicial System
The youth court is part of the court of first instance and can consist of one or more chambers. The size of the *arrondissement* determines the number of chambers. Brussels, for example, counts 14 chambers, while several small *arrondissements* have only one chamber. In every chamber one specialized youth court judge has his seat. The only access to the youth court is through the public prosecutor's office, except for possible revisions of measures already taken.

As mentioned earlier, the judge plays an important role in the investigative phase: he can have a social and personality investigation done (by the social service at the youth court and/or by a private agency), and he can order provisional measures. In the 1965 YPA, the duration of the provisional measures was not set. In practice, they were often extended over long periods, and used in fact as real educative measures. The later formal judgement then implied termination of the 'provisional' measure. Whereas the 1965 act only provided legal assistance in the definitive court trial, many measures against juvenile delinquents were in fact imposed without any due process safeguards. The amendments of 2 February 1994 corrected this anomaly, by setting a time limit to the investigative phase and by providing legal assistance beginning at this phase.

The minor and his parents appear personally before the youth court for the final judgement. A lawyer should always represent minors. The complete file (data about the minor, environment and facts) can be consulted by the parents and the lawyer (not by the minor). The legal arguments are public. As this is not always thought advisable, tricks are used to get around this rule (e.g., by leaving the door of the courtroom open, but not allowing anyone in).

Possible Measures Taken by Youth Court

According to the *Youth Protection Act*, all measures taken by the youth court with regard to the minor are "measures of care, protection and education," and their size and content have no relation to the fact or the behavior that brought the minor before the court. In principle, only the needs of the minor, defined on basis of his/her personality and social environment, determine the nature of the measure. This is in theory, of course. In practice a connection exists between the seriousness of the case and the measure imposed. Most judges do not deny that repressive intentions can play a role in their sentencing.

Except for the unofficial warnings that are usually accompanied by formally registration of the offence without prosecution, the youth court can take the following definitive measures by judgement:

1. A reprimand, which is officially registered in the criminal record;
2. A supervision order, putting the minor under supervision of the court, leaving the minor in his original environment. It is carried out in the same circumstances as in the provisional supervision order, and here also, conditions can be added. One of the conditions used increasingly is community service. Especially in the French community of Belgium, specialized private services for the monitoring of community services have been funded, which provoked a steep increase in its use. Due to the increasing confidence of many youth court judges, community service is now applied more and more to severe offenders also, as alternatives to residential measures (Walgrave and Geudens, 1996);
3. Residential placement in a foster home, or in a private institution authorized for the protection and education of children and juveniles. These are the same homes and institutions as those which are open for the provisional placements. The placement cannot exceed the duration of one year, but it may be extended annually till the age of majority; and
4. Placement in the public facility for supervised observation and education, as mentioned already under the provisional measures. The conditions for placing juveniles by judgement differ from the conditions for

placement as a provisional measure. First, only juveniles of more than 12 years can be admitted by judgement, except for "very exceptional cases." Second, the judgement must specify whether the placement intended is in an open or closed section of the facility. Third, the judgement must also specify the maximum duration of this placement, which, as in point 3, cannot exceed the duration of one year. However, a new judgement may repeat the decision till the age of majority.

In principle, all measures imposed by the youth court end at the age of majority, 18 years old. However, this would make educative measures pointless for juveniles who commit an offence shortly before their eighteenth birthday. Therefore, the duration of the measure can be extended till the age of 20, provided that the youth court renders a judgement to this effect specifying the exact duration of an extension before the youth turns 18.

As a special measure, the youth court can give up its authority over an offending minor, and refer the youth to the public prosecutor, to be tried by a penal court of common law. This referral may already have been requested by the public prosecutor and decided by the youth court pending the criminal investigation. The court can decide upon such a referral when it considers the existing measures of youth protection to be inadequate, under the conditions that a) the minor is at least 16 years old, and b) that a medico-psychological examination has been carried out, or the minor obviously refuses to undergo such examination, or the juvenile re-offends by some type of very serious offence.

Once a juvenile has been referred to the common law procedures, they remain under the competency of the adults' jurisdiction for possible subsequent offences.

After the judgement the youth court will supervise the implementation of the measures directly, or via his/her social service.

The public prosecutor and the parties involved can appeal against the judgement at the youth chamber of the Court of Appeal.

Revision (amendment) of the judgement is always possible on the initiative of one of the involved parties.

Conclusions

As balanced as the Belgian juvenile justice system might appear to be, it has been criticized for its welfare orientation as well as for being hypocritical and unworkable. The system in fact leads not to a justice without punishments, but to punishments without guaranteed justice. Also the efficacy of the YPA has never been demonstrated (see Box 2.2).

> **Box 2.2: YPA**
>
> "The YPA of April 8, 1965, introduced a protection model without distinction in treatment between the endangered child and the offending child. Such a system leads to the exercise of discretionary power by the judicial authorities who submit the legal safeguards of the children to the interests of therapeutic treatment. Such a system does not take into account the need of juveniles to be acknowledged as actors in community life..." (National Commission for the Reform of the YPA, Final Report, 1995. This commission was set up by the minister of justice, and was composed of youth court judges and public prosecutors, chaired by an attorney general of the Court of Appeal.)

Partly due to the pressure of the reform of the Belgian state into a federal system, a complete renewal of the judicial response to juvenile delinquents is under way. In the meantime, more superficial modifications have been made to the Law of 2 February 1994, while the communities have already defined their role of assistance and prevention.

SPECIAL ASSISTANCE TO YOUTH AND PREVENTION

As mentioned before, the Belgian communities were granted jurisdiction over the so-called "social youth protection" by the reform of the Belgian state in 1980 and 1988.

The communities have embraced modern ideas on prevention, and give more attention to the broader social welfare and the socio-economic and cultural backgrounds of those marginalized, as well as of those who are involved in delinquency. Prevention is given a broader interpretation, ranging from relatively focused measures concerning specific groups and for high-risk situations, to more general measures for promoting the juvenile's welfare and integration into society. Though the three communities have elaborated their own decrees, the basic concepts and the institutional elaboration are in fact very much the same. Both the French and the Flemish communities of Belgium begin with a concept of emancipating work, aiming at autonomy and sense of responsibility; stress family-oriented work; consider special support for youth to be subsidiary to the general welfare work, among other related areas. In essence, they focus very much on socially-based prevention strategies.

Though the decrees ultimately created different institutional organizations, it appears superfluous to describe at length the systems of the three communities separately. This is especially true because they in fact deal only marginally with the treatment of juvenile delinquency. In this section, we shall therefore describe only the decree of the Flemish community, in so far as it is important to understand the social reaction to juvenile crime in Belgium.

The legal framework of the **Special Youth Support** (SYS) in Flanders consists of three decrees[8] that are brought together in the Order of the Flemish Executive of April 4, 1990, co-ordinating the decrees on special youth support.

The SYS is composed of several basic agencies:

1. In each administrative *arrondissement* a "committee for special youth care" is founded, composed of volunteers. Each committee is divided in a "bureau for special youth care" and a "prevention cell." The bureau has three tasks:

    *   To organize care and assistance in what are called "problematic educative situations." The bureau co-operates closely with the differentiated net of general welfare services. The intervention is voluntary. It does not depend on only the parents' approval, but also on the consent of the minors themselves, if they are 14 years old and more.

    *   To guarantee that assistance will be offered to (though not imposed on) children and families who have been referred by the judicial system. This is to motivate public prosecutors and youth court judges to refer their cases to the system of SYS and to try to avoid the judicial circuit as much as possible.

    *   To try to set up voluntary assistance in problematic educative situations, wherein the youth court has already taken urgent measures of placement. The court may, at the request of the public prosecutor, take an urgent provisional measure of residential placement when the "physical or psychological integrity of the minor is severely threatened" and urgent measures are considered necessary. However, such provisional measures may not exceed a period of 45 days. If the placement does not succeed, the court will start a procedure for the commission for mediation (see (3) below).

2. The fieldwork of both the bureau and the cell is carried out by the social service for the SYS. The Flemish decree establishes this service per *arrondissement*, and it is divided into two sections, of which one is put at the disposal of the youth court, and the other works for the committee for special youth care. It consists of a team of professional consultants who may have a degree in social work, criminology, or the like.

    The clients of the committee (parents, minors themselves, or others) in fact have contact only with the professional consultants. The consultants try to help by means of advice, referrals, or by means of a concrete offer of assistance, taking into account the diversity of the available facilities. The official members of the bureau in fact only act as relatively distant supervisors and for decisions with financial consequences.

3. The commission for mediation exists in every judicial *arrondissement* and consists of six voluntary members, chosen from experienced welfare workers and lawyers with experience in youth cases. The commission for mediation serves as a last chance for reconciliation concerning the voluntary assistance, when the parties disagree about the proposals for settlement concerning a problematic educative situation.

   The commission for mediation tries to reach a consensus between the conflicting parties. When a voluntary agreement cannot be reached, the commission decides either to simply stop the case or to refer it to the public prosecutor in view of a request to the youth court for a judicially enforced educational measure.

   The Flemish decree then enlists 13 possible measures that may be imposed by the youth court. Several of them coincide with the possible measures imposed on young offenders, even including placement in a closed facility, as described in the former section.

4. The communities acknowledge and subsidize private facilities, and also coordinate public institutions for the SYS. They receive the children and juveniles referred by the youth court and by the committee for special youth care. The minors can be placed there under the protocol for "offending juveniles," as described in the former section, or as minors in "problematic educative situations" as defined by the Flemish decree as well. Minors known as juvenile offenders are thus mixed in the same institutions with children and juveniles in need of welfare assistance. It illustrates again the pure welfare character of the judicial response to juvenile offending.

Figure 2.1 displays the most important trajectories that individual cases can run through in Flanders, and shows how the judicial system and the special support system are linked to each other. In order to preserve clarity, only the most important lines are drawn and the detailed enumeration of the possible measures is left out. More details, nuances and exceptions are described in the text.

TRENDS AND PATTERNS OF JUVENILE DELINQUENCY IN BELGIUM

Data on juvenile delinquency mostly come from two sources: police and judicial registration, and self-reports.

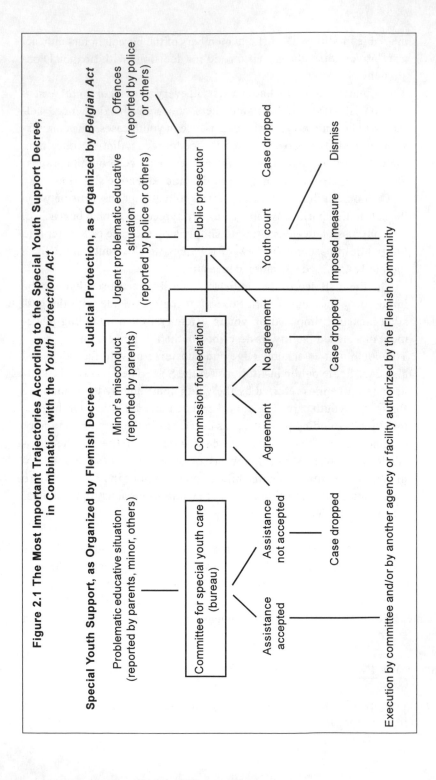

Figure 2.1 The Most Important Trajectories According to the Special Youth Support Decree, in Combination with the *Youth Protection Act*

Registered Delinquency

Gathering good statistics on documented juvenile crime in Belgium is a very frustrating undertaking. Even before 1989, the quality of the statistics was poor, because of irregular provision of basic data by the court administrators, the sloppy way these data were reported, and unclear and overlapping statistical categories, among other factors. After the partial "communitarization" of the Belgian youth protection system in 1988, the central office for statistics did not gather the data anymore, and it was expected that the communities would do the job. The Flemish community collected the figures for the Flemish *arrondissements*, but the French community of Belgium did not. In 1993, the Flemish community stopped collecting, because the Ministry of Justice was to establish a new central office for statistics. At the time of writing, this office is still not really functional. In the meantime the National Institute for Criminalistics and Criminology has been working on the topic. They too, however, are confronted with the lack of interest on the part of the basic data providers, and with insurmountable biases in the available figures. In a recent internal notice, the Institute provides some general reflections, and what we could call a pilot study on the *arrondissement* of Brussels, based on its own detailed exploration of the basic data and on some extrapolations to fill in missing data (Vanneste et al., 1999).

As Belgium has a strictly legalistic system, the police are not given discretionary power for handling juvenile crime, but are obliged to send all reports on crime to the public prosecutors' office. Theoretically, statistics on the cases referred to the public prosecutor will cover all documented crime.

Table 2.1 displays the numbers of juveniles reported to the public prosecutor in the 1980s, when the figures were still collected for the whole of Belgium.

At first glance, there seems to be an important increase from 1980 to 1981, but this is due to the lack of data for 1980 on several *arrondissements* that normally report high numbers of juveniles. Also, the seeming decrease of 1988 must be attributed to the missing of data on several important *arrondissements*. We must, therefore, exclude these years from our analysis. In the other years, only one, or only smaller, *arrondissements* did not deliver the figures, so that what's missing would not change the available data very much. Only the years 1981 and 1983 are complete. This demonstrates the serious difficulties in working with Belgian statistics on youth crime. From 1981 till 1987 only large and systematic shifts in the data might indicate some real changes on the field. Moreover, these numbers not only include referrals for offences, but also referrals for other kinds of misconduct, status delinquency and "children in

Table 2.1: Minors Reported to the Public Prosecutor: 1980-1988			
Year	N reported to public prosecutor	% of Belgian minors reported to public prosecutor	% of Belgian minors reported for offences
1980	85,581	3.4	2.2
1981	103,212	4.2	2.7
1982	106,359	4.4	2.9
1983	104,396	4.4	2.9
1984	97,575	4.2	2.8
1985	92,775	4.1	2.9
1986	99,711	4.4	2.9
1987	100,359	4.5	3.0
1988	69,924	3.1	2.2

Source: National Statistics Institute.

danger" (remember the purely rehabilitation-oriented character of the Belgian system).

The second column relates the number of referred minors to the total number of minors in Belgium. These figures can be considered as an index of "interventionism" by the police towards those aged less than 18, and provide a basis for possible comparison with other countries. All in all, the fluctuations between 4.2 and 4.5 do not indicate clear-cut tendencies from 1981 until 1987. There could be some fluctuations, but no systematic increase or decrease.

The third column is about the referrals for delinquent acts *sensu stricto*, related again to the total number of minors in Belgium. Here, a slightly increasing tendency seems to appear, from 2.7 in 1981 until 3.0 in 1987. Deeper statistical analysis leads to the assumption that this tendency is not due to a growing amount of delinquent behavior, but to a change in the qualification policy by the public prosecutor. As indicated earlier, the *Youth Protection Act* of 1965 allowed the public prosecutor to interpret an offence as an indication of an "endangered situation," and to qualify it as such. A comparison of the development in numbers of "children in danger" with those of referrals for offences shows that they are reciprocal to each other. When the numbers of offences increase, those of endangered situations decrease, and vice versa (Walgrave et al., 1998). It seems, therefore, to be more the qualification policy that has changed, and not the amount of offending behavior.

Figure 2.2 repeats some of the same data, but they are now limited to the Flemish *arrondissements*, for which we can continue the exploration till 1992.

In absolute numbers, the number of referrals evolves from 52,358 in 1982 to 36,189 in 1991. In relation to the total population of minors, this is a decrease

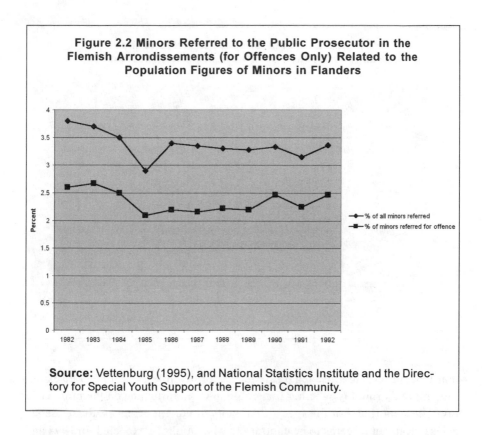

Figure 2.2 Minors Referred to the Public Prosecutor in the Flemish Arrondissements (for Offences Only) Related to the Population Figures of Minors in Flanders

Source: Vettenburg (1995), and National Statistics Institute and the Directory for Special Youth Support of the Flemish Community.

from 3.7% in 1982 to 2.9% in 1991. With regard to offences *sensu stricto*, there is a decrease from 2.6% of the total population of minors in Flanders to 2.2%. With the exception of 1985, when the data on Antwerp are missing, the data are now relatively complete, and the least we can conclude is that the eighties and the beginning of the nineties did not show an increase in juvenile delinquency.

Finally, there are also some partial data on Brussels (Vanneste et al., 1999). These statistics are not representative for the whole of Belgium. Not only is Brussels the biggest and the most urbanized *arrondissement*, it is also the area with the most heterogeneous population, including the highest proportion of immigrant families, and with the highest mobility.

Figure 2.3 displays the development in numbers of offences committed by minors referred to the public prosecutors' office, and the development of referred "offences against persons" (in general, violence).

The tendencies are much clearer now. After a steady increase in the total number of offences reported, a sharp decrease has occurred since 1994. It is difficult to explain this. Of course, the *Youth Protection Act* was changed in

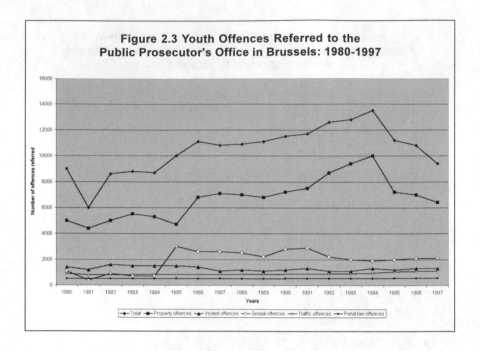

Figure 2.3 Youth Offences Referred to the
Public Prosecutor's Office in Brussels: 1980-1997

that year, providing more legal safeguards for juveniles, but it must be examined more thoroughly whether that could have an influence on the number of juveniles reported. For the specific category of violent offences, the tendency is less clear, but it seems to be contrary to what might be expected. In 1994 and 1995, there was an increase, followed by a stabilization on that higher level. But the changes are not big enough to exclude the possibility that the augmentation reflects changes in qualification strategies rather than in real violent behavior.

Self-Report

In recent years, several self-report studies have been undertaken on offences committed by segments of Belgian youth (Born and Gravey, 1994; Vettenburg, 1998; Vercaigne et al., 2000; Goedseels, 2000). Due to differences in questionnaires and in samples, comparisons are very difficult. The largest and most representative study has been undertaken by Goedseels as part of a larger project on youth in Flanders.

In 1998, a research team questioned a representative sample of 4,829 students of secondary schools (age 12 to 17 years old, and a few older students who committed more than one type of offence) on a broad spectrum of issues, including their self-reported delinquency. Table 2.2 displays the results.

**Table 2.2: Self-reported Delinquency by
Secondary School Students in Flanders (in % of sample)**

	Boys	Girls	Total
Dodge fare	28.5	22.6	25.5
Theft	29.1	18.1	23.4
Vandalism	31.9	9.8	20.6
Drug use	21.5	13.5	17.4
Physical violence	19.6	5.8	12.7
Carrying a weapon	22.2	3.4	12.6
Running away from home	6.8	6.3	6.5
Selling of drugs	8.5	3.0	5.7

N=2,375 N=2,435 N=4,829

As the questions asked are selected (and slightly adapted) from an international study on self-reported delinquency (see Junger-Tas, 1994), some comparisons are possible. These comparisons must be made very carefully, because of the modifications to questions and differences in samples. It seems nevertheless that Flemish juveniles are, all in all, not all that different from Dutch, English, Welsh, Portuguese, Swiss or Spanish young offenders. In that study, property offences varied between 16% and 33.5%, vandalism between 12.6% and 17% (England and Wales 3.5% only), carrying a weapon between 8.4% and 15.4%. In the same study, separate city samples show variance between 7% and 19.9% in drug use.

The prevalence rate was 52.2%. More than half of the Flemish sample thus reported having committed at least one of the questioned offences in the last year. These 52.2% admitted an average of 2.3 offences in the last year. In the international study, the prevalence rate varied between 44% and 72.2%.

The age distribution shows a systematic raise until the age of 16, followed by a slight decrease. This tendency is confirmed in the international study.

Conclusion

With regard to statistical data on youth crime, Belgium is really a problem country. Based on the very few available data, clear-cut developments are not visible. In that regard, Belgium seems not to be atypical of the other European countries (Junger-Tas, 1996; Estrada, 1999). But the question remains whether it is in any way possible to gather good and reliable data on the amount of juvenile offending, and to construct meaningful comparisons among countries and over time. The literature does mention several mechanisms that may influence the fluctuations in registrations. They include such influences as changes in public concerns (focused policies against drugs, for instance). Changes in legal dispositions, new facilities, or new types of sanctions may have an impact on documentation. They all demonstrate how relative the figures are and how difficult they are to interpret.

Nevertheless, the general picture of stability is in fact surprising. Recent decades have witnessed deep social changes from which one should expect effects on juvenile delinquency and its documentation. All over Europe, living conditions and prospects for young people are changing, including urbanization, immigration and unemployment; time and again, decline in family life is mentioned as affecting the quality of socialization; the school system is said to fall short in its educative task. There are also far-reaching institutional changes. Youth culture is "mediatized" and commercialized; public talks and complaints about juvenile misconduct are ongoing; situational criminologists point to the increase in opportunities to commit crimes, partly due to the increasing availability of attractive objects to be stolen or vandalized, and to the decreasing informal social control. We do not see eye-catching results of all that in the crime statistics. How can that be explained?

Several hypotheses may be advanced. Maybe the so-called "deep social changes" are partly a myth, or their influence on juveniles and their (delinquent) behavior has been gravely exaggerated. Maybe the stability in the records does not reflect a real increase in offending on the streets. Indeed, in contrast to the above-mentioned reasons why statistics could be overestimating the real increase, we can also advance arguments in the opposite direction: some factors or dynamics may contribute to an underestimation of the changes through official statistics. The control system may be so burdened that it has reached its maximum of processing capacities, becoming incapable of registering and handling the increase in real crime. The police may handle more cases unofficially, influenced by "diversionary" motives, or by some kind of "norm erosion." The public could lodge fewer complaints with the police, either because it has become more tolerant, or because it has lost its belief in the adequacy of police interventions.

We must therefore conclude that we cannot measure the amount of juvenile delinquency nor its increase or decrease with certitude (van Kerckvoorde, 1995). The officially recorded data on juvenile crime are not good indicators of the rise or fall of juvenile offending. They just give impressions, which should be very critically read and used. It is only when systematic and very obvious shifts are documented that we could possibly conclude that something really had happened in the criminality level. This is certainly not the case in relation to the European figures on juvenile crime in general.

DISCUSSION

Youth Crime as a Hot Issue and a Pressure for More Repression

For the time being, juvenile crime is a hot issue. Especially in the bigger cities like Brussels, Antwerp, Liège, Ghent or Charleroi, a debate is going on about the so-called "increasing unsafety" on the streets. It is largely attributed to youths hanging around in the streets, especially those from the Moroccan or Turkish ethnic minorities. The debate has been fuelled by some sensationalist media outlets (especially in Flanders), and an extremist right wing political party. In light of its considerable electoral success, the other political parties are dragged into espousing panicky positions with regard to street crime and immigration. For example, in the last election campaigns of June 1999 (for Parliament) and October 2000 (for municipalities) unsafety caused by youth crime and street crime was a central theme. Politicians of several parties say they want to get "tough on youth crime" and gain more control over the "youth gangs in the inner cities." It has led to local police initiatives such as curfews for children and juveniles under the age of 14, *streetrazzias* and local imitations of zero-tolerance policies. Public prosecutors' offices and police forces set up special sections for dealing with youth gangs or with collective youth violence. Proposals have been made for special prisons or "detention houses" for juveniles or for making the waivers of minors to the adults' courts easier. Insurance companies even offer special insurance policies for teachers victimized by school violence. One can expect that such a climate will carry a lot of weight in the coming reforms of the juvenile justice system.

As mentioned earlier, this focal concern with youth crime is not supported by the statistics. There is a paradox in the fact that there is so much concern about so-called "increasing youth crime," while the judicial and political authorities show almost no interest in providing reliable basic data on it. In fact, we do not have reliable data to demonstrate any systematic increase in youth crime in recent years. Besides the judicial data briefly reported in the earlier section, police figures also are very incomplete, and show very diverse pictures for each municipality or district. They often also reveal decreases in documented crime. Moreover, it is unclear whether the fluctuations are due to the public's changing degrees of tolerance or of confidence in police, to a change in effectiveness in police record-keeping, to norm erosion, or to real changes in criminality. Statistics at the level of the public prosecutor's office display the same diversities and weaknesses. In any case, the available statistics certainly do not display the kind of dramatic increases which could possibly justify the "moral panic" on street crime by (immigrant) youth (see Box 2.3). Moreover, close scientific research does uncouple street crime from ethnicity.

Box 2.3: Street Crime among Immigrant Youth

In an intensive research program in Brussels, 4,347 minors were questioned, and 2,580 dossiers of youthful offenders selected at the public prosecutor's office were analyzed. A superficial quantitative comparison reveals indeed an overrepresentation of ethnic minority groups, especially Moroccans, in self-reported and in registered crime. After a series of statistical multivariate analyses, however, the ethnicity variable was absorbed completely by the socio-economic variables and by school variables. Ethnicity as such did not appear to be the problem, but socio-economic and educational exclusion, which especially hits children from Moroccan families. It appeared also that, holding constant the seriousness and type of crime committed, the risks of being arrested by the police were more then three times higher for Moroccan boys than for boys of Belgian origin (Vercaigne et al., 2000).

Obviously, the public rhetoric on "increasing youth crime, committed especially by ethnic minority youths" is not supported by firm and reliable data demonstrating increasing criminal behavior, or an increasingly violent character to the crime. This apparent (at least partial) independence of public concerns from statistical facts seems to be true also in other European countries (Mehlbye and Walgrave, 1998). It brings us to the hypothetical conclusion that the concerns are stirred up by a general cultural climate, characterized by existential uncertainty and loss of mutual understanding, leading to more intolerance. The question is how far such a climate is a good base for developing constructive preventive and interventionist policies.

Which Kind of Juvenile Justice Reform?

Since the end of the 1980s, Belgium has been engaged in an ongoing process of juvenile justice reform. After the transfer of a lot of competencies to the Belgian communities, the federal state was left with the responsibility for organizing the youth courts and of indicating specific measures (or sanctions) against juvenile offenders.

Minimal adaptations of the YPA were made in 1994, but, as things stand now, one can expect that more fundamental changes will happen. In 1995, the Commission for the Preparation of the Reform of the YPA published its final report (Cornelis, 1995). The proposals took into account the many criticisms about the loss of legal safeguards in the old act, and tried to conform to the available international standards.[9] The model of pure protection was left behind and so-called "educative sanctions" were proposed. The proposals were meant to be a compromise between an educative measure and one of punishment. The report was subjected to criticism: abandoning the protection model did not lead to a coherent new approach. There were some procedural improvements, but the report still paid lip service to the value of educational approaches, and the potential of the restorative approach was exploited insufficiently.

In 1996, we were invited by the minister of justice to write a new report on how a juvenile justice system would look if it were based on the principles of restorative justice (see Geudens, Schelkens, and Walgrave, 1997). Our report could rely on the strengthening international trend toward **restorative justice**, based on practice, research and theorizing, and on the growing experience in Belgium with victim/offender mediation and community service (see Box 2.4). Moreover, an exploration of recent reforms in most European juvenile justice systems reveals a general tendency to consider juvenile offenders more responsible than is usual with the protective approach, to focus more attention on the victim's harm and suffering, and to avoid the purely repressive response which is dominant in the traditional criminal justice approach.

Most European countries turn to modalities of restorative response, like restitution or mediation and/or community service, to formalize these tendencies (Schelkens, 1998). We therefore proposed a system wherein priority would be given to voluntary settlements, outside of the judicial system but under its control, and wherein judicial coercion, if needed, would be exerted primarily in service of possible restitution or compensation. Therefore, within the frame of restorative actions or sanctions, reintegration of the offender would be the most important additional goal. Only in the case of very serious threats to public safety would the restorative foundations would be subordinated to incapacitation.

Box 2.4: The Restorative Justice Movement

In recent decade, restorative justice has emerged as a very important issue in the debates on criminal justice and juvenile justice reform. There is a growing body of practice, empirical research, and theoretical and ethical reflection from all over the world which justifies increasing confidence in the restorative response to crime. According to the restorative justice paradigm, the primary function of the social reaction to an offence should not be to punish, nor even to (re)educate, but to set the conditions for repair or compensation for the harm caused by that offence. This option has used been extensively with young offenders. In fact, restorative models have penetrated juvenile justice systems in most Western countries, with New Zealand's as the system that has gone the farthest to implement such a model. One of the most important international sources for exchange and discussion of these experiences is the International Network for Research on Restorative Justice for Juveniles. Its annual conference brings together the world's most authoritative scholars with prominent practitioners and policy makers. (For related works, see Zehr, 1990; Galaway and Hudson, 1996; Van Ness and Heetderks Strong, 1997; McCold, 1997; Braithwaite, 1998; Bazemore and Walgrave, 1999).

Our report was taken seriously, and it was one of the basic documents for a ministerial working group preparing a proposal for reform. The group made good progress. In 1999, however, a new government came into power and we acquired a new minister of justice. The earlier proceedings were abandoned and a new proposal has been prepared. It is unclear when the proposal will be published or what kind of impact it will have. We suspect it will likely represent a hybrid project, wherein the option for a restorative foundation will give way to more repressive aspects, with a residue of treatment orientation.

All in all, it remains uncertain when the reform of the juvenile justice system will find a new foundation in a new legal text. It is direly needed, because social problems and youth problems have changed considerably since 1965, and the cultural, administrative and structural context of dealing with youth crime is no longer comparable to the situation when the YPA was accepted. Meanwhile, "creativity" and the good will of judges and practitioners keep the system working, but without a coherent set of adequate legal guidelines. The problem, in fact, is that Belgium has to rebuild its system. The country was indeed one of the very few in the world to provide a purely rehabilitative system for its young offenders. While pure protection has lost now a great deal of its credibility, the belief in returning simply to a traditional punitive system for juveniles also is very low. Belgian authorities are now confronted with a vacuum in principles upon which to base a coherent new system. There exists a struggle between adopting a **restorative justice model** (promoted mainly by Flemish politicians, practitioners and academics), a revised model of **rehabilitative justice** (defended especially in the French-speaking part of Belgium), and a tendency to favor a more punitive and repressive model for what is called "serious" youth crime. This latter model is demanded by some populists in both parts of the country.

Maybe there is only one thing almost certain for the moment. The new system will be less purely welfare-oriented or protective but will be based on a concept of accountability of the offender. As such, the new system will very probably provide more (restorative and/or punitive) sanctions, and focus more on the victims' harm and suffering caused by the offence.

SUMMARY

For a small and relatively young country, by European standards, Belgium's juvenile justice model has undergone significant change in recent years. It has been impacted by both political and cultural differences that exist within the country.

In 1965 the YPA implied a significant prevention orientation. "Committees for the protection of youth" offered voluntary aid and assistance to children and adolescents (up to 21) in "risk situations" and to their families. If they refuse such assistance, the youth court could impose measures "in the best interest of the child." These dispositions were included in the act to promote timely detection and remediation of risk situations, which would prevent later criminality. Since then, however, two developments have complicated the prevention scene.

The "committees" strived for more autonomy from the judicial system, because their aid and assistance to children and their families was motivated not only by a desire to prevent crime but by a focus on improving the welfare of their clients. This tendency has been reinforced by the reform of the Belgian state in 1980 and 1988, which transferred jurisdiction over the committees to the Belgian communities. As described earlier in the historical review, the communities transformed the committees into autonomous welfare-oriented agencies which were maximally integrated into the ordinary welfare system, and kept only a few links with the judicial system. The Flemish system of special youth support, for example, offers assistance and support to children and families for the sake of welfare in its own right. Possible preventive impact on crime reduction is now only a secondary goal, because it is believed that improving the welfare of individuals and families will as such reduce criminality.

Under the pressure of the increasing concern about crime and feelings of insecurity, the federal government developed measures to try to reduce these phenomena. From the 1990s on, the Ministry of Internal Affairs (responsible for police matters) took initiatives in prevention, which initially had an almost exclusively police and situational approach. Soon, the awareness emerged in police circles also that balanced crime prevention must include the tackling of social exclusion and the promotion of social welfare. The concept of integrated prevention on a local level was strongly supported. The Ministry of Internal Affairs and local police forces began to support local initiatives in drug treatment, street corner work, youth work, and campaigns in schools. However, this was not well accepted by the community authorities responsible for welfare work and education, who considered this as a thwarting of their own welfare and education policy.

For several years now, prevention in Belgium has been a chaotic field of overlapping, competing, isolated, disparate initiatives and projects, dependent on several federal, community or local authorities. In some municipalities, one can discover a laborious search for bridging contradictions between welfare-oriented work in the longer term and the short-term safety-focused crime prevention. This kind of multi-agency approach mostly has difficulties in finding common grounds for cooperation (Goris, 2000).

It is hoped the several authorities will find a way to design a coherent framework for a prevention policy that recognizes the need to balance different approaches between well-being, social exclusion, feelings of threat, and crime. Such a framework must respect the autonomy of welfare work and social work, based as they are on social ethics, and recognize them at the same time as the necessary ground for a balanced policy in crime prevention. Indeed, the need for social support of the socially excluded part of the population must be responded to as a genuine need, and cannot simply be translated into a need for more secure feelings on the part of the integrated part of the population. While the future of juvenile justice in Belgium remains something of an enigma, it might bode well for the country to embrace input from scholars within the country, and to examine what other countries have done to address their juvenile justice concerns.

Lode Walgrave is a professor of youth criminology at the University of Leuven (Belgium), and director of the Research Group on Youth Criminology. Recent publications are on youth crime in general; urbanization, social exclusion of youth and streetcrime; violence and unsafe feelings in schools; crime prevention; juvenile justice; and, especially, on several theoretical and empirical topics in the field of restorative justice for juveniles. Lode Walgrave coordinates the International Network for Research on Restorative Justice for Juveniles and is a member of several policy-oriented workshops and commissions.

HELPFUL WEBSITES
There are no specific web sites on juvenile justice in Belgium. The following may be of general interest.
www.flanders.be Offers general information on the Flemish government and administration (English).
www.cfwb.be Similar to the Flemish government site, but this one addresses the French-speaking part of Belgium. (English version available, but no information about juvenile justice or juvenile crime).

KEY TERMS AND CONCEPTS
Youth Protection Act   Legalistic Judicial System
Arrondissements   Welfare Model
Special Youth Support   Restorative Justice (model)
Rehabilitative Justice

STUDY QUESTIONS
1. At what age can Belgians be punished by the justice system? What do you consider the strengths and weaknesses of the Belgium juvenile justice model to be?
2. How would you describe the role of the police with regard to youth crime? How does it differ from other countries?
3. What are the main consequences of the Belgian option to consider youth crime

mainly as a welfare problem, rather than as a criminal problem per se?
4. Is youth crime a serious problem in Belgium? How does it compare to other countries?

NOTES

1 Highlights of the working paper provided by L. Walgrave. See Box 2.2 for further details.

2 A more elaborated version of this historical part in L. Walgrave, 1993.

3 <<*Le domaine de la délinquance juvénile a cessé d'être un terrain réservé aux seuls pénalistes, pour subir également la contrôle des pédagogues, des médecins, des psychologues et des travailleurs sociaux. La* maxime <nulla poena, nullum crimen sine lege> *ne perdait-elle pas sa raison d'être dans un système qui se déclarait non répressif, mais éducatif et protectif?*>>

4 An *arrondissement* is a judicial district. The number of inhabitants per arrondissement can vary from 200,000 to 1.5 million.

5 The law on the state reform of August 8, 1980, recognizes three communities in Belgium: the Flemish community, the French community of Belgium and a (small) German community. These three were given autonomy in the organization of what were considered "personal matters." Obviously, culture, education and welfare belonged to these. The law also recognized two regions, the Flemish and the Wallonian (later on, a separate Brussels Metropolitan Region was acknowledged, functioning in a special way). The Flemish community and the Flemish region decided to fuse their organs into one single Flemish council and a Flemish executive. The legislation of regions and communities are called decrees. Their governments are called "executives."

6 In-depth descriptions of the Belgian system in J. Smets, 1996, and in F. Tulkens and T. Moreau, 2000.

7 The original 1965 act spoke of not finding an appropriate placement, and did not specify that the measure was only applicable once in a procedure. Consequently, this measure was used a lot more and in a way other than was foreseen by the legislator of 1965. Often, judges used this opportunity in a punitive way, and got around the time limit by placing youngsters elsewhere for one day after two weeks and then placing them in the penitentiary again for a new period of 15 days maximum. This carousel was repeated again and again. It was this practice that was condemned by the European Court of Human Rights (Bouamar judgement of 29.02.1988). The amendments of 1994 made this practice impossible.

8 June 27, 1985; June 4, 1986; March 28, 1990.

9 Such as the *United Nations Standard Minimum Rules for the Administration of Juvenile Justice* (1985), the *United Nations Standard Minimum Rules for Juveniles Deprived of Their Liberty* (1990) and the *Recommendation of the Council of Europe with Regard to the Social Reactions to Juvenile Crime* (1987).

REFERENCES

APSD. *Een overzicht van de geregistreerde criminaliteit in Belgie 1997-1998.* (1999). Brussels: APSD, Ministry of Inner Affairs.

Bazemore, G., & Walgrave, L. (Eds.). (1999). *Restorative juvenile justice: Repairing the harm of youth crime.* Monsey, NY: Criminal Justice Press.

Born, M., & Gavray, C. (1994). Self reported delinquency in Belgium. In J. Junger-Tas, J. Terlouwand & M. Klein (Eds.). *Delinquent behavior among young people in the Western world* (pp. 131–155). The Hague/Amsterdam: RDC/Kugler.

Braithwaite, J. (1998). Restorative justice. In M. Tonry (Ed.), *The handbook of crime and punishment* (pp. 323–344). Oxford/New York: Oxford University Press.

Cornelis, P. (1995). *Eindverslag van de Nationale commissie voor de hervorming van de wetgeving inzake jeugdbescherming.* Brussels: *Ministerie van Justitie.*

Estrada, F. (1999). Juvenile crime trends in postwar Europe. *European Journal of Crime Policy and Research,* 7 (1), 23–42.

Galaway, B., & Hudson, J. (Eds.). (1996). *Restorative justice: International perspectives.* Monsey, NY: Criminal Justice Press.

Geudens, H., Schelkens, W., & Walgrave, L. (1997). *Op zoek naar een herstelrechtelijk jeugdsanctierecht in België: Een denkoefening in opdracht van de Minister van Justitie.* Leuven: Onderzoeksgroep Jeugdcriminologie, K.U.Leuven.

Goris, P. (2000). *Op zoek naar krijtlijnen voor een sociaal rechtvaardige veiligheidszorg.* Ph.D.thesis, Criminology, University Leuven.

Goedseels, E. (2000). Delinquentie. In H. De Witte, J. Hoogeand & L. Walgrave (Eds.). *Jongeren in Vlaanderen: gemeten en geteld* (pp. 210–235). Leuven: Leuven Universitity Press.

Junger-Tas, J. (1994). Delinquency in thirteen Western countries: Some preliminary conclusions. In J. Junger-Tas, J. Terlouw & M. Klein (Eds.), *Delinquent behaviour among young people in the Western countries* (pp. 370–380). The Hague/Amsterdam: RDC/Kugler.

Junger-Tas, J. (1996). Youth and Violence in Europe. *Studies on Crime and Crime Prevention,* 1, 31–58.

McCold, P. (1997). *Restorative justice: An annotated bibliography.* Monsey, NY: Criminal Justice Press.

Mehlbye, J., & Walgrave, L. (Eds.). (1998). *Confronting youth in Europe.* Copenhagen: AKF Forlaget.

Schelkens, W. (1998). Community service and mediation in juvenile justice legislation in Europe. In L. Walgrave (Ed.), *Restorative justice for juveniles: Potentials, risks and problems for research* (pp. 159–183). Leuven: Leuven University Press.

Smets, J. (1996). *Jeugdbeschermingsrecht.* Antwerp: Kluwer, A.P.R. reeks.

Tulkens, F., & Moreau, T. (2000). *Droit de la jeunesse. Aide, assistance, protection.* Brussels: De Boeck et Larcier.

Van Kerckvoorde, J. (1995). *Een maat voor het kwaad*? Leuven: Leuven Universitity Press.

Van Ness, D., & Heetdreks Strong, K. (1997). *Restoring justice.* Cincinnati: Anderson.

Vanneste, C., Amrani, L., Minet, J.F., & Neyt, N. (1999). *Evolution de la délinquance des mineurs: Analyse des données statistiques existantes.* Brussels: *Institut National de Criminalistique et de Criminologie.*

Vettenburg, N. (1998). *Zelfgerapporteerde delinquentie bij jongeren uit het Beroepsonderwijs.* Leuven: *Onderzoeksgroep Jeugdcriminologie.*

Vettenburg, N. (1995). Jeugddelinquentie stijgt?! In G. Decockand & P. Vansteenkiste (Eds.). *Naar een nieuw jeugdsanctierecht* (pp. 87–96). Gent: Mys en Breesch.

Vercaigne, C., P. Mistiaen, Chr. Kesteloot, and L. Walgrave (2000). *Verstedelijking, sociale uitsluiting van jongeren en straatcriminaliteit.* Brussel: DWTC.

Walgrave, L. (1993). The making of concepts on juvenile delinquency and its treatment in the recent history of Belgium and the Netherlands. In A. Hessand & P. Clement

(Eds.), *History of juvenile delinquency* (vol. 2., pp. 655–692). Aalen (Germany): Scientia.

Walgrave, L., & Geudens, H. (1996). The restorative proportionality of community service for juveniles. *European Journal of Crime, Criminal Law and Criminal Justice*, 4 (4), 361–380.

Walgrave, L., Berx, E., Poels, V., & Vettenburg, N. (1998). Belgium. In J. Mehlbyeand & L. Walgrave (Eds.), *Confronting youth in Europe* (pp. 55–95). Copenhagen: AKF Forlaget.

Walgrave, L., & Vercaigne, C. (2000). La délinquance des autochtones et allochtones à Bruxelles. In F. Réa (Ed.), *Mon origine, mon délit*. Brussels: De Boeck.

Zehr, H. (1990). *Changing lenses: A new focus for crime and justice*. Scottsdale, PA: Herald Press.

Chapter 3

Juvenile Justice and Young Offenders: An Overview of Canada

John A. Winterdyk
Department of Justice Studies, Mount Royal College

FACTS ON CANADA

Area: 3,851,792 sq. miles or approx. 10 million sq. km. Canada covers six time zones. **Population**: In excess of 30 million in 2000. Outside of the province of Quebec approximately 80% of Canadians are English-speaking, 6% French, with other first languages including Chinese, East Indian, Ukrainian, and German. Seven out of ten citizens are urban dwellers. Approximately 85% crowd into a 200-km. wide strip along the United States-Canadian border. Major cities include Montreal, Toronto, and Vancouver. Ottawa is the nation's capital. Canada's population characteristics are changing rapidly and will continue to do so well into the future. For example, in 1986 the average life span of a Canadian was 73.3 years while by 1996 it had risen to 78.6. According to the most recent census results, the relative proportion of the population constituted by youth between the ages 12 and 17 has increased slightly through the 1990s, to approximately 9%. By 2016 it is estimated that young persons (ages 15 to 19) will total just over 2.1 million, or 17% of the estimated population. **Climate**: Varies widely by region and latitude. Winters are cool to cold (avg. 0° C to -15° C) while summers can average temperatures from 18°C to mid 20s°C. **Economy**: Hosts a wide range of natural resources: fishing, pulp and paper; farming; mining (e.g., gold, silver, zinc, coal, asbestos, uranium, hydroelectricity, etc.) as well as manufacturing. **Government**: A federal parliament and ten provincial legislatures and three territories. In November 2000 the Liberal Party won the federal election for the third consecutive term. Other major parties include: The Canadian Alliance, New Democrats, Bloc Québécois, and the Progressive Conservatives. The ruling party can hold office for up to five years.

... every juvenile delinquent shall be treated... as a misdirected and misguided child...—Juvenile Delinquents Act, *1908.*

... young persons who commit offences should... bear responsibility... —Young Offenders Act, *1984.*

... the principle goal of the youth criminal justice system is to protect the public by: preventing crime by addressing the underlying circumstances... subjecting young persons to meaningful consequences for their offence, and focus on rehabilitating and reintegrating them into society... —Youth Criminal Justice Act, *2001(proposed).*

Although not the youngest nation to be presented in this text, by international standards Canada is a fairly young nation. It is also one of the few countries in the western hemisphere that gained nationhood without a revolution. It was first permanently settled by Europeans in 1608 by Samuel de Champlain of France, and then by the English later in the 1600s in Newfoundland and around the Hudson Bay area. Although England and France were interested in colonization, their primary investment in the 'New Land' was fur trading. Within a few years the rivalries over trading routes and territory began to escalate. This culminated in the Seven Years War (1756 to 63) in which the French were defeated. To preserve social and political stability, the *Quebec Act* of 1774 granted permission for Catholics in Quebec to hold public office, legitimized French civil law, and granted a certain amount of political autonomy to the province. However, the act stipulated that English criminal law was to continue in force.

Since these early times, Canada has been influenced by the different political orientations of its European heritage. And while the Canadian criminal justice system was primarily influenced by England, remnants from the French accusatorial model are still felt. For example, Quebec has retained its French legal heritage by modeling its Civil Code after the French 1804 Code of Napoleon. Another legal area of note concerns jurisdictional powers. In accordance with the **British North America Act** in 1867 (replaced by the **Constitution Act**, 1982, which includes the Canadian Charter of Rights and Freedoms), Canada adopted a political model in which there is a demarcation between federal jurisdiction and provincial jurisdiction. This division of power has had a profound impact on the administration of juvenile justice in Canada.

I will begin by tracing the historical development of the juvenile justice system in Canada. After presenting an overview of the *Juvenile Delinquents Act*, an outline of the tumultuous transition that led to the current legislation for young offenders, the *Young Offenders Act* (YOA) in 1984, will be presented. Here the key elements of the act will be covered before providing an overview of the new proposed legislation—the *Youth Criminal Justice Act* (YCJA), first proposed in March of 1999.[1] From here I will describe some of the past and present trends and patterns of youth crime. This will be followed by an overview of how young offenders are officially handled by the major elements of the young offenders system. Special attention will be given to the similarities and differences between the YOA and YCJA. The chapter will conclude with a discussion of some of the major legislative and social issues currently confronting the handling of young offenders in Canada today.

THE BIRTH OF JUVENILE JUSTICE IN CANADA

Creating the Juvenile Delinquents Act (JDA)

During the early pioneer days, Canada's young people were likely granted considerable freedoms, given the frontier spirit that prevailed. However, due to economic and physical hardships, life was difficult for families and youth. As Carrigan (1998) notes, numerous young persons were being either abandoned, abused, or simply neglected. However, prior to Confederation in 1867, some young offenders were regularly punished in the same manner as adults. In fact, records show that children were even hung for relatively trivial offences such as theft. Over time, these wayward youth became a growing concern until the mid-1880s, when the government found it necessary to intervene. One of the first steps taken in an attempt to control the problem involved making school attendance compulsory in 1871. However, growing urbanization and dramatic increases in the number of "homeless British waifs and street urchins" only helped to fuel the youth problem during the late 1800s (West, 1984:29).

Sutherland (1976) reported that towards the end of the 1890s people felt that more drastic measures were required. The public felt that somehow the state needed to abandon its Puritan beliefs and attempt to ensure that rehabilitation principles could be enforced for the benefit of those involved in delinquent behavior. Although the state was initially somewhat reluctant to interfere in family matters, the efforts of the child-saving movement, combined with the philosophical and practical shifts towards a more benevolent attitude toward children, resulted in the *Youthful Offenders Act* being passed on 23 July 1894. It represented a measure to permit the state to intervene when families failed to raise their children "properly" (Carrigan, 1998). The essence of the legislation was that a juvenile delinquent should not be treated as an adult criminal in need of punishment "but as a misdirected and misguided child." This reform and family-centered system led to the development of children's court. The intention was to keep young persons away from the influence of the adult judicial process. Given the varying sentiments at the time little was done until 1908 when, primarily through the stewardship of J.J. Kelso and W.L. Scott, the *Juvenile Delinquents Act* was passed.

In addition to setting out the guidelines for juvenile courts, the JDA encompassed a number of key philosophical elements that strongly reflected its treatment philosophy. This treatment philosophy is widely referred to as *parens patriae*.[2] It embodied the essential elements of the positivist school of criminology and is described as representing a **welfare model** (Corrado, Bala, Linden, and LeBlanc, 1992). For example, Section 2 of the JDA defined a juvenile delinquent as:

> *any child who violates any provision of the Criminal Code or any federal or provincial statute, or any by-law or ordinance of any municipality, or who is guilty of sexual immorality or any similar form of vice, or who is liable by reason of any other act to be committed to an industrial school or juvenile reformatory under any federal or provincial statute...*

The general features of the JDA can be summed up as follows:
- Informality of handling (e.g., while the minimum age of delinquency was seven the upper limit varied among provinces from 17 to 18); individualized sentencing (i.e., provincial responsibility), and indeterminate sentencing—based on the rational of *parens patriae*.
- Reliance on childcare experts, social workers, and probation officers.
- Emphasis on diagnosing problems (e.g., social, family, school, personal, and physical environment).
- Preference for individualized treatment over punishment. For example, Section 38 of the JDA stated: "the care and custody and discipline of a juvenile delinquent shall approximate as nearly as may be that which should be given by his parents."

And while the act was revised in 1929 and had a number of amendments made to it in subsequent years, criticism grew over whether the principle of *parens patriae* violated basic constitutional rights (Currie, 1986). This issue drew widespread attention after 1967 when the United States Supreme Court heard the case of *In Re Gault*, the first juvenile case to be decided on constitutional grounds. Furthermore, throughout the 1960s and into the early 1970s, there was increasing disillusionment over the rehabilitative philosophy of the Canadian juvenile system and its programs. This general sentiment was epitomized in Robert Martinson's classic 1974 paper in which he proclaimed "nothing works" in the area of community-based corrections. Subsequent support for this view came from Empey (1982), Lundman (1994), and Trojanowicz (1978). Also during this time a number of researchers called for greater accountability of young offenders (e.g., Wilson, 1975). The seeds for reform had begun to germinate. But, as deMause (1988) has questioned, were the seeds planted in the interest of the youth in conflict with the law, or did the reforms simply represent a tactic for extending state control (i.e., net-widening) over our youth? This is a pedagogical issue for which there is no clear answer but one which is identified in several other contributions in this text.

The Long Road to Reform

The following synopsis offers a chronological overview of the major legislative proposals that led to the proclamation of the *Young Offenders Act* in 1984.

- 1965: the Federal Committee on Juvenile Delinquency began to actively campaign to reform the JDA.
- 1970: Bill C-192 introduced a measure to repeal the *Juvenile Delinquents Act*.
- 1975: "Young Persons in Conflict with the Law" proposals were circulated. Each province was asked to review elements for the new act. Key elements included: title of the act (*Young Offences Act vs. Young Offenders Act*); ages (12 to 17); jurisdiction of administration; the importance of diversion and use of alternative social and legal measures; detention and general matters pertaining to sentencing and custody; setting the minimum age for transfer to adult court from 14 to 16; legal representation; and federal/provincial financial implications.
- 1977: the *Young Offenders Act* was first introduced. However, between 1977 and 1981 it was revamped several times.
- 16 February 1981: The Young Offenders Bill was tabled in the House of Commons. Seventy-three years after the JDA, then Solicitor General of Canada, Bob Kaplan, tabled the new act declaring the existing act (JDA) "was seriously out of date with contemporary practices and attitudes regarding juvenile justice and inadequate to meet the problems presented today by young people in conflict with the law" (Solicitor General, 1981).
- 1982: the YOA was passed by Parliament with unanimous support from all three major political parties.
- 1 April 1984: the YOA was proclaimed law.

CREATING THE *YOUNG OFFENDERS ACT* (YOA)

As noted above, the transition from the JDA to the YOA was a drawn-out process. And while the political argument was that delinquency rates had been increasing significantly throughout the 1960s and 1970s, several Canadian researchers suggested that any increase might be largely attributable to more effective police surveillance and a greater determination to bring young people to justice (McDonald, 1969). Furthermore, the period was marked by high unemployment rates and other social problems such as role ambiguity which, in accordance with the **General Strain Theory** (see Agnew, 1992), generates stresses and strains that can leave adolescents feeling lost when they are unable to meet or attain the basic goals common to others in their age group (e.g., owning a television or having stylish clothing—hence the term a "lost generation"). Some youths may feel that the only way to resolve their anger, frustrations, and other adverse emotional states is by resorting to deviant and criminal acts.[3] Agnew (1992) identifies three sources of strain:

1. strain resulting from the failure to achieve positively valued goals (e.g., wealth, fame, and social acceptance);
2. when a youth's positively valued stimuli are removed (e.g., the loss of a friend, moving to a new town, and the divorce or separation of parents) strain can result; and
3. strain arising with the presentation of negative stimuli (e.g., child abuse, criminal victimization, and school failure).

The combination of dramatic social changes, public pressure for accountability of young offenders, the frustration of police with youth courts because they felt the courts interfered with their work, and the political momentum behind the need for reform finally brought the new act to fruition. The new act brought new legal principles and fundamentally different philosophies for handling juvenile offenders into force. The act represented a shift from the positivist school and a welfare model to the neo-classical school and the **modified justice model** (Corrado et al., 1992) which Hagan, Alwin, and Hewitt (1979) generally described as a "loosely coupled system" (see Box 3.1; see also Hagan, 1995).

The most important provisions of the YOA may be summarized as follows:

- The YOA (Section 2[1]) defines a "young person" as someone who is 12 to 17 years of age, inclusive. All jurisdictions are required to comply with this uniform age range in applying the act.
- Those youth under 12 years of age are not to be dealt with by the criminal justice system. Each province maintains its own child welfare legislation to handle any youth requiring special attention. (In most provinces the two bodies work closely together—see Bala, Hornick, and Vogl, 1991, for a sound review).
- Youthful offenders are now referred to as young offenders rather than juvenile delinquents to reflect the change in status and philosophical orientation.

Box 3.1: Defining Juvenile Justice in Canada

Corrado et al. (1992) have described the Canadian young offender justice system as a **modified justice model**. The general philosophy emphasizes due process balanced by informality in trial proceedings. The former point is intended to recognize that certain transgressions require sanctioning and accountability, while the latter point is designed to reflect the fact that some youths may be unable to understand adult criminal proceedings.. The system is considered "modified" in that it resembles a dual handling process. For less serious offences, youth are typically diverted out of the formal justice system into alternative programs or their cases are dismissed due to a lack of evidence or some other technical matter. Hence, the overall task of the YOA is to strike a balance between diagnosing problem-based delinquency and administering the appropriate sanction. Therefore, the key agencies within the system include lawyers, child/youthcare workers, and various "experts" who can attest to the youth's culpability (see Figure 3.1). For the more serious young offender, there is a greater emphasis on accountability and punishment.

While the model might be theoretically described as a modified justice model, Hagan (1983) described its operation as being "loosely coupled." Later Hagan (1995) demonstrated how the communication and networking between the major actors within the formal system, while responsive to one another, still maintain considerable independence—especially when compared to such systems as found in France (see Box 5—Introduction) and Austria (see Chapter 1). This, according to Hagan, has resulted in "the type of communication that encourages…greater attention to rituals and procedures…" (p. 405) than to the needs of the young offender. The proposed *Youth Criminal Justice Act* (see below) is intended to address many of these shortcomings.

- As recommended under Rule 1.3 of the UN Standards (1986)[4], young offenders under the YOA are entitled to due process, and ideally the process should be conducted informally.
- Like adult offenders, youth crimes are considered criminal in nature and are handled in a similar manner. Youth found committing less serious offences should be dealt with less punitively (e.g., diversion or community service work) than more serious offenders (e.g., confinement). These principles appear under Rule 25 of the UN Standards (1986).
- Young offenders who are suspected of violating any federal legislation, such as the Criminal Code, the *Food and Drugs Act*, and the *Narcotic Control Act*, come under the jurisdiction of youth courts.
- Youth Court may also hear the cases of young persons accused of provincial offences such as traffic violations.
- Sentencing should be determinant with a minimum and maximum range. This principle can also be found under Rule 3.1 of the UN Standards (1986).

- Because of their special status, offending youth should be entitled to childcare/youth care experts as well as lawyers for counsel.
- Sentencing should reflect a greater level of accountability than under the JDA. Hence, under the YOA there is a greater emphasis on accountability. However, due to their age, immaturity, and short history of offending behavior, delinquent youth are not generally accountable in the same manner as adults. These concepts are also found in the UN Standards (1986) under Rule 13.1 and 19.1.
- The primary purpose of intervention is a balance between penalizing criminal/deviant behavior and providing appropriate treatment.
- The primary objective of the act is to provide greater accountability while still respecting the individual's rights and taking into account their "special needs."
- In order to address the needs of young offenders, a system of separate and specialized youth courts and correctional programs is maintained. Although not specifically identified, this general principle can also be found under Rule 14 of the UN Standards (1986).

In essence, the shift has been towards due process of law and, as Ted Rubin in 1976 noted (cited in Milner, 1995:67), "The future is clear: law and due process are here to stay in juvenile court... rehabilitation efforts will be pursued in a legal context." However, as indicated above, as controversial as the YOA has been, it does include many of the guidelines put forth by the United Nations (1986) and other international agreements.

Calls for New Reform

In the early 1990s a number of sensational violent cases involving young offenders attracted considerable media attention. In 1994, a 13-year-old youth shot and killed his neighbor after his father refused to allow him to purchase chewing tobacco. In 1995, Sylvain Leduc, 17, and two other teens were kidnapped as a result of a street-gang incident. Leduc was choked to death by a group of youths and five female friends were sexually violated and beaten. In 1997, 14-year-old Reena Virk was bullied and eventually killed by seven young females and one male. In 1998, a 16-year-old **Clayton McGloan** was stabbed at a house party after he tried to shut the party down. However, it was the case of **Ryan Garrioch**, who in 1994 was stabbed and killed in a schoolyard altercation, that started the latest call for reform (see Box 3.2). A virtual one-person campaign, Garrioch's father—in combination more recently with campaigns by the McGloan family—has played a significant role in fueling public outrage with the existing youth justice system. By August of 2000 the "Friends of Clayton McGloan Foundation" had amassed over "900,000 signatures on its petition, in an effort to unite the small pockets of YOA protest into one large voice" (Dumont, 2000). This in spite of the fact that youth crime dropped throughout most of the 1990s (see below). Finally, researchers from the Canadian Resource Centre for Victims of Crime reported not only that youth violence was increasing but that there was an increase in weapons use among youths. Their report followed on the heels of a spate of violent offences involving children across the country (Woodward, 2000) and results from the 1999 General Social Survey which showed that, contrary to a moderately less punitive attitude towards sentencing adult offenders, both males and females "are equally likely to prefer a prison sentence in most cases involving young offenders" (Tufts, 2000, 1). And all this was punctuated by the November 2000 federal elections where most of the major parties said that they would pursue reform to the existing legislation for young offenders.

Box 3.2: Public Pressure Prompts Calls for Tougher Laws

On 11 May 1992 in Calgary, Alberta, 13-year-old Ryan Garrioch was stabbed to death while on his way to school. His assailant was a 15-year-old youth. Not only did the YOA protect the identity of the killer but, in accordance with the act, the youth received a maximum penalty of three years in prison. The incident attracted national attention. The Garrioch family started a national petition campaign to have the act toughened. In partial response to growing public pressure, Bill C-12 was introduced in 1994. The bill increased the maximum sentence for first degree murder from three to five years. The bill also relaxed the criteria for transferring young offenders to adult court. Several other high profile cases prompted further revisions to the Act with Bill C-37 in 1995. In addition to several other YOA amendments, the bill again raised the maximum sentence for first degree murder, this time from five to 10 years (in contrast to the 25 year minimum imposed on adults). However, the Standing Committee of Justice Legal Affairs concluded that "this increase in the penalty structure will not... reduce juvenile violence and will not reduce juvenile recidivism" (CCJA, 1994:3). Rather, it might be more prudent to have serious offences dealt with more seriously in youth court. However, as Leonard and Morris (2000: 135) have noted, "our government appears happy to implement simple solutions to social problems and claim to do this both in our best interest and at our request, but with limited consideration of what is in the best interest of young offenders."

These and several other high profile cases have provided the driving force behind the recent call for legislative reforms which has also been targeted by Opposition critics in Parliament. While the public is calling for tougher sentencing and greater accountability, the government has used public forums to both address public concerns as well as show that a new act would need to continue to respect the special needs of young persons while introducing certain measures to hold the more serious young offender accountable.[5] Finally, in May 1998, the federal government released its Youth Justice Renewal

Initiative, an ambitious plan for the renewal of the youth justice system. This is a tall order given the relative effectiveness of the JDA and the YOA.

CREATING THE *YOUTH CRIMINAL JUSTICE ACT* (YCJA) [6]

"Adult crime? Adult time."—Ontario Attorney General Jim Flaherty, 6 February 2001.

"Quebec considers this reform to be costly and useless."—Quebec Justice Minister Linda Goupil, 6 February 2001.

The *Youth Criminal Justice Act* (Bill C-3) was first introduced in March of 1999 and then introduced again in the House of Commons on 14 October 1999, before it died on the Order Paper just prior to the federal election. After the Liberal government won the election in 2000, the bill (i.e., Bill C-7) was reintroduced on 5 February 2001. The new bill, which retains the overall direction and key elements of the original bill, is intended to replace the current YOA. In its effort to address many of the shortcomings of the YOA and to restore public faith in the youth justice system, the new act is not only twice as long as the YOA but has been expanded from 83 sections to 197 sections (the JDA had 45 sections).[7] The YCJA represents a key element of the Youth Justice Renewal Initiative. The initiative represents the government's strategy to revamp the failing youth justice system and to make it more consistent with national and international human rights.

The 2001 bill (i.e., Bill C-7) has a number of important focuses:

- Prevention, to address the causes of crime and encourage community efforts to reduce crime;
- Meaningful consequences that hold all young people accountable for their actions, and help them to understand the consequences of the harm they have done;
- Rehabilitation and reintegration back into their community; and
- Flexibility for the provinces. While intended to be a federal act, the bill allows for a degree of flexibility for the provinces "to choose options in some areas that best meet their needs and suit their system" (Canada's Youth Criminal Justice Act, 2001:2).

The Youth Justice Renewal Initiative calls for a cooperative, integrated approach to youth justice. In order to support the restructuring of Canada's youth justice system, the federal government has adopted several strategies for use during the implementation period. Reference groups will be convened and consulted on implementation issues. The government will work closely with all relevant levels of the youth justice system to provide consultation and training in implementing the new system. In addition, the government will include a series of public information sessions and regular national reports during the implementation process. Finally, the federal government has committed $206 million over the three years of implementation and will establish a five-to-six-year implementation phase to enable all federal, provincial, and territorial agencies and services to work together towards ensuring that the act is implemented in a constructive manner.[8]

The new act, although sharing elements of the modified justice model, attempts to embrace characteristics of the welfare model: It attempts to reduce youth crime by modifying the major environmental factors thought to cause delinquency (i.e., social inequality). Reid and Reitsma-Street (1984) describes this general approach as a **Community Change Model.**

Having presented an overview of the past, present, and future legislative measures used to address young offenders, we will now examine some of the trends and patterns of youth crime. After that, I will provide an overview on how the key actors of the youth justice system handle young offenders.

THE DIMENSIONS OF THE DELINQUENCY PROBLEM

*Many Canadians, afraid and frustrated, succumb to the temptation of quick fixes served up by ever willing politicians and the media. Lock them up and throw away the key! Send them to boot camp! Bring back the cane! Zero tolerance! Adult time for adult crime! (*Youth Justice...*, 1994)*

In collaboration with the provinces and territorial departments responsible for youth courts, the Canadian Centre for Justice Statistics (CCJS) currently collects information on young persons in Canada's justice system.[9] Until 1991 Ontario and the Northwest Territories did not submit data. Also because of variations among provincial reporting practices, data are considered suggestive rather than definitive.[10] Notwithstanding these qualifiers it is possible to present a general picture of youth crime in Canada that comes to the attention of the police, and of how the cases are disposed of. In accordance with Stanton Wheeler's observation in 1967, a "three-way interaction between an offender, victim or citizens, and official agents" will be followed (p. 319). That is, in addition to examining official statistics, where possible, reference will be made to self-report and victimization studies in order to provide a more realistic account of the "true" juvenile crime picture.

What are the Official Trends?

As illustrated in Table 3.1, official counts of the youth crime rates dropped for the seventh consecutive year in 1998/99, driven by the steep decline in the rate of crime against property. This converts to a decline from 6,259 offences per 100,000 youth in 1991 to 4,363 in 1998 (CCJS, 2000, 20(4)). This figure represents approximately 21% of the total caseload. Yet, while the decreasing youth crime rate of the 1990s may appear promising, it is important to note that the decline in the youth crime rate occurred during a time period when most provinces experienced a decrease among the adolescent population. Further-more, in 1981, the federal Ministry of the Solicitor General conducted the first national survey of victims—the Canadian Urban Victimization Survey (CUVS)—which revealed that Canadians are more concerned about youth crime now than they have been in the past.[11] More recently, the General Social Survey, conducted annually, shows that the public continues to hold a negative atti-tude toward young offenders.

Based on their extensive analysis of youth crime data, Markwart and Corrado (1995:84) conclude that there is "clear evidence of a real and substan-tial increase in youth violence in recent years." In particular, Table 3.1 shows that while the incidents of property crime have decreased since 1991, the rate of violent crime among youths slightly increased until 1995/96 when there was a 2% drop over the previous year followed by very little change throughout the rest of the '90s (Kids and Crime, 2000). For example, property offences fell from 271 per 10,000 youth in 1992/93 to 186 per 10,000 in 1998/99. In contrast, violent crimes increased by 8% between 1992/93 and 1994/95 before tapering off by the late 90s (Kids and Crime, 2000). And while the violent crime rate may not have changed much in recent years (i.e., a 2% increase between 1992/93 and 1998/99), it is worth noting that nearly one-half of these offences involve common assaults (e.g., pushing, slapping, and verbal threats) and these of-fences have been on the increase (CCJS, 2000, 20[2]).

While the overall number of violent crime cases decreased throughout the late 1990s, it was still 125% higher than in 1986/87; this compares to an in-crease of 41% among adult offenders over the same time period. In the face of this overall recent decrease, the group from 12 to 13 years of age demonstrated a noticeable increase, the largest of any youth age group, up 6% over the previous year (CCJS, 1999, 19[13]). Although some of the increases over the years have been attributed to expanding police forces, improved crime fighting technology, and increased sensitivity to youth crime, Carrington and Moyer (1994) argue that these explanations for the increase in violent crime cannot account for the entire rate of increase. The most dramatic increase involved drug convictions—up 49% over the previous year.

Overall, the percent of youth charged with a Criminal Code offence in 1998/99 fell 7% from 1992/93; however, the percent of the youth population also declined 6% between 1991 and the end of 1995. Therefore, depending on how one chooses to read official statistics on youth crime in Canada, you can

Table 3.1: Rates of Youth Charged with Violent and Property Crimes 1992/93 to 1998/99						
	1992/93	1993/94	1994/95	1995/96	1996/97	1997/98	1998/99

	1992/93	1993/94	1994/95	1995/96	1996/97	1997/98	1998/99
Violent crimes: Per 10,000	94	100	98	97	95	97	96
Percent rate change 1992/93 – 98/99:							2.3
Property crimes: Per 10,000	271	254	225	221	214	203	186
Percent rate change 1992/93 – 98/99:							-31.4

Source: CCJS. (2000. 20(2)). Youth Court Statistics, 1998/99 Highlights. P. 13.

end up with mixed messages. Recognizing the growth in serious crime over property crime prompted Leschield and Jaffe (1995:427) to conclude, "that the deterrence-focused dispositions of the YOA seem not to have the same effect of reducing crime as did the treatment disposition within the JDA."

Types of Crimes Committed

For the fiscal year 1998/99, 106,665 cases were processed in the youth courts. This represents a 4% decrease over 1997/98 and a 7% decrease over 1992/93 (CCJS, 2000, 20[2]).[12] In spite of the recent declines in the number of cases heard in youth court, this is significantly up from 1986/87 when 96,443 cases were heard but still down from 1993/94 when 115,949 cases were in youth court. Geographically, four of the provinces (Prince Edward Island, New Brunswick, Saskatchewan, and British Columbia, along with the Yukon) experienced declines in excess of 10% over the previous year. Overall, there has been a 13% drop in youth court cases since 1992/93 (CCJS, 2000, 20[2]). As was noted earlier, the decrease is in part due to the declining number of youths in their adolescent years; however, it also reflects a growing trend towards the increased use of **alternative measures** that do not involve being formally processed (see below).

Since 1986/87 the breakdown of offences committed by young offenders has remained comparatively similar. Most of those youth who commit crime in Canada, as in the past, still continue to commit minor offences. For 1998/99 property convictions accounted for 43% of all youth crime cases while violent crime made up 22%. Meanwhile, drug-related offences made up 4% of the cases while other Criminal Code offences accounted for 18% of the cases for 1998/99 (CCJS, 2000, 20[7]). It is interesting to note however that the number of drug-related cases has doubled since 1992/93, but the rate still remains low at 19 per 10,000 criminal offences. The vast majority of the drug offences involve cannabis. However, some recent findings have raised concern about whether official statistics are providing a realistic picture of the extent and nature of youth crime (see Box 3.3). Table 3.2 presents a comparison between 1986/87 and 1998/99 statistics.

In summary, since the introduction of the YOA, official counts of youth crime continued to escalate until the early 1990s when we began to witness a steady decline in the number of both violent and property offences processed in youth court. In spite of the declining rates, the nature of youth crime is becoming generally more serious, and the average age at which young persons are becoming involved in delinquent activity is getting lower. As has been the case since the enactment of the JDA, these mixed trends continue to pose unique challenges for legislators.

Box 3.3: Victimization in the Schools

Delinquency in schools in not new. West (1984) reported that over 90% of Canadian high-school boys reported committing some delinquent act. But, in recent years delinquency and victimization is schools is seen as an increasingly serious problem (see Day et al., 1995). Statistics Canada revealed that young persons are twice as likely to be victims in school as their representation in the population. Although the results are considered largely exploratory, a major victimization survey conducted on 962 (approx. 2%) of the public and Catholic junior and senior high school students in Calgary during 1994 revealed that 28% of the respondents have carried weapons, 2.6% have packed handguns, and 81.5% have been victimized in the past 12 months, often by having something stolen or damaged (Stewart, 1995). In spite of these statistics, data show that 96% of students said they felt safe in school (Violence in Schools, 2000).

Bullying/intimidation/threats and physical attacks or fights without weapons are the most reported offences in schools. In response, a growing number of schools are incorporating varying types of security measures to curb the problem. These include suspension to expulsion of problem students, controlling access to school buildings, full-time guards, metal detectors, and in some cases closed circuit television. Based on their survey results, Day et al. (1995) recommend that any measures need to be founded on policies that are internally consistent, multifaceted, prevention-oriented, and have a community focus.

Profile of Young Offenders

For 1998/99 eight out of 10 young offenders were male. This has been a typical pattern since the turn of the twentieth century in Canada. What has been changing in recent years is the age at which youth are commencing their

Table 3.2: Percentage Breakdown of Official Youth Crimes: 1986/87–1998/99

Category	Year	
	1986/87*(a) Percent	1998/99**(b) Percent
Theft under $1000**	24.6	15
Break and enter	24.7	11
YOA offences	7.4	12
Minor assaults	8.7	10
Fail to appear	5.2	11
Possession of stolen property 6.1	5	
Mischief	6.5	5
Theft over $1000**	4.1	2
Aggravated assault/weapon	2.0	7
Drug offences/possession	3.0	4
Robbery	1.8	3
Escape/unlawful at large	N/A	N/A
Frauds	2.2	2
Sexual assault	1.2	2
Impaired driving	3.4	1
Take vehicles w/o permission	0.003	2
Against the person and rep.	N/A	1

* Percentages calculation based on raw data and rounded to nearest decimal, so that they may not add to 100%.
** In 1995 theft over/under was changed to $5000 from $1000.
(b) CCJS. (2000, 20(2)). Youth Court Statistics, 1998/99 Highlights. p. 5.
Source: (a) *Decisions and Dispositions in Youth Court,* Nov., 1990. The year 1986-87 was chosen since it was the first year after the implementation of the YOA that data became standardized.

criminal activities. While, for 1998/99, one-half (i.e., 51%) of youth court caseload involved 16- or 17-year-olds (25% and 26% respectively); 21% involved 15-year-olds; while 12- to 14-year-olds showed proportionately less involvement (3%, 8%, and 15% of cases). There was a 3% decrease in caseloads from 1992/93 to 1998/99 (Canadian Criminal Justice Association, 2000a).

Female young offenders, until recent years, have been under-represented in the young offender population. In recent years, however, their numbers have been increasing, especially for minor assaults (Reitsma-Street and Artz, 2000). Between 1989 and 1999, the rate of female youths charged with violent crimes has increased twice as fast (+127%) as that of young males (+65%).[13] Between 1992/93 and 1998/99 the relative proportion of females sentenced went from 16% to 20% (Canadian Criminal Justice Association, 2000c). However, as with males, the proportion of females sentenced varies substantially across the country, with the NWT having the highest conviction rate (27%) compared to 9% in Quebec (Canadian Criminal Justice Association, 2000c).

Typically, young females are charged most frequently with shoplifting offences, mischief, and administrative offences (e.g., failure to comply with decisions of youth court, failure to comply with decisions of the youth justice). Also worthy of note is the fact that females are more likely than males to receive less severe sentences for the same type of offence (Canadian Criminal Justice Association, 2000c). These trends are not dissimilar from those expressed in other chapters throughout this book.

A popular explanation for female under-representation in the official statistics draws on three related factors: sex role socialization, differential social control, and variations in opportunity (Hagan, Simpson, and Gillis, 1979). Yet, referring to official data, Reitsma-Street and Artz (2000) note that there still exist discriminatory sanctioning practices against offending girls. They suggest this is due to the fact that the youth justice system fails to acknowledge the "complex varied situations in which girls live" (Reitsma-Street and Artz, 2000, 78).

Theories of Delinquency

Why do young people break criminal rules and commit status offences? This is a question asked and studied not only by many Canadian criminologists but by scholars around the world. The range of explanations can often appear overwhelming. In this section, I will only focus on studies conducted on Canadian young offenders.

If one can use Canadian textbooks and Canadian journal articles as an indicator of theoretical preference, then it would appear that the sociological/ macro perspectives are the most popular. Factors that have been studied to explain delinquent involvement include:

- Based on the **social learning theory** (Akers, 1985), peer influence and peer pressure have been studied by some scholars in Canada. Using secondary data Brownfield and Thompson (1991) were able to support the social learning/control theory. They concluded, "measures of peer involvement in delinquency are strongly and positively associated with self-report delinquency" (p. 57).
- The conceptualization of class and family focuses on the power relations in the workplace and the home. Hagan, Simpson, and Gillis (1987) argue that delinquency rates are a function of class differences and economic conditions that in turn influence the structure of family life. Their **power-control theory** has been reasonably effective in explain-

ing the relative increase in female delinquency since it recognizes the effects of social changes such as the decline of the patriarchal family and changing sex-roles.

- Drawing on ecological concepts and presuming the rationality of offenders, the **routine activity theory,** developed by Cohen and Felson in 1979, has attempted to link the increase in delinquency to increased suitability of targets and a decline in the presence of "guardians" (e.g., friends, family, and neighbors). In Canada, Kennedy and Baron (1993) demonstrated that choices, routines, and cultural milieu interact to affect one another to create opportunities for delinquency.

- Gottfredson and Hirschi's recent **general theory of crime** (earlier version entitled propensity-event theory) has also received recent attention in Canada. This approach represents an attempt to integrate classical and positivist principles into a general model of crime. The theory represents a revision of Hirschi's **control theory**. The new version suggests that people naturally act in a self-interested fashion. However, our socialization can affect our level of self-control. Delinquency is largely a result of low self-control. However, unlike Hirschi's earlier theory, the new model focuses more on the individual traits than external sources of control. In his study on delinquency and school dropouts, Creechan (1995:238) found the "general theory of crime produced a remarkably accurate prediction of who is normal."

- During the late 1980s and into the 1990s, there appeared to be a return, in some circles, to the positivist/medical model involving factors such as nutrition, chemical imbalances, and neurological problems which may cause a youth to become prone to deviant and violent behavior (Winterdyk, 2000a, Ch. 2).

- The recent research conducted by Richard Tremblay and his colleagues at the University of Montreal has received considerable attention. Their research embraces an interdisciplinary and integrated approach to the development of young persons. Their work focuses on the relationship of various prenatal and early childhood experiences within varying socio-demographic environments and how such situations may, or may not, contribute to future delinquent behavior. In addition to studying possible causal links to future delinquency, they also explore a variety of intervention and prevention strategies (see Pagani et al., 1998).

- Other factors commonly studied and used to explain Canadian youth crime include substance abuse (Hendrick and Lachance, 1991), abuse and neglect (Horner, 1993), breakdown in values and norms, and various personality problems (see Romig, Cleland, and Romig, 1989: 28-29 for a summary of causes and related studies).

- One recent study, which has received considerable press, was headed by Dr. Mark Genuis, Executive Director of the National Foundation for Family Research and Education. Their national survey revealed that parental neglect is the leading cause of youth problems. A number of the other key points discussed in the study relate strongly to Hirschi's control theory. The findings revealed that the suicide rate among Alberta children aged ten to fourteen has risen 146% since 1970 and one-fifth of all adolescents are clinically or emotionally ill (Verburg, 1995).

The cause(s) of youth crime in Canada might best be illustrated in a quote from the Canadian Criminal Justice Association, which in 1992 concluded, "causal relationships among these behaviours cannot be determined accurately, nor can we affirm which comes first in time or importance" (CCJS, 1992:3).

Therefore, while the phenomenon of youth crime has been around since Europeans first began to colonize Canada, our legal efforts and theoretical approaches have not had a positive impact on decreasing youth crime rates. This has been reflected in our youth crime data as well as in our recidivism counts.

Repeat Offenders/Persistent Offenders[14]

Until recently, regular statistics were not kept on recidivism rates among young offenders. Resource and methodological problems were the primary culprits. However, due to a growing concern over crime and a general improvement in data collection with the formation of the Canadian Centre for Justice Statistics in 1982, the center's mandate has been streamlined to better address social, political, and academic concerns (Winterdyk, 1996). Such rates, however, are considered a reasonable measure of how effective the juvenile justice system is in deterring and rehabilitating young offenders. As noted earlier, Leschield and Jaffe (1995) suggest that the current emphasis on crime control does not appear to be having a deterrent effect. This observation is also reflected in police data, which reveals that from 1989 to 1993 police reported that incidents involving young persons rose by 24% (Young, 1994). In 1998/99, 42% of all convictions involved repeat offenders of which 25% had three of more prior convictions and approximately 2% had six or more prior convictions (CCJS, 2000, 20[2] and 20[7]). Collectively, repeat offences represent 12% of all cases brought before the court.

Based on 1990/91 data, Moyer (1992) found that in 19% of youth court cases, the accused had already had five or more previous convictions. It was also revealed that most repeat offenders commit the same types of crimes. That is, about two-thirds were charged with property offences. Based on 1998/99 data, the relative proportion fell to 14% for those with three or more prior convictions (CCJS, 2000, 20[7]). In addition, as reflected in various public opinion polls, repeat offenders tend to commit more serious offences, and the seriousness of their crimes escalated during subsequent offences. Still, a majority (58%) of youth court cases involved first-time offenders.

Persistent offenders tend to commit more serious crimes and tend to be somewhat older (50% were 17 years of age) and they tend to be more criminally active than first-time offenders (Doherty and de Souza, 1995). The study also found that the average elapsed time between offences was eight months unless the young offender had three or more priors, then the interval between offences was less than four months. Given the fact that re-offenders receive harsher penalties than first- or second-time offenders, their continued involvement in delinquent activity raises further doubts about the effectiveness of the YOA and, more particularly, our modified justice model. Males are more likely (58%) than females (50%) to receive custody dispositions (Ibid).

Although data from five of the 12 jurisdictions were excluded because of low numbers, for those provinces which did report, the mean length of dispositions for repeat offenders was actually less than the mean length of dispositions for first-time offenders. For example, for secure custody dispositions first-time offenders received a mean sentence length of approximately 120 days while those youths with three or more convictions received a mean sentence length of around 110 days (Moyer, 1992). This trend is also reflected in the official 1998/99 data that also shows that 66% of those with two or more convictions are likely to receive a custody term versus 14% of those cases involving first-time offenders (CCJS, 2000c). Contrary to public opinion (see Tufts, 2000), with almost half of those youths sentenced to custody for non-violent offences, it does not appear that such punishment represents a mere slap on the wrist. However, the sentence length increase, for repeat offenders, has only slightly increased in the 1990s. Therefore, given the recidivism trends, and as already noted in this section, it is questionable whether the modified justice model is being applied effectively. Using a slightly different orientation, Hackler (1996) arrives at a similar conclusion in his comparative discussion of juvenile justice. The question remains as to whether the proposed YCJA can effectively address the implied shortcomings of the existing youth justice legislation.

Court Dispositions

In 1997/98 Canada's adult inmate incarceration rate is higher than the rates in Western European countries but lower than those in the United States (*Basic Facts about Federal Corrections*, 1999). With an incarceration rate of around 129 per 100,000 it is higher than that of England (120) but lower than that of the United States (649). This is in sharp contrast to how many Canadians view our criminal justice system. In fact, based on a smaller international sample (N=8), the 1999 edition of Corrections in Canada indicated that Canada ranked third amongst the countries listed.

With the passing of the YOA, youth court judges have been provided with a wide array of sentencing dispositions. These include absolute discharge, fines, restitution, community service orders, probation, and open and closed custody.

Approximately two-thirds (i.e., 67%) of all the cases which appeared before youth courts across Canada for 1998/99 resulted in findings of guilt. Only 29% had their proceedings stayed or withdrawn. For the remainder of cases (3%) not guilty verdicts were reached (CCJS, 2000, 20[2]).

Although Canada might be described as being more punitive than many other Western nations (see other contributions), for 1998/99 the bulk (approximately 48%) of case dispositions resulted in probation. This proportion has steadily increased in the 1990s. The medium length of this disposition was one year. Of the remaining cases, 35% resulted in some type of custody (18% open custody and 17% secure custody), 7% of the youths charged received community service orders, and the balance were given fines (6%). Again, these figures reflect the general pattern of dispositions since the Act came into effect.

In Canada it is also possible for offending youths to receive **multiple dispositions**. While nearly 47% of all cases in 1998/99 involved only one disposition, 39% resulted in two dispositions and a small percentage (i.e., 14%) involved three or more. The most frequent combination includes probation and community service (28%) (CCJS, 2000, 20[2]). The latter type of disposition reflects not only the principles of the modified justice model described earlier but also the increase throughout the 1990s in the percent of cases involving two or more dispositions. What has not been determined is the relative effectiveness of these types of dispositions. Yet, they do reflect the guidelines identified by the UN (1986).

Since the enactment of the YOA, there has been considerable debate about whether young offenders are being held more accountable for their offences. Between 1986/87 and 1992/93, Leesti (1994) reported a 41% increase in the number of youth cases receiving custody as the most serious disposition. And while there has been little change in custody proportion, the rates for both open and secure custody increased the same amount—from 10 to 14 per 10,000. However, as will be elaborated upon shortly, while the use of dispositions have gone up, the average length of a disposition, specifically for first-time offenders, has decreased in recent years. This would appear to reflect the intention of the proposed YCJA as well as a strong movement towards the use of alternative measures.

From 1986/87 until the mid-1990s the proportion of young females receiving a custodial disposition has remained consistent at around 14%. However, by 1998/99 the proportion jumped to 28%. The change has been less dramatic for young males. There was a 41% increase in the number of cases receiving custody between 1986/87 and 1992/93 (CCJS, 1995, 15[7]). By 1997/98 the rate for custody dispositions was 182 per 10,000 cases. Although a slight increase over 1992/93 (CCJS, 2000b), the use of alternative measures appears to have absorbed any decline in cases receiving custody throughout the late 1990s (1999, 19[8]). This is especially true for cases involving property-related crimes.

What is interesting to observe, as it reflects different provincial judicial discretionary practices, is that the custody rates vary considerably across the country. For example, open custody is more commonly used in Eastern Canada than in the Western provinces. Young females more commonly have charges laid against them in the Western provinces than those in the Eastern provinces (Reitsma-Street and Artz, 2000). This may be due to the fact that the act's enforcement is a provincial responsibility and, due to variations in resources and political agendas, uniformity in the administration of juvenile justice is not possible. As noted earlier, Hagan (1983) has aptly described this phenomenon as a "loosely coupled system." In addition, an issue that has not been adequately addressed but which is reflected in the negative sentiments of the public, is the lack of an efficient and effective model of juvenile justice. As Hackler (1996) has observed, Canadian policy-makers might be suffering from a "smugness about our system."

Since 1986/87, while the use of custodial dispositions have increased slightly, the duration of the dispositions have tended to result in shorter terms. For example, in 1986/87, 56% of the custodial dispositions were three months or less in duration. For 1998/99 the proportion had increased to 75%. Furthermore, the proportion of cases receiving six months or more decreased from 22% in 1986/87 to 16% in 1992/93 (22% vs. 16%) and down to 7% in 1998/99 (Leesti, 1994; CCJS, 2000a).

This trend reflects the complexity of the YOA principles. The sentencing practices appear to acknowledge the need for accountability but also recognize the importance of reintegration and resocialization of young offenders. In essence, this may be viewed as "short sharp shock" intervention, which received considerable attention during the late 1970s "Scared Straight" program. Lundman (1994) reports that this model of intervention did not prove to be an effective mode of treatment. An additional consequence of the increased caseload has been the increased processing time in youth court. By 1998/99 the median length of youth court cases climbed to 63 days from 23 days in 1989/90. Violent crimes average 103 days while drug cases average 58 days. In addition to wide variation between the provinces, cases involving males tend to last longer (63 days) than those for females (59 days).

According to Corrado and Markwart (1994), the trend towards greater accountability but shorter sentences may in part be explained by the fact that there is a placement shortage in most provincial containment facilities across the country. Courts must entertain alternative disposition options. Based on various provincial statistics, this observation would appear to be valid. Therefore, the question is whether the Canadian juvenile justice model is one of design or necessity? It is the author's opinion that, based on historical trends of juvenile justice practices in our country (see Carrigan, 1998; Smandych, Dobbs, and Esau, 1991) and the implementation of its legislation, the modified justice model may have evolved out of necessity rather than being founded on sound theoretical and empirical evidence. A number of prominent Canadian criminologists have argued that, to date, Canadian criminology has not faired well in blending criminological ideas with political agendas (Winterdyk, 2000b). Hence, in addition to Hagan's notion of a "loosely coupled system," our juvenile justice system could also be described as a philosophically fragmented model.

Transfers to Adult Court

One of the major changes between the JDA and YOA pertained to the issue of transfers to adult court for youths found committing serious offences. This provision comes under section 16 of the YOA and pertains to youths of 14 years of age or older who have committed an indictable offence. Since the introduction of the new act there had been a slight but steady increase each year until 1997/98 in the number of youths transferred to adult court. In 1991/92, only 71 cases were transferred from youth court to adult court, while for 1994/95, 123 cases were transferred (Doherty and de Souza, 1996). Then in 1997/98 the number of cases that were transferred dropped to 79 (*The Daily*, 1999). Of those cases being considered for transfer, almost half spend four or more months in youth court prior to the decision to transfer.

In recent years there have been a number of extreme, violent crimes involving youths that have drawn considerable media and public attention. As noted earlier, the case of Ryan Garrioch attracted considerable public pressure and eventually resulted in a change in the maximum sentence for murders committed by young persons.

Even though the number of transfers to adult court currently represents less than 1% of all youths charged with a crime, conditions for transfer are not uniformly applied across Canada. For example, in 1998/99, only four regions employed the transfer option (i.e., Nova Scotia, New Brunswick, Alberta, and British Columbia). The differences appear to be related to social and political variations that not only reflect a loosely coupled system but also a fragmented philosophical model that places societal interests above those of our youth. It is also interesting to note that, according to one report, youths are choosing transfer to "avoid the discipline and structure of a youth custody facility" (Doherty and de Souza, 1996:7). It will be interesting to see whether Section 91 (transfer to adult facility) of the proposed YCJA will have any significant impact on transfer trends. The proposed act has some noticeable differences regarding the criteria for transferring youth to the adult system (see the Plena Helpful Web Links for information on comparison between the YOA and YCJA).

The Financial Burden of Juvenile Justice

One of the concerns the provinces had throughout the 1970s regarding the proposed changes to the YOA was the increased cost to the provinces to provide the services needed under the new act.

The concerns appear to have been warranted. Between 1988/89 and 1992/93 government spending on the justice system increased 34% to $9.57 billion, which equates to approximately $300 per Canadian per year. The per capita cost had risen to $337 (total budget almost $10 billion) for the fiscal year 1996/97 (CCJS, 1999, 19[12]). After adjusting for inflation, this represents a real growth of around 12%, or an average annual constant dollar increase of 3.2%. The total justice budget represents nearly 3% of total government spending. And while politicians point out that the rise is consistent with the rise in other sectors of the government, given the growing concern with fiscal restraint in Canada and more specifically the provinces, some suggestions that have been forwarded recommend that the provinces divert funds from institutional budgets to community alternatives. However, the CCJS notes that realistically this could only be accomplished if both Parliament and the provinces act to enhance YOA funding (CCJS, 1994). Finally, in 1999 and coinciding with the proposed YCJA, the federal government has earmarked several million dollars that will be directed to community-based resolutions to youth crime. Many of the ideas are part of the Youth Renewal Initiative.

The largest allotment for juvenile justice went to youth corrections, again reflecting the move towards embracing a harsher stand on youth crime in this country. For example, in Ontario about 77% of the $118 million spent on young offenders in 1992/93 was for secure custody/detention—approximately $128,000 per youth under 16 years of age. These costs rise even more when youth over 16 are included (CCJS, 1996). Although justice service cost increased throughout most of the '90s, in 1996/97 total expenditures were down 2% over the previous year (CCJS, 1999, 19[12]). An article on youth justice in Alberta showed that it cost the province between $70 to $80 per day to place a youth in custody, or just over $25,000 per year (Dempster, 1996).

The area which has been most impacted by the YOA has been legal aid. Since young offenders are entitled to legal representation but are often unable to retain their own counsel, they become dependent on legal aid—one of the reasons for its inception. Between 1988/89 and 1992/93, legal aid expenditures went up 70.3%. By 1994/95 expenditures for legal aid were greater than that for young offenders. In fact, the federal government became so concerned that in the early 1990s it placed a ceiling on how much legal aid lawyers could charge per type of case (Hung and Bowles, 1995). By 1998/99 legal aid expenditures had dropped 15% over the previous three years, but their expenditures were still slightly greater than those for youth corrections. And although official expenditures have been decreasing in recent years, community-based initiatives have absorbed some of these expenses. Overall, the expenditures reflect the legalistic orientation of the justice system and its efforts to address crime control through community involvement. This observation is reinforced in the principles of the newly proposed (i.e., February 5, 2001) YCJA.

THE YOUTH JUSTICE PROCESS

The Canadian criminal justice system can generally be characterized as lacking coordination (Larsen, 1995). Critics point out that the criminal justice system does not share a common goal, a common philosophy, or a centralized decision-making authority. And while it can be argued that the system does share the generic goal of crime control and protection of society, there is little agreement as to how these goals can be attained. This general lack of coordination is also apparent in the young offender system.

Unlike the adult justice system, juvenile justice in Canada is administered by the provinces, even though the legislation which identifies jurisdictional powers, the *Young Offenders Act* (YOA), is a federal act. Articles appearing in the book edited by Corrado, Bala, Linden, and LeBlanc (1992) have identified several of the key problems both within and between provincial and territorial jurisdictions. They range from transfer issues, to appropriate dispositions, and the general effectiveness of the act in having its objectives implemented.

Figure 3.1 provides a graphic illustration of what happens once a youth comes into contact with the young offender system. As noted earlier the his-

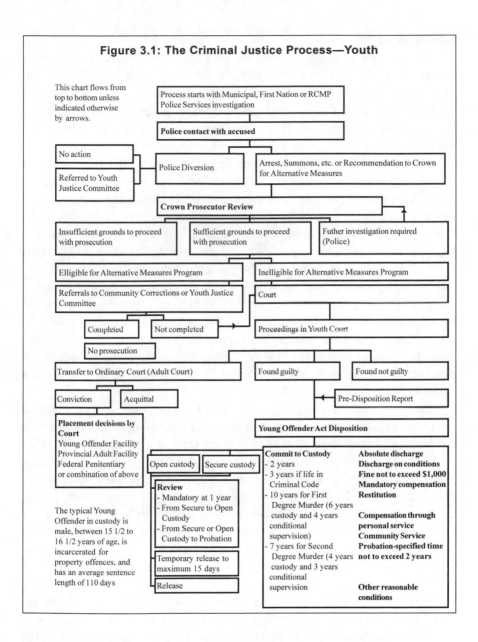

Figure 3.1: The Criminal Justice Process—Youth

tory of the juvenile justice system in Canada has undergone a number of dramatic changes in recent years. Today the model reflects a due process model in which an accused youth is entitled not only to legal representation but special consideration, hence the description "modified justice model."

Initial Contact

The police are usually the first representatives of the formal system that youths encounter. Under the YOA, all Criminal Code provisions from the point of arrest to applying for bail apply equally to young persons. The act and Section 10(a) of the Charter of Rights and Freedoms provide that all youths suspected of committing an offence must be informed about their rights by the attending police officer before they are apprehended and/or arrested.

Given that most of the crimes committed by young offenders are minor in nature, discretion is often exercised when handling such cases—again, the notion of *parens patriae*. But, as Doob and Chan (1982) discuss in their article, in whose best interests are discretionary measures taken? In a post JDA study, Carrington and Moyer (1994) found that since the new act, police are less likely to divert 16- and 17-year-old suspects than 12- to 15-year-olds. This discretionary handling appears to be due to police practices rather than a direct consequence of the act. Those youth between ages 12 to 15 tend to commit less serious crimes and are more likely to receive reprimands, be warned of future consequences should they re-offend, or be returned to their parent(s).

Should the incident warrant formal measures, the police will then use a formal document recommending the laying of a charge. Again, because of provincial jurisdictional authority, the extent to which discretion is exercised varies considerably.

The final decision on the admissibility of statements rests typically with either the police or the Crown. However, other persons in authority and who are involved in the arrest, detention, examination of a young offender (e.g., probation officers and corrections staff) may also be involved in the decision process. Again, it varies across jurisdictions. What is consistent, however, is that Section 56 of the YOA provides the safeguard that a youth, before giving a statement to the police, is entitled to be advised of his/her legal rights and due process, and has the option of having a lawyer or a parent/guardian present. This special provision is intended to ensure that there is no improper questioning by authorities. Under Section 44(1) of the YOA, a youth charged with an offence in which an adult may be fingerprinted and photographed may be subjected to the same measurement. The new proposed act (S. 176) would empower the court to order forensic DNA analysis for certain offence types.

While the basic tenets of the criminal law are entrenched into the YOA, sections such as 3(1)(f) have raised considerable debate as to how much discretion/accountability can be exercised. Section 3(1)(f) refers to the young person's "right to the least possible interference with freedom." Hence, given that enforcement of the act rests with each province and police department, the use of informal procedures varies widely between provinces and even between police jurisdictions within provinces. This practice is virtually unchanged from how youth were handled under the JDA.

Youth Court Proceedings

As was the case under the former JDA, legal proceedings under the YOA are conducted in specially designated youth courts. Depending on the jurisdiction, in some provinces it is the family court, while in others, a branch of adult provincial court.

Ontario and Nova Scotia (eastern provinces) are exceptions to the above scenarios in that they both use a two-tier youth court model. 12- to 15-year-olds are dealt with in family court while 16- to 17-year-olds are proceeded with in provincial court.

While the YOA (s. 52) stipulates that proceedings in youth court approximate those rules governing summary conviction offences in adult court, the proceedings for indictable offences are less complex and are intended to be more expeditious. For example, unlike in the adult system, there are no preliminary inquiries, and all trials are conducted by a judge (there are no jury trials in family court/provincial Court). However, the CCJS (1994), in their review of Bill C-37, strongly endorsed the right to jury trial in murder cases.

Relatively few cases actually end up in youth court. For a majority of those that do end up in youth court, they are the product of a "plea bargain."[15] The youth is "encouraged" to enter a plea of guilty with the understanding that the sentence will be less severe. What kind of message does this send to young offenders? Again, whose best interests are being served?

Should a young offender be required to attend court, Section 11 of the YOA requires that they be advised of their rights, and that if they cannot afford to retain counsel one will be provided by the state. And although it is possible to have a guardian or parent attend in place of a lawyer, given the formal legal procedure and potential risk for punishment youths are encouraged to seek legal counsel.

In Canada, even though young offenders are meant to be held accountable for their actions, there are provisions under the act (e.g., S. 38[1.5]) that do not allow the youths' name or identity to be published unless they are considered at risk of causing injury to themselves or others, and where such information "is relevant to the avoidance of the risk." Also, other provisions (S. 45) require that all criminal records be destroyed five years after the completion of a disposition for an indictable offence and three years after the completion of a disposition for summary offences. Furthermore, potential employers may not ask whether the potential employee has ever been convicted under the YOA. Such measures reflect the limited accountability young persons are afforded during their adolescent years. In accordance with Section 44.1(k), judges may allow for the disclosure of records between and before the non-disclosure period. This option is seldom exercised.

SENTENCING OPTIONS

As noted above, the court is able to draw from a wide variety of disposition options. One of the newest options available to the courts is the use of DNA testing (see Box 3.4). In accordance with Section 20 of the act, available dispositions include:

a) an absolute discharge;
b) an order for restitution or compensation;
c) an order for up to 240 hours of community service work;
d) a fine up to $1000;
e) an order for up to two years' probation;
f) an order for treatment for up to three years; and
g) an order for remand, secure or open custody for up to six years.[16]

Box 3.4: DNA Testing for Young Offenders

With the increasing demand for accountability of serious young offenders and serious adult offenders, a June 1995 bill was passed that now allows judges to issue a warrant authorizing a peace officer to obtain samples of bodily substances through officially prescribed means for forensic DNA analysis. The bill was, in part, fuelled by a public campaign spearheaded by the family whose 15-year-old daughter (Tara Manning) was smothered and raped while in her Montreal home. The amendment to the YOA is added to subsection (2.1) and includes a sub-clause (2). In accordance with the amendment, three investigative procedures are identified as acceptable. They include: hair sampling, taking of a buccal swab, and taking of blood by pricking the skin with a sterile lancet. Young offenders, unlike adults, will be entitled to have the sample taken in the presence of counsel or other appropriate adult. The justice minister backed his decision by pointing out that 20 or more American states already have such provisions, and DNA testing is also available in England, Australia, and New Zealand.

In 1998 the new *DNA Identification Act* empowered the court, on application by the Crown, to make an order authorizing the taking of DNA samples of one or more bodily substances from a young offender found guilty of an offence under the YOA.

Although the options may appear straightforward, there is considerable variation between jurisdictions as each province tries to consolidate its disposition philosophy for young offenders. For example, following the enactment of the act there was a significant increase in the number of custodial dispositions, but it varied between provinces (Corrado and Markwart, 1994). A 1991

Gallup poll found that 48% of the respondents supported the notion that young offenders be tried before the same court as adult offenders—in Quebec an overwhelming 71% supported the notion. However, given the number of articles and appeals surrounding the use of this disposition, it is clear that the legal system has not yet found its "comfort zone" in the use of custodial disposition (Kopyto and Condina, 1986) and the recurring themes of a "loosely coupled system" and "fragmented philosophical model" come to mind.

This controversy is perhaps most evident in the area of transfer to adult court. If a youth is transferred to adult court because of the seriousness of the offence, then s/he will be tried as an adult and all the relevant adult rules of law will apply equally to the youth—including sentencing options. Thus, although under the YOA a youth having committed murder can only receive a maximum of five years in secure custody, under the adult Criminal Code s/he could receive a maximum of life.[17] Milner (1995:384) has observed that there "has been considerable judicial disagreement about the appropriate interpretation of the YOA's standards for transfer, the interest of society... having regard to the needs of the young person."

Post Sentencing.... "Corrections"

On any given day 4,900 youths are in custody in Canada (Dempster, 1996). It has hopefully become clear that the YOA, although intended to ensure due process and accountability of young offenders, has endeavoured through its various provisions to ensure that criminal justice personnel will still be granted reasonable discretion in the handling and disposing of cases. Since its enactment the act has drawn considerable attention. In 1994, the July issue of the *Canadian Journal of Criminology* printed two articles discussing the pro and cons of the act—ten years after its ascension to law.

As noted above, approximately 35% of cases result in custody dispositions while the balance result in some type of alternative measure—a non-custody disposition. This consistent pattern reflects the desire of the YOA to recognize that young offenders may have special needs; it therefore provides provisions that the court can use when deciding a case. Even though alternative measures are popular, Griffiths and Hatch (1994) have observed that, as in adult corrections, there has been no methodologically strong evaluation demonstrating the effectiveness of such programs. In fact there have been concerns expressed about the net-widening tendencies of many community-based programs (see Japan for similar views). One review study found very modest success in the programs they evaluated in Ontario (Hundley, Scapinello, and Stasiak, 1992). The researchers were quick to point out that this does not mean that nothing works. These cautionary observations were largely based on the fact that many of the studies were methodologically weak.

Nevertheless, public sentiment and social policy would appear to suggest that Canada has not recovered from the post-"nothing works" syndrome of the 1970s. In fact there seems to have been an increased emphasis on punishment in spite of the fact that both academics and the Canadian Criminal Justice Association point out that there are major drawbacks to making youth justice policies punishment-oriented. As Griffiths and Hatch (1994:625) observed: "In the coming years, the YOA may come to be viewed as representing less of an enlightened approach to youth crime and young offenders and more of an impediment to addressing the needs of youths, victims, and the community." With the recent initiatives found in the Youth Justice Renewal Initiative and the proposed YCJA, it appears the government is attempting to find a balance between public concerns and its signatory obligations to the United Nations declaration on the rights of children.

CURRENT ISSUES FACING CANADIAN YOUTH TODAY

It seems that every generation and every country has its issues. Canada is no exception. Today Canadian youth are involved in several forms of behavior that are either a concern for criminal justice personnel or society as a whole. For example, data from the 1993 General Social Survey suggest a small but measurable increase in the level of fear of crime victimization compared to the 1988 survey results (Hung and Bowles, 1995).

The following summaries are not exhaustive; rather, they simply serve to provide a synopsis of some of the key "problem" areas Canadians are facing in the new millennium regarding young offenders.[18]

Youth Gangs

While street/youth gangs have existed in Canada since the late 1920s, during the late 1980s and into the 1990s we have witnessed a flurry of gang activity, which has been accompanied by a number of articles in an otherwise sparsely covered topic (Gordon, 1995). Recent studies suggest that, notwithstanding definitional problems, the problem has escalated and diversified. For example, since the mid-1980s Asian organized crime groups (e.g., triads and tongs) have become a growing concern (Prowse, 1994). Aside from being more violent than "traditional" youth gangs, they engage in a wide variety of crimes ranging from home invasion/robbery to extortion, protection rackets, and distribution of drugs. Aboriginal youth gangs have also presented problems in several major cities in recent years. However, Mathews (2000:234) notes that "most youth-gang configurations are not violent or crime-focused." Yet Carrigan (1998) cautions that a number of the modern youth gangs are both sophisticated and just as profit-oriented as their American counterparts.

The primary attraction to gang activity seems to be related to material and psychological rewards, and because of these temptations some youth seem to "drift" (Matza, 1964) into gang-related activities. As a result of their associations, they learn techniques that enable them to neutralize the values and beliefs taught by law-abiding citizens. Mathews (2000) suggests that marginalization of communities from social influences and political power can also create conditions for gang formation. Both explanations speak to a situation where social controls (formal and informal) are less well established. To date most gang activities seem to be limited to major metropolitan areas, and many metropolitan police forces have established special youth gang units to monitor and counter this growing problem.

Runaways and Homeless Youth

Even though being a runaway is not a crime in Canada, the number of youths running away from home has increased significantly over the past three decades (MacLaurin, 2000). A national survey conducted in four major Canadian cities estimates the number of missing children and youth at around 12,500 (CCJS, 1998, 18[2]). The highest risk category are those youth between the ages of 14 and 15 (McDonald, 1994). Due to a lack of employment opportunities, limited social and employment skills, an increasing number of these youths are turning to youth crimes, prostitution, substance abuse, and militant groups as a means of trying to survive on the streets.[19] Girls are more likely than boys to run away, and in a substantial number of cases those who run away from home have done so more than once (McDonald, 1994). These chronic runaways and homeless youth become vulnerable to being victimized physically and sexually, especially when in certain parts of the country there is a dearth of resources available to offer adequate intervention approaches. And in March of 2000, when the proposed YCJA was being studied by the House of Commons, references were made to some recent homelessness initiatives that included homeless youth announced by the federal government. This was extremely timely, as members of ECPAT (End Child Prostitution, Pornography and Trafficking) recently pointed out that Vancouver, British Columbia, has become a popular spot for sex tourists who prey on children. They attribute the increase to rising levels of homeless youth (Edmonds, 2000).

In February 1999, Alberta became the first province in Canada to introduce controversial legislation to combat child prostitution. It gave police and child welfare officials authority to apprehend young persons believed to be involved in prostitution, and to detain them for up to 72 hours to conduct an assessment.

Teenage Suicide

In spite of the general findings of the National Longitudinal Survey of Children and Youth (NLSCY), in 1996/97, which reported that most youth said they have a happy and positive outlook on life (Daily, 1999), suicide among Canadian youth has become a growing concern. In 1998, Canada had the third highest teen suicide rate in the world. In Alberta alone, suicide among teens (ages 10 to 14) has risen 146% since 1970 and 695% for youths aged 15 to 19 since 1955 (Verburg, 1995). This growth in the absolute number of youth suicides is staggering, and according to some they are a reflection of the turmoil and emotional distress many youth are experiencing. For example, the NLSCY noted that 7% of all 12- and 13-year-olds reported they had seriously considered suicide in the preceding 12 months. Hence, the "problem" is seen as a barometer of youth in conflict or at risk. They may then choose to act out in deviant ways to draw attention (e.g., dropping out of school, teenage pregnancy, alcohol and substance abuse, etc.). Suicide rates may also be linked the number of youth at risk, those who are vulnerable to the negative consequences of school failure, substance abuse, poor job prospects, early sexuality, and the pressures to assume greater responsibility at earlier ages.

Female Delinquency

In 1895 Cesare Lombroso and William Ferrero wrote the first book on female offenders, *The Female Offender*; however, Gomme (1993, chap. 9) observed that this area has received little attention in Canada. One explanation for the apparent lack of official involvement may be sexism within the Canadian juvenile justice system. Nevertheless, self-report studies reveal the gap between male and female involvement is not as great as reflected in the official data (Hagan, 1985). Reitsma-Street and Artz (2000) report that there has been a marked increase in the number of charges for noncompliance with the administration of youth justice by females since the late 1980s. They also observed that the rate for minor assaults has also increased noticeably during the early 1990s. Official statistics show that the rate of violent crime charges among young persons rose from 80 per 10,000 in 1987/88 to 130 per 10,000 in 1998 (1999, 13[13]). The rate of increase in violent crime charges for females is higher than that of males (Fisher, 1993). In addition, female youths committing violent crime tend to be younger (peaking at 17 for boys and 14 to 15 for females) than male youths (CCJS, 1999, 19[13]). However, overall, the rate at which youth have been charged with violent crimes has declined slightly since 1996.

While some researchers suggest the increase is due to the applied stereotyped concept of the proper role for women, others more accurately argue the increase is "part of active struggles within a changing social order in which power and privilege are unequally distributed and frequently contested"

(Reitsma-Street and Artz, 2000:83). With increasing role convergence and changing social values, it is anticipated that the numbers of young females offenders will increase.

Youth Violence

As noted earlier, official statistics and self-report studies reveal that while property crime may have declined slightly during the early 1990s, violent crime has increased. By the end of the 90s, violent crime was 77% higher than in the late 80s. By contrast, violent crime among adults only increased by 6% (CCJS, 1999, 19(13)). These trends have also been reflected in two separate self-report studies, one in Ontario (Youth violence..., 1993) and the other in Alberta (Smith, Bertrand, Arnold, and Hornick, 1995). In 1998, one in five youths charged was accused of a violent crime. These trends, while imposing, need to be weighed against a multitude of factors in an effort to answer the questions: "Why is this happening and what can be done about it?" and "Why does it appear to be an international phenomena?"

Replacing the Young Offenders Act?

As noted throughout this chapter, the YOA has drawn considerable backlash from all fronts. It does not appear that the intended principles of balancing special needs with accountability are being implemented. Instead, with the proposed new YCJA, there would be a shift towards greater protection of society and accountability for deviant behavior, albeit with some reflection of the work of the House of Commons Standing Committee on Justice and Human Rights. Yet there continues to exist a major rift between the public outcry for better accountability and the realization that changing the act alone cannot prevent youths from committing crimes. Reitsma-Street (1993) has gone so far as to suggest a moratorium on YOA changes. However, with the June 1995 amendment to Section 3(1)(a) of the act under Bill C-37, provisions have now been included which emphasize crime prevention and multi-disciplinary approaches. This is an element strongly endorsed by the UN minimum standards (see Introduction) for the administration of juvenile justice. Should the new act come into effect, it would address many of the apparent shortcoming of the YOA. Initial debates have raised some doubts as to whether new legislation alone can address social issues, however, and at the time of preparing this chapter a federal election was imminent.

SUMMARY

Canada is a relatively young nation with an even newer legislative act for the handling of young offenders—formally referred to as juvenile delinquents.

This current federal Act, the *Young Offenders Act*, which is administered by the provinces and territories, has been described as a **modified justice model** (see Figure 1—Introduction) that attempts to balance the perceived special needs of young people with a measured degree of accountability. However, unlike the birth of our nation, it was observed that the act's implementation has not gone smoothly. In fact, after being in effect for only 13 years, there is considerable pressure to revise the act, especially as it pertains to the age of responsibility, publication of names, and accountability for serious offences such as murder and aggravated assault. The system has been described as being "loosely coupled" and "fragmented philosophically." For example, Ontario, Manitoba, and Alberta have introduced strict discipline programming (e.g., work or boot camps) for those youth who show a flagrant disregard for the law. What appears to have transpired since the act came into being is that our system is filtering humanity out of the process. At the time of preparing this chapter, a new act, the *Youth Criminal Justice Act*, has been tabled (for the third time in February 2001) in Parliament as a suitable replacement of the existing act and one that claims to have addressed many of the criticisms leveled at the YOA.

In the second section of the chapter it was shown how, since the enactment of the YOA in 1984, the overall youth crime rate modestly increased until the early 1990s, when it began to steadily drop. The decline is largely due to the falling property crime rate, while violent crime has either remained stable or gone up slightly. While the increases cannot be assumed to be directly attributable to the YOA, this socially disturbing trend has raised considerable debate about the effectiveness of the YOA. For example, headings sampled from local newspapers reflect the sentiment which currently prevails: "Youth law weak, say teens," "Youth court a real nightmare for everybody," "No end seen to spiraling teenage crime," and "Young criminals taking a holiday." It seems quite clear that the act has borne the brunt of public discontent. But evidence continues to question whether punishing someone who hurts another is an effective way to demonstrate that hurting is wrong. This is a fundamental issue that all societies must confront.

The third major section of the chapter provided an overview of how youth justice is administered by the major actors in the system. Although cases follow a similar legal format from one province or territory to another, what is significant is the difference among the jurisdictions in the way the YOA is administered. As this section of the chapter suggested, these variations, while understandable to an extent, reflect differing cultural, political, and social views about the objectives of the act as well as the varying financial realities within the provinces and territories.

This overview of the current Canadian youth justice system has painted a somewhat bleak picture. However, it should be noted that with the amendments to the new YCJA bill and various provincial initiatives, there are alternative programs that reflect a more humanitarian/welfare model approach to youth justice. For example, in Ontario there are several communities experimenting with dispute resolution programs that involve pre-trial mediation between the offender and the victim. Manitoba is fairly proactive in using youth justice committees to assist in crime prevention and public education initiatives. A variation of the youth justice committee in Alberta is an experimental community committee that has a mandate to deal with non-violent, first-time offences. The committee can hand out individual sentences ranging from 30 hours of community service to restitution orders up to $1,000. In the Yukon a project is modelled after old Native justice principles. Sentencing circle projects involve a young offender being informally tried in the midst of a circle of individuals consisting of a judge, police, lawyers, and community members, which can include people supporting either the victim or the offender. And Corrado and Markwart (1994) note that Quebec's system of service delivery, which involves multi-disciplinary assessment and intervention, may represent the most progressive interpretation of the YOA across Canada. They suggest that other provinces in Canada should look more closely at the Quebec system. However, given the aggressive nature with which the proposed YCJA is being promoted as the viable replacement for the YOA, it may come to pass that Canada will have a more uniform model of justice and one that will receive greater financial support in its implementation.

While the majority of Canadians' attitudes seem to be oriented towards due process and accountability, there is a growing movement of individuals and organizations such as the Church Council of Justice and Corrections, the Canadian Criminal Justice Association, and individual research efforts whose findings strongly suggest that we may have gone in the wrong direction. We may need to turn back and trade our conventional concepts of (juvenile) justice, guilt and punishment for models based on prevention, education, diagnosis, and treatment. The YCJA includes provisions for such measures, and the government has already begun to allocate resources to facilitate the implementation of more community-based programs. While the YOA encompassed many of the minimum standards for the administration of juvenile justice as identified by the UN, the proposed legislation appears to have further refined the level of attention given to the UN guidelines. Yet only time will tell whether the new model will be able to fill the void left by the YOA.

We concluded the chapter by looking at some of the current issues confronting young persons and young offenders in Canada. While some of the trends have changed (for the better) since the first edition, they continue to remain important issues.

What lies ahead for the administration of youth justice in Canada is not clear. For example, in 1998 the Canadian Criminal Justice Association cautioned that the YCJA will not likely accomplish all that it claims, and it may further undermine the public view of youth justice unless it is accompanied by a strong public education component. In the meantime, it might serve us well to look beyond our limited frame of reference to examine what other countries are doing, to perhaps provide alternative political and etiological insights. The youth are our future and they deserve our fullest attention and support.

John Winterdyk, Ph.D., has been teaching in the Department of Justice Studies at Mount Royal College in Calgary since 1988. In addition to his broad range of journal publications, his recent academic works include: co-editor: *Diversity and Justice in Canada* (1999), *Canadian Criminology* (2000); editor: *Issues and Perspectives on Young Offenders in Canada, 2nd ed.* (2000); editor: *Corrections in Canada: Social Reactions to Crime* (2001); co-author: *Canadian Criminal Justice Today: An Introductory text for the Twenty-first Century* (2000). He is currently preparing a Canadian text on research methods as well as editing a comparative text on adult correctional systems. Winterdyk is also the book review editor for the *Journal of Comparative Criminology* as well as the co-author of a successful health and fitness book: *The Complete Athlete: Integrating Fitness, Health, and Nutrition* (1998).

HELPFUL WEBSITES

Home.istar.ca/~ccja/angl/youth.html A report prepared by the Canadian Criminal Justice Association that comments on the government's proposed new youth justice law.

www.statcan.ca/english/pgdb/state/justic.htm Home site for Canadian justice and crime statistics.

www.usask.ca/nativelaw/jah_ajln.html This site offers a wide range of information on Aboriginal justice issues and strategies.

www.plena.org Public Legal Education Network of Alberta. Provides updates on the Youth Justice Renewal Initiative as well as other information related to youth justice.

KEY TERMS AND CONCEPTS

British North America Act	Constitution Act	Parens patriae
General Strain Theory	*Juvenile Delinquents Act*	*Young Offenders Act*
Alternative measures	Welfare model	Modified justice model
Youth Criminal Justice Act	Community change model	Social learning theory
Multiple dispositions	Routine activity theory	General theory of crime
Power-control theory	Clayton McGloan and	
Control theory	Ryan Garrioch	

STUDY QUESTIONS

1. How does the current *Young Offenders Act* differ from the former *Juvenile Delinquents Act*? How, if in any way, do the changes reflect the recommendations identified in the Beijing Rules?
2. Does the proposed *Youth Criminal Justice Act* compliment the recommendations of the United Nations? If so, in what ways? How does the proposed act represent an 'improvement' over the existing legislation?
3. How do the three acts appear to be socially and politically based as opposed to reflecting the true welfare of young persons?
4. How do the delinquent trends and patterns compare with those of other countries covered in this text?
5. How does youth justice within Canada compare to that in other countries and the world?
6. What are the comparative strengths and weaknesses of the modified justice model?

NOTES

1   In November 2000 Canada had a federal election. The Liberals were successful in winning re-election and their political platform stated that they were prepared to go ahead and reintroduce the act once the new cabinet had been struck. The latest proposed date for enactment of the new Act is April 2003.
2   A Latin expression which means the state has the power to act on behalf of the child and provide care and protection equivalent to that of a parent. The term reflects a paternalistic philosophy which emphasizes treatment and sees delinquent youth as misguided and in need of special consideration and help (Griffiths and Hatch, 1994).
3   This theme was reiterated in a feature article of the "Alberta Report". Dr. Genuis, Executive Director of the National Foundation for Family Research and Education in Edmonton, Alberta, was quoted as saying: "There is also a cultural crisis among teens... Too many of their other anti-social behaviours are on the rise to believe they are not also committing more crimes" (Verburg, 1995: 31).
4   The United Nations Standard Minimum Rules for the Administration of Juvenile Justice contain 30 rules that reflect the aims and spirit that all nations should strive to embrace within their juvenile justice systems.
5   For an interesting comparison on the role of the media in forging legislative reform see Chapter 5 (Juvenile Delinquency in the U.K.), specifically the James Bulger case.
6   In November of 2000 a federal election was held. And, although the Liberals were re-elected, at the time of completing this chapter it was unclear as to whether Bill C-3 would reintroduced. Interested readers can follow the status of the Canadian juvenile legislation by accessing one of the websites provided at the end of this chapter.
7   Copies of the three acts can be found in Winterdyk (2000b)—Appendices A-C.
8   You can follow the progress of the new act by visiting http://canada.justice.gc.ca
9   In 1962 the federal government introduced nationwide the Canadian Uniform Crime Report (UCR) system. This measure helped to minimize many of the limitations of the previous approach. The Canadian UCR was modelled after the American UCR system. In the late 1980s Statistics Canada created a national institute, the Canadian Centre for Justice Statistics, which is now responsible for collecting,

aggregating, and disseminating official crime statistics. The first reports were published in 1991. This model is similar to what the Home Office does for England and Wales.

10 Moreover, the minimum age requirement for charges under the YOA became 12 in 1984, and in April 1984 the maximum age of 17 (inclusive) was established across all of Canada. Because of the significance of these changes, and the time needed to adapt to them, reliable comparisons under the YOA cannot be made prior to about 1986/87.

11 The results of this massive study have been published in a series of federal publications ranging from 1983 through 1986.

12 In 1998 there were 2.5 million Criminal Code incidents. This equates to 8,102 incidents per 100,000 population. This rate has steady declined throughout the 1990s. Yet a 1998 public opinions survey shows that 75% of Canadians feel crime is getting worse (CCJS, 20(4)).

13 This trend is also evident among adult females (CCJS, 1999, 19(13)).

14 Statistics Canada uses the term "persistent offender" to denote young persons who have been convicted of three or more offences.

15 Plea bargaining has been described as one of the most controversial, and perhaps least understood, aspects of the Canadian criminal justice system (Griffiths and Verdun-Jones, 1994). Public surveys show that Canadians feel plea bargaining leads to excessively lenient sentences. In essence, plea bargaining in Canada "is concerned with reaching an agreement to secure a concession from the Crown in return for the accused pleading guilty" (Griffiths and Verdun-Jones, 1994:318).

16 First degree murder carries a maximum custodial sentence of six years, followed by four years of conditional supervision. Second degree murder carries a maximum sentence of four years followed by three years of conditional supervision. Recent amendments to the YOA allow for sentences of three years if the crime would normally carry a maximum penalty of life imprisonment in adult court or involves multiple offences.

17 Not since 1962 has a Canadian been hung for murder. In 1976 capital punishment was officially abolished. Between 1867 and 1962 Canada hanged 693 men and 13 women. The 1994 Canadian Police Association Survey revealed that 76.6% of the respondents supported the return of capital punishment for first degree murder.

18 For example, the problem of drug abuse and alcohol abuse, sexual assault, abductions, and sexual abuse are not covered. For a general overview see Winterdyk (2000c).

19 One recent Canadian study found that some 75% of children and youth engaged in the sex trade were victims of sexual abuse before they became prostitutes. A majority of these children also had a history of poverty and low socio-economic status.

REFERENCES

Agnew, R. (1992). Foundation for a general strain theory of crime and delinquency. *Criminology*, 30, 47-87.

A graphic overview of crime and the administration of criminal justice in Canada. (1996, May). Ottawa: Canadian Centre for Justice Statistics.

Akers, R. (1985). *Deviant behavior: A social learning approach.* Belmont, CA: Wadsworth.

Bala, N., Hornick, J.P., & Vogl, R. (Eds.). (1991). *Canadian child welfare law*. Toronto: Thompson Educational.
Basic Facts About Federal Corrections. (1999). Ottawa: Correctional Service Canada.
Brownfield, B., & Thompson, K. (1991). Attachment to peers and delinquent behaviour. *Canadian Journal of Criminology*, 33(1), 45–60.
Canadian Criminal Justice Statistics (CCJS). Ottawa, ON.
Canadian Criminal Justice Association Bulletin, Nov. 15, 1992.
Canadian Criminal Justice Association Bulletin, Sept. 15, 1994.
Canadian Criminal Justice Association Bulletin, Jan. 16, 1996.
(1995). Youth Custody and probation in Canada. 15(7).
(1998). Missing and Abducted Children. 18(2)
(1999a). Alternative Measures for Youth in Canada. 19(8).
(1999b). Justice Spending in Canada. 19(12).
(1999c). Youth Violent Crime. 19(13).
(2000a). Youth Court Statistics, 1998/99 Highlights. 20(2).
(2000b). The Justice Factfinder, 1998. 20(4).
(2000c). Sentencing of young offenders in Canada, 1998/99. 20(7).
Canadian Police Association Year Book 1994, pp. 27–29. Ottawa: Canadian Police Association, Canadian Badge in Uniform (publication).
Carrigan, D.O. (1998). *Juvenile delinquency in Canada: A history*. Concord, ON: Irwin.
Carrington, P.J., & Moyer, S. (1994). Trends in youth crime and police response, pre- and post-YOA. *Canadian Journal of Criminology*, 36(1), 1–28.
Cohen, L.E., & Felson, M. (1979). Social change and crime rate trends. *American Sociological Review*, 44, 588–605.
Corrado, R.R., Bala, N., Linden, R., & LeBlanc, M. (Eds.). (1992). *Juvenile justice in Canada*. Toronto: Butterworths.
Corrado, R.R., & Markwart, A. (1994). The need to reform the YOA in response to violent young offenders: Confusion, myth or reality? *Canadian Journal of Criminology*, 36(3), 343–378.
Creechan, J. H. (1995). A test of the general theory of crime: Delinquency and school dropouts. In J.H. Creechan & R. A. Silverman (Eds.), *Canadian delinquency*. Scarborough, ON: Prentice Hall.
Currie, D. (1986). The transformation of juvenile justice in Canada: A study of Bill C-61. In B. D. MacLean (Ed.), *The political economy of crime*. Scarborough, ON: Prentice Hall.
The Daily. (1999, July 6). National longitudinal survey of children and youth: transition into adolescence. Ottawa: Statistics Canada.
Day, D.M., Golench, C.A., MacDougall, J., & Beals-Gonzalez, C.A. (1995). School-based violence prevention in Canada: Results of a national survey of policies and programs. Ottawa: Solicitor General Canada.
Decisions and dispositions in youth court, 1986/87 to 1989/90. *Juristat*, 10 (19). Ottawa: Statistics Canada, Canadian Centre for Justice Statistics.
deMause, L. (Ed.). (1988). *The history of childhood*. New York: Peter Bedrick Books.
Dempster, M. (1996, January 19). Young Offenders Act: Crime and punishment. *Calgary Herald*, p. B4.
Doherty, G., & de Souza, P. (1995). Recidivism in youth court 1993/94. *Juristat*, 15 (16). Ottawa: Statistics Canada, Canadian Centre for Justice Statistics.
Doherty, G., & de Souza, P. (1996). Youth court statistics 1994/95. *Juristat*, 16 (4). Ottawa: Statistics Canada, Canadian Centre for Justice Statistics.

Doob, A.N., & Chan, J.B. (1982). Factors affecting police decisions to take juveniles to court. *Canadian Journal of Criminology*, 24 (1), 25–37.

Dumont, M. (2000, August 08). YOA petition close to one million signatures. *Calgary Herald,* p. B6.

Edmonds, S. (2000, November 21). Vancouver branded a haven for pedophiles. *The Toronto Star.* Available online: www.thestar.com

Empey, L.T. (1982). From optimism to despair: New directions in juvenile justice. In C.A. Murray & L.A. Cox Jr. (Eds.), *Beyond probation: Juvenile corrections and the chronic delinquent.* Beverly Hills, CA: Sage.

Fisher, M. (1993, May 19). Rising crime linked to girls. *The Calgary Sun*, 29.

Gomme, I. (1993). *The shadow line: Deviance and crime in Canada* (Ch. 9). Toronto: Harcourt Brace Jovanovich.

Gordon, R.M. (1995). Street gangs in Vancouver. In J.H. Creechan & R.A. Silverman (Eds.), *Canadian delinquency.* Scarborough, ON: Prentice Hall.

Griffiths, C., & Hatch, A. (1994). The Canadian youth justice system. In C. Griffiths & S. Verdun-Jones (Eds.), *Canadian criminal justice* (2nd ed.; pp. 595–631). Toronto: Harcourt Brace.

Griffiths, C., & Verdun-Jones, S. (Eds.). (1994). *Canadian criminal justice* (2nd ed.). Toronto: Harcourt Brace.

Hackler, J. (1996). Anglophone juvenile justice. In J. Winterdyk (Ed.), *Issues and perspectives on young offenders in Canada* (Ch. 12). Toronto: Harcourt Brace.

Hagan, J. (1983). *Victims before the law.* Toronto: Butterworths.

Hagan, J. (1985). *Crime, criminal behavior, and its control.* New York: McGraw-Hill.

Hagan, J. (1995). Good people, dirty system: The Young Offenders Act and organizational failure. In N. Larsen (Ed.), *The Canadian criminal justice system* (pp. 389–418). Toronto: Canadian Scholars' Press Inc.

Hagan, J., Alwin, D., & Hewitt, J. (1979). Ceremonial justice: Crime and punishment in a loosely coupled society. *Social Forces*, 58, 506–527.

Hagan, J., Simpson, J., & Gillis, A.R. (1987). Class in the household: A power-control theory of gender and delinquency. *American J. of Sociology*, 92, 788–816.

Hagan, J., Simpson, J., & Gillis, A.R. (1979). The sexual stratification of social control: A gender based perspective on crime and delinquency. *British Journal of Criminology*, 30, 25–38.

Hendrick, D., & Lachance, M. (1991). A profile of the young offender. *Forum on Corrections Research*, 3 (3), 17–21.

Horner, B. (M.P. Chairman). (1993, February). *Crime prevention in Canada: Towards a national strategy, 12th report of the Standing Committee on Justice and Solicitor General.* Ottawa: Solicitor General of Canada.

Hundley, J.D., Scapinello, K.F., & Stasiak, G.A. (1992). *Thirteen to thirty: A follow-up study of young training school boys.* Ottawa: Corrections Branch, Solicitor General of Canada.

Hung, K., & Bowles, S. (1995). Public perception of crime. *Juristat*, 15(1). Ottawa: Statistics Canada, Canadian Centre for Justice Statistics.

International data. (1995, March–April). *CJ International*, 11(2), 17.

Kennedy, L. & Baron, S.W. (1993). Routine activities and a subculture of violence: A study of violence on the street. *J. of Research in Crime and Delinquency*, 30 (1), 88–112.

Kids and Crime. (Summer, 2000). Official Newsletter of PLENA's Youth Justice Renewal Initiative, Vol. 1 (1). Red Deer, Alberta.

Kopyto, H., & Condina, A.M. (1986). Young Offenders Act means more frequent custody terms. *Lawyers Weekly*, 6, 8.

Larsen, N. (Ed.). (1995). *The Canadian criminal justice system: An issues approach to the administration of justice.* Toronto: Canadian Scholars' Press Inc.

Leschield, A.W., & Jaffe, P.G. (1995). Dispositions as indicators of conflicting social purposes under the JDA and YOA. In N. Larsen (Ed.), *The Canadian criminal justice system.* Toronto: Canadian Scholars' Press Inc.

Leesti, T. (1994). Youth custody in Canada, 1992/93. *Juristat*, 14 (11). Ottawa: Statistics Canada, Canadian Centre for Justice Statistics.

Leonard, C., & Morris, T. (2000). Changes in the Young Offenders Act: Principled reform? In J.A.Winterdyk (Ed.), *Issues and perspectives on young offenders in Canada* (Ch. 5). Toronto: Harcourt Brace.

Lundman, R.J. (1994). *Prevention and control of juvenile delinquency* (2nd ed.). Oxford University Press.

MacLaurin, B. (2000). Youth on the street in Canada. In J. Winterdyk (Ed.). *Issues and perspectives on young offenders in Canada* (2nd ed.; Ch. 8). Toronto: Harcourt-Brace.

Markwart, A., & Corrado, R. (1995). A response to Carrington. *Canadian Journal of Criminology*, 37 (1), 74–87.

Mathews, F. (2000). Youth gangs. In J. Winterdyk (Ed.), *Issues and perspectives on young offenders in Canada* (2nd ed.; Ch. 9). Toronto: Harcourt-Brace.

Martinson, R. (1974). What works?—Questions and answers about prison reform. *The Public Interest*, 35, 22–54.

Matza, D. (1964). *Delinquency and drift.* New York: Wiley.

McDonald, L. (1969). Crime and punishment in Canada: A statistical test of the "conventional wisdom." *Canadian Review of Sociology and Anthropology*, 6: 212-36.

McDonald, R.J. (1994). Missing children. In *Canadian social trends* (Vol. 2; pp. 213–216). Toronto: Thompson Educational.

Milner, T. (1995). Juvenile legislation. In J.H. Creechan & R.A. Silverman. (Eds.), *Canadian delinquency.* Scarborough, ON: Prentice Hall.

Moyer, S. (1992). Recidivism in youth courts, 1990–91. *Juristat*, 12 (2). Ottawa: Statistics Canada, Canadian Centre for Justice Statistics.

Pagani, L, Tremblay, R.E., Vitro, F., & Parent, S. (1998). Does preschool help prevent delinquency in boys with a history of prenatal complications? *Criminology*, 36 (2,: 245–267.

Prowse, C.E. (1994). *Vietnamese gangs.* Calgary: Calgary Police Services.

Reid, S.A., & Reitsma-Street, M. (1984). Assumptions and implications of new Canadian legislation for young offenders. *Canadian Criminology Forum*, 7, 334–52.

Reitsma-Street, M. (1993). Canadian youth court charges and dispositions for females before and after implementation of the *Young Offenders Act. Canadian Journal of Criminology*, 35 (4), 437–58.

Reitsma-Street, M., & Artz, S. (2000). Girls and crime. In J.A. Winterdyk (Ed.), *Issues and perspectives on young offenders in Canada* (Ch. 3). Toronto: Harcourt Brace.

Romig, D.A., Cleland, C.C., & Romig, L.J. (1989). *Juvenile delinquency: Visionary approaches*. Columbus, OH: Merrill.

Smandych, R., Dobbs, G., & Esau, A. (Eds.). (1991). *Dimensions of childhood*. Winnipeg, MB: Legal Research Institute of the University of Manitoba.

Smith, R.B., Bertrand, L.D., Arnold, B.L., & Hornick, J.P. (1995, March). *A study of the level and nature of youth crime and violence in Calgary*. Report prepared for the Calgary Police Service by the Canadian Research Institute for Law and the Family. Calgary: University of Calgary.

Solicitor General of Canada. (1981, February 16). *News release. Young Offenders Bill tabled in House of Commons*. Ottawa: Solicitor General of Canada.

Stewart, M. (1995, May 16). Weapons in schools are a major concern for police. *Calgary Herald*, p. B1.

Sutherland, N. (1976). *Children in English-Canadian society: Framing the twentieth century consensus*. Toronto: University of Toronto Press.

Trojanowicz, R. (1978). *Juvenile delinquency: Concepts and control*. Englewood Cliffs, NJ: Prentice Hall.

United Nations (1986). *United Nations standard minimum rules for the administration of juvenile justice*. New York: U.N. Dept. of Information.

Tufts, J. (2000). Public attitude toward the criminal justice system. *Juristat*, 20 (12), 1-3.

Verburg, P. (1995, May 1). Rebels without consciences. *Alberta Report*, 30–36.

Violence in Schools. (2000). Wysiwyg://10http://7-12educators....ators/library/weekly/aa041800a.htm

Walker, R. (1996, December 13). Drop in health concerns seen. *Calgary Herald*, p. A9.

West, G. (1984). *Young offenders and the state: A Canadian perspective*. Toronto: Butterworths.

Wheeler, S. (1967). Criminal statistics: A reformulation of the problem. *Journal of Criminal Law, Criminology and Police Science*, 58, 317–24.

Wilson, J.Q. (1975). *Thinking about crime*. New York: Vintage Books.

Winterdyk, J. (1996, April/May). The looking glass: Canadian Centre for Justice Statistics. *Law Now*, 14–18.

Winterdyk, J. (Ed.). (2000a). *Issues and perspectives on young offenders in Canada* (2nd ed.; Ch. 2). Toronto: Harcourt Brace.

Winterdyk, J. (2000b). *Canadian criminology*. Scarborough, ON: Pearson Educational.

Winterdyk, J. (2000c). Younger offenders. In F. Schmalleger, D. MacAlister, P, McKenna, & J. Winterdyk. (Eds.), *Canadian criminal justice today: An introductory text for the twenty-first century* (Ch. 14). Scarborough, ON: Prentice Hall.

Woodard, J. (2000, December 1). Youth violence soaring. *Calgary Herald*, p. B12.

Young, G. (1994). Trends in justice spending, 1988/89 to 1992/93. *Juristat*, 14 (16). Ottawa: Statistics Canada, Canadian Centre for Justice Statistics.

Youth justice: A better direction for our country. (1994, Fall). Ottawa: The Church Council of Justice and Corrections.

Youth violence is on the rise. (1993, March 2). *Calgary Herald*, p. A8.

Chapter 4

Youth justice in China

Liling Yue
China University of Political Science and Law, Beijing

FACTS ON CHINA

Area: at 9.6 million sq. km. China is the largest of the Asian countries and has the largest population of any country in the world. **Population:** 1.2481 billion (1998 statistics) with a growth rate of approx. 0.93%. **Climate:** varies widely by region and latitude. In fact, China has one of the world's widest array of ecological niches. In winter, the lowest average temperature for a northern city could be −19 C; in summer, the hottest average temperature for a southern city could reach 30.1C. **Culture:** officially atheist but Taoism, Buddhism, Islam, and Christianity are practiced. Mandarin is the main language with many local dialects, and 92% of the population is Chinese. **Divisions of Administrative Areas:** China has 23 (including Taiwan[1]) provinces, 5 autonomous ethnic regions, 4 municipalities (Chungking, Peking, Shang-hai, and Tientsin), and 2 special administrative regions (Hong Kong and Macau). Beijing (formerly Peking) is the capital. **Government:** China's Constitution was signed 4 December 1982, and its government is communist party-led with 8 minor parties. China is a centralized country for which the People's Congress has legislative authority. Provincial and local people's congresses have authority to make provincial and local laws or regulations. **Economy:** the Gross National Product in 1998 was 7.801.800 million yuan. The average annual growth rate (from 1991-1998) was 10.5%. The government revenue in 1998 was 987.600 million yuan while the government expenditures in 1998 was to 1,079,820 yuan (1 US$ = approx. 8.3 yuan).

"If there is radiance in the soul it will abound in the family. If there is radiance in the family it will be abundant in the community. If there is radiance in the community it will grow in the nation. If there is radiance in the nation the universe will flourish" – Lao Tzu, sixth century BC.

China, officially referred to as the People's Republic of China, is unique among nations in its longevity and history. China boasts a recorded history that dates back some 4,000 years and in spite of the frequent political and social upheavals the country has flourished culturally and economically. With the exception of the introduction of Buddhism from India, China's cultural development has remained relatively unaffected by outside influences. Chinese culture has been heavily influenced by Confucianism (see Box 4.1). However, China's relative isolation left it ill-prepared to adapt and adjust to the technological changes that swept most other parts of the world from the mid-fifteenth century. Not only did China, under the Qing dynasty, experience social strife, economic decline, and dramatic population growth, but it was also subjected to an onslaught of Western penetration and influences (e.g., the Opium War in 1849; forcible occupancy by Britain, the United States, and other western countries; Hong Kong was ceded to Britain in 1842). The end result of the traumatic change was a revolution that began in the early twentieth century against the old regime and culminated in the establishment of a Communist government on October 1, 1949, under the leadership of Mao Zedong. Since then China has gradually re-established itself among the more powerful and influential countries in the world.

Box 4.1: Confucianism and cultural influence

While China has remained relatively isolated from foreign influences, traditional **Confucianism** has and continues to shape the fundamental values that define Chinese social relations. Although it is impossible to construct a reliable picture of Confucius, it is possible to outline some of the major tenets of the social order that date back to around 200 BC. Confucianism emphasizes family and loyalty to group, friends, and rulers. It shares a number of similarities with socialism today in that it promotes collective interests and community welfare. An emphasis on education or remolding is seen to serve a common good. These ideals have helped to reinforce the **participatory** aspects of the Chinese juvenile justice model. However, under the influence of recent social and political change, we see the degree to which legalism or a **justice model** has infiltrated China's approach to juvenile justice.

In 1958, Mao broke off his ties with the Soviet model when he introduced the "Great Leap Forward" program. The program was designed to increase industrial and agricultural production. The program failed because of poor planning and bad weather, which resulted in widespread famine.

Until Mao's death in September 1976, China underwent numerous political upheavals which did little to reinstate Chinese culture and politics to its former stature. Finally, at the Third Plenum in 1978, the leadership; under Deng Xiaoping, adopted social and economic reforms that slowly initiated positive changes.

The period has been referred to a "second revolution". Members of Mao's reform movement were removed from politics allowing for new social reforms to take hold. Deng's policies reflected an openness while still embracing socialist ideas. However, the change did not go smoothly as inflation, mass urban migration, and various social problems (among them an increase in crime and delinquency) ensued. Students began to publicly demonstrate and call for the changes to happen more quickly.

The resurgence of the conservatives under the leadership of Deng Xiaoping in 1992 helped to finally put China back on a path of social, economic, and cultural recovery. And as we enter the new millennium under the leadership of President Jiang Zemin and Premier Li Peng, China seems committed to continued growth.

LEGISLATION ON JUVENILE JUSTICE

China still has not adopted special legislation that can be followed when handling juvenile delinquent cases. There are but a few provisions in criminal law, criminal procedure law and in prison law that are related to juvenile crime and delinquency. It is still a widely observable practice in China to handle a large percentage of minor juvenile delinquency cases under administrative law or **administrative regulations**. This is due to Chinese criminal law, which requires that criminal acts exhibit a certain degree of seriousness in order to qualify as criminal offences and therefore be treated before criminal courts. Petty offences, for example, which do not qualify as criminal offences fall under the authority of administrative regulations and administrative interventions (for details see below).

Some of the legislative efforts on juvenile justice were initiated in the 1980s after China had been suffering for more than 30 years from political turmoil. In the beginning, the creation of laws and regulations on juvenile justice started from the provincial level. Before the *Law on Protection of Minors* came into force on 4 September 1991, there were 17 local or provincial regulations on the protection of minors (see Box 4.2). The first main source of law concerning juvenile justice is the *Law of Protection of Minors* (LPM). The goal of this law is to protect juveniles in all aspects of life and it can be characterized as a **legalistic** or **justice model** (see Figure 1—Introduction). The LPM covers protection by family, school, and society, and it includes chapters on judicial protection and legal responsibility. The definition of minors, as outlined in the LPM, declares all those who are under 18 years old to be juveniles. The provisions of this law, however, are quite general and can also be characterized as sharing elements of the **participatory model** (see Figure 1—Introduction) since the act encourages the involvement of citizens and agencies outside the formal legal arena. These provisions contain rather vague principles in that, to be implemented, the law relies on other laws or regulations, such as criminal law, criminal procedure law, marriage law, civil law, etc. For example, in Chapter 5, titled "Judicial Protection," some principles have been provided for the protection of juvenile delinquents in criminal proceedings, which are missing in criminal procedure law. Within the chapter we find provisions that juvenile suspects should be detained separately from adult suspects during pre-trial detention. There are also provisions that prohibit disclosure of information on juvenile suspects and accused juveniles by print or other media before a final judgement has been made. Collectively, these provisions are consistent with the United Nations' and other international agreements on the handling of juvenile cases. The problem with the implementation of this law is that there are no specific proceedings available for filing a lawsuit in order to appeal against violations, nor are there any administrative or criminal sanctions available. No cases can be found during the last nine years that have been brought to the courts under this law.

Box 4.2: The First Law of Juvenile Justice

The *Law on the Protection of Minors* (adopted on 4 September 1991 and effective as of 1 January 1992) is the first individual law for addressing juvenile issues in China. The law was designed to protect young persons under the age of 18 who have committed an offence. In practice, legal responsibility for matters covered by this law have been diverted to other laws, such as civil, administrative, and criminal laws. Over the years we have seen that some of the responsibilities could not be enforced properly. During the process of legislation, some experts have suggested that nationwide institutions for the protection of minors should be set up to supervise the implementation of this law, and that various institutions should be involved. However, these suggestions have not yet been accepted and, by default, the Communist Youth League (CYL) (a non-government body) has taken up the task. According to information provided by the CYL, in 1999, 31 provinces and cities amended their local laws in an effort to ensure protection of minors. In addition, some 28 provincial governments have set up organizations to assist in support these initiatives.

In response to a growing social and political concern with a perceived increase in delinquency, and in particular an increasing level of violence, a second source of juvenile law has been implemented, the *Law on Prevention of Juvenile Crimes*.[2] The process of drafting this law started in 1994. To help direct policy-makers, a number of research studies on juvenile crime and delinquents had been conducted. Research findings demonstrated that quite a number of juvenile delinquents lacked basic knowledge required for complying with the law. In an effort to address this trend, various initiatives have been taken to focus on educative and crime prevention efforts. The age of juveniles in this law has been limited to 14 to 18; it is the same age range provided in the criminal law. By the time the law was adopted on 28 June 1999, China had 70 million juveniles within this age range.

This new law includes a chapter on education for the purpose of preventing juvenile crime, correcting improper juvenile behavior, strengthening juvenile self-control, preventing relapse into crime as well as promoting legal responsibility. The law has been launched to guide schools and various institutions entrusted with the education and training of youth. It also directs the family in regards to its responsibilities and tasks in preventing juvenile crime.

Regulations of juvenile justice pertain to those internal rules that are created by the Supreme Court, the Supreme Procuratorate, or the Ministry of Public Security (headquarter of police). Among such regulations, we find "Rules on Proceedings in Juvenile Cases" (Supreme Court, 26 January 1991); "Establishing Internal Special Responsibilities for Handling Juvenile Cases" (provided by the Supreme Court, the Supreme Procuratorate, the Ministry of Public Security, the Ministry of Justice, 1 June 1991); "Interpretation of Application of Laws on Juvenile Cases" (Supreme Court, 2 May 1995), "Rules on Handling Juvenile Delinquent Cases" (Ministry of Public Security, 23 October 1995).

In order to understand the Chinese system of juvenile justice, it seems important to add some other information on the particulars of Chinese criminal law. Chinese criminal law excludes from criminal offences such behavior that— although formally falling under an offence statute—is seen to be of a minor and non-dangerous nature, and therefore does not reach the level of seriousness required for establishing a criminal offence. Such behavior may then fall into two other categories of deviance that may be responded to by way of administrative sanctions. One of these categories covers administrative offences (i.e., petty crimes) for which administrative penalties (fines or detention of up to 15 days) may be imposed (in an administrative procedure). The second category involves behavior that is deemed to be more serious than simple administrative offences, in particular from the viewpoint of the victim, but it still does not reach the level of seriousness required to be considered a criminal offence. However, for behavior falling under the latter category, re-education through labor for a period of up to three years applies, which means being detained in a labor camp. Re-education through labor may be imposed only on juveniles who have reached the age of 16.

CRIMINAL RESPONSIBILITY OF JUVENILE DELINQUENTS

The legal basis for juvenile criminal responsibility is found in the *Code of Criminal Law* (article 17). According to the law, the age of criminal responsibility starts at 14, but juvenile offenders who fall between the ages of 14 to 16 can be held criminally responsible only when they commit certain crimes that are specified by the law. These crimes concern intentional homicide, intentional assault to cause serious injury or death, rape, robbery, drug trafficking, arson, causing an explosion and poisoning. Juvenile delinquents who have reached the age of 16 are fully responsible, but the law provides that juvenile delinquents who have reached 16 but are under the age of 18 should get mitigated punishment and should not be sentenced in the same manner as adult offenders.

In an effort to address the previous point, the Supreme Court has set up some conditions under which juvenile delinquents may not be convicted and sentenced as adults. These conditions concern:

1. Older juveniles (between the ages of 14 to 16) who have bullied younger juveniles by threatening them or strong-arming them for money or personal possessions;
2. Juveniles between the ages of 14 to 16 who have committed theft (even if the amount of property has exceeded those limits which would make offenders eligible for a harsher sentence) but are not repeat offenders or who have stolen something from their relatives;
3. Male juveniles who have sexual relations with girls under the age of 14 without any serious consequences; and
4. The Supreme Court has also suggested that, if juvenile offenders are forced, seduced or instigated by adult offenders to commit crimes, then—even though they should be convicted—the juvenile offender should be exempted from punishment.

In summary, these conditions reflect the intention of our juvenile justice system to honor the international rules and standards that focus on the welfare of young persons in conflict with the law, but not without a degree of measured accountability.

EXTENT AND TRENDS OF JUVENILE DELINQUENCY

Official statistics in the legal field are poorly developed in China. Analysis of youth crime usually is based on police data[3] and official statistics of courts and several other sources. For example, the " Law Yearbook of China" is one of the main sources of legal statistics (the first issue was published in 1987). Unfortunately, earlier issues do not include data on juvenile delinquency. For periods before the yearbook was published, some experts conclude that there had been three peaks in youth crime since 1949 in the People's Republic of China (see Figure 4.1). The first peak was observed in the period of 1949 to

1951; then, the rate of crime committed by young people increased to some 20 to 30% of the total of crime recorded by police. The second peak occurred in the period 1959 to 1962. During this period, China was going through a period of economic crisis and over 30% of all police-recorded crimes were perpetrated by juvenile delinquents. Most of these cases were theft and the rate of serious crimes was not considered to be high. The third wave of juvenile crime started in the mid-1970s. During this wave, the proportion of crimes accounted for by juvenile delinquents reached some 70% of all recorded crimes. Because of poor data collection methods, and the nature of our political system prior to the social reforms, most Chinese scholars assumed that a real increase in juvenile crime took place only from the mid-1970s to the mid-1980s.

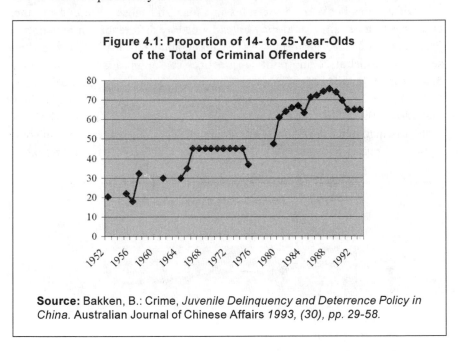

Figure 4.1: Proportion of 14- to 25-Year-Olds of the Total of Criminal Offenders

Source: Bakken, B.: Crime, *Juvenile Delinquency and Deterrence Policy in China. Australian Journal of Chinese Affairs 1993, (30), pp. 29-58.*

Since 1990, separate statistics on criminal convictions of juvenile offenders (14 to 17 years old) are available (see Figure 4.2). From one of the reports provided by the police, for the period between 1985 to 1995, it can be seen that, contrary to public and political perceptions, youth crime did not fluctuate a great deal between 1988 and 2000. In fact, the relative proportion of youth crime to adult offending dropped from 23.8% in 1985 to 10.5% in 1995 (Yisheng, 1998). Between 1988 and 2000, a total of 11 million suspects have been investigated and among them there were 1.5 million juveniles. This represents 14.6% of all known suspects. It is also of interest to see that the rate of juvenile suspects is quite different from the rate of conviction (see Figure 4.3). Comparing the trends in the rates of 14- to 24-year-olds on the one hand and rates of 14- to 17-year-olds on the other hand, it becomes very clear that the actual increase was caused by the young adults. One explanation might be found in particulars of Chinese criminal law which parcels out of criminal acts those behaviors not exceeding a certain degree of seriousness. For example, theft involving loss of property of not more than 500 to 2000 yuan according to Chinese criminal law does not establish a criminal offence, but is dealt with by way of alternative administrative sanctions. As we know from criminological research, children and juveniles commit offences which are primarily in the area of petty offences such as small thefts and other property crimes.

Differences between crime rates in China and those observed in other countries to a certain extent may be explained by differences in registration practices and crime definitions. As is well documented in Western-based research, administrative and political practices can dramatically influence the quality and reliability of official crime statistics. However, given the diversity and range in the crime rates there must be other explanations. For example, it may also be that China's informal control mechanisms, which tends to be more extensive than in most Western and industrialized countries, account for some of the differences in crime rates. This is an area that requires further research.

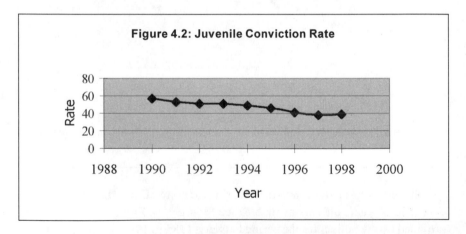

CHARACTERISTICS OF JUVENILE DELINQUENTS KNOWN TO POLICE AND COURTS

Gender

Seen from a gender perspective, juvenile delinquency is almost exclusively male. The proportion of male delinquents lies at 98% and that of females

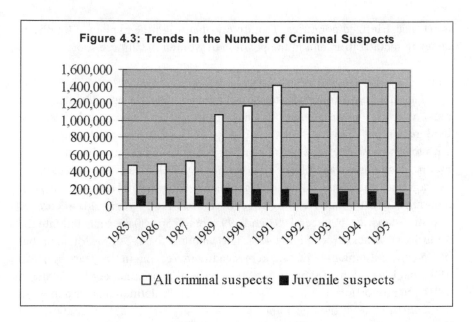

Figure 4.3: Trends in the Number of Criminal Suspects

□ All criminal suspects ■ Juvenile suspects

at only 2% (see Table 4.1). However, as noted in other countries covered in this text, the number of female delinquents seems to be on the increase, although on a level which is certainly far below those observed in Western societies. For example, in the first year of 1999 in Shanghai, 20 female juvenile offenders had been charged with criminal offences. This represents a 58 percent increase over the same period in 1998. In the special region of Macau, statistics show that between 1989 to 1992 only 6.3% of juvenile delinquents were female, but in 1996 the rate increased to 43%. However, in 1998 the proportion decreased again to 26.7%.

Table 4.1: Gender and Juvenile Crime

	1991	1992	1993	1994	1995
Male	184,586	139,277	159,974	158,691	148,988
% male	97.6	97.8	98.2	97.9	97.5
Female	4,617	3,078	3,018	3,401	3,787
% female	2.4	2.2	1.8	2.1	2.5

Source: MPS data.

From a comparative perspective we may note that the juvenile crime rate at large is well under those rates observed in Western societies. As well, the proportion of female juvenile offenders lies markedly under what is reported in most industrialized countries. Tentatively, that might be explained by differences in socialization and in the position of women in Chinese society.

Age

The data drawn from official statistics indicate that the age at which young persons engage in delinquent acts has been declining since the 1950s. One explanation put forward is that the quality of life has improved rapidly and, with that, so have the expectations on the part of young people. Juveniles now mature at an earlier age physically, but not psychologically. Since 1990, the average age of juvenile delinquents has been getting lower. However, the peak age range for criminal offending concerns those 14 to 17 years old. According to police statistics, between 1991 and 1995 some 250,000 suspects fell into the 14 to 15 age bracket (see Figure 4.4). This amounts to 31% of the total number of juvenile delinquents; the rate kept steadily increasing in the years between 1991 and 1995, with an average annual increase of approximately 1%. While in 1991 the proportion of 14- to 15-year-old juvenile delinquents amounted to some 29%, in 1995 the rate stands at 33.4% (see Table 4.2). Other statistical data indicate that, from 1991 to 1995, 98,000 juvenile delinquents under the age of 14 were counted. Although offenders that young cannot be held responsible, police information systems keep track of them and show that they account for some 1.4% of all criminal offenders; the proportion—although rather small—has been increasing. Between 1992 and 1995, the number of child suspects has increased every year by an average of 18.3%.

In the metropolitan area of Shanghai, in the first half of the year 1999, prosecutors had charged 478 juvenile delinquents with criminal offences. Among them, 42 were 14 to 16 years old; in the same period of 1998 only 32 juveniles between 14 and 16 years old had been brought to court. Thus, in relative terms, there was an increase of 31%. In the special region of Macau, too, the average age of juvenile offenders between 1989 and 1993 had been calculated as 15 years of age; however, during the period of 1994 to 1998, the average age dropped to 13.5 years.

Other Characteristics of Juvenile Delinquents

Official statistics show that, of those juvenile delinquents registered in police information systems, a large percentage consists of juveniles who live in rural areas (35%–40%). However, this does not come as a surprise, as farmers, who still account for 80% of the population, dominate China's population structure. Aside from this rural factor, the situation in China otherwise corresponds to what can also be observed for European or North American societies: juvenile crime tends to concentrate in urban milieus. The rate of juvenile

Table 4.2: Developments in the Age Structure of Juvenile Delinquents

	1991	1992	1993	1994	1995
14-15 years old	55,166	43,077	50369	50,598	51,023
%	29.2	30.3	30.9	31.2	33.4
16-17 years old	1134,037	99,278	116,623	111,594	101,752
%	70.8	69.7	69.1	68.8	66.6

Source: MPS data.

Figure 4.4: Developments in Convictions along Age Groups

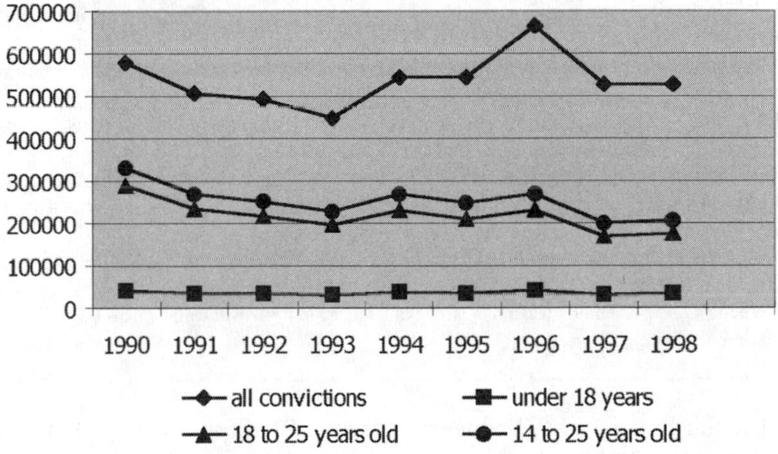

delinquents coming from rural areas has even been decreasing in the nineties. In 1991 delinquents coming from rural areas represented 41% of the total of juvenile offenders; in 1995 the rate had fallen to 36%. This corresponds to the decrease in the total number of juvenile delinquents in rural areas, which has dropped from 77,000 in 1991 to 54,000 in 1995.

The second largest group of juvenile delinquents are students (see Box 4.3). Their proportion as a "group" of juvenile offenders has varied between 28% and 31% from 1991 and 1995. Among students, middle school students (falling in the 13 to 15 age bracket) form an even larger proportion. These students are in their adolescence, and there are many special physical and psychological changes that affect juveniles in this age period. In China a system of nine-year-free education applies. In comparison with students in high school and universities, the students in middle school exhibit a higher rate of delinquency (see Table 4.3).

Box 4.3: The Special School for Problem Teenagers

In 1955 the Beijing government followed the educational theory and experience of a former Soviet Union expert who founded three special schools. These institutions provide educational programs for those teenagers who had violated the law, committed minor crimes, or whose families and schools felt it was too difficult to offer them further education. The schools were called "work and study schools." Here students continued their normal education while also being involved in work-related activities such as workshops or farms located within the school grounds. The intention of these programs was to provide the youth with skills that they could use upon leaving the school.

The schools existed for 11 years before the onset of the "Cultural Revolution" in 1978. During this time the school received 1,028 students. Reports indicated that most of the students had benefited from the regiment of the school setting.

After the "Cultural Revolution" prototypes of the schools were resumed. In 1981, a government program for the school was published. The school could only take problem teenagers who were between 13 to 18 years old. It was also recommended that parents give consent to the educational program and pay most of the accommodation and study fee. If parents could not pay, students could apply for a stipend. Applications by students to attend had to be reviewed and approved by the local education bureau. The school term is two years.

Statistics show that until 1987 there were 96 variations of the schools throughout China. Collectively they dealt with some 30,000 students. The "success" rate was between 85–95%. The criteria of "success" was based on students' good behavior and whether they re-offended.

The third group of delinquents consists of "idlers." Their rate has been increasing from 19.8% in 1991 to 22.6% in 1995. Most of them are individuals who have left or have graduated from school but don't want to get further education (see Table 4.3).

Finally, the majority (95%) of China's juvenile delinquents are (officially) first-time offenders. Only a small fraction of juvenile delinquents therefore have received either criminal or administrative punishments before re-offending.

THE STRUCTURE OF JUVENILE CRIMES

According to official police data the most common type of offence committed by Chinese youth is theft (see Table 4.4). Between 1986 and 1995, theft accounted for between 68% and 81% of all recorded delinquencies. The proportion of robbery has continually increased from some 6% in the mid-1980s to

Table 4.3: Young Delinquents Broken Down by Type of School

	1991	1992	1993	1994	1995
Preliminary school (%)	7.2	7.2	7.1	6.9	7.0
Middle School (%)	18.7	21.2	21.6	20.5	21.3
High School (%)	2.3	2.6	2.8	2.8	2.8
University (%)	0.1	0.1	0.1	0.1	0.1

Source: MPS data.

17% in the mid-1990s. By contrast, violent crime such as assault, rape and homicide have remained fairly stable in their proportions as is the case of incidence rates for fraud. Local statistics from Tianjing (one of those municipalities directly under the authority of the central government) show that in the first half of 1999 the rate of violent crime increased. In particular, the incidence of robbery among juvenile offenders was 26%, whereas it only accounted for 10% of crimes committed by juveniles in 1996 ("Analysing," 1999). What is noticeable, therefore, is the increase in the proportion of robberies during the 1990s. This trend is certainly similar to what can also be observed in European countries and North America. However, it is not possible to analyze data as regards the victims of such robberies and to answer the question of whether the victims of such robberies belong mainly to the same age group as the offenders.

In the 1990s there have been other significant changes in juvenile crimes that are certainly related to the transformation China is currently undergoing on its way to becoming a modern society based on socialist market mecha-

Table 4.4: Distribution of Offence Categories Among Juvenile Offenders

	Homicide	Assault	Rape	Robbery	Theft
1986	0.8	3.6	5.4	4.2	80.8
1987	0.8	3.7	4.9	6.5	78.9
1988	Na	Na	Na	Na	Na
1989	0.6	2.3	2.6	8.7	81.4
1990	0.8	2.7	2.7	8.5	79.5
1991	0.2	3.1	2.8	9.9	77.4
1992	0.9	3.9	3.4	15.7	68.7
1993	0.8	3.5	2.8	16.7	68.9
1994	0.8	3.4	2.5	17.1	68.4
1995	0.8	3.2	2.3	17.1	68.1

Source: MPS data.

nisms. More juveniles evidently commit crimes outside their social network and more and more juveniles commit crimes in groups. Crime statistics show that in 1991, 5.5% of juvenile offenders known to police had committed crimes outside their social network. In 1995 the percentage had increased to 8.3%. The percentage of juveniles who had committed crimes in groups has increased from 25.3% in 1991 to 31% in 1995. Furthermore, there is evidence that juvenile crime is becoming more violent, adult-like and sophisticated.

Drug Problems among Juveniles

In China, when discussing drug problems related to juveniles, the focus is usually on young people under the age of 25.

Since the late 1980s, the problem of drug use and drug-related crimes has been getting more and more serious in China. Surveys have been conducted in some metropolitan areas. For example, in Kunming's[4] center of drug addiction between February 1990 and December 1995, 12,104 persons were admitted as drug addicts; among them, the proportion of young people under the age of 25 amounted to 61.4%, with the youngest drug addict being 12 years old. The survey has also shown that drug problems among young people are becoming more and more serious.

There are several characteristics displayed in this trend:

1. Youth drug use is increasing rapidly and the areas affected by drug use are expanding. A survey carried out in Guangzhou (the capital city of Guangdong Province) showed that in 1990 police had identified 781 juvenile drug users. By 1994, the number had increased to 3,147 juveniles booked by police for use of controlled drugs. Juvenile drug users today are not only found in the southwest of China, where access to drugs—in particular heroin—is easier as it is close to the "**Golden Triangle**"; drug-using young people today are found and documented in almost every province of China.

2. Among youthful drug users, the proportion who are school or university dropouts or unemployed is very pronounced. According to statistics from Shenzhen (a commercial and industrial center located close to Hong Kong), in 1993 among young drug users 57.4% were either unemployed or had dropped out of school or university.

3. The number of young female drug users is on the increase. Police data indicate that before the mid-1980s the number of female drug users were few—reflecting social and cultural values. In recent years, however, female drug users have made up some 20% of drug users known to police.

4. Traditionally, the drug most commonly used by juveniles was usually heroin; however new types of drugs—such as amphetamines and ecstasy—have been found to be used by young people, and
5. statistics show that young persons tend to use drugs in group settings. Four among five drug users booked by police have used the drug together with others, thus displaying a common trend in drug subcultures.

The causes for the increase in drug problems among youth begin with the impact the nationwide drug problem has had on the whole of Chinese society. Drugs—in particular heroin—started to spread from the southwest of China, where the Golden Triangle served to increase the accessibility of drugs, during the 1980s. Then, according to a survey carried out in Guangxi province, it was found that 50% of youthful drug users started using drugs out of curiosity; 30% of youth drug users were induced by peers, or by friends who belong to drug subcultures. So, the basic mechanisms which explain the spread of drug use in many other parts of the world are also operative in China. It is structural processes which influence the supply of drugs, and peer-group-related processes that explain individual drug use.

CRIMINAL PROCEDURE AND THE YOUNG OFFENDER

As described earlier, until recently China still had not adopted a specific law which would provide for separate legal proceedings for juvenile delinquents. There are only several general provisions in the *Law of Protection of Minors* (Chapter 5, "Judicial Protection") that are related to criminal proceedings in some cases. In practice, some internal rules concerning juvenile criminal procedure have been adopted by the Supreme Court, the Supreme Procuratorate and the Ministry of Public Security (headquarter of police).

According to Chinese legal tradition (and as was already mentioned above), illegal acts are divided into two categories: violations of law and criminal offences. The former acts are dealt with and punished under the *Administrative Penalties for the Public*. The act is part of administrative law and administrative procedures. Criminal offences are dealt with by applying criminal law and criminal procedure law — reflecting aspects of the **justice model.** Therefore, whether an illegal act falls under administrative or under criminal jurisdiction is crucial. Definition falls to the responsibility of the police who, when investigating a case, have to make a decision about whether it should be dealt with administratively or whether it should go to criminal prosecution services. If the illegal behavior of a juvenile qualifies as an administrative offence then administrative punishments may be imposed. Such administrative punishment—

including warning or cautioning, administrative detention, fines and rehabilitation—reflects elements of a **participatory** approach (see Figure 4.5).

Figure 4.5 The Juvenile Justice Process in China

Police Investigation
- Police discretion—dismissal of minor offences with admonition, or request parents provide further education
- Apply certain administrative laws—juvenile delinquents who are between 14 and 18 are subject to Administrative Penalties for Public Security; police could impose administrate penalties: warnings, fines and detention. According to another act, police could decide to impose the administrative punishment of "correction through labor."
- For juvenile offenders who are suspected of committing serious crimes, police should file an application for prosecution and transfer files and evidence to the prosecutor's office after the investigation.

Prosecutor decision
- Prosecutors have the discretion to discharge cases. They may also suggest giving the juvenile delinquents administrative punishments.
- Prosecutors must decide how to proceed with the charge and submit their indictment to the court that has jurisdiction.

Court Trial
- Juvenile cases tried in youth chambers without a public hearing.

Correction
- Youth offenders who receive a disposition of imprisonment are generally sent to juvenile rehabilitation institutions.[5]

Also, as described above, delinquents who are 14 or 15 can be held criminally responsible only for those (serious) crimes which are identified by law. If juvenile delinquents cannot be held responsible because of their age, police then may decide to issue an order to their parents or guardians and ask them to discipline the delinquents themselves. In fact, such a transfer of responsibility is an example of a system that can place responsibility for administering any punishment in the hands of a parent or guardian. In fact, an informal approach is strongly encouraged, especially if such informal responses are better suited to the young delinquent than judicial interventions. The government can also order (i.e., Article 17 of the *Criminal Law*) young delinquents to take residence in rehabilitative institutions (see Box 4.4).

Criminal procedure law and internal rules (of procedure) have established some requirements for the investigation of cases of youth crime. These particulars include the principle of separating young suspects from adult suspects in places of pretrial detention (according to the Beijing Rules and U.N. Minimum Rules, as well as the Child Convention) and applying methods of

> ### Box 4.4: The Management of Juvenile Rehabilitation Institute
>
> On 7 January 1986, the Ministry of Justice published a regulation on the management of juvenile rehabilitation institutes. This regulation provided that the institutions should take and hold youth offenders who are between 14 and 18 years old and have received a life or fixed-term imprisonment sentence. Provisions also include the ability to detain those youth offenders who are under 16 years of age who have committed a crime but according to Criminal Law, could not be punished, but rather should be held and given educative instruction.
>
> These regulations offer options for the management of young offenders that differ from those for adult offenders. It was not possible to locate specific statistics on how many of these institutions exist in China. However, based on the Ministry's directives, it is speculated that every province and city directly under the central government is likely to have a rehabilitative institute.

interviewing juvenile suspects deemed to be more appropriate than regular methods of interrogation. There is an ongoing discussion on whether special measures should be introduced as alternatives for pre-trial detention. At present, if juvenile delinquents have committed a relatively serious crime, the coercive measures which are imposed on adult suspects will also be imposed on juvenile suspects. Although if convicted juvenile suspects are detained in separate detention places, there are still concerns about whether being held in detention will result in greater social harm for them. Moreover, in some areas, juvenile suspects still run the risk of being detained with adult suspects. Detention certainly may have negative impacts on juveniles, an impact that in Chinese is labeled "crime pollution."

Serious delinquent cases are handed over to the public prosecutor after the investigative stage of proceedings. Since the *Law on Protection of Juveniles* went into force, juvenile prosecution divisions have been gradually set up in various prosecutors' offices. Although there is no special legal provision authorizing prosecution discretion over juvenile delinquents, prosecution policies have been initiated which hold that decisions made about prosecution should be based on the principle of reeducation and rehabilitation of the young delinquent. Since the Supreme Court has issued guidelines on sentencing the juvenile delinquent, prosecutors should also take these guidelines into account. When prosecutors opt for a decision of non-prosecution in juvenile cases, they can also suggest to responsible authorities that they impose administrative punishment (e.g., cautioning, fines or short term detention). This means that juvenile delinquents who are not charged with criminal offences can be sent to rehabilitative institutions.

As was outlined earlier, no youth court act exists which would provide for special trial proceedings for juveniles, and the recently (1998) amended *Crimi-*

nal Procedure Law also lacks a chapter regarding juvenile delinquents. However, the "Rules on Handling Juvenile Criminal Cases" which have been issued by the Supreme Court, in fact have this function, and these rules have been respected as principle regulations of youth court proceedings. These internal rules have established special standards for handling juvenile cases in the trial stage. They say that courts at every level (local, provincial, central) must have a youth chamber, and judges and lay assessors assigned to these chambers should be experts in handling juvenile cases. In 1984 the first youth trial chamber was set up in Shanghai, and as of 1994 there were 3,600 youth trial chambers throughout the country. The chambers have jurisdiction over cases where the juvenile defendant's age is under 18, or where the principle offender or the majority of defendants (if more than one defendant is involved) is under 18 years old. However, certain problems have emerged with these rules. According to Chinese Criminal Law, the age of criminal responsibility starts at the age of 14, and juveniles are defined as 14 to 17 years old. However, in Chinese criminal procedure law, the status of a juvenile is determined by his or her age when the case comes to trial. The problem is then that, if the juvenile was under 18 when he or she committed the crime, s/he is to be treated as a juvenile according to substantial criminal law, but according to procedural law the offence will treated as an adult case if the young delinquent has reached the age of 18 before the case goes to court. This issue affects some of the juvenile delinquent's procedural rights such as whether a defence council must be appointed for trial proceedings.

There are other principles provided by Chinese *Criminal Procedure Law* and the rules issued by the Supreme Court to protect juvenile offenders' rights. For example, it is absolutely forbidden to have public hearings in cases where the juvenile offender's age is 14 to 15. In general, there are also no public hearings for cases where juvenile offenders are between 16 and 17 years of age (Article 152 of *Criminal Procedure Law*).

According to *Criminal Procedure Law*, the juvenile cases should be tried without public hearing, but the judgement should be announced in public. There is a debate going on over this issue. Some legal experts think that this legislation and judicial practice do not comply with the Beijing Rules and other international standards on juvenile justice issues.

The juvenile delinquents' right to have counsel is protected by *Criminal Procedure Law*. The law provides that in cases where the juvenile defendant has no defence lawyer, the court must appoint one. The law also provides that, in addition to the defence lawyer, the young offender may also have his or her legal representative(s) (e.g., parents) attend the trial.

The form of trial in juvenile cases is different from that applied in adult cases. The rules issued by the Supreme Court provide for special forms for juvenile trials:

- judicial police should not be present during trial, as would be the case in ordinary proceedings;
- juvenile defendants—even if they are charged with serious crimes— should not be forced to wear handcuffs or anklets when attending trial;
- courtrooms reserved for juvenile cases should be designed in a way different from adult courts, better suited for juveniles;
- judges should not wear robes or uniforms but ordinary clothing;
- the manner of talking and interviewing, etc., during trial proceedings should adopt the style of everyday discussions, so that the accused can readily understand the proceedings; and
- there are quite a number of second instance courts that have set up special appeal chambers for juvenile appeal cases. However, this has not yet become general practice. Most juvenile appeal cases are still tried by adult chambers.

Sentencing of the Juvenile Offender

There are no specific provisions in the basic Chinese criminal code to guide sentencing in juvenile cases. However, in 1995, the Supreme Court published an "Interpretation for Application of Criminal Law in Juvenile Cases." Section 3 of these interpretative rules provides for special sentencing principles to be adopted in cases of juvenile delinquency. The rules emphasize that the purpose of sentencing the juvenile offender is mainly education; punishment is a secondary goal only. According to the interpretative rules, the following principles should be taken into account:

1. If the young offender has no previous criminal record and s/he has only committed a minor offence, the juvenile defendant should be exempted from punishment. The court should ask the young offender to make an apology to the victim or to compensate the victim. The court may also suggest diversion of the case to administrative proceedings and administrative punishment.
2. If there are elements in the case that speak in favour of imposing lighter penalties for juvenile delinquents, the court should in fact choose the lightest punishment from the range of penalties provided for the criminal offence in question and also choose the shortest term of imprisonment. If legal grounds for mitigating the sentence exist, then judges should give the lightest punishment prescribed by law.

3. If the juvenile delinquent is sentenced to a penalty of criminal deten-
    tion or to imprisonment of less than three years, and if the defendant's
    family can provide favorable conditions and if the young offender will
    not pose risks for society, then the detention or imprisonment should
    be suspended. Exceptions from these rules concern the young of-
    fender who has a prior criminal record or who was the principle of-
    fender (in a case where several offenders are involved). Under such
    conditions suspension of a prison sentence should not be granted.
4. Deprivation of political rights is considered a supplementary punish-
    ment provided under criminal law; it is enforced when there is a prison
    sentence involved. While life imprisonment in principle can be im-
    posed in case of juvenile offenders, except for life imprisonment, a
    juvenile offender should not be deprived of his or her political rights.

According to the revised criminal law (1997), the death penalty may not be
imposed on young offenders (under the age of 18 when having committed the
offence) nor suspended merely until they come of age. China respects the
standards that are expressed in the Child Convention and in other international conventions.

Given that China acknowledges the merits of the international rules and
guidelines for young offenders, there is ongoing discussion as to whether the
criminal record of a one-time juvenile delinquent should be erased after a certain number of years. Up to now there have been no time limits for keeping
criminal records.

REFORM OF JUVENILE OFFENDERS AND JUVENILE RECIDIVISTS

Official data showing imprisonment rates for juveniles or the number of
juvenile offenders who are subject to administrative punishment, such as correction through labor or reform in rehabilitative institutions, are not available.
Until recently there were also no data that showed rates of juvenile re-offending. A study carried out in Shanghai, however, shows the rate of juvenile re-
offenders to be 20% (Pan, 1999). The study found that recidivists can be
categorized into one of the four following groups:
*   those whose main original offence was theft;
*   those whose punishment was an imprisonment term of less than three
    years (some 70% of convicted juveniles are sentenced to a maximum of
    three years' imprisonment);
*   those who could not find a job after release from prison (some 70% of
    released juvenile offenders are unemployed); and
*   those (23.8%) who come from a single parent family.

The law on "prevention of juvenile delinquency" has provided several principles to better prevent juvenile relapse into crime. However, it lacks special institutions and measures to guarantee these principles are carried out in practice.

Summary

Although the People's Republic of China has a rich and long history, our juvenile justice system is quite new when compared to many described in this text. In fact, it can be said that China's juvenile justice system is just emerging.

For the first 10 years after the People's Republic of China was founded (from 1949 to 1959), the crime rate in the whole country was extremely low. During 10 years of Cultural Revolution (the largest political movement in China) the social order and legal structures were disturbed a great deal. The Cultural Revolution stopped almost all possibilities for social, cultural and legal developments. Youth could not grow up in a proper way because of the social and cultural upheaval the country experienced—a form of **anomie** and/or **social disorganization**.

After the Cultural Revolution ended in 1976, the juvenile crime rate began to increase. Juvenile crime has become a serious social problem in China, although compared to western countries juvenile crime rates still are rather low. The responses to youth crime problems have also pushed new developments in the field of juvenile justice. The **Chinese Juvenile Delinquency Association** was founded in 1981 (see Box 4.5). Since 1979 research on juvenile crime and juvenile justice has been initiated in a number of areas.

Legislation of juvenile justice stills needs to be improved. The main sources of juvenile law are very general, found in adult criminal law and criminal procedural law. The implementation of juvenile justice policies is mainly based on

---

Box 4.5: China Juvenile Delinquency Association (CJDA)

The CJDA was founded in June 1982. During the 1980s they carried out several domestic surveys in China. These include studies that have focused on the causes of juvenile delinquency, juvenile delinquency in rural areas, young female offenders, and violent crime among juvenile offenders. They also organized experts who specialized in juvenile justice to write academic works. They organized conferences, seminars and workshops on specific topics relating to juvenile justice. They also established a journal, *Study on Juvenile Delinquency*, in 1990. The CJDA also established sub-associations at the provincial level. In addition, the CJDA has organized and fostered international contacts. Since the early 1990s numerous research projects have been undertaken to assist in addressing the various challenges young offenders present throughout China. A detailed account of CJDA activities and publications can be found in the *Law Yearbook of China*.

administrative regulations and internal rules. There is, therefore, an urgent need to have a juvenile act in which special institutions related to juvenile justice, the court proceedings, sentencing and corrections are dealt with comprehensively.

Statistics on juvenile justice and juvenile crime are poorly developed in China. Moreover, statistics on juvenile delinquency are not always published by police or other legal institutions and are therefore not accessible for research. Where available, in some cases data on juveniles is not separated from adult data. Therefore, it is still difficult to analyze trends in juvenile delinquency in China properly.

However, various studies suggest that the crime rate among youth is nationwide and on the increase. As China covers a large territory, there might be varying trends in different regions, but this has not yet been examined. However, some experts estimate that juvenile delinquency increases by some 5% on the average per year, while the average age of offenders is decreasing. The rate of female offenders is increasing, though on a rather small scale. Young offenders are involved in group crimes more frequently than they used to be. The crime that is dominating juvenile delinquency is theft (and property crime at large). In recent years, the number of juvenile drug users and offenders who committed drug crimes has been increasing.

Although some internal rules have been established and adopted by legal institutions, and special juvenile divisions have been set up in prosecutors' offices and in courts, there is still a strong demand to regulate procedures for handling juvenile delinquents cases on a statutory basis.

According to basic criminal law, sentencing in the case of young offenders is not different from sentencing adults, except for the exclusion of the death penalty for juvenile offenders. However, there is a lack of alternatives to imprisonment. The sanctions made available in Chinese criminal law are imprisonment and fines. The possibility of imposing life imprisonment for 14- to 17-year-olds has until now not been challenged.

In conclusion, we may note that the study of juvenile delinquency and the establishment of an autonomous juvenile justice system is a work in progress. Therefore, it is not possible to provide a real picture on its extent and trends. However, coinciding with recent social, cultural, and political reforms, there are clear signs that promising ways of improving juvenile justice are going forward.

Liling Yue is an associate professor working at China University of Political Science and Law. She is a member of the board of directors at the Center for Criminal Law and Justice where she is responsible for international research projects. At the university she teaches in the areas of criminal procedure, evidence law, and comparative criminal justice. Her publications in English and German have focused on the reform of criminal justice in China.

HELPFUL WEBSITES
www.state.gov/www/current/debates/china/html Department of State for China. Various information is available in English.

www.qis.net/chinalaw/info1.htm This link provides an English version of criminal law in China. Other law links also available at this site.

(in Chinese)

www.lawbook.com.cn China Law Book. Presents information on various juvenile justice projects.

www.hkfyg.org.hk

www.youth.china1law.com Chinese law as it pertains to young offenders.

www.ycp.gov.cn

KEY TERMS AND CONCEPTS
Golden Triangle	Administrative Regulations
Chinese Juvenile Delinquency Association	Legalistic Justice Model
Law on Prevention of Juvenile Crimes	Anomie
Confucianism	
Participatory Model	

STUDY QUESTIONS
1. How has China's past affected the development of its juvenile justice system?
2. How do China's laws for juveniles compare with other parts of the world?
3. One of the peaks of delinquent activity appeared between the 1980s through to the late 1990s. Some have suggested rapid social, economic, cultural, and even political change may account for the increase in delinquency. What kinds of policies and strategy could be made to control and prevent juvenile crimes? How might China benefit from examining other countries' models? What factors and/or issues might need to be taken into consideration?
4. What factors might China need to take into account in trying to balance the rights of young offenders while still protecting the members of society at large?

NOTES
1   Taiwan is an island province that has been under separate administration since 1949.
2   This law was adopted on 28th June, 1999, and is effective as of November 1, 1999.
3   As collected in provincial police reports.
4   The capital city of Yunan Province. This province is close to the Golden Triangle, where drug production and drug trafficking has posed serious problems for decades.
5   This is also translated as "correction and education through labor." A person who is punished by imposing reeducation through labor can be detained in a rehabilitative

institution for a maximum of three years. This type of administrative punishment has been criticized because of the lack of external (in particular judicial) control and its reliance on internal controls.

REFERENCES

Analysing ten years of development if juvenile delinquency in Tianjing. (1999). *Research on Juvenile Delinquency*, No, 11–12.

Chen, X. (1999). Research on juvenile mass: violent behaviors in Macao. *Research on Juvenile Delinquency*, No.5–6, 30–36.

Guo, X. (1997). Juvenile delinquency: The United Nations regulations and Chinese legal Measures. *Research on Juvenile Policies*, 7, 13–19.

Law Yearbook of China 1987–1999. (2000). Beijing.

Pan, Z. (1999). The problems of the juvenile re-offender, *Research on Juvenile Delinquency*. No.2.

Sun, Q., & Huang, H. (1998). Juvenile justice system. *Legal System and Social Development*. No.4, 43–48.

Tan, X. (2000). Changing the punishment system for juvenile delinquents. *Research on Juvenile Delinquency*. No.1, 58–61.

Tian, J., & Fu, S. Y. (1998). Analysis of drug problems among youth in Shenzhen. *Research on Juvenile Delinquency*, No.5–6, 17–21.

Wang, Y. D., & Bao, S. X. (Eds.). (1997). *The research on the issues of current juvenile delinquency*. Beijing: The Publisher of China Prosecution.

Chapter 5

Comparative Juvenile Justice: England and Wales

Loraine Gelsthorpe and Vicky Kemp
Institute of Criminology, University of Cambridge
Cambridge, England

FACTS ON THE UNITED KINGDOM

Area: 244,820 sq. km. Britain comprises of Great Britain (England, Wales and Scotland) and Northern Ireland. It's full name is the United Kingdom of Great Britain and Northern Ireland. It is one of the 15 member states of the European Union, which it joined in 1973. **Population**: Britain is densely populated. A total population of over 59 million people ranks it 17th in the world. The capital, London, has a population of just over 7 million. Other major cities include Birmingham (1 million), Leeds (727,000), Sheffield (531,000), Liverpool (461,000), Edinburgh (440,000) and Manchester (430,000). Although the population has remained relatively stable over the last decade, it has aged considerably. In 1991, nearly 19% of the population were over the normal retirement ages (65 for men, 60 for women) compared with 15% in 1961. Life expectancy for men is 73 years and for women 78. Significantly, there has been a concomitant decline in the number of people under the age of 18. Between 1983 and 1993, the number of young people aged between 10 and 17 fell by 19%. **Ethnicity**: Over the centuries many people from overseas have settled in Britain, either to escape political or religious persecution or in search of economic opportunities. It is worth noting, however, that since 1981 there has been a tightening of immigration law, something that has made it much more difficult for foreign nationals to settle in Britain. In the 1991 census just over 3 million people (5.5%) described themselves as belonging to an ethnic group other than the 'white' group. **Religion**: Although Britain has been predominantly Christian since the early Middle Ages, today most of the world's other religions are represented. Britain's Jewish, Hindu and Sikh communities each number around 300,000; the Muslim community is around 1 million. **Economy**: Although historically Britain was one of the leading industrialized countries, in recent years, however, the economic and industrial pattern has altered considerably. Service industries have become increasingly important and now account for over two-thirds of employees. Financial and other business services have also grown in significance, particularly during the 80s. **Government**: Britain is a parliamentary democracy with a constitutional monarch - currently Queen Elizabeth II - as head of State. Unlike many other parliamentary democracies, it has no written constitution outlining the rights and obligations of government or citizens. Instead, it is ruled according to laws passed by Parliament, decisions made in the higher judicial courts, and (perhaps most importantly) tradition. Parliament, Britain's legislature, comprises of the House of Commons, the House of Lord's and the Queen in her constitutional role. General elections to choose Members of Parliament must be held at least every five years. The last general election was held in May 1997 and led to a new Labour Administration after 18 years of Conservative rule. The Government is formed by the party with the majority support in the Commons. The Queen appoints its leader as Prime Minister. The second largest party forms the official Opposition, with its own leader and shadow cabinet. The Opposition has a duty to challenge government policies and to present an alternative program.

In the little world in which children have their existence, whosoever brings them up, there is nothing so finely perceived and so finely felt, as injustice.
Charles Dickens, 1812-1870.

This chapter is primarily concerned with youth justice in England and Wales though we include a brief outline of the legal framework and issues in another jurisdiction of the United Kingdom—Northern Ireland (see Box 5.3). Occasionally Parliament passes similar legislation in respect of all its jurisdictions, but, as we hope to make clear, different arrangements exist for dealing with young offenders in the three jurisdictions: Scotland, Northern Ireland, and England and Wales. (See Chapter 15 for a full discussion of Scotland.)

OVERVIEW OF THE JUVENILE JUSTICE SYSTEM IN ENGLAND AND WALES

In order to provide a reference point for the discussion of English and Welsh juvenile justice, Figure 5.1 shows the main decision points in the system which predominated in the 1980s and 1990s up to the 1998 *Crime and Disorder Act*.

One of the most striking features of juvenile justice in England and Wales is the range of agencies which are involved, and it may be described as an **open system** (Singer and Gelsthorpe, 1996). The system emerged on an *ad hoc* basis over the past hundred years, growing out of the criminal justice system more generally. As with so many things, a historical approach is perhaps the best way of understanding the form of the contemporary system. It will also highlight another striking feature of juvenile justice, namely the range of competing approaches to the problem of youth crime within the system itself.

FIGURE 5.1: OUTLINE OF THE YOUTH JUSTICE SYSTEM IN ENGLAND & WALES: Pre 1998

APPREHENSION & CHARGE

Parents are expected to come to the police station. If they do not, social workers may intervene following an arrest to act as an "appropriate adult" during police interviews to protect the rights of young people.

The police apprehend, or have reported to them, young people suspected of committing criminal offences. No national data is available on the numbers of such referrals or apprehensions.

BAIL

Social Workers or Probation Officers may intervene to try to secure the release of a young person on bail. Intervention may include the provision of "bail support" (i.e. temporary accommodation and/or short-term supervision).

Most young offenders who are arrested are bailed by the police (i.e. they return home). Some young people are remanded in custody (national facilities: age 15+ only) or local authority accommodation, which may be secure.

DIVERT

Some local areas have multi-agency diversion panels to advise the police whether a formal prosecution is necessary.

Probation officers, social workers and education welfare officers (but not parents or victims) had been involved in multi-agency diversion panels.

The police decide whether to prosecute or divert a young person. Over 80% of known 10- to 13-year-old offenders are formally cautioned. Over 60% of known 14- to 17-year-old offenders are formally cautioned.

Instead of a formal caution a young person may get an "informal warning" or "no further action" may be taken. No national data is available on these disposals.

PROSECUTE

Young people "in need" (including offenders) may be referred to social workers as welfare cases. Most such young people are dealt with under a voluntary agreement between the family and the SSD, but some cases may be taken to the family proceedings court.

If (and only if) the police decide it would be right to prosecute, papers are passed to the Crown Prosecution Service (CPS). Of those young people referred to the CPS by the police for prosecution, over 25% are discontinued (on evidential insufficiency or public interest grounds).

YOUTH COURT

Parents are required to attend the youth court.

The Probation Service or the Social Services Department may be asked to complete a pre-sentence report.

Legal representation is allowed, and is standard practice in more serious cases.

Many young people appear in court on two or three occasions before sentence. Between court appearances the young person may be bailed, or remanded to local authority accommodation or custody (see above).

SENTENCE

Custodial Sentences	Community Services			Other Sentences
	Probation Service	Social Services Department	Other Bodies	
Detention in a young offender institution	Probation orders* Supervision orders* Community service orders Combination orders	Supervision orders*	Attendance centers	Fine Absolute or conditional discharge Bind over Compensation
15 years + only		10- to 17-year-olds	10- to 17-year-olds	
Secure training orders		* May contain additional specified requirements	Curfew orders	10- to 17-year-olds
12- to 14-year-olds	16- to 17-year-olds		16- to 17-year-olds	

THE HISTORICAL DEVELOPMENT OF JUVENILE JUSTICE, 1908 - 1997

Historical Background

Prior to the nineteenth century there was relatively little formal differentiation between adult and juvenile offenders. However, over the course of the nineteenth century a number of developments occurred which changed this. Firstly, there was the emergence of a discourse on juvenile delinquency as a distinct social problem. The second development involved the expansion of summary jurisdiction; that is, an extension of the ways in which juveniles could be dealt with in the lower courts. This meant that young offenders no longer had to be detained in adult prisons—awaiting trial at the Assizes.[1] Thirdly, the reformatory and industrial schools arguably had educational principles at their core, though in a context of a need for a disciplined, trained, emollient work force (Carlebach, 1970). It was not until the 1908 *Children Act*, however, that the principle of dealing with juvenile offenders separately from adult offenders was finally established. Essentially, the new act was founded upon three principles that are often taken to mark the beginnings of a **welfare** perspective within British juvenile justice:

- Juvenile offenders should be kept *separate* from adult criminals and should receive *treatment* differentiated to suit their special needs;
- Parents should be made more responsible for the wrongdoing of their children; and
- The imprisonment of juveniles should be abolished.

But the introduction of the juvenile court[2] reflected a primarily *symbolic* change in attitudes towards the juvenile offender. Juvenile courts remained *criminal* courts and the procedures were essentially the same as for adults. Close scrutiny of matters suggests that the act reflected ideas and principles derived from concerns about criminal justice and crime control. From its inception, conflict and ambivalence were embedded in the concept of the juvenile court. Even the abolition of the imprisonment of juveniles should not be seen to be an unalloyed reflection of humanitarian ideals. It was said that "imprisonment would destroy the deterrent value *if used too soon*" (emphasis added; Hansard, 1908).

The juvenile courts retained their original character and structure until the *Children and Young Persons Act* 1933 when there were some significant developments, namely that there be a specially selected panel of magistrates to deal with juveniles, and that the age of criminal responsibility be raised from the age of seven to eight. The act also dictated that magistrates were to have regard to "the welfare of the child." The juvenile court was to act in *loco parentis*, establishing itself as the forum capable of adjudicating on matters of family socialization and parental behavior, even if no "crime" as such had been committed (see Morris and McIsaac, 1978; Rutherford, 1986).

A combination of **crime control** and **welfare** perspectives thus informed juvenile justice. These competing considerations were reflected in other developments in the period prior to the Second World War. Borstals,[3] for example, under attack because of allegations of brutality, gradually became detached from their penal roots and were increasingly modeled on public schools. They took a new welfare/treatment direction and this philosophy was promoted throughout the 1930s (Hood, 1965). At the same time, however, other types of institutions were increasingly used. The number of juveniles in approved schools (established in 1933—and providing education and training for juvenile offenders) rose, as did the number in remand homes.

By the end of the 1930s, there was evidence of a revitalized emphasis on punishment. In particular, the Magistrates' Association[4] seemed determined to keep alive their idea for a new sentence of "young offenders detention" that was intended to provide a sentence "midway" on the continuum between borstal and probation. Further support for this came from a governmental committee on corporal punishment that could only conceive of abolishing corporal punishment if it were to be replaced with other measures to strengthen the authority of the courts.

Juvenile Justice 1945 to 1970

Between 1945 and 1970, Britain experienced both Labour (1945 to 51 and 1964 to 70) and Conservative (195 to 64) administrations. One might assume that this led to a radical shift from one set of policies to another. However, the closing years of World War II saw the development of a broad political consensus. One feature of this consensus was the creation of a post-war welfare state. This involved state intervention in the economy in order to maintain full employment, with supporting policies on housing, unemployment and sickness benefit, and health and child care (Marshall, 1975). Although there are some variations with regard to what was emphasized, these policies were shared between the two main parties.

The period was marked by major social change with increases in the Gross Domestic Product and personal incomes; low unemployment rates; changes in housing away from largely privately rented accommodation to both local authority housing and owner-occupied housing; and increases in the number of married women working and young people entering higher education. At the same time, the rate of births to teenage mothers rose; divorce became easier to obtain; church attendance declined and cars and televisions increasingly became regular features of family life (Halsey, 1988; Marwick, 1982).

This was the context for a new phase in juvenile justice. A broad political consensus provided a backdrop for consensus with regard to criminal and juvenile justice policy. Nevertheless, despite the emergence of a welfare perspective in general and a sympathetic, child-oriented perspective in particular (Rose, 1989), the war years had seen a new clamor for an unequivocally punitive perspective towards young offenders. In 1942, for example, John Watson, widely regarded as a progressive juvenile court chairman, called for a new type of punishment to bring offenders to their senses and to act as a deterrent. A concern for the welfare of the child co-existed with a tougher outlook (i.e., **crime control model**).

Key events in the post-war history of juvenile justice included the call from penal reformers, social work thinkers and others for "the urgent need for re-orienting the social services towards the maintenance of the family," not least because they believed juvenile crime often resulted from family breakdown. They called for the setting up of a government-led committee of enquiry whose terms would be broad enough "to include all causes of family breakdown, with positive recommendations for their prevention and alleviation." Their letter was followed up by a delegation to the Home Office.

At the same time, the Magistrates' Association pressed the Home Office for a review of the procedure in juvenile courts and the treatment of juveniles coming before them. The Home Office responded by setting up a departmental committee (the Ingleby Committee) in 1956 to consider the issues posed by both groups. The **Ingleby Report** was one of four major reports that influenced the direction of juvenile justice in the post-war period, the others being the Longford Report and two Labour Party white papers. The main points of these documents can be summarized as follows:

1. The *Ingleby Report* (Home Office, 1960) endorsed the existing structure of the juvenile court, though there were recommendations to strengthen the powers of the court by allowing magistrates to sentence young persons directly to borstal. The Committee also proposed that the age of criminal responsibility be raised from eight to 12, however, thereby replacing criminal with care proceedings for the younger age group. In 1963, as a legislative compromise, the age of criminal responsibility was raised to 10 in the *Children and Young Persons Act*. Criticisms of this led eventually to the publication of a Labour party report described below.

2. *Crime—A Challenge to Us All*, the report of a Labour Party study group (known as the Longford Report) was published some months before the Labour Party came to power in 1964. A fundamental principle underlying the report was that "delinquents are to some extent a

product of the society they live in and of the deficiencies in its provision for them" (Labour Party, 1964: 28). It also argued that the machinery of the law was reserved for working class youth and that those from other social classes were dealt with by other means. The report's proposals, therefore, were that "no child in early adolescence should have to face criminal proceedings" (1964: 24), that criminal proceedings were "indefensible" where the offence was trivial (1964: 24) and that serious offences were themselves indicative of "the child's need for skilled help and guidance" (1964: 24). One further issue was clear: juveniles had no personal responsibility for their offences. The report's aim, therefore, was to take juveniles out of the criminal courts and the penal system and to treat their problems in a family setting through the establishment of family advice centers, a family service and, for a minority, a family court.

3.   The subsequent white paper *The Child, the Family and the Young Offender* (Home Office, 1965) proposed the abolition of the juvenile court and its replacement by a non-judicial **family council**, linked to a unified **family service**. But there was concerted opposition to these proposals (from magistrates, lawyers and probation officers who, commentators believe, did not want to lose the chance of working with young offenders in their fast-developing professional service (Rutherford, 1986; Harris and Webb, 1987; Pitts, 1988).

4.   In response to this opposition, the Labour Government produced a second white paper *Children in Trouble* (Home Office, 1968). In this second attempt to promote reforms, the government leaned heavily on the expertise of the Home Office Child Care Inspectorate (Pitts, 1988) and, as a result, the language used changed. The appropriate response was one that depended on such phrases as "observation and assessment," "a variety of facilities for continuing treatment," "increased flexibility," and "further diagnosis."

The culmination of this period of activity was the *Children and Young Persons Act* 1969. The 1969 act dictated that juveniles under 14 were not to be referred to the juvenile court solely on the grounds that they had committed offences (thus bringing Britain into line with many other European countries). Rather, where it could be established that such juveniles were not receiving the care, protection and guidance a good parent might reasonable be expected to give, it was proposed that "care and protection" proceedings should be brought. Criminal proceedings were to be possible against juveniles aged 14 to 16 who had committed offences, but only after mandatory consultation had

taken place between the police and social service departments. The expectation was that these juveniles would also, in the main, be dealt with under care
and protection proceedings.

Integral to these proposals was an increase in the role of the local authority social worker. There was to be mandatory consultation between the police
and local authority social services prior to proceedings in the juvenile court,
and increased social work with families and juveniles on a compulsory and
voluntary basis. Moreover, considerable power was to be placed in the hands
of social workers to vary and implement the dispositions made by the magistrates. Magistrates were no longer to make detailed decisions about the kind of
treatment appropriate for juveniles; instead, this task was to be given to social
workers.

A second main thrust of the act was an attempt to curtail magistrates'
power to make use of custodial sentences. Prior to the act, magistrates had
been able to remit juveniles of 15 and over to the Crown court with a recommendation that the judge impose a sentence of borstal training. Magistrates
had no direct power to sentence juveniles to substantial periods in custody.
The act sought to prevent all those under 18 from being remitted to the Crown
court in this way. Further, detention centers and attendance centers were to be
replaced by a new form of treatment—intermediate treatment—and the form
which this would take was also to be determined by social services (Bottoms et
al., 1990).

Overall, the general aim of the act was to make the commission of an
offence no longer a sufficient ground for intervention—that is, to **decriminal-
ize** the court's jurisdiction; to reduce the number of juveniles appearing before
the juvenile court—that is, to *divert* juveniles wherever possible; and to abolish detention centers and borstals and replace them with community measures—that is, to encourage *deinstitutionalization*. Put very simply, the juvenile
court was to become a welfare-providing agency, but also an agency of last
resort: referral to the juvenile court was to take place only where voluntary and
informal agreement could not be reached among social workers, juveniles and
their parents (Morris and McIsaac, 1978).

Juvenile Justice in the 1970s: The Eclipse of Welfare?
Having witnessed the development of a consensus, albeit a fragile one,
the 1969 Act brought latent tensions to the surface. The breakdown of this
issue-specific consensus reflected the breakdown in the broader political consensus achieved in the immediate post-war years. The stage was set for a very
different conception of social order and of the appropriate response to juvenile offenders. The writings of the Conservative Party (see, for example, Coo-

per and Nicholas, 1963 and 1964) depict the law-breaker as choosing to commit offences and as doing so from personal iniquity and from "demands" or "desires" exacerbated by the welfare state rather than from social inequality.[5] Neither psychological nor social conditions were viewed as relevant to understanding criminal behavior. Consequently, juvenile offenders were viewed as personally responsible for their actions although, depending on their age, parents might share in this responsibility, in that they had failed both to discipline their young and to inculcate in them basic values. Thus a key role in preventing and controlling crime was assigned to the family which, it was believed, had been systematically undermined by socialism because it had taken away the responsibility from families to provide for its members. Thus "family responsibility" was given a different force and meaning from that found in comparable Labour Party writings. Deficiencies in the family were to be remedied through discipline and external controls, not through support and services. Parents were to be held responsible for the offences of their children by making them pay, quite literally. The appropriate response to the delinquent was correction through discipline and punishment. The role of the courts was also viewed as important in preserving respect for the law, ensuring parental responsibility, and making juvenile offenders accountable for their actions.

As a result, sections of the Conservative Party were always opposed to the philosophy underlying the *Longford Report*, the 1960s white papers and the 1969 act. In making sense of Conservative ideology about crime, we find its roots in the core values of Conservatism. According to Durham (1989, p. 50), Conservatism rests on a belief in "human fallibility"—humans, as a result of their "proneness to evil," need government—and on a reliance on tradition. Conservatism is also said to uphold both authority and liberty. In essence, Conservatives prefer to limit state controls, to cut government spending, to expand free enterprise and to privatize (eventually) even essential services. Through these strategies, societies are believed to be better off, both materially and morally, as they encourage competition, and competition means progress. Substantial government intervention is viewed as socially disruptive, as wasteful of resources, as promoting economic inefficiency, and as removing individual freedom. There is an acceptance of the government's role in the provision of certain services but this is as a last resort, a safety net, and only for those in real need.

What is significant in this context is that these ideological struggles impinged on the practice and practitioners of juvenile justice, too. On the right, alliances were drawn between the Conservative Party and the Magistrates' Association (and to some extent the Police Federation); and on the left, alliances were drawn between the Labour Party, social workers and liberal reform groups. Ideological differences provided the ammunition: policies for equality of opportunity were posed against those for achieving equality of results; the responsibility of juvenile offenders was set against their need for help; measures of punishment were contrasted with measures for treatment. Under the banner of "the best interests of the child," these ideological and professional differences were provided with a public forum.

The proposed 1969 act, then, represented an attempt to bridge this divide. It offered a compromise between concern with the welfare of the offending child on the one hand, and the retention of the full machinery of courtroom adjudication on the other. The latter was a sop to those who saw juvenile offenders as responsible, and who therefore believed in the symbolic and deterrent value of legalistic appearances. Yet the consequence of this compromise was that the competing conceptions collided at key points in the process (i.e., prosecution, adjudication, determination of the disposition, and implementation of the disposition). What is more, a Conservative Government replaced the Labour one in 1970 and the Conservatives made it clear that they would not fully implement the act. When the Labour Party were re-elected in 1974, it was no longer politically or popularly viable to implement the act in full. Thus new welfare measures were added *on to* but did not replace the old punitive ones.

More broadly speaking, two opposing trends—first, an increase in punitive dispositions generally and in custodial dispositions in particular, and second, an increase in the use of diversion—occurred in the 1970s. Neither are overtly linked with welfare; the opposite, in fact. But both were undoubtedly created by the consequences of perceptions of welfare or, more accurately perhaps, by perceptions of those promoting welfare practices. A third and paradoxical trend also occurred—a decline in the use of welfare-oriented dispositions despite the intentions underlying the act (see Gelsthorpe and Morris, 1994, for details of the use of custody and welfare over this period).

Juvenile Justice in the 1980s: The "Moment" of Crime Control

In the 1980s in England and Wales, as elsewhere, there was an explicit revival of traditional criminal justice values (**crime control**). It is no accident that this coincided with and was fuelled by the electoral campaigns and eventual election of a Conservative Government with a large majority. The need to stand firm against crime was especially apparent in the electoral campaigns of the Conservative Party in 1979 where it presented itself as the party who could and would take a strong stand against crime, in contrast to the Labour Party, which was presented as excusing crime and as being sympathetic to offenders.

The message used in this 1979 campaign was the need to protect victims from offenders irrespective of their age, the need to reduce the high level of recorded crime, and the allegedly increased seriousness of crime, particularly among juveniles. Specifically, the political rhetoric referred to "young thugs" who were to be sent to detention centers for a short, sharp shock; secure places for juveniles were to be increased, and the number of attendance centers expanded. And later that year, after they had won the election, the new home secretary made good some of the electoral promises: two detention centers were, on an experimental basis, to have tougher regimes.

The Conservative government's *Criminal Justice Act* 1982—hit at the root of the social welfare perspective underlying the 1969 act, although there was some endorsement for the expansion of diversion and a reduction in the minimum period of custody for which a boy could be held in a detention center. Clearly, there were moves towards the notion of personal responsibility, punishment, and parental responsibility. In brief, the 1982 act made available to magistrates three new powers of disposal: youth custody, care orders with certain residential requirements and community service. Further, there were three major changes to existing powers: periods in detention centers became shorter, restrictions on activities as part of supervision orders became more common, and it was to become normal practice to fine parents rather than the juvenile.

In the light of these changes two significant trends occurred:

1. *Limiting custody and residential care.* Against the predictions of academic commentators (see, for example, Morris and Giller, 1979), the number of 14- to 16-year-old boys found guilty of indictable offences and sentenced to custody declined dramatically during the 1980s (most dramatically between 1988 and 1989). Also, the proportionate use of custody hardly changed until 1989 (remaining at about 12%)—and only fell to 9% in 1989 and then 7% in 1990.

Decreases in the number of care orders imposed on boys and in their proportionate use occurred too. Similar decreases in the use of custody and care orders occurred for girls (though there was an initial increase in the use of custody for girls between 1979 and 1984).[6]

How is this decline in the use of custody and care orders and the rate of decline to be explained? Early research on the impact of the criteria introduced in the 1982 *Criminal Justice Act*, which had been intended to restrict the use of custody, showed magistrates failed to follow statutory procedures (Burney, 1985; Parker, 1981). Gradually, however, case law emerged on what amounted to an offence sufficiently serious to warrant custody. Lawyers in certain areas took a more active stance, and the criteria used in justifying custody were further tightened up in the *Criminal Justice Act* 1988 (see Stanley, 1988; Dodds, 1986 and 1987; Allen, 1991, for a description).

Changes in the 1982 *Criminal Justice Act* also required changes in social work practice. They forced social workers and probation officers to reconsider the provision and content of social enquiry reports (court reports) and to reform the provision and content of intermediate treatment (IT). Though the original form of IT continued to be available (as part of a supervision order) a new format was also introduced in the 1982 act—the supervised activity requirement. The significance of this was that the control and content of the order shifted to magistrates. This was an explicit attempt to increase the magistrates' confidence in such orders as realistic alternatives to custody.

At the same time, according to Bottoms et al. (1990), intermediate treatment practitioners were evolving a new style of working which meant a move away from a concentration on meeting the social and emotional needs of juveniles, towards a perspective which focused more on the offence. They also began to focus more on the provision of IT as a sentencing option specifically aimed at those at risk of residential care or custody. Thus IT gradually (in the 1980s) developed into a mechanism geared to solve some of the consequences of the ideology which had produced it—for example, to reduce the number of care orders imposed.

The decline in the use of custody and care can also be partially explained by the impact of diversion (cautioning) practices; the increased use of fines, compensation and community service orders; and the introduction of criteria to restrict the use of custody, or the increased legal representation of young offenders that reduced custody.

2. *The continued expansion of diversion.* Throughout the 1980s, diversion was repeatedly affirmed in government documents (for example, Home Office, 1980), consultative documents (Home Office, 1984), Circulars to the police (for example, Home Office Circular 14/1985) and in the Code of Practice for prosecutors (Crown Prosecution Service, 1986). In these various documents, it was made clear that prosecution should not occur unless it was "absolutely necessary" or as "a last resort," and that the prosecution of first-time offenders where the offence was not serious was unlikely to be "justifiable" unless there were "exceptional circumstances." Prosecution was to be regarded as "a severe step." This principle was echoed in local police force procedures. Thus the proportion of boys cautioned for indictable offences increased enormously over this period. As a consequence, the government then became concerned about net-widening, and encouraged the use of no further action or informal warnings instead of formal cautions, and the number of juveniles brought into the juvenile justice system *did* then decline. But net-widening probably declined for other

reasons too—because of a declining youth population (with fewer young people coming to the attention of the police) and because inter-agency consultation as to what action to take for particular juvenile offenders developed (which may have limited police intervention), for example. Also, many police areas developed "multiple cautions" (though this practice was never as widespread as believed—see Evans and Wilkinson, 1990—and prosecution remained the norm after one or two cautions except in exceptional circumstances). But the major reason for the reduction in the number of juveniles subject to official processing was perhaps the expansion of informal cautions in some police force areas.

We can sum up the 1980s in this way. In 1979, the Conservative Party made crime a major election issue. The emphasis was on re-establishing Victorian values in opposition to the legacy of the supposed permissiveness of the 1960s and its soft approach to crime and all its unwelcome, politically unpalatable effects. In such a supposedly de-moralizing culture, crime and violence were seen as "out of control": hence the need for "law and order" policies to reassert the virtue and necessity of authority, order and discipline, and for attempts to realign relationships between the state and civil society as a whole.

Juvenile Justice in the 1990s: The Return to Consensus?
The first significant event of the 1990s was the implementation of the 1989 *Children Act* that came into force in October 1991. This represented a major structural alteration to the law concerning the welfare of juveniles and covers an enormous range of matters previously dealt with in different legislation. The law affecting juveniles who offend is only touched upon, but the resulting changes, together with the act's underlying sentiments about the nature of the relationship between the state, children and their parents, have significant implications for juvenile offenders.

The most important of these was the cessation of the use of the care order as a disposal available to the court in criminal proceedings, and the removal of the offence condition in proceedings justifying state intervention in the life of a family. These changes at once recognized the enormous decline in the use made of the care order, the inappropriateness of a care order in criminal proceedings, the principle of determinacy in sentencing and the importance that the government gave to parental responsibility. New rules also provided for the transfer of care proceedings from the juvenile court. These are now heard in a renamed "family proceedings" court; the newly named youth court deals only with criminal proceedings.

Since the beginning of the 1990s there have been a number of other new developments in youth justice. These include:

- An increase in the maximum age limit of cases dealt with by special courts for young people—renamed as youth courts following the 1991 *Criminal Justice Act*. The court now deals with 10- to 17-year-olds (inclusive).
- The deliberate creation of a so-called "overlapping jurisdiction" of community orders for 16- and 17-year-olds found guilty, for it is intended that courts should choose the most appropriate orders for defendants on an individualized basis, taking into account the maturity of the individual offender. (Hence, probation orders became available for 16-year-olds, supervision orders for 17-year-olds, and the maximum number of hours of community service that could be imposed for 16-year-olds was changed to 240—as opposed to 180, the previous limit).
- There was also an attempt to enhance parental responsibility for children's offending (especially those under the age of 15). This was done by strengthening the requirement for parents to attend the youth court whenever their children appear, and by giving the court powers to "bind over" parents with regard to their children's future behavior. If the children continued to offend, the parents could be fined for not exercising proper control and for being in breach of the binding-over condition.
- The 1991 *Criminal Justice Act* also increased the minimum age for detention in a young offender institution for males from 14 to 15 (this was the minimum for females prior to the act).

The nature and form of youth justice has also been influenced by the *Criminal Justice and Public Order Act* 1994. There were four main provisions of this Act which affected the sentencing of young offenders:

1. The introduction of the secure training order—a new custodial sentence for persistent juvenile offenders aged 12 to 14 inclusive;
2. extending to 10- to 13-year-olds the existing powers of long-term detention (under the *Children Young Persons Act* 1933, s.53) available in respect of 14- to 17-year-olds (such orders were previously only available to 10- to 13-year-olds if they had committed murder or manslaughter); and
3. allowing 10- to 15-year olds to receive long-term detention for offences of indecent assault against a female (this provision was previously only available for 16- and 17-year-olds).

This line of "toughening up" penalties for young offenders was also re-flected in the increase in the maximum length of a sentence of detention for an offender 15 to 17 inclusive, in a young offenders institution from 12 months to two years. Finally, the *Criminal Justice and Public Order Act* 1994 made fur-ther attempts to strengthen parental responsibility by making clear that in a parental bind-over the parent should ensure that the offender complies with the requirements of a community sentence.

Three other points are worth noting in this brief review of developments in the 1990s. The first concerns the idea of "Boot Camps" for young offenders. The government considered the introduction of a pilot project in one young offender institution based on the "high impact incarceration programs" — more commonly referred to as "Boot Camps" (military style camps). The idea was that a tougher, more physically demanding regime might have impact on young offenders' criminal propensities. Research in the United States on the effectiveness of boot camps is unpersuasive in the claim that they will lead to a reduction in crime by young people (Mackenzie and Souryal, 1994). This being so, it was difficult to understand the then government's interest in such regimes—except in terms of political rhetoric to seduce voters into thinking that crime can be under control with a Conservative government.

The second point concerns the age of criminal responsibility. As a result of court cases in 1994 and 1995 (most notably the case of the two boys aged 10 and 11 who were tried for killing two-year-old James Bulger) the principles governing the criminal responsibility of children between the ages of 10 and 13 were reviewed. As previously stated, the age of criminal responsibility in En-gland and Wales is 10-year-olds, and children under that age could not be found guilty of a criminal offence. Children between 10 and 13 were presumed in law to be **doli incapax** (incapable of criminal intent) and this presumption must be rebutted by the prosecution before they can be convicted. In order to rebut the presumption, the prosecution must show beyond all reasonable doubt that the child appreciated that what he or she did was "seriously wrong" as opposed to merely naughty or mischievous. Nevertheless, following the re-view, the principle of *doli incapax* was upheld on the grounds that there is wisdom in protecting young children against the full rigour of the criminal law because of the need to acknowledge varying rates of child development and maturity.

The age of criminal responsibility in England and Wales is unusually low in comparison with most countries of western Europe (see other contributions in this text and Figure 5.1), in which offenders under 14 are dealt with by civil proceedings. The seeming lack of differentiation between the political mani-festos relating to the 1992 election (Conservative Political Centre, 1992; Labour Party, 1992) led many to believe that there was a new consensus on youth crime and punishment. Further, in both rhetoric and practice, the formal arrangements for youth justice at the beginning of the 1990s were increasingly becoming linked with other social institutions and processes (e.g., schools, the family, neighborhood, work), and there was ostensible concern among political parties and politicians to make strong connections amongst these processes, where preventative and healing resources were perceived ultimately to reside.

The Shape of Youth Justice to Come: the 1998 Crime and Disorder Act

Throughout their opposition years 1979 to 1997 the Labour party argued that youth crime and youth justice would be a priority of the next Labour government. Having produced a paper *Tackling Youth Crime, Reforming Youth Justice* (Labour party, 1996) as they contemplated the weightiness of the ballot box, the newly elected government were exceedingly quick off the mark to produce further documents. Three consultation papers, *Tackling Youth Crime* (Home Office, 1997a), *Tackling Delays in the Youth Justice System* (Home Office, 1997b), and *New National and Local Focus on Youth Crime* (Home Office, 1997c) appeared within six months of Labour's election to power in May 1997. This came as no great surprise, and proved to be central to the government's approach to youth justice. The home secretary also appointed a multi-agency "Youth Task Force" in June 1997 which itself produced a report a year later to reinforce many of the points made in the consultation papers.

The general tenor of these documents was to make proposals "to improve the effectiveness of the Youth Justice system in preventing, deterring and punishing youth crime" (Home Office, 1997a, 2). The white paper containing the main framework for the legislation was published in November 1997, its title giving a telling clue to what lay within (*No More Excuses: A New Approach to Tackling Youth Crime in England and Wales*) (Home Office, 1997d) and signified that tough measures were on the way (see Box 5.1).

Box 5.1

Home Office White Paper: *No More Excuses: A New Approach to Tackling Youth Crime in England and Wales* —"An excuse culture has developed within the youth justice system. It excuses itself for its inefficiency, and too often excuses the young offenders before it, implying that they cannot help their behavior because of their social circumstances. Rarely are they confronted with their behavior and helped to take more responsibility for their actions" (Home Office, 1997d, 1).

The *Crime and Disorder Act* 1998 which followed was described as a "comprehensive and wide-ranging reform programme" (Home Office, 1997a:1) and as "the biggest shake-up for 50 years in tackling crime" (Travis, 1997). This flagship law-and-order legislation received royal assent on 31 July 1998;

many of its provisions are explicitly aimed not only at young offenders, but at young people more generally. The legislation appears to favor punishment to signal society's disapproval of criminal acts and deter offending. At the same time, however, it remains faithful to its commitment to be "tough on crime, tough on the causes of crime" by referring at times to social factors which contribute to crime, and by proposing to prevent re-offending through an interventionist, welfare approach reminiscent of interventions in the 1960s and 1970s. The act also contains provisions that underline support for the government's belief in restorative justice principles (though reparation orders, for instance). Therefore, it can be said that, while our juvenile justice model largely represents a **corporatist model** (see Figure 1—Introduction),* it is unclear where the balance lies between crime control and welfare.

In a way, none of this was unexpected. If the mood of the early 1990s can be characterized by the public response to the James Bulger case and fears about persistent young offenders, the shape of the 1998 act reflects a concern to control crime, to strike at the causes of crime through preventative measures and at the same time address the needs of victims.[7] But there is also a sense in which the 1998 legislation (and indeed the concomitant *Youth Justice and Criminal Evidence Act* 1999) might be characterized by eight key themes in criminal justice thinking which have come to dominate (Gelsthorpe and Morris, 1999; James and Raine, 1998; Bottoms, 1995) (see Box 5.2).

The *Crime and Disorder Act* 1998 included key measures to ensure the effective functioning of the system (through, for example, the introduction of a national Youth Justice Board) to give strategic direction to, set standards for, and measure the performance of, the youth justice system as a whole. It also incorporated various measures to speed up the punishment process. Thus it fulfilled various *managerial* aspirations.

There are also new measures in this act to ensure that offenders address their offending behavior and reduce *risk* to the community (through, for example, warnings—which trigger interventions from youth offending teams, action plan orders, and drug treatment and testing orders). Other measures ensure protection of the community (through, for example, anti-social behavior orders) as well as of individual victims (through, for example, reparation orders) which serve to address *community interests* and *restorative justice* values. *Risk assessment* and *actuarial justice* with strong notions of taking anticipatory action on the basis of the probability of offending are reflected in the 1998 act's child safety orders. Such safety orders are issued for children under the age of ten if they have done something that, if performed by some-

---

*   The model, as identified, has been provided by the editor and does not necessarily reflect the views of the authors.

Box 5.2 Key themes that characterize criminal justice thinking in the late 1990s

- *Just deserts*—an approach to sentencing that focuses on proportionality and consistency, but which in the public mind is linked to retributivism. Just deserts thinking has been increasingly influential over the last quarter century and is epitomized in the 1991 Criminal Justice Act:
- *Managerialism*—an ethos which places emphasis on "the system," inter-agency cooperation, strategic plans, and the delivery of services, and which is frequently referred to as underpinning the three "Es" of economy, efficiency and effectiveness;
- *Risk assessment and "actuarial justice"*—notions which involve an emphasis on the statistical probabilities of future crime (based on offence seriousness, previous offending and offenders' social characteristics) and taking anticipatory action on the basis of these;
- The incorporation of the *community*—which means a new focus on community penalties, and more intrusive controls in the community (for example, electronic tagging);
- *Public voice and participation*—that is, participation based on consumerism and rights, especially the notion of victims' rights;
- *Active citizenship*—which means encouragement for the shared responsibility for crime and crime prevention;
- *Restorative justice*—the central tenet of which is that crime should be seen primarily as a matter concerning the offender and victim and their immediate families, and thus should be resolved by them through constructive effort (reparative measures) to put right the harm that has been done; and
- *'Populist punitiveness'*—an ideology which involves not just a reflection of public opinion, but also politicians tapping into, and using for their own purposes, what they believe to be the public's punitive stance.

one older, would be considered an offence. Children may also receive a safety order if they have acted in a manner that has caused, or is likely to cause, harassment, alarm or distress, or if they have contravened a ban imposed by a curfew order (see below). Similarly, a safety order may be issued if such an order is considered necessary to prevent offending. Under the same act, local curfew orders apply to all children under the age of ten in a specific area, and prevent them meeting in specified public places between 9 P.M. and 6 A.M. unless accompanied by a parent or responsible adult. Local authorities can impose these curfews on the assumption that children are "at risk" of committing offences.

The theme of *active citizenship*, it may be argued, is reflected in a number of ways—notably through the 1998 act's parenting orders. These require guidance or counselling sessions once a week for up to 12 weeks, and can be imposed on parents whose children are on a child safety order, an anti-social behavior order or a sex offender order. A parenting order is especially likely when it is believed that a child under 16 may re-offend unless the parents are instructed in how to take greater responsibility for their offspring's behavior. Anti-social behavior orders (ASBOs) that encourage neighbors to report on the perceived troublesomeness of local residents (the "neighbors from hell") also reflect the theme of *active citizenship*.

Some of the signal themes, particularly *active citizenship* and *restorative justice*, are rehearsed in the 1999 *Youth Justice and Criminal Evidence Act* which introduces a new primary sentencing disposal for 10- to 17-year-olds pleading guilty and convicted for the first time. The disposal involves referral orders, which means that the offender is referred to a local youth offender panel where a contract will be arranged with the young person to prevent further offending. Significantly, panel members may include members of the public as "community panel members," and contracts will include reparation to the victim or the wider community as well as a program of activity designed to prevent further offending.

As for *populist punitiveness*, the Labour government's agenda for criminal justice following its election to power arguably involves a shift to the right in order to challenge the Conservative party on its own ideological territory. Indeed, in the early election promises it became clear that New Labour wanted to establish itself in the public's mind as the party best equipped to introduce tough and effective measures to deal with offenders (Brownlee, 1998). The main tenor of Labour's criminal justice legislation between its coming to power in May 1997 and the time of writing (January 2001) does not, therefore, mirror the party's sympathetic thinking from the 1960s about "children in trouble" and so on. Rather, it indicates a melting pot of contradictory ideas and ideologies. These may militate against each other instead of serving the notion of clear and consistent sentencing (Fionda, 1999). They might even result in an ideological shift in favor of punishment and crime control. Such a shift would be reminiscent of Cohen's "punitive city" (Cohen, 1979; 1985) in which more and more people, including children, are brought into the criminal justice system for an ever-expanding range of criminal or troublesome behavior (Gelsthorpe and Morris, 1999). There are very mixed views on this. (See Figure 5.2, which shows changes to the decision-making process with regard to young offenders after the 1998 *Crime and Disorder Act*.)

Following the 1998 *Crime and Disorder Act*

Criminal liability—Under criminal law children under 10 cannot be liable for a criminal offence at all. As described above, in the past there was a well-established presumption that children between the ages of 10 and 13 were not criminally liable (the doli incapax rule applied), though this rule was rebuttable. In 1998 this rebuttable presumption was repealed by s. 34 of the *Crime and*

Figure 5.2: Outline of Changes to the Youth Justice System in England and Wales Following Implementation of the *Crime and Disorder Act* 1998 and the *Youth Justice and Criminal Evidence Act* 1999

APPREHENSION & CHARGE

Parents are expected to prevent their children from committing offences and, in the circumstances, if their child does offend they can be placed on a "parenting order" under which they are required to attend parenting classes (they can be fined or imprisoned for failing to attend).

In addition to the police apprehending or having youngsters reported to them, children under ten who have broken a local curfew or committed an offence can now be dealt with under a child safety order in the family proceedings court and such an order can lead to care proceedings.

BAIL

The contents of bail support programs vary. Support can include programs which seek to reintroduce youngsters back to school or assist in finding training or employment. The lack of accommodation is generally recognised as a major factor influencing bail, with some teams seeking to increase provision.

The 1998 act requires that every local authority must ensure, to such extent as is appropriate for their area, that there is provision for the support of children and young persons remanded or committed on bail whilst awaiting trial or sentence.

DIVERT/PROSECUTE

On issuing a warning, the police will refer the case to the YOT for an assessment, and an intervention is normally expected. This can be by way of a "change program" and/or a restorative caution.

Doli incapax is no longer available for young offenders aged 10 to 13.

The statutory final warning scheme replaces the former cautioning scheme for 10- to 17-year-olds.

The police decide whether to reprimand, warn or prosecute.

Pre-court decisions do not need parents' consent.

YOUTH COURT SERVICES

Community Sentences		Civil/criminal orders		Custody	Others
Action plan[1]	Drug TT order[1]	ASBO[1]	10–17 years	Detention and training order[3]	Referral order[4]
Supervision order[2]	Probation order[2]	Sex offender order[1]			Reparation[1]
Attendance centre	Community service	Child safety order[1]	Under 10s	For 10–17 years	Fine Discharges[5]
Curfew order	Combination order	Parenting order[1]	For parents or guardians		Compensation
For 10–17 years	For 16–17 years				Bind over
					For 10–17 years

1 Contained in the *Crime and Disorder Act* 1998, these new orders were implemented in June 2000.
2 These orders may contain additional specified requirements.
3 Detention and training orders were included in the 1998 act and implemented on April 1, 2000, replacing young offender institutions and secure training orders. The orders can be for 4 to 24 months with half the order served in custody and the other half under supervision (only effective for 12- to 17-year-olds at present). Section 53 CYPA 1933 is retained.
4 The referral orders were implemented in 2002-2003.
5 A conditional discharge is not available if the offender had carried out a program of work as directed by the YOT.

Disorder Act 1998. In this respect children aged 10 and above are now treated like adults. British (excluding Scotland) children are almost alone in Europe in being regarded as criminals at the age of 10! Based on the models presented in Figure 1 (see Introduction) the new act no longer shares the pure characteristics of a corporatism model. Walgrave and Mehlbye (1998) describe the latest approach as a **juvenile penal law system**.

The pre-court system - If a child, or young person between 10 and 17, is believed to have committed an offence, the police have two main options: formal action, or giving an informal warning or "telling off" on the street. Before taking formal action, the police must interview the young person (with at least one parent or guardian present).

If it is not possible for a parent or guardian to be present, then the police must arrange for "an appropriate adult" (e.g., social worker) to accompany the child. Following the interview, if the offence is denied, the police must seek to prove the case in court or drop the matter. Where the police believe that there is a case against the child or young person, and where that child or young person admits the offence, they can decide to take *no further action* or *pursue formal action*. "No further action" is only likely to be used where the offence is minor. In terms of formal action, the police may decide to give the offender a **reprimand** or a final **warning** where the young person has admitted the offence. A final warning will initiate a referral to the local youth offending team (YOT) for an assessment of what intervention may be required to reduce the likelihood of offending. The YOT[8] will provide such programs of rehabilitative intervention. A first offence will be thus met with a reprimand, a final warning, or criminal charges depending on the seriousness of the offence. Following one reprimand, any further offences will lead to a warning or to a charge. Any further offending following the final warning will normally be dealt with in court. A second warning will only be given in very limited circumstances where the latest offence is not serious and more than two years have passed since the final warning was given. Reprimands and warnings are issued by a police officer, and where the young person is under 17, in the presence of an appropriate adult. These actions are formally recorded and may be cited in court if the young person offends again in the future.

The post criminal court system involves a range of sentences:
  • **Bind-over** - The ancient power to bind over persons to "be of good behavior and keep the peace" is used to mark offending or misbehavior which might lead to a breach of the peace in the future—a method known as "preventive justice." The power can be used on its own or in

connection with criminal offences, in addition to any penalty. At the time of going to press, this penalty had been declared void following a European Convention of Human Rights ruling in 2000, but there was no English legislation to indicate that it was to be abolished.[9]

- **Reparation Order** - Reparation orders were established by the 1998 *Crime and Disorder Act*. The orders apply to 10- to 17-year-olds and require reparation to be made in kind, up to a maximum of 24 hours of work within a period of three months. The reparation might involve writing a letter of apology, apologizing to the victim in person, cleaning graffiti, or repairing criminal damage. The victim's views must be sought before such an order is imposed. The reparation order is not a community sentence and therefore may be used in respect of an offence that is not yet serious enough to justify the passing of a community sentence. Before making such an order, the court is required to obtain and consider a report from a probation officer, social worker or a member of a youth offending team indicating the type of work that is suitable for the young offender and the attitude of the victim(s) to the requirements to be included in the order.

- **Referral Order** - The referral order was introduced by the *Youth Justice and Criminal Evidence Act* 1999 and confirmed as a sentence of the youth court by the powers of the *Criminal Courts (Sentencing) Act* 2000 for those offenders under 18. They must be first-time offenders who plead guilty and for whom the court is not intending to impose a custodial sentence, hospital order or absolute discharge. In order to qualify for such a sentence the young person must also never have been bound over to be of good behavior and keep the peace, and the offences must not be ones for which the sentence is fixed by law.

  Essentially, the referral order involves the young offender being referred to the "youth offender panel" within the local YOT. The panel, comprising a person from the YOT and two lay persons, the offender, the offender's parents, the victim (if s/he wishes to attend), the offender's friend (any person over 18—including a lawyer, although there is no provision for legal aid), the victim's friend, and any person thought "capable of being a good influence on the offender," would seek to reach an agreement with the offender for a program of activity to prevent re-offending by the young person

  This "youth offender contract" may require the offender to be at home at specified times, to attend school/work, to attend specified programs, to make financial or other reparation to the victim, and/or to attend victim-offender mediation schemes, and/or to perform unpaid community work/service. If the panel and the offender cannot agree on a contract, the case returns to the youth court for sentence, but otherwise the panel has continuing jurisdiction for the length of the contract. These orders were implemented in April 2002.

- **Discharges** - An *Absolute Discharge* usually signifies a technical offence or extreme "triviality." It puts matters at an end, and involves the offender in no further obligations or liability. Legally, there is an offence, but this does not count for any other purpose. That is, it does not rank as a conviction for the purpose of a criminal record. A *Conditional Discharge* can be imposed for up to three years. The condition is that he or she does not commit another criminal offence in that period. Provided that no new offence is committed, the conditional discharge lapses and does not count for any other purpose. A new offence during the period means that the offender can be sentenced afresh for the original offence. Thus the defendant may face a sentence for two matters: the new and the old.

  The *Crime and Disorder Act* 1998 limits the court's use of conditional discharge when sentencing a young offender who, within the past two years, already has received a warning. In the circumstances a conditional discharge cannot be used unless there are exceptional circumstances relating to the offence or the offender which justify it, and if so the reason should be stated in open court.

- **Fines and compensation**—The standard scale of fines ranges from £200 to £5000, but there are limits on certain age groups and on certain offences. Parents or guardians can be ordered to pay fines and compensation imposed upon a juvenile. Compensation orders are at a fixed sum decided by the court. They may relate to injury, loss or damage, but not normally where this arises from a motor accident. The purpose is to provide recompense to victims, rather than to punish the offender.

- **Community Sentences**

  Community Service Orders (now called Community Punishment Order)—these can be made in respect of persons aged 16 or over for between 40 and 240 hours. The main purpose of such an order is to reintegrate the offender into the community by compelling him or her to perform positive and demanding unpaid work in a disciplined manner. When possible, the work should be socially useful, making reparation to the community for the damage done by the offence.

  Combination Orders (now called Community Punishment and Rehabilitation Order)—this is a mixture of a probation order and a community service order. The probation part of the mix must be for not less than 12 months and the community service part of the mix must be for not less than 40 hours and not more than 100 hours. ***Curfew Orders***—new powers to impose curfew orders on offenders of or over 16 years of age were introduced by the *Criminal Justice Act* 1991. The curfew order may specify different places or different periods of curfew in respect of different days, but the curfew cannot last for longer than six months from the date of making the order, and must not involve curfew periods of less than two hours' duration or more than 12 hours' duration in any one day during that period. A curfew order may, in addition, include requirements for securing the electronic monitoring of the offender's whereabouts during the curfew periods specified in the order. ***Probation Orders*** (now called Community Rehabilitation Order)—can be made for six months to three years in respect of persons 17 or over. This places the offender under the supervision of a probation officer or a YOT member. Standard conditions are normally attached to the order (e.g., to report to the probation officer as required, to reside in an approved hostel, to attend a probation center for up to 60 days or evenings, to take part in specified activities such as an "anger control group" or an "alcohol offender group" or a "sexual offender group"). ***Attendance Center Orders***—are available for 10- to 20-year-olds, though the centers dealing with 10- to 17-year-olds are known as "Junior Attendance Centers." The orders can be imposed for up to 24 hours for those between 10 and 15, and up to 36 hours for those between 16 and 20 (though those between 15 and 17 will serve their hours in a Junior Attendance Center and those over this age in a senior attendance center. Offenders are required to report to a center on a weekly basis (often on a Saturday afternoon) for a range of activity including military drill, gym, social skills training and creative skills (e.g. woodwork or metalwork). ***Supervision Orders***—may be imposed on 10- to 17-year-olds. Offenders have to report to a social worker, probation officer, or a YOT member. Supervision frequently involves certain conditions such as intermediate treatment that involves up to 90 days activity and instruction in social, community, domestic and creative skills. Another condition concerns "specified activities," that essentially means that the court can dictate which activities the young offender is to engage in as part of the order. ***Drug Treatment and Testing Orders***—have been devised within the 1998 *Crime and Disorder Act* to direct drug users away from criminality and into treatment. The order can be imposed on offenders 16 and over who are dependent on, or have a propensity to misuse, drugs, and whose condition requires (and is likely to be susceptible to) treatment. Orders can be made for between six months and three years. *Action Plan Orders*—established under the 1998 *Crime and Disorder Act*, are applicable to offenders aged 10 to 17. The action plan order lasts three months and is described as a short intensive program of community intervention combining punishment, rehabilitation and reparation to change offending behavior and prevent further crime. Before making such an order, the court is required to obtain and consider a report from a probation officer, social worker or a member of the youth offending team which indicates the requirements which that person proposes to include in the order, and the "therapeutic" rationales.

- **Custodial Sentences—Detention and Training Orders** may be imposed on 10- to 17-year-olds (only implemented with 12- to 17-year-olds at present). Those under 14 (and indeed, up to 18) may be detained under Section 53 (2) of the 1933 *Children and Young Persons Act* if they have committed an offence punishable with 14 years' imprisonment, or indecent assault on a woman.

- **Ancillary Orders**—include such matters as driving disqualification, penalty points endorsements, forfeiture orders and restitution orders in respect of stolen property.

- **Special Powers**—special powers allow sentencers to deal with cases when problems arise from the defendant's mental condition. These include hospital orders, guardianship orders, and conditions of treatment attached to probation orders.

- **Additional Civil/Criminal Orders**—other orders, or powers, which are available otherwise than as a sentence following conviction include: the *Child Safety Order,* which can be imposed by a family proceedings court on a child under ten, involving supervision from a responsible officer (a local authority social worker or member of a YOT) for up to 12 months; a *Local Child Curfew* which involve curfews within specified public areas for up to 90 days, placing a ban on unsupervised children under 10 between 9 P.M. and 6 A.M.; an *Anti-Social Behavior Order* is a civil court order, applied for by the local authority and police in consultation with each other, against an individual (aged 10 and above) whose behavior is anti-social, that has effect for a minimum of two years (with breach being punishable by imprisonment or age-related alternatives); and a *Sex Offender Order* (for all aged 10 and above) which can be used to restrict the movements and activities of anyone whom the police (upon application to the court) believe to pose a threat of serious harm to the public.

- **Parenting Orders** are also an invention of the 1998 *Crime and Disorder Act* and involve powers in the youth court and Crown court (a higher court) as well as in the family court. Such courts may require a parent or guardian of a person 10 to 17, who *inter alia* has been convicted of an offence, to attend counselling or guidance sessions and to comply with certain specified requirements. The parent can be required to attend counselling sessions not more than once a week and for no longer than three months overall. The specified requirements (e.g., ensuring that the child is accompanied to school each day and is indoors by a certain hour in the evening) may remain in force for up to 12 months (see Chapter 15 on Scotland and Box 5.3 on Northern Ireland for a contrasting perspective).

Box 5.3 Juvenile Justice in Northern Ireland

Juvenile justice in Northern Ireland is largely governed by the *Children and Young Persons Act* (Northern Ireland) 1968, the Children (Northern Ireland) Order (1995), and more recently the Criminal Justice (Children) Order 1998. The juvenile court (now the youth court) remains the judicial forum in which any statutory intervention into the lives of children and young persons takes place. The age of criminal responsibility in Northern Ireland is 10, as it is in England. The youth court is presided over by a magistrate who has at least six years' experience as a practicing lawyer, assisted by two members of a lay panel. Dispositions available to the court include: fines, absolute and conditional discharges, committal to juvenile center orders, supervision or probation orders, attendance center orders, a period in a young offenders' center, and community service (for those juveniles who have reached the age of 16). A review of legislation and services relating to the care and treatment of young people (chaired by Sir Harold Black, the report being published by the Department of Health and Social Services et al. in 1979; see Gelsthorpe and Morris, 1994) made some radical suggestions, including the separation of juvenile justice and welfare systems (as in England; see Gelsthorpe and Morris, 1994), determinate sentencing, and for a fixed number of custodial places (in a secure unit as opposed to training schools). Many of Black's recommendations appear to have been recently incorporated in the Children (Northern Ireland) Order (1995), and the Criminal Justice (Children) (Northern Ireland) Order (1998), and there are a range of new proposals outlined in the "Review of the Criminal Justice System in Northern Ireland" (Criminal Justice Review Group, 2000).

Principal amongst these is the development of restorative justice approaches for young offenders and the setting up of the "youth conference." Such a conference involves a coordinator, the offender, the offender's parents, the victim (if he or she agrees) and the victim's supporters, significant others relevant to the offender (for example, a teacher), a defence lawyer (where this is wished) and, where appropriate, professionals such as probation and social services. In essence, it is recommended that the Northern Ireland system focus on reparative justice (to meet the needs of victims) and rehabilitative justice (in order to prevent re-offending) and generally make much less use of custody than hitherto. At press time it was unknown how many of these broad recommendations would be adopted (see O'Mahony and Deazley, 2000, for further details of the review of the Northern Ireland Youth Justice System).

JUVENILE CRIME: TRENDS AND PATTERNS

Having outlined the development of juvenile justice within England and Wales and indicated some of the differences in Northern Ireland, it is worth pausing to consider the nature and extent of the problem which the system has set out to deal with. In this section, we will therefore examine recent trends and patterns in juvenile crime. The following statistics are drawn from *Criminal Statistics, England and Wales*, published by the Home Office, the government department which deals with domestic matters. It is worth noting that the age categories changed in 1993, following the 1991 *Criminal Justice Act*. As we noted in the previous section, one consequence of this act is that 17-year-olds are now dealt with in the youth court and not the magistrates' court. The age groupings of the statistics have thus changed, from 14 to 16 to 14 to 17, and from 17 to 20 to 18 to 20.

It is also important to note that the statistics of recorded crime do not necessarily portray the full picture of crime. The 1998 British Crime Survey (a government-inspired national victim survey carried out at regular intervals), for example, suggests that of all offences committed, less than half are reported to the police and only a quarter are recorded. For a variety of reasons, many offences are not reported to the police and, of those that are reported, some go unrecorded, and this picture varies considerably between different offences. Of all offences that were recorded in 1998/99, only 29% were cleared up, that is, prosecuted or resolved in some other way (as reported in the Home Office, 1998 Criminal Statistics).

Figure 5.3 offers some indication of extent of the crime problem within England and Wales since 1978.

Although absolute comparisons between criminal justice statistics in different countries are difficult, comparisons based on general trends suggest that during 1998 crime rose on average by 4.7% in the 29 countries covered,

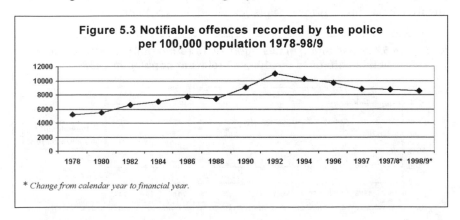

Figure 5.3 Notifiable offences recorded by the police per 100,000 population 1978-98/9

* *Change from calendar year to financial year.*

including Western Europe, the USA, Canada and Japan, although in England and Wales there was a slight fall of 1%. This continues the trend of falling crime rates in England and Wales, after they had the highest increase, 35%, between 1987 and 1994 (as reported by the Home Office Criminal Statistics, 1994). The subsequent fall of 13% was one of the highest recorded (Home Office, 2000).

What is particularly significant in this context is that offending is particularly prevalent among young people. In a self-report survey produced by the Home Office, John Graham and Ben Bowling (1995) found that among 14- to 25-year-olds, one in two males and one in three females admitted that they had committed an offence at some time. The majority of offenders commit no more than one or two minor offences. Property offending was found to be more common than violent offending —with 49% of males and 28% of females admitting committing property offences compared to 28% of males and 10% females admitting violent offences.

One in four males and one in eight females admitted committing an offence in 1992; of these, about a quarter of male offenders and one in 10 female offenders admitted committing more than five offences. According to Graham and Bowling, about 3% of offenders accounted for approximately a quarter of all offences.

It is important to note, however, that the number of young offenders aged 10 to 17 known to have committed an indictable offence in England and Wales has fallen in recent years. In 1997, 9,192 young offenders (aged 10 to 17) were found guilty or cautioned for indictable offences per 100,000 of the relevant (age-related) population. This compares with 13,647 in 1977, a fall of 33%—although there was an even wider gap in the mid-1990s. The fall in the number of known young offenders is only partly accounted for by the decline of the juvenile population. As stated earlier, between 1983 and 1993, the number of young people aged between 10 and 17 in the population fell by 19%. For a more detailed breakdown of these statistics see Figures 5.4 and 5.5.

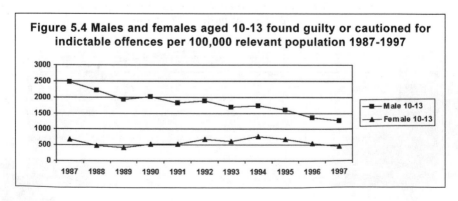

Figure 5.4 Males and females aged 10-13 found guilty or cautioned for indictable offences per 100,000 relevant population 1987-1997

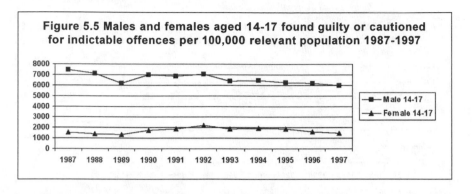

Figure 5.5 Males and females aged 14-17 found guilty or cautioned for indictable offences per 100,000 relevant population 1987-1997

In 1998, of all young offenders found guilty or cautioned for indictable offences, the most common type of offence committed by both males and females was theft and handling. This comprised 59% of offences committed by males aged 10 to 14, and 84% of those committed by females aged 10 to 14. Of those aged 15 to 17, 42% of male offences and 65% of female offences were theft and handling. The second most common offence committed by females was violence against the person (8% of girls aged 10 to 14, and 14% of those aged 15 to 17). For females aged 10 to 14, burglary was the third most common offence (5%), but for those aged 15 to 17 it was drug offences (6%). For males aged 10 to 14, burglary was the second most common offence (17%) followed by offences of violence (10%), but for males aged 15 to 17 it was drug offences that were the second most common offence (17%), with offences of burglary and violence accounting equally for 13% of all offences.

Having considered the rate and nature of offending, let us now turn to an examination of what happens to offenders within the system.

As Figures 5.6 and 5.7 show, a significant number of offenders are cautioned, which essentially means that they are given a formal warning by the police. There is no doubt that there has been an enormous expansion in the use of cautioning. The 1970s marked its first growth period. This trend continued into the 1980s and the 1990s but can be seen to have abated following the Cautioning Circular 18/94 (a policy statement issued by the Home Office, 1994b) which sought to limit the use of cautions to only one except in cases where the subsequent offence was trivial. We should add that it is very difficult to interpret cautioning rates because some police force areas have used informal warnings to a greater extent than others and these have not been recorded in a systematic fashion.

There has also been a change over the past 10 years in the types of sentences used by the courts for indictable offences—with fines declining significantly for both males and females. There has also been a general increase in the use of community penalties and a recent increase in the use of custodial

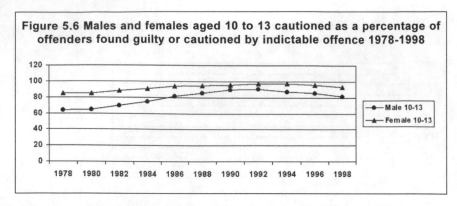

Figure 5.6 Males and females aged 10 to 13 cautioned as a percentage of offenders found guilty or cautioned by indictable offence 1978-1998

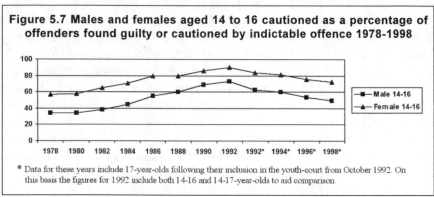

Figure 5.7 Males and females aged 14 to 16 cautioned as a percentage of offenders found guilty or cautioned by indictable offence 1978-1998

* Data for these years include 17-year-olds following their inclusion in the youth-court from October 1992. On this basis the figures for 1992 include both 14-16 and 14-17-year-olds to aid comparison.

penalties. This increase is somewhat surprising given the overall decline in the number of young people cautioned or found guilty for indictable offences and suggests a move towards greater punitiveness. Moore (2000) notes an increase of over 30% (for those under 21) between 1993 and 1996, and the trend towards custodial sentences has continued to the point where custody is once again a primary sentence for young people. This is all the more significant when one realizes that 10% of children remanded in custody are homeless, 29% have been excluded from school, and numerous others face multifarious social problems (Children's Society, 1998/9). These changes are reflected in Figures 5.8 and 5.9.

Girls, Crime, and Criminal Justice

The official Criminal Statistics published annually by the Home Office suggest that more males than females are dealt with by the criminal justice system. In 1998, for example, only 17% of 1.7 million known offenders were female. The gap is notably smaller for younger age groups, however, and whilst self-report studies (notably Graham and Bowling, 1995) confirm the general

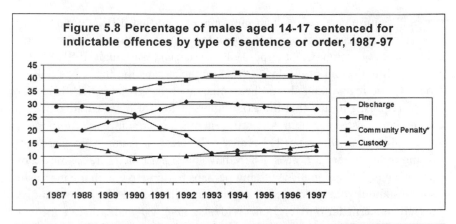

Figure 5.8 Percentage of males aged 14-17 sentenced for indictable offences by type of sentence or order, 1987-97

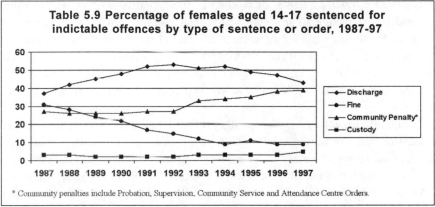

Table 5.9 Percentage of females aged 14-17 sentenced for indictable offences by type of sentence or order, 1987-97

* Community penalties include Probation, Supervision, Community Service and Attendance Centre Orders.

point that fewer females than males appear to commit crime, they indicate too that the gap is perhaps smaller than is imagined.

In the 1992/3 survey reported by Graham and Bowling (1995), 31% of females and 55% of males aged 14 to 24 reported that they had committed an offence. They describe that young men are about two-and-a-half times more likely than young women to admit to ever having committed a crime, and that the ratio widens the more serious the crime. For example, young men are about twice as likely to have taken drugs, but about five times more likely to have taken heroin. To judge from this self-report survey, the most common offences committed by young women are handling stolen goods, shoplifting, fighting and vandalism. From the official statistics, theft and handling is the most common offence, with violence following second, and drugs third. The peak age for female offending is 18, the same as for males.

Anyone looking at the treatment of girls and young women within the juvenile justice system would not fail to notice an evident ambivalence about appropriate responses. Indeed, there is a long standing belief that girls "in trouble" require care rather than punishment, and that difficult and deviant behavior of adolescent girls is but a symptom of problematic sexuality requiring welfare regulation (Gelsthorpe, 1989; Carlen and Wardaugh, 1991; Worrall, 1999). While the end of the 1980s brought the suggestion that custodial sentences for young women should be abolished on the grounds that there were so few requiring it, and that the existing provision for them would suffice, a decade later custody nonetheless still remains a common response to young female offenders. This is partly because of beliefs that young women are committing more violent offences. There have been periodic moral panics about girls and gangs (Campbell, 1995) but perhaps nothing to match the increasing concerns about young women and violence in the late 1990s, though the expressed concerns far outweigh the evidence. Over 10 years, there appears to have been a 4.5% increase for women in the proportion of violent to other offending (alongside an apparent 11.6% decrease for men). However, on raw figures alone, the number of women convicted of violent offences has increased by 21% (Home Office, 1998). Much of this increase can be attributed to young women (14 to 17), but close examination of the evidence suggests that the biggest increase has been in *minor* rather than *serious* offences of violence.

Overall, however, it is exceedingly difficult to make sense of the criminal statistics because they are beset with confusion and ambiguity; because of traditional views of females as non-offending, even the smallest increases can become exaggerated so that the figures reflect *perceptions* of changes in young women's behavior as much as real changes. But if there are real increases, then these as likely as not indicate increasing social divisions and young women's impoverishment in the sense of seeing no future for themselves—as with young men, the economic and social marginalization which follows widens the pathway towards crime (see discussion below).

The overall criminal statistics certainly suggest that the problems caused by girls are periodic rather than pressing (despite increases in violence), but Graham and Bowling (1995) found that some offending is relatively "normal" for girls, with one in three having committed an offence at some time in their early teens. Their criminal activity correlates with the same combination of social circumstances that appear to be relevant to troublesome boys—namely low parental supervision, poor relationships with at least one parent, poverty, truancy and delinquent associates (Farrington, 1997).[10]

CONTEMPORARY CONCERNS REGARDING PROBLEM YOUTH

Having outlined the emergence and development of juvenile justice within England and Wales and pointed to trends and patterns in youth crime over the last 20 years, we now want to examine contemporary concerns about youth. It is clear that anxieties about juveniles extend well beyond the "facts and figures" of the statistics. Indeed, it is arguable that specific aspects of youth crime have become the focus of a disproportionate amount of media and political attention. It is these specific anxieties about youth crime that have often fuelled policy changes. The notion of "three strikes and you're out" which started in the U.S., for instance, quickly received media and political attention in England—as a vote catcher it seems—with the result that burglars and others who commit offences of a specific sort attract deterrent-based minimum custodial sentences of at least three years under the *Crime (Sentences) Act* 1997.

In this section, we will examine three aspects of youth crime which have provoked, and continue to provoke, considerable anxiety, namely the emergence of a drugs-dominated and "rave" sub-culture, joy riding and car theft, and nuisance or anti-social behavior. Although discussion of these issues will be brief, we hope it will provide some kind of context for understanding the construction of problem youth within modern Britain. In essence, alongside avowed attempts to be "tough on crime, tough on the causes of crime," the Labour government's approach to young offenders may be described as being one of "zero tolerance."

Drugs
According to John Graham and Ben Bowling's study of juvenile crime, drug use is "widespread" amongst young people today; every other male and every third female have used drugs at some time (1995:2). This is mostly confined to cannabis, which is consumed regularly (i.e., at least once a week) by one in three male and one in five female users. "Other drugs" are consumed less regularly, although 13% of male users and 19% of female users did so at least once a week. Miller and Plant's (1996) survey of 7,722 youths aged 15 and 16 found that 94% had drunk alcohol, a third had smoked cigarettes in the past 30 days, and that 42% had at some time used illicit drugs, mainly cannabis. Similarly, data derived from the British Crime Survey estimated that around one in two young people has tried a prohibited drug at some time (Ramsey and Spiller, 1997). Drawing on various Schools Health Education Unit surveys a NACRO report (NACRO, 2000) suggests that the figure is more like one in every three young people trying drugs by the time s/he is 15—but that this indicates a sixfold increase since 1987, and there is a worrying trend that higher numbers of younger children are trying illegal substances than ever before. The percentage of 12- to 13-year-olds who had tried drugs in 1996 is actually higher than the percentage of 15- to 16-year-olds who had tried drugs in 1987 (Balding, 1998).

Studies have also revealed the close links between drug abuse and crime (particularly theft—as young people steal to finance the habit) though there are more suggestions about links than there is evidence. It is commonly thought that drug use leads to violent criminal behavior, for instance, and whilst there is evidence to indicate this sort of link for a small number of people, it is by no means widespread. Evidence suggests that young offenders have higher rates of drug use and misuse in comparison with the general public (NACRO, 2000) and that drug use and delinquent behavior may be mutually reinforcing—as drug use increases so does the likelihood of other problem behavior.

There are links too with youth sub-culture. The dance scene in the 1990s in particular encouraged the use of amphetamines, LSD and ecstasy (referred to as "designer drugs") which to some extent became the focal point of general cultural anxieties about drug use amongst young people in the 1990s. Concerns about "ecstasy" are intimately linked to the emergence in the late 1980s of a new youth subculture that revolves around all-night, illegal dance parties or "raves." Ecstasy—between £15 to £25 for a non-addictive, energy-enhancing rush—is the drug of choice amongst a generation of young people who attend raves. Since the late 1980s, "rave culture" has emerged as the nadir of respectable society, a clandestine and highly dangerous world of teenage drug use and bacchic pleasures.

These kinds of fears first emerged in the late 1980s when raves first surfaced in the public consciousness. They resulted in legislation which increased fines from £2,000 to £20,000 for "rave organizers" who failed to obtain local authority permission. Organizers could also receive a six-month prison sentence, and have all their equipment (i.e., sound systems) confiscated. The early rave parties followed a quite distinct pattern: phoning numbers from flyers or pirate radio, waiting in motorway service stations, traveling in a convoy of cars to a secret location. But tighter legal regulation of the events themselves has meant that the focal point of public anxieties about the rave subculture have focused exclusively on the question of drug use, particularly "mind-altering" drugs such as ecstasy.

Yet, as anyone familiar with post-war youth history would say, drug use in youth sub-cultures is nothing new. In fact, each generation appears to have its own favorite chemicals: Mods used amphetamines, hippies LSD, and punks sniffed solvent. Perhaps what is unnerving is the ever-increasing sophistication in drug use among young people. Many have their own favorite cocktail, a post-modern collage of illegal pleasure. It is this kind of sophistication in drug use, not to mention the extent of drug use, which has made the rave subculture so problematic for respectable society.

Taking such drugs is an offence under the *Misuse of Drugs Act* 1971. This legislation seeks to achieve the broad objectives of the control of dangerous or otherwise harmful drugs and the prevention of their abuse, though there have been subsequent refinements to the legislation in order to increase penalties. The government appointment of a national "drugs tsar" gives an indication of perceptions of the seriousness of the problem.

Joy Riding and Urban Youth

Car crime, that is to say, theft from or of a motor vehicle, consistently accounts for about a quarter of crimes committed by young males. Curiously, however, it is a particular type of car crime—what is known as "joy riding"—which periodically dominates public discussion of this problem. What is interesting is that joy riding is almost always perceived as a youth problem; more specifically, a problem of deprived, urban, male youth.

In an account of the joy riding phenomenon, Beatrix Campbell (1993) links the upsurge in this kind of crime to the decline of the inner city within contemporary Britain. Long-term economic decline has meant that unemployment has become the norm amongst working-class youth. For the first time, a generation of young people face the possibility of a life time without stable employment. Social and economic deprivation thus leads to the expression of a kind of masculinity in its purest form. It is this celebration of masculinity which in Campbell's view explains the attractions of crime. Other means of achieving recognition—of being "real men"—are denied to these young people. Violent and dangerous criminal activity becomes the only means of acquiring the mantle of manhood.

The Yob Culture

The third theme to mention here is that of the "yob culture" (Box 5.4). The predominance of young men within the youth justice system is unmistakable, notwithstanding evidence from self-report studies which suggests a narrower gap than commonly supposed. (In 1998, for instance, 10,142 males but only 3,008 females in the 10 to 17 age group were found guilty or cautioned for indictable offences per 100,000 of the age-related population.) There has been growing public and political concern about the apparently increasing anti-social behavior of the young urban male.

Box 5.4 The yob culture

Yob is a species of young white working class male which, if the British public is to be believed, is more common than ever before. The yob is foul-mouthed, irresponsible, probably unemployed and violent. The yob hangs around council estates where he terrorizes the local inhabitants, possibly in the company of his pit-bull terrier. He fathers children rather than caring for them. He is often drunk, probably uses drugs and is likely to be involved in crime, including domestic violence. He is the ultimate expression of macho values: mad, bad and dangerous to know. (Coward,1994: 32)

Media attention to the yob culture suggests that there is an increasing number of marauding, mindless hooligans, though closer scrutiny of the issues would seem to indicate that not only is the violence seemingly not "mindless" but takes place in specific places (e.g., in the vicinity of football grounds, for instance), and is particularly visible amongst those who do not rank highly in educational and occupational status. In other words, proper analysis of the topic would lead us to consider not only how violent and anti-social behavior is linked to masculinity, but how marginalized working class young males as a group achieve status within an ever-declining economic market. "Yobbish barbarism" therefore perhaps has its roots in social divisions and inequalities in contemporary British society (Muncie, 1999; Brown, 1998). In this way, we can see that media and popular representations of the field of youth and especially of youth crime reflect the perspective taken; that perspective in turn reflects historical, economic, cultural and political circumstances, institutional priorities and interests.

SUMMARY

This chapter provides an historical account of the emergence of changes within the English and Welsh system. The main points can be summarized as follows:

- The emergence of a distinct system of juvenile justice is a relatively recent phenomenon, dating from the early part of the twentieth century. Prior to this development juvenile offenders were subject to the same legal processes and punishments as adult offenders. A distinct system of juvenile justice was institutionalized by the 1908 *Children Act*, a legislative instrument that marked the introduction of a welfare approach to the problem of youth crime. The period between 1908 and the mid- to late 1960s was marked by a broad political consensus in the treatment of juvenile offenders. A concern for the **welfare** of the child co-existed with a tougher, more punitive outlook (i.e., **justice model**—see Figure 1—Introduction).

- The 1960s was a period of intense activity culminating in the 1969 *Children and Young Persons Act*. The Labour Party promoted ideas that blurred the distinction between the deprived and the depraved child, and that insisted that young offenders should be dealt with by way of care and protection proceedings rather than criminal proceedings. The general aim was to divert young offenders from the formal criminal justice system or, where it was absolutely necessary to send them to court, to treat young offenders rather than punish them. Whilst a welfare perspective blossomed in the 1960s, the 1970s saw the eclipse of such ideas within the courtroom, with the reinstatement of the Conservative Party and a more punitive perspective which saw the use of custody rise. The theme was essentially that the appropriate response to the delinquent in the courtroom was correction through discipline and punishment. The idea of diversion persisted, though, so that the period of the 1970s reflected a curious mixture of increasing reliance on custodial sentences and on police cautions.

- The 1980s was a period which saw the explicit revival of traditional criminal justice values, policies and practices which hit at the root of the Labour Party social welfare perspective of the 1960s. It was a period of law and order and **crime control** with policies that were designed to reassert the virtue and necessity of authority, order and discipline. The 1982 *Criminal Justice Act*, for example, made three major changes to sentencing provisions to toughen and tighten up sentencing options. Interestingly, despite these efforts, there was a gradual decline in the use of custody (with some notable variation—in the use of custody for young black men, for example). The decline can at least in part be attributed to the emergence of case law in relation to the criteria for custody introduced in the 1982 act, along with an increase in diversionary practices (cautioning), an increased use of fines and compensation, and an increased use of community service orders.

- The 1990s witnessed a number of developments which, taken together, seem to suggest that the arguments are clearly no longer about welfare, crime control or justice. The new philosophies, where discernible amongst practitioners, cannot be allied to the political right or left as they once could. The Labour government's radical overhaul of the youth justice system resulted in the continuation of the Conservative's hard line on offenders, but has added new dimensions. Now there is an emphasis on restorative (or reparative) elements, new forms of constructive intervention linked to reprimands and warnings through programs developed by local youth offending teams and through referral orders to youth offender panels, parents' responsibility for their children (with new powers to punish parents if their children get in to trouble), and new restrictive and punitive orders. In the Introduction to this collection of readings, it is suggested that the model throughout most of the 1990s could be described as representing a **corporative model** (see Figure 1—Introduction; also see Hong Kong for a comparative approach) but has also been described as a "juvenile penal law system."

In essence, we have seen the development of a **mixed model** of juvenile justice in this period. The provisions mean that crime is to be treated as a serious issue, and that those who commit offences are to be made to confront the unacceptable nature of their behavior; at the same time, it is claimed that the social roots of offending behavior are to be seriously tackled by the government. Thus the government's mandate to be "tough on crime, and tough on the causes of crime" is expressed in a model of juvenile justice which mixes corrective, punitive, welfare, interventionist, and restorative principles.

Recent trends in the official recording and punishment of juvenile crime were then highlighted. It was suggested that while these statistics are important, they represent only part of the story. Specific aspects of youth crime have become the focus of a disproportionate amount of media and political attention, and it is these specific anxieties which often fuel policy changes. Drugs and youth crime, the "rave" subculture, the problem of car crime in the inner city, and the seeming development of a "yob culture" all feature highly here. The intention of this discussion was to provide a context for understanding the construction of problem youth within modern Britain and the background against which all changes within the system of juvenile or youth justice have take place.

One key thing we can learn from history and the development of policy in relation to juvenile or youth crime is that it has to be understood in a social and political context. Moral panics about youth crime also mask more general fears about modern society, so that the evidence is sometimes tangential to the direction that policy takes (Pearson, 1983; Goode and Ben-Yehuda, 1994). Putting this another way, concerns about contemporary youth cannot be taken at face value, for they may signify other concerns about social life and social order.

Loraine Gelsthorpe is one of Britain's leading commentators on youth justice issues. She has published extensively on juvenile justice, but has broader interests too which include notions of discretion and discrimination (with a particular focus on race and gender issues), issues relating to community penalties, and social exclusion, crime and justice. As well as teaching and carrying out research within Cambridge University she has served in an advisory capacity on a number of governmental committees. She plays an active part in the development of the field, and currently chairs the British Society of Criminology's Professional and Ethical Committee.

Vicky Kemp was formerly the criminal policy advisor at the Legal Aid Board responsible for advising the Lord Chancellor's department on policy development and implementation in respect of criminal legal aid. She represented the board on the Trial Issues Sub-Group responsible for implementing the Home Office "reducing delays at court" pilot project and was an advisory group member of the Justice Restoring Youth Justice report chaired by Lord Hope of Craighead. Vicky gained experience as both a practitioner and policy officer, having worked initially for the

Home Office Safer Cities Unit and then as Northamptonshire County Council's community safety coordinator.

HELPFUL WEBSITES

www.homeoffice.gov.uk Home Office of England. Source of numerous reports and of crime and delinquency data.

www.cabinet-office.gov.uk/seu/ Site of the Social Exclusion Unit.

www.youth-justice-board.gov.uk Site of the Youth Justice Board.

www.nayj.org.uk Site of the National Association of Youth Justice.

www.narco.org.uk NACRO (National Association for the Care and Resettlement of Offenders).

www.homeoffice.gov.uk/rds/cjspub1.html A useful introductory guide to the criminal justice system in England and Wales. Originates from the Home Office.

KEY TERMS AND CONCEPTS

Welfare Model	Crime Control Model
Crime and Disorder Act	*Doli Incapax*
Reprimand	Warning
Family Council	Family Service
Decriminalize	Justice Model
Yob	Corporatist Model
Juvenile Penal Law System	Mixed Model
Open System	Ingleby Report
Bind-over	Reparation Order
Referral Order	discharges
fines and compensation	community sentences
custodial sentences	ancillary orders
parenting orders	

STUDY QUESTIONS

1. Why do welfare and diversionary reforms always appear to be partial, ambiguous and politically contested?
2. In what ways might the "melting pot" of ideologies within youth justice which emerged at the end of the 1990s in the *Crime and Disorder Act* 1998 within England and Wales militate against their effectiveness?
3. What prospect do the new changes within the English and Welsh system hold out for "being tough on crime, tough on the causes of crime"?
4. What are the comparative strengths and weaknesses of the English and Welsh, Scottish and Northern Ireland systems?
5. How does youth justice within Britain compare with youth justice in European countries and with systems in other parts of the world?

NOTES

1   The Assizes are a periodical county court session for the administration of criminal justice.
2   Juvenile courts were initially special sittings of the magistrates' court from which the public were excluded.

3   Borstal schools were training schools for 16 to 21 year olds designed to facilitate the offender's reformation and the repression of crime.

4   The Magistrates' Associations represent an organization to which lay magistrates or justices of the peace as they are sometimes known (members of the public who are approved and then trained to serve—in a very part-time, non professional capacity—in the magistrates' courts (lower courts) belong.

5   The Conservative Centre Office published two influential reports in the 1960s which are clear statements of Conservative Party policy on crime. These are *Crime and Punishment,* published in 1961, and *Putting Britain Right Ahead* in 1965. In addition, the Conservative Political Centre also published a number of reports and papers in the 1960s on crime that can be broadly taken as indicative of party thinking (Conservative Political Centre, 1961).

6   The actual number of girls involved in the courts was much lower, of course.

7   In January 2001 the High Court granted Robert Thompson and Jon Venables, the killers of James Bulger, life anonymity. The decision banned any publicity about the two boys' identity or whereabouts after their release. The court ruled the decision was consistent with the *Human Rights Act.*

8   A YOT is usually comprised of at least a social worker, probation officer, police officer, person nominated by the local health authority, person nominated by the local education authority and a YOT manager.

9   Besides passing a sentence on the young person, the courts can impose a bind-over on the parents to prevent further offending. Parents or guardians are bound over to take proper care of him/her and to exercise proper control over him/her, to ensure that the child complies with the requirements of the community sentence (with forfeiture of up to £1000 if the young person reoffends or does not comply with the requirements of the sentence).

10 But young women also seem to "grow out of crime" more successfully than young men do. Young women seem to be much more successful than young men in making the transition from adolescence to the responsibilities of adulthood.

REFERENCES

Allen, R. (1991). Out of jail: the reduction in the use of penal custody for male juveniles. *Howard Journal*, 30, 30–53.

Balding, J. (1998). *Young people and illegal drugs in 1998.* London: Schools Health Education Unit, University of North London.

Bottoms, A.E. (1995). The philosophy and politics of punishment and sentencing. In C. Clarkson and R. Morgan (Eds.), *The politics of sentencing reform.* Oxford: Oxford University Press.

Bottoms, A. E., Brown, P., McWilliams, B., McWilliams, W., & Nellis, M. (1990). *Intermediate treatment and juvenile justice: Key findings and implications from a national survey of intermediate treatment policy and practice.* London: HMSO.

Brown, S. (1998). *Understanding youth and crime.* Buckingham: Open University Press.

Brownlee, I. (1998). New Labour—New penology? Punitive rhetoric on the limits of managerialism in criminal justice policy. *Journal of Law and Society*, 25 (3), 313–335.

Burney, E. (1985). *Sentencing young people.* Aldershot: Gower.

Campbell, A. (1995). Creating a girl gang problem. *Criminal Justice Matters*, 19, 8–9.

Campbell, B. (1993). *Goliath: Britain's dangerous places*. London: Methuen.

Carlen, P., & Wardaugh, J. (1991). Locking up your daughters. In P. Carter, T. Jeffs, & M. Smith (Eds.), *Social work and social welfare yearbook 3*. Milton Keynes: Open University Press.

Carlebach, J. (1970). *Caring for children in trouble*. London: Routledge and Kegan Paul.

The Children's Society. (1998/9). *Annual reports of the National Remand Rescue Initiative 1997 and 1998*. London: The Children's Society.

Cohen, S. (1979). Notes on the dispersal of social control. *Contemporary Crises*, 3, 339–63.

Cohen, S. (1985). *Visions of social control: Crime, punishment and classification*. Cambridge: Polity Press.

Conservative Political Centre. (1961). *Crime and punishment*. London: Conservative Political Centre.

Conservative Political Centre. (1965). *Putting Britain ahead*. London: Conservative Political Centre.

Conservative Political Centre. (1992). *The best future for Britain, Conservative party manifesto*. London: Conservative Political Centre.

Cooper, B., & Nicholas, G. (1963). *Crime in the sixties*. London: Conservative Political Centre.

Cooper, B., & Nicholas, G. (1964). *Crime and the Labour party*. London: The Bow Group.

Coward, R. (1994, September 2). Whipping boys. *Guardian Weekend*, p.5.

Criminal Justice Review Group. (2000, March). *Review of the criminal justice system for Northern Ireland (Research Report 17)*. Belfast: Northern Ireland Office.

Crown Prosecution Service. (1986). *Code of practice for prosecutors*. London: Crown Prosecution Service.

Dodds, M. (1986, June 7). The restrictions on imposing youth custody and detention centre sentences. *Justice of the Peace*, pp. 359–362.

Dodds, M. (1987, September 19). The restrictions on imposing youth custody and detention centre sentences. *Justice of the Peace*, pp. 597–600.

Durham, M. (1989). The Right: The Conservative party and conservation. In L. Tivey & A. Wright (Eds.), *Party ideology in Britain*. London: Routledge.

Evans, R., & Wilkinson, C. (1990). Variations in police cautioning policy and practice in England and Wales. *Howard Journal*, 21, 123–135.

Farrington, D. P. (1997). Human development and criminal careers. In M. Maguire, R. Morgan and R. Reiner (Eds.), *The Oxford handbook of criminology* (2nd ed.). Oxford: Clarendon Press.

Fionda, J. (1999, January). New Labour, old hat: Youth justice and the Crime and Disorder Act. *Criminal Law Review*, pp. 36–47.

Gelsthorpe, L. (1989). *Sexism and the female offender*. Aldershot: Gower.

Gelsthorpe, L. R., and Morris, A. (1994). Juvenile Justice. In M. Maguire, R. Morgan and R. Reiner (Eds.), *The Oxford Handbook of Criminology*. Oxford: Clarendon Press.

Gelsthorpe, L., & Morris, A. (1999). Much ado about nothing: A critical comment on key provisions relating to children in the Crime and Disorder Act 1998. *Child and Family Law Quarterly*, 11 (3), 209–221.

Goode, E., & Ben-Yehuda, N. B. (1994). *Moral panics*. Oxford: Blackwell.

Graham, J., & Bowling, B. (1995). *Young people and crime, Home Office Research and Statistics Department, Research findings* (no. 24). London: HMSO.

Halsey, A. (1988). *British social trends since 1900* (2nd edition). London: Macmillan.

Hansard. (1908). *Parliamentary Debates*, Vol. 183, Columns 1435-1436.

Harris, R., & Webb, D. (1987). *Welfare, power and juvenile justice*. London: Tavistock.

Home Office. (Annual Reports). *Criminal statistics England and Wales*. London, HMSO.

Home Office. (1965). *The child, the family and the young offender* (Cmnd. 2742). London: HMSO.

Home Office. (1968). *Children in trouble* (Cmnd. 3601). London: HMSO.

Home Office. (1980). *Young offenders* (Cmnd. 8405). London: HMSO.

Home Office. (1984). *Cautioning by the police: A consultative document*. London: HMSO.

Home Office. (1994a). *The cautioning of offenders* (Circular 18/1994). London: HMSO.

Home Office. (1994b). *Criminal statistics England and Wales, 1994* (Cmnd. 3010). London: HMSO.

Home Office. (1996). *Drug misuse declared: Results of the 1994 British crime survey* (Research Study 151). London: HMSO.

Home Office. (1997a). *Tackling youth crime* (Consultation paper). London: HMSO.

Home Office. (1997b). *Tackling delays in the youth justice system* (Consultation paper). London: HMSO.

Home Office. (1997c). *New national and local focus on youth crime* (Consultation paper). London: HMSO.

Home Office. (1997d). *No more excuses: A new approach to tackling youth crime in England and Wales* (Cmnd. 3809). London: HMSO.

Home Office. (1998). *Criminal statistics England and Wales 1998* (Cmnd. 4649). London: HMSO.

Home Office. (2000). *International comparisons of criminal justice statistics 1998* (Statistical bulletin 04/2000). London: HMSO.

Hood, R. (1965). *Borstal reassessed*. London: Heinemann.

James, A., & Raine, J. (1998). *The new politics of criminal justice*. London: Longman.

Labour Party. (1964). *Crime: A challenge to us all. Report of a Labour party study group, chaired by F. Longford*. London: Labour Party. ("The Longford Report").

Labour Party. (1992). *It's time to get Britain working again, Labour party election manifesto*. London: Labour Party.

Labour Party. (1996). *Tackling youth crime, reforming youth justice: A consultation on an agenda for change*. London: Labour Party.

Mackenzie, D., & Souryal, C. (1994). *Multi-site evaluation of shock incarceration*. Washington, DC: National Institute of Justice.

Marshall, T. (1975). *Social policy*. London: Heinemann.

Marwick, A. (1982). *British society since 1945*. Harmondsworth: Penguin.

Miller, P., & Plant, M. (1996). Drinking, smoking and illicit drug use among 15- and 16-year-olds in the United Kingdom. *British Medical Journal*, 313, 394–397.

Moore, S. (2000). Child incarceration and the new youth justice. In B. Goldson (Ed.), *The new youth justice*. Lyme Regis: Russell House.

Morris, A., & Giller, H. (1979). *What justice for children?* London: Justice for Children.

Morris, A., & McIsaac, M. (1978). *Juvenile justice?* London: Heinemann.

Muncie, J. (1999). *Youth and crime: A critical introduction*. London: Sage.

National Association for the Care and Resettlement of Offenders. (2000). Young people, drug use and offending. In *Briefing*. London: National Association for the Care and Resettlement of Offenders.

O'Mahony, D., & Deazley, R. (2000, March). Juvenile crime and justice. In Criminal Justice Review Group (Eds.), *Review of the criminal justice system for Northern Ireland* (Research report 17). Belfast: Northern Ireland office.

Parker, H. (1981). *Receiving juvenile justice*. Oxford: Blackwell.

Pearson, G. (1983). *Hooligan: A history of respectable fears*. London: Macmillan.

Pitts, J. (1988). *The politics of juvenile justice*. London: Sage.

Ramsey, M., & Spiller, J. (1997). *Drug misuse declared in 1996:Key results from the British crime survey* (Home Office research findings no. 56). London: HMSO.

Rose, N. (1989). *Governing the soul: The shaping of the private self*. London: Routledge.

Rutherford, A. (1986). *Growing out of crime*. Harmondsworth: Penguin.

Singer, S., & Gelsthorpe, L. R. (1996, July). Criminalization and open contemporary systems of juvenile justice: The case of the United States and the United Kingdom. Paper presented to the Law and Society meeting, Glasgow, Scotland.

Stanley, C. (1988, Oct. 8). Making statutory guidelines work, *Justice of the Peace*, pp. 648–650.

Travis, A. (1997, September 26). Straw to combat crime-breeding excuse culture. *The Guardian*, p. 9.

Worrall, A. (1999). Troubled or troublesome? Justice for girls and young women. In B. Goldson (Ed.), *Youth justice: Contemporary policy and practice*. Aldershot: Ashgate.

Chapter 6

Juvenile Crime and Juvenile Law in the Federal Republic of Germany

Hans-Jörg Albrecht
Director Max Planck Institute for Foreign
and International Criminal Law in Frieburg

Facts about Germany

Area: 356,733 sq. km. **Population:** As of 1999, 82,037,000 or 230 per sq. km. Eighty-six percent live in urban areas. After German re-unification in 1990, some 15.4 million live in the east of Germany in the so-called "New Bundeslaender." The size of the population now (2000) is at approximately 82 million, including some 7.4 million foreigners (9.0 %). **Climate:** A mild continental climate. Average lows in winter hover around -1° C; the summer average is approximately 19° C. **Economy:** A highly industrialized country—56% service industry and 40% industry. **Government:** The political system of Germany is federal in nature, with sixteen states (Bundeslaender). The division of legislative and administrative powers between the federal level and the state level is laid down in the German constitution which gives the federal Parliament a strong position in legislation. (In fact, the major fields in which state parliaments possess almost exclusive competence concern police and education, while most other legislation—e.g., adult criminal law, juvenile criminal law, juvenile welfare law—falls within the competence of the federal Parliament). On the other hand, implementation of laws or administration is entrusted (with some exceptions, e.g., defence) to the "Länder." With respect to criminal justice (i.e., basic criminal law and procedural criminal law) virtually all statutes are federal statutes, while the single states are empowered to implement justice administration (including public prosecution, criminal courts and criminal corrections, in particular prisons).

The adolescence that occurs without stress and strain is too unusual to be called normal.—Reuter, The Sociology of Adolescence, American Journal of Sociology, *1937, 43, p.414.*

THE HISTORY OF JUVENILE CRIMINAL LAW

In 1923 the **Youth Court Law** (*Jugendgerichtsgesetz*) came into force in Germany. The Youth Court Law signaled a profound change in dealing with young offenders. It provided for a different legal framework for criminal cases involving juveniles (14- to 17-year-olds). Until then juvenile offenders (12 to 17 years) fell under the jurisdiction of the adult system, although being of minor age led to mitigated penalties (Eisenberg 1995).

The *Youth Court Law* was the first significant result of rehabilitative thinking in modern German criminal legislation. The idea of rehabilitation was expressed by the so-called "modern school of criminal law" which was opposed to the classical doctrine of punishment and the use of punitive sanctions in favor of behavior-modifying rehabilitative measures. The leading figure of the "modern school of criminal law," Franz von Liszt (1905, p. 346), put it this way: "If a juvenile commits a criminal offence and we let him get away with it, then the risk of relapse in crime is lower than the risk we face after having him punished." The development of the "modern school of criminal law" coincided partially with the emergence of the "youth court movement," which also stressed the impact of rehabilitating juvenile offenders. In addition, the movement stressed the need for a completely different system of justice for juvenile offenders, which it envisioned as a system of education. The "youth court movement" relied heavily on the thinking of the North American child-saver movement as well as on North American experiences with juvenile courts. In 1908 Frankfurt became the first German city to establish a special department for juvenile offenders. The first juvenile prison opened in 1911.

One year before the enactment of the *Youth Court Law*, another youth law, namely the *Youth Welfare Law* (*Jugendwohlfahrtsgesetz*, 1922), became effective. The *Youth Welfare Law* was aimed at youth under the age of civil responsibility, which then commenced at the age of 21 (today 18), in need of care and education. The development of German youth laws has been based on those basic beliefs that have characterized the emergence of youth laws in virtually all Western juvenile justice systems (Empey, 1982; Klein, 1984). These basic beliefs are embedded in the positivism-based perception that juveniles are different from adults in terms of psychological and physiological properties. As well, juveniles are assigned a particular social status, creating particular sources of stress and conflicts during a limited developmental period between childhood and adulthood. A belief prevailed that juvenile criminal behavior indicated the need for mediated legal intervention because of the juveniles' particular social and psychological status.

Juvenile criminal law and juvenile welfare law are part of a bipartite approach to youth problems that separates the juvenile criminal offender from otherwise endangered children and juveniles. Both of these approaches were based upon the idea that the failure of parents in raising their offspring and in providing adequate education must have the consequence of public education, organized either by youth departments (in case of criminal behavior of the juvenile) or by the juvenile criminal court. However, a basic difference lies in the input requirements. Admission to the criminal justice system and to the juvenile criminal court requires suspicion and indictment because of a criminal offence. Admission to the juvenile welfare system requires establishing the need for care and education with no minimum age requirements. The *Youth Court Law* amendments of the twentieth century (1943, 1953 and 1990; see Kerner, 1990) adhered to the principle of education, although in 1943, under the influence of German fascism (Kerner and Weitekamp, 1984), a special amendment concerning juvenile felons introduced the possibility of the transfer of juvenile offenders 16 years and older to adult criminal courts with adult criminal penalties (including the death penalty). Furthermore, the age of criminal responsibility was lowered and set at 12 years for juveniles having committed serious crimes. This law was abolished immediately after World War II. The amendment of 1953 brought important changes in terms of the opportunity to sentence young adults as juveniles and the possibility of placing juvenile offenders under probation supervision in the case of a suspended sentence of youth prison (see Box 6.1). With the latest *Youth Court Law* amendment of 1990, among other changes, the indeterminate sentence of youth imprisonment was abolished; diversion and victim-offender mediation have been widened; and important restrictions on placing juveniles in pretrial detention have been introduced.

Box 6.1: Member of Parliament Demands Decreasing the Age of Responsibility to Twelve

In the 1990s the media and police have drawn considerable attention to a group of young people (ages 11 to 13) who have been heavily involved in delinquent and criminal activity. They drew specific attention because German juvenile criminal law does not deal with youths under the age of 13. They are dealt with by the juvenile welfare system, which since the early 1970s no longer provides for closed and secure juvenile custody. The police in particular have argued that nothing can be done to stop this group of delinquent children from committing serious crimes. Responding to this a member of the federal Parliament declared on 12 September 1995, that from the age of 12 most youth are cognitively developed enough to understand the wrongfulness of any criminal actions. The plea failed to receive any support from either the federal Parliament or the federal government. However, as reflected in Table 1 (Introduction), many other countries do have a lower age limit, raising the question as to what constitutes an appropriate minimum age of responsibility.

JUVENILE CRIMINAL LAW BETWEEN
ADULT CRIMINAL LAW AND YOUTH WELFARE LAWS

The creation of the *Youth Court Law* focused on the educational and rehabilitative needs thought to be indicated by the criminal offence of juvenile offenders. But German juvenile justice was never dominated by a social welfare model; the idea prevailed that both punishment and education should be reconciled within the framework of juvenile justice. Strict separation of the juvenile offender from children and juveniles who are in need of care and education can be observed throughout the (short) history of juvenile laws. Throughout this century voices have been raised in favor of a "unified" **welfare** approach to "delinquent" children and juveniles. But juvenile criminal law never deviated far from general criminal law (i.e., **justice model**—see Figure 1—Introduction). It remained bound to the rule of law with respect to the "triggers" of public intervention and to a compromise between punishment and education. Hence, it remains a subsystem in the general criminal justice system.

The criminal justice system in Germany classifies individuals into four categories according to age. Under the age of 14 no criminal culpability exists. The onset of criminal responsibility is now at 14 years (sec. 19, German Criminal Code). But as criminal law is based on the assumption that full criminal responsibility is the product of a fully completed process of socialization and moral development, a particular system of juvenile criminal justice responds to criminal offences committed by juveniles (Kaiser, 1993a). Furthermore, section 3 of the *Youth Court Law* demands full proof that a juvenile offender was mature enough to be aware of the wrongfulness of an illegal act and was capable of behaving according to such awareness. However, criminological research shows that juvenile court practice does not comply fully with section 3, but only pays lip service, while routinely assuming criminal responsibility of juvenile offenders. Full criminal responsibility commences at the age of 18. Young adult offenders (18 to 20 years old) are presumed to be adults, and therefore they are presumed to be fully responsible in the case of criminal offending; however, under certain conditions (sec. 105, *Youth Court Law*) young adults may be prosecuted as if they had been juveniles when committing the crime. With sections 3 and 105 it was acknowledged that the concept of adolescence requires flexibility in assuming criminal culpability because of considerable variation in the process of maturation, social and moral development and integration into the world of adults.

Children (up to the age of 13) and juveniles (14 to 17 years old) who are defined to be in need of care and education are handled by youth welfare departments set up under the *Juvenile Welfare Law* (now *Kinder-und*

Jugendhilfegesetz). Although general youth problem behavior does not justify juvenile court proceedings, a criminal offence committed by a child may be
used as an indicator of the need for care and education. In general, public
youth welfare is understood as a last resort with private youth welfare having
priority over public interventions.

The links between the *Youth Court Law* and the **Juvenile Welfare Law** are
visible in a certain overlapping of measures that may be initiated on the basis
of mere welfare considerations. Educational measures may be imposed as a
consequence of a criminal offence committed by a juvenile. Furthermore, the
Youth Court Law requires specialization of the juvenile criminal court, insofar
as judges should have special (psychological and sociological) knowledge of
youth. As a general rule, judges in juvenile criminal courts should at the same
time be appointed as a family judge (*Vormundschaftsrichter*) responsible for
applying juvenile welfare law in the family court.

The Definition of Juvenile Crime

The definition of juvenile crime does not differ from that of adult crime.
Juvenile criminal procedures may be initiated only if there is sufficient reason
to assume that a juvenile has committed a criminal offence. The same standards as in adult criminal procedures apply. Decisive for the definition of juvenile crime is the age of the perpetrator at the time of the offence. So criminal
offences as defined in the German Criminal Code apply to juveniles as well as
to adults, as do the basic rules that must be followed when establishing criminal responsibility. The differences between juveniles and adults lie in the type
and the range of penalties that can be imposed. Procedural rules referring to
the organization of juvenile criminal prosecution and juvenile criminal courts
as well as to juvenile criminal trials also differ.

Contrary to other justice systems, especially North American systems of
juvenile justice, German youth laws do not provide for so-called "status offences," nor does the *Youth Court Law* provide for waivers of juvenile rights
and the possibility of transferring juvenile offenders to adult criminal courts.
On the contrary, as has been pointed out above, young adults (18 to 20 years)
may be transferred to the juvenile justice system instead of being tried in an
ordinary criminal court. On the other hand, a specific set of youth protection
laws spells out criminal offences (i.e., offences more serious in nature) that are
subject to punishments similar to those for adults who commit the same offences. Although there are no youth-specific types of behavior which could
serve as a trigger for juvenile criminal justice measures, a debate goes on
about the question of whether offences laid down in the basic criminal statutes
for juveniles and adults should be adapted in some respects to the particulars

of the world and lifestyles of young people. Here it is argued that criminal offence statutes like fraud or forgery, as well as certain aggravating circumstances, are perhaps well suited for judgements on adult behavior, but are perhaps too complicated to be fully understood by a 14- or 15-year-old juvenile (Ostendorf, 1992). Furthermore, certain juvenile behavior patterns, such as forcefully taking items belonging to opposing soccer fans, are assumed to be triggered by expressive motivations and do not reflect the instrumental reasons at the center of legal considerations in framing offence statutes like robbery or theft.

The Principle of Education

The major difference between juvenile criminal law and juvenile justice on the one hand and adult criminal law on the other can be found in the general orientation of the two systems. While the offence itself is the center of adult criminal law, youth criminal law emphasizes the offender. Youth criminal law is bound to the goal of education and rehabilitation of the young offender. Although a juvenile is held legally responsible for a crime (*mens rea* must be proven), the primary goal of juvenile criminal justice concerns education and rehabilitation. Juvenile criminal law does not emphasize the criminal offence or the seriousness of the offence but the offender and his or her rehabilitative needs. This orientation has led to an ongoing conflict about the relationship between punishment and education. The debate began shortly after the enactment of the *Youth Court Law* and the general discussion around the lack of uniformity in its wording. While the "modern school of criminal law" pushed for a rehabilitation-oriented system, partisans of the punishment approach expressed the fear that the principle of education could serve as a "Trojan Horse," ultimately undermining criminal law in general (Heinz, 1992, p. 123). The wording of the *Youth Court Law* is not uniform. With respect to the sanctions provided in the *Youth Court Law* the term "educational measure" is used in conjunction with the term "punishment" (*Jugendstrafe*). This allows for several interpretations; the reading depends on whether the criminal offence or the educational needs of the juvenile offender are emphasized.

However, the adoption of the principle of education as well as the disregard for general prevention, general deterrence, and seriousness of the offence as a guiding rule in sentencing does not mean that the general principle of **proportionality** is never applied. The principle of proportionality (*Verhältnismäßigkeit*) is derived from the German constitution and requires that the state must comply with the legal requirements that the "educational measure" chosen must be:

    1. sufficient to reach the goal which is pursued by the intervention,

2. the least severe measure among several which are equally suited to attain the goal envisaged, and
3. proportional to the goal to be achieved.

This principle also serves to set an upper limit to legal intervention in juvenile criminal cases. Therefore, while any disposition has to be proportional to the offence committed, it is also guided by the goal of education. The meaning of education has also been involved in an ongoing debate. Streng (1994), among others, suggests that the meaning of education in the context of juvenile criminal law should not go beyond the prevention of individual relapse into crime. Moreover, any meaning of education extending to the manipulation of the motivation of norm compliance, attitudes, and general behavior patterns is likely to violate constitutional rights (of the juvenile offender and his or her parents) and, in practical terms, overestimates the capabilities of any justice system.

EXTENT, STRUCTURE, AND DEVELOPMENT OF YOUTH CRIME

General Trends in Youth Crime

Analyses of the development of youth crime in the Federal Republic of Germany can be based on police crime statistics as well as on criminal court statistics. In German criminal procedure the finding of guilt and sentencing are not split into two decisions. The finding of guilt and the sentence are produced in a single decision. Unlike the situation in a number of other countries, German police statistics count "suspects," they do not refer to arrested offenders. Suspicion of a criminal offence does not necessarily lead to a formal arrest.

Longitudinal self-report studies and victimization surveys are not available for the Federal Republic of Germany. Reliance upon police-based statistics in the analyses of youth crime means that analysis extends to the legal response to the youthful offender. Since crime statistics reflect the investigative work done by police and the general mechanisms of social control, we have to take into account that official accounts of crime are dependent on the public's willingness to report crimes.

As Figure 6.1 demonstrates, a considerable increase in the relative figures of juvenile suspects took place during the 1960s and 1970s. Throughout the mid-1980s these figures stabilized, but by the end of the decade and the beginning of the 1990s there was again a marked increase in juvenile crime which continued until 1998. Parallel movements in the figures of juvenile crime can be observed in virtually all countries of Western Europe (Kaiser, 1989). On the other hand, demographic changes lead to a considerable decrease in the pro-

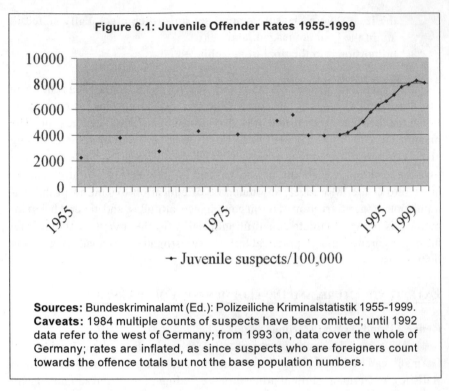

Figure 6.1: Juvenile Offender Rates 1955-1999

⎯•⎯ Juvenile suspects/100,000

Sources: Bundeskriminalamt (Ed.): Polizeiliche Kriminalstatistik 1955-1999.
Caveats: 1984 multiple counts of suspects have been omitted; until 1992 data refer to the west of Germany; from 1993 on, data cover the whole of Germany; rates are inflated, as since suspects who are foreigners count towards the offence totals but not the base population numbers.

portions of child, juvenile, and young adult suspects in the population of suspects as a whole. While juveniles accounted for approximately 15% of all known suspects in 1980, their share dropped to 9.5% in 1991. Children accounted for 6.3% of all known suspects in 1980 and 4.4% in 1991. During the same period the proportion of young adult suspects (18 to 20 years) decreased from 13.5% to 10.2%. However, during the 1990s the proportions of children, juveniles and young adults have been increasing again (due to a baby-boomerang effect on the one hand and immigration on the other hand) and stand now (1999) at 6.7% for children, 13.1% for juveniles and finally 10.6% for young adults. However, the increase in juvenile offender rates over the last five decades can to a large extent be explained by an enormous increase in the rates of petty theft.

Crime data for the east of Germany are available from 1993 on. In general we find that there is an increase in crime at large as well as in juvenile crime in particular. As was expected, the trend in the east moves towards convergence with crime rates in the west. However, crime rates among the young in the east of Germany in some offence categories far exceed those in the west. In particular, rates for assault and robbery in the east have been skyrocketing, although rates for these offence categories in the east still are slightly lower than those

observed in the west. Figure 6.2 demonstrates the trends of aggravated assault for the second half of the 1990s. It has been argued that young people in
the east of Germany are far more exposed to those risks thought to contribute
to crime and therefore far more involved in committing crime—in particular
street crime and auto theft (Frehsee, 1995; Kerner and Sonnen, 1997). It might
also be that police and the public in the east of Germany still differ from the
west in terms of control styles and crime reporting patterns vis-à-vis young
people.

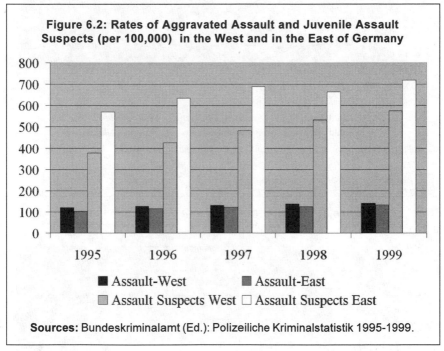

Figure 6.2: Rates of Aggravated Assault and Juvenile Assault Suspects (per 100,000) in the West and in the East of Germany

- Assault-West
- Assault-East
- Assault Suspects West
- Assault Suspects East

Sources: Bundeskriminalamt (Ed.): Polizeiliche Kriminalstatistik 1995-1999.

Serious crimes, especially serious violent crimes, represent rare events in
younger age groups. Figures 6.3 to 6.5 show the trends in (relative) murder,
robbery, and aggravated assault figures during the last two decades for children (8 to 13 years old), juveniles (14 to 17 years old) as well as young adults
(18 to 20 years old).

For murder and robbery it is obvious that clear distinctions can be made
between children and juveniles on the one hand and young adults on the other
hand. Young adults are more heavily involved in serious crimes than are children and juveniles, where theft accounts for a large proportion of crime involvement. However, the peak in the numbers of murder suspects which emerges
during the 1990s for juveniles and in particular for young adults may tentatively explained by:

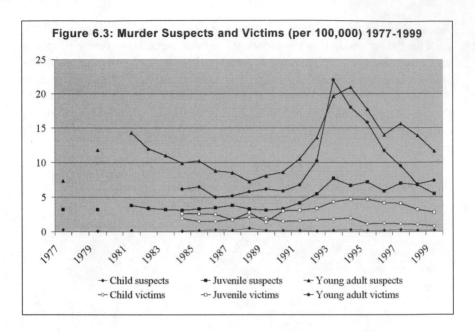

Figure 6.3: Murder Suspects and Victims (per 100,000) 1977-1999

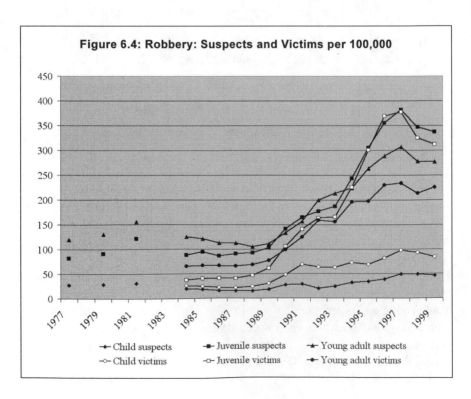

Figure 6.4: Robbery: Suspects and Victims per 100,000

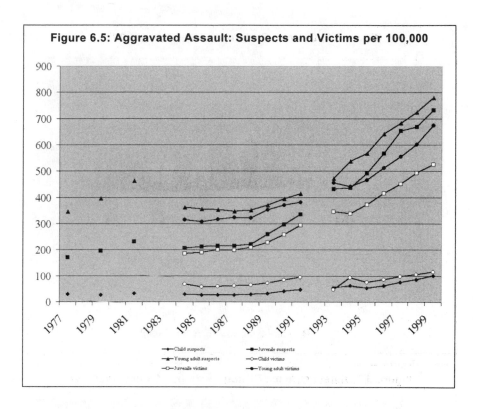

Figure 6.5: Aggravated Assault: Suspects and Victims per 100,000

First: the shootings and killings taking place at the West German-East German border prior to re-unification. To a certain extent, those that have been investigated and prosecuted since the beginning of the 1990s involved young adults as suspects (former soldiers of the NVA/National Peoples Army) and young adults as victims (those trying to cross the border); and

Second: by prosecuting and sentencing arson committed by throwing Molotov cocktails into houses of refugees, etc., as attempted or completed murder (changes occurred after the case of Mölln, where several Turkish citizens were killed by fire caused by a Molotov cocktail; see Neubacher, 1999).

Trends in the rates of child, juvenile, and young adult victims of violent crime parallel very closely those of the offender rates in these age groups, which suggests a considerable degree of overlapping in offender and victim roles. Research on self-reported crimes and victimization has indeed revealed that those juveniles and young adults ranking very high on scales of self-reported crime are those with the highest risk of being victimized (Villmow and Stephan, 1983).

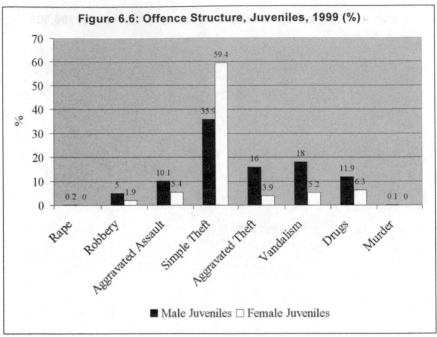

Figure 6.6: Offence Structure, Juveniles, 1999 (%)

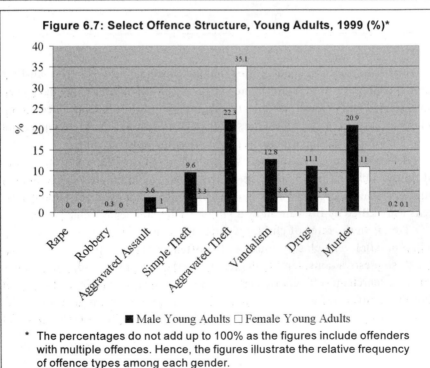

Figure 6.7: Select Offence Structure, Young Adults, 1999 (%)*

* The percentages do not add up to 100% as the figures include offenders with multiple offences. Hence, the figures illustrate the relative frequency of offence types among each gender.

Figures 6.6 and 6.7 give some insight into the structure of crimes committed by juveniles and young adults. Property and non-violent crimes such as simple theft outweigh other offence types in the population of female offenders. Female juveniles' share of police recorded crime was 21% in 1999, while for female young adults it was 18%. And while there has been no qualitative change in the amount of female crime, the proportion of female crime has increased somewhat during the last decades (see Albrecht, 1987a).

In general the structure of criminal offences committed by male juveniles is determined through theft and criminal damage. Serious violent offences and drug offences play a minor role. Drug offences become more important in the group of young adults (and even more so in the adult population). Although Figure 6.6 points to considerable proportions of aggravated theft (which includes burglary), robbery and other violent offences for male juveniles are significantly lower in seriousness compared to young adult and adult crimes of the same category (Dölling, 1992).

Furthermore, the picture of youth crime emerging from the analysis of official crime data indicates that criminal behavior may represent rather normal behavior, even in terms of police recorded crime and court dispositions. A study of male birth cohorts found that as many as one third of their members had a criminal record before they reached the age of 24 (Kaiser, 1988). Analysis of data from four birth cohorts (1970, 1973, 1975 and 1978) from the state of Baden-Wurttemberg show that, when reaching the age of 17, approximately 15% of male juveniles of German descent have been suspected at least once of having committed a crime (Grundies, 1999; see also Karger and Sutterer, 1988). The corresponding rates for immigrant male youth, as well as ethnic Germans who immigrated from the former Soviet Union (for details, see Grundies, 2000) amount to some 40% in the case of the 1978 birth cohort (see Figure 6.8).

Conflicting Explanations

The various increases in officially recorded crime has received much attention in criminology and criminal politics. The assessment of these trends in the development of youth crime remains a controversial issue. Three conflicting positions may be identified:

1. It is argued that rising crime rates among children and juveniles point to a growing menace to society and require strong preventive and (partially) repressive action (Pfeiffer et al., 1998).
2. The increase in youth crime is exaggerated by the media, police and politicians. The increase should be regarded as an artificial product resulting from an increase in police attention paid to children and juveniles and also reflects a net-widening effect, and particularly an in-

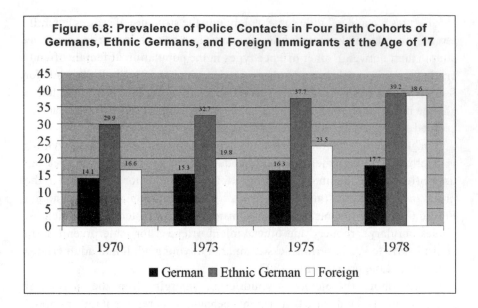

Figure 6.8: Prevalence of Police Contacts in Four Birth Cohorts of Germans, Ethnic Germans, and Foreign Immigrants at the Age of 17

crease in the efficiency of police crime investigation (P.A. Albrecht, 1993).

3. There was actually an increase in youth crime, but this increase was mainly due to an increase in crime of a non-serious nature, which should not be overdramatized (Heinz, 1997; Kerner and Sonnen, 1997).

Research on the "causes" of juvenile crime carried out in the 1950s and 1960s pointed to the relevance of the broken family, bad parenting, school problems, and unemployment (Villmow and Kaiser, 1974). Since the mid-1960s, results from self-report surveys on delinquency and crime indicate a shift from etiological concepts in explaining crime to labelling theory, which leads to new perspectives on juvenile delinquency and delinquency prevention. The finding that delinquent behavior is ubiquitous in youth populations, while official criminal-law-based interventions concentrate on a rather small proportion of those who could be the target of legal interventions, gave rise to the assumptions that:

- juvenile crime represents "normal" behavior; and
- juvenile criminal behavior alone is not sufficient to justify public intervention in terms of education and/or punishment pursuing the goal of rehabilitation.

From these perspectives, prevention serves to discriminate against marginal and deprived youths augmenting the risks of deepening disintegrative processes. Although in-depth studies on the relationship between undetected and known crime among youths revealed that the assumption of ubiquity of crime holds true only for petty or trivial offences, while serious crimes and repeated criminal offences are restricted to a rather small group of juveniles, the argument became decisive in designing youth criminal policy in the 1970s and 1980s.

Conclusions drawn from these studies supported the view that a juvenile offence is not a signal demanding official intervention and public education. Longitudinal research on offence patterns shows that as many as 70% of juvenile offenders are one-time offenders (Krüger, 1983; Grundies, 1999). These findings lead to the conclusion that prevention of juvenile delinquency should rely heavily on non-prosecution and diversion rather than the use of youth prison and other punitive measures. The 1980s saw an increasing use of diversion and community-based measures such as community service, social training courses and, most recently, restitution, conflict mediation, and reconciliation schemes. Informal sanctions and informal systems of control as represented by the family, peer groups, and schools currently outweigh formal systems of control. In turn we observe a renewed criminological interest in family, school, religion, and employment as decisive elements in the prevention of juvenile delinquency (H.-J. Albrecht, 1991). This renewed interest also corresponds to a shift in theoretical thinking about juvenile delinquency and its prevention from stress and labelling theories to control theories of juvenile crime (Kaiser, 1993a).

On the macro level, research turned to the question of how large-scale changes in the roles and functions of the family, school, and religion in post-industrial societies could be related to changing patterns of juvenile crime. It is argued that the potential of the family, the school, and the neighborhood for providing bonds between juveniles and society has diminished steadily. However, it is also argued that probably nothing has changed in terms of behavior patterns of juveniles; rather, systems of informal control have broken down, thus exposing children and juveniles to formal control systems with respect to behavior that would have been handled informally in the past. Both explanations point to a common perspective for prevention: strengthening the role of the community, the neighborhood, family, and school in handling problem behavior. The focus of current research is on the feasibility of replacing formal juvenile court responses to juvenile delinquency through restitution and victim-offender reconciliation schemes. Restitution and victim-offender mediation receive strong support outside and inside the criminal justice system (Schöch, 1992).

Particular Problem Groups and Particular Risks

In the 1980s two subgroups of juvenile delinquents attracted considerable attention from German criminological research. These subgroups comprise ethnic (or foreign/immigrant) minority youth and chronic juvenile offenders. Research has pointed out that substantial proportions of police-recorded crime and self-reported delinquent acts can be linked to a disproportionally small group of juveniles (Krüger, 1983; Karger and Sutterer, 1988; Grundies 1999). This observation has led to a growing interest in identifying early signs of chronic offending, but G. Albrecht (1990) concludes that it will not be possible to convert the retrospective finding of high-rate juvenile offenders into ethically and economically feasible prospective prevention strategies.

Ethnic and foreign minority juveniles are also targeted for preventive reasons. The most important group of foreign youth in quantitative terms are the Turks. Official statistics suggest that crime rates among certain ethnic and foreign minority groups are two to four times greater than rates observed in the majority group (H.-J. Albrecht, 1987b, 1997; Karger and Sutterer, 1990). Time-series data for foreign offender rates and foreign population rates demonstrate clear trends that might be interpreted as the result of changes in behavior patterns of second and third generations and of changes in migration patterns. Disproportionate involvement of foreign minority members in police recorded crimes can be observed especially in the age-bracket of 18- to 20-year-old suspects. In 1999, 27.6% of the suspects were traced to foreign minority members (19.8% of all juvenile offenders and 18% of children) (Bundeskriminalamt, 2000). Walter (1995) suggests demographic characteristics may account for the increase in crime participation among foreign populations. In addition, the number of foreign suspects was certainly inflated by the influx of asylum seekers, peaking in 1993 and then decreasing considerably after significant changes in asylum laws. For example, in the state of Northrhine-Westfalia between 1984 and 1993 the crime rate among young foreigners more than doubled (from 6,651 to 13,614), while the increase among young Germans was from 4,075 to 5,038. Conversely, between 1984 and 1993 the crime rate among "guest-workers" (e.g., transient workers) and immigrant workers did not change much (Bundeskriminalamt, 1995). A tentative explanation could be that first generation immigrants experience improved conditions of living, housing, and medical care which outweigh existing differences between minority and majority groups (Kunz, 1989; H.-J. Albrecht, 1997a).

Most self-report surveys do not include ethnic or foreign minorities, but samples are regularly drawn from the German resident youth population (H.-J. Albrecht, 1988). However, evidence derived from those surveys that include immigrant minority youth is not conclusive. At the beginning of the 1980s research based on self-reports from the city of Bremen concluded not only that a larger involvement in delinquency on the part of foreign juveniles did not occur but that those foreign juveniles interviewed seemed to be remarkably conformist (Schumann, Berlitz, Guth, and Kanlitzki, 1987; H.-J. Albrecht, 1997). Self-report surveys carried out in the nineties show higher crime participation rates of certain minority and immigrant youth (Albrecht 1998) which could reflect changes in immigration patterns and increasing problems of marginalization among certain segments of immigrant and ethnic minority youth (see Grundies, 2000).

As we observe segmentation in society along ethnic lines, we may assume that the lowest segments of society are increasingly filling up with immigrant groups that are most likely to be affected by unemployment, bad housing, poverty, insufficient education and vocational training. The research questions, which in the 1960s and 1970s highlighted class, crime, and justice issues, will in the 1990s and in the decades to come be replaced by ethnicity and crime. Therefore, in general, crime and delinquency among minority youth should be explained by the same theories that are applied to the majority group (Kube and Koch, 1990). Although bonding theories fit the sensitive situation of second and third generation immigrants who actually live between two rather distinct cultures (e.g., Turkish juveniles), this position creates particular problems in terms of conflicts between traditional norms valued by parents and those values and norms of the peer group (Mansel and Hurrelmann, 1993).

Economic recession in the 1970s, exposing the young to unemployment, created at the beginning of the next decade renewed interest in the possible links between youth unemployment and youth crime (Münder, Sack, Albrecht, and Plewig, 1987; Kaiser, 1993b). Despite considerable increases in unemployment rates among juveniles and young adults, the proportion of those unemployed and suspected of having committed a criminal offence decreased. These diverging trends do not suggest a causal relationship between these variables on the micro level, but point to a re-enforcing impact of unemployment.

Youth gangs attracted scientific attention in the late 1970s with soccer hooliganism (Heitmeyer and Peter, 1988; Kersten, 1993). In the 1990s, after German re-unification, the problem of right-wing extremist violence towards immigrants and other minorities committed by groups of juveniles and young adults arose (Viehmann, 1993). Most of these bias-motivated violent offences were and are committed by juveniles or young adults: 70% of offenders fall into the age bracket of 14 to 20 years, 3% of the offenders are 30 years of age or older (Bundesamt für Verfassungsschutz, 2000). Part of the hate violence is linked to youth subcultures like skinhead groups that are concentrated in the east of Germany where more than half of violence-prone skinheads are located (while just one-fifth of the population at large lives in the east (Bundesamt für Verfassungsschutz, 2000). However, the proportion of bias-motivated violence of all violent crimes committed by youth is rather small; furthermore, most inter-ethnic violence obviously is not linked to racism or hate but to conventional triggers of violent behavior (Solon, 1994).

In recent years youth violence has been targeted as an eminent social and policy problem. A dilemma arises as demands for "get tough" approaches to right-wing juveniles conflict with educational demands put forward by the *Youth Court Law*. The answer to the dilemma seems to lie in the conception of youth violence. Youth violence may be conceived as indicative of **anomie** and **social disintegration**; youth violence may also be understood as being part of a much broader violence-prone political radicalism. Finally, youth violence may be explained as a specific transitional phenomenon of male youth associating in gangs (Kersten, 1993). Dependent on these conceptions, youth violence against foreign and ethnic minorities may be the product of social turmoils, representing "hate-crimes," and therefore deserving of repressive action or indicative of mere changes at the surface of ordinary violent gang activities. However, the prevalent approach in explaining youth violence towards minorities refers to the traditional hypothesis of frustration-aggression (Rommelspacher, 1993; Bliesener, 1992).[1]

JUVENILE CRIMINAL LAW AND JUVENILE CRIMINAL PROCEEDINGS

Processing the Juvenile Offender

Although the basic principles of criminal law apply to juvenile offenders, *Youth Court Law*'s basic orientation extends towards educating the young offender. No special juvenile offences exist in German criminal law.

Criminal prosecution in Germany commences regularly with investigation of the crime by police (see Figure 6.9). Police have no discretionary power to dismiss criminal cases but have to refer every suspect (be it an adult or a juvenile) to the public prosecutor's office, where a decision is made whether a charge should be filed or not. Without a formal indictment by the public prosecutor's office no juvenile case can be brought to the juvenile criminal court.

After criminal proceedings have been initiated, investigators will begin to gather information on personal and social circumstances relevant for evaluating the personality of the juvenile offender and for the choice of sanction (sec. 43 *Youth Court Law*). Immediately after initiation of criminal proceedings against a juvenile offender the Juvenile Court Aid (*Jugendgerichtshilfe*) has to be notified. From here a social worker investigates the personal and social

Table 6.1: An Abbreviated Model of the Young Offenders Legal Process				
Input:	Crime Investigation	Indictment/Dismissal	Trial	Juvenile Corrections
Victim's complaint (ca. 90% of cases)/ **Proactive policing** (e.g., drug offences, ca. 10% of the cases)	**Police: No discretionary powers.** Investigaton of juvenile crimes Information of juvenile court aid Transfer of case files and evidence to the public prosecutor's office In some German states (Bundeslaender) police now are empowered to eg. caution the juvenile offender and thus prepare a decision of non-prosecution/ diversion by the public prosecutor	**Public prosecutor's office (juvenile branch):** Decision-making on whether to dismiss/divert or indict criminal cases; Monopoly on bringing cases to juvenile criminal courts; Principle of Legality applies (with certain exceptions). **Discretionary options: §45.** Dismissal of case without any further action (petty crimes); Dismissal of case if sufficient responses to the juvenile offender have been made by others (e.g., family, school); Dismissal of case if the juvenile public prosecutor thinks that imposition of mediation, restitution, or community service by the juvenile judge is sufficient (and if the juvenile offender complies with the order imposed). **Indictment to:** – juvenile judge (single judge); if only educational or disciplinary measures are expected to be the outcome. – juvenile court; (Schöffengericht); – juvenile court (district court); in case of murder/homicide	**Criminal courts (juvenile branch)** Adjudication and sentencing, supervision of juvenile corrections Procedural options of the juvenile Court 1. Dismissal of the case (§47) 2. Simplified trial 3. Full trial Sentencing Options Educational measures ⇒ Disciplinary measures – Restitution, fine, etc. ⇒ – Short-term detention ⇒ – Youth imprisonment min./max.: 6 months to 5 years – Suspended ⇒ – Unsuspended ⇒	Supervision of Juvenile Corrections at large through the **Juvenile Judge** Decision-making on parole and on appeals against orders/ action of youth prison administration Juvenile Court Aide Juvenile Court Aide Juvenile Judge Probation Services Director of the Youth Prison
	Juvenile Court Aid: Investigation of the juvenile of-fenders´ person-ality and social environment; Providing infor-mation for the public prosecu-tors´ decision on diversion/indict-ment as well as on pretrial detention.		**Juvenile Court Aid:** Presenting a pre-sentencing report in the trial (including proposals for disposition and sentencing)	

circumstances of the juvenile offender for the prosecutor in order to provide information about which sanction seems appropriate for the juvenile offender. The court aid has the right to be present during trial. The juvenile court has no discretion in admitting the social inquiry report prepared by the aid. The court must hear the report in order to comply with the general procedural rule that any evidence relevant for the finding of guilt and the appropriate sentence must be heard in trial (for a summary see Laubenthal, 1993). Other than the parents of the juvenile offender, court hearings are not open to the public (including the media).

In recent years the position of the victim has been strengthened beyond those rights. Today, the victim has the right not only to be present during the trial but also to act as a "prosecutor" (*Nebenklage*—"side-prosecution"). Finally, in a major criminal law reform in 1987, a series of victim's rights were added to the Code of Criminal Procedure (among them the right to have access to the court files, the right to be informed about the outcomes of the criminal trial, etc.). All these options available for the victim of an adult offender are not valid in juvenile court proceedings according to the leading doctrines (see Schaal and Eisenberg, 1988). As the victim's rights are still highly valued, the debate is now on whether the particular goal of juvenile justice, that is education, actually may justify restricting the victim's rights.

The right to appeal against a verdict of guilt is restricted for juvenile offenders. Juvenile offenders must choose between two options. They have the right of a full re-trial or the right to have their case reviewed on legal grounds.

The use of pre-trial detention is also restricted in juvenile proceedings. For juvenile suspects aged 14 to 15, escape risks may only be assumed on the grounds that the juvenile has made an attempt to escape or that the juvenile has no permanent place of residence in order to justify pre-trial detention (sec. 72 II *Juvenile Court Law*). None of the reasons valid for adult offenders may be introduced as satisfactory legal grounds to justify pretrial detention. In addition, when deciding on pre-trial detention in a juvenile case, the court has to consider whether it is sufficient to place the juvenile offender in a foster home. In the case of an order to place the juvenile offender in pretrial detention, the court aid has to be informed (sec. 72a *Juvenile Court Law*) in order to assure that all information relevant for the decision on pretrial detention, including information on possible alternatives such as foster care, can be made available. Contrary to the way adult detainees are handled, juvenile pre-trial detention must be organized in a way that favors education. As a consequence, when placed in a pre-trial detention center the young offender is obliged to work.

Criminal Penalties

Each offence in the German Penal Code carries its own penalty with a minimum and a maximum range. The penalty ranges provided in the criminal penal code, however, do not apply to juvenile offenders. The *Youth Court Law* contains a specific system of sanctions or measures that are divided into three categories.

a. Educational Measures

Educational measures cover a range of orders that can be imposed in a juvenile court. Educational measures shall, according to section 10 of the *Youth Court Act*, have a positive impact on the behavior patterns of juvenile offenders in terms of securing and enhancing conditions of socialization. A catalogue of specific orders is annexed to section 10. Among the orders listed there we find community service, participation in social training courses, participation in victim-offender mediation, participation in traffic education, supervision by a social worker, attendance at vocational training, etc. The assistance provided by the children and youth welfare law may also include placement in a home or a foster family. Table 6.1 gives some insight into the use of short-term detention. It is obvious that very rare use is made of this type of enforcement. The power to enforce educational measures through short-term deprivation has provoked a debate on whether the order to do community service then violates the German constitution (which prohibits forced labor outside the prison system). But the procedure was recently upheld based on the argument that it was the educational nature of community service imposed on juvenile offenders under the *Youth Court Law* (*Bundesverfassungsgericht* [Constitutional court] 1991).

b. Disciplinary Measures

The second category of juvenile sanctions concerns **disciplinary measures** (*Zuchtmittel*, s. 13 *Youth Court Law*). Disciplinary measures are classified in three subcategories:

- Cautioning by the juvenile judge. This is a formal verdict that is entered into the criminal record.
- Fulfilling certain conditions (e.g., paying a fine), doing community service (the maximum number of hours of community service is not prescribed by law but is limited by the general principle of proportionality), compensating the victim of the offence and making a formal apology to the victim.
- The most severe disciplinary measure concerns short-term detention (*Jugendarrest*) which may last for up to four weeks or may be imposed

during weekends or spare time. Short-term detention means placement
in a special unit (separated from youth prison) for juvenile offenders.

c. Youth Imprisonment

As defined in section 17, Youth Court Law, youth imprisonment is the only
juvenile criminal penalty in the strict sense of the word. Although official
records provide for two separate court information systems, one for juvenile
sanctions and the other for adult penalties, a verdict of youth imprisonment is
entered into the adult criminal record when the juvenile offender has reached
the age of 18. All other juvenile measures are kept exclusively in juvenile
records. The minimum sentence for youth imprisonment is six months and the
maximum is five years. With respect to those offences for which the Criminal
Code provides a maximum term of imprisonment of more than 10 years, the
maximum youth imprisonment may be 10 years. The reason to set the minimum
term of imprisonment at six months (in adult criminal law the minimum is one
month) lies in the belief that treatment and education of a youthful offender is
only efficient if a certain minimum term of secure placement is available. As is
the case in adult criminal law, a sentence of youth imprisonment may be suspended if the juvenile offender is regarded to be a low risk and if the sentence
does not exceed one year. A juvenile offender serving youth imprisonment
may be paroled after having served one-third of the sentence, while in adult
criminal law the minimum term that has to be served before being eligible for
parole is half of the prison sentence.

The Choice among Different Sanctions

With respect to the choice between these different types of measures the
focus is on educational needs. Section 5 of the *Youth Court Law* says that
disciplinary measures may be applied only if educational measures are not
sufficient in responding to the educative needs displayed by the juvenile offender. Moreover, section 17 II of the *Youth Court Law* states that juvenile
imprisonment may be imposed only if educational or disciplinary measures are
not sufficient to educate the juvenile offender or if the offence requires criminal punishment.

Young Adults and Juvenile Justice

Young adults (18 to 20 years old) are basically presumed to be adults and
thus may be tried and sentenced according to adult criminal law. But as a
general rule, section 105 of the *Youth Court Law* requires that a young adult be
adjudicated and sentenced as a juvenile:

- if a psychological evaluation reveals that the young adult offender shows a typical youthful personality in terms of intellectual and emotional maturity, or
- if the offence in question concerns typical juvenile misbehavior according to the type, the circumstances, or the motives of the offence.

With regard to the treatment of adolescent offenders, virtually all adolescents adjudicated on the basis of the most serious offences are sentenced according to the *Youth Court Law*. An exception involves traffic offences. A substantial proportion of adolescent offenders are processed through the adult criminal justice system.

The proportion of young adult offenders tried and sentenced as juveniles has increased steadily during the last decades. On average, slightly more than 60% of all young adults are sentenced as juveniles. Virtually all young adults are sentenced as juveniles in the case of robbery (corresponding rates can be observed for first and second degree murder). An explanation of the considerable variation in referring young adults to juvenile criminal courts may be found in the rather high minimum penalties which juvenile court judges evidently are very reluctant to impose on young offenders. The minimum penalties are one year for robbery, five years for aggravated robbery, two years for rape, and five years to life for murder. The minimum penalty for murder is dictated by the circumstances surrounding the homicide.

The system of juvenile justice and the practice of treating young adults as if they were juveniles recently came under pressure with the enormous increase of bias-motivated violent crimes committed almost exclusively by juveniles and young adults. The debate on how to develop juvenile criminal law in the future centers today around three suggestions:

- The abolition of the choice available today in the *Youth Court Law* with respect to handling young adults and the legal difference between juveniles and young adults. Young adults of 18 to 20 years should, according to this opinion, fall under the category of juveniles.
- Amendment of section 105 *Youth Court Law* so as to reduce the number of young adults adjudicated and sentenced significantly, and to make this option an exception to the rule that young adults should be sentenced as adults (motion of the Christian Democratic Party as of April 12, 2000, BR-Drucksache, 14/3189).
- Keep young adults completely in the adult system but cut by half the minimum and maximum penalties available for adult offenders (such a system has been adopted in Austrian juvenile criminal law).

What can be learned from the experiences of the German criminal justice system with respect to young adult offenders is that there exists a youth-specific system of justice, which is located between a juvenile welfare system and adult criminal justice. Secondly, besides a welfare approach to juvenile delinquency or juvenile problem behavior, a justice approach to juvenile crime that can be extended to young adults is feasible. Since the transitional periods have been prolonged and the entrance to the adult world has been made more difficult for certain subgroups of juveniles, if the differences between young adults and adults are not respected, then an instrumental character of criminal law is prevailing that precludes justice for young offenders.

Decision-making in the System

Contrary to common law systems where the public prosecutor has full discretion in deciding whether a formal indictment should be filed or not, the German system of prosecution in the field of juvenile criminal justice is based on the principle of "legality." This means that as a general rule the public prosecutor is obliged to file a charge in every case where there is reasonable evidence that the offender has committed a crime. Nevertheless, there are important exceptions from the general rule of legality laid down in the Code of Criminal Procedure that permit the dismissal of cases in the field of petty offences (sections 153 and 153a of the Code of Criminal Procedure). Even more important are those exceptions made in *Youth Court Law*.

In criminal proceedings against a juvenile offender, a public prosecutor is allowed to dismiss the case on those grounds that justify case dismissal in adult criminal proceedings, that is, the offence was a misdemeanor of a minor or trivial nature and the personal guilt of the offender was negligible. In addition, section 45 of the *Youth Court Law* empowers the public prosecutor to dismiss any case if an adequate educational measure has been carried through by some other institution or by individuals such as teachers, parents, or other relatives. If the public prosecutor has filed a formal charge, then the juvenile judge may dismiss the case (with the concurrence of the juvenile public prosecutor) on the same reasons mentioned above (sec. 47 *Youth Court Law*). This type of diversion has been considerably extended during the 1980s based upon the idea that the average juvenile offender does not need education and the attention of the juvenile court but will grow out of crime and stay out of crime when diverted by the public prosecutor. The German legislature in the *Youth Court Law* amendment of 1990 has explicitly adopted this position and thus supported the idea that juvenile court procedures should be a "last resort."

THE SYSTEM IN ACTION

Adjudication and Sentencing

Despite the increases in the number of offenders during the 1960s and 1970s, there was only a slight increase in the adjudication and sentencing rates. But during the 1980s the conviction and sentencing rates declined from approximately 1,500 juvenile offenders per 100,000 youth per year at the end of the 1970s to slightly more than 1,000 in 1990 (Heinz, 1990a); the rate increased again during the 1990s to some 1,200 per 100,000 in 1998, but is still well below adjudication rates observed in the 1970s. Research on public prosecutors' decision-making patterns revealed that dismissals of criminal juvenile cases are rather frequent and that every second juvenile offender has his or her case dismissed through the juvenile public prosecutor (Heinz, 1989; Heinz, 1990a). In fact, diversion by the juvenile public prosecutor has become a major dispositional alternative to formal measures according to juvenile court law in the last decade. In recent years strong voices have been raised to set victim-offender mediation as a prerequisite for dismissals. A considerable number of victim-offender mediation schemes have been established which have been evaluated positively, although proper evaluation designs are observed rarely and obviously minor offenders are the dominant target (H.-J. Albrecht, 1990). It is then interesting to note that the pronounced increase in juvenile and young adult suspects has not been followed by a corresponding trend in adjudication and sentencing. The rates of adjudication and sentencing are rather stable. This means that most of the increase in police recorded juvenile crime is dealt with by way of non-prosecution or dismissals through the public prosecutor (Heinz, 1997).

The proportion of the most severe dispositions (i.e., youth imprisonment) has remained fairly stable in the 1970s—approximately 8% of all youth court dispositions. Even though the number of juvenile suspects has increased steadily. During the 1980s and '90s the rate decreased to some 6% of all youth court dispositions; the average length of incarceration has increased slightly. Conversely, there has been a marked increase in the number of educational measures requiring community service and social training by the juvenile offender. This trend reflects a growing concern within the juvenile justice system for community-based responses to juvenile offenders, while short-term detention (*Jugendarrest*) continues to be on the decline (from 24% in 1976 to 18% in 1998). Approximately half of sentences for juvenile imprisonment fall into the range of up to one year and some 64% of all youth prison sentences are suspended.

Correctional Supervision

The rate of juvenile and adolescent sentenced offenders incarcerated since the late 1960s has been steadily declining (approximately 40 per 100,000 in 1961 to 10 per 100,000 by 1989). However, in the '90s imprisonment rates increased again, standing in 1999 at 24 per 100,000. A corresponding decline and increase can be observed in prisoner rates for young adults (18 to 20 years) as well as for the age group of 21 to 25 years. Prison rates for adults 26 years and older have remained fairly stable throughout the 1970s and 1980s.[2]

Comparing the rates demonstrates that throughout the 1980s and 1990s the ratio of juvenile pre-trial detainees and juvenile prisoners is 1:1. The corresponding ratio for young adults is 1:2 and for adults 1:4. This occurs despite the statutory requirement that pre-trial detention be used only in those cases where there is reason to believe that the juvenile offender will either not attend court hearings or will receive a long youth prison sentence. The disproportional use of pre-trial detention in cases of juvenile offenders may be understood as a strategy of the juvenile justice system using pre-trial detention as a "short, sharp shock" immediately after the offence has been committed, or as a means of crisis intervention (Gebauer, 1987; Heinz, 1987; Heinz ,1990b).

Despite the long-term decrease in the use of youth imprisonment, the proportion of juveniles placed under some type of judicial control increased considerably since the 1960s. The rate climbed from 200 per 100,000 in 1965 to 400 per 100,000 in 1989. With establishing and expanding intermediate sanctions such as probation and parole, the significance of imprisonment changes from immediate physical control to a last resort, strengthening the deterrent impact of sanctions based on supervision and control outside the prison but nevertheless backed up by the threat of imprisonment. The assumption of greater elasticity of probation and parole as well as the reduction of the use of prison to a symbolic level is supported by changes in criteria for revoking probation. In the 1960s the offender population put on probation was characterized by low risk (as measured by prior record) and a limited need for control (no prior record and a stable work record had been major pre-conditions for granting probation). However, since the mid-1970s the target group for probation parallels a group that formerly had been sent to prison.

In juvenile pre-trial detention, the proportion of foreigners is rather pronounced. Depending on the region, foreign youth in correctional facilities comprise up to 57% of the youth inmate population. Enormous differences in rates of young prisoners may be observed in Western Europe.[3]

Problems in Sentencing Juvenile Offenders

As has been pointed out earlier, reliance on the principle of education in the juvenile justice system is accompanied by discriminatory decision-making, in that disadvantaged youth are more likely to be sentenced to intensive types of sanctions. In addition, other problems are currently being discussed which refer to differential treatment compared to the adult criminal justice system and to enormous regional variations in the type of dispositions used in juvenile cases.

Criminological studies revealed that juvenile judges make considerably more use of sanctions involving deprivation of liberty than do their counterparts in the adult system (Heinz, 1990a). While unconditional prison sentences amount to approximately 5% of all adult offenders sentenced, the rate of juvenile offenders sentenced either to an unconditional term of youth prison or to short-term detention is approximately 25%, despite the fact that average seriousness of juvenile crimes is well below that of adult crimes. Juvenile offenders are thus treated more harshly than their adult counterparts (Heinz, 1992). Differential treatment can be observed with respect to the length of prison sentences. The average juvenile prison sentence is longer than adult prison sentences in comparable offence categories (Pfeiffer, 1991).

Moreover, studies on decision-making have shown that considerable regional variation exists with respect to the disposition of juvenile offenders, which cannot be explained by differences in characteristics of offences or offenders (Heinz, 1990c). Obviously, these extremely different styles of implementing educational policies reflect differing court traditions that ultimately provoke the problem of equal treatment. Equal treatment seems to be rather difficult to attain when basing decision-making on the principle of education.

Does the Youth Prison Meet the Promise of Education and Rehabilitation?

In summing up research on treatment in juvenile correctional institutions, pessimistic assessments prevail. There is no empirically sound reason to belief that efforts focusing on the offenders' vocational skills or other treatment options are accompanied by lower recidivism rates. If differences in rates of recidivism between differentially treated groups are observed, these are usually rather small and may reflect *a priori* differences between the groups treated differently (Geissler, 1991). In general we may assume that the possibly positive effects of treatment or support offered are outweighed by negative influences of "prisonization" and the prison subculture. Comparing dispositional alternatives in the juvenile justice system such as short-term detention, suspension of prison sentence, community service, cautioning and imprisonment, evaluation has to be based on research using natural variation in decision-making between different juvenile court districts. The results of such research lend support to the conclusion that different types of juvenile court measures have similar effects in terms of rates of recidivism as well as the general toll of juvenile crime in those court districts relying on different dispositional strate-gies (Heinz, 1990c). Variation in the intensity of intervention is not associated with juvenile criminal behavior nor with juvenile crime. And even though other Western European countries rely on rather different policies vis-à-vis juvenile crime and juvenile offenders, they face similar crime and delinquency problems (Kaiser, 1989).

SUMMARY

Juvenile criminal policy in Germany underwent some important changes in the last decades. These changes may be described in terms of a shift from institutionalization to de-institutionalization and community-based as well as intermediate responses to youth crime, from formal proceedings to diversion and from a welfare-based model to a justice model.

As far as the future development of the juvenile justice system is con-cerned, it may be pointed out that, contrary to the recommendations of the UN Beijing Rules (see Box 1—Introduction), there has been a shift from advocat-ing a unified juvenile welfare law to keeping a separate criminal law for juvenile and young adult offenders. This coincides with the growth in distrust of reha-bilitation and education as major goals of juvenile welfare and juvenile criminal justice. While in the 1970s, and until the beginning of the 1980s, the focus of juvenile law reform was on rehabilitation and treatment—a youth welfare ap-proach to juvenile crime— the 1980s and 1990s are characterized as emphasiz-ing the need to grant juvenile offenders the same rights in terms of due process and fair trial as adult offenders in the adult criminal procedural law. The latest juvenile court law amendment (1990) brought some important changes in this respect, although some critical issues in *Youth Court Law* were not touched at all. The indeterminate youth prison sentence was abolished and the position of intermediate sanctions was strengthened. Moreover, with victim-offender mediation, a new perspective was introduced which places less weight on the offender's person but puts the focus on the impact the offence had on the victim and on society. On the other hand, Parliament did not follow sugges-tions to abolish short-term detention and to amend the conditions for impos-ing youth imprisonment. As recent proposals for youth law amendments suggest, decriminalization and diversion will continue to be among the promi-nent topics of reform (*DVJJ-Kommission zur Reform des Jugendstrafrechts*, 1992). However, at the turn of the century, as the discourse on increasing juvenile crime and the still-intensifying political debates on safety continue, voices grow louder that demand a more repressive approach to juvenile and young adult offenders, even to criminalize children. In 2000, several motions have been introduced that cover youth legislation which would bring upon significant changes (if accepted by the federal Parliament). The Christian Democratic Party/Christian Social Union have introduced a proposal (*BR-Drucksache*, 14/3189 as of 12 April 2000) which is supported in parts by various German states and seeks to:

- make it an exception that young adult offenders are adjudicated and sentenced as juveniles,
- introduce sentencing powers which would allow combination of short term detention of up to four weeks (arrest) with a suspended sentence of youth imprisonment,
- increase maximum imprisonment for young adults if they are sentenced as juveniles to 15 years,
- introduce a new supervision order which would allow tight controls on the free movement of juveniles,
- give new powers to the family or youth court to impose in case of delinquent or criminal children a range of restrictive (and punitive) orders (such as participation in a social training course, victim-offender-mediation, community service as well as restrictions on visiting places or meeting other persons) which correspond to what is found in the *Youth Court Law* as a response to juvenile crime; with that, criminal responsibility of children— although statutorily not established— would be introduced by switching labels in the *Children and Youth Support Law* (*Kinder- und Jugendhilfegesetz*), and
- strengthen powers of family courts to respond to parents who allegedly have failed in supervising and controlling their delinquent or criminal offspring.

As a consequence of German reunification in 1990, the criminal justice system, including juvenile justice, actually had to be established according to West German standards in the east of Germany. As all parts of the justice system have to be either reorganized or completely built up (as the socialist system did not provide the required social services), the burden of cost weighs heavily. As in Russia and Hungary, Germany is experiencing some transition. Recent social and political trends have tended to be conservative, as we continue to embrace the justice model in an effort to respond to the increases in youth crime patterns. This in turn may lead to shortages and budget cutting in the east as well as in the west for a certain period of time.

Just as the initial formation of our juvenile justice system was influenced by developments in North America, it may be timely to examine other foreign trends. The challenge for the new century is to address the issues associated with chronic offenders, ethnic and immigrant groups, re-unification, and how we might accommodate the UN recommendations. These issues cannot be studied solely within the narrow framework of juvenile justice system reforms.

Hans-Jörg Albrecht has been the director at the Max Planck Institute (MPI) for Foreign and International Criminal Law in Freiburg, Germany since March 1997. He teaches criminal law, criminal justice and criminology at the University of Freiburg. He studied law at the universities of Tübingen and Freiburg. At Freiburg University he completed a Ph.D. in 1979, and in 1991 obtained the *venia legendi* for criminal law, juvenile criminal law, criminology, and prison law. From 1977 until 1991 Albrecht was a research fellow at the MPI. Between 1991 and 1997 Albrecht taught criminal law and criminology at the law faculty of the University of Konstanz and also served as the chair for criminal law, juvenile criminal law and criminology at the University of Dresden (1993-1997).

Albrecht's research interests cover various legal, criminological and policy topics ranging from sentencing theory, juvenile crime, drug policies, environmental crime and organized crime, evaluation research and systems of criminal sanctions.

Albrecht has published, co-published and edited various books, among them volumes on sentencing, day-fine systems, recidivism, child abuse and neglect, drug policies, research on victimization, etc. He is co-editor of the journals "*Monatsschrift für Kriminologie und Strafrechtsreform*," "European Journal of Crime, Criminal Justice, and Criminal Law," the series "Crime and Justice in Europe," and for the journal "*Déviance et Société*."

HELPFUL WEBSITES

Juvenile Politics:

www.bmj.bund.de/ Site of the federal Ministry of Justice. The ministry provides basic information on legislation (English home page) as well as an English edition of the German Criminal Code Book. (download available: pdf files).

www.bmfsfj.de/ Site of the federal Ministry for Families, the Aged, Women and Youth. The ministry provides information on youth-related legislation and youth-related programs and policies, as well as research funded by the ministry.

Police and Court Data:

www.bka.de/ Site of the German Federal Police (Wiesbaden). The BKA provides national police data on juvenile crime (downloads available: pdf files).

www.statistik-bund.de/basis/d/recht/rechueb1.htm Site of the Federal Bureau of Statistics. Basic data on adjudication and sentencing of adult and juvenile offenders are provided (no downloads yet available; partially a pay site).

Legal and Social Science Research:

www.dji.de/ Site of the *Deutsches Jugendinstitut Muenchen* (German Institute for Research on Youth). The institute was established to carry through research on all aspects of youth as well as to serve as a documentation center for youth research.

www.iuscrim.mpg.de Site of the Max Planck Institute for Foreign and International Criminal Law Freiburg. The institute is engaged in a variety of youth justice and youth crime-related research projects including research on the implementation of minimum standards of juvenile detention, on self-reported juvenile crime in Germany, Switzerland and France and research on contextual effects on youth crime (downloads available: pdf and doc files).

www.uni-bielefeld.de/ikg/eng/index.html *Institut fuer interdisziplinaere Konflikt- und Gewaltforschung* (Interdisciplinary Institute for Conflict and Violence Research). The institute covers topics such as youth and violence, xenophobia, urban milieus and violence.

www.uni-konstanz.de/FuF/Jura/ *(Forschung – Institut fuer Rechtstatsachenforschung – Konstanzer Inventar - Sanktionsforschung [KIS])* Institute for socio-legal studies. The institute provides data on the German criminal justice system including the juvenile justice system and sentencing.

KEY TERMS AND CONCEPTS

proportionality	*Youth Court Law*
welfare model	justice model
Juvenile Welfare Law	anomie
disciplinary measures	educational measures
social distinction	

STUDY QUESTIONS

1. Why can young adults (18 to 20 years old) be adjudicated and sentenced as juveniles in Germany? What do you think of this provision?
2. How did the German criminal justice system respond to increases in juvenile crime during the nineties?
3. What are the major differences between processing adult criminal offenders, in Germany, and processing the juvenile criminal offender, and how are these differences justified? How does the process differ from other countries covered in this text?
4. What are the major differences between substantial juvenile criminal law and substantial adult criminal law and which are the common features?
5. Which youth and juvenile crime-related topics are focused upon today by German politics and German socio-legal research, and what are the differences compared to the situation in North America?

NOTES

1 Furthermore, the mass media, especially video, have been singled out recently for particular attention in this respect. It is assumed that the presentation of violence on video and television (facilitated by easy access to video and television) contributes considerably to youth violence (Glogauer, 1991; Jung, 1993), such assumptions have not been, until now, supported by scientific evidence.
2 Very few females are detained in youth prisons. As of March 31, 1999, 26 sentenced female juveniles (14 to 17 years old) have been detained in German youth prisons.
3 The rate of imprisoned young offenders (up to 21 years) varied between approximately 30 per 100,000 (Italy, Netherlands, and Greece) and approximately 300 (England and Wales) in the 1980s.

REFERENCES

Albrecht, G. (1990). Möglichkeiten und grenzen der prognose "krimineller Karrieren." In Deutsche Vereinigung für Jugendgerichte und Jugendgerichtshilfen (Eds.), *Mehrfach Auffällige—Mehrfach.* *Betroffene. erlebnisweisen und reaktionsformen,* pp. 99–116. Godesberg: Forum Verlag.

Albrecht, H.-J. (1987a). Die sanfte minderheit: mädchen und frauen als straftäterinnen. *Bewährungshilfe,* 34, 341–359.

Albrecht, H.-J. (1987b). Foreign minorities and the criminal justice system in the Federal Republic of Germany. *The Howard Journal,* 26, 272–286.

Albrecht, H-J. (1988). Ausländerkriminalität. In H. Jung (Ed.). *Fälle zum wahlfach kriminologie: Jugendstrafrecht, strafvollzug* (2nd ed., pp. 183–204). Munich: Beck.

Albrecht, H.-J. (1990). Kriminologische perspektiven der wiedergutmachung. In A. Eser et al. (Eds.), *Neue wege der wiedergutmachung im strafrecht* (pp. 43–72). Freiburg: Max-Planck-Institut für Strafrecht.

Albrecht, H.-J. (1991). Bilan des connaissances en Republique Federale d'Allemagne. In Ph. Robert (Ed.), *Les politiques de prevention de la delinquance: A l'aune de la recherche* (pp. 43–56). Paris: L'Harmattan.

Albrecht, H.-J. (1993). Ethnic minorities: Crime and criminal justice in Europe. In F. Heidensohn & M. Farrell, (Eds.), *Crime in Europe* (pp. 84–102). London, New York: Routledge.

Albrecht, H.-J. (1997). Ethnic minorities, crime, and criminal justice in Germany. In M. Tonry (Ed.), Ethnicity, crime, and immigration: Comparative and cross-national perspectives. *Crime and justice: A review of research* (Vol. 21). Chicago, London: The University of Chicago Press.

Albrecht, H.-J. (1998). Jugend und gewalt. *Monatsschrift für Kriminologie und Strafrechtsreform,* 81, 381–398.

Albrecht, P.A. (1993). *Jugendstrafrecht* (2nd ed.). Munich: C.H. Beck.

Arbeiterwohlfahrt Bundesverband e.V. (Ed.). (1970). Vorschläge für ein erweitertes jugendhilferecht. Denkschrift der arbeiterwohlfahrt zur reform und vereinheitlichung von jugendwohlfahrtsgesetz und jugendstrafgesetz. *Schriften der Arbeiterwohlfahrt,* No. 22: (3rd ed.). Bonn.

Bliesener, T. Psychologische hintergründe der gewalt gegen ausländer. In DVJJ-Regionalgruppe Nordbayern (Eds.). *Ausländer im jugendstrafrecht. neue dimensionen* (pp.15-32). Erlangen.

Bundesamt für Verfassungsschutz. (2000). *Verfassungsschutzbericht* 1999. Berlin: BfV.

Bundeskriminalamt. (1995). *Polizeiliche Kriminalstatistik 1994.* Wiesbaden: Bundeskriminalamt.

Bundeskriminalamt. (2000). *Polizeiliche Kriminalstatistik 1999.* Wiesbaden: Bundeskriminalamt.

Bundesministerium der Justiz (Eds.). (1987). *Verteidigung in jugendstrafsachen.* Bonn: Burg Verlag.

Bundesverfassungsgericht (Constitutional court). (1991). *Neue Juristische Wochenschrift* (p.1043).

Dölling, D. (1992). Die bedeutung der jugendkriminalität im verhältnis zur erwachsenenkriminalität. In Bundesministerium der Justiz (Eds.). *Grundfragen des jugendkriminalrechts und seiner neuregelung* (pp. 38–59). Godesberg: Forum Verlag.

Dünkel, F. (1990). *Freiheitsentzug für junge rechtsbrecher: Situation und reform von jugendstrafe, jugendstrafvollzug, jugendarrest und untersuchungshaft in der Bundesrepublik Deutschland und im internationalen vergleich.* Bonn: Forum Verlag.

DVJJ-Kommission zur Reform des Jugendkriminalrechts. (1992). Für ein neues jugendgerichtsgesetz. *DVJJ-Journal,* 1–2, 4–39.

Eisenberg, U. (1995). *Jugendgerichtsgesetz mit erläuterungen* (6th ed). Munich: Beck.

Elsner, E., Steffen, W., & Stern, G. (1998). *Kinder- und jugendkriminalität in München.* Munich: Bayerisches Landeskriminalamt.

Empey, L.T. (1982). *American delinquency: Its meaning and construction* (2nd ed.). Homewood, IL: The Dorsey Press.

Frehsee, D. (1995). Sozialer wandel und jugendkriminalität. *DVJJ-Journal* 3–4, 269–278

Gebauer, M. (1987). *Die rechtswirklichkeit der untersuchungshaft in der Bundesrepublik Deutschland.* Göttingen: Schwartz.

Geissler, I. (1991). *Ausbildung und arbeit im jugendstrafvollzug: Haftverlaufs- und rückfallanalyse.* Freiburg: Max-Planck-Institut für Strafrecht.

Glogauer, W. (1991). *Kriminalisierung von kindern und jugendlichen durch die medien* (2nd ed.). Baden-Baden: Nomos.

Grundies, V. (1999). Polizeiliche registrierungen von 7- bis 23jährigen: Befunde der freiburger kohortenuntersuchung. In H.-J. Albrecht (Ed.), *Forschungen zu kriminalität und kriminalitätskontrolle am Max-Planck-Institut für Ausländisches und Internationales Strafrecht in Freiburg i.Br* (pp. 371–402). Freiburg: Max-Planck-Institut.

Grundies, V. (2000). Kriminalitätsbelastung junger aussiedler: Ein längsschnittvergleich mit in Deutschland geborenen jungen menschen anhand polizeilicher registrierungen. *Monatsschrift für Kriminologie und Strafrechtsreform,* 83, 290–305.

Heinz, W. (1987). Recht und praxis der untersuchungshaft in der Bundesrepublik Deutschland: Zur disfunktionalität der untersuchungshaft gegenüber dem reformprogramm im materiellen strafrecht. *Bewährungshilfe,* 34,.5–31.

Heinz, W. (1989). Jugendstrafrechtsreform durch die praxis—Eine bestandsaufnahme. In Bundesministerium der Justiz (Eds.), *Jugendstrafrechtsreform durch die praxis* (pp.13–44). Bonn: Burg Verlag.

Heinz, W. (1990a). Gleichheit vor dem gesetz in der sanktionspraxis? Empirische befunde der sanktionsforschung im jugendstrafrecht in der Bundesrepublik Deutschland. In H. Göppinger (Ed.). *Kriminologie und strafrechtspraxis: Tagungsberichte des kriminologischen arbeitskreises* (Vol. 7, pp. 171–209). Tübingen: Aktuelle Probleme der Kriminologie.

Heinz, W. (1990b). Die jugendstrafrechtspflege im spiegel der rechtspflegestatistiken: Ausgewählte daten für den zeitraum 1955–1988. *Monatsschrift für Kriminologie und Strafrechtsreform,* 73, 210–276.

Heinz, W. (1990c). Mehrfach auffällige—mehrfach betroffene: Erlebnisweisen und reaktionsformen. In Deutsche Vereinigung für Jugendgerichte und Jugendgerichtshilfen (Eds.), *Mehrfach Auffällige—Mehrfach Betroffene* (pp.30–73). Bonn: Forum Verlag.

Heinz, W. (1990d). Diversion im jugendstrafverfahren: Aktuelle kriminalpolitische bestrebungen im spiegel empirischer untersuchungen. *Zeitschrift für Rechtspolitik,* 23, 7–11.

Heinz, W. (1992). Abschied von der "erziehungsideologie" im jugendstrafrecht? Zur diskussion über erziehung und strafe. *Recht der Jugend und des Bildungswesens,* 40, 23–143.

Heinz, W. (1997). Jugendkriminalität uwischen verharmlsoung und dramatisierung. *DVJJ-Journal,* 3, 270–293.

Heitmeyer, W., & Peter, J.I. (Eds). (1988). *Jugendliche fußballfans: Soziale und politische orientierungen, gesellungsformen, gewalt.* Weinheim, Munich: Juventa.

Hupfeld, J. (1993). Zur bedeutung des erziehungsgedankens und des richterlichen spezialisierungsgrades in der jugendstrafrechtspraxis. *DVJJ-Journal,* 1, 11–17.

Kaiser, G. (1988). *Kriminologie* (2nd ed.). Heidelberg: C.F. Müller.

Kaiser, G. (1989). Jugenddelinquenz im internationalen Vergleich. In Innenministerium Baden-Württemberg (Ed.). *Jugend und Kriminalität.* Innenministerium Baden-Württemberg: Stuttgart, pp. 13–48.

Kaiser, G. (1993a). Jugendstrafrecht. In G. Kaiser et al. (Eds.), *Kleines kriminologisches wörterbuch* (pp. 199–204). Karlsruhe: C.F. Müller.

Kaiser, G. (1993b). *Kriminologie* (9th ed.). Heidelberg: C.F. Müller.

Karger, T., & Sutterer, P. (1988). Cohort study on the development of police-recorded criminality and criminal sanctioning. In G. Kaiser & I. Geissler (Eds.), *Crime and criminal justice* (pp.89–114). Freiburg: Max-Planck-Institut für Strafrecht.

Karger, Th., & Sutterer, P. (1990). Polizeilich registrierte gewaltdelinquenz bei jungen ausländern. *Monatsschrift für Kriminologie und Strafrechtsreform,* 73, 369–383.

Kerner, H.J., & Weitekamp, E. (1984). The Federal Republic of Germany. In Klein, M.W. (Ed.), *Western systems of juvenile justice* (pp.147–170). Beverly Hills, CA: Sage.

Kerner, H.J. (1990). Jugendkriminalrecht als "vorreiter" der strafrechtsreform? Überlegungen zu 40 jahren rechtsentwicklung in rechtsprechung, lehre und kriminalpolitik. *DVJJ-Journal,* 133, 68–81.

Kerner, H.J., & Sonnen, B.-R. (1997). Jugendkriminalität und jugendstrafrecht. *DVJJ-Journal* 158, 339–345.

Kersten, J. (1993). Das thema gewaltkriminalität in kulturvergleichender sicht. *DVJJ-Journal,* 1, 18–26.

Klein, M.W. (Ed.). (1984). *Western systems of juvenile justice.* Beverly Hills, CA: Sage.

Krüger, H. (1983). Rückfallquote: rund 30%. *Kriminalistik,* 37, 326–329.

Kube, E., & Koch, K.-F. (1990). Zur kriminalität jugendlicher ausländer aus polizeilicher sicht. *Monatsschrift für Kriminologie und Strafrechtsreform,* 73, 14–24.

Kunz, K.-L. (1989). Ausländerkriminalität in der schweiz—Umfang, struktur und erklärungsversuch. *Schweizerische Zeitschrift für Strafrecht,,* 106, 373–392.

Laubenthal, F. (1993). *Jugendgerichtshilfe im strafverfahren.* Cologne..

Liszt, F.v. (1905). Die kriminalität der jugendlichen. In F.v. Liszt, *Strafrechtliche Aufsätze und Vorträge* (Vol. 2, pp. 331–355). Berlin: Gutlentag.

Mansel, J., & Hurelmann, K. (1993). Psychosoziale befindlichkeit junger ausländer in der Bundesrepublik Deutschland. *Soziale Probleme,* 4, 167–192.

Münder, J., Sack, F., Albrecht, H.J., & Plewig, H.-J. (1987). *Jugendarbeitslosigkeit und jugendkriminalität.* Neuwied: Luchterhand.

Neubacher, F. (1999). Die fremdenfeindlichen brandanschläge nach der vereinigung. *Monatsschrift für Kriminologie und Strafrechtsreform,* 82, 1–15.

Ostendorf, H. (1992). Ansatzpunkte für materiell-rechtliche entkriminalisierungen von verhaltensweisen junger menschen. In Bundesministerium der Justiz (Eds.), *Grundfragen des jugendkriminalrechts und seiner neuregelung* (pp.194–204). Godesberg, Bonn: Forum Verlag.

Pfeiffer, C. (1991). Wird nach jugendstrafrecht härter bestraft? *Strafverteidiger,* 11, 363–370.

Pfeiffer, C., Delzer, I., Enzmann, D., & Wetzels, P. (1998). Ausgrenzung, gewalt und kriminalität im leben junger menschen. Hanover: DVJJ.

Rommelspacher, B. (1993). Männliche jugendliche als projektionsfiguren gesellschaftlicher gewaltphantasien: Rassismus im selbstverständnis der mehrheitskultur. In W. Breyvogel, (Ed.), *Lust auf randale: Jugendliche gewalt gegen fremde* (pp. 65–82). Bonn: Verlag Dietz.

Schaal, H.-J., & Eisenberg, U. (1988). Rechte und befugnisse von verletzten im strafverfahren gegen jugendliche. *Neue Zeitschrift für Strafrecht*, 8, 49–53.

Schöch, H. (1992). *Empfehlen sich änderungen und ergänzungen bei den strafrechtlichen sanktionen ohne freiheitsentzug?* Munich: C.H. Beck.

Schumann, K.F., Berlitz, C., Guth, H.-W., & Kanlitzki, R. (1987). *Jugendkriminalität und die grenzen der generalprävention.* Neuwied, Darmstadt: Luchterhand.

Solon, J. (1994). Jugendgewalt in München—Ausdruck deutscher fremdenfeindlichkeit oder unvermeidbare ethnische konflikte. *Der Kriminalist*, 26, 73–79.

Streng, F. (1994). Der erziehungsgedanke im jugendstrafrecht. *Zeitschrift für die Gesamte Strafrechtswissenschaft*, 106, 60–92.

Stümper, A. (1973). Die kriminalpolitische bewertung der jugendkriminalität. *Kriminalistik*, 49.

Viehmann, H. (1993). Was machen wir mit unseren jugendlichen gewalttätern? *DVJJ-Journal*, 1, 26–29.

Villmow, B., & Kaiser, G. (1974). Empirisch gesicherte erkenntnisse über ursachen der kriminalität. In Der Regierende Bürgermeister von Berlin (Ed.), *Verhütung und Bekämpfung der Kriminalität*. Berlin: Berliner Senat.

Villmow, B., & Stephan, E. (1983). *Jugendkriminalität in einer gemeinde: Eine analyse erfragter delinquenz und viktimisierung sowie amtlicher registrierung*. Freiburg: Max-Planck-Institut für Strafrecht.

Walter, M. (1995). *Jugendkriminalität*. Stuttgart, Munich, Hanover: Boorberg.

Chapter 7

Juvenile Delinquency in Hong Kong

Harold Traver
Department of Sociology, Hong Kong University

FACTS ABOUT HONG KONG

Area: 1098 sq. kilometers. **Location and Climate**: Hong Kong is located on the coast of southern China and directly adjoins Guangdong province, which is part of the People's Republic of China. Hong Kong's climate is subtropical. **Population**: At the end of 1999 the total population stood at 6,974,800 (overall density 6,480 people per sq. km). Hong Kong qualifies as one of the most densely populated places in the world. The Kwun Tong District has 55,020 people per sq. km. The population is 95% Chinese. **Economy**: Because of a land shortage, Hong Kong imports much of its food supply. Its economy is heavily dependent on international trade. Hong Kong ranks as the ninth largest trading entity in the world and it operates the world's busiest container port. Since the 1980s the service sector of the economy has expanded to the point where it now contributes over 85% of GDP. Telecommunications, financial and business services including banking, insurance, real estate and a wide range of professional services play an increasingly important role in the economy. Hong Kong's stock exchange is the second largest in Asia. It is also the ninth largest banking center in the world and has extensive trade and investment ties with China. **Government**: Hong Kong was occupied by Britain in 1841 and was formally ceded by China the following year. Hong Kong became a Special Economic Region (SAR) of the People's Republic of China on 1 July 1997. As a SAR Hong Kong continues to have its own government and legislature and is allowed a considerable degree of autonomy, except in those areas that relate to foreign affairs and defence, for the next 50 years.

"Whilst thy father lives study his wishes; after he is dead study his life. He who for three years makes no change in his father's ways may be called a good son." Confucius (Lyal, 1925:2).

Since the 1960s there have been a series of "moral panics" in Hong Kong in regard to youthful misbehavior and apparent dramatic increases in juvenile delinquency coming to the attention of the police (Gray, 1991). The facts, however, are not always what they appear to be. As with any other social problem our perception of delinquency is conditioned by prevailing social and cultural norms. In order to fully understand delinquency one must first understand the theory and practice of juvenile justice, and then be able to place this understanding within its proper historical and cultural context. Consequently, this chapter devotes considerable attention to examining the possible effects of Chinese cultural values on the development of juvenile justice in Hong Kong, the emergence of young people as a distinct segment within Hong Kong society, and the subsequent creation of youthful misbehavior as a social problem.

Only by taking into account the cultural and historical forces that have shaped our conception of delinquency can one hope to arrive at some understanding of the nature and extent of delinquency in society. In the case of Hong Kong this means understanding why there has been continued public concern over increased involvement of young people in a variety of criminal offences, ranging from serious assault and robbery to shop theft and other forms of petty theft. This chapter considers several possible explanations which may account for the apparent increase in delinquent behavior:

First, changing social and economic conditions in Hong Kong have helped to produce a real increase in crime and delinquency. In this case public concern merely reflects what is actually occurring in society.

Second, the increase in delinquency is due to an increased willingness to report crime and delinquency. In actual fact, however, there may have been no significant change in crime or delinquency.

Third, there is also the possibility that criminal justice policy may shift in such a way that an increasing number of people enter the criminal justice system. Once again, arrest and prosecution rates may change without there being any real change in the volume of crime or delinquency.

As the term is used here, juvenile delinquency refers to violations of the criminal law, or what could be called "juvenile crime," and not to status offences such as truancy or running away from home. Status offences are unquestionably more common than "juvenile crime." However, since this chapter relies on official delinquency statistics, it will focus on "juvenile crime" figures. Moreover, to a large extent the existence of the juvenile justice system is justified on the basis of the prevention and control of "juvenile crime." Consequently, for these reasons, this chapter devotes the bulk of its attention to juvenile crime.

DELINQUENCY AND CHINESE CULTURE

In many respects juvenile delinquency in Hong Kong means very much the same thing as it means in the West. In Hong Kong delinquency essentially involves a failure on the part of the youth to conform to standards of behavior laid down by adult institutions (e.g., family, school, police and the courts). Moreover, in line with most contemporary Western societies, Hong Kong has an extensive juvenile justice system, which attempts to separate juveniles out from adults and places more emphasis on therapeutic programs than on punishment.

Despite its many similarities to the West, it should always be kept in mind that Hong Kong is still predominantly a Chinese society. Traditional Chinese society was organized on the Confucian principle that the perfect society was one in which individuals acted according to the duties imposed on them by their status in society (Lui, 1972). In **Confucian society** the family was the primary economic, social and religious unit. The concept of **filial piety,** the obligation of children to show deference and respect towards their parents, represented the most fundamental social relationship in society and personified the correct attitude towards all forms of authority. Filial piety was seen to be the driving force for the maintenance of the stable hierarchical social order that lay at the very heart of Confucian society.

The concept of juvenile delinquency as a pervasive social problem suggests a degree of independence and separateness of children from adults that would be almost unthinkable in Confucian society. Therefore, when youthful misbehavior was discovered it was treated as a family matter and as such was to be confined to the family, rather than submitting the juvenile to a justice system which was easily capable of administering arbitrary and harsh forms of punishment (Cohen, Edwards and Chen, 1980; Ch'u, 1965).

Hong Kong, however, can hardly be characterized as a traditional Confucian society. Since World War II industrialization and urbanization has meant a rapid decline in informal family-based systems of control. More parents are working away from the home and even more children spend most of the day in school in the company of their peers. Under such conditions it is reasonable to suppose that the family may not be fulfilling its socialization and control functions as effectively as it did in the past.

At the same time, some things have not changed that much. Filial piety continues to exercise a lingering hold over Hong Kong society. For instance, in 1986 a survey of 539 persons in the Kwun Tong District of Hong Kong over the age of 18 found that 85% of the respondents were willing to financially support their aging parents. In the same survey, 86% of the respondents "agreed" or "strongly agreed" with the idea that the government should enact laws to force children to take care of their elderly parents, and 89% believed that filial piety was essential for a good society (Lau and Kuan, 1988:59, 139).

Despite a Confucian stress on mediation and social harmony and a general de-emphasis on the role of law, the respondents were willing to use law to support filial piety, a central feature of Confucian philosophy. For example, according to a 1988 social indicator survey involving a sample of 1662 adults drawn from the general population, 65% of the respondents stated that they trusted judges and lawyers, and 67% agreed that the "law was an efficient means of conflict resolution" (Kuan, Lau and Wan, 1991:216, 218).

In the 1986 Kwun Tong survey, as well as in a larger 1988 social indicator survey, the "youth problem" was ranked as the most serious of 12 different kinds of problems facing Hong Kong (Lau and Wan, 1991). In both surveys a concern for the youth problem exceeded that shown for such problems as pollution, transportation and public order. The degree of concern shown for youthful misbehavior suggests that while informal family-based systems of control may have declined, conduct norms continue to demand a degree of conformity from juveniles that would be more characteristic of Confucian society than Western society.

What has changed is not so much the nature and extent of illegal behavior among juveniles as the perceptions of parents and the authorities about the desirability of handing juveniles over to the juvenile justice system for formal processing. Whether or not a juvenile is judged to be delinquent depends less on the existence of a particular system of juvenile justice and more on how that system is perceived and used by the various sectors of adult society. The same observation also applies to specific forms of illegal behavior. What may be taken as an indication of a serious act of delinquency in Hong Kong in another cultural context may be perceived merely as an example of normal youthful exuberance or experimentation.

THE CREATION OF JUVENILE DELINQUENCY

In the West the notion that youthful misbehavior is a specific type of socially undesirable behavior emerged in the late nineteenth century as people increasingly came to view childhood and adolescence as relatively distinct and critical phases in the individual's transition to adulthood (see Hagan and Leon, 1977, Sutton, 1988). The final result of this evolutionary process was the creation of the concept of juvenile delinquency and the development of a juvenile justice system (see Figure 7.1).

The Origins of Juvenile Justice in Hong Kong

In contrast to Western societies, the development of juvenile justice in Hong Kong was not the result of a gradual evolutionary process. Instead,

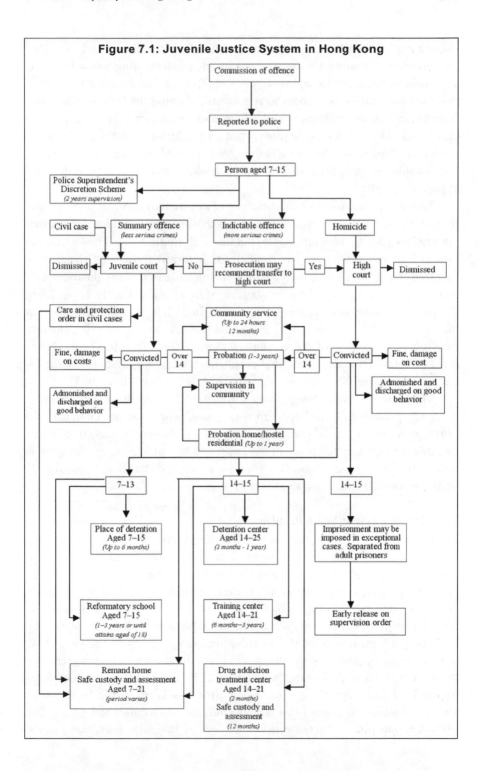

Figure 7.1: Juvenile Justice System in Hong Kong

Hong Kong's juvenile justice system emerged fully developed in 1932 when the *Juvenile Offenders Ordinance* was enacted establishing juvenile courts and probation officers to deal with juvenile offenders. In the same year reformatories and industrial schools were established under the Industrial and Reformatories School Ordinance. Most of the laws which currently affect juvenile (aged 7 to 15) and young offenders (aged 16 to 20); namely, the Juvenile Offenders, Probation of Offenders, Training Schools and the Industrial and Training Schools Ordinances, have been on the books in one form or another since at least the 1950s.

The motivation for the establishment of a system of juvenile justice came from the British colonial administration which was legally obligated to see that laws in Hong Kong were more or less in line with English law. The 1932 *Juvenile Offenders Ordinance* was basically transferred from English law and "grafted" into Hong Kong society and law with little or no thought about how well it might fit with local circumstances. More specifically, the Hong Kong *Juvenile Offenders Ordinance* was based on English legislation, in particular the *Children's Act* of 1908 and the *Probation of Offenders Act* of 1908, and also took into account some of the recommendations of the Committee on the Treatment of Young Offenders 1927 that eventually were incorporated into the *English Children and Young Persons Act* 1933 (Allison and Giller, 1983).

The basic outline of Hong Kong's system of juvenile justice clearly predates any public or official concern with young people, or any evidence of a growing volume of delinquency in Hong Kong society. In fact, in 1954/55 juvenile delinquency fell to an all time post-war low of 333 arrests, and, while arrests and prosecutions tended to increase gradually after that date, juvenile delinquency still continued to attract little attention.

The Discovery of the "Youth Problem"

One of the earliest mentions of delinquency appears in the Hong Kong Report for 1960 when, in the course of discussing the opening of two new magistracies during the year, it was observed that, "An increasing number of juveniles are now being remanded for at least a week so that probation officers may make inquiries" (Hong Kong Government, 1961, p. 176). The Social Welfare Department, which was, and continues to be, responsible for overseeing probation orders, also noted that in order to cope with the increased use of the remand home in Kowloon the maximum accommodation had been increased from 54 to 70 (Social Welfare Department, 1961). It should perhaps be mentioned here that even though adult probation has been on the books since 1956, probation continues to be largely confined to juveniles and young first offenders. Despite an increase in the number of juveniles on remand in the early 1960s, the authorities never raised the possibility that delinquency might represent an emerging social problem in Hong Kong. During this period, when crime became the object of attention it was only to note that there had been a reduction in crime known to the police, which presumably included delinquency, and that this was "particularly impressive in the face of the steady growth of the population" (Hong Kong Government, 1961, p. 192–193).

Such apparent complacency was not destined to last for long. Events began to take shape during the 1960s that would profoundly affect the perception of delinquency in Hong Kong. The authorities, as well as the public, were just beginning to become aware of the fact that nearly 50% of the population of Hong Kong was under the age of 21. The Hong Kong Report for 1961 for the first time called attention to the pressing problem of assessing the "interests and requirements of this segment of the population." The fact that the number of juveniles on probation had increased from less than 300 at the end to 1960 to about 500 at the end of 1961 is cited as evidence of declining standards of behavior among young people. The report concludes its discussion of delinquency by noting that:

> (T)he experience of other Asian territories has shown that, where the energy and enthusiasm of youth are misdirected or not given constructive outlets, they will find expression in teenage violence and other anti-social behavior (Hong Kong Government, 1962:187).

In 1964 developments in Hong Kong added additional weight to the notion that young people posed a potential problem to the community. That year saw considerable publicity being given to the "*ah fei*" (teddy boy) problem in the local press. As the term was used in Hong Kong, the *ah fei* problem referred to young hooligans and criminals, usually under 23 years of age. A number of educational, religious and Kaifong (charitable) associations demanded that the government adopt more stringent measures to control the problem.

Public concern over the *ah fei* problem was sufficiently strong that the governor ordered the colonial secretary to set up a working party to examine "whether present legislation...enables the Courts to deal adequately with crimes of violence by young persons" (Hong Kong Government, 1965, p. 1). A few months later the Working Party produced the first official report dealing with juvenile delinquency in Hong Kong. The report concluded that, while the activities of youth gangs would need to be closely watched in the future, there was nothing to indicate an "extraordinary upsurge" in juvenile crimes of violence. Even though the overall tone of the report was even-handed and reassuring, for the first time juvenile delinquency was publicly identified as a social problem.

A year later in April 1966 a fare increase for the Star Ferry that transported passengers between Hong Kong Island and Kowloon sparked what came to be called the Star Ferry Riots. Young people were unquestionably involved in the leadership of the demonstrations against the fare increases as well in two nights of "violence and looting" in Kowloon that month. Once again young people were in the news. The Kowloon Disturbances, as they were officially called, again produced an official commission of inquiry and an official report which gave special attention to the prominence of young people aged 15 to 25 in the disturbances. As a result of the *ah fei* problem and the Star Ferry Riots, by the end of the 1960s delinquency and youthful misbehavior were well on there way to becoming established social problems in Hong Kong.

During the 1960s several characteristic features of Hong Kong's conception of delinquency were beginning to take shape. First, there was tendency to discount the possible "political" content of delinquency and view it instead as a manifestation of individual frustration over limited opportunities for achievement and youthful exuberance. In the absence of a radical overhaul of the existing economic system and the redistribution of economic rewards, there was very little that the authorities could hope to do about improving the availability of economic opportunities. An inability to control emotions and surplus energy, however, did not present the same problems. Here the authorities could safely come out in favor of more varied opportunities for recreation and leisure time activities.

Second, as might be expected there was (and is) a strong emphasis on prevention and diversion from being officially processed. The juvenile justice model is comparable to the **corporatist model** (see Figure 1—Introduction). The root causes of delinquency, and there are many, may be seen to be poverty, poor home environment, the influence of triad societies, or even compulsory education, but in all cases the solution is likely to be the same, namely, a better youth policy and more youth facilities (Fight Crime Committee, 1981; Fight Violent Crime Committee, 1973; Hong Kong Council of Social Service, 1981; Ng, 1975). In the past this was likely to mean more recreational facilities, although as professional social workers began to enter the juvenile justice system there has been a growing emphasis by juvenile justice specialists on responding to the developmental problems that young people face (Chow, 1987; Law, 1986).

Third, in those cases where prevention has failed, the means advocated for dealing with delinquency and youth crime reflect the general view that it may be desirable to treat and rehabilitate (i.e., retrain) offenders rather than punish them. For instance in 1990/91 around 75% of those on probation in Hong Kong were below the age of 21 (Social Welfare Department, 1991). In

Hong Kong the juvenile justice system continues to be firmly based on the doctrine of *parens patriae,* which sanctions the right of the state to assume the role of parent when a child's natural parents are unwilling or unable to act in the child's best interests (Jensen and Dean, 1992).

Finally, there is a conception of delinquency that can best be termed a **reservoir theory** of deviance. This refers to the idea that there is a large amount of potential juvenile delinquency just waiting to engulf the community if steps are not taken to stem the flow. The community, of course, is never engulfed, but the authorities and the public continue to maintain a vigilant and anxious eye for possible signs of impending trouble.

Delinquency and Social Organization

In sociological terms, delinquency is related to society's social organization and its culture. A number of writers (Cohen, 1985; Ferdihand, 1989; Wilkins, 1965) contend that formal control efforts play a significant role in amplifying deviance in society. In so-called traditional societies, where formal attempts to control deviance are largely lacking, deviance has been observed to be relatively underdeveloped, spontaneous and transitory. In contrast, modern industrial societies such as Hong Kong are characterized by highly developed and elaborate formal systems of control and treatment. In such societies crime and delinquency are inclined to become established and intransigent social problems.

This may well be true, but if Hong Kong is anything to go by it would seem that formal control mechanisms in themselves do not automatically result in an amplification or intensification of deviance (see Box 7.1). In Hong Kong a juvenile justice system was in place for thirty years before there was any widespread concern either about the problem of delinquency or the possibility that a youth culture was developing whose values were contrary to those held by adult society.

As seems to have been the case in most of the countries covered in this reader, a growing feeling that young people might pose a threat to adult society accompanied social and economic changes. Unlike most other countries, these conditions emerged much later in Hong Kong—the 1960s and 1970s. For instance, the government introduced compulsory universal primary education in 1971 and universal junior secondary education in 1978. From 1978 onward all children by law were required to be in full-time education between the ages of 6 to 15 years. Today, most children now spend most of their day in school and in the company of their peers (see Box 7.2). The result of all this was the creation of a distinct age segment of society that had not previously existed. It is probably no accident that this period saw the emergence of widespread

> ### Box 7.1: Juvenile Crime: An Educated Guess?
>
> It is perhaps ironical that compulsory education is being cited for the surprising sudden surge in juvenile crime. Because one reason for launching compulsory schooling by stages to up to form three in 1978 was that it would "take the kids off the street." And hence reduce the risk of their becoming criminals.
>
> Admittedly, the report of the working group formed by the Fight Crime Committee to probe the rise in juvenile delinquency stresses that the delayed effects of introducing compulsory education is only a contributing factor...
>
> But it is convinced that we are paying the penalty for "inflicting" compulsory education without implementing any of the refinements. And it should have been obvious from the start that simply laying down the law that you will go to school until 15 was not enough.
>
> Of course there should be no suggestion of turning back the clock. Compulsory education to form three level must stay on the books. To think otherwise would be a ridiculously retrograde step...
>
> But we must give serious consideration to the wisdom of extending compulsory education beyond form three. Youth at that age should be allowed to choose whether they remain at school or go out and seek a job. They must be given the option. It should not be forced on them.
>
> One of the disturbing aspects of the surge in juvenile crime is that it has happened when recreational facilities are mushrooming. That is not to say that we provide sufficiently healthy outlets for a youngster's energies. But the quality of life in this area has improved dramatically in recent years. Yet more young people are turning to crime.
>
> *South China Morning Post*, 4 April, 1981, p.2.

concern about the possibility of **triad** infiltration of schools. From this point onwards, what was once likely to be dismissed as merely "gang bullying" or "schoolyard intimidation" now is likely to be interpreted as an indication of triad activities.

In the years since, the problem of triad infiltration of schools has become an almost permanent social problem in Hong. Students themselves apparently hold this view of triads as well. A 1998 survey of 2,930 students in ten secondary schools in Hong Kong which asked students to rank their "biggest challenges" found that the threat of triads topped the list. Pornography, drugs, and sex abuse ranked second, third and fourth as the most serious problems facing teenagers (South China Morning Post, 1998).

Over the years the police have also responded to this problem by organizing a wide variety of programs designed to prevent students and young people from being harassed by "bad elements" or enticed into a life of crime. This may take the form of increased patrols by anti-triad units to prevent gang activities, police visits to schools, and lectures and seminars on a regular basis to educate students on triad-related matters (South China Morning Post, 1997).

Box 7.2: Kids on Curfew

Thirteen-year-old Ah Bun is tired of studying, but not staying out late. The Tai Po resident...has skipped school for days after falling out with one of his teachers and now spends his time hanging out on the streets with fellow teenagers.

In Tai Po and some other parts of the New Territories, where young families have flocked to new housing estates and often both parents commute long distances to work, the ranks of wandering youth like Ah Bun have grown, prompting police to slap a midnight curfew on children under the age of 16.

The six-month trial scheme, imposed in mid-September, aims to combat juvenile crime by giving frontline officers the right to bring to the police station youngsters considered to be in moral or physical danger when found on the streets between midnight and 6 A.M. Parents are then called and asked to take their children home. If a youngster is picked up three or more times, police may apply to court for a care-and-protection order, which would establish arrangements for extra supervision by the child's parents, most likely in conjunction with a social service agency.

Tai Po has a large under-16 population and faces an especially serious juvenile problem, mostly non-violent theft and burglary. In the first half of this year, 432 juveniles were arrested there, up from 379 in the same period last year. The Tai Po Police district...includes about 20% of the SAR's under-16 population but accounts for about 30% of juvenile arrests.

Two weeks ago, Ah Bun and about 20 other teenagers were hanging around open areas between blocks at Fu Sin public housing estate, where Ah Bun lives, when police turned up at about four in the morning. Still, he is not worried about being on the street late at night, nor does he see anything wrong with the nocturnal and risky lifestyle he and his friends have adopted.

"I am not afraid of being lured [into trouble] by criminals. I can protect myself. I don't need police to protect me."

.... No one was taken to a police station—although 13 youngsters have been taken off the streets and brought to police stations since the scheme was introduced in Tai Po.

... Officers were mentors to almost 1,000 boys and girls last year, and juvenile crime dropped. Unfortunately, however, the programme became a victim of its own success and was scrapped this year.

Social workers support such crime prevention schemes in principle but are concerned about the potential for abuse of power by frontline officers. "A balance needs to be struck between preventing crime and protecting personal freedom," says Charles Chan Chi-kwong, who supervises care services for young people at Cariats, the Catholic social service agency.

... Social workers believe that even though picking kids up off the street might reduce juvenile crime, it does little to curb juvenile delinquency. This is attributed to a much deeper problem: family disintegration.

... Al Bun, for example, still lives at home but is unwilling to talk about his parents and two sisters. "We don't have much to say to each other," he says in a low voice, his face devoid of emotion.

Youth workers say Ah Bun and his peers have plenty of company. Youth Outreach, which scours the streets for wandering youths late each night, estimates 50,000 to 60,000 neglected teenagers in the SAR alternate between home and street life over the course of a year. This is double the figure of a decade ago...

South China Post, 28 October 2000, p. 15.

Another area that has attracted considerable attention over the years is the question of increasing drug abuse among young people in Hong Kong. Is there a growing problem of drug abuse among young people in Hong Kong? What evidence there is regarding the abuse of drugs among young people comes from a series of government-sponsored school surveys of Hong Kong students in secondary schools and technical institutes carried out in 1987, 1990, 1992 and 1996 (Narcotics Division, 1988, 1991, 1993 and 1997). In the School Survey 1987 it was estimated that 1.1% of all secondary students had at some time abused psychotropic substances and that, of these, 42% (0.5% of all students) were regular users. However, the percentage of students who reported to have ever abused psychoactive substances, excluding heroin, decreased from 3.1% in 1992 to 2.7% in 1996. Moreover, the percentage of those students who had abused psychoactive substances in the 30 days prior to the survey decreased from 0.8% in 1992 to 0.6% in 1996. Cough medicines, tranquilizers and marijuana are the main types of drugs abused. The percentage of students who reported ever having abused heroin increased from 0.4% in 1992 to 2.1% in 1996. The percentage of students who had abused heroin in the 30 days prior to the survey also increased from 0.1% in 1992 to 0.8% in 1996. By international standards these figure are low, and, with the exception of heroin abuse, the figures are decreasing.

DELINQUENCY AND YOUTH CRIME

For nearly the last 30 years the authorities and the public have been acting as if Hong Kong has a serious delinquency and youth crime problem on its hands. However, our perception of the nature and extent of delinquency and crime normally derive not from firsthand experience but instead from the official crime statistics. Unfortunately, the observation that these statistics are probably the "most unreliable and most difficult of all social statistics" (Sutherland and Cressey, 1966:27) is especially true for delinquency and youth crime statistics insofar as the age of the offender can only be determined when the offender has been arrested by the police or prosecuted by the courts.

Even though arrest and prosecution statistics may tell us something about the rate at which the police process offenders or the volume of traffic passing through the courts, the bulk of delinquency and crime goes either undetected or unreported. Furthermore, possible variations in police policies and court procedures upset any hope that these statistics will maintain even a constant ratio with the "true rate" of delinquency and crime—whatever it is.

Legal Definition

Discussions of juvenile delinquency are further complicated by the fact that in Hong Kong there are a variety of legal definitions as to what constitutes a "juvenile" as opposed to a "child" or an "adult" (Leung and Sihombing, 1999). For instance, under the *Juvenile Offenders Ordinance* a "child" is defined as any person under the age of 14 and a "young person" is anyone "14 years of age or upwards and under the age of 16 years." The age of criminal responsibility begins at seven. No child may be imprisoned and detention is only possible for serious (indictable) offences such as attempted murder or manslaughter. For youths aged 14 to 16, imprisonment may only be ordered if there are no suitable alternatives, and in all such cases the young person is not allowed to associate with adult prisoners. The *Criminal Procedures Ordinance* also requires that, before imposing a prison sentence on a person aged 16 to 20, the court must obtain and consider all relevant information about the person and the circumstances of the case, so as to be certain that there are no other suitable methods of dealing with the person. Official crime statistics are reported on the basis of the 16 to 20 age criterion specified in the *Crimes Procedure Ordinance*. Consequently, in the official statistics a juvenile delinquent is anyone aged 7 to 15 and a young offender is any person aged 16 to 20. It should be noted here that serious consideration is being given to increasing the age of criminal responsibility from the old common standard of seven. The exact age of responsibility has yet to be determined but will probably be somewhere in region of 16 years of age. This is in the future. Primarily because it uses official statistics as its main source of data, this chapter adopts the "statistical definition" of juvenile delinquency.

Observed Trends

Has there been a real or significant change in the volume of juvenile delinquency (aged 7 to 15) and youth crime (aged 16 to 20)?

First, it is worth noting that despite growing alarm over the youth problem in the 1960s, between 1961/62 and 1973/74 the prosecution rate for juveniles (aged 7 to 15) declined from 236 per 100,000 to 158 per 100,000. However, during this same period the prosecution rate for young offenders (aged 16 to 20) increased from 512 per 100,000 to 1111 per 100,000. The juvenile prosecution rate only experienced significant increases after 1978. In 1979 the rate increased to 310 per 100,000 as compared with 187 per 100,000 in the preceding year. In the years since, the prosecution has fluctuated from a high of 620 per 100,000 in 1989 to a low of 359 per 100,000 in 1982. In 1997 the juvenile prosecution rate stood at 448 per 100,000. Figure 7.2 also shows that the arrest rates for juvenile and young offenders have also displayed a similar pattern of increasing in the 1980s and then declining in the 1990s. For instance, in 1999 the juvenile arrest rate stood at 704 per 100,000. This is considerably in excess of the 1976 figure, which stood at 212 per 100,000, but well below what is was in

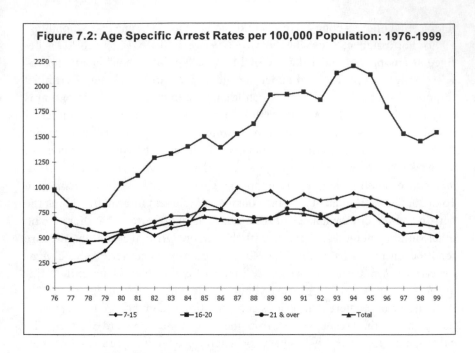

Figure 7.2: Age Specific Arrest Rates per 100,000 Population: 1976-1999

1987 when it peaked at 997.0 per 100,000. The arrest and prosecution rates for juveniles have always been well below that for young offenders. The gap between the two age groups has, however, narrowed over the years. In comparison with juveniles, in the mid-1970s young offenders were approximately six times as likely to be prosecuted but by the mid-1980s the margin between the two age groups had narrowed to around three times as likely and it has remained at this level in subsequent years.

Second, Figures 7.3 and 7.4, which show the rates for supervision under the Police Superintendent's Discretion Scheme, the prosecution rate, and the **offender rate** (combined rate for supervision and prosecution) for juvenile and young offenders, provide a somewhat different picture. One thing that immediately stands out in this figure is that the use of supervision for juveniles increased dramatically between 1980 and 1987 (see Figure 7.3). As a result of this increase the offender rate for juveniles, the combined rates for prosecution and supervision, also increased significantly. This increase, however, was almost exclusively due to an increased use of supervision. In fact, between 1985 and 1987 more juveniles were being supervised than prosecuted. Few young offenders are eligible for supervision but even this age group experienced an increase in the use of supervision (see Figure 7.4). The increased use of supervision for juveniles means that more juveniles are being processed by the juvenile justice system, which in turn helps to foster the notion that there

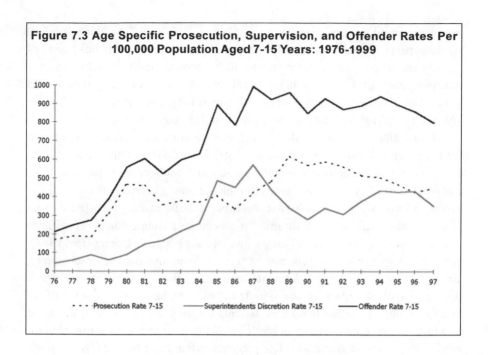

Figure 7.3 Age Specific Prosecution, Supervision, and Offender Rates Per 100,000 Population Aged 7-15 Years: 1976-1999

- - - Prosecution Rate 7-15   ——— Superintendents Discretion Rate 7-15   ——— Offender Rate 7-15

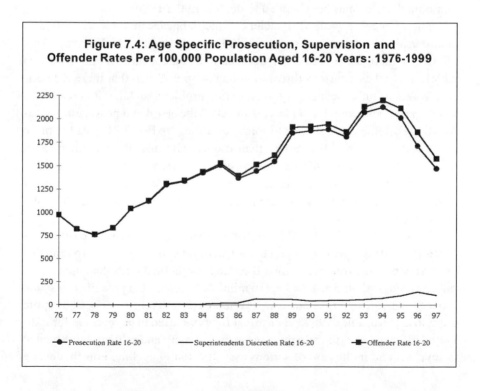

Figure 7.4: Age Specific Prosecution, Supervision and Offender Rates Per 100,000 Population Aged 16-20 Years: 1976-1999

—●— Prosecution Rate 16-20   ——— Superintendents Discretion Rate 16-20   —■— Offender Rate 16-20

has been a rapid expansion in delinquent behavior. Figure 7.3 also shows that, while supervision rates have tended to decline since 1987, this has been accompanied by corresponding increases in the prosecution rate. This suggests that more juveniles are now being prosecuted where previously they would have been placed on supervision. Be this as it may, the net result is that the volume of delinquency has remained more or less constant since 1987.

Third, alarm over a possible increase in juvenile delinquency appears to find support in Table 7.1 which shows that, in comparison with young offenders, juvenile involvement in serious assault and robbery increased dramatically between 1976 and 1988. Even though the young offender rates for these offences have always been higher than the juvenile rates, juvenile involvement in these offences has supplied a reoccurring theme for many official discussions of delinquency in Hong Kong (see Fight Crime Committee, 1981). However, despite continued concern over juvenile involvement in violent crime, Table 7.1 shows that since 1989, when arrest rates first started to be published, juvenile involvement in serious assault and robbery has tended to level off or even decline. The other thing that is apparent in Table 7.1 is that the most common crimes committed by juveniles are shop theft and other forms of theft. Both types of crime are non-violent property offences. It should also be noted that both these crimes have tended to decline in the 1990s.

The offence of "unlawful society" which appears in Table 7.1 refers to membership in a triad society, which in Hong Kong is in itself illegal. This offence is included in Table 7.1 because recruitment into triad societies is widely viewed as a serious threat to young people. Given that there are periodic waves of public concern about the triad problem, and that it is relatively easy to arrest someone for "unlawful society," the arrest and prosecution rates for young offenders are subject to some variation (see Box 7.3). This has more to do with shifts in police policy than it does with any possible changes in triad membership. In contrast, the arrest and prosecution rates for juveniles have remained more or less constant over the years. However, these do not tell how many of these persons were placed on supervision as opposed to being prosecuted.

What does all this tell us? First, the prosecution rate for young offenders (aged 16 to 20) is typically several times that of juveniles (aged 7 to 15) and this observation holds true even when the rate is combined with the supervision rate. Second, it should also be kept in mind that because the juvenile arrest and prosecution rates started out low any increase is likely to appear as quite dramatic. Third, since 1989, when arrest figures started to be reported for individual offences, the juvenile rates for serious assault and robbery have tended to level off and in the case of serious assault actually decline. Fourth, despite

Table 7.1: Prosecution and Arrest Rates for Selected Offences per 100,000 Age Specific Population: 1976-1999

	Serious Assault		Robbery		Shop Theft		Other Theft		Unlawful Society		Total	
	7-15	16-20	7-15	16-20	7-15	16-20	7-15	16-20	7-15	16-20	7-15	16-20
Prosecution Rates:												
1976	10.4	104.6	16.6	74.6	-	-	69.1	167.6	19.5	275.5	169.9	972.7
1977	10.5	109.2	18.3	55.7	-	-	92.6	194.8	10.7	146.8	189.9	823.2
1978	22.1	130.1	11.3	56.0	-	-	83.1	195.1	9.5	95.9	186.7	761.3
1979	23.6	128.8	26.4	75.9	-	-	145.6	211.9	12.3	52.9	314.3	834.1
1980	28.3	157.1	42.9	99.8	-	-	221.7	290.4	13.2	45.4	469.9	1044.9
1981	29.9	156.8	56.0	98.9	-	-	204.2	318.9	15.6	38.2	459.9	1122.6
1982	33.2	156.5	33.2	108.9	31.2	64.0	119.5	283.0	13.8	42.1	359.4	1296.9
1983	37.6	166.4	40.9	92.7	53.6	110.0	98.4	263.4	12.5	25.3	381.9	1336.8
1984	43.7	164.1	42.8	88.6	39.6	108.6	93.7	316.4	14.4	45.3	374.2	1425.8
1985	40.1	173.0	55.4	104.6	59.4	156.3	77.3	280.0	23.5	68.4	408.0	1506.0
1986	39.3	202.0	48.4	74.7	40.8	137.7	75.4	255.0	11.3	28.9	334.7	1368.8
1987	39.4	160.2	69.5	103.3	64.3	126.9	81.9	238.3	17.8	30.2	421.4	1445.5
1988	46.4	163.3	91.8	114.7	55.1	108.3	106.9	270.9	17.3	32.4	485.0	1546.9
Arrest Rates:												
1989	58.9	180.0	127.0	169.7	330.0	153.9	249.1	348.3	26.3	43.1	962.0	1914.7
1990	52.5	136.1	96.6	171.7	220.6	164.6	182.7	350.2	26.8	50.7	849.5	1921.1
1991	59.6	152.5	127.3	185.6	228.8	144.2	201.5	321.3	31.3	61.1	928.9	1944.0
1992	52.8	138.1	121.1	176.5	215.2	160.0	186.5	332.8	34.0	59.0	871.1	1864.7
1993	66.8	170.2	102.3	213.1	225.4	221.9	206.9	366.0	28.2	66.2	891.9	2134.3
1994	82.7	166.4	89.1	190.7	256.8	256.7	216.4	392.4	35.1	68.7	942.4	2203.4
1995	90.1	189.2	52.7	141.2	284.6	245.6	184.9	367.0	29.1	78.6	897.7	2116.4
1996	102.0	168.2	44.4	102.3	281.0	228.9	164.6	297.5	28.8	58.0	860.2	1861.9
1997	91.1	165.9	34.4	67.2	268.0	185.6	151.6	273.3	27.3	45.8	799.8	1579.1
1998	86.3	159.3	42.4	74.8	268.7	158.9	139.7	252.8	25.8	46.2	782.9	1510.5
1999	83.1	166.6	40.5	86.7	217.1	162.6	147.7	266.4	28.9	59.8	730.4	1606.8

Box 7.3: When Only the Brave Are Prepared to Speak Out

Triads are preying on students and infiltrating schools, according to parents and teachers. But the authorities are anxious to dismiss such notions as exaggerated. Who is telling the truth?...

Kwok-wai, a Form One student, bumped into a gang of teenagers after school, was kicked a few times and then forced to hand over $10. He never reported the incident to the school authorities because he feared they belonged to the Sun Yee On Triad society.

It is one of many incidents that go unreported in the territory's schools and highlights a problem that principals and teachers say is growing. Triads are becoming a worrying menace in the schools which are perfect recruitment grounds, according to school authorities. But there is little they can do...

Among the principals of 11 schools interviewed...all had students claiming to be triad members. And all had reported incidents of triad intimidation during the past year.

"We can't say for sure whether the teenagers who hang around our school are really triads or not," said one school principal who asked not to be named. "They don't wear school uniforms and they don't go to work, yet they still have money to spend, what else can that be?"...

Tuen Mun is typical of the territory's bustling new towns. It also has one of the biggest juvenile populations in the territory. According to Deputy District Commander, Senior Superintendent Ian Seabourne, about 60% of the district's 330,000 population is under 16. That means two out of every three are youngsters and potential triad targets.

But according to Superintendent Seabourne, there is no evidence of triad infiltration in the schools. "There is no indication of a real effort by triads to recruit students here. I don't think the students are of any use to them. It is no use building up a gang of people who are too small to fight," he said.

But he admitted that the gangs that prey on the schools were ripe for Triad membership. "Yes, it is fair to say that these loose gangs of 17-year-olds may become triads one day. If kids think this is an easy way to earn a living and they want some money to spend, especially when most of the kids come from working class families, which make up the core of the population here, they may be attracted to it."

Pseudo-triads—as Superintendent Seabourne described the 17-year-olds hanging around outside schools or video game centers—are involved in robbery, blackmail and intimidation of a smaller scale, and petty crimes. "They may bully other kids, threaten and take money from them, using the name of triads. We are receiving more and more reports but we rarely charge them of claiming to be triads. We don't believe them. They are just gangs," he said...

Most principals blame the problem on the nine-year compulsory schooling. "Children don't have to study hard to get promoted. Life is easier for them now than it was for us...And we are not allowed to expel any bad children, unless permitted by the head of the Education Department," he said.

Another principal...blamed the remote location and age range of his school. "We are a new town. There is nothing around us, except construction sites. And the fact that we are new means we don't get the best students...And if these children are fed up with schooling because of their bad academic results, they will be easily led astray by these guys we see hanging outside of school," he said.

Superintendent Seabourne admitted that the number of complaints from schools was increasing, as were the number of juvenile crimes...

South China Morning Post, 1 April 1990, p. 13.

any possible increases, juvenile serious assault and robbery rates typically account for only 10% and 15% of the overall rate of delinquency respectively. A similar observation applies to young offenders. It is still correct to say that in most cases the juvenile delinquency involves petty property offences such as shop theft (i.e., shoplifting) and other relatively minor infractions of the law. Finally, there is a distinct possibility that even apparently serious offences such as assault and robbery may in actual fact entail relatively minor degrees of violence normally associated with bullying or intimidation in schools and playgrounds.

Increased Reporting

One source of information that avoids some of the pitfalls associated with official statistics is a series of victimization surveys that have been conducted in Hong Kong. There have been six such surveys since the first one was conducted in 1978 (Census and Statistics Department, 1979, 1982, 1987, 1990, 1995, 1999). Two things stand out from these surveys: First, the possibility that there may be an increased tendency to report crime finds clear support in the results of these surveys. The percentage of violent crime (assault and robbery) reported to the police increased steadily from 28% in 1978 to 45% in 1989, declined to 34% in 1994 and declined again in 1998 to stand at 31.3%. The reporting of household crimes (various theft offences) has shown a more consistent tendency to increase. Between 1978 and 1989 household crimes reported to the police increased from 18.7% to 24.2% and then declined slightly in 1994 and 1998 to 22% and 20% respectively (Census and Statistics Department, 1995, 1999). Second, any increased tendency to report tends to be most marked for those offences most commonly associated with juvenile or young offenders, that is, relatively minor offences involving the theft of property. Between 1978 and 1989 the percentage of "personal crimes of theft" (e.g., snatching, pickpocketing and other personal theft) reported to the police jumped from just under 10% to 41% while the figure for 1998 stood at 38%. In short, the one type of crime that juveniles are most likely to be associated with also has the highest level of increased reporting.

These surveys also lend little support for the notion that delinquency and youth crime are on in the increase in Hong Kong. In terms of crimes of violence where the victimization involved a single offender, the figures for those offenders estimated to be under the age of 21 have fluctuated between a high of 25% in 1981 to a low of 11.7% in 1998 (Census and Statistics Department, 1979, 1999). By way of contrast the 1994 Victim Survey found that 23% of the offenders were estimated to under 21 years of age (Census and Statistics Department, 1995).

Victimizations involving multiple offenders tell a somewhat different story. Since 1981, the proportion of crimes of violence involving multiple versus single offenders has fluctuated from 53% to a low of 37% in the 1998 survey. What has really changed is the proportion of personal crimes of violence victimization involving multiple offenders under the age of 21. In the 1978 and 1981 victim surveys around 24% of all personal crimes of violence involving multiple offenders were found to be committed by offenders estimated to be under 21, while in 1994 this figure had increased to 46%. In the 1998 survey this figure declined to 39%, although this change may have more to do with a change in the coverage of crime types in the 1998 survey than it does with the characteristics of the offender (Census and Statistics Department, 1979, 1982, 1995, 1999).

This apparent increase may not be as serious as it might first appear. In 1994, 85% of all violent crime and 100% of all robbery victimizations involving victims between 12 and 19 years of age were committed by multiple offenders who were all aged under 21. In the 1998 survey this figure declined but it still stood at 75% of all violent crimes and 71% of all robberies. Comparable figures for single offender victimization for 1994 and 1998 are 55% and 56% respectively. In other words, the usual situation involves a group of young offenders victimizing members of their own age group. Indeed, the data suggests that many personal crimes of violence are likely to be relatively minor affairs involving local youths extorting lunch money and similarly small sums of money from other, less aggressive youths in the area. If this is the case, a great deal of "serious" juvenile delinquency and youth crime may not be as serious as the official statistics would have us believe.

Amplification and Net-Widening

It has often been observed that diversion, or community-based programs, do not necessarily always work to keep offenders from entering the justice system. Instead such programs may actually end up extending control over persons who otherwise would not have entered the justice system. This observation especially applies to juvenile and young offenders who typically have no prior record and who have committed relatively minor offences. Whereas in the past many of these persons would have been dealt with informally and released outright, they are now likely to be placed in diversion programs simply because they are there. This phenomenon is commonly referred to as **net-widening**. There is a distinct possibility that in Hong Kong an increase in the number of youths entering the official statistics as juvenile delinquents or young offenders may well have something to do with an overall increase in the services and resources available to criminal justice agencies. If net-widening does occur it means that the juvenile offender rate is as much subject to police discretion as it is to established rules of due process.

In Hong Kong the possibility of net-widening can be clearly seen in the Superintendent's Discretion Scheme (see Gray, 1991; Chong, 2000). Police supervision has been around since 1963 when a Juvenile Liaison Section in the Police was set up to deal exclusively with the guidance of juvenile offenders. Its main goal was to supervise first offenders and improve parental control "rather than following the more drastic step of instituting criminal proceedings" (Hong Kong Government, 1964:213). During the 1980s when police supervision started to play an important role, nearly half of the juvenile offender rate (1984 to 1988) came from the use of supervision and not prosecution (see Figures 7.3 and 7.4). This pattern has continued throughout the 1990s. A policy decision in 1985 to extend police supervision to youths up to the age of 17 and include second- and third-time offenders in the scheme contributed to the significant increase in police supervision.

The fact that many offences committed by young people consist of relatively minor infractions of the law often means that they are more a matter of definition than fact, in that they are more subject to changes in police policy or the public's willingness to report crime. As evidenced in the 1981 "Fight Youth Crime" campaign, juvenile involvement in shop theft is an example of such an offence. Things started to change soon after the campaign. According to official statistics, between 1982 (when shop theft cases started to be separately reported) and 1985 the number of juvenile (aged 7 to 15) shop theft cases in which juveniles were prosecuted or placed under the Superintendent's Discretion Scheme had increased from 759 to 2,926 (95.9 to 377.3 per 100,000). By 1985, 42% of the juvenile offender rate was attributable to shop theft as compared with only 18% in 1982. Shop theft peaked in 1987 when 2,640 (342.6 per 100,000) juveniles were placed on supervision and another 498 (64.3 per 100,000) were prosecuted. During the same period similar increases were observed for young offenders (aged 16–20). Figures are lacking for the 1990s, but there is no reason to believe that this situation has changed dramatically in the following years.

Why the dramatic increase in shop theft in the 1980s? The proliferation of shopping centers and supermarkets as well as the general increase in the use of open and enticing store displays is one explanation offered by the police (Royal Hong Kong Police Force, 1987, 1988). Improved security arrangements, an increased tendency to report shop theft to the police, or even an inexplicable decline in moral standards are other possible explanations. However, none of these explanations entirely accounts for the dramatic increase in juvenile shop theft. Another possibility is that many juveniles accused of minor first offences, which includes most cases of shop theft, were being diverted into supervision instead of simply being released with a warning or not even brought to the attention of the police. If this actually occurred, the juvenile "crime wave" of the 1980s may well have been at least partly a product of the increased use of police supervision for shop theft.

Arriving at any conclusion about possible net-widening effects is extremely difficult using official statistics. Chong (2000) found that for juveniles between 1976 to 1997 the correlation between the arrest rate and the supervision rate was higher than that between arrest rate and the prosecution rate. Chong interprets this as suggesting that the increasing use of supervision has resulted in more juveniles being arrested, and that supervision was not used as an alternative to prosecution. If this interpretation is correct it would indicate that net-widening has in fact occurred in Hong Kong. In contrast, no such relationship was found for young offenders, which in turn suggests that supervision really is used to divert young offenders away from prosecution (Chong, 2000:182-183). Figure 7.3 shows that throughout the first half of the 1990s the increase in the supervision rate was accompanied by equally rapid declines in the prosecution rate. To a much lesser extent the arrest rate also declined during the same period. This does not necessarily provide evidence for net-widening but it would certainly suggest that supervision was a popular option to prosecution, and that it may have served to amplify the volume of delinquency and youth crime entering into the official statistics.

SUMMARY

Which of the three possible explanations of delinquency best fits the facts? In trying to answer this, it is worth pointing out that there are several things that make crime and delinquency in Hong Kong different from that found in many Western societies. For example, Hong Kong:

- Lacks racial or ethnic ghettos characteristic of many cities in the West.
- Is culturally and linguistically homogenous. With 96% of the population being Chinese, there are no minority groups in Hong Kong which are perceived to constitute a threat to law and order.
- Has experienced remarkable economic development which has been sufficiently widespread to preclude the development of an underclass. This has remained true even though Hong Kong's economic fortunes declined in the late 1990s as result of the Asian economic crisis that started in 1997.

These characteristics of Hong Kong society have meant that crime has not been politicized in the way it has in many Western societies. Instead, crime is normally seen to be committed by deviant individuals, not representative of oppressed and possibly dangerous racial or economic minorities. It may be for this reason that a **corporatist model** has remained in place since Hong Kong's juvenile justice system was first established. However, some of its parameters differ from those found in England and Wales (see Ch. 5). This is in part due to the possible effects of Chinese cultural values which preceded English influences.

The same is not necessarily true for delinquency. One of the most significant and clearly visible divisions in Hong Kong society is in terms of age. Throughout the 1960s and 1970s just under half of the population was under the age of 21. Since then the proportion has declined but it still stands at around 25% of the total population. As the only obvious major social division in Hong Kong society, juveniles become the focus for the community's concerns about order, stability and continuity. These concerns may be especially strong in a society that, to some degree, still adheres to a Confucian view that children should be subservient to the will of their parents and serve their needs. Quite possibly a society may place relatively higher standards of behavior on children if it believes, as Hong Kong appears to, that the maintenance of parental power is fundamental to the continued maintenance of social order.

The above refers to perceptions of juvenile delinquency. What about real changes in the volume of delinquent behavior? Throughout this chapter evidence has been provided lending support to the notion that delinquency has increased over the last three decades. However, the official statistics also indicate that the situation is probably far less serious than is widely supposed and certainly far more complex than that presented in the media or by the authorities.

First, as mentioned above, the period under study has quite literally seen the creation of childhood as a distinct phase in the individual's development, and the emergence of "young people" as a separate segment of society.

Second, economic development and urbanization in Hong Kong has meant, among other things, that there is now quite simply more time, as well as opportunity, to get into trouble. In addition there are also likely to be fewer informal family-based control mechanisms to keep the juvenile out of trouble.

Third, victim surveys also support the idea that there has been an increase in the tendency to report crime and delinquency. Whether it be the result of increased public confidence in the authorities' ability to maintain law and order, or simply the fact that the police are becoming the only alternative control mechanism available as parents progressively lose the power to control the lives of their children, the end result is more delinquent behavior coming to their attention of the authorities. (Refer to other contributions in this textbook for similar observations).

Fourth, there is good reason to believe that in most cases delinquency involves relatively minor offences. This is obviously the case for petty offences such as shop theft, but the same observation may well apply to apparently more serious offences such as assault or robbery. Fifth, this chapter has suggested that there is good reason to believe that an expansion of diversionary programs has contributed to recent increases in the official rates of delinquency. It is entirely possible that an increasing number of juveniles are being introduced into the juvenile justice system who previously either would have been merely released with a warning or would not have come into contact with the system in the first place.

Finally, it should be noted that the creation of a juvenile justice system preceded by several decades any widespread concern that juvenile delinquency might pose a threat to adult society. Such things as net-widening and **deviance amplification** appears to have contributed to increases in the delinquency rate, but it is also obvious that any such effects do not automatically come into play. Instead the juvenile justice system only began to be utilized when certain social and economic conditions occurred that changed public and official perception of the position that young people occupy in society. Once again this is in line with the idea that there has been a decline in informal control mechanisms.

What about the future of juvenile justice in Hong Kong? At first glance it seems as if it was in for some major changes, given that on 1 July 1997, the People's Republic of China resumed sovereignty over Hong Kong. However, contrary to what one might expect (see Gitting and Chan, 1996) this did not produce any significant changes in juvenile justice in Hong Kong. First, while Hong Kong is unquestionably an inalienable part of the People's Republic of China, it is also a special administrative region (SAR) within China. As a SAR, Hong Kong continues to enjoy a high degree of autonomy. The only exception to this is in the areas of foreign affairs and defence. The various policies governing the transference of the territory are stipulated in the Sino-British Joint Declaration and in the Hong Kong Basic Law. Among other things, these two documents provide that the existing judicial system and all laws previously in force in Hong Kong shall be maintained for 50 years after China resumed sovereignty over Hong Kong. If all goes as planned the juvenile justice system of Hong Kong should continue to be firmly based on the rule of law and currently existing policies of treatment and rehabilitation.

Second, it should also be kept in mind that, in terms of basic principles of juvenile justice, the People's Republic of China (see Chapter 4) and the Hong Kong SAR share many things in common. In fact, there are more similarities than there are differences. Both systems emphasize treatment over punishment and both go to great lengths to see that children and young offenders avoid entry into the adult criminal justice system. Consequently, what the future has in store for the juvenile justice system in Hong Kong is more likely to be continuity rather than dramatic change.

Harold Traver is an associate professor in the Department of Sociology at the University of Hong Kong. He received his Ph.D. from the University of California at Santa Barbara and has taught in the University of Hong Kong since 1971. He has a long-standing interest in criminology and criminal justice studies. Among others things, he was responsible for establishing the department's master of social science (M.Soc.Sc.) degree program in criminology, and developing of the diploma in criminal justice offered by the School of Professional and Continuing Education at the University of Hong Kong. Most recently, he has directed the development of the bachelor of criminal justice degree program that is jointly offered by the School of Professional and Continuing Education and the Department of Sociology, and has played an active role in the establishment of the Centre for Criminology in the University of Hong Kong. His research interests include the study of crime trends, drug abuse, policing, and juvenile delinquency in Hong Kong. He has published extensively on these topics.

HELPFUL WEBSITES
www.info.gov.hk/police/ Hong Kong Police Force.
www.info.gov.hk/police/cpb/english/ Crime Prevention Bureau, Hong Kong Police Force.
www.hku.hk/crime/ Centre for Criminology, University of Hong Kong.
www.icac.org.hk/ Independent Commission against Corruption.
www.info.gov.hk/nd/beat/3.htm Narcotics Division, Hong Kong Government Secretariat.
www.hkfyg.org.hk/ Hong Kong Federation of Youth Groups.
www.hkfyg.org.hk/yrc/chinese/yr-jys1-2-abs.html Journal of Youth Studies in Chinese with English abstracts.
www.info.gov.hk/swd/html_eng/index.html Social Welfare Department.

KEY TERMS AND CONCEPTS

Net-widening	Corporatist Model
Filial piety	Triads
ah fei	Reservoir theory
Deviance Amplification	Confucian society

STUDY QUESTIONS
1. What factors contributed to the development of Hong Kong's juvenile justice system? Are any of these contributing factors different from those found in Western societies?

2. What role, if any, does culture play in contributing to our conception of juvenile delinquency as a social problem? When answering this refer to Hong Kong and Chinese cultural norms.
3. Based on the Hong Kong experience, in what way have such things as economic development and urbanization contributed to the emergence of juvenile delinquency as a social problem?
4. Assuming that "net-widening" is becoming an increasingly common feature of juvenile justice in Hong Kong, what implications does this have for the future of juvenile delinquency in Hong Kong?
5. Discuss the difficulties involved in proving that there has been a "real" or "absolute" change in the delinquency rate.
6. What factors contributed to the emergence of young people and youthful misbehavior as social problems in Hong Kong?
7. What are the characteristic features of Hong Kong's conception of delinquency? Are these any different from those found in many Western societies?

REFERENCES

Allison, M., & Giller, H. (Eds.). (1983). *Providing criminal justice for children.* London: Arnold.

Census and Statistics Department. (1979). *Crime and its victims in Hong Kong 1978.* Hong Kong: Government Printer.

Census and Statistics Department. (1982). *Crime and its victims in Hong Kong 1981.* Hong Kong: Government Printer.

Census and Statistics Department. (1987). *Crime and its victims in Hong Kong 1986.* Hong Kong: Government Printer.

Census and Statistics Department. (1990). *Crime and its victims in Hong Kong 1989.* Hong Kong: Government Printer.

Census and Statistics Department. (1995). *Crime and its victims in Hong Kong 1994.* Hong Kong: Government Printer.

Census and Statistics Department. (1999). *Crime and its victims in Hong Kong 1998.* Hong Kong: Government Printer.

Chan, Q. (1996, Oct. 16). Hong Kong to sign child custody treaty. *South China Morning Post. (Online).*

Chong, Wai Kei. (2000). *The Police Cautioning Diversion Scheme: Participant observation of post-caution visits in Hong Kong.* Hong Kong: Master of philosophy thesis, Department of Sociology, University of Hong Kong.

Chow, W.S.N. (1987). *A comparison of delinquent youth and non-delinquent youth on the aspects parental supervision and schooling: A follow-up study on unruly youth in Tsuen Wan, Kwai Chung and Tsing Yi.* Hong Kong: Kwai Chung and Tsing Yi District Board.

Ch'u, T.S. (1965). *Law and society in traditional China.* Paris: Mouton and Company.

Cohen, J., Edwards, R.R., & Chen, F.M.C. (Eds.). (1980). *Essays in China's legal tradition.* Princeton, NJ: Princeton University Press.

Cohen, S. (1985). *Visions of control: Crime, punishment and classification.* New Brunswick, NJ: Transaction Books.

Ferdinand, T.N. (1989). Juvenile delinquency or juvenile justice: Which came first? *Criminology,* 27 (1), 79–106.

Fight Crime Committee. (1981). *Report of the working group on juvenile crime.* Hong Kong: Government Printer.

Fight Violent Crime Committee. (1973). *Interim progress report by the sub-committee on the social causes of crime.* Hong Kong: Government Printer.

Gitting, D.G., & Chan, Q. (1996, Oct. 2). Crime bill dropped in handover rush. *South China Morning Post.* (Online).

Gray, P. (1991). Juvenile crime and disciplinary welfare. In H. Traver & J. Vagg (Eds.), *Crime and justice in Hong Kong* (pp. 25–41). Hong Kong: Oxford University Press.

Hagan, J., & Leon, J. (1977). Rediscovering delinquency: Social history, political ideology and the sociology of law. *American Sociological Review,* 42 (4), 587–598.

Hong Kong Council of Social Service. (1981). *Report on the prevention of delinquency by the ad hoc working group on the prevention of juvenile delinquency.* Hong Kong: Hong Kong Council of Social Service.

Hong Kong Government. (1961). *Hong Kong report for 1960.* Hong Kong: Government Printer.

Hong Kong Government. (1962). *Hong Kong report for 1961.* Hong Kong: Government Printer.

Hong Kong Government. (1964). *Hong Kong report for 1963.* Hong Kong: Government Printer.

Hong Kong Government. (1965). *Report to governor in council by working party on the adequacy of the law in relation to crimes of violence committed by young persons.* Hong Kong: Government Printer.

Jensen, G.F., & Dean, G.R. (1992). *Delinquency and youth crime* (2nd ed.). Prospect Heights, IL: Waveland Press.

Kuan, H.C., Lau, S.K., & Wan, P.S. (1991). Legal attitudes. In S.K. Lau, M.K. Lee, P.S. Wan, & S.L. Wong (Eds.), *Indicators of social development: Hong Kong 1988* (pp. 207–223). Hong Kong: Hong Kong Institute of Asian-Pacific Studies, the Chinese University of Hong Kong.

Lau, S.K., & Kuan, H.C. (1988). *The ethos of the Hong Kong Chinese.* Hong Kong: the Chinese University Press.

Lau, S.K., & Wan, P.S. (1991). Attitudes towards social problems. In S.K. Lau, M.K. Lee, P.S. Wan & S.L. Wong (Eds.), *Indicators of development: Hong Kong 1988* (pp. 25–40). Hong Kong: Hong Kong Institute of Asia-Pacific Studies, the Chinese University of Hong Kong.

Law, C.K. (1986). *A study on the behaviours and attitudes of youths in Kwun Tong.* Hong Kong: Working Group on Problem Youth, Kwun Tong District Board.

Leung, E.O.E., & Sihombing, J.E. (1999). The law relating to children. In M.M. Tsoi & N.A. Pryde (Eds.). *Hong Kong's children: Our past, their future.* Hong Kong: Centre of Asia Studies, University of Hong Kong.

Lui, W.C. (1972). *Confucius: His life and time.* New York: Philosophical Library.

Lyall, L. (1925). *The sayings of Confucius.* London: Longmans, Green and Company.

Narcotics Division. (1988). Survey of abuse of psychotropic substances among students in secondary schools and technical institutes. Hong Kong: Narcotics Division, Government Secretariat Hong Kong Government.

Narcotics Division. (1991). Survey of abuse of psychotropic substances among students in secondary schools and technical institutes. Hong Kong: Narcotics Division, Government Secretariat Hong Kong Government.

234

Narcotics Division. (1993). Survey of abuse of psychotropic substances among students in secondary schools and technical institutes. Hong Kong: Narcotics Division, Government Secretariat Hong Kong Government.

Narcotics Division. (1997). 1996 Survey on drug use among students in secondary schools and technical institutes: Executive summary. Hong Kong: Narcotics Division, Government Secretariat, Hong Kong Government.

Ng, A. (1975). *Social causes of violent crimes among young offenders in Hong Kong.* Hong Kong: Social Research Centre, the Chinese University of Hong Kong.

Royal Hong Kong Police Force. (1987). *Annual review 1987.* Hong Kong: Government Printer.

Royal Hong Kong Police Force. (1988). *Annual review 1988.* Hong Kong: Government Printer.

Social Welfare Department. (1961). *Annual departmental report, 1960/61.* Hong Kong: Government Printer.

Social Welfare Department. (1991). *Annual department report by the director of social welfare for the financial year 1990–91.* Hong Kong: Government Printer.

South China Morning Post. (1997, September 11). Focus on triad influence in schools, p. 10.

South China Morning Post. (1998, February 23). Triads top teen threat list, p. 12.

South China Morning Post. (2000, October 28). Kids on curfew, p. 15.

Sutherland, E.H., & Cressey, D.R. (1966). *Principles of criminology.* New York: J.B. Lippincott Company.

Sutton, J.R. (1988). *Stubborn children: Controlling delinquency in the United States, 1640–1981.* Berkeley: University of California Press.

Wilkins, L.T. (1965). *Social deviance.* Englewood Cliffs, NJ: Prentice-Hall.

Chapter 8

Comparative Juvenile Justice: An Overview of Hungary

Mária Herczog
National Institute of Criminology
Ferenc Irk
National Institute of Criminology
Budapest, Hungary

FACTS ABOUT HUNGARY

Area: Located in the center of Europe, in its eastern part. The country covers 93,030 sq. km. The area is referred to as the Carpathian Basin. The capital is Budapest (pop. 2 million). **Population**: Hungary is a republic with 10,043,000 inhabitants in 1999 (109 persons per sq. km.). Age breakdown: 17.1% people aged 1 to 14, 63.2% aged 15 to 59, and 19.7% in the age group 60 or older. Hungary is experiencing a rapidly aging population and a decline in child-births. Population growth rate is –0.5. Life expectancy for men is 66.32 and for women 75.13.[1] The majority of the population is atheist. While most of the religious population is Roman Catholic, with large numbers of Protestants and Jews, there are no precise figures available as the census does not contain reference to religious conviction. The number of people belonging to ethnic minorities is also estimated. The principal minorities are Croat, German, Greek, Romanian, Serb, Slovak, and Slovenian. The Hungarian language can trace its origin back to the Finnougric group of languages. **Climate**: Hungary has a continental climate with Mediterranean and Atlantic influences. Average temperature in January is –2° C and 23° C in July. **Government**: In 1990 the former single-party, Soviet-type communist system, termed a people's republic, was replaced by a freely elected multi-party parliament which consists of six political parties. A conservative coalition government emerged in the 1998 elections, replacing the former socialist-liberal one. The parliament has a single chamber with a powerful government and a less dominant president of the republic. The Constitutional Court has a major role in ensuring checks and balances of the branches of power.

In Hungary the trends in delinquency have been turning unfavorable over the past decade. This can be illustrated with the following:

- *In the last 25 years the number of criminal offences has increased fourfold, and between 1988 and 1991 the number of offences doubled. Between 1995 and 1999 there was a 10% increase;*

- *Offences against property represented two-thirds of all cases in 1988, a little more than half in 1995, and 48.3% in 1999;*
- *The most significant change occurred between 1989 and 1992, but there is a growing fear that because of rapid and not readily "absorbed" changes, another crime wave may come within ten years;*
- *In 1990, 8.7% of all offenders were 14- to 18-years-old. In 1995 this number had decreased to 8.4% but increased slightly in 1999 (8.7%), indicating that the proportion of young persons has not changed. It is a much higher number if we include young adults aged 18 to 21, too; and*
- *Since 1987 the means of investigating cases have not kept abreast with the increase in crime. In 1999 less than 60% of all reported cases were investigated.*

The National Crime Prevention Program, 2000.

THE STATE OF JUVENILE DELINQUENCY IN HUNGARY

Even as we enter a new century, the general public in Hungary does not generally believe juvenile delinquency is related to young offenders' social and cultural background, their lack of family care, or their academic ability. Even professional public opinion continues to be divided. These facts combined with a lack of research, programs, and policy evaluation tend to promote emotionally based debates. However, such debates are not common in Hungary. Media attention is limited primarily to crimes, which have a news value, rather than focused on possible solutions, prevention, or professional responsibility. In cases involving brutal criminal offences by young persons—such as a taxi driver's killing or the murder of an 11-year-old child by her classmates (see Box 8.1) —the public is not interested in the complete history and background. Instead, it blames the parents exclusively and wants long-term lock-up, without knowing the possible influence and outcome of such actions.

This apparent lack of concern for juvenile crime and its correlates is reflected in the statistics. In 1999, 11,540 young individuals were accused of having committed offences. Of those, 35.2% (4,906) had their cases dismissed for various reasons. Due more to a lack of adequate resources than a rational model of juvenile justice, an overwhelming majority of juvenile delinquents (4,701 or 88.8%) are released on probation. In 1999, 191 (3.6%) of young offenders were sentenced to a term in a reformatory institute, while those who had committed more serious crimes (2,601 or 29.6%) were given juvenile prison terms. However, due to the lack of resources, 1,493 had their sentence suspended. The majority of juvenile crimes, however, are property-related offences (73.4% of all recorded juvenile offences in 1999). The rest are crimes against public order (15.7% in 1999), against individuals (4.9% in 1999) and traffic crimes (2.1% in 1999). And although representing a comparatively small per-

---

Box 8.1: Youth Violence and Accountability

Recently some killings committed by young persons raised the question of age limits again. Two children, a 14-year-old girl and a 12-year-old boy, murdered their 11-year-old girl classmate in a school for children with special needs. The question in Hungary is not about the possible ways of repairing the harm or helping these children to learn; rather, the intent is to punish them without questioning the effectiveness or the proper method of punishment. Comparisons were made to the Jamie Bulger case in England (see Chapter 5), and the lengthy punishment the offenders received. A couple of months earlier two girls (14 and 15 years old) beat a taxi-driver to death to rob his car. It is clear from the investigation that the girls had offered sexual services to him before they all went to a forest near Budapest where the girls killed the driver. The girls were sentenced to nine to ten years of imprisonment in a prison for adult women, and no one asks whether it would do them any good.

---

centage, there has been a growing number of serious crimes, gang-related crimes, and crimes involving adults contributing to the delinquency of a juvenile. A rapidly growing problem is drug-related crime (3.1% in 1999 compared with 0.12% in 1995).

Since the political change-over in 1990, there has been a sharp increase in the number of juvenile delinquents. This appears to be due to a number of factors, in particular the hiatuses of a structurally and professionally outdated child and juvenile protection system. As reflected in Table 8.1, juvenile and adult crime rates increased between 1975 and 1992, when we witnessed a small decline in the total number of juvenile offences. The recent decrease is partially attributable to the drop in the number of youth. Other explanations for the changing numbers include: the opening up of borders, an unexpected gap between living standards and potentials, and increasing unemployment rates. Finally, it has also been suggested that a lower level of efficiency of police detection and apprehension resulting from the fiscal restraints that arose during the transformation may also partially account for the recent drop in juvenile crime numbers.

As a result of the growing number of crimes committed by children and young juveniles, a growing number of people have demanded that the age limit of culpability (i.e., 14) should be decreased. Fortunately, however, their voice is not very strong. As for the administration of juvenile justice, because of limited resources and qualified manpower, and a lack of concrete objectives, there has been little effort put forth to lower the age limit, let alone adequately address the growing delinquency problem.

Contrary to point 1.1 in the 1984 Beijing Rules (see Box 1—Introduction), there has been no special attention paid to the juvenile delinquency problem.

Table 8.1: Adult and Youth Crime: 1975-1999.		
Year	Total No. of Adult Crimes	Total No. of Juvenile Crimes
1975	72,049	7,268
1980	72,881	6,535
1985	85,766	9,449
1990	112,254	12,848
1991	122,835	14,307
1992	132,644	15,476
1993	122,621	15,001
1994	119,494	14,479
1995	121,121	14,321
1996	122,221	13,544
1997	130,966	13,955
1998	130,966	12,866
1999	131,658	11,540

Source: Statistical yearbook, 2000.

In fact, no major development has taken place since the beginning of the twentieth century, which at the time was highly progressive even by international standards. Very few of the rules laid down in international and United Nations agreements have actually been observed.

Prevention, probation, and follow-up care are in a critical situation. The number of so-called "social patrons" (supportive lay adults) has dropped drastically while that of "official patrons" (helping professionals) has not increased sufficiently. And even though relevant professional training was started in 1994 within the framework of fulltime and postgraduate training for social workers, the results of these programs may not be felt for some time in the juvenile justice system.

In essence, the recent history of juvenile justice in Hungary has not been a promising one. Along with the major social and political changes came a lack of attention to prevention and social work with the families of problem youth, who have become victims of the changes (see Box 8.2).

Social and Legal Definition of Delinquency

The current Hungarian Penal Code was adopted by Parliament in 1978. It has been amended several times, particularly after the political changeover in 1989/1990. According to the Penal Code, "a crime is a voluntary or involuntary act (in cases where the latter is penalized by law) which is dangerous for society and which by law involve a punishment" (Paragraph 1 of Article 10). An act is dangerous for society if it endangers the state, the social or eco-

---

Box 8.2: Delinquent's as Victims of Change

A group of teenagers in Gyor, a Hungarian city near the Austrian border, regularly blackmailed and robbed school-aged children, took their money, stole their jackets and sport shoes, and even took lunch boxes. These incidents occurred over several months during the early 1990s. The children had to pay "protection money." If they failed to do so, the youngsters were often beaten. The victimized children were too afraid to come forward and tell their parents or teachers. The team leader of the youth "gang" was less than 14 years of age and all other members of the group were between 15 and 17. After finally being detected, all the youths were apprehended and placed in custody.

---

nomic order of the Republic of Hungary, and threatens, or infringes upon, the rights of citizens.

Unlike many Western countries, Hungary does not have a separate act for juvenile offenders. Instead, special provisions for juveniles are described in Chapter VII of the Penal Code. Having a separate act for juvenile delinquents would imply making a sharp distinction between adults and youngsters. To do so would make it possible to honor all the legal obligations stipulated and acknowledged under the international regulations (e.g., Beijing Rules). To undertake such changes would, at least, help to clarify how to handle youths under the age of 14, what kinds of preventive and care activities should be taken, and by whom and how. In addition, guidelines for the handling of young adults (ages 18 to 21) could be more clearly defined. Alternatively, however, handling the problems of adults and juveniles together could help spur reforms and enlarge the role of alternative sanctions. A notable lack of separation means that in Hungary both adults and juveniles are treated the same under our Penal Code even though young offenders need a "milder" approach.

In accordance with the relevant provisions in Article 107, a juvenile is a delinquent who is at least 14 years of age but has not reached 18 when committing a crime. A juvenile delinquent may be subject to punishment or to other legal measures as defined within the Penal Code. The primary intent of both forms of sanctions is correction. As stipulated under Article 108, prison sentences can be imposed only in cases where the intent of the punishment or measures cannot be realized in another way. However, under Article 109 a term in a correctional institution can be imposed. Penal substantive law contains a number of other alleviating provisions in the case of juvenile delinquents. For instance:

- The longest term of confinement for a juvenile who is 16 or over when committing an offence is 15 years, in the case of crimes that could involve life imprisonment if committed by an adult; and 10 years in the case of crimes that involve imprisonment of adults for longer than 10 years (Article 110);

- A juvenile who is not yet 16 when committing an offence can be sentenced to a maximum of 10 years in the case of crime that can involve life imprisonment for an adult;
- All juvenile sentences must be served in a juvenile penitentiary institution (Article 111);
- Juvenile delinquents may be sentenced to pay a fine only if they have an income or possess the appropriate funds (Article 114);
- In connection with banishment, Article 116 prescribes that a juvenile who lives in an appropriate family may not be banned from the town/village in which his or her family resides;
- Limiting provisions of probation do not apply to juvenile delinquents. Probation is possible irrespective of the offence committed (Article 117);
- The court may rule that the juvenile delinquent be sent to a reformatory institution when it is believed necessary in the interests of the juvenile's corrective education. Such a ruling may prescribe a term of one to three years. In cases where the term is longer than one year, it is possible for the court to temporarily release the juvenile delinquent (Article 118);
- Juvenile delinquents who receive a suspended sentence can be placed on either probation or parole, or be temporarily released from a reformatory institution (Article 119);
- The entire duration of the pre-trial confinement should count towards the term in the reformatory institution. Consequently, each day of pre-trial confinement reduces the stay in the reformatory by one day (Article 120/B); and
- A juvenile delinquent will be exempted from the disadvantages attached to a criminal record earlier than an adult. Such a measure should be imposed only if the sentence is less serious than in the case of an adult (Article 121).

The provisions are grounded in the **neo-classical school** of criminological thought, which provides for judicial discretion, minimum and maximum sentences, as well as the principle of extenuating circumstances. The model of justice, in accordance with Figure 1 of the Introduction, could best be described as a **crime control model**. These are only assumptions, as there have not been any research or surveys conducted on the subject. However, based on media coverage and public opinion polls, it would appear that both the media and public would like to see more serious punishment and prison sentences administered against juveniles.

The prevention versus punishment dilemma is a very difficult one, as prevention seems to represent an **insecure investment** with its exact costs and effectiveness unknown. In 1996 the Institute for Criminology began an evaluation project designed to assess the cost and effectiveness of prevention and punishment programs for juvenile delinquents in Hungary.

EVOLUTION OF JUVENILE JUSTICE IN HUNGARY

The two most significant documents in nineteenth century Hungarian penal law were the 1843 penal bills and the so-called **Csemegi Code** of 1878, the first Hungarian Penal Code. Neither, however, provided for the criminal liability of juvenile delinquents, as they both reflected the "classical school." Nevertheless, there are records showing that the necessity of different regulations for juvenile delinquents was raised in the committee preparing the 1843 bill on prisons, and a provision was put forth to introduce reformatory schools.

Following the German pattern, the Csemegi Code regarded juvenile delinquents as "little adults" and did not provide for criminal liability differently. However, it still contained formulations that could serve as the basis for less severe sentences in cases of 12- to 16-year-old delinquents.

Legislative Act No. XXXVI, known as the "First Penal Novel," or first penal code (1908), was enacted in the wake of criticism—a change of attitude as a result of increased juvenile delinquent activities. For the first time the criminal liability of juvenile delinquents was handled differently. This was also the first law to introduce the practice of suspended sentences. According to the preamble of the legislative act showing Dutch, Belgian, and American influence, "...it is not restoration but protection and education that should be the guiding principle when facing child and juvenile delinquents" (Lévai, 1994).

The age of juvenile status was determined as between 12 and 18 years. No procedure could be initiated against delinquents younger than 12, although "house discipline" (e.g., incarceration at school) was permitted. The "ability of discretion" was replaced by "intellectual and moral development." Although its range remained undefined, the opportunity to exercise some discretion in sentencing helped the judge. Instead of relying only on short-term imprisonment measures that were the most expedient and suited the character of the young delinquent, judges were now able to make judgements in accordance with the principle of individualization. The maximum term of reformatory confinement was not specified, but it could not extend beyond the delinquent's 21st year of age.

Juvenile delinquents' courts were set up and regulated by Legislative Act No. VII of 1913. The spirit of this act, which was essentially an amendment to the Penal Novel, already reflected the awareness of the relationship between child protection and criminality. In this way delinquents' courts did more than perform mere judicial tasks, and they were the first European courts to involve patrons and patronage associations. On the other hand, the spirit of the law could not always be realized due to the lack of institutional systems for the handling and protection of young offenders.

During the short-lived, 133-day Commune in 1919, the Communists in power regarded juvenile delinquency as a product of capitalism (see Chapter 14 on Russia) and did not consider it justified to penalize young delinquents. Active child protection was proposed based on constructive school programs and education, and topped by a system of judicial child protection (i.e., a **welfare** model), which aimed at solving problems through juvenile education. According to Decree No. LWWII, "...after the necessary temporary measures, children and young people should be passed on to the general health care and educational child protection institutions..."

A fundamental change during the period between the two World Wars was the restoration of the First Penal Novel that had been in force prior to the Commune. It remained in force through 1948 with only minor amendments. Then, after a few basic changes in 1950 and 1951, the 1952 Law Decree No. 34 provided for penal law and penal procedures pertaining to juvenile delinquents. It was based on the principle that, although education is the focus of juvenile penal law, it was still essentially penal law. The age of juvenile status remained 12 to 18 years of age, while the old term "intellectual and moral development" was replaced by the following provision: if, owing to an underdeveloped intellect, the juvenile could not fully recognize the fact that his or her act was dangerous for society, then investigation could be refused, procedure terminated, and exemption could ensue.

Legislative Act No. 23 of 1953 divided juveniles into two groups; those aged 12 to 14 and those aged 14 to 18. The only forms of punishment applicable to the younger age group were admonishment, probation, reformatory education, and special education—a **welfare approach**. Special education as a sanction was a new feature and was applied to mentally handicapped individuals who were unfit for correctional education. As for those aged 14 to 18, the main rule stipulated penalization—a crime control approach. Educational measures could be applied only as a supplement. The shortest term of imprisonment was 30 days and the maximum length five years. In exceptional cases a longer sentence was allowed and even capital punishment was possible. Juvenile courts fell within the structure of the judiciary. The minister of justice appointed the special judges and the court officials. The two lay assessors in the juvenile court included a member from the women's movement and a member from the teacher's trade union.

Legislative Act No. 38 of 1957 relegated social policy decisions to the authorities of local administration. To date this has settled the distribution of tasks: child and juvenile protection and juvenile crime prevention are the duty of the local system while the judiciary controls subsequent intervention.

Act V of 1961, the so-called first socialist Penal Code, did away with the relative autonomy of juvenile delinquents' criminal liability. Provisions that had formerly been codified in a separate decree were included in Chapter VI of the new act. This chapter dealt with juvenile delinquency. The act abolished capital punishment and put correctional education in the focus—a principle set forth under the Beijing Rules. It set the maximum term of confinement at 10 years and created better chances for reintegration into society by the institution of exemption. The act represented a shift away from crime control to a more **participatory/welfare** model (see Figure 1—Introduction).

In response to the inefficiency of juvenile protection inspectors, the minister of education issued a decree in 1970 that created positions for professional probation officers. And while the use of social patrons has not disappeared completely over the past 20 years, the number of probation officers has slowly been increasing. While there were 219 probation officers in 1994, there are no nationwide statistics as to the number of social patrons. But in 1994 there were 13,393 young people seeing probation officers, compared to 2,056 under the care of social patrons.

Preparation of Bill VI of 1978, the Penal Code, commenced in the early 1970s. By then a mass of new research information had accumulated and criminology had emerged as an area of study in Hungary. Heads of the justice administration, however, did not intend to change the concept or details of earlier regulations, and all codifying committees were of the opinion that the criminal liability of juvenile delinquents should be considered as criminal liability in the strictest sense. Consequently, the new act contained only minor changes, the most important being the abolition of remedial education as a separate category of measures. For example, Article 37 of the Penal Code stipulates the objective of penalization for all delinquents is "…with a view to the protection of society, preventing the perpetrator or other persons from committing another offence."

In spite of repeated 'tinkering' with the legislation, it did not provide the solution to countering the ravages of the economic and political chaos that dominated Hungary during the late 1980s and into the 1990s. For example, in 1994 there were 1,069 instances of fighting and rioting and 535 robberies. With the exception of public disorder offences, the number of these offences has been nearly the same since 1988 (see Table 8.2). In 1995 spiralling juvenile delinquency rates, combined with the failures of a cumbersome judiciary, helped to bring about changes through the passing of Act XLI. The act also represents an attempt to align Hungarian standards of juvenile justice with those of its European neighbors. Some of the key elements include:

- Imprisonment of a delinquent young person is only allowed if the objective of punishment cannot be reached in any other way.
- The term of confinement to a reformatory institution is no longer indefinite, and the duration of pre-trial confinement should be considered as part thereof.
- Pre-trial confinement beyond the basic conditions stipulated by law can only be justified by the extreme severity of the offence.
- Juvenile delinquents should preferably be confined to a reformatory institution prior to their trial.
- In cases involving imprisonment of less than five years the prosecutor may suspend prosecution for a probation period of one to two years in order to give the juvenile delinquent the chance to develop in the right direction.

These measures represent another (legal) step towards embracing a more **paternal/welfare** model of juvenile justice in Hungary. In practice however, as we will see in the next section, the intent of the provisions has not been actualized.

ROLE OF THE KEY ACTORS IN THE ADMINISTRATION OF JUVENILE JUSTICE

Although there is a broad social safety net for juvenile offenders in Hungary, ranging from social workers to community work and alternatives to punishment, it plays a marginal role. This is largely due to the former ideological and political practice, the lack of professional debates, a weak sense of advocacy on the part of the delinquents and their helpers, and the lack of research and evaluation on the outcomes of various ways of dealing with juvenile offenders. In fact, only a very limited circle in Hungary knows foreign trends and practices. The entire field is not a prime subject of research and publication.

Mediation and restorative justice have only been recognized by a few academics in Hungary. In October of 1999 Paul McCold and Ted Wachtel of the United States ran the first training course. Since then, in one of the detention centers for boys at Aszod, newly sentenced younger offenders are asked to write a letter to their victim—if they wish—and there is an opportunity for them to send it. They may even take part in a conference, meeting their victim(s) and the victim's supporters. Two law faculties are introducing a special course on mediation and restorative practices such as those used by the Police Academy in Budapest starting in 2001.

When a young offender comes to the attention of the police, their actions are regulated by the Penal Code. Criminal and procedural matters were discussed above. Criminal procedures are provided for by the much-amended Act I of 1973. Specifically, Chapter XIII described the most important differences between how juveniles and adults are treated. Some of the key aspects include:

- The rules of criminal procedure against juvenile delinquents are still applicable for a person of juvenile age who has acquired adult status by marriage or has turned 18 after committing a delinquency.
- Provisions of Chapter XIII do not apply for those who committed the offence shortly before and shortly after reaching 18 years of age (Article 292).
- A juvenile delinquent cannot be forced to pay a fine without a trial.
- A juvenile prosecutor appointed by the supervisory prosecutor should undertake prosecution. The juvenile prosecutor is obliged to be involved in all the phases of the trial. A juvenile delinquent cannot be subject to (private) accusation (Article 295).
- In the case of trials for first- and second-time offenders (with the exception of trial by the Supreme Court) the court is appointed by the minister of justice and acts as a juvenile court. One of the lay assessors for first-time offenders should be a teacher (Article 296).
- A defence attorney is obliged to participate in procedures against juvenile delinquents (Article 298).
- The juvenile delinquent's guardian should be summoned as a witness so that the character, the level of intellectual development, and general background of the juvenile can be better revealed (Article 301).
- Pre-trial confinement of a juvenile delinquent is justified only in exceptional cases. Juvenile delinquents should be separated from adults during such confinement (Article 302). This is an open process where the media and the public are allowed to attend juvenile proceedings unless the court (i.e., judge) rules otherwise.
- The court may pass a sentence to confine the juvenile delinquent to a reformatory institution. The sentence, however, does not stipulate that the delinquent is guilty (Article 305).

For criminal procedures the interior minister's precept regarding investigation (Precept No. 40 of 1987 of the interior minister) is followed. Some of key procedural elements include:

- In Hungary culpability begins at age 14. Those 18 years of age and over are culpable as adults, not juveniles.
- Penal law considers those under 14 to be children. The status of child excludes criminal liability; therefore in such instances investigation should be denied or stopped and the local authority should be notified so that it can initiate protective measures.
- Rules pertaining to juvenile delinquents are applicable to suspects who have married or reached 18 years of age after committing a delinquency.
- If the juvenile delinquent has no defence attorney the police are obliged to call one in and ensure that the defence attorney be present at the first hearing.
- During the procedure the juvenile's legal representative (usually the parent) has the right to speak on behalf of the youth. In cases where the legal representative should be excluded from speaking on behalf of the youth (e.g., when the representative is deemed an unsuitable parent, or has a criminal record), the investigative authority should appoint a case guardian through the local guardianship authority.
- In juvenile criminal procedures the suspect's age, character, intellectual development, and living conditions are significant subjects of evidence.

To this end:
- The child's custodian should testify as to the conditions of the child's upbringing. No such testimony can be refused.
- A case survey should be prepared which provides a truthful picture of the juvenile's character and living conditions.
- Reports should be requested from the school and the employer.
- In case there is an indication or antecedence of mental disorder, the expert opinion of a psychologist or special education teacher should be obtained.
- The legal representative of the juvenile delinquent and, if needed, a psychologist or another expert, may be present at the hearing.
- In case the juvenile suspect is seriously endangered the juvenile should be taken temporarily to a state child and juvenile protection institution.
- In the event of confinement, the family or legal representative should be separated from adult criminals.
- A child, or juvenile person, who is found loitering should be taken to the nearest police station if their home is not closer or if they can not be handed over to their legal guardian.

- In case the criminal procedure against a juvenile delinquent reveals an infringement in connection with the youth's education, employment, or other relevant activity, the relevant authority should be notified in accordance with Article 117 of the relevant decree of the interior minister.
- Upon release from a prison or reformatory institute, the offender is entitled by decree to support.

Collectively, the above points embrace some of the fundamental **corporatist** views, especially with reference to their general features, tasks, and objectives. This is partially due to financial constraints as evidenced by the lack of sufficient staff, automobiles, and time to address the caseloads. In addition, the rules are not taken seriously and the delinquents and their families are seldom aware of their rights. Therefore, only in a few cases are the regulations followed. This is possible since there is no monitoring system or regular supervision. Even in the known and reported cases the general response is: "theoretically it is alright, but the circumstances are inadequate to meet the standards." Consequently, our system functions perhaps as a crime control model more out of necessity than by design.

The Actors
As can be seen from the above description, the intent of the Ministry of Justice and the Ministry of the Interior is not only to hold juveniles accountable for their action but to provide special support. To this end there are literally hundreds of associations and foundations lawfully registered to address these needs. Unfortunately, these intentions remain unfulfilled. Nevertheless, it can be argued that the Hungarian judiciary system essentially conforms with the minimum standards stipulated by the Beijing Rules. In particular, the relevant laws in force provide for the special treatment of juvenile delinquents in terms of material, procedural, and punitive respects. However, on the basis of Hungarian legal material, legal application and correctional practices, it can be said that our penal judiciary system is an attenuated variation of the same system relating to adult offenders. In practice the juvenile system does not represent a separate system as is characterized by other modern social states (Lévai, 1994) (see Figure 8.1 for a graphic illustration of the Hungarian juvenile justice system).

As noted above, the law provides that juveniles be treated differently from adults when being investigated by the police. Unfortunately, police investigations very often do not observe the rules relating to the notification and presence of the legal representative or the guardian or the involvement of

Figure 8.1

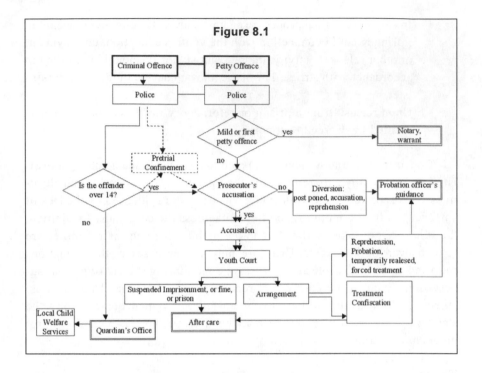

a defence attorney. In fact, there is often no real connection between the social protection system and the investigators and procedure officers during the investigation and the criminal procedure. Therefore, contrary to the stated objectives, juveniles seldom have a chance to obtain professional help. Even the probation officer, who should be notified immediately after a youth has been charged, usually does not find out about the case until after the charge has been laid. In this way the probation officer is in no position to provide early assistance to either a released suspect or to a suspect held in pre-trial confinement.

So, contrary to Beijing Rule 1.3, the Hungarian model of juvenile justice does not provide adequate support for juvenile offenders. In fact some schools expel the student at even the slightest suspicion and stigmatization almost automatically occurs. At the same time, due to the underdeveloped local supply system, real family assistance stands no chance against this premature reaction, nor indeed, at any later stage. Overburdened probation officers and patrons, the lack of professional standards, and the scarcity of assistance reduce the efficiency of protective efforts.

Although no data exist, on the basis of the social and cultural background of the perpetrators, we can say that the defence attorney plays only a marginal role in protecting the rights of suspected juvenile offenders. A defence attorney is called in only when families cannot provide their own attorney. As for the police, the number of convictions they obtain indicates their efficiency. The police have no vested interest in giving the juvenile suspect any opportunity to prove his or her innocence.

Before youths even get to court their basic rights are often dramatically compromised. The juvenile court judges further undermine the situation. Judges receive no special initial or in-service training; nor do they consider it their duty to explore areas beyond the scope of general law. Finally, specially trained probation officers, patrons, and social workers are few and far between; therefore, the preparation of cases and the exploration of circumstances is highly arbitrary.

Pre-trial

Pre-trial confinement takes place with only a few of the delinquents. In 1999, 4.1% of the juvenile suspects (N= 477) were subject to confinement. In accordance with the international agreements signed by Hungary, Act XLI of 1995 stipulates that after 1 July 1996, wings and units suitable for pre-trial confinement of juvenile delinquents would be set up in three reformatory institutions and a special children's home. A former detention center, a special children's home and a wing of the girls' reformatory school were transformed and modernized to fulfill this requirement. The manner in which the detainees are treated is determined by a well-designed educational and re-socialization model.

As the length of time is not predictable, only special programs apply. This is an important issue because pre-trial confinement is very often prolonged. Many juvenile suspects spend six to 12 months in confinement, and they previously had no access to a meaningful occupation or education during this period.

Despite the newly available accommodations, placement into an appropriate facility is usually accidental. It depends on the police and their "comfort," given the need for regular hearings or other reasons why the young person should be readily available. In accordance with the Beijing Rules promulgated in Hungary by Act LXIV of 1991, the signatory states should make every effort to "… take steps towards the handling of the suspect or guilty child's case without a judiciary procedure, while maintaining full observance of human rights and legal guarantees" (Paragraph 3 of Article 40 of UN Resolution 40/33/ 1985). Accordingly, young delinquents should be treated in accordance with their situation and the crime they committed—"the principle of proportionality."

The intent is to focus on the needs of the youth as opposed to exacting "just desserts." This, unfortunately, is by no means fully implemented in Hungary. This is particularly true of the lack of protection, guardianship, control, counselling, release on parole, family care, general professional educational programs, and non-institutional solutions. Moreover, not only is there a lack of institutions, professional experts, and financial resources; professional conviction and attitude are likewise non-existent.

Juvenile (In)justice

Owing to the excessive burdens on the police and courts, the investigation and trial of cases are highly prolonged. It is not infrequent for two or three years to elapse between the delinquency and the court ruling; therefore, any educational impact involved in the ruling is dissipated. Moreover, the juvenile delinquent who is 18 years of age and over can no longer be confined in a reformatory institution.

Until recently, the practice of adjudication was influenced by the fact that the duration of pre-trial confinement did not count towards the term of reformatory confinement. On 1 July 1996, the rule was changed. Until then judges generally felt that juveniles were at a disadvantage and therefore often passed sentences that allowed for immediate release. A direct consequence of this attitude was the extremely low number of delinquents referred to reformatory institutions.

Probation and patronage of young adults extend beyond the time when they reach adulthood. This is partly justified by the relevant provisions in force (e.g., the Penal Code increased the age of probation and patronage from 18 to 24 years). The best example is the fact that young adults in state care can remain in the relevant institution until they are 24 years old. This, unfortunately, marked the low level of efficiency of the system and a lack of professional insight. And even though point 3.3 of the Beijing Rules stipulates that provisions pertaining to juvenile delinquents should be expanded to so-called young adult perpetrators, Lévai (1994:343) notes: "The psychological traits and social position of a young person around 20 are closer to those of a 17- or 18-year-old than to those of an adult if only a few years older."

Nevertheless, it would be inexpedient to increase the upper age limit from the point of view of criminal policy, as the institutional system that serves for resocialization would thereby be extended to incorporate criminally active, sociologically and criminologically heterogeneous groups. If 21 years of age were the threshold of adulthood in Hungary, the authorities would have to "deal with 15,000 more juvenile delinquents per year" (Lévai, 1994).

Another major area confronting the proper handling of juvenile cases concerns probation, suspension of confinement, parole, and provisional release from a correctional institution, which involves a probation officer commissioned by the court. Aside from a general lack of proper training, there has been much debate within the judiciary about the role of probation. Foreign models of probation differ and there are several different approaches in Hungary. The most problematic weakness of the former system was eliminated with the introduction of the new *Child Protection Law* (XXXI/1997) in November 1997, and since then the employer of the probation officer is a county guardianship office. Unfortunately, their work is still not smoothly integrated with that of the local government and the court. The probation officers are still not working according to a formalized protocol, regulated by professional standards and responsible together with family social workers, local child welfare services, and the schools. Their respective responsibilities, perspectives and hierarchy are not clear. Even if one of the parties is in favor of cooperation, this cannot be forced, so the problem tends to go unaddressed and the responsibility to one another left unfulfilled. Despite of all the efforts made by the policy makers there is hardly any progress in jointly assessing, planning and evaluating their work.

Getting an education and finding a job and a place to live are objectives that are difficult to achieve under the current social and political environment in Hungary. This has been particularly true since the late 1980s. Earlier, being unemployed was in itself illegal ("penal idleness," punishable by 30 days imprisonment until 1989). Another handicap to efficient probation is the inadequate number of social service agencies. They have a limited scope of activity and lack the cooperation to manage this complex problem. Consequently, probation is arbitrary and dependent on the persons involved. Family assistance is generally not part of probation planning and is extended only in a limited way even if other problems (e.g., social and child safety) are involved in a case.

Correctional education takes place in one of the two reformatory institutions. One is for boys while the other is an old educational institute used for female offenders. The reformatories all come under the auspices of the Ministry of Welfare, but they perform their tasks in relative isolation. Therefore, it is not a surprise that they are able to provide only marginal re-socialization services and provide only a very limited chance of not going back to the unchanged harmful environment.

By international standards the average length of incarceration could be severe. With confinement averaging one-and-a-half years, their educational value is questionable. Contacts with the local social system are arbitrary and lack professional protocol. Juvenile delinquents in state custody are often "forgotten" by their former protection institution and their current local county child and juvenile protection institute. Since the introduction of the child protection legislation in November 1997, all newly formed local child welfare services are supposed to provide the needed assistance and care to both the offender and his or her family.

Those formerly in care have almost no chance to find proper housing, education or employment. For them, rehabilitation is almost hopeless as most of them have nowhere to go and their family ties are uncertain or non-existent. While they are still in custody, escapes are frequent, and many escapees commit easily detectable offences while "on the lam." They escape and re-offend in order to prolong the confinement, for once they are released they have no home, no job, and no food. The number of those who would like to live there has been increasing while fewer of them are capable of leaving. And while the centers have a beneficial correctional educational impact on the youth, many experts question their location. One of the facilities is located in Budapest and the other on the outskirts of the city. In general, the lack of similar facilities in the rest of the country means that family contact and other opportunities for rehabilitation are very difficult. Furthermore, a lack of resources makes it difficult to allow weekend leave.[2]

In addition to a large number of juveniles classified as mentally challenged, underprivileged and undersocialized young persons are also overrepresented among the juvenile offender population. Romany ("Gypsy") youths (see Box 8.3) are also overrepresented. For political reasons this has remained a delicate issue, since they have not been officially recognized for the past 40 years. While there is no official data describing the size of the Romany population, it is a well-known fact that 60% of this group live below the poverty line. As most of them are unskilled, they were the first to lose their jobs as a consequence of the industrial crisis. The number of Romany juveniles who drop out of school is higher than the national average.

The proportion of Romany children in child protection institutions varies significantly from county to county, from a low of 25% to about 80%. One reason for the great variation is that as a result of forced assimilation, Romany identity and culture were never emphasized, and masses of children come from families where everyday customs and education differ from "the good Hungarian practice." The risks for criminalization in these instances are very high. As a result they become marginalized and lose the protection of a community.

Furthermore, because of social and cultural isolation, many Romany youths lack proper family socialization. In fact many Romany delinquents are considered by psychologists to be mentally handicapped although it is merely the consequence of their social deprivation. Their problem is not solved by probation or correctional education; quite the contrary. Prejudices are tangible and almost impossible to prove. On the other hand, special care and assistance are not provided. Nor is there any affirmative action in theory or in practice. Equity before the law inevitably recreates inequalities.

Box 8.3 The Romanies in Hungary[3]

According to the work of a German philologist in 1780, the Romanies appear to have originated from India around 1000 A.D. By the late 1400s most Europeans knew them as vagabonds, fortune-tellers, singers, dancers, and charming tricksters. Unlike in many other countries, the Romanies were never ostracized in Hungary until more recently. Today the Hungarian government wants to punish those families whose children do not attend school regularly. Instead of forming "child-friendly" and "Gypsy-friendly" school environments, the government tries to financially control or even punish the parents. Data shows that schools try to get rid of "unpleasant" children and form special "Gypsy" classes. In this manner the government and schools exclude children in a discriminatory manner which in turn tends to lead to problems with these youth in the community. Nevertheless, there have been calls for specific programs for Romany children that can address their unique needs.

RECENT DEMOGRAPHIC TRENDS

The number of offences committed prior to the age of culpability (i.e., in childhood, rather than at juvenile age from the point of view of penal law) is an indication of the future trend of juvenile delinquency. But first, in order to have a basis of comparison for juvenile offence rates, it is necessary to provide a sense of crime trends in the general population.

In Hungary, the number of offences involving public indictment was 120,880 in 1975. In 1993 this number increased to 400,935 (an increase of 231.7%). In 1975 the number of known perpetrators of offences involving public indictment was 72,049, while in 1993 the same figure was 122,621 (an increase of 70.2%). There are two possible explanations for the delinquency rate changes from 1975 to 1993. First, the number of those who committed multiple delinquencies has increased, and secondly the efficiency of detection may have decreased, thereby enabling youth to commit multiple offences.

Meanwhile, Gönczöl (1995) suggests that the increase in delinquency may be a by-product of the new market economy of the early 1990s and all the social problems it created (e.g., unemployment, and the loosening of social bonds as both parents entered the work force).

Child Delinquency

The number of child delinquents increased from 2,557 in 1975 to 4,128 in 1993 (an increase of 61.4%). The increase was 13.2% in 1990-1991 and peaked in 1992 with 4,492 delinquents. In 1996, 3,689 children committed crimes as opposed to 4,133 in 1999. Most of the young offenders tend to carry out their crimes with other young offenders. As evidenced in most countries, the most common offences committed by children are property-related offences. Since 1990 property-related offences have constituted approximately 90% of all offences committed by child delinquents, a 138.8% increase between 1975 and 1995. Similarly, the number of child delinquents involved in fighting and rioting grew from 97 in 1990 to 212 in 1996 (see Table 8.2). The other major delinquent activity areas include theft and burglary involving stealing. In recent years, 60 to 70 young persons have been charged with assault-related offences.

As indicated in Tables 8.2 and 8.3 offences against persons have been increasing in recent years. In addition, there are more and more criminal cases where children are involved together with adults and/or young persons. Altogether 7,737 such cases have been recognized above and beyond the ones committed by the children on their own, of which 80% were against property, and 8% sexual abuse cases.

Juvenile Delinquency

The number of juvenile delinquents increased from 7,258 in 1975 to 14,321 in 1995, dropping back to 11,540 in 1999 (see Table 8.3).[4] This is a significantly higher increase than that of the number of adult perpetrators. And while the proportionate rate of increase when compared to the entire delinquent population was not as extreme (i.e., from 10.1% in 1975 to 12.2% in 1993, and 8.7% in 1999), the absolute numbers can be significantly higher, as the rate of detection of juvenile delinquents dropped significantly between 1975 and 1999 (see Table 8.4).

The number of juvenile delinquents per 10,000 juvenile inhabitants was 161 in 1985 and increased to 217.4 by 1994, and 225.9 by 1999. The differing rate of increase is due, in part, to the fact that the increase followed the general demographic upswing, which peaked as a result of two successive demographic interventions (in 1950 to 54 and 1972 to 76). Consequently, the juvenile population peaked at the turn of the 1980s and the early 1990s. This demographic asymmetry has its primary impact in the high number of young adult delinquents.

Finally, as is the case in most other parts of the world, youth crime in Hungary has been increasing at an uncomfortable rate. And while the specific indicators may vary somewhat, the primary causes reflect a lack of social control, lack of conformity and uniformity, as well as a general condition of social upheaval—a state of **anomie**. Furthermore, it would appear that little progress has been made in adopting a **social welfare model** of juvenile justice. This has been reflected in the police data that indicate an increase in more violent be-

Table 8.2: The Number of Children Delinquents and Percentages According to Criminal Actions

Number and Rates of Children Delinquents

	1990		1994		1996		1998		1999	
	Number	%	Number	%	Number	%	Number	%	Number	%
Total	3,744	100.0	4,168	100.0	3,689	100.0	3,864	100.0	4,133	100.0
Against Persons	76	2.0	128	3.1	95	2.58	93	2.41	105	2.54
Manslaughter	2	0.1	3	0.1	4	0.11	1	0.03	3	0.07
Bodily Harm	52	1.4	94	2.3	63	1.71	66	1.71	78	1.89
Traffic Crime	75	2.0	94	2.3	89	2.41	113	2.92	118	2.86
Against Moral	34	0.9	55	1.3	17	0.46	16	0.41	39	0.94
Sexual Abuse	6	0.2	12	0.3	6	0.16	5	0.13	10	0.24
Fighting and Rioting	97	2.6	249	6.0	212	5.75	237	6.13	282	6.82
From this: Rioting	46	1.2	130	3.1	86	2.33	106	2.74	103	2.49
Against Property	3,457	92.3	3,640	87.3	3,270	88.64	3,384	87.58	3,566	86.28
From this: Stealing	1,835	49.0	1,904	45.7	1,761	47.74	1,822	47.15	2,000	48.39
Break in	1,026	27.4	1,062	25.5	880	23.85	865	22.39	827	20.01
Robbery	100	2.7	151	3.6	126	3.42	147	3.80	166	4.02
Other	5	0.1	2	0.0	6	0.16	21	0.54	23	0.56

Table 8.3: The Number of Young Delinquents and Percentages According to Criminal Actions

Juvenile Delinquents' Number and Rates

	1990		1995		1997		1998		1999	
	Number	%	Number	%	Number	%	Number	%	Number	%
Total	12,848	100.0	14,321	100.0	13,955	100.0	12,866	100.0	11,540	100.0
Against Persons	849	6.6	829	5.79	731	5.24	641	4,98	564	4.89
Manslaughter	31	0.2	20	0.14	24	0.17	33	0.26	32	0.28
Bodily Harm	613	4.8	652	4.55	527	3.78	489	3.80	425	3.68
Traffic Crime	713	5.6	540	3.77	344	2.47	403	3.13	239	2.07
Against Moral	145	1.1	113	0.79	120	0.86	111	0.86	84	0.73
Sexual Abuse	55	0.4	35	0.24	36	0.26	28	0.22	18	0.16
Fighting and Rioting	862	6.7	1,593	11.12	1,616	11.58	1,764	13.71	1,814	15.72
From this: Rioting	643	5.0	1,047	7.31	846	6.06	825	6.41	800	6.93
Against Property	9,955	77.5	11,017	76.93	10,953	78.49	9,691	75.32	8,582	74.37
From this: Stealing	5,160	40.2	5,327	37.20	5,566	39.89	5,252	40.82	4,555	39.47
Break in	2,690	20.9	3,739	26.11	3,467	24.84	2,913	22.64	2,324	20.14
Robbery	409	3.2	546	3.81	546	3.91	406	3.16	399	3.46
Other	324	2.5	229	1.60	191	1.31	256	1.99	257	2.23

Table 8.4: Juvenile Delinquency 1985-1999

Year	All known delinquents	If 1985= 100.0 %	Number of Delinquents /10,000 inhabitants	Juvenile Delinquents		If 1985 =100.0	Delinquen/ 10,000 juvenile inhabitants	Number of childe delinquents	If 1985 =100.0 %
1985	85,766	100	80.5	9,449	11.0	100.0	161.0	3,745	100.0
1986	93,176	108.6	87.6	10,554	11.3		179.5	4,064	108.5
1987	92,643	108.0	87.2	9,887	10.7	104.6	168.0	3,302	88.2
1988	82,329	96.0	77.6	8,667	10.5		146.4	3,652	97.5
1989	88,932	103.7	84.0	9,661	10.9	102.2	154.8	3,723	99.4
1990	112,254	130.9	108.2	12,848	11.4	136.0	191.6	3,744	100.0
1991	112,835	143.2	118.6	13,508	11.0	143.0	192.5	4,240	113.2
1992	132,644	154.7	128.3	15,476	11.7	163.8	214.5	4,488	119.8
1993	122,621	143.0	118.9	15,001	12.2	158.8	213.9	4,128	110.2
1994	119,494	139.3	116.3	14,479	12.1	153.2	217.4	4,168	111.3
1995	121,121	107.90	118.22	14,321	11.82	111.46	226.74	4,168	111.32
1996	122,221	108.88	119.68	13,544	11.08	105.42	226.30	3,689	98.53
1997	130,966	116.67	128.72	13,955	10.66	108.62	246.73	4,287	114.50
1998	130,966	116.67	129.22	12,866	9.82	100.14	240.97	3,864	103.21
1999	131,658	117.29	130.46	11,540	8.77	89.82	225.86	4,133	110.39

havior. The lack of preventive programs at schools and in the community limit the chances of such an approach being readily adopted.

Child and Juvenile Victims of Crime

In Hungary victimization data on juvenile crime has only been collected since 1988. In that year, 105,532 offended parties were registered, of whom 2,000 were children, and 3,876 were of juvenile age. The number of offended parties increased to 230,915 by 1993 (an increase of 118.8%), of whom 2,626 (30.8%) were children and 7,160 (84.7%) of juvenile age. While the total number of offended parties was highest in 1991, the number of offended children was highest in 1990 and the number of offended juvenile parties has increased steadily since the beginning of the period under examination.

Examining the victims of particular offences, it can be stated that:

- The number of offended parties involved in crimes against sexual morals was 445 in 1988, 412 in 1993, and 608 in 1999. Between 1988 and 1999 there has been a steady increase in the number of offended parties who were children (16.9% vs. 19.8%). Meanwhile, the same figures for offended juvenile parties have declined since 1988 from 20.7% to 19.3% in 1999.
- Offended parties involved in manslaughter or attempted manslaughter numbered 398 in 1988 and 464 in 1993. The rate of offended children was 11.6% in 1988 and 5.8% in 1993, while the same figures for offended juvenile parties were 1.8% and 1.3% respectively.
- The number of parties offended in intended bodily harm cases totalled 5,580 in 1988 and 8,181 in 1993. Children offended constituted 2.4% in 1988 and 1.7% in 1993, while the same figures for offended juvenile parties were 4.5% and 5.5% respectively.

Examination of the relationship between juvenile perpetrators and offended parties reveals that most of them are not acquainted with each other. Those who are acquainted are predominantly schoolmates or related as parent and child.

CURRENT AND PROJECTED TRENDS

Future Directions:

There are three major factors that influence the image of delinquency in Hungary:

1. The proportion of the population consisting of youth from the ages of 14 to 18;

2. The legal definition of a juvenile offender. While the current lower age limit is 14 there has been much debate about lowering it to 12, and
3. The response of society and the state. How will the state choose to respond to the growing sense of insecurity and anger towards young offenders as well as adult offenders?

The first item pertains to demographic issues that cannot be affected by criminal policy or by general crime prevention. The second factor is subject to debates on codification that are greatly influenced by the attitude taken towards the third point. At the same time there is a growing number of crimes being committed by youth between the ages of 12 and 14. This trend had prompted many to call for legal reforms.

In our opinion young offenders should be separated from adults, as the underlying causes of their offences are basically different. Aggressive and brutal crimes, which undermine the system of values of society and the stability of the legal system, should be handled entirely differently from other types of crimes. Here the principal task is to protect the integrity of the legal system and its underlying values.

Those delinquent acts that do not harm or endanger life or that involve theft not motivated by financial gain should be treated separately by society. On the other hand, when crimes result in public harm or are motivated by financial gain, individuals should be held criminally responsible. Each type of crime reflects a different causal relationship and demands suitable responses that are in conformity with the legal norms. Nonetheless, we believe that juvenile offenders from all three classifications could be handled appropriately with the new restorative justice techniques.

Potential developments and changes currently being considered by Hungary are measured against the country's efforts to be a full member of the European Union and meeting the requirements of the Council of Europe. As a signatory of a number of international agreements, Hungary has undertaken adherence to, and promulgation of, all the contracts and conventions adopted by the developed world (Beijing Rules, Riyadh Guidelines, UN Rules regarding the support of juvenile delinquents in confinement, Convention on the Right of Children). However, there is still a significant discrepancy between the provisions of these agreements and Hungarian legal practice. Nonetheless, on the whole the most up-to-date and widely accepted trend is to increase the necessity of legal intervention. The challenge to develop sensitivity to human dignity and embrace the basic liberties of the individual will require the adoption of special laws and procedures. In addition, it will require the establishment of special authorities and institutions and favors problem management that excludes court procedure. It seems to be a very slow process despite what numerous foreign research studies have shown. Should Hungary be able to embrace these, its model of juvenile justice would be more in keeping with the UN recommendation that all countries adopt a social welfare model, and the Council of Europe recommendation on the introduction of mediation.

It is encouraging to see the shift from criminal accountability towards providing education and resocialization. Similarly, prevention has become more empathic, as has the use of alternative programs to incarceration. Some of these include: a renewed probation system, co-operation with the supply system (school, local government, family services and other service providers), and the modernization and differentiation of juvenile confinement institutions.

Unfortunately, because of the economic recession and transformation in the wake of the political changeover, many of the above objectives will remain conceptual dreams for a long while. Our "prematurely born welfare state" has exceeded the load-bearing capacity of the Hungarian economic situation since the 1990s. Furthermore, since the media tend to focus on shaping public opinion by offering biased coverage that concentrates primarily on the scandalous aspect of youth's behavior, the public is not likely to be sympathetic to the plight of young people. These circumstances are further undermined by the social problems that have emerged after the introduction of the market economy. Overall, it is questionable when and to what extent the justice administration and the parliament will be prepared to implement full-fledged reform. For example, the bill on child protection that was passed in 1997 after 10 years of proverbial political "ping-pong," while considered good in many ways, has been met with considerable controversy (see Box 8.4).

Therefore while initiatives are slowly being introduced it appears that change and acceptance will be slow in coming. However, given the international agreements mentioned above, there is an obligation for legislators to move towards honoring international conditions and standards. The need to embrace the agreement is perhaps best conveyed in the following note:

> The penal system of juvenile delinquency in itself is incapable of offsetting the unfavorable social and economic processes, the disturbances of the child protection system and the lack of social policy measures and institutions to prevent juvenile delinquency (Lévai, 1994:345).

SUMMARY

Hungary, while a small country, has a long history of being a tenacious survivor. It has survived attacks from the Tartars, Turks, Habsburgs, and Rus-

---

Box 8.4: The Law on the Protection of Children

After 96 years of working with an outdated law on the protection of children, in April 1997 the Hungarian Parliament passed new legislation which came into effect 1 November 1997. The new law is in accordance with the UN Convention on the Right of the Child and follows all the relevant international standards and guidelines regarding the needs and interests of children. The law guarantees the right for children to be brought up in a non-abusive environment, a right to proper living conditions which include proper shelter, food, education, as well as respecting their religious and ethnic identity.

The new law was accompanied with the establishment of child welfare services for all cases. The aim of these services is to provide needed information for families and co-ordination of service provisions to ensure the needs of children are properly dealt with.

The new law further provides for the establishment of foster and residential care facilities, and there are clear guidelines as to how children can and will be placed. Priority is given to placement with extended family who become eligible for financial assistance.

Unfortunately, the new legislation has been meet with some difficulties. The primary problem is a lack of financial resources and enough professionally trained staff. And while the intentions are thought to be good, there is considerable skepticism as to whether the new legislation can live up to its billing. In the interim, an assessment and outcome measurement system, designed in England and used in many other countries, has been introduced to monitor the new legislation.

---

sians. Hungarian history and character are best exemplified in our national anthem, which describes Hungarians as "people torn by fate."

After the Soviet army liberated the country in 1945, the Communists quickly gained power and eliminated free elections and subjected Hungarians to various atrocities. Then in 1956 there was a revolution against Stalinism—and there are still harsh debates after ten years of political transition about whose revolution it was and what its aims were—which failed after ten days. Although the uprising was defeated by Soviet troops, Janos Kadar promised democratic socialism. However, it was not until 1990 that the Communist party voluntarily gave up its autocracy. The people of Hungary are often upset because their dreams of democracy and freedom are far from the current realities. One of the many by-products of the struggle appears to be the steady growth in crime and delinquency rates, although analysts say that it is still far from the Western average. An increasing number of Hungarian scholars also believe that the crime and delinquency problem has been triggered by the breakdown of society and the inability of the state to respond in any concrete way.

As the realities of the economic, political and social transition in Hungary play a major role in the everyday operation of juvenile justice administration, it should be noted that point 1.5 of the Beijing Rules or the UN Convention on the Rights of Children acknowledges that international agreements can only be implemented within such a context. And even though Hungary has agreed to move towards a social welfare model, the politicians do not take this move seriously. Since there is no strong advocacy, research and evaluation are almost non-existent, and scandals are investigated only within a limited circle and are considered as isolated instances. In this way there is little chance of influencing public opinion and decision-makers. Therefore, it is anticipated that, like many social issues in Hungary, the plight of young offenders will receive only token attention for the near future.

It was also shown in this chapter that delinquency in Hungary is closely linked to social and cultural status (e.g., education, housing, income, and lifestyle). This is particularly evident with the Gypsy population, but it has also been found to be true of most poverty-stricken areas throughout the country. Since 1988 delinquency rates have increased and the incidence of violent crime has grown most dramatically. Gönczöl (1995:13) reports that, when compared to a half-dozen Westernized countries, Hungary offered "the least to the young in terms of long-term prospects."

The contributing factors to delinquency in Hungary fit some classical sociological indicators found in most textbooks on the subject. Most criminology scholars in Hungary are gradually recognizing the breakdown in social bonds and the sense of anomie. But these perspectives were not commonly known and accepted prior to the transition in 1989. The social, cultural and political price has been great. Nevertheless, we believe that we cannot return to the punitive and oppressive regime of the past. Rather, Hungarians must recognize they have endured many "storms" and this is but one more challenge that we must rise above. Through bringing into effect the agreements signed and through discussion with other countries we can, and must, begin to systematically introduce comprehensive social policy to meet the general aim of promoting juvenile welfare.

Maria Herczog is a senior researcher with the National Institute of Criminology. She is also the head of the Department of International Programs at the National Institute of Family and Social Policy.
Ferenc Irk is the director at the National Institute of Criminology and head of the department for the Police Academy in Budapest.

HELPFUL WEBSITES
www.okri.hu This is the homepage for the National Institute of Criminology in Hungary. It includes a range of information including some on juvenile offenders.

http://eurochild.gla.ac.uk This site is dedicated to the protection of children's rights. It includes documents from the Council of Europe's Program for Children. In addition, it includes a wide array of information on juvenile delinquency throughout Europe. Although not specific to Hungary, it does offer some information on delinquency in Hungary.

KEY TERMS AND CONCEPTS

anomie	corporatist view
crime control model	Csemegi Code
insecure investment	neo-classical school
participatory/welfare	Romany
welfare approach	paternal/welfare model

STUDY QUESTIONS

1. What are the key elements of the Hungarian juvenile justice system? How do they compare with other European countries?
2. Based on the discussion around the use of alternative measures and restorative elements in Hungary, how successful and effective do you think Hungary will be? Based on the efforts of other countries covered in this text, what recommendations might be offered?
3. How would you describe and characterize the different actors in the Hungarian juvenile justice system? Address such aspects as their impact on social-, health-, education-, and justice-related matters.
4. How do the youth age categories in Hungary compare to those in other countries? Should they be changed? Clarify your answer.
5. As Hungary docs not have a separate juvenile justice system, what do you consider to be the strengths and/or weaknesses of how the formal agencies deal with juvenile offenders?

NOTES

1 This figure is very low by international standards—even by East European standards.
2 From an organizational perspective it has been questioned whether these correctional institutions should belong to the Ministry of Justice, the Ministry of Education, or the Ministry of Welfare. The argument revolves around who should be responsible for the welfare of juvenile delinquents whose problems are professionally considered to be social problems that are similar to those of children.
3 For a comprehensive review of Romany youth you can view a report prepared by the United Nations Interregional Crime and Justice Research Institute in Turin, Italy at: www.unicri.it/html/rromani_youths.htm
4 This is a higher increase than that of the number of adult perpetrators (from 72,049 in 1975 to 122,621 in 1995 and 131,608 in 1999).

REFERENCES

Criminal statistics. (2000). Budapest: National Institute of Criminology.
Gonczol, K. (1995). Anxiety over crime increase. *CJ Europe,* 5 (1), 9–16.

Levai, M. (1994). *A fiatalkoru bunelkovetokkel szemben kiszabhato szankciok reformja.* Reform of sanction applicable for juvenile delinquents. *Magyar Jog,* 6, 341.

National Crime Prevention Program. (2000). National Institute for Criminology and Criminalistics. Budapest.

Program 3 of article 40 of UN Resolution 40/33/1985.

Statistics yearbook. (2000). Budapest: National Statistics Office.

placed as apprentices into a trade. The *Reformatory School Act* of 1876 was the next landmark in dealing with juvenile delinquents. The act empowered local governments to establish reformatory schools and, in accordance with the *Indian Penal Code Act* (1860), exempted all children under 12 years of age from all criminal offences. The act also gave them protection: under the Act, the sentencing court could keep the child for two to seven years in a reformatory school if he or she was under 18 years of age. However, youth placed in reformatories could leave such schools if they found gainful employment. The Code of Criminal Procedure (1898) included provisions to place youth up to the age of 18 in reformatory schools and then have them placed on probation until their 21st birthday.

The Indian Jail Committee (1919 to 20) appointed by the government of India under British rule submitted a detailed report of its observations and suggestions. The committee condemned the practice of sending juveniles to adult court. The committee further recommended the establishment of separate children's courts for hearing cases dealing with children and young offenders. The committee also suggested that imprisonment of offenders should be prohibited, and that children committing offences should be sent to remand homes and certified schools. Finally, it was also suggested that children could be released on the basis of good conduct with supervisory provisions after their release.

Following the suggestions made by the Indian Jail Committee, Madras, Bengal and Bombay enacted their *Children Acts* in 1920, 1922, and 1924 respectively. All these acts were closely related to the *Children Act*, 1908 of England. Though the Madras *Children Act* was enacted in 1920, it was not enforced properly until 1928. In Madras, the first juvenile court was set up in 1939 on the premises of the Madras Children's Aid Society. By contrast, in Bengal the juvenile court had been established in 1914 in Calcutta, long before the enactment of the Bengal *Children Act* of 1922. Apart from Madras, Calcutta and Bombay, other provinces of India did not have any separate legislation for dealing with children. It was only in 1960 that the central government enacted the ***Children Act*** for the protection and care of children in the union territories. Though after independence practically all states and union territories had their own children acts to address the problem of delinquent youth, it was found that no minimum standard for basic needs, living conditions and medical services were provided for under these acts. Thus, a uniform legislation, which could provide for all this and more, was needed. This gave rise to the *Juvenile Justice Act* of 1986 for the care, protection and rehabilitation of neglected children and juvenile delinquents. The government of India, in addition to the implementation of the *Children Act*, has also enacted the following social legislation for the protection of children:

1. *Child Marriage Restraint Act* (1929)—with a view to preventing child marriage.
2. *Children (Pledging of Labour) Act* (1933)—to prohibit the pledging of the labor of children and the employment of children whose labor has been pledged.
3. *Immoral Traffic (Prevention) Act* (1956)—for suppression of immoral traffic in women and girls.
4. *Young Persons (Harmful Publications) Act* (1956)—to prevent the dissemination of publications that are harmful to young persons.
5. *Probation of Offenders Act* (1958)— to restrict courts in imposing imprisonment on offenders less than 21 years of age and to order the removal of all disqualification attaching to juvenile conviction.
6. *Orphanages and Other Charitable Homes (Supervision and Control) Act* (1960)—to provide for the supervision and control of orphanages, homes for neglected children and like institutions and to penalize those who exploit children in such settings.
7. The *(Central) Children Act* (1960) [meant for union territories only but which was also supposed to serve as model legislation for other states]—to deal with separating destitute children from juvenile delinquents by providing specialized institutions for each (it was amended in 1978 to make it more viable and effective).
8. *Child Labour (Prohibition and Regulation) Act* (1986)—to ban employment of children in specified occupations and processes.

As can be seen from the legislation just summarized, India has introduced numerous acts since the 1920s, each dealing with a different issue of how juveniles should be treated. The most recent of these changes is the *Juvenile Justice Act* (JJA) in 1986 and in 2000. The changes reflect a welfare model objective in that it attempts "to provide for the care, protection, treatment, development and rehabilitation of neglected or delinquent juveniles and for the adjudication of certain matters relating to, and disposition of, delinquent juveniles" (No. 53). The JJA applies to all of India's states and union territories except Jammu and Kashmir[4] The JJA with its welfare model approach is illustrated in Figure 9.1.

DEFINITION

From the legal point of view, delinquency is called a pattern of behavior which is disapproved of by the law. It is a very simple concept involving ungovernable, unmanageable or incorrigible behavior, running away from home and association with anti-social elements. The age of the person is the com-

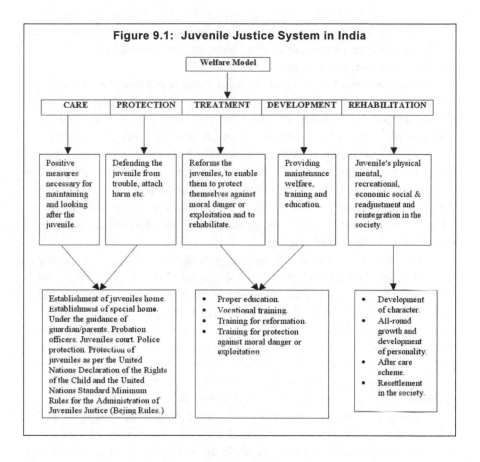

Figure 9.1: Juvenile Justice System in India

mon criterion adopted in judging whether a person is a juvenile or not. In most countries, laws dealing with juvenile delinquency set an upper age limit and only those who are within that age limit are considered to be juveniles (see Figure 1—Introduction). For example, the majority of European countries have fixed the upper age limit at 16 years. A "child" is defined differently in the various states of India in their *Children Acts*. For instance, in Madhya Pradesh and Telangana, a child means a person under 16 years, in Gujarat and West Bengal under 18 years, and in Andhra Pradesh outside Telangana, under 14 years. In the union territories of India, a child is defined as a boy under 16 years or a girl less than 18 years of age.

There is also a legal and conceptual difference between delinquency and crime. In the case of crime there is a definite motive or purpose, a capacity for skillful judgement of the act, while delinquency includes any type of wrongdoing whether motivated by material gain or not. A delinquent child can be defined as a wayward, incorrigible or habitually disobedient child. It can, therefore, be concluded that what is an offence for a juvenile is not an offence for an adult. For example, running away from home or smoking cigarettes is not considered an offence when an adult does it.

The etymological meaning of the word juvenile is a young person, having or retaining the characteristics of youth, and the meaning of the word delinquency is failure in duty. The *Children Act*, 1960 (sec. 2[f]) defines juvenile as one who is found to have committed an offence. However, the nature and extent of juvenile offences varies considerably from one society to another. In India, juvenile delinquency is somewhat different in nature as compared to other societies. The Indian concept of juvenile delinquency is much narrower than the English (see Chapter 5) or the American concept (see Chapter 18), which is much wider in scope and includes a number of behaviors in addition to violations of the penal statutes.

There may be a number of factors responsible for juvenile delinquency in India. The first factor which might spur delinquent behavior is an unfavorable family environment, including weakening of family ties, disruption of previous relationships, or the breakdown of consensus and loyalty. Such family environments may predispose young persons to become involved in delinquency, as they are less likely to be capable of carrying out their prescribed functions properly. In addition to the family factors, some authors (e.g., Rao, 1965; Sethna, 1971) have suggested that bad companionship and poor neighborhoods develop non-normative propensities among children.

Poverty in India has also been associated with predisposing youth to delinquent behavior. One of the research studies (National Institute of Social Defence, 1996) stated that most juvenile delinquents belong to low-income households. Poverty provokes a juvenile to go astray and commit illegal acts. Besides, if the parent or the guardian of the child is unable to check the behavior of the child then he or she may become wayward or disobedient.

Finally, another important factor that contributes to our youth becoming delinquent is the rapid industrialization and urbanization which, in turn, has given rise to new housing problems like slum-dwelling and overcrowding, as well as lack of paternal control, family disintegration, lack of proper employment scope and so forth (Wani, 1999). Industrialization and urbanization have raised the demands of people but the means to fulfill these demands are limited. The expensive cost of living in urban areas makes it necessary even for women to take up jobs outside the home to support their families financially, with the result that their children are left all alone at home without any parental control. Moreover, the craze for modern luxuries of life prompts youngsters to resort to wrongful acts to satisfy their wants. All these factors cumulatively lead to an enormous increase in juvenile delinquency in urban areas. Juveniles who are not mature enough to understand the consequences of their actions are the people who are most prone to all this; they take the easy way out to keep pace with their rising demands and expectations.

THE JUVENILE JUSTICE (CARE AND PROTECTION OF CHILDREN) ACT, 1986 (JJA)

The JJA was enacted on December 3, 1986, and came into force on 2 October 1987, throughout the country. In 2000, the most significant amendment to the act was the increase of the upper age limit of male juveniles from 16 to 18. The act contains 63 sections and seven chapters. The first chapter deals with various definitions. The second chapter outlines competent authorities and institutions for juveniles. The provisions of the third and fourth chapters deal with neglected and delinquent juveniles respectively. Chapter five addresses issues of procedure to be followed by authorities and the process for appeals and revision of orders from such authorities. Chapter six describes what legally constitute juvenile offences. The final chapter outlines miscellaneous provisions.

Objectives of the JJA

The main objective of the JJA is to protect, care for, rehabilitate, educate and give vocational training to children who are delinquent as well as to make services available to those children who have been neglected. The act deals with children in a very scientific manner. Consistent with the **welfare** model, the JJA is intended to facilitate rehabilitation and resocialization by attending to the youths' needs. However, Ved Kumari (personal communication with John Winterdyk, March 1996) characterized the JJA as representing the **modified justice** approach with elements of the justice and crime control models (see Figure 1—Introduction, and Figure 9.1).

Under the JJA after-care homes have been provided where juveniles who are in need of additional help can continue to stay even after they have been discharged from their juvenile homes or special homes, as the case may be. The law also recognizes the important role of voluntary organizations in helping institutions (and the machinery of such institutions) in the proper disposal of cases. Some institutions run by the voluntary organizations can also be recognized as observation homes, juvenile homes, and special homes, or after-care homes.

The JJA is designed to ensure that children who come into conflict with the law are treated in a humane way. Formal interventions (e.g., the police or jail authorities) are intended to be used minimally. Whenever juvenile courts and welfare boards do not exist, the Ministry of Social Justice and Empowerment and the National Institute of Social Defence pressure the authority responsible to develop the infrastructure as early as possible. The National Institute of Defence also organizes special training programs for officials dealing with children.

Under the JJA efforts are made to rehabilitate juveniles within the precincts of the family itself. A great emphasis is placed on the individualized handling through case study and diagnosis. The Ministry of Social Justice and Empowerment has circulated a scheme for prevention and control of juvenile maladjustment under which financial provision is available for setting up observation homes, juvenile homes/special homes, upgrading existing institutions, and training people to handle the work. UNICEF-sponsored programs (e.g., intensive programs for school drop-outs, adult and non-formal education, health awareness programs, nutrition programs, vocational and career guidance, etc.) are available to the state governments. UNICEF provides financial help for the vocational training of destitute children. It has been observed that children who are generally homeless or have lost ties with their families are economically forced to commit petty offences like theft, robbery, and snatching.[5]

FEATURES OF THE JJA

The main objects of the Act are:
- To lay down a uniform legal framework for juvenile justice in the country so as to ensure that no child under any circumstance is incarcerated or placed in police lock-up. Establishing juvenile welfare boards and juvenile courts is ensuring this.
- To provide for a specialized approach to the prevention and treatment of juvenile delinquency in its full range in keeping with the development needs of the child found in any situation of social maladjustment.
- To spell out the machinery and infrastructure required for the care, protection, treatment, development and rehabilitation of various categories of children coming within the purview of the juvenile justice system. Establishing juvenile homes and special homes, observation and after-care homes for delinquent juveniles.
- To establish norms and standards for the administration of juvenile justice in terms of investigation and prosecution; adjudication and disposition; and care, treatment and rehabilitation.
- To bring a juvenile justice system into operation. The term "neglected juvenile" has been defined in section 2(1) of the JJA as a juvenile who:

1. is found begging;
2. is found not to have any home or settled place of residence, or any means of subsistence, and who is destitute;
3. has a parent or guardian who is unfit or incapacitated to exercise control over the youth;
4. lives in a brothel or with a prostitute or frequently goes to any place used for the purpose of prostitution, or is found in such association as is likely to lead to an immoral, drunken or deprived life; or
5. who is being or is likely to be abused or exploited by others for any illegal gain. The Juvenile Welfare Board has the jurisdiction to deal with such neglected juveniles.

The juvenile justice system in India has within itself a number of functionaries to discharge its duties effectively (see Figure 9.2). They are, first, the officers who bring juveniles to the notice of the law, for example, police. Second, judicial and quasi-judicial bodies are also important as they determine the facts and take appropriate action. Third, institutions that cater to the needs of such neglected and delinquent juveniles, in conformity with the United Na-

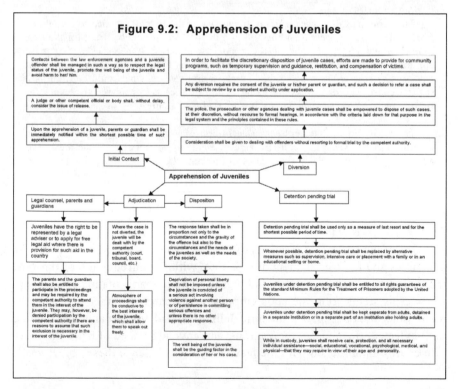

Figure 9.2: Apprehension of Juveniles

tions Standard for Minimum Rules for the Administration of Juvenile Justice (see Box 1—Introduction).

In addition, the act also protects juveniles from having their names published. The act further provides that a young offender cannot be: sentenced to death; imprisoned; or kept in a prison in default of: i) payment of fine, or ii) furnishing surety.

With the recent amendments to the JJA, the upper age limit for the classification "juvenile" is now 18 for both boys and girls[6] (see Box 9.1). Prior to the change, the upper age had been 18 for girls and 16 for boys. The lower age limit for juveniles was, and remains, seven. Children under the age of seven are not considered to have attained sufficient maturity to understand the nature and consequences of their conduct and cannot be dealt with as juvenile delinquents as they are incapable of committing an offence as provided by the Penal Code (i.e., *mens rea*).

Box 9.1 Supreme Court clears doubt in JJA

The Supreme Court of India has clarified a major ambiguity in the Juvenile Justice Act by ruling that a juvenile would be tried by a regular court if s/he was arrested after turning 16 years of age.

The Supreme Court was clearly of the view that the Juvenile Justice Act would be applicable if the competent authority found the person brought before it for the first time to be under 16 years of age (18 years in case of a girl). It means even if a person committed an offence while being a juvenile but is brought before the competent authority after s/he has crossed the age of 16 or 18 years, s/he would be tried by a regular court. The date of commission of the offence is considered irrelevant for finding out whether the person is a juvenile within the meaning of section 2 (H) of the Act.

The Court noted that neither the definition of juvenile or any other provision contained in the Act specifically provides the date by reference to which the age of a boy or girl has to be determined so as to find out whether s/he in a juvenile or not.

Source: *The Hindustan Times*, June 14, 2000.

Critical Analysis of the JJA

One of the important elements of the JJA that causes conflict between its principles and their implementation is that, with the introduction of the JJA, the definition of a delinquent child focused on more than violators of the Penal Code. This stems from the act's emphasis on treatment rather than punishment. Since the concept of a juvenile delinquent had now expanded to include the neglected, the abused, the vagrant, and anyone in need of help, the juvenile court was burdened with the task of trying to balance these objectives.

Another limitation of the JJA is the fact that there is a general lack of awareness and familiarity with the legislation by those who were/are responsible for its implementation. Furthermore, insufficient resources confound the situation; administrative lethargy and slackness are other factors that hinder the operation of the system. For example, in Table 9.1 we can see how limited the states and territories are in providing resources for young offenders.

Table 9.1: Institutions under the Juvenile Justice Act, 1986, with Total Capacity of All Institutions

State/union territory	Observation homes	Juvenile homes	Special homes	Aftercare inst.	Total	Total capacity
Andhra Pradesh	9	5	2	1	17	2010
Arunachal Pradesh*	1	1 *	1 *	-	2	N.A.
Assam	7	25	1	1	34	250
Bihar	10	8	5	2	25	1340
Goa	2	2	2	-	6	125
Gujarat	25	5	2	14	46	2243
Haryana	3	3	1	1	8	250
Himachal Pradesh	-	1	1	-	2	70
Karnataka	22	19	-	11	52	3640
Kerala	12	5	2	-	19	1750
Madhya Pradesh	22	2	3	1	28	1600
Maharashtra	45	101	3	3	152	10095
Manipur	1	2	1	-	4	175
Meghalaya	1	-	-	-	1	40
Mizoram	3	3	-	-	6	45
Nagaland	-	1	1	-	2	30
Orissa	12	2	-	-	14	425
Pubjab	7	2	1	2	12	850
Rajasthan	11	4	1	-	16	525
Sikkim	1	-	-	-	1	N.A.
Tamil Nadu	14	17	3	3	37	N.A.
Tripura	1	1	-	-	2	75
Uttar Pradesh	59	10	1	-	70	3450
West Bengal	7	19	4	6	36	2315
Andaman and Nicobar	-	-	-	-	-	-
Chandigarh	1	1	1	-	3	30
Dadra and Nagar Haveli	-	-	-	-	-	-
Daman and Diu	-	-	-	-	-	-
Delhi	3	11	-	-	14	1740
Lakshadweep	-	-	-	-	-	-
Pondicherry	1	1	1	1	4	150
TOTAL	280	253	37	46	613	123,223

Note: The Act is not implemented in the State of Jammu and Kashmir.
N.A. = Not available.
*Juvenile homes and special homes are common.
Source: Annual Report 1998-1999. Ministry of Welfare, Government of India, New Delhi.

According to Jayaram (1999) the JJA was nothing but a replica of the *Children Act* (CA) of 1960 in so much as all the provisions in the new act were taken from the old act. It is important to note, however, that the CA applied only to the union territories whereas the new act applies to the whole of India except Jammu and Kashmir. Further, the term "child" in the old act is replaced by the term "juvenile" in the new act. Thus the JJA simply represents an administrative shift in which India now has moved toward a uniform law governing juveniles throughout the country.

The government claims that the failure of the old act to effectively deal with children led to the creation of the JJA. However, the question that comes to one's mind is that, if the CA of 1960 was really a failure, then how could the JJA be its total replica (Jayaram, 1986)?

On the other hand, different critics of the JJA (e.g., Jayaram [1986] and Rao [1965]) argued that the procedures that are actually followed by the authorities to deal with juvenile delinquents are not really based on the welfare model. They believe that it is not as reformative as claimed. The key provisions of the new act may exemplify these claims substantially. The court constituted under sec. 5(2) of the 1960 act is a criminal court, and the session judge can transfer a case pending in children's court under sec. 528 (I-c) of the Code of Criminal Procedure (Cr.P.C). The new act (sec. 6[3]) also says that a person with adequate training and knowledge regarding how to deal with a juvenile should be appointed as a member of the welfare board or a magistrate of the juvenile court. To this extent, the act (sec. 4[4]) requires the appointment of at least one woman member, and that a woman magistrate is compulsory on the juvenile welfare board and on the magistrate bench of juvenile court respectively. Unfortunately, this requirement is not strictly adhered to. In fact, in some places such qualified magistrates, due to lack of sufficient boards and juvenile courts, do not even try juveniles.[7]

As per the new act, a police officer who takes charge of a neglected or delinquent youth is required to bring such a youth before a board within 24 hours of a charge being laid. Until brought before the board no juvenile shall be charged with, or tried for, any offence. But in practice the police will barely produce the juvenile before the board within 24 hours. Moreover, since the child is kept in police custody till they can be brought before the court or board, they are generally kept with other adult offenders—a rather common practice. This trend can be attributed to lethargy in implementation and to the callousness of the police officials (Rao, 1965).

Further, where no juvenile welfare board/juvenile court has been constituted, either the district magistrate or subdivision magistrate or any magistrate of the first class can exercise the power conferred on a board or juvenile court (sec. 7[2]), and any person aggrieved by an order of competent authority under the act may prefer an appeal to the court of sessions (sec. 37[1]). Even the enquiry against a juvenile will be made according to the procedure for trial in summary cases. Sections 7(2) and 37(2) of the CA also had a similar provision. This indicates that both old as well as new acts are penal in nature and not fit to deal with children.

The other important drawback lies with the implementation of section 27(2) of the act. Under this section, the proceedings against juveniles have to take place in different buildings from that of civil and criminal courts, or at least at different times from that of the ordinary shift of such courts. In practice the proceedings against delinquent juveniles are not conducted in camera; usually the trial is conducted in an open court that is meant for adult offenders, in contravention of the Beijing Rules.

Similarly the JJA prohibits the publication of names and photographs of delinquent juveniles in newspapers and magazines (sec. 36[1]). But unfortunately it is still the practice to publish photographs of such juveniles in places like railway stations and bus depots. Because of these defects the object of the new act has not been achieved to the expected extent. What should be evident is that India, while having juvenile legislation similar to many Western nations is less effective at enforcing these practices. This is mainly due to inherent defects in the act and the system, social instinct and a degree of political apathy.

BENEFITS OF THE JJA

Though a majority of the experts (e.g., Ved, 1993) in the field agree that there are no major differences between the old act and the new act, the latter has four important features not found in the former. These are: 1) uniform legislation, 2) separate handling of delinquent and non-delinquent children, 3) juvenile welfare boards and development of community-based welfare agencies, and 4) protection and rehabilitation of maladjusted children.

The scheme for prevention and control of juvenile social maladjustment which the ministry has been operating since 1986/87 (JJA) was also revised, with a view to strengthening the implementation of the act and bringing about a qualitative change in the services provided under the scheme to both neglected as well as delinquent children. The salient features of the revised scheme, which is called "A Programme for Juvenile Justice" are as follows:

- Establishment of a national advisory board (NAB) on juvenile justice to advise the government on matters relating to the implementation of the JJA in the country, including the quality of infrastructure and the staff available under this act. The chairperson of the NAB is the secretary, Ministry of Social Justice and Empowerment. The board also has representation from other ministries—both central and state, juvenile welfare board, juvenile courts, schools of social work, law schools and non-government organizations,

- Creation of a juvenile justice fund,
- Establishment of a secretariat for the national advisory board,
- Constitution of a social audit party (SAP) comprising of five to six juvenile justice facilities across the country,
- Appointment of an observer to report upon implementation of the act in different states and union territories,
- Institution of a chair on juvenile justice at the Child and the Law Centre of the National Law School of India at Bangalore,
- Institution of awards for the best-maintained juvenile justice institution in each state and at the national level,
- Training, orientation and sensitization of judicial, administration, police and non-governmental organizations responsible for implementation of the JJA,
- Provision of one hundred percent financial assistance to states and union territories, and voluntary organizations to facilitate creation of infrastructure prescribed under the act in hitherto uncovered districts of the country,
- Financial assistance to bring about a qualitative improvement in the existing infrastructure,
- Expansion of non-institutional services such as sponsorship, foster care, probation, etc. as alternatives to institutional care, and
- Provision of scholarship to children being prosecuted under the act for excelling in academics or extracurricular activities.

Hence, while India is confronted with a number of pragmatic issues that hinder a comprehensive administration of the JJA, some of the inherent defects of the act have already been addressed by the government (see Box 9.2).

Overview of Juvenile Crimes

The total number of juvenile delinquents in the country is not known as many of their activities go unregistered. However, to ascertain the extent of the problem, we rely on the official figures of the National Crime Records Bureau (NCRB) that comes under the Ministry of Home Affairs. The data on delinquency incorporated here are mainly taken from the NCRB publication entitled "Crime in India" (1998).

Box 9. 2 Government plans to amend the Juvenile Justice Act

The Union government plans to amend the JJA to protect the interest of the child. Rather than amend the definition of "juvenile" it intends to remove the confusion over the applicability of the legislation in criminal trials involving young offenders. Union Social Justice and Empowerment Ministry proposed that the amendment would bring the Act in conformity with the UN Charter on the Rights of the Child. The existing Act does not provide for rehabilitation and after-care of the child. The Ministry wants the neglected child to be treated differently by the various agencies including the police. The amended Act would help rehabilitate and empower the neglected children—consistent with the **welfare model**. The National Institute of Social Defence has been training the officials associated with the juvenile justice system to enable them to work in the street with the children.

Source: *The Hindustan Times*, 30 May 2000.

The proportion of offences committed by juveniles out of the total Indian Penal Code (IPC) crimes reported in the country between 1988 and 1998 are presented in Table 9.2.

The table indicates that the country has shown a declining trend since 1988, notwithstanding the fact that there is an appreciable increase in the population of the country.

The role and performance of police on juvenile crimes is governed by:

Table 9.2: Incidence And Rate Of Juvenile Delinquency Under Ipc (1988-98)

Year	Incidence of Juvenile Crimes	Total Cog.* Crimes	Percentage of Juvenile Crimes to Total Crimes	Estimated Mid-Year Population (100,000s)	Rate (Incidence of Crime 100,000 of Population
1988	24,827	1,440,356	1.7	7,966	3.1
1989	18,457	1,529,844	1.2	8,118	2.3
1990	15,230	1,604,490	0.9	8,270	1.8
1991	12,588	1,678,375	0.8	8,496	1.5
1992	11,100	1,689,341	0.7	8,677	1.3
1993	9,465	1,629,936	0.6	8,838	1.1
1994	8,561	1,635,251	0.5	8,999	1.0
1995	9,766	1,695,696	0.6	9,160	1.1
1996	10,024	1,709,576	0.6	9,319	1.1
1997	7,909	1,719,820	0.5	9,552	0.8
1998	9,339	1,779,111	0.5	9,709	1.0

Source: Crime in India 1998, NCRB, Government of India, R.K. Puram, New Delhi.

* **Cognizable Crimes:** means an offence in which a police officer may arrest without warrant in accordance with the first schedule of the Code of Criminal Procedure 1973 or under any other law in force at the time.

a) The Indian Penal Code, 1860, and
b) The special law (vide sec. 41 of IPC) which is applicable to a particular
    subject, and local law (vide sec. 42 of IPC) which is applicable to a
    particular part of India (SLL).

The NCRB figures show that the proportion of crimes committed by juveniles relative to the total IPC crime in the country since 1988 has shown a
declining trend. The relative proportion of juvenile crimes went from 1.7% in
1988 down to 0.5% in 1998 (see Table 9.2).

Table 9.3: Juvenile Delinquency (Ipc) Under Different Crime Heads 1998

Crime	1993	1994	1995	1996	1997	1998
Murder	297	288	253	270	316	251
Attempt To Commit Murder	182	166	208	202	147	161
C.h. Not Amounting To Murder	15	19	23	21	25	22
Rape	168	176	174	157	163	194
Kidnapping & Abduction	184	95	152	132	72	153
(i) Of Women & Girls	140	51	66	43	48	134
(ii) Of Others	44	44	86	89	24	19
Dacoity[1]	51	32	56	44	20	35
Preparation & Assembly For Dacoity1	5	23	3	0	1	2
Robbery	98	49	76	87	50	53
Burglary	1138	1294	1285	1315	1162	1293
Theft	2404	2346	2835	2356	1975	2152
Riots	1023	637	955	856	513	574
Criminal Breach Of Trust	15	17	33	33	16	19
Cheating	63	24	54	60	43	33
Counterfeiting	1	3	1	0	1	0
Arson	*	*	8	33	40	26
Hurt	*	*	791	1395	1242	1642
Dowry Death	*	*	27	42	49	78
Molestation	*	*	86	117	131	138
Sexual Harassment	*	*	27	13	25	37
Cruelty By Husband And Relatives	*	*	192	166	154	248
Other Ipc Crimes	3821	3392	2527	2740	1764	2228
Total Cognizable Crimes Under Upc	9465	8561	9766	10024	7909	9339

1 "Dacoity" Is Robbery Perpetrated By Armed Gangs
Source: Crime In India 1998, Ncrb, Government Of India.

Figure 9.3 Fluctuations in IPC crimes: 1997-98	
INCREASE (IPC CRIME HEADS) (Percentage change in 1998 over 1997)	DECREASE (IPC CRIME HEADS) (Percentage change in 1998 over 1997)
Rape (19%)	Murder (-20.6%)
Kidnapping and abduction of women and girls (179.2%)	Culpable homicide not amounting to murder (-12%)
Dacoity (75%)	Kidnapping and abduction (other than women and girls) (-20.8%)
Preparation and assembly for dacoity [armed robbery by gangs] (100%)	Cheating (-23.3%)
Burglary (11.3%)	Counterfeiting (-100%)
Riots (11.9%)	Arson (-35%)
Criminal breach of trust (18.8%)	
Hurt (32.2%)	
Dowry deaths (59.2%)	
Sexual harassment (48%)	
Cruelty by husband and relatives (61%)	
Other IPC crimes (26.3%)	

Table 9.3 depicts the juvenile delinquency (IPC) under different crime heads and various percentage changes from 1993 to 1998. And in Figure 9.3, one can see which ICP-recorded crimes increased versus decreased between 1997 and 1998.

On the other hand, **special and local laws** (SLL) cases registered against juveniles, like IPC crime, also went up; they increased by 36.2% during 1998 compared to 1997. Unfortunately, it is not possible to attribute the dramatic fluctuations in the data strictly to changes in the incidence of crime itself. As noted in the Introduction ("Problems with Comparative Studies"), a variety of reporting, recording and administrative factors can affect the fluctuations in IPC crimes. Notwithstanding these shortcomings, the data presented in the various tables offer tentative insight into the official juvenile crime picture in India.

Table 9.4 presents the picture of delinquents acts (SLL) under different crime heads with percentage variation in 1998 over 1997. Juvenile delinquency declined considerably under the *Arms Act* (55.4%), *Excise Act* (42%), *Indian Railways Act* (42.3%) and *Protection of Civil Rights (PCR) Act* and *Essential*

Table 9.4: Juvenile Delinquency (SII) Under Different Crime Heads And Percentage Variation 1998 Over 1997

Crime Head	Number Of Cases Reported During		Percentage Change In 1998 Over 1997
	1997	1998	
Arms Act	101	45	-55.4
Narcotic Drugs & Psy. Substances Act	11	18	63.6
Gambling Act	97	277	185.6
Excise Act	212	123	-42.0
Prohibition Act	152	1313	763.8
Explosives & Explosive Subs. Act	1	0	-100.0
Immoral Traffic (Prevention) Act	83	226	172.3
Indian Railways Act	26	15	-42.3
Registration Of Foreigners Act	18	15	-16.7
Protection Of Civil Rights Act	6	3	-50.0
Indian Passport Act	8	5	-37.5
Essential Commodities Act	2	1	-50.0
Terrorist & Disruptive Activities Act	1	0	-100.0
Antiquity & Art Treasure Act	0	0	-
Dowry Prohibition Act	3	4	33.3
Child Marriage Restraint Act	1	3	200.0
Indecent Representation Of Women (P) Act	0	0	-
Copyright Act	0	0	-
Sati Prevention Act *	0	0	-
Sc/St (Prev. Of Atrocities) Act+	15	16	6.7
Forest Act	0	5	-
Other SII Crimes	3671	393	.7.2
Total Cognizable Crimes Under SII	4408	6005	36.2

Source: Crime In India 1998, Government Of India.
*Sati - Sacrifice Of Wife At The Time Of The Death Of Husband.
+Sc/St - Scheduled Caste And Scheduled Tribe As Per The Constitution Of India.

Commodities Act (50% respectively). No delinquency case was registered for the *Explosives and Explosive Substance Act* and Terrorist and Disruptive Activity (TADA) during the year, compared to one such case in the previous year (1997). Minor increases were noticed in cases of the *Prohibition Act* (763.8%) and *Child Marriage Restraint Act* (200%).

The distribution of juvenile offences (IPC) by state under various crime heads is of great importance here. Being a vast country with a number of states/union territories (UT), and different types of religions, subcultures and communities, the offences also vary in magnitude and nature. For example, Madhya Pradesh and Maharashtra reported the highest incidence of juvenile crime (i.e., 2,349 and 2,254 incidents respectively). The above two states together registered 49.3% of the total incidence (9,339) recorded in the country. Theft (2,152), hurt (1,642) and burglary (1,293) constituted 54.5% of total juvenile IPC crimes. Of 251 cases of murder registered against juveniles, Madhya Pradesh and Maharashtra reported 65 and 46 cases respectively, which accounted for 44.2% of the total incidence of murder across India.

By contrast, data from the SLL show that in 1998 Tamil Nadu (south eastern corner of India) reported the highest number of cases (3,398, or 56.7% of all cases) in the country. Other leading states were Maharashtra (1,104), Gujarat (528), Madhya Pradesh (289) and Karnataka (204). During 1998, offences reported against juveniles in connection with SLL cases were mainly under the *Prohibition Act* (1,313), *Gambling Act* (277), *ITP Act* (226), and *Excise Act* (123).

Karnataka registered the highest number of cases (97) under the *Immoral Traffic (Prevention) Act* against delinquents, while incidence of such crimes in other states was negligibly small. Haryana registered more cases (53) under the *Excise Act*. Maharashtra reported more cases (748 and 208) against juveniles under the *Prohibition Act* and *Gambling Act* respectively.

Table 9.5 provides details on juveniles apprehended by gender and by age groups from 1988 to 1998. The table reveals that the number of juveniles apprehended has been gradually declining over the years. But it is noticed that there was an increase of 6.6% in the juveniles arrested in 1998 over the figures of 1997. The number of girls apprehended in 1998 went up by 41.1% when compared with the figures of 1997. Juveniles in the age group of 12 to 16 were more likely to commit crime under both IPC and SLL cases, and more juveniles were arrested in this age group (61.0%) in 1998. The juveniles in the age group 16 to 18 constituted 21.4% of the total arrests in 1998. Juveniles in the age group 7 to 12 comprised 17.5% of the total share of juveniles arrested in the country in 1998. Juveniles arrested in the age groups 7 to 12 and 16 to 18 increased by 21.1% and 41.3% respectively in 1998 as compared to corresponding figures for 1997. However, in the case of juveniles in the age groups 12 to 16, there was a decline of 4.9% in the number of arrests. (Crime in India, 1988).

As noted earlier, the number of juveniles being apprehended has been declining in recent years. The percentage of juvenile awaiting trial in 1996 was 39.4%, dropping to 36.2% in 1998. Of the total juveniles apprehended in 1998, 13.8% were disposed of after advice and admonition; 20.5% was placed under care of parents/guardians; 4.4% were sent to institutions; 9.2% to special homes; 4.8% were fined, and 11.1% were either acquitted or otherwise disposed of.

The distribution of juveniles apprehended (IPC+SLL) on the basis of economic background is an important aspect of the problem that needs elaboration. Table 9.6 shows the percentage of juveniles from different income groups.

Table 9.5: Juvenile Apprehended under IPC and SLL Crimes by Gender and Age-Group (1988-1998)

Year	Boys	Girls	Percentage of girls	7-12 years	Percentage to total	12-16 years	Percentage to total	16-18 years	Percentage to total	Total
1988	33065	5103	13.4	3446	9.0	31098	81.5	3624	9.5	38168
1989	24777	11615	31.9	4812	13.2	21028	57.8	10552	29.0	36392
1990	25269	5547	18.0	3681	11.9	23580	76.5	3555	11.5	30816
1991	23201	6390	21.6	5837	19.7	18887	63.8	4867	16.4	29591
1992	17474	3884	18.2	3435	16.1	14793	69.3	3130	14.7	21358
1993	16391	3676	18.3	3929	19.6	13437	67.0	2710	13.5	20067
1994	13852	3351	19.5	3694	21.5	11053	64.3	2456	14.3	17203
1995	14542	4251	22.6	3377	18.0	12013	63.9	3403	18.1	18793
1996	14068	5030	26.3	3490	18.3	11378	59.6	4230	22.1	19098
1997	14282	3514	19.7	2747	15.4	12171	68.4	2878	16.2	17796
1998	14005	4959	26.1	3327	17.5	11570	61.0	4067	21.4	18964
Percentage of change in 1998 over 1988			41.1	-3.5		-62.8		12.22		-50.3
Percentage of change in 1998 over 1997			41.3	21.1		-4.9		41.3		6.6

Source: Crime in India 1998, NCRB, Government of India.

Table 9.6: Percentage Distribution of Juveniles Apprehended (IPC+SLL) by Economic Background during 1994 to 1998						
Income Group	Income (in rupees per month)	1994	1995	1996	1997	1998
Low	≤ 500	54.1	52.9	48.7	45.3	52.1
Lower/Middle	501 to 1000	28.1	29.2	32.9	31.9	26.6
Middle	1001 to 2000	11.6	11.4	11.2	15.4	14.4
Upper Middle	2001 to 3000	3.6	4.1	5.9	5.6	5.4
Upper	> 3000	2.1	2.4	1.3	1.8	1.5

Note: one U.S. dollar is approximately equivalent in value to 46 rupees.
Source: Crime in India 1988, NCRB, Government of India.

As expected, the share of juvenile delinquents belonging to the low-income group (up to 500 rupees per month; 1 U.S. dollar = 46 rupees) steadily declined from 1994 till 1997 (see Table 9.6). Its share of 54.1% in 1994 declined to 45.3% in 1997, but it again went up to 52.1 in 1998. The share of juvenile delinquents belonging to the middle income group went down (14.4%) in 1998. A marginal decrease in the case of the upper middle-class is noticed in 1998 (5.4%) in comparison to 1997 (5.6%). In case of the upper class the same trend is noticed as in the case of the upper-middle class. In 1998, the percentage of such juveniles arrested was 1.5% whereas in 1997 it was 1.8%.

In conclusion, it can be stated that officially the problem of delinquency in India is not a serious issue. However, although the delinquency level has gradually declined since 1996 there was a marginal increase in the trend of IPC crime in 1998. By contrast, based on the number of crimes against SLL cases, there was a significant increase between 1997 and 1998. Finally, it should be noted that since only official data sources are available, and considering the level of attention given to juveniles in India, the trends should not be taken at face value. As reflected in other contributions in this text, self-report data can sometimes present a very different picture. This is an area Indian scholars and juvenile justice agencies should consider using when trying to construct a picture of youth crime in our country.

Rehabilitation of Juvenile Delinquents in India

Rehabilitation of juvenile delinquents in India is done primarily by sending them to correctional facilities such as juvenile and special homes. Section 9 of the JJA empowers the state government to establish and maintain juvenile homes for the treatment of neglected juveniles. The section further states that a juvenile home to which a neglected juvenile is sent under this act shall not only provide the juvenile with accommodation, maintenance and facilities for education, vocational training and rehabilitation, but also provide facilities for the development of character and abilities.

The act also provides for giving necessary training for protecting against moral danger or exploitation and such other facilities as are necessary for the all-round growth and development of personality. Section 15 and 21 of the JJA empower the welfare boards and juvenile courts to commit the children to juvenile homes and special homes respectively.

Generally, in correctional institutions (juvenile/special homes) two types of programs are offered. On the one hand, basic amenities like accommodation, food, clothing, health and recreation are provided, and, on the other hand, various types of education and vocational training are imparted through trained instructors. In addition, cultural meetings, parents-inmates-staff meetings, community contacts, and visits to outside institutions are used to facilitate socio-cultural development.

Community-based Rehabilitation Programs

Non-institutional or community-based rehabilitation programs for juvenile delinquents mainly include probation, release on license, after-care, and juvenile service/guidance bureaus. We will examine each of these a little more closely.

Probation:

Sections 19 and 21 of the JJA deal with the subject of probation. Under these provisions, the probation officer is expected to obtain information regarding the family of the juvenile and other information which might be necessary for the juvenile court in conducting an enquiry. On the basis of this enquiry, the juvenile court may punish the child or place the youth on probation of good conduct and place him/her under the care of a parent/guardian or a sanctioned institution.

The court may order the youth to pay a fine if s/he is over 14 years of age and has an income. Depending upon the case, in the interest of the juvenile, the court may place the juvenile under the care and protection of a probation officer for a period not exceeding three years. The probation officer's specific assignment includes preventing recurrence of the child's delinquent behavior, preventing long-time deviate or criminal careers and assisting the child to achieve his or her potential as a productive citizen through measures provided by the probation service.

Release on License/After-care:

The philosophy underlying after-care is that each juvenile must be able to adapt to the open community after s/he is rehabilitated in institutions. Since the juvenile has followed the schedule of the institution in a restricted environment, s/he may find it difficult to adjust in the open community. While the juvenile is in after-care, it is generally within the precincts of a home. Release on license is also known as "statutory after-care" and sometimes as "after-care."

The difference between statutory after-care and after-care (non-statutory) is that, in the former case, the juvenile is released on supervision on the condition that s/he will be returned to the institution if s/he violates the conditions of release. With non-statutory after-care, there is no legal binding, as s/he has already completed the entire term before being released from the institution. Section 49 of the JJA deals with the release of the juvenile on license. Section 12 (a, b) of the JJA empowers the state government to make rules to establish or recognize after-care organizations for the purpose of taking care of juveniles after they have been released from juvenile or special homes.

Juvenile Service/Guidance Bureau:

Juvenile services/guidance bureaus, in a strict sense, are not really for the rehabilitation of juvenile delinquents. Rather, they have been established to prevent juvenile delinquency. However, released juveniles can also make use of them. The juvenile services guidance bureaus are functioning in very few states at present in India.

There are 41 juvenile guidance centers in the state of Maharastra, of which four are run by the government at the divisional headquarters of Bombay, Pune, Nagpur and Aurangabad, and the remainder are managed by voluntary agencies. Besides, the Juvenile Aid Police Unit runs 11 centers in Bombay. The Children's Aid Society's Juvenile Service Bureau, Bombay, was established in 1954, with the financial assistance given by the Central Social Welfare Board.

Since 1988, the bureau has received further impetus owing to the funds provided by UNICEF. The objectives of the bureau are to:
1. focus public attention on health and welfare needs of socially and physically handicapped children,
2. provide consultative services in guidance, counseling and therapy,
3. provide referral and diagnostic services to schools, teachers, parents or guardians and other agencies,
4. maintain, in cooperation with other welfare agencies, central social exchange agencies,
5. cooperate with civic and educational institutions and welfare agencies in evolving suitable programs for children's physical, mental and educational growth, and

6. conduct and promote scientific research and work with factual data to determine the special needs of children in difficult circumstances.

An Integrated Program for Street Children:

The scheme for the welfare of street children was updated in 1998 by the Ministry of Welfare (now called Ministry of Social Justice and Empowerment) and is now called an "integrated program for street children." The salient features of the revised program are as follows:

- The basic aim of the program is to prevent destitution of children and facilitate their withdrawal from a life on the streets;
- Under the program a wide range of initiatives relating to street children have been enforced which cater to their shelter, nutrition, drinking water, proper education, recreational facilities, protection against abuse, and exploitation;
- In addition to voluntary organizations, under the revised program, state governments, union territory administrations, local bodies, and educational institutes are also eligible for financial assistance;
- The target group of this program is essentially children without homes and family (i.e., street children and children especially vulnerable to abuse and exploitation, such as children of sex workers and children of pavement dwellers);
- The government of India will cover up to 90% of the cost of each project undertaken, although in the case of union territory administration 100% of the cost can be covered for operating a project; and
- This program requires participation of organizations having experience with working for children, although this clause can be disregarded in certain circumstances.

Again, in addition to the integrated program for street children, a child-line service was also introduced. The child line is a 24-hour free home service that can be accessed by dialing 1098 on a telephone.[8] Child line provides emergency assistance to children who are in need. The service focuses on children living alone on the streets, child laborers working in unorganized sectors of the labor market, domestic workers, and the sexually abused.

As a part of the Ministry of Social Justice and Empowerment's plan of action for strengthening and improving facilities for children, a project was launched seeking participation of the corporate sector for providing additional facilities in observation/juvenile/special homes. In 1991, a pilot project was initiated with the help of an external agency entitled "Advantage India." The purpose was to conduct a needs assessment of all the homes in Bihar and

Delhi. The possible areas of intervention and help by the corporate sector in these homes were identified with the help of staff deployed in the homes.

Initiatives Taken by the National Human Rights Commission (NHRC)

Under section 12(c) of the *Protection of Human Rights Act* (1993), the National Human Rights Commission has been entrusted with the responsibility of visiting any jail or any other institution under the control of the state government where persons are detained or lodged for purposes of treatment, reformation, or protection, and of studying the living conditions of inmates and making recommendations for improvement.

In March 1997, the commission undertook a nationwide initiative to bring about comprehensive improvements in various custodial and other probation homes set up in different states. At the onset detailed questionnaires were prepared and dispatched to the state governments seeking information on the working conditions in such institutions. The questionnaires sought to elicit information on the following five categories of institutions: 1) observation/juvenile/special homes set up under the JJA; 2) probation homes set up under the *Probation of Offenders Act*; 3) short stay homes/*nari niketans* set up under the *Immoral Traffic (Prevention) Act*; 4) reception centers/beggars homes set up under the *Prevention of Beggars/Begging Act*, and 5) borstal institutions set up under the *Borstals Act*. The information sought from the states under some 26 sub-heads includes, among other things, details regarding statutory requirements, the number of institutions, the profiles of inmates, matters connected with accommodation and living conditions, medical facilities, facilities for education, training, recreation, information concerning supervisory arrangements and cooperation with non-government organizations. The final outcome is yet to come out. We may expect concrete and fruitful findings, as the commission had already cautioned that it would take a serious view if the information sought for the survey is found to be improper (Tiwari, 1998).

Role of the Police and Other Agencies

Often being the first formal point of contact for juvenile delinquents (see Figure 9.2), the police play an important role in combating juvenile delinquency. Prior to Indian independence, the role of the police was indeed questionable as they were treated as an agency that used to suppress people who refused to obey (Ram, 1999). The current role emerged after newly independent India became a welfare state in January 1950, and various legislation was passed to protect children. This shift also resulted in changes in the duties assigned to the police. (Note, however, that it has been reported that in India the police have not been able to give adequate attention to the subject of juvenile delinquency owing to their preoccupation with law-and-order duties [Ram, 1999].)

Given their responsibilities, it is necessary that even in such routine matters as arrest and interrogation, care should be taken by the police official to make them less traumatic to the child. In accordance with the JJA and its modified justice orientation, the action of the police should be planned in such a way that it does not cause irreparable damage to the tender mind of the child. However, the manner in which the police handle young offenders has been the subject matter of much study by criminologists and administrators alike since such approaches have not been part of traditional practices (Rao, 1965).

Today the role of police in community coordination is to develop overall crime prevention programs. To do so, the police work in coordination with other agencies (e.g., non-governmental organizations working in a related sphere for the prevention of juvenile delinquency).

In 1952, the government of India invited Walter C. Reckless, a prominent American criminologist and U.N. expert on social defence, to assist in defining the role of police in India. According to Reckless, the police should exercise a liberal attitude towards children, taking children to their parents and rendering any other possible help. Only in extreme cases should the police take the juvenile to remand homes or produce them before court. The seminar on "Juvenile Delinquency—Role of Police," organized by the Central Bureau of Investigation in 1965, felt that the police must play a positive role in preventing juvenile delinquency and treat juvenile delinquents with sympathy. It was also felt that the police should leave the juvenile delinquent on probation so that s/he can grow up in the community milieu. In 1970, a similar recommendation was made by the seminar on "People's Role in Social Defence" organized by the Central Institute of Research and Training in Public Cooperation, and in 1971 by the National Correctional Conference on Probation and Allied Measures.

The National Police Commission in its second report in 1970 recommended that juveniles becoming wayward, taking drugs, or pilfering objects out of bravado could be officially warned and their parents duly advised. Persons in danger of falling into the clutches of criminals could be brought to notice of social welfare organizations. Counseling and warning should be deemed legitimate police crime prevention activities, and recognized as such in law. The commission further recommended that the police be properly trained in service-oriented functions, including the counseling of persons in distressful conditions, which the commission recognized as "service par excellence."

The same commission in its fifth report in 1980 recognized the importance of women police in dealing with women and juvenile delinquents. They are now attached to city police stations and juvenile aid police units.

The Juvenile Aid Police Unit in Bombay was set up as part of the vigilance section of the Criminal Investigation Department to function under the general guidance and control of the Deputy Commission of Police. The unit undertook the responsibility of identifying the breeding areas for juvenile delinquency, determining the problems of these juveniles and recommending institutional care wherever necessary. Subsequent to this, juvenile aid police units or bureaus were established in Calcutta (1956), Hyderabad (1958), Madras (1960), Patna and Ranchi (1961), Calicut (1970), and Bhilai, Indore and Jabalpur (1974). The third five-year plan took note of the good work done by these units and recommended establishing specialist units in all cities having a population of 100,000 or more. Today it is generally agreed that the specialist units should be part and parcel of the general police function, and their work should be fully integrated with normal police work.

The observations made by the Rustomji Committee in 1954 on the problem of juvenile delinquency are worth mentioning. In its report, the committee observed that the police needed to be confronted directly about their handling of the subject. What was needed was a change of outlook, so that an average constable would not consider a juvenile offender a hardened criminal but a child deserving protection. Then as now, a systematic and planned effort to educate the rank and file of the police about their proper role in identifying pre-delinquent children and about the correct methods of dealing with them was a pressing need. Senior police officers should ensure that the dealings of their subordinates with juveniles are in conformity with this new spirit.

The police also have a major role to play in juvenile courts under the various children acts. Police are enjoined not to appear before the child in uniform. Children are not to be handcuffed. It is also provided in the act that as soon as the child is arrested or bailed out, the police officer should inform the probation officer of the area, the name, and the address of the parents, and other particulars of the child.

Police officials also play a very important role in after-care. Very thoughtful efforts are necessary to resettle youths to make a new beginning in their lives. This task again lies with police officials. The *Children Act, Borstals School Act*, and *Probation of Offenders Act* all provide that there is no disqualification attached to conviction under these acts. An institutional term spent in certified schools or in schools under the *Borstals School Act* should not pose an obstacle when the juvenile reintegrates into the community.

From the above discussion it becomes evident that police officials should be given proper training regarding their role in preventing and controlling juvenile delinquency. Systematic training courses in correctional work are also necessary. The National Police Academy has already introduced such courses for senior police officials. It has also been recommended by the Central Bureau of Correctional Services that all state police training colleges and schools should also introduce lectures on criminology, correctional legislation, treatment of offenders, and similar subjects.

Since the approach towards delinquency is rehabilitative in nature rather than punitive, the role of **legal practitioner** is not considered more valuable than that of magistrates or probation officers. However, the legal practitioner participates in the proceedings of the juvenile courts and provides relevant legal information and advice to the court and the juvenile so as to assist the court in reaching a constructive resolution to each case.

While social and cultural factors play a vital role in rehabilitating juveniles in India, these factors are not well addressed within the juvenile justice system. The basic problem lies in the awareness of the general public of the principles and modalities of the system. For example, the nomenclature "juvenile" is unknown not only to the common person, but even to police and the literate class of the society. Hence, the attitude of the public towards juveniles may be regarded as deplorable. The situation is further complicated and compounded by the lack of funds and the apathetic attitude many administrators display towards the establishment of such homes. Nevertheless, there have been a number of local and state initiatives that show promise in creating a social awareness and demonstrating a degree of commitment to helping juvenile offenders.

Finally, it is widely believed that the **correctional institutions** are mostly not able to achieve even the legislatively prescribed objectives of reformation and rehabilitation of the juvenile delinquents institutionalized in them (Bedi, 1976). In fact, most institutions are suffering from chronic handicaps like the problematic background of their inmates; lack of, or inadequate, staff training; insufficient treatment and after-care facilities, and unsystematized and irregular functional routines. Collectively, these hindrances only serve to widen the gap between the modern philosophy the state is attempting to incorporate and its ability to fulfill these goals (Bedi, 1976).

SUMMARY

While India is steeped in history and culture when compared to most Western nations, the evolution of juvenile justice has been slow. However, in 1986 various initiatives culminated in the JJA which, while representing a modified justice approach, contains elements of the welfare model of juvenile justice. The act includes provisions that attempt to organize efforts to prevent and treat juvenile social maladjustment in keeping with the rights and interests of the children and young persons involved. A comprehensive approach towards the JJA brings within its purview not only children who come into conflict with the law but also children who have the tendency to drift into criminal behavior due to situational triggers.

In fact, juvenile justice in India is a social justice issue that has to define itself within the care and protection of children generally. There is universal acceptance of the principle that a juvenile offender cannot be compared to an adult criminal in terms of maturation and responsibility and accountability for his or her deeds. Accordingly, the JJA, with its welfare philosophy, plays a pivotal role in bringing the delinquent or neglected juvenile back into the mainstream of social life. This has led to the emergence and progressive refinement of a separate system of juvenile justice distinct from the one that regulates adult offenders.

To sum up, it is clear from the above that in modern times the approach to the problem of juvenile delinquency is based on assumptions that are markedly different from traditional ones. In varying degrees, this is reflected in juvenile legislation and services as well as in the processing of delinquents. This notwithstanding, the problem is growing. This ominous trend could safely be attributed to a variety of environmental changes. In view of this juvenile legislation, police, courts and institutional and non- institutional services—all need to be further streamlined.

In an orientation program that took place in June of 2000, Delhi police personnel gathered to discuss ways to engender a more sensitive approach towards juveniles and delinquents. Among the recommendations that emerged from the meeting, it was suggested that exploitation of a child, induction of a child into begging and other criminal activities should be severely dealt with. Children are coerced into these activities by their parents in most cases and so the problem must be discussed not in isolation but with an eye to the large picture. A ray of hope was seen when the government decided to amend the existing *Juvenile Justice Act*. However, compared to many Western countries, our juvenile justice system needs an infusion of internal support on all levels, and it has been suggested that we could benefit from the support and experiences of other countries that take a philosophical approach to the handling of juvenile delinquents similar to India's.

Tapan Chakraborty at present works as an analyst in the Bureau of Police Research and Development under the Ministry of Home Affairs, Government of India. After completion of a master's degree in economics in 1975, he worked in the National Sample Survey Organisation (Field Operation Division) under the Ministry of Planning, Government of India. He then switched over to his present department. He is about to complete his Ph.D in police science from Choudhury Charan Singh University, Meerut.

   Shri Chakraborty's main field of interest is crime and criminology with a focus on participatory approaches. He has published research papers on policing in various parts of India as well as presented an array of scholarly works on policing and victimology.

Shri Chakraborty has been nominated as one of the expert members of UNICRI, Italy, for the Asia-Pacific region. He is also a member of Asia-Crime Prevention Foundation, Japan.

Helpful Websites

www.louisville.edu/library/ekstrom/govpubs/international/india/indiacrime.html Located at the University of Louisville in Louisville, Kentucky. This site provides a number of links on Indian culture, including criminal justice.

http://www.bprd.org. A weblink of the Bureau of Police Research and Development, Ministry of Home Affairs, Government of India. This site is under construction. It will provide details of research activities on police science and the criminal justice system of India.

www.ncrbindia.org This site will soon provide statistical figures of crime in India.

Key Terms and Concepts

Juvenile Justice Act   welfare model
modified justice model   National Human Rights Commission
Indian Penal Code   special and local laws
Children Act   legal practitioner
correctional institutions

Study Questions

1. What are the far-reaching effects of the *Juvenile Justice Act* of 1986?
2. What are the important features of the *Juvenile Justice Act* of 1986?
3. How is the *Juvenile Justice Act* of 1986 different from legislation to prevent juvenile delinquency in your country?
4. How do the juvenile homes and the special homes contribute to the overall development and rehabilitation of neglected and delinquent juveniles?
5. Compare and contrast the various years, with the help of the statistical data provided, and show whether juvenile delinquency is on the increase or on the decrease in India.
6. According to you, is the total eradication of juvenile delinquency possible without altering the infrastructure of your country?

Notes

1   The author is indebted to Ms. Roweena Soloman, Research Scholar, JNU, New Delhi for her sincere assistance in completing this project.
2   The 1991 census was not undertaken in Jammu and Kashmir—the most north-westerly state in India.
3   Depending on the source used, the total number of languages and dialects ranges between 179 and 188 languages and between 49 and 544 dialects.
4   The exclusion of Jammu and Kashmir (JandK) does not discriminate against the children of JandK because the *JandK Children Act* 1970 is in *pari materia* with the *Children Act* 1960 which, in turn, is similar to JJA.
5   Theft - Whoever intending to take dishonestly any moveable out of the possession of any person without that person's consent, moves that property in order to such taking, is said to commit theft [sec.378, (p. 531)], Robbery - In all "robbery" there

is either theft or extortion... Snatching - Whoever assaults or uses criminal force to any person, in attempting to commit theft of any property which that person is then wearing or carrying, shall be punished with imprisonment of either description for a term which may extend to two years, or with fine, or with both (sec. 356, p. 488) (Source: The Indian Penal Code [1999]).

6 The differential definition in age of responsibility was introduced by the *Children Act* of 1960. The definition had two presuppositions. First, that 16 was the appropriate age for granting protection, and second, girls needed protection for two more years because of social circumstances (Kumari, 1993).

7 In such conditions, juveniles are kept sometimes under the supervision of a probation officer or sent to an observation home.

8 In India, the free home service is available in ten major cities. Since its inception in October of 1998 until July 2000, there have been 200,000 phone calls for varying types of services. The calls include calls for: a) medical assistance (7620), b) shelter (6899), c) missing children (2918), d) protection from abuse (1016), and e) emotional support and guidance (18735). "Butterfly" Green Park, Mandiwala Gali, New Delhi).

REFERENCES

Bedi, M. S. (1976). *Socially handicapped children: A study of the institutional changes*. Jodhpur: Jain Brothers.

Bhatnagar, R. (2000, June 28). Govt. plans to amend Juvenile Justice Act. *The Times of India*, p. 7.

Chakraborti, N .K. (1999). *Juvenile justice in the administration of criminal justice*. New Delhi: Deep and Deep Publishers.

Chandrachud, Justice Y.V., & Manohar, V.R. (1999). *The Indian Penal Code* (28th ed.). New Delhi: Rajindra Book Agency.

Department of Women and Child Development. (1999). *Annual report 1998-1999*. New Delhi: Ministry of Human Resources Development.

Department of Women and Child Development. (2000). *Annual report 1999-2000*. New Delhi: Ministry of Human Resources Development.

First report of the National Police Commission. (1970). New Delhi: Government of India.

Gokhale, S.D. (1982, Sept.). Juvenile delinquency, social change, 12, 3, 22–25.

Jayaram. C. (1999). A critical analysis of juvenile justice act. In N.K. Chakraborti (Ed.), *Juvenile justice in the administration of criminal justice* (pp. 51–57). New Delhi: Deep and Deep Publishers.

The Juvenile Justice Act. New Delhi : Government of India.

Kumari, V. (1993). *The treatise on Juvenile Justice Act, (1986)*. New Delhi: Law Centre, Faculty of Law, University of Delhi.

Ministry of Home Affairs. (1954). *Report of the Committee of the Inspector General of Police Conference*. New Delhi: Government of India.

Ministry of Home Affairs. (1984). *The Jail Reforms Committee (1980–1983)*. New Delhi: Government of India.

Mishra, B.N. (1991). *Juvenile delinquency and juvenile justice*. New Delhi: Ashish Publishing.

National Crime Records Bureau. (1999). *Crime in India: 1998*. New Delhi: Government of India.

National Institute of Social Defence. (1970). *Juvenile delinquency—A challenge: Care and protection services for children under the children acts*. New Delhi: Ministry of Welfare, Government of India.

National Institute of Social Defence. (1979). *Towards delinquency control*. New Delhi: Ministry of Welfare, Government of India.

National Institute of Social Defence. (1996). *Control of juvenile delinquency*. New Delhi: Ministry of Welfare, Government of India.

Need felt to handle juvenile crimes sensitively. (2000, May 30). *Hindustan Times*, p. 4.

Newman, C. L. (1973). *Source book on probation, parole and pardons*. Springfield, IL: Charles C. Thomas.

Panakal, J.J. (1955). Aftercare. *The Indian Journal of Social Work,* 16 (1). Cited in N.K Chakraborti, (Ed.), (1999), *Juvenile justice*. New Delhi: Deep and Deep Publication.

Pitts, J. (1988). *The police of juvenile crime*. New Delhi: Sage.

Ram D. (1999). *Role of various agencies in combating juvenile delinquency*. New Delhi: Bureau of Police Research and Development, Ministry of Home Affairs, Government of India.

Rao. S.V. (1965, November 25–27). *Working paper on the seminar on juvenile delinquency: Role of the police*. New Delhi: Central Bureau of Investigation, Ministry of Home Affairs, Government of India.

Roy J.G. (1965). *Role of voluntary agencies in prevention and control of juvenile delinquency* (pp. 17–18). New Delhi: National Institute of Social Defence, Ministry of Welfare, Government of India.

Second report of the National Police Commission. (1979). New Delhi: Government of India.

Sethna, M.J. (1971). *Society and the criminal* (3rd ed.). Bombay: N.P.Tripathi Pvt. Ltd.

Singh, H. (1999). United Nations standards for juvenile justice. In N.K. Chakraborty, (Ed.), *Juvenile justice in the administration of criminal justice*. New Delhi: Deep and Deep Publishers.

Srimad Bhagwat Gita. (2000; Sri P.K. Siddarth, Trans.). Gorakhpur, Uttar Pradesh (India): Geeta Press.

Srivastava, S.P. (1989). *Juvenile justice in India: Policy, programme and perspective*. New Delhi: Ajanta Publishers.

Supreme Court clears doubt in JJA. (2000, June 14). *Hindustan Times*, p. 12.

Tappan, P.W. (1949). *Juvenile delinquency*. New York: McGraw Hill.

Third Report of the National Police Commission. (1980). New Delhi: Government of India.

Tiwari, A. (1998). Administration of juvenile institutions in India: An overview. *Indian Journal of Criminology*, 26 (1&2): 46–54.

Trojanowicz, R.C. (1983). *Juvenile delinquency: Concept and control* (3rd Ed.). Englewood Cliffs, NJ: Prentice Hall.

Walker, R.N. (1973). *Psychology of young offenders*. Cincinnati: Thomas.

Wani, A.L. (1999). Juvenile delinquency in India. In N.K. Chakraborti (Ed.), *Juvenile justice in the administration of criminal justice* (pp. 28–41). New Delhi: Deep and Deep Publishers.

Chapter 10

Comparative Juvenile Justice:
An Overview of Italy

Uberto Gatti
Alfredo Verde
DI.ME.L — Section of Criminology and Forensic Psychiatry
University of Genova

FACTS ON ITALY

Area: 301,303 sq. km. **Population**: 57,910,000 in 1995. The capital is Rome (pop. 2.7 million). Other main cities include Milan, Naples, Turin, Genoa, Palermo, Venice, Florence, and Bologna. Population density is 192 per sq. km. **Economy**: Throughout Italy's 130-year history as a nation-state, its various regions have undergone widely differing patterns of development. In very approximate terms, the north of the country is economically and industrially well developed, while the south lags far behind, as a result having fewer industries and a higher rate of unemployment. The post-war period in Italy witnessed a considerable economic boom (60% employed in service industry and 32% in industry), which prompted copious migration from the south to the north and from the rural areas to the cities (71% of the pop.). In recent years the new phenomenon of immigration from non-E.E.C. countries has appeared in Italy, giving rise to a wide range of problems that our society was unprepared to tackle. **Government**: Parliamentary republic, with a House of Deputies and a Senate, divided into twenty regions, with limited autonomy from the central government. A wide constitutional and political reformation is taking place, but it is still too early to say what its results will be. Main political parties: Forza Italia, Alleanza Nazionale (Casa delle libertà), Partito Democratico della Sinistra and allies (Alleanza dell'Ulivo), Rifondazione Comunista.

The most certain method of preventing crime is to perfect the system of education.

C. Beccaria, On crimes and punishments *(1963:65).*

THE BIRTH OF THE JUVENILE JUSTICE SYSTEM IN ITALY

Juvenile courts in Italy, unlike many of their Western counterparts, were not established until 1934. The courts' jurisdiction covers all minors and is divided into three sectors: penal, civil, and the particular sector of "administrative" or rehabilitative jurisdiction.

The juvenile court is made up of four individuals who preside over the cases that come before the court. They include an appeals court judge who presides over the court proceedings; a court magistrate and two citizens, one man and one woman, whom act as assistants and consultants in the case. The citizens are chosen from among experts in the fields of biology, psychiatry, criminal anthropology, education, and psychology. They must have distinguished themselves in community service and be at least 30 years of age (art. 2, R.D. n°1404/1934).

Article 97 of the Italian Penal Code states that a person who has not reached the age of 14 at the moment when he or she commits a crime must not be punished.[1] Article 98, sub-section 1 of the penal code states, in turn, that a person who has reached the age of 14 but not 18 at the time of committing a crime and who is "capable of understanding and willing" (*capace di intendere e di volere—mens rea*) must be punished, but the punishment may be reduced. At the age of majority, 18 years old, the person becomes fully responsible for his or her crimes. Between the ages of 14 to18 the ability to understand and to form mental intent must be clearly ascertained in each case by the presiding judge. Unlike in the adult system, juvenile court judges are not bound by specific technical methods of investigation. The system recognizes that the cognitive inability of a juvenile to understand and to form intent is not necessarily the same as that of an adult. In this respect the courts have established the concept of "immaturity": a condition of inadequate physical, psychological, or even social development.

In practice, the presiding guidelines have been interpreted in very different ways, to the extent that some juvenile courts (especially in the north of Italy) have, in the past, frequently acquitted minors on the grounds of immaturity, while others have applied this provision very sparingly. At the present time, acquittal on the grounds of immaturity appears to find limited application. The magistrates prefer to take advantage of the wide range of solutions made available by the new penal procedure for minors.

Since minors under the age of 14 are not responsible, they are automatically acquitted. Minors between the ages of 14 to 18 may be given a custodial sentence, which is usually reduced to two-thirds of the sentence that would have been imposed on an adult offender for the same crime. Usually, however, once having been deemed responsible, they will be offered the benefit of a diminished punishment.

THE EVOLUTION OF THE JUVENILE JUSTICE SYSTEM IN ITALY

After World War II, the first substantial modification of the juvenile justice system was enacted by legislation in 1956. This modification was oriented towards a *rehabilitative* approach, and in 1962 a whole range of assistance services were established. These included a social service for minors, which was to work in close coordination with the juvenile court and whose task was to provide technical support in the penal field, as well as carrying out a range of interventions to help and support minors in the civil and "administrative" fields.

Before 1956 magistrates in the juvenile courts had mainly made use of penal measures (e.g., crime control and the justice model), though these were tempered with rehabilitative elements. This was in keeping with the thinking of the day, which attributed an important correctional function to the sentence imposed. After 1956, however, juvenile delinquency was tackled from a rehabilitative standpoint by means of a dialectic liaison between the courts and social services. Thus, the 1956 model combined penal intervention and assistance, punishment, and welfare. The program came under the auspices of the juvenile courts and the centralized social services department of the Justice ministry. However, in practice the rehabilitative institutions (which housed minors defined as "wayward in behavior and character" under the terms of the so-called "administrative" jurisdiction) did not differ greatly in organization or atmosphere from penal detention centers (Senzani, 1970). According to Betti and Pavarini (1985), the overall effect of this set of provisions was to create a correctional continuum inspired by the need for social control, whether or not the minor had committed any crime. Hence the model was essentially a blend of the **crime control** and **justice model**, as described in Figure 1—see Introduction.

Indeed, the years following 1956 saw a robust expansion in the administrative sector, which became the most commonly used means of dealing with juvenile problems. In spite of the face-lift they had been given by the new rehabilitative ideology, institutions for the rehabilitation of minors remained starkly backward—without trained staff and housed in ancient buildings which were uncomfortable and often lacked adequate sanitation. For example, a number of the institutions included old monasteries, convents, and outdated boarding schools. The backwardness of these structures, which distinguished Italy from neighboring countries such as France, contributed to an upsurge of scathing criticism of the system in the 1960s. The problems related to juvenile justice, which until then had been the exclusive province of specialists, for the first time came in for scrutiny and discussion by protest movements, the mass media, and the general public, as did the psychiatric institutions of the day. In this climate of protest, the authorities undertook initiatives to open rehabilitative institutions to the outside world. This was nevertheless accompanied by an increased use of penal structures.

In summary, the birth of juvenile justice in Italy did not follow a similar path to that of many Western countries. In fact, its genesis was in response to academic, public, and social criticism. For a country which has a rich history in criminological thought and justice reform (e.g., for formulation of a Civil Code, Beccaria (1963), and Lombroso (see Martin, Mutchnick, and Austin [1990]), this may seem out of character. However, the situation speaks to the general diversity of juvenile justice around the world and the merits in examining such a complex and diverse issue.

JUVENILE JUSTICE AFTER THE DECENTRALIZATION AND REFORM OF THE WELFARE SYSTEM

In 1977 a presidential decree (D.P.R. n°616, 24/7/1977) on administrative decentralization brought about a sweeping transformation in the practical workings of the juvenile justice system. The legislation transferred executive authority over decisions taken in the civil and administrative fields, from the social services department of the Justice ministry to the social services departments of local authorities. Though still imposed by the juvenile courts, rehabilitative measures now took on a completely different meaning. Local authorities, especially in the large cities of northern Italy, fostered the development of alternative social policies, inserting minors from the juvenile justice system into the general social welfare processing system for minors and their families. The model deeply transformed justice procedures as there was a shift towards community intervention and small residential structures (such as group homes). This reform, however, gave rise to numerous conflicts between magistrates in the juvenile courts and local authority administrators. In many cases the magistrates demanded greater control over young deviants, including the use of closed, more coercive institutions (Ricciotti, 1982). This was juxtaposed to the local authorities, which stressed the roles of assistance and rehabilitation in their intervention. This latter approach was aimed at improving compliance and avoiding the stigmatization and exclusion associated with closed institutions. This was done by placing problem juveniles in non-specialist programs designed for all minors.

A particular area of conflict arose regarding the measures to be imposed on problem juveniles. The new legislation had created the conditions for possible clashes between resources and decisions. Indeed, under the provisions of D.P.R. n°616/1977, the measures to be imposed on deviant minors were to be decided by the juvenile courts. However, the provisions were to be implemented by the local authorities. This meant that the local authorities were, in effect, able to organize alternative forms of intervention that would remove minors from the penal-administrative system and, thus, effect a progressive separation between the justice and welfare systems. This separation, which stemmed from the assignment of jurisdiction to two different bodies (Justice ministry and local authorities), led to clashes between magistrates of the juvenile courts and local authority social service departments (Gatti and Verde, 1988). The implementation of the court-imposed measures depended on the structures that the local authorities had provided. Consequently, magistrates were considerably hampered in their work since they could only request intervention that was actually available. Before that time the problem had been less acutely felt, as magistrates and rehabilitation structures both belonged to the same environment (that of the Justice ministry). Under this model the values and ideologies were less divergent.

In reply to the criticism leveled at them by the magistrates, the local authorities cited their constitutionally recognized right to autonomy in their intervention. This claim was later given a solid juridical basis by an important pronouncement of the Constitutional Court (n°174/1981). The amendment upheld the local authorities' right to make decisions regarding the means of handling juvenile-related problems. Subsequently, as the new system came to be accepted, conflict diminished even though a few penal social workers and magistrates held onto their familiarity with the justice model and subsequently continued to call for more stringent laws and institutions.

THE NEW JUVENILE PENAL PROCEDURE

The approval of D.P.R. n°448/1988, which introduced a new juvenile penal procedure, effected further important changes within the broader context of penal procedure code reform. In the shift from an inquisitorial to an accusatory model, a profound change was brought about in the judicial context and penal proceedings concerning juveniles, and it is within this context that the current system is set.

The process is divided into three phases. The first of these, the so-called preliminary investigation, conducted by the public prosecutor through the criminal investigation department of the police (under the supervision of the magistrate for preliminary investigations) is not really a judicial phase at all. A preliminary hearing then follows, during which the judge assesses the investigations carried out and, after hearing the arguments put forward by the public prosecutor and the defending attorney, decides whether to dismiss the case or order a trial. The third phase concerns the trial itself, during which the evidence is scrutinized and debated.

Within this general context, the norms governing juvenile penal procedure have undergone a series of adjustments in order to apply the new principles to minors in such a way as to protect the minors themselves. The adjustments also endow the trial with a rehabilitative character, while still guaranteeing the individual's rights, such as the presumption of innocence and right to legal assistance. In this framework plea-bargaining is not an option for minors, but there are comparable provisions, such as:

- An "abbreviated" trial. This can occur when the accused asks for a preliminary hearing to be regarded as definitive. The accused is then entitled to a one-third reduction in his/her sentence.
- An "immediate" trial has no preliminary hearing as such. The case goes directly to trial.
- An "accelerated" trial is conducted when the minor has been arrested *in flagrante* or else confesses. For minors a personality assessment must be carried out.

Under the terms of D.P.R. n°449/1988, the preliminary investigation is headed by a magistrate of the juvenile court, while the preliminary hearing is carried out by one professional magistrate and two honorary magistrates (one man and one woman). The trial itself takes place in the juvenile court in its ordinary composition. The case is prosecuted by the public prosecutor who is attached to the juvenile court (see Figure 10.1).

The magistrate in charge of preliminary investigations is responsible for ensuring that the investigations are carried out in a proper and timely fashion, as well as safeguarding the freedom of the person under investigation. Within the sphere of the preliminary hearing, the magistrate can decide to commit the minor for trial, find "no grounds for prosecution," place the youth on probation, or may apply an alternative sanction to detention. During the trial, which is not usually public, the accused is questioned directly by the presiding magistrate; in order to avoid any trauma, the minor is not cross-examined. A verdict is then reached.

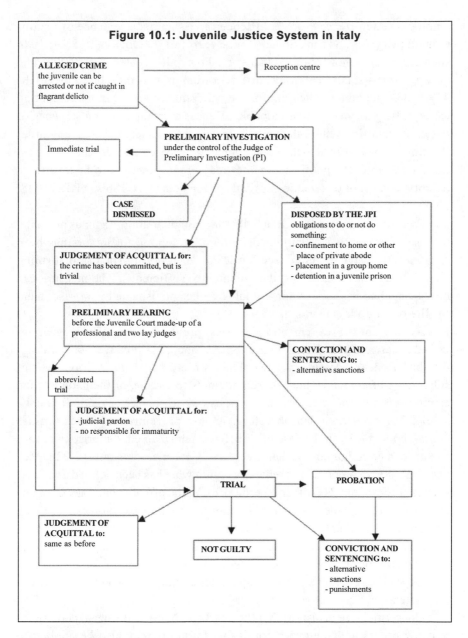

Figure 10.1: Juvenile Justice System in Italy

ALLEGED CRIME
the juvenile can be
arrested or not if caught in
flagrant delicto

Reception centre

PRELIMINARY INVESTIGATION
under the control of the Judge of
Preliminary Investigation (PI)

Immediate trial

CASE DISMISSED

DISPOSED BY THE JPI
obligations to do or not do
something:
- confinement to home or other
  place of private abode
- placement in a group home
- detention in a juvenile prison

JUDGEMENT OF ACQUITTAL for:
the crime has been committed, but is
trivial

PRELIMINARY HEARING
before the Juvenile Court made-up of a
professional and two lay judges

CONVICTION AND SENTENCING to:
- alternative sanctions

abbreviated
trial

JUDGEMENT OF ACQUITTAL for:
- judicial pardon
- no responsible for immaturity

TRIAL

PROBATION

JUDGEMENT OF ACQUITTAL to:
same as before

NOT GUILTY

CONVICTION AND SENTENCING to:
- alternative
  sanctions
- punishments

Sentencing Options

We shall now examine the provisions relating to the arrest and detention of minors. A minor can be arrested *in flagrante* if caught in the act of committing a crime eligible for preventive detention (art. 16 sub-section 1 D.P.R. n°448/1988). In any case, a minor may be detained if suspected of having committed a non-culpable offence. Such an offence carries a prison sentence of a minimum of two years and a maximum of nine years (art. 17 D.P.R. n°448/1988). In such cases, the minor is housed in a special reception center (*Centro di prima accoglienza*)—small institutions different from prisons introduced by D.P.R. 448/1988—pending the hearing for the validation of arrest. In the remaining cases of flagrancy (e.g., non-culpable offences carrying a prison sentence of not more than five years), the bailiffs or law-enforcement officers may order the minor to be confined to the family home. If the parents are absent or deemed to be unreliable, the public prosecutor may order the minor to be taken to a reception center or to a public or private group home (art. 18bis D.P.R. n°448/1988).

Even though section D.P.R. n°448/1988 sought to limit, as far as possible, the use of preventive detention for minors, the option for minors has been subsequently extended under section D.P.R. n° 12/1991. The original ruling was deemed not to safeguard the community sufficiently. The measure can now be applied in cases of non-culpable crimes punishable by imprisonment for life or for no less than nine years.

Apart from the aforementioned cases, preventive detention may be invoked in cases of aggravated theft, robbery, rape, extortion, weapons or drug-related offences. Detention can only be ordered if there is grave risk of subversion of evidence, the accused attempts to escape, or the nature of the crime is considered to represent a serious risk to society or the individual's safety. The magistrate can, therefore, impose preventive measures (*misure cautelari*), but only in the case of an offence punishable by imprisonment for life or for a period of no less than five years. Such measures (art. 19-22 D.P.R. n°448/1988) are ordered hierarchically within what has been defined as a "correctional continuum" (Gatti and Verde, 1991). The offender can pass from one level to another in the event of non-compliance (the harshest measure being preventive detention in prison for a maximum period of one month). These measures are constituted by *prescrizioni* that involve ordering the minor to carry out study or work activities, "confinement to home or other place of private abode," placement in a group home, and the aforementioned preventive detention.

Concerning the decisions that the court can impose, the penal code states that the orders and sentences applicable to adults may also be applied to minors (e.g., suspended sentence, non-registration of the conviction in criminal records, rehabilitation, alternative sanctions) with considerable latitude and reductions, as well as the particularities specifically designed for minors. These latter are worth examining in detail:

- Judicial pardon: this is a form of depenalization applicable only once. The magistrate deems that a sentence may be imposed which restricts personal liberty for a period of no more than two years. A pardon may be applied when, having assessed the gravity of the offence and the individual's potential for delinquency, the magistrate presumes that the minor will not commit any further offences (art. 169 penal code and art.19 R.D. n°1404/1934). The measure remains on the minor's criminal record until s/he reaches the age of 21 years.

- Dismissal on the grounds of inability to understand and to form intent (*mens rea*) (*incapacità di intendere e di volere*). As mentioned above, this depends on the ascertainment of a condition of immaturity.

- Dismissal on the grounds of the insignificance of the offence (*irrilevanza del fatto*): art. 27 of D.P.R. 448/1988 states that, "if the offence is petty and the behavior out-of-character, and when to proceed with the case would jeopardize the minor's education," the public prosecutor may ask the magistrate to dismiss the case on the grounds of insignificance of the offence.

- Suspension of the trial and imposition of probation (*sospensione del processo e messa alla prova*): operated by the social services department of the Justice ministry. This measure can be adopted either at the preliminary hearing or during the course of the trial. The probationary period may be as long as three years for a particularly serious crime.

  The magistrate may also impose *prescrizioni*, which are aimed at making amends for the consequences of the offence and promoting reconciliation with the victim. This latter provision marks a new tentative orientation on the part of the Italian juvenile justice system. It represents a slight move towards a *restorative* model of justice that is similar to those countries employing a modified **welfare model**. If the period of probation is successfully completed, the offence is written off and the verdict is not registered in the juvenile's criminal record. If, on the other hand, the outcome is negative, and at the same time the offender's behavior and character development are assessed negatively, the minor is sentenced.

- Custodial sentence: this is usually reduced by one-third and is served in special prisons for minors (*prigione-scuola*). At any stage of the sentence, the minor may be conditionally released, regardless of the established duration of the sentence.

For young offenders, including those under the age of 14, a provision is made for the application of a special security measure (*misura di sicurezza*) involving confinement to a judicial reformatory (*riformatorio giudiziario*). Such measures are applied when the individual is regarded as "socially dangerous," that is, when the youth is deemed likely to commit further crimes, even if s/he has been judged to be non-responsible. The provisions are imposed after the custodial sentence has been served, or, in the case of diminished responsibility, as an alternative to punishment. The new code provides that control in the community (*libertà vigilata*) be applied in conformity with articles 20 and 21 (which refer to *prescrizioni* and confinement to home). Placement in a reformatory is to be applied "in conformity with article 22," which refers to *prescrizioni* and placement in a group home—and only in cases concerning crimes punishable by imprisonment for more than 12 years as a maximum term (art. 36, sub-sections 1 and 2). The reformatory is therefore replaced *de facto* by the group home.

The administrative jurisdiction of the juvenile court tended to be legalistic in orientation and did not readily embrace the notion that young offenders as minors be deemed to be "wayward in behavior or character"—beyond social control (*irregolarità della condotta o del carattere*) (art. 25 R.D. n°1404/1934, as modified by law n°888/1956). The measures applicable in such cases have progressively fallen into disuse since the new code for penal procedure came into effect and are now rarely applied.

The civil jurisdiction of the juvenile court concerns itself with the various forms of supportive intervention (e.g., adoption, limitation or withdrawal of parental authority, and fostering) invoked in cases of absence of the family, mistreatment, or moral or material abandonment of the minor. Moreover, with a view to discourage the exploitation of minors by criminal organizations or by adults in general, the law n°203/1991 has recently reformulated articles 111 and 112 of the penal code. The articles made provisions for increasing punishment for anyone who induces a person who is not responsible or unpunishable to commit a crime.

Having presented an overview of the juvenile justice administrative scheme, let us now take a look at some of the trends and patterns of youth crime in Italy.

YOUTH CRIME AND ITS CHARACTERISTICS

Analysis of the data on juvenile delinquency in Italy is hindered by many problems and limitations. While some of the obstacles are similar to those expressed by other countries covered in this collection, several are unique to the Italian context. First of all, officially based statistical analyses of delinquency often reflect the action of social control agencies rather than the real numbers and features of delinquent behavior. Secondly, the system for gathering crime figures in Italy works rather poorly, often being unreliable and invariably out of date as reflected in the data presented in the figures below. Further-more, only recently has Italy begun to employ alternative methods such as self-report studies and victimization surveys (Gatti et al., 1991a; 1991b; 1994; ISTAT, 2000). In spite of these drawbacks, it is possible to glean useful infor-mation from the statistical analyses of the data available.

With reference to the types of juvenile crimes that are reported, property offences are the most commonly recorded type of offence while violent crimes are rather unusual—not dissimilar from most countries covered in this text. In 1998, 15,559 (37%) of the global amount of 42,107 reports of juveniles to the public prosecutor (*Procura della repubblica*) were thefts, and 3,177 (7.6%) receiving stolen goods. In the same year 4,145 (9.8%) reports for drug selling, 3,169 (7.5%) reports for damages to goods, and 1,503 reports for resistance and outrage to authority were registered. As concerns offences against the per-son, in 1998, 2,986 reports for personal damage (*lesioni personali volontarie,* i.e. a sort of aggravated assault), 1,507 for private violence and threat, and a small number (47) of reports for murder were registered. In the same year, the reports for robbery were 1,534.

These kind of reports (classified in the statistics as "reports to the Procura della Repubblica") are mandatory, but the cases are frequently dropped, either because the offender is under the age limit (14 years) and cannot be punished, or because the proceeding authority (public prosecutor) does not consider the incident as an offence, or because it lacks a complaint by the victim, necessary for the exercise of penal action by the prosecutor (the so-called *querela di parte*). For all these reasons, in 1998 the reports were 42,107, as mentioned above, but the number of prosecutions was lower (24,138).

In Figure 10.2 are reported the data concerning the total number of reports and of prosecutions, from 1971 to 1998 (data regarding reports between 1976 and 1985 are not available).

The figures for the total number of cases reported to the public prosecutor were relatively stable between 1971 and 1978, but there was a sharp fall from 1979 onwards. The drop in the number of minors charged after 1979 may be seen in relation to the enactment of D.P.R. n°616/1977. Indeed, the fact that many responsibilities were shifted to the local authorities radically transformed the ideology and the procedures of preventive and rehabilitative intervention. This meant that, in practice, a great many problem cases were handled by the local authority social services departments instead of the penal system. It may also be speculated that this new perspective might have influenced all the other agencies of social control, thus eliciting a new style of intervention, which saw a greater use of welfare instruments and a consequent reduction in penal proceedings.

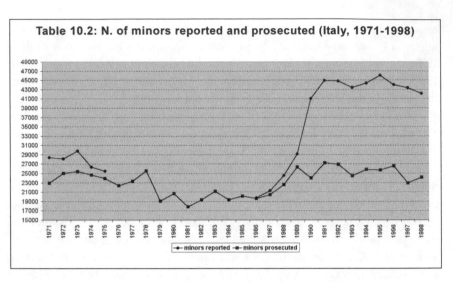

Table 10.2: N. of minors reported and prosecuted (Italy, 1971-1998)

After 1988, this new approach ran into trouble as the number of reported cases began to increase again. By 1991 the number charged had more than doubled since 1987. However, the trend remained relatively stable in the following years. A number of hypotheses can be put forward in order to explain such a phenomenon. For example, the crisis of the welfare state, which is linked to the more general economic depression, undermined the quality and functioning of social services. The economic recession resulted in financial cutbacks, a decline in motivation, enthusiasm, and operational capacity, and a shrinkage in personnel due to policies of non-replacement.

From the point of view of criminal phenomena, moreover, we have witnessed an undeniable increase in violent crime in Italy on the part of both adults and minors. This increase is often linked to organized crime, though there has also been a rise in offences connected with the recent phenomenon of non-EC immigration and with the increased presence of Gypsies or Romani youth (Viggiani and Tressanti, 1992): the relative percentage of offences committed by **foreign juveniles** increased from 18% in 1991 to 26% in 1998. However, many of the foreign minors are less than 14 years of age and are not prosecuted. The presence of a large number of foreign minors under 14 explains the strong divergence witnessed in recent years between the number of reported juveniles and the number of prosecuted ones. Such juveniles mainly come from the former Yugoslavia, and, smaller numbers, from Morocco and Albania. Among reported foreign juveniles, one can observe that females account for 36% of all offences, while Italian females only account for 14% of the Italian counterparts.

The large number of reported foreign juveniles can be seen as a consequence of two different causes: firstly, immigrant minors live in a very difficult social situation (clandestine immigration, irregular families, school problems, poverty), which entails a growing risk of marginality and their involvement in delinquent and criminal pathways. In some cases foreign juveniles are recruited by criminal adults who employ them, for example, for crimes such as drug-selling. Secondly, their socio-economic and cultural circumstances results in greater vulnerability to penal reaction. In other words, they have a greater possibility of being reported, prosecuted, and incarcerated than their Italian counterparts, as has been shown by Barbagli (1995), who reports that a foreign minor caught in a supermarket stealing has twice the possibility of being prosecuted as an Italian boy.

Given their particularities and the crisis of their culture, Gypsy juveniles should be dealt with in a different manner. Changes in society and the processes of modernization have deeply affected traditional occupations upon which Gypsy culture depended. This situation has resulted in devastating consequences such as a loss of economic autonomy, a cultural identity crisis, and a growing involvement in marginal and criminal activities. In particular Roma communities have suffered all of these changes, given the fact that the war in Yugoslavia has pushed many Roma groups to our country.

Finally, the rise in the number of minors charged might also be related to the changes brought about by the new juvenile penal procedure (D.P.R. n°448/ 1988), which came into effect at the end of 1989. As has already been observed, the new norms modernized and rationalized the system by relegitimizing a whole range of correctionally-oriented penal interventions that had previously been abandoned in favor of social intervention after the introduction of D.P.R. n°616/1977 (Gatti and Verde, 1991).

As one regards the evolution of various categories of offence (here we shall consider only data regarding prosecuted juveniles), one can observe that while prosecutions for theft follow the general evolution of juvenile crime, marked by a diminution at the end of the seventies and a growth from the end of the eighties onwards, such trends in serious violent crime as robbery, personal damage (*lesioni personali volontarie*) and homicide follow a different path. The rationale for this phenomenon is that the growth rate begins much earlier, in the early 1980s, and is very sharp for personal damage and robbery, three times higher at the end of the century. Prosecutions for homicide are stable, even if not on a regular basis, from the 70s to date; but homicide is not frequent among Italian juveniles (it is never higher than 100 cases, and on average it amounts to about 50 cases a year) (see Figure 10.3).

In recent years, the rate of juveniles prosecuted for drug-selling has been growing, increasing from 50 per 100,000 juveniles at the beginning of past decade to more than 100 per 100,000 in 1998.

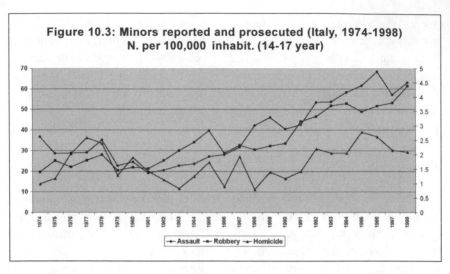

Figure 10.3: Minors reported and prosecuted (Italy, 1974-1998)
N. per 100,000 inhabit. (14-17 year)

The analysis of such data indicates that, while the general trend is influenced by the two deep transformations of juvenile justice mentioned above (D.P.R. 616/1977, introducing the role of local authorities, after which the number of prosecutions fell, and D.P.R. 448/1988, containing new procedural norms for juveniles, after which the number of prosecutions rose), serious crimes and drug crimes appear to have risen, not only in official statistics, but even in reality, according to a trend observed in nearly all European countries. According to Pfeiffer (1998), after a comparative analysis of data regarding juvenile violent crime in Europe, such a phenomenon does not reflect just a change in tolerance by society, a shift confirmed by victim surveys conducted in England, Sweden, Holland and Germany. Rather, the rise in crime also demonstrates deeper social changes that have occurred in recent years, which have sharply modified conditions for juveniles in Europe. The rise in juvenile violence would be a product, in this view, of the spreading condition of anomie and alienation resulting from the problems of mass immigration, the growing number of idle juveniles, and finally the dissolution of local communities in urban neighborhoods, nowadays in decline, but once characterized by working-class culture (Dubet and Lapeyronnie, 1992).

Further considerations can be elicited by the analysis of the regional distribution of prosecutions for different crimes in our country (rates per 100,000 juveniles resident in Italy of the mean values for the period 1994 to 1998). As reflected in Figure 10.4, homicide is the most variant crime, according to the regional distribution: rates are particularly high in certain regions (Sicily, Calabria, Puglia), over five prosecutions per 100,000, a rate 10 times higher than the rate of Lombardia, Marche, Umbria, Molise, where it is below 0.5 prosecutions per 100,000 juveniles.

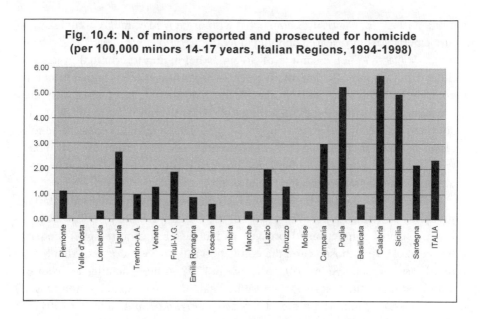

Fig. 10.4: N. of minors reported and prosecuted for homicide (per 100,000 minors 14-17 years, Italian Regions, 1994-1998)

Rates for robbery are, even with some irregularity, also higher in the southern regions (about 50 per 100,000 juveniles, compared to 35 per 100,000 in the northern regions and 44 per 100,000 in the central regions). The reason for such disequilibrium can be traced both to economic factors such as unemployment (constantly related to homicide by world criminological research) and to cultural factors, linked to a more general acceptance of violence in the southern part of the country. Rates for theft, on the contrary, scarcely vary across the different parts of Italy: we found higher rates in some northern and central regions as Liguria, Tuscany and Lazio.

While foreign juveniles are concentrated mainly in northern and central Italy, the involvement of juveniles in organized crime is typical of southern Italy, particularly in Campania, Calabria, Puglia, and Sicily. According to juvenile judges, and other local scholars, such involvement is empirically supported by the growing number and the typology of some juvenile crimes, such as blackmail, possession of illegal weapons and explosives, and drug-selling on a commercial basis. Data in this direction has already emerged from field research, such as that conducted by LABOS (1991) on southern Italian metropolitan areas. The research indicated that in some deteriorating neighborhoods of southern towns many juveniles were exposed to Mafia models and ideals, and as a result completely adhere to criminal values and lifestyles, in the hopes of aspiring to roles in the criminal organization. The socialization process in such neighborhoods would thus facilitate the shift of juveniles from a generic deviant lifestyle to activities connected with organized crime. A complex picture emerges from research conducted by the *Ufficio centrale per la giustizia minorile* (1998) upon a sample of juveniles belonging to criminal organizations. Findings indicate that involvement in organized crime is higher in southern Italy, but is present also in northern Italy. In northern Italy, criminal activities are mainly constituted by drug-selling (94% of self-reported crimes), while in southern Italy criminal activity begins at an earlier age and is constituted to a lesser extent by drug-selling (25% of self-reported crimes). There exists a higher frequency of reports for robbery and blackmail, illegal use of weapons, and attempted and actual homicide in the south.

The data concerning the way in which minors are dealt with by the Italian juvenile court show a peculiar aspect of the Italian juvenile justice system: a low percent of convictions. However, an increase has occurred over the past ten years. During those years, the conviction rates have increased from 8.5% of all cases prosecuted in 1991, to 15.9% in 1998. A more detailed analysis of data relating to the measures imposed reveals that the most common reason for dismissal is "judicial pardon" (*perdono giudiziale*), applied in 40 to 50% of all prosecutions at the beginning of the decade, and in 30 to 40% at the end. An increasing number of cases are put on probation and subsequently discharged. The total number of probation cases has risen from 788 in 1992 to 1249 in 1998 (almost exclusively Italian juveniles).

Reception Centers: Pre-conviction

Some important features of the Italian justice system can also be deduced from the data on placements in juvenile penal institutions and in reception centers. In interpreting the overall figure presented in Figure 10.5 for juvenile imprisonment, data regarding both of these institutions must be taken into account since reception centers play an important role as filters.

In 1998, about one-quarter of the minors taken into reception centers subsequently proceeded to preventive detention (De Leo, Patrizi, Donato, and Scali, 1993). The figure shows that the number of minors entering juvenile penal institutions fell markedly at the end of the 1980s and reached an all-time low in 1990, the year after the new procedural norms came into effect. These norms markedly reduced the possibility of imposing preventive detention. The following year, however, as mentioned above, these norms were modified to permit a broader use of such measures; subsequently, there is a rise in the number of admissions to the penitentiary circuit, especially to reception centers. Drug users constituted the largest proportion of detainees. In 1990 they accounted for 25.4% of the juvenile penal population, while in 1991 their proportion dropped to 19.4%, and in 1998 to 20% (ISTAT, 2000).

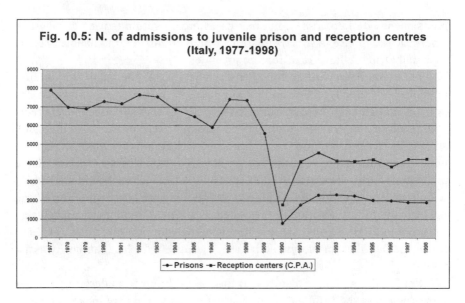

Fig. 10.5: N. of admissions to juvenile prison and reception centres (Italy, 1977-1998)

Closer inspection of the data presented in Figure 10.5 on minors detained in penal institutions reveals a clear upward trend in the total number of foreigners. Their representation in juvenile penal institutions went from 11.2% in 1983 to 30.7% in 1991 and 53.2% in 1998. The figures for reception centers are similar, reaching 54.6% in 1998. Another clear trend, which is linked to the previous one, is seen in the percentage increase in detained females, which rose from 3.6% in 1983 to 17.0% in 1991 and to 20.2% in 1998. For reception centers, the female percentage reached 24.4% in 1991 and 23.4% in 1998. As already stated, the two above trends are linked, in that foreign females are disproportionately over-represented in the juvenile penal system. In 1998, for example, female foreigners detained in penal institutions constituted 39.9% of the total inmate population vs. 3.69% for Italian female detainees. For the most part, these foreign females are nomads charged with property offences.

Imprisonment: Post-conviction

Prison as punishment, in the strict sense, is inflicted on an extremely limited number of minors. In 1998, for example, the daily average of minors placed in juvenile prisons (*prigione-scuola*) was 176.

Implications

All of the data reported point to a few conclusions regarding the trends which have emerged in recent years. It can be seen that the penal system tends to avoid incarcerating minors. Detention is used almost exclusively as a preventive measure, one which in some cases represents a sort of anticipation of punishment (De Leo, 1981). In other cases incarceration is used as a sort of emergency response to social situations which are difficult to handle. This is especially true in the case of foreign juveniles.

The statistics regarding foreigners can be seen as the manifestation of a phenomenon already observed in many juvenile justice systems, which has been called **bifurcation**. According to this notion, the modernization and reorganization of the system, implemented through such measures as diversion and alternatives to detention (as in Italy after D.P.R. n°448/1988), generate an undesired spinoff. The result is that the new opportunities are made available to the more fortunate sectors of the target population, while the old methods— which are not abandoned completely in that they are the expression of the intrinsically punitive nature of the system as a whole—end up as a receptacle for those individuals who are less fortunate, like foreign juveniles. Added to this is the fact that foreign juveniles are not eligible for local authority assistance.

Finally the statistics also reveal that, in addition to undergoing greater repression than their Italian counterparts, foreign minors are incarcerated for committing comparatively less serious crimes (Verde and Bagnara, 1989). And although the problem of foreign minors in Italy has several unique characteristics, the reader is likely to observe that "minority/foreign" groups in other countries experience similar difficulties. This general trend would appear to deserve both national and international attention, both from an etiological and a political perspective.

CURRENT AND PROJECTED TRENDS

The transformation recently brought about by the new norms of juvenile penal procedure (D.P.R. n°448/1988) was the expression of a process of rationalization and modernization advocated by an authoritative group of juvenile magistrates. The provisions of D.P.R. n°448/1988, which, strictly speaking, should regard only procedural aspects, in reality also introduced substantial modifications.

Basically, the new juvenile justice system represents the results of a compromise among various ideologies. It represents an attempt to pursue a whole range of objectives that are difficult to reconcile: safeguarding the rights of the minor, increasing the minor's responsibility by means of punishment (De Leo, 1985), obtaining rehabilitation through personalized social programs, pursuing depenalization options and release from imprisonment by reducing the terms of preventive detention. Clearly there are many points of contrast between the treatment-oriented view, for instance, and the position based on depenalization. The reform introduced a norm which allows for the depenalization of any type of offence on the grounds of insignificance; at the same time, however, it allows a whole range of preventive measures of a therapeutic nature, some rather harsh (*misure cautelari*), to be imposed on a minor who might be acquitted during the preliminary hearing or trial. This almost suggests a desire to "teach the minor a lesson" even before the trial begins. The format is somewhat analogous to the "scared straight" programs popular in the United States during the 1980s (see Finchenauer, 1982).

In general, the new norms seem to favour extending the intervention aspect of the juvenile justice system by restoring functions that had been transferred over the years to the local authorities. These norms make provision for a range of psycho-social interventions within the penal system, while at the same time reintroducing into that system the intervention of the local authority services, albeit in a subordinate position. In this respect article 6 of D.P.R. n°448/1988 constitutes a complete turn-about in the policy of separation of roles established by D.P.R. n°616/1977 on administrative decentralization: "At any stage of the proceedings, the judicial authority may avail itself of the juvenile services of the Justice department. It may also avail itself of the welfare services instituted by the local authorities." This concept is restated unequivocally in art. 28 sub-section 2 of D.P.R. n°448/1988, which establishes that when probation is imposed, " the magistrate is to entrust the minor to the juvenile services of the Justice department in order to implement suitable measures for supervision, treatment and support, if necessary enlisting the collaboration of the local authority services."

In other words, the new provisions seem to have been aimed at providing a response within the penal system to problems more closely connected with social intervention. This could be seen as an attempt to make up for the inequalities that have grown at a national level between the north, where social services were beginning to reach European standards, and the south, which remained enmeshed in archaic social policies that held the rights of minors in scant regard. The early results seem to indicate that the norms have been applied very differently in various geographical areas, not least on account of the varying standards of the local authority social services.

An interesting new approach, introduced in recent years on an experimental basis in some of the most open and dynamic juvenile courts (Milan, Turin, Bari, etc.), is that of mediation schemes between the perpetrator and the victim of a crime, together with community service orders (Gatti and Ceretti, 1998). In every court mediation offices have been constituted, relatively independent from the court, composed of educators, psychologists, and criminologists. The mediation process attempts to manage and solve the conflict between author and victim of crime by using psychosocial instruments and, when successful, juveniles are kept away from the penal system and the case is dismissed.

Current Theoretical "Bias"

The 1991 upturn in crime among minors has been attributed to various recent developments in the phenomenology of juvenile delinquency. The increased presence of foreign immigrants, often illegal, has been implicated, as has the greater involvement of minors in drug-related crime (Ponti and Merzagora, 1991). The progressive and dramatic decline of certain areas of the country, due to the economic recession, has also been cited. In these areas worsening social problems have been accompanied by the further consolidation of criminal fraternities, which offer young people a means of gaining notoriety or earning a living when legal employment is difficult to obtain (Occhiogrosso, 1992-1993; Viggiani and Tressanti, 1992). This thesis is also sustained by Merzagora and Paolillo (1991), who compared the official statistics for minors involved in crimes of extortion and drug trafficking in the regions of Campania, Sicily, Calabria, and Puglia with the national totals. Their figures showed that a large proportion of such crimes (almost 50% for extortion) are committed in these four regions, which strongly suggests that the minors involved are working for organized crime syndicates. The phenomenon is not new and, in fact, dates back to at least the middle of the 1980s.

SUMMARY

At the present time, the areas of juvenile deviance which are attracting the greatest attention on the part of citizens, the mass media, and public authorities in Italy are those which concern foreign minors, especially Gypsies and North Africans. The involvement of minors in organized criminal activities is also a major concern. The real magnitude of these phenomena, however, appears to be extremely difficult to assess in that empirical research is still sorely limited.

Public alarm about juvenile crime is a fairly recent phenomenon in Italy and a clear response on the part of the juvenile justice system has yet to be evinced. Indeed, while the number of minors charged with offences has increased greatly, the number of referrals to reception centers and penal institutions has remained relatively low. In the last decade, other types of measures, such as probation, have been adopted to a broader extent, and reparative measures, which under Italian law can only be imposed in connection with probation, have consequently found a more frequent application; thus reflecting a *modified* **welfare** orientation.

The world of juvenile justice appears to still be hesitating before the complexity of the problems facing it, and the different means of intervention: the tendency to centralize via penal instruments has contrasted with new local forms of social intervention in the preventive field.

The re-centralization of penal intervention has been perceived as a risk which may be accentuated by the current economic difficulties that are taxing the resources of local authority social services. In addition, problems of financing have hindered programs for prevention, which now seem chiefly oriented towards containing the phenomenon of drug addiction and its related pathologies. The welfare of young offenders in Italy would appear to be caught between the chaos. It is time that we recognize the global importance of youth justice.

Uberto Gatti, born in 1941, is full professor of criminology in the University of Genoa, and director of the post-graduate school in clinical criminology of the same university. He has written and published extensively in the area of juvenile justice.
Alfredo Verde, born in 1956, is associate professor of criminology in the University of Genoa and a psychoanalyst in private practice.

HELPFUL WEBSITES
Data and statistics on Italian juvenile justice system:
http://www.giustizia.it/misc/STATISTICHE.htm
Restorative justice and mediation in Italian juvenile justice system:
http://www.giustizia.it/studierapporti/mediazione

KEY TERMS AND CONCEPTS
welfare model	crime control
justice model	foreign juveniles
reception centers	bifurcation

STUDY QUESTIONS
1. Why has juvenile justice in Italy developed so late?
2. How was it shaped at the beginning and how does it differ from today? How might this change be explained and how does our model relate to international standards?
3. When was probation introduced in the system and how much is it applied at the present time? How does our probation system differ (if at all) from that of other countries covered in this text?
4. How are foreign juveniles managed by the system? Does their treatment differ from that of their Italian counterparts?
5. What does the term "bifurcation" mean and how could it be applied to the Italian juvenile justice system?

NOTES
1 Minors under 14 years of age and minors between 14 to 18 who are not considered "capable of understanding and willing," are usually transferred by the judge to the

general welfare system (local authority). There are exceptions, such as when the minor is judged as "socially dangerous." They can then be maintained inside the penal system by the adoption of a "secretary measure" of "judicial reformatory," or "control in the community."

2   For further discussion on nomadic youth and the problems they pose for juvenile justice, see:

www.unicri.it/html/body_rromani_youths.htm

REFERENCES

Barbagli M. (1995). *L'occasione e l'uomo ladro. Furti e rapine in Italia*. Bologna: Il Mulino.

Beccaria, C. (1963). *On crimes and punishments*. (Henry Paolucci, Trans.). New York: Bobbs-Merill.

Betti, M., & Pavarini, M. (1985). Potere giudiziario e governo locale nell'amministrazione della giustizia minorile: il quadro normativo e le ipotesi interpretative. In M. Bergonzini and M. Pavarini (Eds.). *Potere giudiziario, enti locali e giustizia minorile*. Bologna: Il Mulino.

De Leo, G. (1981). *La giustizia dei minori. La delinquenza giovanile e le sue istituzioni.* Turin: Einaudi.

De Leo, G. (1985). Responsabilità: definizioni ed applicazioni nel campo della giustizia minorile. In G. Ponti (Ed.). *Giovani, responsabilità e giustizia*. Milan: Giuffré.

De Leo, G., Patrizi, P., Donato, R., & Scali, M. (1993). L'interazione fra servizi sociali e autorità giudiziaria in alcuni interventi innovativi del processo penale minorile. In G. De Leo & A. Dell'Antonio (Eds.). *Nuovi ambiti legislativi e di ricerca per la tutela dei minori*. Milan: Giuffré.

Dubet, F., & Lapeyronnie, D. (1992). *Les quartiers d'éxiles*. Paris: Editions du Seuil.

Faccioli, F. (1990). Devianza e controllo istituzionale. In Consiglio Nazionale dei Minori (Ed.). *Il minore in Italia*. Milan: Angeli.

Finchenauer, J.O. (1982). *Scared straight and the panacea phenomenon*. Englewood Cliffs, NJ: Prentice-Hall.

Gatti U., & Ceretti A. (1998). Italian experiences of victim-offender mediation in the juvenile justice system. In Walgrave (Ed.), *Restorative Justice for Juvenile Potentialities, Risk and Problems*. Leuven, Belgium: Leuven University Press.

Gatti, U., Fossa, G., Lusetti, E., Marugo, M.I., Russo, G., & Traverso, G.B. (1994). La devianza giovanile in Italia: un'indagine sui comportamenti illeciti autorilevati in un campione di studenti di scuola media superiore. *Rassegna Italiana di Criminologia*, 5.

Gatti, U., Fossa, G., Marugo, M.I., & Materazzi, V. (1991a). Le inchieste di vittimizzazione: problemi metodologici e primi risultati di uno studio-pilota condotto nella città di Genova. *Rassegna Italiana di Criminologia, 2*, 363.

Gatti, U., Malfatti, D., Marugo, M.I., & Tartarini, E. (1991b). La diffusione dei comportamenti devianti fra i giovani: una ricerca sulla popolazione genovese mediante la tecnica dell'autoconfessione. *Rassegna Italiana di Criminologia, 2*, 387.

Gatti, U., & Verde, A. (1988). S'éloigner du système pénal: un approche du problème de la délinquance juvénile en Italie. *Revue internationale de criminologie et de police technique, 41*, 49.

Gatti, U., & Verde, A. (1991). The dividing line between punishment and help: New questions, old answers. In J. Junger-Tas, L. Boendermaker, & P. van der Laan P. (Eds.). *The future of the juvenile justice system*. Leuven, Belgium: ACCO.

ISTAT. (2000). *Statistche giudiziare 1998*. Rome: Istituto Nazionale di Statistica.

LABOS. (1991). *Giovani a rischio nelle aree metropolitane*. Rome: Edizioni TER.

Martin, R., Mutchnick, R.J., & Austin, W.T. (1990). *Criminological thought: Pioneers past and present*. New York: Macmillan.

Merzagora, I., & Paolillo, D. (1991). Il coinvolgimento dei minori nella delinquenza organizzata: Un tentativo di indagine quantitativa. *Marginalità e società*, 20, 30.

Occhiogrosso, F. (1992-1993). Introduzione. Anche per i minorenni è necessaria una "Nuova Resistenza." *Minori Giustizia* (nuova serie), 4-1, 9 (numero speciale dedicato a "Ragazzi della mafia").

Pavarini, M. (1992-1993). Più o meno carcere. *Minori Giustizia* (nuova serie), 4-1, 357 (numero speciale dedicato a "Ragazzi della mafia").

Pazé, P. (1991). Una legge inadeguata per proteggere i minori dalla droga. *Il bambino incompiuto*, 8, 3, 17.

Pfeiffer, C. (1998). Juvenile crime and violence in Europe. In M. Tonry (Ed.), *Crime and justice: A review of research*, Vol. 23, 255-328. Chicago: University of Chicago Press.

Ponti, G., & Merzagora, I. (1991). Il minore tra responsabilizzazione, pena rieducativa e delinqunza organizzata. *Marginalità e società*, 20, 14.

Ricciotti, R. (1982). *Il diritto minorile e dei servizi sociali: gli interventi amministrativi e penali*. Rimini: Maggioli.

Senzani, G. (1970). *L'esclusione anticipata. Rapporto da 118 case di rieducazione per minorenni*. Milan: Jaca Book.

Ufficio per la Giustizia Minorile, Ministero di Grazia e Giustizia. (1995). Rome: ISTAT.

Ufficio per la Giustizia Minorile, Ministero di Grazia e Giustizia. (1998). Rome: ISTAT.

Verde, A., & Bagnara, F. (1989). L'utilizzazione delle strutture penitenziarie minorili in Italia. *Rassegna di Criminologia*, 20, 317.

Viggiani, L., & Tressanti, S. (1992). Indagine sulla delinquenza minorile. *Esperienze di giustizia minorile*, 39, 1, 35.

Chapter 11

Juvenile Justice and Juvenile Crime: An Overview of Japan

Minoru Yokoyama
Faculty of Law, Kokugakuin University

FACTS ON JAPAN

Area: 377,854 sq. km. Japan is composed of five main islands from north to south: Hokkaido, Honshu, Shikoku, Kyushu, and Okinawa. It is located from latitude 24° N to 45° N. It has one time zone. **Population**: Approximately 126.5 million in 1998 (pop. density 339 per square km.), of which 99.8% were Japanese. Population growth rate per 1,000 amounted to 2.5. Koreans made up 42.2% of the non-Japanese population, followed by the Chinese at 18%. 64.7% of the population lived in urban settings in 1995. Thirteen major cities institute a ward system, of which Tokyo is not only the largest but is also the nation's capital (pop. 11.9 million). Persons between birth and fourteen years of age decreased from 29.8 million in 1955 to 19 million in 1998, while those of 65 and over has increased from 4.7 to 20.5 million over the same time period. **Climate**: Although mostly temperate, the climate varies from north to south. For Tokyo, the average monthly temperature is 5.2° C in January and 27.1° C in August. Heavy snowfall is common along the Japanese Sea in winter.

Economy: Since World War II, Japan has evolved from an agricultural and primary industry oriented nation to an industrialized and manufacturing nation. More recently, as Japan has become more developed, many people work in the tertiary industries. In 1998, 31.4% of the workforce was employed in the construction and manufacturing sectors, while only 4.9% remained in an agricultural setting. **Government**: Under the constitution enacted in 1946, the Emperor is a symbol of the state—a hereditary title. The sovereign power rests with the people, who elect both a member of the House of Representatives and of the House of Councillors. The members of the Diet designate a prime minister, who organizes a cabinet. Between 1955 and 1993, the Liberal Democratic Party (LDP) ruled the government. After a major political scandal in 1993, the LDP lost its parliamentary majority. In 1994 it returned to power under a coalition with the Socialist party. The autonomy of local governments remains limited.

There is no school equal to a decent home and no teachers equal to honest virtuous parents — Mohandas (Mahatma) Gandhi

Japan's History

According to ancient Chinese literature, the Japanese state existed at the latter half of the third century AD. Since the end of the sixth century, emperors ruled our country. In 604, the first Japanese constitution with 17 articles was proclaimed, which were maxims influenced by Buddhism. At the beginning of the eighth century, a legal system was established in imitation of that in Tang China. Some of the key periods include:

1. **Nara** period (710 to 793 AD): saw the widespread influence of Buddhism under the reign of powerful emperors, although many Japanese remained believers of Shinto, the core of which is the worship of nature and ancestors without a creator or bible like other main religions.

2. **Heian** period (794 to 1191): witnessed the emperor being deprived of political power, which resulted from the internal fights between the court nobilities. Then, as a result of this internal fighting, warriors gained political power.

3. **Kamakura** period (1192 to 1333): two legal systems co-existed; one for the court of the emperor and another for the military government of warriors that was founded by the Minamoto Shogun.

4. For over one hundred years from 1467, many wars occurred with the decline of the manor system. In 1543, the Portuguese were the first Europeans to come to Japan, and they introduced Christianity and guns.

5. **Edo** period (1603 to 1867): saw the establishment of a rigid caste system under the feudal lords. To eradicate believers in Christianity, the government of Tokugawa Shogunate banned any further contact with Spain or Portugal. Only the Dutch and the Chinese were allowed to trade at an artificial island in Nagasaki Harbour. In 1742 the Tokugawa Shogunate compiled the Criminal Code of One Hundred Articles. Ordinary people had to comply with a sentence without knowing the laws. In the middle of the nineteenth century, Japan was pressured by Russia, England, and the United States to abandon its isolation policy. This led to considerable internal squabbling over how to address the response to these pressures. Consequently, the low-ranking warriors succeeded in overthrowing the Tokugawa Shogunate, and restored the court of the emperor.

6. After the **Meiji Restoration** in 1868, Japan began introducing a Western legal system. In 1873, **Gustave Boissonade**, an associate of the

University of Paris, was invited to help with the transition of the legal system. He succeeded in enacting the Penal Code and the Code of Criminal Procedures. The short-lived French model of the Penal Code was replaced by a new Penal Code in 1907, after the positivist model advocated in Germany.

7. With the defeat of Japan in World War II (1945), the emperor's regime collapsed, Japan was stripped of its empire, and the criminal justice system was democratized at the direction of the Allied Powers. Following the enactment of a new constitution in 1946 and the revisions of the Penal Code in 1947, a new Code of Criminal Procedures was enacted in 1948. The code was modelled after the American system to guarantee due process, while its fundamental framework remained under the legal models found in most of Western Europe.

DEVELOPMENT OF JUVENILE JUSTICE

Criminal Responsibility

Since the eighth century, the criminal laws for the court of the emperor had some prescriptions to exempt juveniles from penalty or to reduce sentences. It was the case even in the criminal laws for the court of warriors. For example, the Criminal Code of One Hundred Articles of 1742 allowed for the mitigation of criminal punishment for juveniles 15 and under.

After the **Meiji Restoration**, Western systems for juveniles were introduced. In 1872, compulsory education was instituted. In 1880, the Penal Code was enacted, which included several provisions for juvenile offenders. For example, Article 79 defined the minimum age of culpability as 12.

Emergence of Juvenile Facilities

The Prison Rules and its illustration of 1872 provided for the establishment of reformatory prisons. They were modelled after the English-style prison system used in Hong Kong and Singapore. Although the intention was to provide educational programs, limited resources restricted such provisions.

Around 1880, after learning more about the use of reformatory schools in Western countries, some volunteers introduced a reformatory school (Tsujimoto, 1990). In 1883, a female priest in a sector of Shinto founded a school for the first time. The priests of conventional religions such as Shinto and Buddhism played an important role in establishing these reformatory schools. In this movement, Japan saw the start of the participatory nature of its juvenile justice system.

Enactment of the Reformatory Law and Juvenile Law

Given the strong support for the private reformatory schools, the Reformatory Law was proclaimed in 1900 to endorse their activities. Although the law encouraged the establishment of public reformatory schools, by 1908 only five prefectural reformatory schools were opened.

In 1907, the current Penal Code was promulgated. Article 41 prescribes that anyone under the age of 14 shall not be held criminally responsible. Confinement to the reformatory prison was abolished. In 1908, the Reformatory Law was amended to treat juveniles who had been confined in reformatory prison.

After nine years of debate, the first drafts of the Juvenile Law and the Correctional School Law were completed in 1919. However, Shigejiro Ogawa, who had contributed to drafting the Reformatory Law, pointed out that in Japan there was not the same urgent need for a juvenile law as in the United States. Ogawa further suggested that offenders under the age of 14 should not be adjudicated under the juvenile law, and that a correctional school similar to a juvenile prison should not be instituted in place of the well-functioning reformatory school.

In spite of such opposition, both acts passed in 1922. However, owing to budgetary restraints between 1922 and 1934, the Juvenile Law was only enforced in some large cities near Tokyo and Osaka. In 1933, the Juvenile Training and Education Law was enacted in place of the Reformatory Law to coordinate with the system under the Juvenile Law (see Box 11.1).

Box 11.1: Family School established by Kosuke Tomeoka

In 1983, the national government removed the ban on Christianity. Kosuke Tomeoka, a Christian, became a chaplain at Sorachi Penitentiary in Hokkaido, the northern island of Japan, in order to improve the treatment in the prison (Correctional Association, 1984). He later went to the United States to learn about the Elmira Reformatory system. After returning to Japan, he founded a reformatory school in Tokyo in 1899 after the model of that in western countries.

His reformatory was called a family school—Katei Gakko. A teacher and his family lived together with about ten juveniles in an independent house. The setting was very nurturing under the affection of a married couple. For a long time, the basic model of this family school was maintained at many child education and training homes (Kyogoin Homes), at which the Christian atmosphere was lost. However, the system of rearing by a married couple has been gradually abandoned (see Hattori, 1996, for further discussion on the history and development of family schools).

CHARACTERISTICS OF THE CURRENT JUVENILE LAW

Shortly after the Second World War there was a sharp increase in juvenile crime in Japan. This prompted discussions of enacting a new Juvenile Law.

Being heavily influenced by the Allied Powers, Japan was expected to place greater emphasis on child welfare for realization of democracy in the future.

The new Juvenile Law, enacted in 1948, followed the principle of *parens patriae* like the old law. However, to guarantee juvenile rights at the adjudication, the family court was founded in the place of the semi-judicial agency for adjudication. On the other hand, to expand the welfare model, the range of cases under the juvenile law was widened. The age of juveniles applied to the law was lifted from under 18 to under 20. The public prosecutors lost their power to screen juvenile cases, and were not qualified to appear at the family court. Under the current principle of *parens patriae*, Japanese juvenile law is designed to provide educative measures for juvenile delinquents that will enable them to develop their individual abilities.

After the war, the opinion of new classicists, stressing human rights in the criminal justice system, was prevalent. They insisted that criminal policy should be carried out under the principle of legality (Yokoyama, 1994). However, the Juvenile Law has been interpreted since 1922 as following the **welfare** and **rehabilitation models** on the basis of the doctrine of *parens patriae* (Yokoyama, 1992a). Sawanobori (1994) insists that the Juvenile Law is a welfare law because of its paternalistic orientation, while guaranteeing due process as a procedural law. In addition, referring to Figure 1 (see Introduction), the Japanese model might also be described as representative of the **participatory model**, as many citizens have participated as volunteers in activities to realize the purpose of the Juvenile Law.

The most important provisions of the Juvenile Law include:

- The purpose of the law is to help ensure that juveniles are raised soundly. To this end, the law provides for protective educative measures. Article 24 of the law prescribed three measures: putting juveniles under probation; committing them to a home for dependent children, or a home to support children's independence; and committing them to a juvenile training school.
- "Juveniles" are defined as those under the age of 20, although the Child Welfare Law is applied to those under 18 years of age.
- The family court has jurisdiction over three kinds of juveniles: juvenile offenders between the ages of 14 and 19; lawbreaking children under the age of 14; and pre-offence juveniles under the age of 20 who are prone to committing some criminal offence. The latter category is justified by paternalism, though it is contradictory to the principle of legality.
- Chapter 2 of the law prescribes procedures and dispositions for the protection of juveniles. In principle, they stress informality and the

absence of a confrontation between the defendant and the prosecutor. The hearing at the family court shall be performed in a congenial atmosphere.

- All cases must be referred to the family court. However, the family court judge has the discretion to refer a case back to the public prosecutor. This would be analogous to transferring a youth to adult court in Western countries.

- Chapter 4 pertains to procedures and punishment in juvenile criminal cases. The procedures are more protective than for adult offenders. In addition, the criminal punishment imposed on juveniles can be mitigated.

Movement for Revision of Juvenile Law

Soon after the enforcement of the new Juvenile Law in 1949, the Ministry of Justice and the public prosecutors began to discuss the revision of the law to restore their strong power under the old law. One main purpose of the revision was to lower the age applied by the law from under 20 to under 18. Another was their acquisition of the power to express their opinion from the perspective of the maintenance of the public order at the family court. Under the initiative of the Ministry of Justice, some drafts of the revised Juvenile Law were made out. However, these drafts were met with the severe opposition of many people, such as scholars of criminal law, lawyers, members of the labor union, and members of the Opposition Party, who supported the welfare model under the law. Even the Supreme Court expressed opposition against the draft of 1966, which prescribes that the age applied to the Juvenile Law be lowered to under 18 years of age, while reserving the possibility of offering the protective measures to youths between 18 and 23 years of age. After the publicity of the interim report of the Legal System Council in 1977, Japan did not see any active movement for the revision of the Juvenile Law until the late 1990s, although it saw the highest peak of juvenile delinquency in 1983.

In the 1990s lawyers participated as attendants in cases, in which juveniles were referred to the family court for some false charge. Under the current Juvenile Law based on the doctrine of *parens patriae*, there is no appropriate system to find facts on criminal behaviour because of the absence of a confrontation between the defendant and the prosecutor. There are no provisions for formally declaring innocence for juveniles who are found to be innocent in the adjudication. Therefore, lawyers began to think about the revision of the Juvenile Law to guarantee juveniles' rights sufficiently. However, as they respect the welfare and rehabilitation models, they are reluctant to advocate the introduction of criminal procedures that guarantee the same rights as those afforded to adult defendants. To revise the Juvenile Law, the Supreme Court, the Ministry of Justice, and the Japan Federation of Bar Association began to exchange opinions in November, 1996.

In 1997, a boy of 14 years of age living in Kobe killed two children and injured three others. The mass media reported one case especially, in which he murdered a boy of 11, mutilated his body, and put his severed head on the gate of a school. Starting with this case, the mass media continued to report several murder cases committed by boys between 15 and 17 years of age as big news. By receiving the sensational report on juvenile crimes such as murder and robbery, a growing number of people are of the opinion that these heinous offenders should be harshly punished to prevent such crimes (see Canada for a comparison on the role of the media).

Another factor impacting the tough policy against juvenile offenders has been the upsurge of the movement for the crime victims. Until recently, the support system for victims was poor. It was not until the late 1990s that the movement for victim support began to appear in the spotlight. Some crime victims (e.g., families who had a child killed) began to insist that their rights are neglected, while offenders' rights, above all, juvenile offenders' rights, are respected too much.

In the above-mentioned background, more people criticize the Juvenile Law for offering lenient protective disposition to spoiled juvenile delinquents. Therefore, the ruling LDP began to advocate the revision of the Juvenile Law, calling for tougher measures against juvenile offenders. Under the pressure from the LDP the Legal System Council discussed the draft for six months and submitted it to the Ministry of Justice in January, 1999. However, this draft did not pass the Diet. Then, members of three ruling parties submitted a new draft to the Diet. It was enacted at the end of November, 2000.

The Revision of the Juvenile Law in 2000

The main characteristics of the revised Juvenile Law of 2000 are the following:

1. The revised Juvenile Law adds a purpose of adjudication at the Family Court. During the hearing, all participants are expected to make a juvenile offender reflect on his/her offence. The Family Court is also expected to make the parent(s) or guardian(s) realize their responsibility for the offence. The Family Court judges can give an instruction and a warning to parent(s) or guardian(s). Although the above-mentioned practice has been carried out, it is clearly declared as a purpose by the revised law. The conservative place an emphasis on the responsibility

of a juvenile offender and their parent(s) or guardian(s) rather than the protection of the offender.

2. The new law guarantees the victim's right to know the result of adjudication at the Family Court. Before the adjudication, a victim can talk to the Family Court judge or the Family Court probation officer about his/ her opinion and feelings on a juvenile offender. However, s/he is not allowed to appear in court in consideration of the protection of the offender. In response to victim's request, the Family Court informs him/her of the name and address of a juvenile offender, and of the result of a disposition and the brief reasons for this disposition. By victim's request, with some adequate reason, the Family Court can permit him/her to see and copy the original record of the result of adjudication. However, the scope of the record being opened to him/ her is limited to facts concerning to an offence and the motivation to commit it. From the viewpoint of the protection of the juvenile offender, the record on his/her personality and background is not opened.

3. The new law has some provisions to improve procedures to find the facts on a juvenile delinquent. In an urgent case, a court composed of three judges can adjudicate. The maximum term of the custody in the juvenile detention and classification home is changed from four to eight weeks. The Family Court can permit the public prosecutor to appear at the court in the case of a heinous offence such as murder or robbery. In this case, a legal counsellor has to appear at the court as an attendant for the juvenile offender. To maintain the welfare model, the public prosecutor is allowed to question and to state his/her opinion only about facts on criminal behaviour. The public prosecutor can appeal to the high court, if s/he has a claim against the recognition of facts on criminal behaviour by the Family Court.

4. The revision of the Juvenile Law focuses on accountability. The minimum age of a juvenile offender who can be referred back to the public prosecutor for a criminal charge has been lowered from 16 to 14. In cases involving a juvenile over 16 years of age who has committed a homicide or a malicious offence resulting in death, the Family Court is obliged in principle to refer back to the public prosecutor. However, the maximum age of a juvenile to whom the Juvenile Law applies is not changed, because juveniles of 18 and 19 years of age have not committed any heinous offence like that being paid attention by the mass media.

Although the revised Juvenile Law aims in part for accountability, the fundamental system under the welfare model is maintained (Yokoyama, 2001).

We expect the practice not to shift drastically towards a **justice**-oriented **model,** since most of those working in the juvenile justice system respect the welfare model.

THE DIMENSIONS OF DELINQUENCY

The national government has strong executive power, and is able to collect various data uniformly from all over the country. Notwithstanding the obvious limitations of official statistics, the government's statistics are considered more reliable than those in de-centralized countries like the United States. Because of the government's stable bureaucratic system, the data are rarely influenced by the results of elections. Consequently, self-report and victimization surveys, unlike in Europe and North America, are not well funded, and are carried out only sporadically (see Fujimoto, 1994).

We have several primary sources of formal criminal justice statistics: the National Police Agency compiles crime statistics; the Ministry of Justice produces annual data on prosecution, correction, and rehabilitation; and the Supreme Court publishes judicial statistics on an annual basis. In addition to these reports, the National Police Agency, the Ministry of Justice, and the Administrative Affairs Agency publish white papers on police, crime, and juvenile offenders respectively.

Delinquency Trends after World War II

There have been three major peaks of juvenile delinquency since World War II (Yokoyama, 1986a). The first occurred in 1951, when the rate of juvenile Penal Code offenders was 9.5 per 1,000 population of between 10 and 20 years of age. Given that the police had been decentralized under the decree of the Allied Powers, it seems that this figure only showed the tip of the iceberg. The highest rate of juvenile delinquency probably occurred in the chaos immediately after World War II, when there were many poor and orphaned children. These juveniles often committed property crimes such as theft and robbery because of absolute poverty (Yokoyama, 1985).

The second peak happened in 1964, when the rate rose to 11.9 per 1,000. In the early 1960s, attention is drawn to violent offences being committed by juveniles born during the baby boom after World War II.

The third peak occurred in 1983, when the rate climbed up to 17.1 per 1,000. Although there were a large number of investigations, most of them were for minor offences. The rise may reflect the net-widening of guidance activities of the police (Yokoyama, 1989).

After the third peak, the rate of juvenile Penal Code offenders declined to 12.1 in 1995 then, rose to 15.0 in 1998. To understand the current situation, I would like to compare selected crime statistics from 1964, 1983, and 1995 with those of 1998.

Delinquency Trends and Patterns

The main characteristics of juvenile delinquency may be described as follows:

- As indicated in Table 11.1, the increase in the number of thefts contributed to forming the third peak in 1983; it represented the drastic increase between 1964 and 1983. In 1998, the percentages of shoplifting, motorcycle, bicycle, and other theft were 54.1%, 17.2%, 15.4%, and 13.3% respectively *(White Paper on Crime in 1999)*. Unlike many Western countries, motor vehicle theft (1.8%) and break-and-enters (1.2%) are infrequent. Perhaps unique to Japanese youth culture, motorcycle theft is more common than motor vehicle theft. *The White Paper on Crime in 1994* notes that only 0.5% of the thefts were motivated by poverty, while 67.6% were motivated by greed and 25.9% for play.

- Since 1964, there has been a sharp increase in the number of embezzlements (See Table11.1). In Japan, this refers to crimes involving the taking of a lost or deserted thing, most of which is riding a lost or deserted bicycle without the owner's permission. The net-widening of police guidance might bring this drastic increase.

- Table 11.1 indicates the dramatic decrease in murder and robbery, as well as a reduction of other violent crimes during the period from 1964 to 1995. The decline in all types of violent crime might be due to a very proactive campaign against violence, which was initiated in the early 1960s. Recently, we witnessed an increase in the total number of robberies. One of reasons for this phenomenon is the prevalence of "daddy hunting," that is, casually gathered youngsters attack a middle-age male to take money for play. Another reason is that the police adopted a tough policy, especially after the murder case in Kobe in 1997 (Hamai, 1999). They arrest juveniles more frequently on a charge of the more serious offences. For example, those who might be previously charged for thcft and injury are arrested for robbery causing injury (Terao, 1999).

- Around 1964, school violence was a big social problem. Beginning in 1985, "bullying" activities, that is, minor violence in schools, drew national media attention when several victims of bullying committed suicide. It is generally felt that bullying increased as a result of gloomy competition in the examination ordeal. However, I believe that bullying became a social concern because people's tolerance levels for violent behavior have declined with the decrease of serious violent crimes. Around 1995, the bullying drew attention again, when the police arrested or guided a total of 534 juveniles *(White Paper on Police in 1999)*. However, by the late 1990s, media attention had shifted away from bullying, and the number of reported cases dropped to 268 in 1998. While an interesting observation, it should be noted that most bullying incidents go unreported. In reality, bullying may not have increased even at the time, when mass media drew attention.

- Sex crimes such as rape and indecency decreased drastically during the three decades since 1964 (see Table 11.1). Again, the campaign against violence seems to have had a positive impact on reducing sex offences. Another explanation may be that with the development of the economy, more youngsters have their own money—enough to buy the services of a prostitute, pornographic literature, and so on, to satisfy their sexual appetite (Yokoyama, 1995). However, recently, the total number of rapes has increased. In the late 1990s, the support system for crime victims began to be improved. Therefore, more victims of rape might report to the police.

- "**Hotrodders**," that is, groups of youth who enjoy driving motorcycles and cars while making a loud noise, appeared in the late 1950s (Yokoyama, 1986b). Amendments in the criminal laws towards criminalization were made to address this problem (Yokoyama, 1990a). The criminalization against hotrodders has been carried out by practices within the juvenile justice agencies (Yokoyama, 1990b). As a result, the members of the hotrodder groups decreased from 42,510 in 1982 to 26,720 in 1996 *(White Paper on Police in 1997)*. However, their activities continue to be troublesome.

- In addition to the problems with hotrodders, many juveniles commit traffic offences. In 1998, a total of 817,139 juveniles were charged for some violation of the Road Traffic Law *(White Paper on Crime in 1999)*. Meanwhile, 3,7120 juveniles were charged with professional negligence causing death or bodily injury, because they killed or injured someone as a result of a traffic accident (See Table 11.1).

- The use of hard drugs such as cocaine and heroin is not seen as a serious problem in Japan. Since the end of World War II, however, stimulant drugs composed of methamphetamines have been prevalent. Despite efforts to suppress this contamination through criminalization (Yokoyama, 1991), the police have not succeeded in eradicating the drug abuse, because the Boryokudan (Japanese organized crime gangs, known as Yakuza in foreign countries) dominate the black market for the stimulant drugs (Tamura, 1992 and Yokoyama,

1999b). (Organized gangs similarly control the recent drug trade problem in Russia [see Chapter 15]). Owing to the high price, ordinary juveniles had limited access to the drugs prior to 1990. However, during the Depression some foreigners, above all Iranians, began to sell the stimulant drug even to juveniles at a cheap price (Yokoyama, 1999a). Therefore, we see the shift from the sniffing of thinner or toluene to the abuse of stimulant drugs among juveniles. The total number of juveniles caught on a charge of the Stimulant Drug Control Law increased from 769 in 1990 to 1,069 in 1998, while juveniles on a charge of sniffing of thinner or toluene decreased from 22,366 to 4,496 (*White Paper on Police in 1991* and *1999*).

Table 11.1: Juvenile penal Code Offenders Investigated by the Police

	1951	1964	1983	1995	1998
Total	166,433	238,830	317,438	193,308	221,410
Theft	127,122	135,849	202,028	99,076	121,261
Fraud	4,886	1,781	662	456	673
Embezzlement	3,142	1,123	19,624	26,652	35,847
Robbery	2,197	1,987	788	873	1,566
Extortion	3,635	15,228	8,504	6,339	6,767
Intimidation	461	1,252	158	67	86
Minor violence	3,126	13,881	7,660	1,945	1,847
Injury	8,653	16,669	11,406	8,101	9,914
Rape	1,530	4,242	750	268	460
Indecency	347	1,630	756	461	458
Murder	448	361	87	80	117
Arson	446	535	389	258	236
Professional negligence causing death or injury	10,440*	44,292*	55,804	44,171	37,120
Other			8,822	4,561	5,058

* Professional negligence and Other combined.
Source: White Paper on Crime in 1999: 496-499.

PROFILE OF JUVENILE DELINQUENTS

Delinquency and Gender

During the third peak of 1983, female delinquency increased dramatically. The number of non-traffic Penal Code offenders rose from 11,866 in 1966 to 54,459 in 1983 (*White Paper on Crime in 1975* and *1984*). This increase can be mainly attributed to the change in lifestyle of young girls in Japan. The rate of female juvenile Penal Code offenders per all juvenile ones reached to over 10% in 1971*(White Paper on Police in 1997)*. After 1976, it remained stable at the level of around twenty per cent. However, recently it rose drastically. It amounted to 25.4% in 1998. The increase can be attributed to the decline of tolerance levels towards minor offences by female juveniles under the influence of the adoption of the tough policy by the police (see Box 11.2).

Box 11.2: The "play-type" delinquency or the "incipient-type" delinquency?

In the late 1960s, the serious and violent crime rates dropped. The police were then able to direct their resources to less serious offences, such as bicycle theft, embezzlement of a lost or deserted bicycle, and shoplifting (Yokoyama, 1992b). Most of these crimes were committed for fun or thrills. Therefore, after 1970, the police referred to them as "play-type" delinquency. The play-type delinquency was usually committed by ordinary juveniles from middle- or upper-class families. The net-widening efforts by the police contributed to forming the third peak of juvenile delinquency in 1983.

After the research in 1981 by the National Research Institute of Police Sciences, Kiyonaga (1983) pointed out that juveniles committing minor offences at a younger age were prone to developing a criminal tendency toward committing a conventional theft and/or a violent crime, or engaging in drug abuse. In response, the police renamed the play-type delinquency to "incipient-type" delinquency in the *White Paper on Police in 1982*. Shoplifting, motorcycle theft, bicycle theft and the embezzlement of a lost or deserted thing were categorized under this new label. However, these four offences seem to be committed by juveniles with different criminal tendencies. For example, motorcycle theft can be committed by juveniles who admire hotrodders, while riding a bicycle temporarily without the owner's permission tends to be committed by play-type delinquents (see Yokoyama, 2000e, for the further criticism).

The rate of the above-mentioned incipient-type delinquency among all juvenile Penal Code offenders increased from 36.0% in 1973 to 64.4% in 1984 and to 75.6% in 1998 (*White Paper on Police in 1983, that in 1984* and *that in 1999*). By advocating the category of the incipient-type delinquency, the police have carried out the net-widening activities against juvenile minor offenders with fewer criminal tendencies. In the late 1990s, their activities contributed to giving the public a warning against the increase in a total of juvenile offences. Under the moral panic among the public, the Juvenile Law was revised toward criminalization in 2000.

Of all female juvenile Penal Code offenders in 1998, 78.5% were caught on a charge of theft, followed by 13.8% on the embezzlement of a lost or deserted bicycle *(White Paper on Crime in 1994)*. Most of the thefts are composed of minor shoplifting. The increase in shoplifting coincided with a growth in large-scale department stores and supermarkets that use a self-service system (*White Paper on Police in 1976*).

The use of illegal drugs has also increased among female delinquents in recent years. The percentage of young females caught for sniffing thinner or toluene amounted to 31.8%, while the corresponding percentage for those abusing stimulant drugs was 50.2% (*White Paper on Police in 1999*). The higher percentage of those abusing the stimulant drug corresponds to the increased number of young females working at night. Their increased income enables them to buy stimulant drugs and they are often exposed to risk of contact with members of Boryokudan (Yokoyama, 1991).

Juvenile Delinquents by Age

As indicated in Table 11.2, between 1983 and 1995 the rates of juvenile delinquency among all age groups dropped. The decline may be explained by the fact that after the second baby-boom in the early 1970s, Japan experienced a population decline with low birth rates, and that juveniles reared in a small family have been more protected, or perhaps overprotected, by adults. Recall that Gottfredson and Hirschi (1990) emphasize parental concern for the welfare or behavior of the child as a necessary condition for successful child-rearing.

Since 1966, the highest rate of juvenile non-traffic Penal Code offenders was for those children between the ages of 14 and 15 years. In the third peak this rate climbed up to 29.5 per 1,000. The *White Paper on Police in 1999* reports that junior high school students are more likely to commit minor offences such as theft and the embezzlement of a lost or deserted bicycle (68.6% and 16.2% respectively).

Table 11.2: Rate of Juvenile Non-traffic Penal Code Offenders Guided and Investigated by the Police per 1,000 Population

	All juvenile offenders	Under 14*	14-15	16-17	18-19
1966	9.0	5.0	12.1	11.6	9.7
1983	14.1	8.1	29.5	18.0	7.7
1995	9.3	3.8	17.1	14.9	6.3
1998	12.5	4.9	22.0	20.3	9.0

* Rates of offenders under 14 years of age per 1,000 population between the ages of 10-13.
Source: White Paper on Crime in 1999: 497.

Previously, the high delinquency rate among junior high school students was explained by the heated competition for higher education opportunities (Tokuoka and Cohen, 1987). However, Harada (1995) found that students' maladjustment tends to be short-term in nature. The rate of delinquency in the age group between 16 and 17 drops because many juveniles are liberated from the stress of severe competition after graduation from junior high school. I believe that the high rates among junior high school students around 1983 and 1998 are attributable to the net-widening activities by the police for those found to commit minor offences. Nevertheless, in spite of the net-widening initiatives, Japanese delinquency rates are still among the lowest in the world.

ADMINISTRATION OF JUVENILE JUSTICE SYSTEM

The judiciary is separate from and independent of the central and local governments. As can be seen from Figure 11.1, the flow of the juvenile justice administrative process involves many steps. This section concentrates on some of the major elements in Japan's juvenile justice system.

Preventive Activities in the Community

The participatory nature of Japan's juvenile justice system is conspicuous in the preventive measures against delinquency taken in the community (Yokoyama, 2000a). Rural areas have historically relied on strong, informal control in the family and in the neighbourhood, which prevents juvenile delinquency. And even though the majority of people live in urban settings, informal control still remains even in large cities, contrary to many Western countries. The town associations carry out many activities such as: festivals, athletic meetings, traffic safety, recreational activities for the elderly and children, and so on. These activities help to promote close community ties which in turn have served to help monitor and reduce the incidents of juvenile delinquency (Yokoyama, 1981).

In addition to the village and town associations, many civil groups participate in the movement to raise juveniles soundly. For example, in many communities, organizations such as the mothers' associations are involved with activities for juveniles (*White Paper on Juveniles in 1999)*. The national and local governments, law enforcement agencies, and juvenile justice agencies encourage and support these informal preventive activities in the community (Murai, 1979). These activities serve to supplement formal social control.

Juvenile Guidance Centres

Two **juvenile guidance centers** for delinquents were established for the first time in Kyoto and Osaka in 1952 by the initiative of citizens. By 1963, there were 118 juvenile guidance centers. However, the national government did not subsidize them until 1964, at the second peak of juvenile delinquency. The guidance centers carry out three main activities: patrolling streets in the amusement quarters to guide juveniles, counselling juveniles and their parents, and improving the social environment for rearing juveniles soundly.

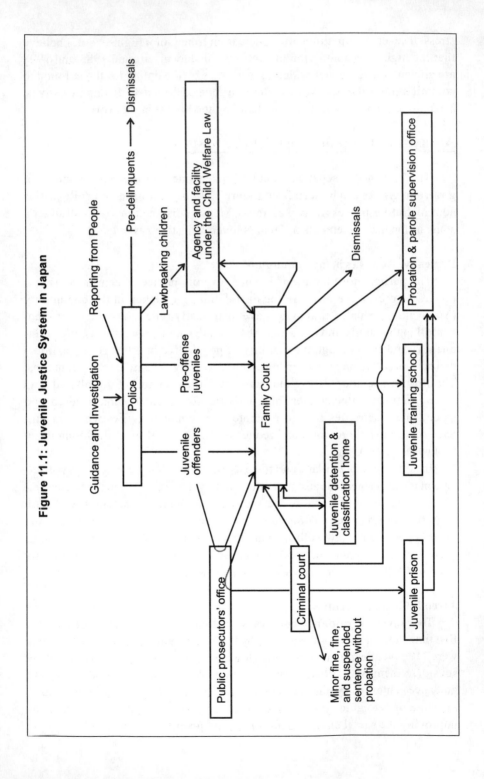

Figure 11.1: Juvenile Justice System in Japan

At the beginning of November, 1998, there were 703 juvenile guidance centres, with approximately 74,000 juvenile guidance volunteers (*White Paper on Juveniles in 1999*). In 1997, the juvenile guidance officers and volunteers gave caution to about 366,000 juveniles while patrolling on the street. The total number of individual counselling cases amounted to approximately 156,000. In small- or medium-sized cities, many juvenile guidance centres are managed by the education department of the municipal government, while in large cities, the department coping with the youth problem administers them. Police departments administer several juvenile guidance centres in larger cities. The centres of the former two types do not have compulsory power for law enforcement.

Preventive Activities by the Police
The police have developed organizations for the prevention of delinquency such as the crime prevention association, the company-police conference, and the school-police conference. Numerous organizations have collaborated with the police in efforts to prevent crime. For example, at the end of 1998, the total number of the liaison houses for crime prevention affiliated with the crime prevention associations amounted to 468,091 (*White Paper on Juveniles*, 1999).

During the second peak of juvenile delinquency in 1964, we directed attention to offences by youths coming from rural areas after graduation from a junior high school. These youths were the main target of the newly established company-police conference. Today, the total number of this conference has decreased to approximately 300 company-police conferences, as companies do not employ many teenagers.

After recovery from the economic difficulties in the aftermath of World War II, Japan began to focus on the large amount of physical violence in junior high schools (Hiyama and Katsumi, 1974). In order to cope with the increase in delinquency of high school students, the school-police conference was organized. By 1969, every junior high school was required to have a teacher in charge of guiding students (Yokoyama, 1981). In 1998, there were approximately 2,400 school-police conferences, in which about 90% of all elementary, junior high, and senior high schools participated (*White Paper on Juveniles in 1999*).

Another police organization in the community included police boxes (Koban) in the urban areas and police houses (Chuzaisho) in rural areas. In 1998, there were about 6,600 Kobans and about 8,100 Chuzaishos (*White Paper on Police in 1999*). The police officers working at a police box or a police house carry out many crime prevention activities in their territory. One of these activities involves patrolling on foot, when police officers often guide juvenile delinquents. In the police station, there is a Department of Community Safety. The police officers belonging to this department and the guidance volunteers patrol the amusement quarters to guide juveniles who are prone to deviant behaviour.

Finally, the police have also established three voluntary systems: the guidance volunteer, the police helper for juveniles, and the instructor for juveniles (Yokoyama, 1989). In 1998, the total number of guidance volunteers amounted to approximately 51,000. In addition, about 1,100 citizens, many of whom are retired police officers, work as police helpers in charge of dispersing the groups of juvenile delinquents. Approximately 6,000 juvenile instructors, authorized by the Law on Regulation of Business Affecting Public Morals of 1985, work to protect juveniles from unsound environments (*White Paper on Police in 1999*). Under the Juvenile Law, the police are not qualified to supervise juveniles after the guidance. However, some of them are invited by the police to receive after-care treatment and to participate in sports.

The police participate in many activities to reduce the risk of delinquency. In 1998, the police counselors visited 10,921 schools, 65.8% of all junior and senior high schools, to speak to students about the prevention of drug abuse (*White Paper on Police in 1999*). The police also invite young persons to join them in various sporting and social events. For example, in 1998 about 1,000 police stations opened their training gym to approximately 70,000 juveniles, where police officers and volunteers instructed in Judo and Japanese fencing (*White Paper on Police in 1999*). The police also provide counselling for juveniles and their parents (Yokoyama, 1992a). In 1998, the total number of those counseling cases amounted to 92,268 (*White Paper on Police in 1999*).

Before the third peak, the police emphasized the necessity of early intervention and early treatment for delinquents. In 1982, the National Police Agency issued a general principle, enabling the police to widen their activities to control juveniles under the name of rearing them soundly (Ayukawa, 1994). Fukuda (1988) suggests that the police have moved towards placing juveniles under total control and surveillance. However, it would be more desirable if most of these activities were carried out by schools or by child welfare agencies. The government should assign more resources to child welfare agencies, such as the child consultation centres and juvenile guidance centres.

In contrast, the police have earnestly campaigned for an increase in the fixed number of police officers and reinforcement of their resources. In addition, every time some heinous crime occurs, the mass media point to defects in the activities of the police. Then, the police succeed in getting more financial resources for improving these defects. As a result, the fixed number of police officers increased from 181,768 in 1972 to 263,402 in 1998 *(White Paper on*

Police in 1973 and that in *1994*). This increase has contributed to their net-widening activities.

Disposition of Cases by the Police and Public Prosecutors

Under the Police Activity Rules of 1960, the police handle juveniles with bad conduct as pre-delinquents. If the police officer or the volunteer patrolling on foot finds a pre-delinquent, they simply give a warning. In 1998, such warnings were given to 928,947 juveniles of which 48.9% and 32.0% concerned smoking and loitering at midnight respectively (*White Paper on Police in 1999*).

According to the Juvenile Law, the category of pre-offence juveniles is defined under the principle of *parens patriae*. This category has been subject to criticism by a number of legal professionals from the viewpoint of the principle of legality. Also under the law, police must refer all cases of pre-offence juveniles to the Family Court or the child consultation center. Therefore, the police are careful when classifying a juvenile as a pre-offence delinquent. In the process of the net-widening of their guidance activities, they prefer guiding juveniles as a pre-delinquent.

In 1998, the Family Court disposed of 1,525 pre-offence juveniles, of which 49.2% were female (*Annual Report of Judicial Statistics for 1998*). Typically, girls who run away from home and associate with members of the Boryokudan are treated as pre-offence juveniles for protective purposes.

Cases of law-breaking by children under 14 years of age are reported to the child guidance centre. If the caseworker in the centre judges that there is a need to impose protective measures under the Juvenile Law, the prefectural governor or the chief of the center refers the child to the Family Court. In 1998, there were only 292 such referrals.

The police must refer all cases of juvenile offenders directly, or via public prosecutors, to the Family Court. Only a small number of cases of minor offences, for which the law does not prescribe severe punishment such as imprisonment or the death penalty, are directly referred to the Family Court. The public prosecutors do not have discretion in screening cases. Therefore, after an investigation, they must refer all cases to the Family Court. At the referral, they can write their opinion. However, they cannot attend the hearing to state their opinion except for the cases of heinous offences, at which the Family Court judges give permission.

Imposition of Criminal Punishment

If Family Court judges find that a juvenile over 14 years of age should be punished, they can refer them back to the public prosecutor. In 1998, public prosecutors prosecuted 11,218 juveniles, of which 97.1% were for offences of the Road Traffic Law or professional negligence causing death or bodily injury (*Annual Report of Judicial Statistics for 1998*).

The total number of non-traffic cases referred to public prosecutors dropped from 3119 in 1965 to 328 in 1995 (see Table 11.3). The trend during the same period was similar to that for heinous offences by juveniles and for offences by older juveniles (see Tables 11.1 and 11.2 above). Recently, more juveniles have been referred back to public prosecutors. Unlike other countries, Japan experienced a long-term trend towards making less use of punishments in juvenile criminal cases. Instead, many youths receive a suspended sentence. However, in the late 1990s, under the influence of the tougher measures adopted by the police, more juvenile offenders are referred back to public prosecutors. Nevertheless, the total number of juveniles newly committed to the prison in 1998 amounted to only 44 (*White Paper on Crime in 1999*). This represents a dramatic drop since 1951 (see Box 11.3).

Box 11.3: Controversy about Restoration of Public Prosecutors' Authority

Under the initiative of the Ministry of Justice, in which public prosecutors monopolize all key positions, several drafts for revision of the Juvenile Law were put forth (Saito, 1986). The main purpose of the revisions was the restoration of the public prosecutors' authority, which had been lost under the introduction of the welfare model by the enactment of Juvenile Law in 1948. However, legal professionals and members of the opposition parties criticized this restoration severely for being crime control oriented.

Under the moral panic among the public in a conservative mood the ruling coalition parties submitted the bill of a revised Juvenile Law to the Diet. In November, 2000, it passed in spite of the opposition of the Communist Party and the Social Democratic Party. By this enactment, the public prosecutors succeeded in acquiring their qualification to appear at the Family Court with the permission of a judge.

Owing to the low number of juveniles receiving prison terms, young adults up to the age of 26 are also being treated in a total of eight juvenile prisons throughout the country (Yokoyama, 1982). These facilities are designed to offer many programs for vocational training and, as is the practice in many Western countries, inmates are usually granted parole before the expiration of their term of imprisonment. These practices reflect the welfare flavour evident in Japan's juvenile justice system.

Family Court Probation Officers and Tentative Probation

Since 1950, Family Courts have used probation officers who are trained in the behavioral sciences. Again, as in many Western countries, probation officers

Table 11.3: Final Dispositions of Juvenile Non-traffic Offenders at Family Courts

	Total	Dismissal without Hearing	Dismissal after Hearing	Referral to Public Prosecutors*	Referral to Child Consultation Centres	Probation	Juvenile Training Schools	Commitment to Facilities under Child Welfare Law
1965	158,475	88,364	39,862	3,119	561	19,262	7,079	228
	(100.0)	(55.7)	(25.1)	(2.0)	(0.4)	(12.2)	(4.5)	(0.1)
1983	198,729	139,368	38,049	1,008	183	15,171	4,758	192
	(100.0)	(70.1)	(19.2)	(0.5)	(0.1)	(7.6)	(2.4)	(0.1)
1995	123,372	90,451	16,954	328	114	11,996	3,335	194
	(100.0)	(73.3)	(13.7)	(0.3)	(0.1)	(9.7)	(2.7)	(0.2)
1998	153,138	115,504	16,293	324	108	15,880	4,791	238
	(100.0)	(75.4)	(10.6)	(0.2)	(0.1)	(10.4)	(3.1)	(0.2)

* Excludes cases referred to public prosecutors due to reaching majority.

Sources: White Paper on Crime in 1984, p.285.
White Paper on Crime in 1985, p.213.
White Paper on Crime in 1997, p.482.
Annual Report of Judicial Statistics for 1998, pp.56—57.

are responsible for processing the case, conducting background research, and providing services while the youth is under supervision.

Before adjudication, Family Court judges can place a juvenile delinquent under **tentative probation,** which is supervised by Family Court probation officers. In some cases these youths are guided by volunteers or accommodated in private houses. In 1998, 13,401 juveniles were placed under tentative probation, of which 2,663, 6,472, and 4,266 were charged with non-traffic offences, professional negligence causing death or bodily injury, and the violations of the Road Traffic Law respectively (*Annual Report of Judicial Statistics for 1998*). The total number of tentative probationary cases declined steadily since 1989. The number of those who were committed to some private house or facility also dropped from 840 in 1984 to 325 in 1998. The tentative probation by volunteers demonstrates the participatory character in our juvenile justice system. However, this system is declining with the change in our society (Yokoyama, 2000b). For example, because of the economic, social, and cultural changes in Japan, it is becoming more difficult to recruit volunteers.

After completing their tentative probation, the youths must appear before the Family Court for their hearings. Usually, the Family Court judges sentence them to dismissal in order to avoid a double penalty (Yokoyama, 1984). In 1998, the Family Courts heard 9,212 juvenile tentative probationers, excluding those charged under the Road Traffic Law. Of these probationers, nearly 80% were adjudicated dismissal, 14.4% were placed on probation, while 2.7% were committed to juvenile training schools (*Annual Report of Judicial Statistics for 1998*).

Juvenile Detention and Classification Homes

If crisis intervention is deemed necessary, the Family Court judges can decide to place the youth in a juvenile detention and classification home administered by the Ministry of Justice. In 1998, there were 52 juvenile detention and classification homes and one branch home. The total number of juveniles newly admitted to the detention and classification homes decreased from 35,341 in 1964 to 10,410 in 1974. Then, it increased to 21,854 in 1983 at the third peak of juvenile delinquency. By 1995, it dropped to 14,265, but it rose again to 19,421 in 1998 (*White Paper on Crime in 1999*). This increase is related to the growing number of arrests against juvenile offenders in the late 1990s. In the juvenile detention and classification homes, specialists in behavioral sciences carry out many kinds of tests on inmates while observing their behaviour. Although the maximum term of custody is eight weeks under the Juvenile Law, the tests and observation are usually finished within four weeks.

Adjudication by Family Court Judges

All judges in lower-class courts are professional. They are appointed by the Cabinet, which follows the recommendation of the Supreme Court. Therefore, the Family Court judges are independent of any public image. They have endeavoured to decide the disposition in the best interests of juvenile offenders, in consideration of the reports from the Family Court probation officer and a specialist at a juvenile detention and classification home. However, after the murder case in Kobe (discussed earlier), many people began to question whether the rights of crime victims are neglected in the juvenile justice system, while the rights of juvenile offenders are given too much attention. In light of this public pressure, it has become difficult for judges to remain objective.

For non-serious cases, the Family Court judges decide the dismissal without hearing from the youth, after screening by the Family Court probation officer. In other cases, the judges may hear from the youth. Then, in consideration of reports from the Family Court probation officer and a specialist at a juvenile detention and classification home, they decide whether or not to impose protective educative measures. Based on the total number of final dispositions of juvenile non-traffic offenders, the percentage of dismissal without hearing amounted to 55.7% in 1965 (see Table 11.3). Then, it increased to 75.4% in 1998, which was almost the same as the growing rate of the so-called incipient-type delinquency in the same year. The increase seemed to reflect the fact that juveniles having committed minor offences, such as shoplifting and bicycle theft, were more frequently caught by the net-widening of guidance activities of the police.

Under the Constitution, Japanese offenders are guaranteed the right to a public trial. However, in juvenile cases the hearing is carried out in a closed court to prevent stigmatizing juveniles. Juveniles and their parent(s) or guardian can employ a legal counsellor as an attendant at the hearing. In almost all juvenile cases, juveniles confess their offences without employing legal counsel.

Recently, lawyers have participated in several cases defending juveniles against a false charge. To obtain a confession, the police interrogators are apt to torture a suspect psychologically for long hours, while confining them in a police station cell as a substitute for regular detention houses (Igarashi, 1989). The lawyers insist on the necessity of defending juveniles from a false charge brought by such interrogation, and campaign for the importance of the legal counsellor as an attendant.

After the hearing, the Family Court judge decides whether or not to impose protective educative measures. Many juveniles are dismissed after receiving a warning and advice at the hearing (see Table 11.3). Only a few are released because of their innocence. However, under the principle of *parens patriae*, 'innocence' is not formally sentenced under the Juvenile Law.

If the Family Court judges admit the necessity of protecting a juvenile delinquent, they will impose protective educative measures. While the old Juvenile Law of 1922 prescribed nine protective educative measures, the current Juvenile Law provides (as mentioned earlier) for only three. Under Article 24 of the current law they include: probation, commitment to juvenile training schools, and commitment to facilities for children of up to 18 years old under the Child Welfare Law.

Facilities under the Child Welfare Law

The Family Court judge can place juvenile delinquents of younger ages in a home for dependent children or a home to support children's independence. The delinquent children placed in such facilities are few in number (see Table 11.3). Almost all of these children are treated in one of 57 homes to support children's independency around the country.

In addition to the compulsory commitment by the Family Court, the majority of the children are accommodated in the home to support children's independence by order of prefectural governor with the consent of their parent(s) or guardian(s). In recent years, however, the percentage of the total number of inmates in the homes per maximum occupancy rate decreased from 58.7% in 1987 to 44.5% in 1991 (Hattori, 1992). It has declined to under 40%, although it increased a little in the late 1990s.

Local governments have been assigning ordinary officers as caseworkers at the child consultation centre. Unfortunately, their knowledge and understanding of the facilities for child welfare is limited, and they often fail to obtain the consent necessary to commit the child to a home to support children's independence (Hattori, 1992). This is one reason why the total number of inmates in the home to support children's independence has decreased. And even though amendments to the Child Welfare Law (1998) can offer treatment to children with behavioral problems, their relative effectiveness has yet to be clearly demonstrated. Furthermore, it has become difficult to maintain this system owing to changes in the social structure of Japan (Hattori, 1996). For example, in accordance with the Labour Law, married couples are prohibited from working with juveniles all day long and/or all year round.

Juvenile Training Schools

Until the early 1960s, juvenile training schools were overcrowded (Yokoyama, 2000c). This problem contributed to the schools having difficulty offering educative treatment programs. Subsequently, judges and probation officers at the Family Court distrusted the treatment in these schools, and referred fewer cases. In addition, serious offences by juveniles decreased after the second peak of juvenile delinquency (see Table 11.1). Therefore, the total number of juveniles newly admitted to juvenile training schools declined steadily from 8,065 in 1966 to 1,969 in 1974 (*White Paper on Crime in 1999*).

In response to the declining youth crime rate, the Ministry of Justice began to reform the system of juvenile training schools (Yokoyama, 1992a). In 1977, the ministry introduced a system of short-term schools for juveniles with less advanced criminal tendencies and for juvenile serious traffic offenders. In response to the reform by the Ministry, the Family Court judges began to place juveniles in the short-term schools. Therefore, the total number of juveniles sent to juvenile training schools increased to 4,758 in 1983 (see Table 11.3). However, after the third peak of juvenile delinquency, the numbers began to decline once again. Subsequently, to accommodate more juvenile delinquents, short-term schools with special training courses were introduced in 1991 in place of that for juvenile traffic offenders. The total number of juveniles newly admitted to the short-term schools increased from 1,678 in 1991 to 2,216 in 1998, or by 32.1%, while the corresponding number of juveniles committed to the long-term schools rose from 2,651 to 3,172, or by 19.7% (*White Paper on Crime in 1999*). For the past few years, juvenile training schools have widened their net to include juveniles who have committed less serious offences (Yokoyama, 2000e).

Previously, juveniles admitted to long-term juvenile training schools were treated within two years. However, as noted earlier, after the murder case in Kobe, the use of short confinement was heavily criticized. In response, the Ministry of Justice established a new course of treatment to deal with those charged with more serious offences. This means that most of inmates in the long-term schools now receive educative treatment for about one year, while inmates in the general short-term schools and those in the schools with the special training courses are released after receiving treatment for six and four months respectively. The schools offer a variety of programmes, including academic education, vocational training, and guidance on living skills.

Probation and Parole
One of the protective educative measures under Juvenile Law is probation. Juvenile probationers can be placed on probation until they are 20 years of age. From 1965 to 1983, the adjudication of probation decreased (see Table 11.3). One of the reasons for this decrease may have been the net-widening of juvenile training schools since 1977. However, we also saw net-widening in the area of probation. For example, in 1994, the Ministry of Justice adopted a new

system of short-term probation of six or seven months to accept more juvenile probationers.

Under the law, professional probation/parole officers are expected to work as specialists with social work training. Most of them have to pass a special examination before they can work with juvenile offenders. Usually the professional officers work only as distributors of cases and supervisors for the volunteer officers, therefore, they tend not to develop their abilities as social workers.

In addition to the professional officers, the Minister of Justice commissions a leader in the community to work as a volunteer probation/parole officer. This is another example of the participatory nature of Japan's juvenile justice system. In 1999, there were 48,815 such volunteer officers (*White Paper on Crime in 1999*). The volunteers guide, supervise, and assist almost all probationers and parolees through their experiences. They may also utilize resources in the community more effectively than professional officers, who are typically transferred to another office every two or three years.

The average age of volunteer probation/parole officers rose from 53.2 in 1953 to 63.0 in 1999 (*White Paper on Crime in 1999*). Therefore, we may see a wider generation gap between volunteer officers and juveniles. Recently, more females have become volunteer officers. The percentage of female volunteer officers rose from 7% in 1953 to 23.3% in 1999. Female volunteer officers are expected to have a good influence on juveniles in a different way from that of male officers.

SUMMARY

After the Meiji Restoration, Japan began to develop the framework for its current juvenile justice system. It was modelled after the system in Western countries. The objective of following the modern juvenile justice system was to provide juvenile delinquents with educative protective treatment to rehabilitate them. In keeping with Japanese tradition and culture, volunteers played an important role—hence, we saw the participatory nature of our juvenile justice system. In 1922, the Juvenile Law was enacted. However, owing to a poor budget, the juvenile justice system under this law was not completely established until 1942.

After World War II, Japan's justice system was democratized. A new Juvenile Law under the complete welfare model was promulgated in 1948. But again, owing to limited resources, juvenile justice agencies had a difficult time meeting with the urgent necessity of protecting many poor juvenile delinquents. However, with the economic recovery in the early 1950s, we gradually improved the resources of juvenile justice agencies.

With the growth of the baby boomers after the war, we saw the second peak of juvenile delinquency in 1964. We directed attention to an increase in violent crimes. As a result, many resources were assigned to delinquency prevention activities. The police were very active with their initiatives. These activities appear to have had an impact, since the number of delinquencies declined in the early 1970s.

By the late 1970s, the police were well equipped to guide and investigate virtually any type of delinquent behaviour. As a result of the net-widening activities of the police, we saw the third peak of juvenile delinquency in 1983, which was committed by the young generation born during the second baby boom. For the next decade, we saw a decrease in juvenile offences. This may be partially due to the fact that young people have come to be excessively protected, guided, and supervised by the surrounding adults in the aging society. However, in the late 1990s, we witnessed an increase in official delinquency rates. This phenomenon may be caused by the fact that the police strengthened their net against juveniles in the moral panic among the public.

After the second peak, heinous and violent crimes committed by juveniles decreased. Therefore, the number of juveniles placed on probation or admitted to juvenile training schools declined. In response, the Ministry of Justice introduced the system of short-term juvenile training schools and short-term probation. This seemed to be another net-widening phenomenon.

Recently, lawyers have been drawing attention to defects in the current juvenile justice system. Their criticisms have focused on the difficulty of guaranteeing due process. However, their challenges fall short of advocating the **just deserts model**. On the other hand, after the Kobe case in 1997 there was moral panic about juvenile crimes among the public. Crime victims began to insist on the guarantee of their rights in the juvenile justice system. Therefore, in 2000, the Conservative government succeeded in revising the Juvenile Law toward partial criminalization. However, the welfare/participatory model, with an emphasis upon rehabilitation, is maintained in principle.

In many respects, our juvenile justice practices complement the recommendations put forth in the Beijing Rules (see Box 1—Introduction). However, we must continue to examine the prescriptions of our Juvenile Law and the practice of our juvenile justice agencies in consideration of the recommendations cited in the Beijing Rules, and those declared at the ninth UN Congress on Prevention and Treatment.

It is anticipated that the population of juveniles will decrease as the nation's birth rate continues to decline. If the current social structures in Japan do not change drastically, the total number of juvenile delinquents is likely to continue declining. If juvenile justice agencies do not adapt to such a situation, they will not be able to maintain their current resources, because the Ministry of Finance will have to curtail their budgets. In order to prevent the progress towards reduction, the juvenile justice agencies are likely to carry out additional net-widening strategies.

Net-widening ventures have produced advantages and disadvantages in Japan. These ventures have likely contributed to the reduction in juvenile delinquency. Early intervention by the police has helped to prevent many juvenile delinquents from developing criminal tendencies. The net-widening of probation and treatment in juvenile training schools has given them the opportunity to receive the educative protective services that are deemed in their best interests.

On the other hand, net-widening may more seriously invade juvenile liberties. By proceeding to the further stage in the juvenile justice system, juvenile delinquents may be stigmatized as well as other negative effects—as labelling theorists point out.

Finally, as the relative proportion of young people in Japan continues to decline, we will likely see juveniles being excessively protected, guided, and supervised by adults. According to Merton's (1968) typology of the modes of individual adaptation, juveniles of the retreatism-type may increase over those of innovation-type, whom we often saw before the second peak of juvenile delinquency. If most of the juveniles become too conformable to conventional norms, and if the juveniles of the retreatism persuasion increase in numbers, then Japan's current rate development would likely be compromised. From this viewpoint, too, we must examine functions of the juvenile justice system in Japan.

Minoru Yokoyama completed his B.A. in Law and M.A. in Criminal Law and Sociology at Chuo University, Tokyo. He is a professor and the former Dean of the Faculty of Law at Kokugakuin University. He is the former second Vice President of the Research Committee for the Sociology of Deviance and Social Control of the International Sociological Association. He is a member of the board of directors and the former president of the Japanese Association of Sociological Criminology. He is the president of the Tokyo Study Group of Sociological Criminology and a member of the board of directors of the Japanese Association of Social Problems. He has presented numerous papers at national and international conferences and symposia, and has published many articles in professional journals.

HELPFUL WEBSITES
* there are very few links in English that specifically address juvenile justice in Japan
www.japantimes.cp.jp/ Japan Times newspaper published in English.

www.npa.gp.jp/ The National Police Agency provides some data on juvenile crime data in English.

www.moj.go.jp/toukei/toukei.htm Ministry of Justice (only in Japanese).

KEY TERMS AND CONCEPTS

Gustave Boissonade	Meiji Restoration
Juvenile Law	Juvenile Guidance Centres
Tentative Probation	Juvenile Training Schools
Welfare model	Participatory Model
Koban	Hotrodder
Justice model	Just Deserts Model
rehabilitation model	

STUDY QUESTIONS

1. How have the trends and patterns of delinquency changed in Japan since World War II? What appear to have been the major contributing factors?
2. What do you consider to be the strengths and weaknesses of the Family Court within the Japanese juvenile justice system? How does it compare to other countries?
3. Japan can be characterized as trying to balance several different juvenile justice models. What are they, and which model is more dominate? What are your impressions of how Japan formally deals it's young offenders?
4. Net-widening initiatives have been used extensively by the police in recent decades, and have allegedly contributed to a decrease in delinquency. Do you think this is an effective approach? How does it compare to other countries?
5. Referring to other countries, how practical do you consider the revisions to the Juvenile Law in 2000 to be?

REFERENCES

Administrative Affairs Agency. (1994). White paper on juveniles in 1994 (written in Japanese). Tokyo: Printing Bureau of the Ministry of Finance.

Ayukawa, J. (1994). *Sociology of juvenile delinquency* (written in Japanese). Kyoto: Sekai Shiso-sha.

Correctional Association. (1984). *Modern development of juvenile correction* (written in Japanese). Tokyo: Correctional Association.

Fujimoto, T. (1994). *Crime problems in Japan.* Tokyo: Chuo University Press.

Fukuda, M. (1988). *A critical analysis of the juvenile justice system in Japan.* Paper presented at the 40th Annual Meeting of American Society of Criminology, Chicago, U.S.A.

Gottfredson, M.R., and T. Hirschi. (1990). *A general theory of crime.* Stanford, CA: Stanford University Press.

Hamai, K. (1999). *The Japanese Juveniles are becoming violent: moral panic or reality?* Paper presented at the 51st Annual Meeting of American Society of Criminology, Toronto, U.S.A.

Harada, Y. (1995). Adjustment to school, life course transitions, and changing in delinquent behavior in Japan. *Current Perspectives on Aging and the Life Cycle,* 4:35-60.

Hattori, A. (1992). Future of the child education and training homes (written in Japanese). *Juvenile Problems* (Japan),198:31-44.

———. (1996). Kyogoin Home in Japan. In C. B. Fields and R. H. Moore, Jr. (Eds.), *Comparative criminal justice.* Prospect Height, Ill: Waveland Press: 573-582.

Hiyama, S., and H. Katsumi. (1974). *History of juvenile crimes after the war* (written in Japanese). Tokyo: Sakai Shoten.

Igarashi, F. (1989). *Coerced confessions and pretrial detention in Japan.* Paper presented at the 41st Annual Meeting of American Society of Criminology, Reno, Nevada.

Kiyonaga, K. (1983). Younger juvenile delinquents—Prediction from 1983 (written in Japanese). *Crime and Delinquency* (Japan), 56:104-129.

Merton, R. (1968). *Social theory and social structure* (Enlarged edition). New York: The Free Press.

Murai, T. (1979). Juvenile delinquency and community. *Hitotsubashi Journal of Law and Politics* (Japan), 8:31-46.

National Police Agency. (1973). White paper on police in 1973 (written in Japanese). Tokyo: Printing Bureau of the Ministry of Finance.

———. (1976). White paper on police in 1976 (written in Japanese). Tokyo: Printing Bureau of the Ministry of Finance.

———. (1984). White paper on police in 1984 (written in Japanese). Tokyo: Printing Bureau of the Ministry of Finance.

———. (1999). White paper on police in 1999 (written in Japanese). Tokyo: Printing Bureau of the Ministry of Finance.

Oda, A. (1999). From the child education and training home to the home to support child's independency (written in Japanese). In N. Araki (Ed.), *Modern Juveniles and Juvenile Law* (Japan). Tokyo: Akashi-shoten. pp.:170-200.

Research and Training Institute of the Ministry of Justice. (1965). White paper on crime in 1965 (written in Japanese). Tokyo: Printing Bureau of the Ministry of Finance.

———. (1975). White paper on crime in 1975 (written in Japanese). Tokyo: Printing Bureau of the Ministry of Finance.

———. (1984). White paper on crime in 1984 (written in Japanese). Tokyo: Printing Bureau of the Ministry of Finance.

———. (1985). White paper on crime in 1985 (written in Japanese). Tokyo: Printing Bureau of the Ministry of Finance.

———. (1994). White paper on crime in 1994 (written in Japanese). Tokyo: Printing Bureau of the Ministry of Finance.

———. (1999). White paper on crime in 1999 (written in Japanese). Tokyo: Printing Bureau of the Ministry of Finance.

Riesman, D. (1961). *The lonely crowd.* New Haven, Conn: Yale U. Press.

Saito, T. (1986). The Japanese Juvenile Law and amendment issues. *Konan Hogaku* (Japan), 26(2 & 3):267-285.

Sawanobori, T. (1994). *Introduction to Juvenile Law* (written in Japanese). Tokyo: Yuhikaku.

Supreme Court. (1994). Annual report of judicial statistics for 1993 (written in Japanese). Tokyo: Hoso-kai.

———. (1999). Annual report of judicial statistics for 1998 (written in Japanese). Tokyo: Hoso-kai

Tamura, M. (1992). The Yakuza and amphetamine abuse in Japan. In H. Tarver and M. Gaylord (Eds.), *Drugs, law and the state*. Hong Kong: Hong Kong U. Press. pp.: 99-117.

Terao, F. (1999). Why do juveniles commit delinquency? (written in Japanese). In N. Araki (Ed.), *Modern Juveniles and Juvenile Law* (Japan). Tokyo: Akashi-shoten. pp.:202-231.

Tokuoka, H., and A.K. Cohen. (1987). Japanese society and delinquency. *International Journal of Comparative and Applied Criminal Justice*, 11(1 & 2):13-22.

Tsujimoto, Y. (1990). The historical development of child saving in Japan. *Bulletin of the Research Institute, Chuo-Gakuin University* (Japan), 8(1):5-27.

Tsutomi, H. (1999). What is a judicial teacher? (written in Japanese). In N. Araki (Ed.), *Modern Juveniles and Juvenile Law* (Japan). Tokyo: Akashi-shoten. pp.:134-168.

Yokoyama, M. (1981). Delinquency control programs in the community in Japan. *International Journal of Comparative and Applied Criminal Justice*, 5(2):169-178.

——. (1982). *How have prisons been used in Japan?* Paper presented at the World Congress of the International Sociological Ass. Mexico City, Mexico.

——. (1984). *Why doesn't Japan have diversion programs for juvenile delinquents?* Paper presented at the World Congress of the International Institute of Sociology, Seattle, Washington, USA.

——. (1985). Criminal policy against thieves in Japan. *Kangwon Law Review* (Korea), 1:191-217.

——. (1986a). The juvenile justice system in Japan. In M. Bursten, J. Graham, N. Herriger, and P. Malinowski (Eds.), *Youth crime, social control and prevention*. Wuppertal: Centaurus-Verlagsgesellschaft-Pfaffenweiler, pp.: 102-113.

——. (1986b). Social control and juvenile traffic offenders in Japan. *Kangwon Law Review* (Korea), 2:142-160.

——. (1989). Net-widening of the juvenile justice system in Japan. *Criminal Justice Review*, 14(1):43-53.

——. (1990a). Criminalization against traffic offenders in Japan. *International Journal of Comparative and Applied Criminal Justice*, 14(1 & 2):65-71.

——. (1990b). Criminalization against traffic offenders in Japanese criminal justice. *Kokugakuin Journal of Law and Politics* (Japan), 27(4):1-27.

——. (1991). Development of Japanese drug control laws towards criminalization (Japan), 28(3):1-21.

——. (1992a). Guarantee of human rights in juvenile justice system in Japan. *Kokugakuin Journal of Law and Politics* (Japan), 30(2):1-30.

——. (1992b). Net-widening in juvenile justice system [written in Japanese]. In the Committee for Celebrating the 70th Birthday of Prof. Kuniyuki Yagi (Ed.). *Modern development of criminal jurisprudence II*. Tokyo: Hogakushoin, pp. 481-512.

——. (1994). Treatment of prisoners under rehabilitation model in Japan. *Kokugakuin Journal of Law and Politics* (Japan). 32(2):1-24.

——. (1995). Analysis of prostitution in Japan. *International Journal of Comparative and Applied Criminal Justice,* 19(1 & 2):47-60.

——. (1999a). Analysis of crimes by foreigners in Japan. *International Journal of Comparative and Applied Criminal Justice,* 23(2):181-231.

——. (1999b). Trends of organized crime by Boryokudan in Japan. In S. Einstein and M. Amir (Eds.), *Organized crime: Uncertainties and Dilemmas*. Chicago: The

Office of International Criminal Justice, the University of Illinois, Chicago, pp. 135-154.

——. (2000a). Activities for prevention of juvenile delinquency in the community in Japan. In Tauber Istvan (Ed.), *Tanulmanyok, Vigh Jozsef, 70. Szuletesnapjara.* Budapest: TLTE Allam-es Jogtudomanyi Kar, pp. 292-307.

——. (2000b). Volunteers' Activities for Treatment of Juvenile Delinquents in Japan. In the Committee for Memorizing the Retirement of Prof. Han-Kyo, Lee (Ed.), *Issues and views of criminal laws in Korea and in Japan.* Seoul: Whasungsa, pp. 681-697.

——. (2000c). Formation of juvenile training schools (written in Japanese). In the Committee for Celebrating the 70th Birthday of Prof. Toshio Sawanobori (Ed.), *Views on Juvenile Law.* Tokyo: Gendaijinbunsha, pp. 291-309.

——. (2000d). *Development of Educative Treatment in Juvenile Training Schools in Japan.* Paper presented at the 52nd Annual Meeting of American Society of Criminology, San Francisco, California.

——. (2000e).*Tendency of Juvenile Delinquency in Japan and Criminalization* (written in Japanese). Paper presented at the symposium on juvenile delinquency, which Korean Research Institute of Criminology organized.

Chapter 12

Juvenile Justice in Namibia—
A System in Transition

Stefan Schulz[1]
Department of Legal Studies, Polytechnic of Namibia

FACTS ON NAMIBIA

Area: Namibia is a vast country of 823,145 sq. km. It is the twelfth largest country in sub-Sahara Africa, lying on the South West Coast of Africa between latitude 17.5^0 and 28.5^0 south and between longitude 12E and 20E. It shares main borders with Angola, Botswana, and South Africa. In the far northeast is the Caprivi Strip, an elongated panhandle consisting of tropical riverina swamplands and bordered by four countries—Angola, Botswana, Zambia, and Zimbabwe. **Population:** According to the last official census (1991), Namibia had a population of just more than 1.4 million and an annual population growth of about 3%. A 1999 estimate puts the population at approximately 1.695 million and the annual population growth at 2.6%. The average population density of the territory is only 1.7 persons per sq. km. compared with 1.5 for Africa and 32.5 per sq. km. for the world. Although Namibia is one of the most sparsely populated regions in sub-Saharan Africa, it has a rich variety of peoples in culture, language, and racial origin. While English is the official language, many languages are spoken in the country. They can be divided in three categories: the Bantu languages spoken by the Owambos, Hereros, Kavangos, Caprivians and Twanas; the Khoi-san languages spoken by the San and Nama/Damara; and the Indo-Germanic languages of Afrikaans, English, and German. The Owambos are the biggest ethnic group; numbering approximately 700,000 in 1991, they represent about 50% of Namibia's population. Windhoek is the nation's capital. Other major municipalities include Ondangwa, Oshakati, Walvisbay, Katima Mulilo, Keetmanshoop, and Oranjemund. **Climate:** Namibia has a dry climate typical of a semi-desert country where droughts are a regular occurrence. Days are mostly warm to very hot, while nights are generally cool. Average day temperatures in the summer vary from 20^0 C to 34^0 C and average night temperatures in the winter from 0^0 C to 10^0 C. Temperatures in the interior are lower because of the altitude, while along the coast the cold Benguela Current has a modifying influence. Average rainfall figures vary from less than 50 mm along the coast to 350 mm in the central and

700 in the far northeastern regions. However, because of the high variability of rainfall, especially in the arid regions, the "annual" rainfall does not necessarily give a true picture. **Economy:** The pillars of Namibia's economy are mining, fishing, tourism, and agriculture; tourism is the fastest growing industry. The largest single contributor to Namibia's GDP is general government, and the largest provider of employment is agriculture. **Government:** Namibia is a unitary state, which is now divided in 13 administrative regions. Namibia is ruled by a multiparty Parliament and has a democratic constitution. The constitution provides for the division of power between the executive, the legislature, and the judiciary.

There is no trust more sacred than the one the world holds for children. There is no duty more important than ensuring that their rights are respected, that their welfare is protected, that their lives are free from fear and want .. .the wellspring of human progress is founded on the realization of children's rights.—Kofi Annan, Secretary General of the United Nations

"Umuntu ngumuntu nagabantu" (Zulu): "A person is a person because of other people. " —Ubuntu is a frame of mind prevalent in sub-Saharan Africa.

Before we begin to examine the juvenile justice system in Namibia, it is prudent for the reader to understand the unique history of the country as it has a direct relationship to its juvenile justice. Namibia is a newly independent state. The territory was proclaimed a German protectorate by Bismarck in 1884. The conquest of German South West Africa by South African troops during World War I resulted in its subsequent administration by South Africa under a 1920 League of Nations Mandate. In December 1946, the United Nations (UN), successor organization of the League of Nations, rejected South African plans to make Namibia part of South Africa. However, South Africa went on with what was in practice an annexation of Namibia. In 1949, South Africa stopped reporting to the UN on how it was administering the country. On 27 October 1966, the General Assembly of the UN decided to end the South African mandate over Namibia, but the South African government refused to carry out this and other decisions of the UN. It was in the same year that the protracted war for national liberation between the occupying South African forces and the Namibian liberation movement South West African People's Organization (SWAPO) started. Finally, in 1989, the implementation of UN Resolution 435 for free and fair elections resulted in SWAPO coming to power. On 21 March 1990, after 106 years of foreign rule, Namibia achieved independence. Dr. Sam Nujoma became the country's first President.

Namibia's social, cultural, and political reality today is largely influenced by the destructive and devastating effects of colonialism and political apartheid. It is true that Namibia was not directly affected by the slave trade and early colonialism that affected many other African nations, but, since Germany declared the territory a protectorate in 1884, land theft and colonial oppression encroached on the indigenous economic and cultural basis with almost the same effects over time. The system of forced labour, introduced by the German colonial administration in 1907, carried on and was sophisticated by the South African administration to a steady destruction of the social and cultural fabric (Nachtweih, 1976). The drain of the workforce represented an ongoing rupture of the organic economic indigenous structures. Unfortunately, social disintegration has not stopped with independence but, rather, has taken an expeditious course (Schulz, 1997). This has become particularly visible in the black community where, before independence, almost any social development had been inhibited by the apartheid regime (Smit, 2000). Whereas on one hand, the advent of independence with the abolition of all discriminatory social and administrative control mechanisms has led to unknown freedom of choice and action, citizens, on the other hand, continue to struggle with the ever-increasing complexity of the social and economic changes that confront them.

It is against this background that we have to assess not only the extent and dimension of juvenile delinquency in Namibia today, but also the shortcomings of the judicial system that has to deal with it. Namibian society, like many other parts of the world, is concerned about a perceived increase in criminality (O'Linn, 1997), but it is difficult to establish whether the dimension of youth crime is alarming, as statistical data are scarce.[2] This chapter will, therefore, deal only to a lesser extent with the interpretation of information on crime and focus on the analysis of the functional framework of the current youth justice system. As will be illustrated, various complaints about malfunctions of the system suggest assessment of prevalence and incidence and their causes and consequences.

We will begin by describing the characteristics of juvenile justice in Namibia. This will be followed by an overview of how young offenders are officially handled by the major players of the criminal justice system as well as a description of some of the patterns of youth crime. Special attention will then be given to the work of the Inter-ministerial Commission on Juvenile Justice which, since 1997, has been working towards creating a cohesive juvenile justice system.

THE YOUTH SYSTEM: NAMIBIA'S NORMATIVE HORIZON AND THE SITUATION ON THE GROUND

With the **Namibian Constitution** (NC) coming into force on the very day of independence, Namibia embraced a political system under constitutional supremacy. The paradigm shift from **parliamentary sovereignty** to constitutional supremacy obligated the government to treat "all members of the community, as individuals, with equal concern and respect." However, the right of the child has found only limited expression in the Namibian constitution. For example, Article 14 (3) provides that the family is the natural and fundamental group unit of society and is entitled to protection by society and the state. Meanwhile, Article 15 (1) states that children have the right to be cared for by their parents; further, Article 15 (5) prohibits preventive detention of children under the age of 16 (Namibian Police *et. al.*, 1997). Article 20 NC provides that primary education is compulsory and will be provided free of charge. In terms of Article 12 (Fair Trial) of the Constitution all the due process rights applicable to arrested, detained, or accused persons also apply to children. However, the Namibian Constitution, unlike Section 28 of the South African Constitution, does not contain any provision that recognizes the right of the child not to be detained except as a measure of last resort and for the shortest appropriate period of time. In essence, under the NC, juvenile justice in our county conforms most closely with the classic **justice model** (see Box 12.3).

In September 1990 Namibia ratified the Convention on the Rights of the Child (CRC), thus accepting the obligation to establish laws, procedures, authorities, and institutions specifically applicable to children in conflict with the law. However, there is no single piece of legislation which reflects the recognition that, due to the special needs of young people who conflict with the law, it is necessary to provide special protection. The legal situation is largely the same as it was in South Africa at the time of Namibia's independence, where no cohesive juvenile justice system was developed (see Chapter 16). By virtue of Article 66 and Article 140 of the NC, much of the law in force prior to independence remains in force. For example, Article 66 NC provides that common law and customary law remain in force, provided such law "does not conflict with this Constitution or any other statutory law." Article 140 NC governs the validity of pre-constitutional statutory law.[3]

All this left Namibia virtually without a real system to manage young people in trouble with the law. Only limited provisions provide specifically for the management of young offenders, and these are spread throughout a number of separate statutes. They include the *Criminal Procedure Act* 51 of 1977, the *Children's Act* 33 of 1960, and the *Prisons Act* 17 of 1998. It can generally be said that the law applying uniformly to adult and juvenile offenders is mostly based on deterrence and retribution (Snyman, 1995). The lack of differentiation between young persons and adults contradicts international standards and does not acknowledge sufficiently that preventive and repressive needs in the case of young offenders are different from those that can be established for adults.

In the next section we will examine the legal provisions as they pertain to age and criminal capacity, legal representation, police procedures, release policy, diversion, juvenile courts, sentencing and monitoring, and some important aspects regarding their implementation (see Table 12.1).

Table 12.1: The Namibian Juvenile Justice System

Police:　　　　　　　　　No discretionary power. Investigation of juvenile crimes. Transfer of case files and evidence to the public prosecutor's office.

Public Prosecutor's Office: *Dominus litis*; decision-making whether to dismiss, divert, or indict criminal cases. Discretionary power: Section 6 *Criminal Procedure Act* 51 of 1979 to stop prosecution, or to withdraw charges.

In practice, though no formal legislative framework yet exists, a decision will consider the recommendation for diversion based on the result of a "screening" of the juvenile by a social worker.

"Juvenile" Courts:　　　　No separate criminal court for juveniles; adult courts double up as juvenile courts. Adjudication and sentencing.

Sentencing options:

1. Imprisonment
2. Periodical imprisonment
3. A fine
4. Committal to any institution established by law
5. Discharge with caution and reprimand
6. Postponement of sentence, unconditionally or with one or more conditions
7. Placement under the supervision of a probation officer
8. Placement in the custody of any suitable person designated by the court

"Youth" Prison:　　　　　No formal legislative framework for juvenile prisons exist. In terms of the *Prisons Act* 17 of 1998, however, children (*Prisons Act*: prisoners of 18 years and younger) are to be kept separate from adult prisoners.

AGE AND CRIMINAL CAPACITY

The definition of a juvenile is related to age. The term juvenile, however, differs from that of a child. The Namibian Constitution (Article 15[5]) defines children as persons younger than 16 years of age. Section 51 of the *Criminal Procedure Act* provides for special procedures in instances where children under the age of 18 are dealt with after arrest and during court proceedings. For example, section 72(3) says that an accused under the age of 18 is entitled to be assisted at criminal proceedings by parents or guardian, and section 153(4) provides that proceedings are to be held in-camera where the accused is under the age of 18. Article 17 of the new *Prisons Act* defines a juvenile as a person of *18 years of age and under*. In Namibia the minimum age of criminal capacity is determined by the *doli capax/doli incapax* rule: below the age of seven, the child is presumed to lack criminal capacity (Snyman, 1995). Along with the South African age limit, Namibia has one of the lowest ages of commencement of criminal capacity in the world (see Table 1 - Introduction). There is a presumption that children under 14 but seven years of age or older are deemed to lack criminal capacity, unless the state proves that the child can, indeed, distinguish between right and wrong and knew the wrongfulness of the offence at the time of commission. Though the presumption was designed to protect children, it does not, in fact, present an impediment to the prosecution and conviction of young people. Criminal capacity, even if a child is under 14, is seldom an issue. In those instances where the prosecution does set out to prove criminal capacity, the test almost always focuses on whether the child knows the difference between right and wrong and not on whether the child had the ability to act in accordance with the knowledge of that unlawfulness.

CHILDREN'S COURT INQUIRY

Notwithstanding problems around the proper application of the *doli capax/doli incapax* rule, Namibian law provides for social welfare investigation and support for very young children who find themselves in trouble with the law. Section 254 of the *Criminal Procedure Act* allows conversion of criminal proceedings into a Children's Court inquiry. Children's Courts are ensured under Article 33 of the *Children's Act* 33. The Act makes provision for various options. However, the opportunity to make use of conversion into a Children's Court inquiry is rarely used —possibly because many magistrates have not been trained in conversion procedure. If conversion takes place, the options actually available to a child in need of care are very limited. A personal communication from the Commissioner of the Children's Court in Windhoek revealed that 1999/2000 saw only a single case of conversion. In general, many Children's Court inquiries cannot be concluded due to the fact that a social worker's report is not presented to the court within a reasonable time. A delay of six months or more from the time the report is initially requested seems not to be uncommon.

Age Determination

A problem related to the *doli capax/doli incapax* rule is the determination of a child's age. It is common for Namibian children to be unaware of their ages and exact dates of birth; in some cases, even the parents of such children are unable to give particulars in this regard. One of the reasons for this phenomenon is that, before independence, children's births were most of the time only registered in church registers and that often children do not have a birth certificate.Currently, however, it is both difficult and time consuming to produce whatever documentary proof of age that might be available. To produce these documents often takes time and necessitates alternative methods, such as examination by the district surgeon—a somewhat subjective and inexact method.

Legal Representation

Apart from the right of an accused to assistance by his or her parents or guardians in criminal proceedings, accused children have, like adults, the right to legal representation from the time of arrest. The Namibian Constitution does expressly guarantee the right of all detained and sentenced persons to have access to a legal practitioner. Section 73(1)of the *Criminal Procedure Act* provides that an accused under arrest "be entitled to the assistance of his legal advisor as from the time of his arrest." It follows that the accused have the right to a fair trial in terms of Article 12 of the Namibian Constitution and that anybody who is arrested should be informed of his right to be legally represented (Legal Assistance Centre, 2000). Due to their youth and immaturity, children facing criminal charges are particularly vulnerable and in need of competent legal representation, assigned by the state and at state expense. However, legal representation is not compulsory, and sometimes children do not have any legal representation as they and their family do not have the means to retain a private lawyer.

Article 29 of the *Legal Aid Act* deals with assignment of a legal aid lawyer. It is unfortunate that children are not particularly mentioned in this Act. Where an accused appears in the High Court and that court is of the opinion that there is sufficient reason to grant the person legal aid, then it may issue a legal aid certificate. Section 9 deals with legal aid in the Magistrates Courts. If the accused are charged with such serious offences as abduction, arson, bestiality, bigamy, rape, or sedition, among others from a schedule provided by the Act, or if the accused are not charged with any of these offences but the court considers that "having regard to all the circumstances of the case, it is in the interest of justice that the accused should be represented," then the court must recommend to the Director of Legal Aid that the accused get a lawyer. In the context of juvenile delinquency, it is noteworthy that offences such as theft, housebreaking, and robbery are excluded from the schedule.

POLICE PROCEDURES

Arrest

Arrest is the primary method of securing attendance of children in court. Other options of the *Criminal Procedure Act* include a written notice to appear (s.56) which can be issued by the police, and the use of a summons (s.54). However, their use has been hindered by reason of the fact that a written notice can only be issued for very minor offences and because of the necessity of locating a parent or guardian before handing over a written notice or summons, so that the parent or guardian may be prepared to attend court proceedings. According to the data recorded by the Juvenile Justice Project for Windhoek, in approximately 27 % of the Windhoek cases, children reported that their parents/guardian were not informed of their arrest.

Although statistics are not available for the rest of the country, it is held that delays in notifying parents and guardians occur throughout Namibia. One reason why parents and guardians are not notified or why such notification involves lengthy delays is related to the problem of delivering the notices.

Pre-trial Detention

International rules provide that children awaiting trial should be detained only as a last resort. Although Namibia is signatory to these international instruments, detention of arrested children is the norm (see Figure 12.1). The *Criminal Procedure Act* includes several mechanisms designed to facilitate pre-trial release once a child has been arrested: a written notice (see above: s.56) can be issued at the police station where minor offences are involved, with the effect of releasing the child from custody; bail, which can be granted either before the first appearance in court at the police station in the instance of certain minor offences (s.59) or by a judicial officer after appearance in the court (s. 60); and release on warning by a judicial officer after first appearance in court (s. 72) into the custody of a person in whose custody s/he is.

The law does not make provision for all arrested children to be kept separately from adults, although there is a standing instruction that all arrested children are to be kept separately from adults. Consequently this does not happen at all police stations, especially not where and when police cells are overcrowded.

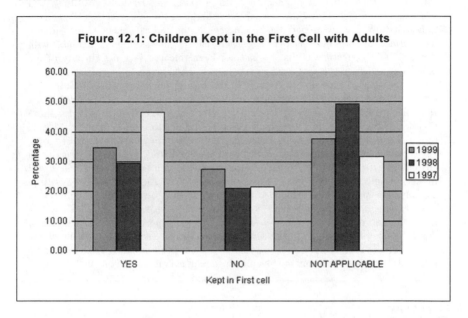

Figure 12.1: Children Kept in the First Cell with Adults

Release Practice

Practice has revealed that there are numerous problems preventing, or hindering, the application of international rules, and, for several reasons, extended periods of pre-trial detention of at least one month or longer can be observed (Albrecht, 1997). The reasons given for long periods in detention include the fact that parents do not wish to take custody of their children, failure to locate parents or guardians, the seriousness of the offence for which the child is arrested, and, the decision of the court to postpone the case and remand the child to custody. It has also been shown, that in many cases, bail amounts being set are such that children (and/or parents) cannot afford to pay (Super, 1999).

The fact that children remain in detention is tantamount then to a denial of bail altogether. The decision on bail seems often to be based purely on the offence. The adverse results of institutionalization and the undesirability of separation of children from their families, which inhibits reintegrating of the child into society, linked with long pre-trial detention periods are reinforced by the fact that most police stations in the country do not run any programs for children (see Box 12.1)

> ### Box 12.1: Practice in conflict with international principles—a serious indictment
>
> The case of B was first mentioned on 7 May 1998 at an Arrest and Awaiting Trial Working Group meeting by the constable in charge of the police cells at Wanaheda Police Station. She mentioned that B had been in the cell at Wanaheda for "quite a long period," and was believed to be a repeat offender who was "always in trouble with the law." Her concern was that he had not been released into the custody of his parents/guardians, and he received no visits and had no clothes to wear. His next court appearance was scheduled for 19 May1998; one of the social workers doing the screening undertook to follow up the case. B's case was also discussed at a Windhoek Juvenile Justice Forum meeting on 13 May 1998. However, it appears that nothing was done, since at the next Juvenile Justice Forum meeting on 17 June1998 it was reported that B had appeared in courtthe day before, but his case was remanded to 17 June1998 when "...the case was handed over to social workers. The boy remains in custody and the case will go to the criminal court. Hopefully the social workers will investigate and request a children's court inquiry." On 13 August 1998, B was still in custody, and his case was remanded to 14 August1998. There were 21 children in custody with B. On 3 September1998 it was reported that B had been sentenced to a term in prison on a charge of house-breaking. He was reported to be 11 years old at the time of committing the offence. On 21 March1999 the social worker at Windhoek Central Prison reported at a Juvenile Justice Forum meeting that B was about to be released (Discussion Document: Juvenile Justice in Namibia, 1999: 65).

DIVERSION

Diversion in Namibia is understood as channelling *prima facie* cases away from the criminal justice system with or without conditions. Conditions can range from a simple caution, or referral, to participation in particular programs, reparation, or restitution (see Figure 12.1). However, the chief referral mechanisms include withdrawal of charges by public prosecutors.[4] There is no formal legislative framework for diversion and a more systematic and general approach to it has been only recently endorsed. Diversion options/programs currently include consensus decision-making (CDM), pre-trial community service (PTCS), and a life-skills program (LSP). The different options are not equally available all over the country. Whereas in Windhoek, for instance, only CDM and LSP are used, problems have been experienced with LSP in the regions, since the program is group-based and there are insufficient numbers in smaller areas to compose a group. The LSP is based on a program devised by the South African National Institute for Crime Prevention and Reintegration of Offenders (NICRO). It is aimed both at instilling a sense of moral responsibility, accountability, self respect, and respect for other people and at empowering young people to make informed decisions about their lives and future actions. Consensus decision-making is a therapeutic process used prior to the diversion of the child. The victim, the offender, and their families are brought together to discuss the offence, their feelings, and the restorative effort that each party can make. A Juvenile Justice Project staff member who acts as a mediator, facilitates the meeting between the parties. It is designed to allow the victim and offender an opportunity to reconcile and mutually agree on reparation.

The procedure applied requires an initial screening of the child. The aims of screening are seemingly comparable to such aims as described in the South African Law Commission (see South Africa Law Commission, 1999).

Screening, which was initiated in 1995, is now a well-established process in Windhoek, although it is still only undertaken during office hours. Screening is carried out three times per week by staff of the Juvenile Justice Project (JJP) (see Box 12.2)—a project of the Legal Assistance Centre (LAC)—and two times per week by social workers from the Ministry of Health and Social Services (MOHSS). MOHSS social workers do the screening in the regions, but in the smaller towns where there are no social workers, no screening is done.

Box 12.2: The Juvenile Justice Project of the Legal Assistance Centre: A humane option for children who come into conflict with the law

The Legal Assistance Centre (LAC) is a public interest law centre, which strives "to make the law accessible to those with the least access, through education, law reform, research, litigation, legal advice, representation, and lobbying, with the ultimate aim of creating and maintaining a human rights culture in Namibia." (Mission statement: Legal Assistance Trust and Human Rights Trust, Annual Report 1999, 2000.)

The Juvenile Justice Project (JJP) is a project of the LAC. It was instituted in 1995, when the LAC was mandated by the newly established Juvenile Justice Forum to implement a pilot (experimental) Juvenile Justice Project. The CRC framework for addressing the situation of children who come into conflict with the law had made it necessary to conduct a survey on Namibia's young offenders. The outcome of the survey, which was done at all prisons in the country in 1994, shocked not only specialists in the field of children's rights but also the Namibian public, as it was found that the human rights of children who had been arrested were being abused. This alarming situation drew the attention of the government, the public, and non-governmental organizations, such as the United Nations Children's Fund (UNICEF) to the urgent need for a juvenile justice system in Namibia that complies with the CRC. Funded by he American government and the Canada Fund, the pilot project was successfully implemented in Windhoek, and the permanent Juvenile Justice Project was subsequently implemented as a special project of the LAC. The JJP has become a centerpiece in the functional framework of the development of a cohesive Namibian juvenile justice system.

Its main aims and objectives are:
- To advocate and lobby for restorative justice instead of retributive justice in cases involving children. This means diverting children (steering them away)

from the criminal justice system and rehabilitating them rather than punishing them by sentencing them to imprisonment or a fine.

- To help ensure that a court's decision in cases involving children is guided by the "best interests of the child" (a fundamental CRC provision) and also by the right of all Namibians to live in a crime free environment.
- To empower young people by assisting them to serve the community, strengthen community networks, and be accountable for their actions.
- To advocate and lobby for the implementation of a Juvenile Justice Policy in Namibia.
- To train all role players in juvenile justice so that the system can be decentralized to all regions of Namibia and to solicit national support for and commitment to the programme.
- To conduct research on juvenile justice issues in order to inform planning and project design.

Current activities of the JJP are:
- Crime prevention: This activity targets school-going children and school dropouts, in particular, and young people in general. The inter-sectoral Youth Crime Prevention Program is aimed at sensitizing the target groups and their communities around youth crime issues, to help them to mobilize themselves against such crime. The JJP and other role players in the program provide training for the school populace and communities throughout Namibia on ways to prevent crime, and develop and distribute reading material on crime prevention.
- Monitoring: This involves visiting police cells reserved for children to monitor the physical cell conditions, as well as the physical and emotional state of the children in the cells. Monitoring also entails administering questionnaires to find out whether the rights of any child were abused at any point of being arrested and while awaiting trial. The JJP helps to ensure that appropriate action is taken if any abuses and/or irregularities are noted. The Namibian police assist with the monitoring, which is overseen by the Arrest and Awaiting Trial Working Group composed of some role-players in juvenile justice.
- Pre-trial diversion: The JJP offers a range of pre-trial diversion options for children who have committed less serious crimes for the first time.

Juvenile Courts

There is no separate criminal court for juveniles in Namibia (see Box 12.3) even in Windhoek where there are sufficient numbers of accused persons under the age of 18 to warrant such courts. There is, however, a special court dealing exclusively with such cases at the magistrate's court; it is referred to administratively as "juvenile" court. At other courts an adult court doubles as a juvenile court.

In the present system, courts at all three levels (magistrate's, regional, and high court) can, and do, have jurisdiction over cases where juveniles are accused. The choice of a forum usually depends on the seriousness of the charge and the sentencing powers of the courts. Magistrates' courts do exercise an increased jurisdiction with regard to juvenile cases linked to the fact that the sentences for juveniles differ from those of their adult counterparts, and it is therefore common for robbery cases involving juveniles to be dealt with by the magistrate's court. Cases may also be referred to the regional court for sentence, especially if the accused has previous convictions, meaning that a sentence in excess of the Magistrate's Court jurisdiction is warranted.

Box 12.3: Defining the (Current) Juvenile Justice System in Namibia

It seems rather difficult to provide a clear definition of our juvenile justice system as it falls somewhere on the continuum of the models presented in Figure 1—Introduction. The difficulty is in part due to the gap between the practical legal ramifications and the situation on the reality of its application. However, it would appear safe to say—notwithstanding even falling short in regard to its professed provisions—that our current juvenile justice system conforms most closely with the **justice model**. General features that can be found in our system not only include "due process" and retribution, but also concern for the educational relevance of any disposition. Our system is based on the assumption of individual responsibility, but it fails to clearly subscribe to the role of prevention as a viable intervention strategy. The fact that young offenders can be sent to a school of industry under the *Children's Act* does not qualify as a preventative measure. Furthermore, where a case is converted into a Children's Court inquiry the child is generally considered not to have criminal capacity or at least diminished criminal capacity. Though in theory the system has provisions for a dual handling approach, our system does not qualify to be called **a modified justice model.** The intervention in terms of the *Children's Act* is still too formal.

It has generally been advocated that the procedure and conduct of our juvenile courts fall short of the minimum standards provided by the international children's rights instruments. It would appear that the courts have not succeeded in promoting the dignity of young people appearing before them, their proper growth and development, and their reintegration into society, as is required by the international instruments. There are a number of specific concerns which have been noted by academics and activists in the field. They relate to procedural problems such as the lack of legal representation of children in the criminal courts, long delays in the finalization of trials involving juveniles, and problems with the separation of young offenders from adult co-accused persons (Super, 1999). In addition, personnel working with young offenders are not specially qualified or trained for this work, and there is a high turnover of staff. Simply put, our legal system for juvenile offenders is fraught with a number of practical and administrative challenges that the country is currently trying to address.

Sentencing

Until now, we have not had a distinctive approach to juvenile justice sentencing, but as a general principle, juveniles are sentenced more leniently than adults. Namibian courts are able to draw from a variety of disposition options (see Figure 12.2). However, it is held that the personal circumstances of the juvenile accused are not always taken into account when sentencing, and the decision on sentencing seems to be based rather on the nature of the offence alone.

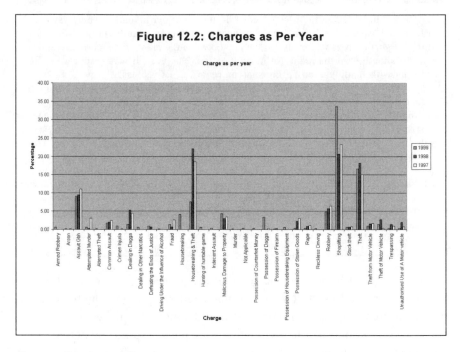

Figure 12.2: Charges as Per Year

Current Sentencing Options

The *Criminal Procedure Act* provides for a range of sentences which may be imposed upon juveniles. They include:

- Discharge with caution and reprimand (s.297):
- !postponement of a sentence, unconditionally or with one or more conditions (s.297);
- suspension of sentence, with or without conditions;
- placement under the supervision of a correctional officer;
- placement in the custody of any suitable person designated by the court;
- a fine, which the court may suspend or allow to be paid in instalments; and

•   sentence to a reform school or imprisonment, including periodical imprisonment.

In s. 297 of the *Criminal Procedure Act* a wide range of options are identified for conditions of suspension or postponement of a sentence. They include compensation, rendering to the person aggrieved of some specific benefit or service in lieu of compensation for damage, performance without remuneration and outside the prison of some service for the benefit of the community under the supervision or control of an organization or institution (community service), submission to instruction or treatment, compulsory attendance or residence at some specified centre for a specified purpose, and good conduct.

Post-conviction Measures, Other than Sentencing, According to Terms of the Criminal Procedure Act

Though virtually never made use of, after conviction it is still possible to convert a criminal matter into a Children's Court Inquiry according to the terms of s.254 of the *Criminal Procedure Act*. The criminal conviction then falls away, and a range of outcomes as provided for in s.33 of the *Children's Act* becomes available. They include placement of the child in the custody of a foster parent, placement in a children's home, sending the child to a school of industry, or return of the child to a parent or guardian under the supervision of a social worker (see Box 12.4).

Pre-sentence Reports

Monitoring of children in detention and children serving sentences has revealed that many children serve terms of imprisonment without a pre-sentence report having been requested or provided (Super, 1999). The situation is similar to that in South Africa, where it has been proposed that pre-sentence reports should be mandatory before a custodial sentence can be imposed (South African Law Commission, 1999).

YOUTHS IN PRISON

In terms of the *Prisons Act* a juvenile is a person 18 years of age or under. The *Prison Act* provides that a juvenile awaiting trial or at the conclusion of his/her trial shall not be detained in prison, unless such detention is necessary and no suitable place of detention as defined in the *Children's Act* (a "place of safety") is available. Therefore, during the pre-trial stage virtually no detention of juveniles takes place in prisons (see Figure 12.3). This is probably a reflex of a literal understanding of the negative effects of imprisonment through labelling. However, given the daunting situation of juveniles in most of the

Box 12.4: *Elizabeth Nepemba* Juvenile Center (Rundu/Namibia)

Following the critical assessment of Namibia's country report submitted by the UN Committee on the Rights of the Childs under terms of Article 44 of the CRC, Namibia endorsed the idea that juvenile (child) prisoners could not be dealt with properly and in line with Namibia's international obligations as long as young offenders were kept together with adult prisoners. With *Elizabeth Nepemba* Juvenile Center, Namibia intends to make a leapfrog towards a modern system of youth imprisonment.

The *Elizabeth Nepemba* Juvenile Center is still being built and is situated 18 km outside Rundu, the regional capital on the Kavango river. On 28 August 2000, there were 34 juveniles between the age of 14 and 18 years and 82 adults at the centre, most of them engaged in its construction. Adult prisoners have been transferred mainly from Windhoek Central Prison and were specifically chosen for the construction project. The idea is that once the center has been completed, it will only accommodate children. Construction is expected to end in 2002/2003 when the center will be able to accommodate 475 juveniles. These juveniles will be accommodated in three standard units of 128 prisoners per unit, an observation unit with a capacity for 64 inmates, and a single cell unit with a space for 27 inmates. Additional facilities for training, education, sport, and recreation will be provided in the future. A section for agricultural activities, a bakery for the production of bread, and vocational training (mechanical, civic, and electrical) are planned. The total number of personnel will be 122 by the year 2003. The personnel structure makes provision for two social workers and two registered nurses.

In 2000, the center managed 44 members, including a nurse. Different rehabilitation programs include the following topics:
- alcohol and (illicit) drugs
- HIV/AIDS
- first aid training
- life skills
- spiritual care, and
- sport and recreation

Until such time as the personnel structure comes into operation in 2003 the center shares the services of the social worker of the Divundu Rehabilitation Centre, situated approximately 200 km east of Rundu. Due to the construction on the site and the fact that prisoners—juveniles and adults—have been selected according to criteria like good behaviour, adaptation to prison life, non-violence, and positive prognosis, the atmosphere is relaxed and informal. This atmosphere, which is most conducive under rehabilitative aspects, in particular as far as juveniles are concerned, will, however, disappear once the center is completed. Close-circuit television, watch towers, and electric fences will then be installed and dominate the scene. It will be seen then whether the center will be able to fulfill its mission: "... to afford young offenders a second opportunity to continue with their studies as well as equipping them with skills that may enable them to lead a productive law-abiding life after being released from prison. This implicates a moving away from a strict punitive system to a rehabilitative approach, with emphasize on unit management approach."

police cells around the country, and the less sceptic report on youths in Namibian prisons, one wonders whether pre-trial detention would not better take place in prisons (Super, 1999). However, in October 2000 there were 295 children/juveniles in Namibian prisons.

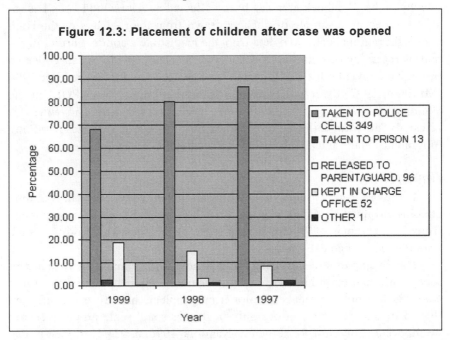

Though the "Discussion Document: Juvenile Justice in Namibia" stresses positive aspects—for instance, special programs run in the children's section at Hardap or a pre-release program at *Elizabeth Nepemba*—it also mentions: "The overstressing of security concerns means that not enough attention is being paid to reintegration and justice concerns." This has certainly to do with the current prison-staff/prisoner ratio. In 1997 the ratio between prison staff and prisoners has been approximately 1:10 (Albrecht, 1997). The situation has since improved, partly due to the incorporation of some 500 ex-combatants employed by the Ministry under the "Peace Project" decided upon by Cabinet in 1999 (Bukurura, 2000).

THE DIMENSIONS OF THE DELINQUENCY PROBLEM

Currently, only scattered information on crime and criminal justice is available for Namibia, and that comes from police information systems. Police data obviously cover information on recorded offences, the type of offences, and whether crimes have been cleared up. More information could be made available by police, although information does not seem to be easily computed but must be manually drawn from files or other documentation. No regularly published crime statistics are available to be used in planning and implementing criminal justice and strategies. However, some statistical information on delinquency in the Windhoek area has been collected by Albrecht (1997). His research relied on a sample of dockets drawn from the registers of the High Court, the regional court and data from the magistrate's courts. Further information regarding juveniles in the Windhoek area has come from data collected through the Juvenile Justice Project of the Legal Assistance Centre since 1996 (Mutingh, 1997; Swarts, 1998). The Namibian police (NAMPOL) in the Windhoek area was requested to fill out a basic form whenever a juvenile was arrested. This form collected information on a number of variables regarding biographic details and alleged offence information.

Official Trends

Due to a virtual absence on any information on youth crime in Namibia, conclusions must be drawn from Albrecht's work and generalizations made from the assessment of Windhoek magistrate's court files. The validity of such undertaking is of course limited.[5]

Namibia up to now has had a rather "snow white" image. In virtually all tourist information guides, crime is either not mentioned or it is noted that Namibia does not experience a major crime problem, that streets are safe, and that visitors should be cautious only insofar as small-scale property crimes might occur (Polyglott-Reisefuehrer Namibia, 1996, p. 93). However, police crime data describe a somewhat different picture; it reveals Namibia as a country with an extremely high rate of violent crime and a rate of property crimes that parallels rates found in industrial countries. Figure 12.4 offers some insight into the magnitude, development, and trends in crime between 1991 and 1998. While not dramatic, the number of recorded youth crimes (with the exception of 1994) shows a steady increase throughout the 1990s.

Types of Crimes Committed

Young offenders are charged with a very wide variety of offences, but it is obvious that the majority of juveniles were charged with property crimes. In the 1999 Windhoek sample, property crime accounted for 72% of all youth crime cases, while violent crime made up 16.6%. Drug-related offences made up 5.3%, of which the vast majority (90%) involved *dagga* (cannabis).

Profile of Young Offenders

For 1999 roughly 7.5 out of 10 young offenders were male. Figures for 1996, 1997, and 1998 show a slightly different ratio of male to female of 86/14,

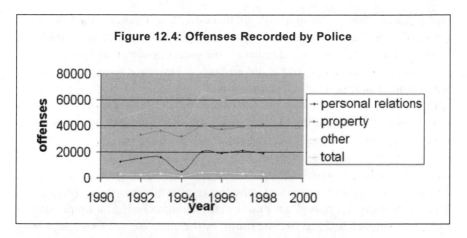

Figure 12.4: Offenses Recorded by Police

85/15, and 84/14, which might indicate that the number of female young offenders has been increasing since the assessment in 1996. The popular explanations used to explain female under-representation include sex role socialization, differential social control, and variations in opportunity.

The age at which youths commence their criminal activities appears fairly stable. Whereas the Windhoek sample shows that, for 1996, 57.4% of juvenile offenders fell in the age group 16 to17 years old, the figures for 1997 and 1998 are 61% and for 1999 is 59%.

THEORIES OF DELINQUENCY

Crime is perceived as one of the most important social problems of our time. Hence, while presenting the Namibian criminal justice system, it seems worthwhile to address theoretical approaches to crime and those assumptions underlying practical steps made in order to contain the problem. As a matter of fact, there was no open debate on the phenomenon of deviance under the Apartheid regime. Only after independence, an atmosphere promoting public discourse on the interpretation of social problems began to emerge. However, genuine criminological research is limited, and scholarly contributions are still rare. Apart from few studies carried out at the University of Namibia, a number of studies have been commissioned by the Namibian government, international organizations like UNICEF, and development agencies such as the Austrian Development Corporation and the German Development Agency *Gesellschaft fuer technische Zusammenarbeit* (GTZ). Because, these studies are mostly carried out within the functional framework of law reform and focus on the malfunctions of the system instead of epistemological issues, their reports seldom addressed the theoretical basis of their recommendations. If one can use them as an indicator of theoretical preferences, then it would appear that the "classic" perspective on crime and delinquency in the tradition of utilitarian proponents like Bentham is the most popular. This does not mean that a sociological perspective is not embraced. However, the influence of the social and structural context on crime and the criminal justice system's response to it appears rather as a second order explanation. This applies in the first place to the combatting of crime in general (O'Linn, 1997); *pars pro toto* here to mention is the motivation of the new legislation on rape.

The new *Combatting of Rape Act* (i.e., Act 8 of 2000) is a commendable piece of legislation, which abolishes a large number of inconsistencies in the former law pertaining to rape and remedies its possibly unconstitutional parts. The fact that the Act provides for minimum sentences reflects a simplistic *just desserts* approach and leaves little room for the more complex view that male identity and sexual violence is also a gender-based crime in a gender-oriented society (Badinter, 1992; Messerschmidt, 1993).

The fact that the judicial system has not developed a special consideration for juveniles bears witness of that mono-dimensional crime model, which was, until recently, applied rather indifferently. Namibia has come to realize that something has to be done to address juvenile delinquency. This insight was not informed through a discourse in the social sciences. Rather, a positivist approach[6] enabled Namibia to realize that something is wrong with its prevalent view on youth deviance. By ratifying the Convention on the Rights of the Child the government is obliged to establish laws, procedures, authorities, and institutions specifically applicable to children in conflict with the law.[7] Following the conclusion drawn (i.e., Articles 37 and 40) by the UN Committee on the Right of the Child at its fifth session in 1994 and in order to be consistent with relevant international instruments such as the Beijing Rules, the Riyadh Guidelines, and the United Nations Rules for the Protection of Juveniles deprived of their Liberty, the Namibian government set up an **Inter-Ministerial Commission** (IMC) on juvenile justice. It is with this background that the *Discussion Document: Juvenile Justice in Namibia* discusses juvenile justice from a legal perspective. However, we can infer from the document that, in its discussion of crime prevention, the most appropriate theoretical approach reflected falls in line with Durkheimian and/or Mertonian theory on **anomie**, on the one hand, and rediscovered thoughts on **social disintegration** as developed by Shaw and McKay (1942), on the other. These ideas are also reflected in the report on the "Workshop on Youth Crime Prevention" organized by the Steering Committee on Youth Crime Prevention and held from 25-26 March 1999 in Katutura (Windhoek), where key causes of crime have been identified as poverty, unemployment, and lack of self-discipline, among other (see Box 12.5).

Box 12.5: Steering Committee on Youth Crime Prevention

The Namibian government and non-governmental organizations have realized the need to incorporate youth crime prevention in juvenile justice. This understanding has been endorsed by the Windhoek Juvenile Justice Forum. In order to stimulate and implement youth crime prevention activities, a Steering Committee on Youth Crime Prevention was formed at the beginning of 1999. The main organizations represented were the Ministry of Youth and Sport, the Change of Life Style Homes Project (COLS), the Namibian Police, and the Juvenile Justice Project of the Legal Assistance Centre, Windhoek. In the meantime other organisations, such as the Department of Legal Studies of the Polytechnic of Namibia, have sent representatives to committee meetings. The rationale behind the incorporation of youth crime prevention in juvenile justice is to ensure that attention is given not only to children who are in conflict with the law, but also to those who may be at risk of committing crimes. The Steering Committee held a first participating workshop with pupils from various Namibian High Schools in 1999.

Finally, another theoretical framework that can be used to explain youth crime in Namibia in light of the empowerment of formerly disadvantaged groups after Independence is the theory that **economic deprivation** affects community crime rates.[8] The majority of Namibian citizens experience absolute and relative economic deprivation. A World Bank study found extreme income inequality for the country as a whole, with the inequality line clearly drawn between races. The white population, which makes up 5% of the population, and the small black elite, another 1%, have average annual per capita incomes of US$16500, while another 39% of the population, blacks who work in the modern sector, have annual per capita income of US$750. The rest of the population, all black, has an annual per capita income of US$85. Thus, the "average" Namibian in economic terms does not exist. Reference to an average income is meaningless. No one has an income anywhere near the average, and virtually everyone has either considerably higher or considerably lower incomes. It is one thing to be poor if everybody else is, but being poor takes on a different connotation if many others are not.

CURRENT ISSUES FACING NAMIBIAN YOUTHS TODAY

Unemployment

One of the biggest challenges for Namibian youth is unemployment and poverty. In May 1999 the government announced that unemployment had mushroomed to 35% of the country's labor force. "When it comes to the issue of youth development in Namibia, the picture is bleak indeed, " said former minister of youth, Richard Kapelwa Kabajani, in remarks to the National Assembly. For example, in 1999, 16,000 school-leavers were competing for 4,000 new jobs. The employment dilemma is a situation that has plagued Namibia since Independence.

The economy is not growing fast enough, and the job market is saturated. Actually the GNP per capita average annual growth rate has decreased by an estimated 1.3%. People are streaming into Windhoek every day from the countryside looking for work. The situation is far worse in the countryside, where there are too few companies setting up business, too few retail outlets, and little, if any, industrial development. Due to a lack of employment opportunities and limited social and marketable skills and competencies, it can be forecast that an increasing number of youth will be turning to crime, prostitution, and substance abuse, among other delinquent activities. Taking into consideration that the per capita average annual growth is negative, it is difficult to imagine how Namibia can afford to allocate sufficient funds for preventive activities in the future.

HIV/AIDS: The demographic factor and economic decline

Although it is beyond the scope of this chapter to provide an in-depth analysis of a very complex issue, it is held that, in general, HIV/AIDS has a direct or indirect impact on economic growth through its effect on labor, depending on whether the national economy is labor or capital intensive, and that HIV/AIDS will increasingly and negatively affect the economy. The latest update 2000 of the UNAIDS/WHO "Epidemiological Fact Sheet on HIV/AIDS" for Namibia reports an estimated number of adults and children living with HIV/AIDS for the end of 1999 was about 160,000. The adult rate, referring to men and women aged 15 to 49, lies at 19.5%.

Prevalence of HIV in pregnant women is a good indicator of levels of HIV in the general female population. HIV prevalence among 15 to 19 year olds tested increased from 6% in 1994 to 12% in 1998. Among 20 to 24 year olds, HIV prevalence increased from 11% in 1994 to 20% in 1998. The demographic impact of HIV/AIDS, according to the United Nations Population Division, is worst in sub-Saharan Africa.

In the 29 hard-hit African countries that are studied, life expectancy at birth is currently estimated at 47 years, seven years less than what could have been expected in the absence of AIDS. The Namibian figures are shown in Figure 12.5. The HIV/AIDS epidemic will play a double role in the future of sub-Saharan African youth, Namibian youth in particular. Apart from the fact that the individual youth faces a high probability of orphanage, HIV/AIDS gains cybernetic momentum (see Figure 12.5).

The demographic consequences of HIV/AIDS will possibly create a severe economic impact. The loss of young adults in their most productive years

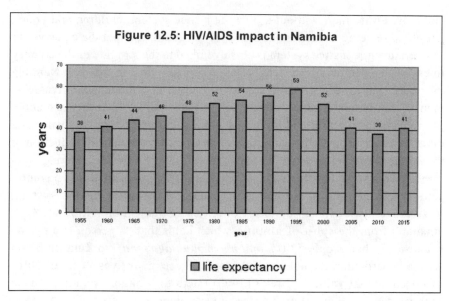

Figure 12.5: HIV/AIDS Impact in Namibia

will affect the overall economic output. AIDS deaths lead directly to a reduction in the number of workers available. The shortage of workers leads to higher wages, which leads to higher domestic production costs. The national economy faces increased expenditure through health care costs, burial fees, training, and recruitment and, at the same time, experiences the incapacitating effect of decreased revenue through absenteeism due to illness, time off to attend funerals, and time spent on training with a higher labor turnover (Bollinger and Stover, 1999). Hence, HIV/AIDS will contribute to an already negative economic environment with its effects on individual choices and vice crime.

In the wake of the HIV/AIDS epidemic. Namibia will not only face ruptures of economic structures but also a steady deconstruction of its social and cultural fabric. In terms of any sociological theory that emphasizes social structure, this means that society becomes a prime breeding place for crime and deviance. On an individual level, the disappearance of parents in the life of a child (orphanage), means less guidance, less control, less personal, and less cultural continuity, which, in accordance with Gottfredson and Hirschi's (1990) **General Theory of Crime**, leads to low levels of self control and subsequently to more crime.

REFORMING THE JUVENILE JUSTICE SYSTEM

In 1994, following the conclusion drawn by the UN Committee on the Right of the Child at its fifth session, the Namibian government became more and more aware that, without a juvenile justice system, children and young people were being treated in the same way as adults and that the endeavor to create a juvenile justice system is closely linked to the struggle of the country to establish a democratic system based on human rights. In that year Namibia introduced juvenile justice work, which resulted in a fundamental reassessment of the criminal justice system in relation to children. Since then, a number of innovative structures and programs with a focus on restorative justice and diversion have become the centerpiece of new initiatives. The introduction of the notion "restorative justice" is a reference criteria for the forthcoming juvenile justice system. It reflects the advent of an *African Renaissance* and represents a cornerstone of an authentic Namibian juvenile justice system. Restorative justice lies at the heart of African adjudication (Hinz, 1998). It emanates from the spirit of **ubuntu**, which holds that "a person is a person because of other people": "*Umuntu ngumuntu nagabantu*" in Zulu. In South Africa in particular, the notion of ubuntu has been invoked as a useful source of constitutional values. Mireku (2000) refers to Mokgoro pointing out in Makwanyane[9] "(ubuntu) embraces the key values of group solidarity, compassion, respect, human dignity, conforming to basis norms and collective unity, in its fundamental sense it denotes humanity and morality. Its spirit emphasises respect for human dignity, marking a shift from confrontation to conciliation" (see Box 12.6).

Box 12.6: Opening Address of the JJP Seminar on Children Involved with the System of Juvenile Justice, by Ngarikutuke Tjiriange, Minister of Justice, September 1998

Namibia ratified the United Nations Conventions on the Rights of the Child in September 1990. It then becomes imperative that the international standards in handling juvenile offenders are applicable. What I want to see as Minister of Justice when the Juvenile Justice Policy is in place is this: 1) The juvenile offender in court should be given preference. The child should be charged, convicted and sentenced in a very short space of time; 2) No child should be detained except as a measure of last resort, in which case the child may be detained only for the shortest appropriate period of time; and 3) More use could be made of the provision of section 297 of Criminal Procedure Act No 51 of 1977. It allows for a postponement in passing sentence and facilities the engagement of NGOs to assist in the placement and supervision of children. This section provides a wide list of sentencing options including community service, instruction of treatment, and correctional supervision.

However, it was soon felt that the development of a juvenile justice system has to deal with an immensely complex scenario, and nobody could ever hope to achieve the goal in a piece-meal approach. The Inter-Ministerial Committee on Juvenile Justice, which is chaired by the Ministry of Justice, was subsequently established to create a comprehensive and sustainable model for a future juvenile justice system in Namibia.

The formation of the Inter-Ministerial Committee (IMC), is regarded as a milestone in government engagement (Super, 1999). The Ministry of Justice envisages the Namibian government taking greater responsibility for juvenile justice service delivery. To this end it understands as one of its responsibilities the development of policy and law to undergird service delivery. The services rendered currently by the Juvenile Justice Project should be channelled to government in order to enable government to establish true ownership of the concept of diversion.

Since its inception the IMC has carried out substantial activities pertaining to the transformation of the juvenile justice system, in particular the compilation of a *Juvenile Justice Program*, which envisages a structured and holistic juvenile justice system. Funded by the Austrian Development Corporation, the program contains a problem analysis and defines and describes possible projects and necessary measures to achieve the intended goals. The *Juvenile Justice Program* is based on a number of project interventions to transform the current system. It aims to reduce juvenile delinquency in Namibia in a sustainable way. The implementation of the program should achieve the following objectives:

- the development of laws to protect and safeguard the rights of children entrenched in the Namibian Constitution and provided for in the international instruments of Human Rights;
- the development of policies and interim guidelines to make the juvenile justice practice uniform;
- the development and expansion of the service delivery system to cater for all children in conflict with the law throughout the country and thus to broaden the net of diversion options to ensure that children are channelled to a program that responds to their needs;
- the design and implementation of pilot projects aimed at empowering and strengthening children, parents, and the community;
- the development of a pool of trained and skilled people to work with children in conflict with the law;
- the systematic and structured approach in the implementation of juvenile justice services;
- the development of a viable system for ongoing evaluation, research, and monitoring; and
- and the role of advocate for preventative and aftercare services for children.

The program is planned over a period of three years, after which an evaluation will be carried out. The most important projects are *Law Reform* and the development of a well-equipped *Service Delivery System*. Both projects are connected in an intricate way by transforming constitutional precepts and those derived from international instruments such as the CRC. Any legal system as a preventative or remedial value has its own inherent limitations. Different factors are contributing to make legal responses good or effective. It is here the Service Delivery System plays a major role.

Law Reform

The current legal system, with its emphasis on **retribution** cannot adequately deal with youth in conflict with the law. A composite piece of juvenile justice legislation that conforms to international standards will be drafted. This comprehensive instrument shall become the focal point for the various actions a role-player in the system may take. The law, apart from its instrumental function in the guidance of the decision-making process of any judicial officer, also symbolizes the public affirmation of such social ideals and norms as entrenched in the Namibian Constitution and the before-mentioned international instruments (Schulz, 1997). The Inter-Ministerial Commission on juvenile justice commissioned the drafting of the Juvenile Justice Bill at the end of 2000. A first draft, submitted in 2001, was not well received. A revised draft is expected to be submitted in in mid 2002; it will be endorsed by the aspiration conference, and thereafter introduced into parliament through the IMC and the cabinet committee on legislation.

Service Delivery System

The intended Service Delivery System is considered the backbone of the upcoming juvenile justice system. It consists of screening services; pre-trial diversion programs; monitoring of the treatment of juveniles at arrest, trial, and sentencing; and aftercare services. At present, screening and pre-trial diversion are taking place in some places throughout the country. Children who are currently not receiving this service will become beneficiaries of a national policy supported by legislation formulated to improve and expand the Service Delivery System. In order to broaden the current service and the net of diversion a number of pilot projects have been identified, inter alia:
- The Referral, Reception and Assessment Centre in Windhoek,
- After Care and Follow-up Project in Windhoek, and
- Community Safe Home Project in Oshakati.

Other aspects include *training,* in order to achieve a wider pool of skilled people by systematically introducing professionalism in the field of juvenile justice via training and capacity building; *evaluation and monitoring* for the production of statistical data to inform planning strategies; *development and evaluation* of the program; and *crime prevention and advocacy* focussing on primary crime prevention oriented towards children between the ages of 10 to 14 years, through inter-sectorial strategies.

SUMMARY

Namibia is a newly independent nation, which in the wake of colonial oppression and foreign rule has yet to develop a comprehensive juvenile justice system. The current criminal justice system is informed by stereotyped common sense concepts of "criminality," and "the criminal." Simplistic views undergirded by utilitarian arguments have put Namibia at odds with international instruments, such as the United Nations Rules for the Administration of Juvenile Justice (Beijing Rules) and the Convention on the Rights of the Child (CRC), which have embraced a holistic perspective on juvenile crime and deviance.

The Youth System section of this chapter provided an overview of how juvenile justice is administered by the major actors in the system. It was shown that the attempt to deal with juveniles caught up in the criminal justice system according to declarative clauses of the Namibian Constitution and obligations derived from international instruments is ineffective. The symbolic meaning of the conventional structures of the current criminal justice system informs too strongly the perception of single actors in the system and the expectation of dealing with juveniles in terms of concepts like prevention, education, diagnosis, and treatment, when the legal ramifications offer conventional wisdom and retributive concepts of justice of guilt and punishment, seems unrealistic.

The overview of the Namibian juvenile justice system has painted a rather bleak picture. However, informed by the same legalistic approach which eventually led to a situation where Namibia (almost) came in breach of its international obligations, and urged by concerned NGOs, the Namibian government has come to understand the necessity of establishing a juvenile justice system in line not only with the formal meaning of international instruments and its own Namibian Constitution, but also with its cultural heritage of truly African provenance. In the spirit of ubuntu, Namibia has set forth to establish a **restorative juvenile justice system**. Since 1997 the Inter-ministerial Commission on Juvenile Justice has commissioned a discussion paper on juvenile justice and held numerous workshops with governmental and non-governmental organizations in order to sensitize all stakeholders in youth justice to the problems and issues.

Based on the proceedings and the recommendation of the discussion paper, the drafting of a *Juvenile Justice Act* as a legislative focal point of juvenile justice has been commissioned. It is now hoped that by 2003/2004 the Juvenile Justice Program, understood as a series of project interventions and not a single individual project, will have been carried out and, in the process, become integrated in the functions of government. We may forecast that the Namibian juvenile justice system will then focus on promoting the best interests of the child within a restorative justice setting, where, wherever possible, community-based diversion program options will be available and where children will only be processed through the justice system if diversion is not suitable. However, it may be learned that honest motives and a noble spirit will not be sufficient to master such a Herculean task. Namibia has a long way to go before it can unlock the huge economic potential with which it is endowed to fuel social justice and finance a modern juvenile justice system from its own resources. Meanwhile Namibia still needs the support from benevolent donor countries like Austria, which has offered through the Austrian Development Corporation financial resources to keep the program going.

Time will show to what lengths Namibian society will go. In the section on *Theories of Delinquency* it was held that sociological perspectives on crime have been less the vehicle of change in the youth system than positivist-legalistic attitudes. The same proponents of a humanitarian/welfare model approach to youth justice revert to "just desserts" policies with regard to (adult) crime in general, as if a silent metamorphosis of the ontological character of crime takes place in the transition from adolescence to adulthood. The program-related friction between the current criminal justice system and the future youth justice system could become virulent when the decline in youth crime which is expected after the introduction of principles of restorative justice will be absorbed by the effects of deteriorating socio-economic conditions, ongoing modernization, urbanization, and subsequent disintegration.

What lies ahead for the administration of youth justice depends on uncertain dimensions. In the section *Current Issues,* the HIV/AIDS impact on demographic projections came into focus. The probable increase in the HIV/Aids related death rate of the age group 15 to 49 will not only leave behind more orphans with all the devastating effects on their upbringing, but also deprive Namibia's economy of a significant part of its workforce. Taking into consideration no other factors then discussed in this chapter, Namibia will, with a high probability, face a rupture of economic structures and a steady deconstruction of its social and cultural fabric. Notwithstanding this daunting outlook, we need to work on a juvenile justice model that is more equitable than the current system for youths of today as well as for the next generation. With the advent of juvenile justice reform, there is a considerable need for research on its impact. The situation of the data currently available in Namibia is insufficient and cannot inform systematic studies. However, without criminological research, Namibian officials will be operating in the dark about the consequences of their ambitious program.

Stefan Schulz is a qualified German lawyer, currently working in the department of legal studies at the Polytechnic of Namibia. His responsibilities entail, among other administrative duties, teaching in the police science diploma program. Prior to his current position, he worked as a public prosecutor with the prosecutor general at Rostock in Mechlenburg/Vorpormmern (one of the 16 member states of Germany), as a summary judge and head of the medical and social services division of the prisons and correctional services directorate in the ministry of the state.

In 1997 he organized a local conference in his German state which focussed on juvenile justice related issues. He also facilitated, in 1999, a project at the Polytechnic of Namibia on the recognition and accreditation of prior learning that assists in admitting learners to an insititution of tertiary education without sufficient formal qualifications. As former head of the department of legal studies he co-organized and co-hosted the joint 2000 University of Namibia/Polytechnic of Namibia conference "10 Years of Namibia Nationhood."

KEY TERMS AND CONCEPTS

Diversion	Namibian Constitution
Parliamentary Sovereignty	retributive/restorative
Inter-Ministerial Commission	African Renaissance
general theory of crime	Ubuntu
Anomie	Durkheim/Merton
Social disintegration	Economic deprivation
justice model	Modified justice model
restorative juvenile justice system	

HELPFUL WEBSITES

http://www.polytechnic.edu.na: Home site of the Polytechnic of Namibia, where the processed Juvenile Justice Project data used for the charts of this chapter can be inspected. A discussion forum, Crime and Society, facilitated by the Department of Legal Studies, is forthcoming (2003). Proceedings of the University of Namibia/ Polytechnic of Namibia conference, "Ten Years of Namibian Nationhood," 11-13 September 2000, SAFARI Conference Centre, Windhoek/Namibia, will be published soon on this site.

http://www.namibian.com.na: Home site of *The Namibian* newspaper. This site offers discussion fora, of which some debate issues of crime and deviance in the Namibian society.

http://www.tfgi.com/ecimaids.asp: The Futures Group International; Economic impact of AIDS in Africa.

http://www.iaen.org/HyperNews/get.cgi/impact.html: IAEN—International AIDS Economics Network; Economic Impact Conferences Discussion Area with interesting contributions on the economic impact of HIV/AIDS on macro- and micro-economic level.

STUDY QUESTIONS

1. Since Namibia obtained its independence (1990) and established constitutional supremacy, the government is obliged to "treat all members of the community with respect, as individuals, with equal concern and respect." However, Namibia has virtually no real system to manage young people in trouble with the law. How can we explain this phenomenon, and can we learn anything from what other countries have done?
2. Comparing and contrasting what is being done elsewhere, how might you describe and characterize the juvenile justice system projects that the Namibian government has initiated?
3. Although Namibia only has police crime data upon which to describe delinquency trends and patterns, how do they compare internationally? Are there any issue or concerns that appear deserving of closer scrutiny? For example, although not a highly industrialized country, Namibia's violent and property crime rates rival those of more industrialized nations.
4. Since Namibia does not have a formal juvenile justice system, what are the strengths and weaknesses of this approach? To what extent are the initiatives that have been taken consistent with international standards and guidelines?

NOTES

1 The author wishes to acknowledge that this contribution is partly based on work on statistical data done by members of the Juvenile Justice Project of the Legal Assistance Centre, Windhoek. Many discussions with members of the Inter-ministerial Commission on Juvenile Justice are hereby also acknowledged. Opinions expressed in this contribution or conclusions arrived at are, however, those of the author.
2 All statistical data used or presented in this chapter have been taken either from the study "Crime, Criminology and Law Reform" (1997), the Statistical Abstract (1999), or the records of the Juvenile Justice Project of LAC (1997-1999).
3 Article 66 (1) Namibian Constitution; Article 140 Namibian Constitution, which applies to statutory law reads: "...all laws which were in force immediately before the date of Independence shall remain in force until repealed or amended by Act of Parliament or until they are declared unconstitutional by a competent Court."
4 Though the present Namibian system regards the public prosecutor as *dominus litis,* it is a matter of fact that the police, too, take a gate-keeping role in the criminal justice system and choose not to charge an arrested person in certain circumstances (for example asking juveniles to move, instead of arresting them for loitering). The dimension of that practice in Namibia is, however, unknown, as no study of informal police decision-making has been carried out yet. The situation in Namibia might not be very different than South Africa's. See, L. Fernandez, "Juvenile diversion through police cautioning," in J. Sloth-Nielsen (ed.), *South African Juvenile Justice: Law Practice and Policy* (forthcoming).

5 There are no separate data for young offenders. Their offences are aggregated with the total number of crimes registered by the police.
6 The effects of a theoretical approach to the understanding of the law in the tripartite relationship between legislature, judiciary, and executive—which until independence was informed uniformly by the linguistic version of positivism—still produce their repercussions and qualify Namibian governmental practice; see: Schulz (2000).
7 This assumption rests on Article 144 of the Namibian Constitution, which reads: "Unless otherwise provided by this Constitution or Act of Parliament, the general rules of public international law and international agreements binding upon Namibia under this Constitution shall form part of the law of Namibia." It is held that the CRC is self-executing and does not require a law to make it operative. The argument is that, since the CRC came into operation after the *Criminal Procedure Act* 51 of 1977 and the *Children's Act* 33 of 1960, it must be taken to have implicitly repealed those provisions which are inconsistent with it.
8 On "ecology and crime," see: Barkan (1997).
9 S.V. Makwanyane (1995). (3) 391 (CC).
10 Publications on Juvenile Justice in Namibia are rare. Most of the material exists in form of studies, reports, etc. commissioned by the Namibian government, NGOs, the Legal Assistance Center, or international organizations. The interested reader should contact the respective organization and request a copy.

REFERENCES[10]

Albrecht, H.J. (1997). *Crime, criminal justice, and law reform*. Windhoek: Ministry of Justice.

Badinter, E. (1992). *XY—De l'identité masculine.* Le livre de poche. Paris: Edition Odile Jacob.

Barkan, S.E. (1997). *Criminology: A sociological understanding.* Upper Saddle River, NJ.: Prentice-Hall.

Blau, P.M., & Blau, J.R. (1982). The cost of inequality: Metropolitan structure and violent crime. *American Sociological Review* 47: 114-29

Bollinger, L., & Stove, J. (1999). The economic impact of AIDS in Namibia. http://www.tfgi.com/ecimaids.asp

Bukurura, S.H. (2000). Namibia prison service and the Constitution: Lesson and experiences, 1990-2000: 13.

Gottfredson M.R., & Hirschi, T. (1990). *A general theory of crime*. Stanford, CA: Stanford University Press.

Hinz, O. (1998). *Customary law in Namibia: Development and practice.* 4th ed. Windhoek: Centre for Applied Social Sciences (CASS).

Hubbard, D. (1991). *A critical discussion of the Law on Rape in Namibia*. Windhoek: Namibian Institute for Social and Economic Research, University of Namibia.

Hubbard, D. (1996). *Should a minimum sentence for rape be imposed in Namibia?* Windhoek: Legal Assistance Centre.

Law Reform and Development Commission. (1997). *Discussion Paper: Law pertaining to rape*. Windhoek: Ministry of Justice.

Legal Assistance Centre, Windhoek. (2000). *Namibian police human rights manual*. Windhoek: Legal Assistance Centre.

Legal Assistance Trust and Human Rights Trust, Namibia. (2000). *Annual Report 1999*. Windhoek: Legal Assistance Centre.

Namibian Police, *et al*. (1997). *Police training manual: A course for trainers of police officials who work with juvenile offenders*. Windhoek: UNICEF. Chapter 7.

Malan, J.S. (1995). *Peoples of Namibia*. Windhoek: Rhino Publishers.

Messerschmidt, J.W. (1993). *Masculinities and crime: Critique and reconceptualization of theory*. Lanham, MD: Rowman & Littlefield.

Mireku, O. (2000). *Underlying values and the spirit of the South African Constitution*. Proceedings of the University of Namibia/Polytechnic of Namibia conference "Ten Years of Namibian Nationhood" (forthcoming).

Muntingh, L.M. (1997). *Report to the Legal Assistance Centre on juvenile cases assessed at the Windhoek magistrate's court in 1996*. Windhoek: Juvenile Justice Project of the Legal Assistance Centre.

Mutingh, L. & Super, G. (1999). *Evaluation of the Juvenile Justice Project of the Legal Assistance Centre*. Windhoek: Austrian Development Cooperation.

Nachtweih, W. (1976). *Namibia: Von der anitkolonialen Befreiungsrevolte zum nationalen Befreiungskampf*. Mannheim, Germany: Verlag Juergen Sendler. 51 ff.

O'Linn, B. (1997). Report of the proceedings and deliberations of the Presidential Commission of Inquiry into legislation for the more effective combatting of Crime in Namibia. (O'Linn Report). Windhoek: Office of the President.

Polyglott-Reisefuehrer Namibia. (1996). Munich.

Prisons Service *et al*. (1994). *A study of young* offenders *in Namibia*. Windhoek: Prisons Service, Legal Assistance Centre, Ministry of Youth and Sport, UNICEF.

Schneider, K.-Guenther, & Wiese, B. (1992). *Namibia und Botswana*. 3rd ed. Landschaftsfuehrer. Cologne: DuMont Buchverlag.

Schulz, S. (1997). *Offenses against/infringement on sexual self-determination by persons in positions of authority or power (sexual exploitation)*. Windhoek: Ministry of Justice.

Schulz, S. (2000). *Legal interpretation and the Namibian Constitution*. Proceedings of the University of Namibia/Polytechnic of Namibia conference, "Ten Years of Namibian Nationhood" (forthcoming).

Shaw, C.R., & McKay, H.D. (1942). *Juvenile delinquency and urban areas*. Chicago, IL: Chicago University Press.

Smit, P. (2000). *The land issue of Namibia: Some environmental, economical, and planning perspectives*. Proceedings of the University of Namibia/Polytechnic of Namibia conference, "Ten Years of Namibian Nationhood" (forthcoming).

South African Law Commission. (1997). *Juvenile justice*. Issue Paper 109, Project 106. Pretoria.

South African Law Commission. (1999). *Juvenile justice*. Discussion Paper 79, Project 106. Pretoria.

Super, G. (1999). *Discussion document: Juvenile justice in Namibia*. Windhoek: Inter-Ministerial Commission on Juvenile Justice.

Swarts, J. (1998). *Report to the Legal Assistance Centre on juvenile cases assessed at the Windhoek magistrate's court in 1997*. Windhoek: Legal Assistance Centre.

Snyman, C.R. (1995). *Criminal law*. 3rd ed. Namibia. 17 ff, 165.

Chapter 13

Youth Crime and Juvenile Justice in The Netherlands

Henk B. Ferwerda
Advice and Research Group Beke

FACTS ABOUT THE NETHERLANDS

Area: The Netherlands is a small country of 41,526 sq. km. (of which 33,882 sq. km. is land) divided into twelve provinces. **Population**: Approximately 15.8 million (1999 estimate), with 3.8 million being under the age of twenty. Population growth ranged from .25% in the late sixties to .70% in 1999. Population density is 465 people per sq. km., which is among the highest in the world. Amsterdam is the nation's capital (population: 731,200) and The Hague (population: 440,900) is the city where the government is seated. The Netherlands is a multicultural nation. The largest groups are of Surinam (with Dutch nationality), Turkish, Moroccan, and Antillian origin. **Climate**: Temperate, marine, cool summers and mild winters. **Economy**: The Netherlands is a modern, industrialized, and affluent welfare-state based on private enterprise. Rotterdam has one of the biggest sea harbours in the world. Unemployment is 3.1% (1999). The Netherlands has a highly sophisticated social service system, which absorbs about one third of the domestic income. **Government**: The Dutch government is based on a parliamentary democracy with a constitutional monarchy.

Killing time, waiting for the bus,
Killing time, like everybody does,
Killing time, you're feeling bad,
Killing time, making you mad!
We're bored! no fucking thing to do.
We're bored! hanging round with the crew.
We're bored! bored with the human race.
We're bored! we're wrecking up this place!
(Rap, written by Thuur Caris, 1992)

THE DUTCH PERSPECTIVE ON JUVENILE DELINQUENCY

Until quite recently, almost everyone who was in some way involved with the phenomenon of juvenile delinquency in Holland saw it as a passing element of puberty or the adolescent stage. While something to pay attention to, it was generally thought to be nothing to worry about. Although this view has faded somewhat, it is still the prevailing sentiment.

This chapter will attempt to shed light on the issue of juvenile delinquency in The Netherlands by presenting an overview as it exists in our country. We will begin by defining youth criminality before examining some of the available statistics on juvenile delinquency, as well as describing some of the trends. The chapter will also offer an overview on the types of measures that have been and are being proposed for the handling of juvenile offenders. Finally, the chapter will conclude with an examination of some of the recent developments in dealing with juvenile delinquency.

DEFINING YOUTH CRIMINALITY IN THE NETHERLANDS

Every day the regional and national media in The Netherlands gives attention to the illegal activities committed by youths, categorically called "**juvenile criminality**." Even though, with some regularity, the media and public policies do not appear to differentiate the nature of illegal activities committed by a 10-year-old different from that of a 22-year-old, in legal terms it is a notable misnomer. There are sharp age limits in The Netherlands when it comes to the question of just what juvenile crime is or is not. The core of the Dutch justice system is that the punitive responsibility increases with age. To sum it up:

- For children under the age of 12 there are no legal provisions for punitive responsibility, nor can such youth be prosecuted for a criminal offence.
- Youth between the ages of 12 to 18 fall into what is referred to as the punitive minor years. Young persons who offend during these years are subject to our juvenile justice system.
- From eighteen years on, the general justice system, also referred to as the adult justice system, applies.

When a youth under the age of 12 commits a punishable crime in The Netherlands, there is, in principle, no statement taken during the arrest[1]. This is the result of the content, in this case the structure, of the juvenile justice system as we know it.

Unlike in North America, it is worth noting that the juvenile criminal law is not a separate law, but a series of legal parameters within the general justice system. The Criminal Law Statute states specific parameters (Articles 77a through 77gg) regarding the category to whom the juvenile justice system applies. Globally[2], these are the criminal minors from 12 to 18 years old.

As mentioned, there is no punitive or criminal responsibility for those youth under the age of 12 . This means that, in principle, juveniles under 12 do not appear in police or judicial statistics, but the report is registered with Child Protective Services as a complaint or child rearing case and not as a punitive case.

The most pure and formal definition of juvenile criminality is the following: "Juvenile criminality refers to behaviour of youths from 12 to 18 years old for whom legally bound parameters of norms are overstepped and for which a punishment stands" (Ferwerda, 1992, p.17).

Like many other European countries, we use a graduated approach to criminal responsibility. For example, it is possible for a juvenile (usually 16 or 17 years old) to be punished under the adult criminal system. This is in cases where it is regarded as necessary, depending upon the suspect and the nature of the crime. Typically, such measures are restricted to those youth who commit serious vice crimes and extremely violent crimes such as homicide (i.e., murder and manslaughter), which are committed in a cold or calculated manner. The converse is also possible; someone 18 or 19 years old can also come under the juvenile criminal system should their offence and character warrant it. Hence, we have what could be described as a **justice model** (see Figure 1 – Introduction).

In spite of having a relatively precise definition for juvenile criminality, the description tends to create a general "dumping station" or "catch-all" term for juvenile criminality. For example, one is just as guilty of committing a juvenile crime whether they're a 14-year-old girl who steals cosmetics from a department store; a group of 13- or 14-year-old boys who vandalize a train car, or a 16-year-old boy who is repeatedly in the police station for breaking and entering.

The concept of juvenile criminality doesn't differentiate between the nature of the crime committed and the type of offender. Later in this chapter, juvenile crime in The Netherlands—as in other countries—will be described as having "more faces than one" (Ferwerda, 1992) (see Box 13.1).

JUVENILE CRIMINALITY IN THE NETHERLANDS

Police statistics

To gain insight into the developments of juvenile crime in The Netherlands, we will first present the numbers originating from police statistics from

1989 through 1998. Firstly, the absolute number of criminal minors concerning offences that were reported and had a hearing[3], and secondly, the absolute number of youths from 12 to 17 years old who lived in The Netherlands[4]. It is notable that in this period, the number of juvenile inhabitants was 1.5 million in 1989 and dropped to 1.1 million in 1998, while at the same time, the number of minor suspects increased from 39,389 in 1989 to 46,372 in 1998.

Figure 13.1 reflects the percentage of the total number of youths who were reported and received a hearing by the police in the period 1989-1998.

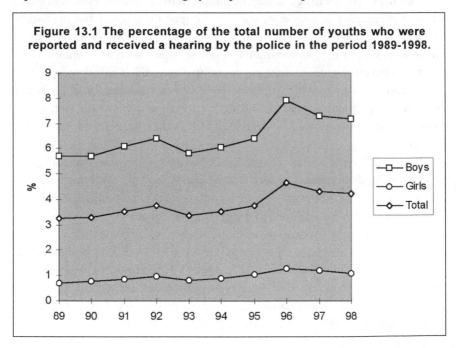

Figure 13.1 The percentage of the total number of youths who were reported and received a hearing by the police in the period 1989-1998.

From Figure 13.1 we see that in the 10 year period, the percentage of criminal minors who have been reported and have had a hearing was between 3.2% and 4.7% (average 3.8%[5]) of all the criminal minors in The Netherlands. Between 1989 and 1998 there was an increase from 3.2% to 4.2% in juvenile crime. We also see from Figure 13.1 that more boys (averaging almost seven times as much during this period) were reported and had more hearings (averaging 6.4%) than girls (averaging 1%). Not unlike many other countries covered in this text, it can be concluded from this that in The Netherlands, juvenile criminality is a predominantly male issue. Regardless of the fact that girls' participation in juvenile criminality is marginal, we can state from Figure 13.1 that this participation is gradually increasing (see other contributions for similar observations).

With respect to the nature of crime, it is important to emphasize that most juvenile delinquency is property crime that mostly involves simple theft and burglary. Table 13.1 shows the distribution and trends of crime[6].

Table 13.1 Juveniles heard by the police by offence for the years 1989 and 1998				
Offence category	1989		1998	
	N	%	N	%
Property offences	25,397	64.5	25,520	55.0
Violence against persons	3,370	8.6	9,136	19.7
Public order	9,011	22.9	10,463	22.6
Other	1,611	4.0	1,253	2.7
Total	39,389	100	46,372	100

What we see in Table 13.1 is that there was a change in the crime pattern between 1989 and 1998. While the number of property offenders remained virtually unchanged, there was a dramatic and extreme increase in the number of violent offenders. Table 13.2 shows the distribution of violent offences in 1998.

Table 13.2 Juveniles heard by the police in 1998 by violent offences	
Violent offences	%
Offences against life and threats	12.9
Sex offences	8.3
Assault	55.2
Theft with violence and extortion	23.6

As is well known, police statistics have their limitations. In fact, the presented numbers are not considered overly representative of the scope of delinquent activity. The police are just not in a position to arrest all young offenders. Assuming that the registration of juvenile criminality between 1989-

1998 is consistent, then the official statistics reflect a limited perspective on development and trends in juvenile criminality (see Box 13.2).

Box 13.2: Crime on the Political Agenda

In the '60s, and even more so in the '70s, The Netherlands, as with so many other Western countries, was confronted with rising crime rates. To a great extent, this rise was caused by offences of a minor nature and were committed mostly by juveniles and young adults. Often these offences are wrongfully referred to as petty or "small" crimes. These crimes include fare dodging in public transport, vandalism, shoplifting, bicycle theft, theft from and of cars, break-and-enter, harassment, handbag snatching, etc. While not violent in nature, they nevertheless cause feelings of unrest among the public and generally result in serious financial damage. Significant financial investments were made by the police, the courts, probation services, and (local) government in order to deal with crime and its perpetrators. For the first time in many years, pressure on the prison system increased. Not surprisingly, crime caught the attention of politicians. Entering the '80s, the issue of crime and dealing with crime became a major political issue (van der Laan, 2000).

Self-report Measures

To supplement police statistics and to illustrate the nature and scope of juvenile crime in The Netherlands, we present a few results from a nation-wide self-report survey. These surveys are often used to supplement official police statistics, as they not only provide information about the nature and scope of juvenile crime but also help to uncover the "dark figure" of crime. The survey has been conducted every two years since 1988 (van der Laan, Essers, Huijbregts, and Spaans, 1998).

From Table 13.3, we can see that the percentage of youths committing at least one offence in any given year is greater than is known and reported in police statistics. On the basis of self-report studies, the percentages are between 34.5% and 40.2%, while we stated earlier that the average annual percentage was merely 3.8% of the criminal minors who are heard and reported to the police. This clearly shows why police statistics offer extremely marginal insights to the nature and scope of juvenile criminality.

Just as with the police statistics, based on the results presented in Table 13.3, there has been an increase in juvenile criminality. The increase has been most notable in cases involving violent offences, vandalism, and shoplifting.

From the police statistics, it appears that juvenile criminality pertains mostly to boys. On the basis of the self-report study, the difference between boys and girls is usually smaller. In 1988, 38% of the boys and 29% of the girls admit to having committed at least one offence. In 1996, these percentages increase to

Table 13.3 Juveniles that Reported an Offence in the Past School Year by Offence and Year in Percentages

Offence	1988 n=994	1990 n=1,006	1992 n=1,038	1994 n=1,096	1996 n=1,083
Fare dodging	14.5	17.0	19.0	15.7	16.7
Graffiti	10.3	8.8	8.6	10.1	11.1
Harassment	9.9	12.0	11.8	14.1	14.6
Vandalism	8.9	9.9	10.5	9.1	14.6
Shoplifting	5.4	7.4	6.6	7.0	10.0
Arson	3.8	5.0	3.8	4.3	5.3
Receiving stolen goods	3.5	4.1	4.0	4.2	8.6
Bicycle theft	2.1	3.0	2.7	1.3	3.1
Beating up	1.9	2.7	2.7	2.7	3.3
Breaking and entering	1.5	1.6	1.3	1.6	1.2
Theft from phone booth/ vending machine	(-)[7]	1.2	1.0	1.1	2.3
Theft from school	(-)	6.5	8.4	7.2	10.1
Involvement in fights or riots	(-)	6.7	8.8	11.6	14.7
Using weapon to injure person	(-)	0.6	0.4	0.4	1.1
Carrying a weapon	(-)	(-)	12.8	20.5	21.5
Extortion	(-)	(-)	0.4	0.3	0.5
Combined offences	34.5	38.2	38.2	37.8	40.2

Note: (-) means that the offence was absent from the survey taken in that year.

a respective 47% and 33%. The ratio of boys: girls in 1996 was the same as in 1988, 1.4: 1[8]. So while boys offend more frequently than girls, participation among females has been gradually increasing.

When we summarize police figures and data from self-report measures, we see that there is a slight increase in juvenile delinquency in the past 10 years. Although it is difficult to draw direct conclusions, one might say that the crime prevention measures that were taken in The Netherlands in this period have had a certain impact.

THE THREE FACES OF JUVENILE CRIMINALITY

In addition to the earlier presented self-report research, other institutions in The Netherlands are performing similar studies on Dutch youth (Angenent, 1991; Ferwerda, 1992; Beke and Kleiman, 1992; Ferwerda, Bottenberg, and Beke, 1999).

From these studies, it appears that most of the offences are of a reasonably benign nature. Yet approximately two thirds of the minors who have been guilty of at least one offence during their adolescence. On the basis of this and the existing damages, we cannot minimize the quantitative nature of juvenile criminality, because every year such crimes result in billions of guilders in damage.

From the self-report studies we can divide Dutch juvenile criminality into three types: "kick behavior," "hardcore behavior," and "psychopathological behavior."

Kick Behavior

Young boys commit most juvenile offences, and it is generally considered "normal" behavior among their peers. Their behavior has been described as **kick behavior** (Ferwerda, 1992). It is characterized by its short duration, and is often the result of opportunity as opposed to planned behavior. Examples of opportunistic criminality are fare dodging, shoplifting, theft at school, and, pre-eminently, vandalism.

This form of juvenile crime is regarded as nuisance crime, and is generally seen as part of a young person's "normal" development as they seek their behavioral boundaries and discover their self-control.

In The Netherlands, the philosophy on responding to this type of offender is to respond quickly and in a pedagogical way. For example, young people who have committed a minor offence are mostly given the opportunity to "pay for their crimes" ("tit for tat") without the intervention of the courts (see Box 13.4).

Hardcore Behavior

As appears to be the case in most countries represented in this book, in The Netherlands there is a small proportion of juvenile offenders who commit more serious offences. They also tend to have longer criminal careers and in some cases become career criminals. This group is referred to as **hardcore** offenders and are almost exclusively young males.

Hardcore juveniles are characterized both by the severity of their offences and by the fact that their acts have both a structural and an operational character (instrumental criminality structure) (see Box 13.3). Structural, because criminality is not just an incidental outburst, but is a part of the youth's life pattern. The behavior is instrumental in nature because it is frequent and clearly serves a purpose (i.e., financial aims).

Fortunately in The Netherlands, hardcore juvenile offenders represent a small percentage of the juvenile population. However, in recent years their numbers have been increasing and pose new problems and challenges for the juvenile justice system. From estimates based on the large-scale self-report studies which began in the 1990s, 2% of criminal minors belonged to the

---

Box 13.3: Drug Policy in The Netherlands

The *Opium Law* of 1919 (revised in 1928 and 1976) states the rules for the production, distribution, and the possession of drugs. A differentiation was made between
drugs with an unacceptable risk (hard drugs such as heroine, cocaine, and LSD) and
cannabis. Possession, dealing, and production are punishable, except for medical,
scientific, and instructive purposes as long as permission is granted.

The Dutch Minister of Public Affairs has introduced directives for tracking and
prosecuting activities considered illegal under the Opium Law. The import and export
of hard drugs has the highest priority. Tracking and prosecuting for the possession of
small amounts of soft and hard drugs for personal use has the lowest priority. In The
Netherlands, this is known as the "tolerance policy". This means that possession of
a maximum of 0.5 grams of hard drugs and a maximum of five grams of soft drugs for
personal use is connived at. The sale of soft drugs occurs, among other places, at
coffee shops where people of at least eighteen years of age can buy a maximum of
five grams of soft drugs.

Coffee shops are legal businesses (with licences) that have to conform to strict
criteria: no advertisements, forbidden sale of hard drugs, sale to minors is prohibited,
the shop may not disturb the peace, and one may not have more than 500 grams of
soft drugs in the shop.

---

hardcore group, while this percentage at the end of the 1990s had increased to
4.5% (Ferwerda, Versteegh, and Beke, 1995; Ferwerda, 2000).

The Psychopathological Juvenile Delinquent

Among the hardcore group, there are a small number of offenders who
suffer from psychological problems and/or psychiatric disorders. This type of
delinquency does not belong to the "normal" adolescent delinquency or with
the hardcore criminality. This group is referred to as the **psychopathological
juvenile delinquent**.

Based on research by Doreleijers (1995), these youths exhibit six to seven
times more psychiatric disorders than any other type of delinquent. Unfortunately, because of a lack of research in the area, we do not have any reliable
indicator of how many Dutch juvenile offenders would be classified as a "psychopathological juvenile delinquent."

The classification pertains to youths who at a young age demonstrate
severely disturbed behaviours. For example, they come across as cold, cruel,
emotionless, and without conscience. Here one thinks of cruelty to animals,
breaking and entering at the age of six, torturing other children, and setting
fires.

What these events have in common is that they are unexplainable or difficult to explain with the current criminological theoretical models.[9] It is often
said of these youths that there's "a screw loose." Because there is little to

nothing known about this group of juvenile delinquents, the offences are often difficult to comprehend. In recent years a number of Dutch researchers have been engaged in studying serious violent offenders (i.e., sexual offenders) in a way that also gives attention to the offenders psychological problems and/or psychiatric disorders (van Wijk, 2000).

In the next section, we will briefly summarize the evolution of juvenile justice in The Netherlands.

BACKGROUND OF THE DUTCH JUVENILE JUSTICE SYSTEM

The following section offers a concise overview of the development of juvenile justice in The Netherlands. The material is based on the work of the well-known Dutch criminologist Professor Josine Junger-Tas (1997).

1613 — First childcare measure in Amsterdam.

1666 — Opening of a special courthouse and two orphanages.

1809 — Dutch criminal code distinguished three categories of juveniles. Children under the age of 12 could not be punished. Children aged 12 to 15 could have so-called children's punishment, and juveniles aged 15 to 18 mitigated adult punishments.

1811 — Replacement of the criminal code by the Code Pénal (Napoleon), which did not make any distinction between children and adults.

1886 — New penal code added that children under the age of 10 could not be prosecuted. In this code was now a separate system of sanctions for adults and children.

1901 — First Dutch Children's Act. This first civil law made it possible to encroach on parental authority in cases where the child was in need of protection. The second (juvenile penal law) abolished the requirement of "discernment between right and wrong" as a criterion for guilt in children, and also abolished any distinction based on age. The law ruled that children could no longer be detained along with adults, but must be placed in separate youth institutions. This law also created three special youth sanctions: reprimands, fines, and placement in a reformatory for a period of no less than one month and no more than 12 months. Juveniles aged 16 to 18 who had committed serious crimes may be sent to prison. Mentally disturbed juveniles may be placed "at the disposal of the government" (TBS) in a treatment institution until their adulthood at the age of 21.

1922 — Introduction of a separate juvenile court in civil and penal matters. The law also introduced the Supervision Order (OTS).

1965 — Major revision of the law, in the sense that the welfare system was introduced in the juvenile justice. Its characteristics were:

    1. large discretionary powers, especially for the juvenile judge, based on the concept of parens patriae, which presumes that the judge always acts in the best interest of the child;

    2. irrespective of the criminal act, the personality and the needs of the child are predominant and dictate the decision;

    3. the emphasis is on treatment and assistance to the family and child instead of on punishment; and

    4. informality of the proceedings—court hearings are not open to the public, all proceedings are of a confidential nature, and there are hardly any procedural safeguards because in a welfare system these are deemed unnecessary.

1980s-1990s — Like many other countries, The Netherlands experienced a recession, unemployment rose, immigration from trouble spots around the world increased, and the future looked insecure to many. One could say that in this period, the post-war economic boom ended and the crime picture changed. The spread of drugs and illegal immigration brought more street crime. For the first time, crime became an important political issue (see Box 13.2). In this period, there was a noticeable shift away from deterministic environmental causes of crime and a belief in education and treatment to a philosophy of free will in which juveniles are considered responsible for their actions. In these years, there is a clear shift in the juvenile justice system from a **welfare model** to a **justice model**. This change resulted in new legislation in 1995.

1995 — New criminal code for juveniles (see Figure 13.3).

FROM A WELFARE TO A JUSTICE MODEL

When we look at the development of the juvenile justice system in The Netherlands, one could say that it changed over a short period of time from a **welfare model** in the 1960s and 1970s to a **justice model** in the 1990s. The change also led to a renewed emphasis on punishment as well as on early detection of troublesome behaviour. This shift is quite contrary to the standards that have been put forth in the 1984 Beijing Rules. The trend may reflect the social political nature of reform and a growing sentiment of conservatism in The Netherlands.

The most important dispositions of the (new) justice model (since 1995) are:

1. the role of the juvenile judge as a kind of welfare actor has been greatly reduced in favour of a judicial role;
2. it has become easier to transfer 16 to 18 year olds to the adult system. Transfer is allowed in cases where only one of the following three conditions is fulfilled: serious crime, serious circumstances, offenders personality;
3. in cases warranting a sentence of more than six months or in cases of mental disturbance, the case can no longer be dealt with by the individual juvenile judge but must be tried in full court by three judges;
4. the use of reprimands and the supervision orders have been removed from the juvenile justice system; and
5. the options for youth custody are enlarged (from maximum six months to 24 months).

REACTIONS TO JUVENILE CRIMINAL BEHAVIOUR: PREVENTION AND REPRESSION

By employing the earlier differentiated "faces" of juvenile crime, we gain insight in the preventative and repressive possibilities to avoid, deter, or even to control juvenile crime behaviour in The Netherlands.

In general, it can be said that the Dutch are reserved when it comes to imposing heavy sanctions such as imprisonment, but rather gravitate towards using alternative measures. The Dutch approach towards a **justice model** tends to emphasize prevention over custody. Therefore, unless the offence committed is serious, the police are inclined to use the so-called **pedagogical sanctions** before using alternative measures service or some other measure.

Since children under the age of 12 cannot be held criminally responsible the police refers them to Child Protection Services. Juveniles, on the other hand, are subject to a wide range of options reflecting the objective of trying to hold young offenders accountable while also recognizing their special needs. Such considerations are consistent with the UN Convention on the Rights of the Child (i.e., Beijing Rules – see Box 2 in Introduction) as well as the European Convention On Human Rights. Therefore, we will now direct our attention to the reactions to criminal behaviour for 12- to 18-year-olds.

Criminality as Kick Behavior

We established earlier that, in regards to this form of youth crime, these juvenile delinquents are opportunistic offenders. This is important in terms of criminality policy. Removing the opportunity to commit crime will bring down the occurrence of this type of criminality. This approach appears to work in practice, providing it's well organized. Examples of such forms of preventative methods in The Netherlands include:

- formal supervision, such as more police in the streets and camera security;
- informal supervision by hiring a concierge in an apartment building, neighbourhood prevention projects, and someone with a supervisory role placed in schools;
- object measures, like closing off entrances, placing urinals, and organizing neighbourhood clean-up action;
- target-group measures, as in setting up social and cultural youth work and youth centres, awareness activities at school, parent courses, and creating youth provisions;
- increasing visibility, by way of extra lighting and the pruning of trees and bushes; and
- registration of a graffiti photo file or the development of an arrest formula for vandalism that could perhaps be used by schools.

Since "criminality as kick behavior" is the most common type of delinquency, the police and courts are better equipped and informed to respond to these type of young offenders. Dutch research (Ferwerda, 1992; Commissie Jeugdcriminaliteit, 1994) has found that it is the opportunistic delinquent who is sensitive to police contact. That is to say, because they are afraid for their future place in society and the reactions of their peers, they tend to respond well to some form of pedagogical sanction. Hence, it is generally believed that the best way to deal with these types of youths is for the police and the judicial system to respond as quickly as possible. Yet, for first-time offenders, the police are most likely to issue a warning, while for recidivist offenders they use more formal sanctions such as unpaid service to the community and/or payment of damages (e.g., HALT; see Box 13.4). However, whether first-time offenders or recidivist offenders, it is considered important to bring the incident to the attention of the youth's parent(s).

Hardcore and Psychopathological Juvenile Delinquents

Unfortunately, the current preventative measures or the mild sanctioning measures—such as those described above—are insufficient for the small group of Dutch juvenile delinquents who are classified as hardcore and/or psychopathological. However, since the establishment of the new juvenile court system in 1995, there has been a greater shift towards using more punitive sanctions in order to ensure greater accountability for the more serious type of offenders.

Through this streamlining and modernizing, the juvenile laws now seem similar to the adult laws. This has lead to a number of changes, specifically heavier juvenile sanctions.

Box 13.4: HALT - An Alternative Sanction

HALT, which means "stop" in Dutch and is an acronym for "Het Alternatief," represents The Netherlands' first experience with diversion techniques. It was introduced in the 1970s, and in 1998 there were 64 HALT programs financed by the municipalities and the Ministry of Justice. The objective of the program is to allow juveniles, during their free Saturday, to work, clean or repair the damage done, and impose them, where appropriate, to pay damages.

It should be kept in mind that the intervention is spread out over time: a first meeting with project staff takes place within weeks after police contact. A second meeting follows and in general it will take about eight weeks before work starts. This means the intervention is more "intense" than it would appear and certainly more intrusive than a simple warning.

HALT has become very popular among the police in The Netherlands. They now have a useful tool that allows them to intervene in a rather light manner. In 1995, HALT was introduced in the new law as a form of police transaction. The police may now propose a maximum of 20 hours of HALT activities as an alternative to prosecution and on a voluntary basis. Both the juvenile and his or her parents have to agree. The police may only do so in the case of a limited and specified number of offences: wanton destructiveness, vandalism, simple theft, hooliganism, and infractions of the firework regulation. Recent evidence showed that HALT is an effective remedy for vandalism in more than 60% of cases.

When this type of young offender comes to the attention of the police and the courts, they attempt to strike a balance between accountability and addressing the needs of the juvenile. The general orientation of the police and courts are consistent with the Beijing Rules, and the European Convention on Human Rights. In spite of the good intentions of the Dutch system, as appears to be the case with many other countries, recidivism rates—between 65% and 75% (Commissie Jeugdcriminaliteit, 1994)—indicate that our system struggles to find the appropriate sanction for hardcore and/or psychopathological offenders.

We will give a short review of the differing types of sanctions for minors, whereby the list begins with pedagogical sanctions and ends with the placement of youths in an institution.

HALT-Sanction: In principle, the HALT-sanction is not meant for hardcore juveniles and psychopathological delinquents, because of the nature and extent of their offences. Within the new youth laws, HALT has gained a legal place and means that the police propose a HALT-sanction for a maximum of 20 hours for HALT-worthy offences. In general, the HALT-sanction consists of performing tasks and repayment of the ensuing damages. If the suspect agrees with the proposal, the warrant is not sent on to the justice officer (see Figure 13.2). Between 1989 and 1998 the number of Halt sanctions increased from just under 5,000 to nearly 21,000 sanctions.

Work and Learning Sanctions: These sanctions, also known as alternative sanctions, can replace a main punishment ([un-] conditional freedom or fines). In fact, combinations of work and learning sanctions can be sentenced with a maximum of 240 hours. The possibilities are:

- doing work of general usefulness (work in parks or in neighbourhood centres),
- working to repair the damages done,
- following a course "victims in focus" (especially for the offenders of violent crimes),
- participation in social skills training,
- following a course "social sexual forming" (especially for offenders of light vice crimes such as violation of virtue), and
- working on a farm in France.

With this intensive combination of work and learning sanctions there is much attention paid to the individual and the group processes.

Financial Fines: A fine can be an independent sanction, but can also be used in combination with another sanction, such as conditional freedom. Depending on the type of crime, the amount of the fine can vary from 5 to 5,000 guilders.

Conditional Freedom Sanction: The conditional freedom sanction is seen as a legal "big stick." This sanction is mostly used in combination with another sanction (e.g., help and support).

Youth Detention: Unconditional juvenile detention can be used in cases of serious offences. The length of juvenile detention varies from a minimum of one day to a maximum of two years in a juvenile hall.

Placement in a Juvenile Institution: Along with the previously mentioned sanctions, our juvenile system has a number of measures. These are meant for minors, who in the court's opinion, not only deserve punishment but also require treatment ("indefinite detention orders" [TBS] and "committal to a centre for special treatment"). The most important criminal measure against minors is placement in an institution for youths. The maximum period a youth can be placed in such an institution is six years (see Figure 13.2).

Mandatory Probationary Contact: In addition to the punishments and measures taken, there is still the instrument of obligatory juvenile probation contact. This regularly used disposition serves as an opportunity for the courts to provide the youth with a level of supervision that is intended to enable the

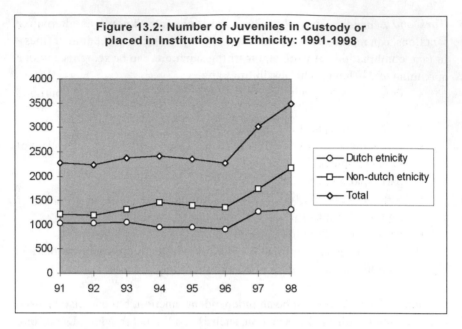

Figure 13.2: Number of Juveniles in Custody or placed in Institutions by Ethnicity: 1991-1998

probation officer to help the young offender deal with his or her problems in a constructive manner. To facilitate the counselling process in these cases, it is possible that an advisory examination occurs, that mandatory supervision (OTS) is used, or that the youth is required to participate in other forms of counselling.

Currently, counselling by juvenile probation is possible before and after the trial. However, there is consideration of extending the use of probation to during and after a task sanction (work and/or learning sanction) as well as after juvenile detention. The counseling can be ordered by the justice officer or the family court judge, but can also be ordered by Child Protective Services. Counselling is performed by the foster care services as long as the juvenile criminal law is applicable to the minor. However, for cases where adult criminal law is applied to 16- or 17-year-olds, then youths come under the jurisdiction of The Dutch Probation Organization, The Salvation Army, or the Consultant Bureau for Alcohol and Drugs.

TRIAL OF YOUNG OFFENDERS IN THE NETHERLANDS

When a criminal juvenile has committed a serious offence, the police will report it directly to the public prosecutor.[10] Public prosecutors are key figures in Dutch law. Based on the information on the offender's background from the Council of Child Protection, they decide whether a case will be prosecuted or dismissed. The public prosecutor can impose an alternative sanction or order

Figure 13.3: The Dutch Juvenile Justice System

The Police	- No future action
	- Dismissal (after hearing parents)
	- Juvenile sent to diversion project
(HALT)	
	- Report sent to prosecutor
Public Prosecutor	- Unconditional discharge
	- Conditional discharge
	- payment to special funds (max. 5000 guilders)
	- fine
	- alternative sanction (max. forty hr, if >twenty hr. Assistance by counsel)
	- supervision by social worker for max. six months
	- Referral to juvenile judge
Juvenile Judge	- Pre-trial detention (in the capacity of judge of instruction)
	- Probation (max. six months)
	- Fine (max 5000 guilders; may be substituted by custody or alternative sanction)
	- Alternative sanction
	- community service
	- reparative work on behalf of the victim
	- special training course
	- Custody (only in cases of crimes)
	- <sixteen years of age: max. twelve months
	- 16-18 years of age: max. twenty-four months
	- sixteen to eighteen years of age: transfer possible to adult court
	- Placement in institution: if serious crime, danger to others, or in need of special help (max. six years)

Source: adapted from the first edition, p. 61.

payment of a fine or damages. It is important to notice that the public prosecutor in The Netherlands has a wide discretion to annul punishments. He or she can, for instance, drop proceedings in return for payments of a fine in cases of certain types of theft or even (petty) violence (Morelli and Wolthuis, 2000). Only 20% of all recorded cases at the public prosecution service are brought to court to the **youth judge** (Central Bureau of Statistics, 1999).

The youth judge is both a civil and penal judge. The Dutch youth judge has wide discretion in selecting type and severity of sentences. The judge decides—after taking into account the offender's character and the nature of the offence—whether to divert the case from criminal proceedings (first offender and/or problematic family background) or to impose alternative sentences, fines, or juvenile sentences.[11]

The youth judge used to have considerable discretionary powers. Under the old law (before 1995), no decision concerning a juvenile could be made without the judge's consent. The new law introduced the formal separation of powers and gave more room to the public prosecutor and less room to the individual youth judge. In cases where custody of more than six months is imposed or in case of a measurement of placement in a treatment institution, the case will be tried by three judges, one of which is the youth judge (Junger Tas, 1997; Morelli and Wolthuis, 2000).

As mentioned earlier in this chapter, the main objective of juvenile criminal law in The Netherlands was to focus on educational sanctions, but in recent years—since the establishment of the new juvenile court system in 1995—there is a shift towards more punitive measures.

When sentencing in the Netherlands is compared to other European countries, such as Germany (see Chapter 6), we notice a great difference in the duration of juvenile sentences available. In the Netherlands, up to a maximum of two years of imprisonment can be imposed, and only one year under the age of 16. In Germany, the maximum amount is 10 years for a juvenile sentence. But in The Netherlands, general criminal law can be applied to 16 and 17 year olds if the severity of the crime is judged to require a higher custodial sentence. For young offenders there is no such option. Under strict conditions placement into child-care institutions can only be ordered for a maximum of up to six years (Morelli and Wolthuis, 2000).

Current Problems in Delinquency and Juvenile Justice

While there has only been a small increase in juvenile crime in recent years, the picture concerning specific types of crime and specific groups of offenders is more complex. For example, as noted earlier, both police data and data from self-report studies show that there has been a steady increase in violent crime in The Netherlands. According to police data, the proportion of violence has more than doubled between 1989 and 1998 (from 8.6% to 19.7%). This development is similar in other European counties (Pfeiffer, 1997).

Violent crimes in the public domain ("street violence") is at this moment one of the most important crime issues for researchers, policy-makers, and politicians in The Netherlands (Ferwerda and Beke, 1998; Ministry of Justice, 1999; Terlouw, de Haan, and Beke, 1999).

Apart from this development, we see that specific groups of offenders are becoming more prominent. Each year the police detain more girls. Compared to boys their numbers are small, but from self-report studies we learn that the involvement of girls in shoplifting, vandalism, and harassment are almost the same as that of boys (Mertens, Grapendaal and Schamhardt, 1998; van der Laan, Essers, Huijbregts, and Spaans, 1998).

A major area of concern involves offences committed by young people from ethnic minorities (i.e., Moroccans and Antillians). A series of research projects (Leuw, 1997; Beke, Ferwerda, van der Laan, and van Wijk, 1998) show that some ethnic groups are seriously over-represented in the child-care system, in the juvenile justice system, and in its institutions (see Figure 13.2). Compared to Dutch juveniles, some ethnic groups are more (three to six times) involved in criminal activities (especially in the use of violence). Although we are not proud to acknowledge it, like in many other countries, The Netherlands has areas in their large and middle-sized cities that are sometimes comparable to the black ghettos in America. In these areas—where rents are low and residents often do not benefit from the favourable economic climate—there is an accumulation of problems, such as relatively high unemployment, concentration of ethnic minorities, unkempt residential environments (litter), youngsters hanging around, alcohol- and drug-related trouble, and all kinds of inconvenience and crime caused by young people (Snel and Ferwerda, 2000).

As has been reported in other contributions in this book, our official data reveal that a small proportion of mostly young male offenders are responsible for a disproportionate amount of rather serious offences. Earlier it was noted that this group represents approximately 4.5% of young offenders. However, depending on which definition is used, the estimate can vary between 6% to 18% of the juveniles arrested by the Dutch police. This group of juvenile delinquents are responsible for 50% to 60% of all crimes committed by young persons (Junger-Tas, 1996).

From several recent longitudinal studies we have learned more about the characteristics of this group and the background of their offending patterns (Junger-Tas, 1996; Ferwerda, Jakobs, and Beke, 1996; van der Heiden-Attema and Bol, 2000). These studies show that these youngsters demonstrate various types of problematic behaviour at a very early age (under the age of 12) and that they are likely to continue to show problematic behaviour as they grow up. The so-called risk factors that play a role in the emergence of problems and problem behaviour include medical and physical conditions, psychological characteristics, familial and school influences, peer-related dynamics, and community/neighbourhood factors. The multiplicity of factors presents a significant challenge in trying to establish prevention policies.

Finally, we want to refer to the phenomenon of group crime (from groups hanging around in public areas to youth gangs) as a recent spearhead of the research and policy in The Netherlands. Schuyt (1993) noticed that group crime was a principle trait in juvenile delinquency. Schuyt also stated that this group "event" is not given enough attention within criminology and sentencing. Given the recent trends, this disregard is unjustified since they are responsible for a great deal of property damage, are regularly involved in acts of football hooliganism, and can pose an emotional threat when milling around in public areas such as shopping malls and parks.

The fact that the phenomenon of group crime has received little attention is, among others, the result of limited sentencing possibilities to approach this specific form of criminal behaviour. Criminal behavior and the sentence given in The Netherlands, is in the first place, an individual matter. This also goes for the sanction package for juvenile crime. The HALT-sanction is an example of such an individual application. Additionally, the (juvenile) criminal law offers little to no room for (preventative) measures at the group level.

The legal deficit is partially explained by the fact that there is little known about the dynamic of juvenile group crime. The current theories from the sociological, social psychological, and criminological terrain are insufficient to say anything reliable about the connection between (juvenile) criminality and group criminality, and the subsequent sentencing possibilities, either preventative or repressive.

With the shocking image of American gangs and the increase—in a number of areas—of juvenile criminality, the Dutch Ministry of Justice found it necessary in 1998 to gain more insight in the phenomenon of group crime committed by youths. One wanted not only insight in the scope and nature of the crime committed in groups, but also an accentuated look at the way to deal with it.

In 1998, this lead to the first exploratory study of the phenomenon of group criminality (Hakkert, van Wijk, Ferwerda, and Eijken, 1998). In mid-year 1999—at the request of the Ministry of Justice—a national study was started, wherein a quantitative inventory of criminal juvenile groups is being undertaken as well as a qualitative analysis of which processes and mechanisms are in play within these groups (Beke, van Wijk, and Ferwerda, 2000). It is expected that in the coming years, the (disposition) possibilities will be expanded to deal more efficiently with criminality committed in groups (see Box 13.5).

Recently, in the framework of EURO 2000—the European Football Championship, which took place in The Netherlands and Belgium—an advance was made in the form of a new policy measure ("**managed detention**") through which it was possible to deal with any group overstepping the boundaries.

Summary

This chapter presented an overview of the Dutch juvenile justice system and provides an account of the extent and development of juvenile criminality

---

Box 13.5: Managed Detention

As a result of the diverse large-scale public disturbances, the necessity for supplementary options has arisen to help deal with large groups who disturb the public order. The goal of the measure, which was instated in May 2000 referred to as **managed detention**, is to prevent the occurrence of (further) disturbances. Moreover, it deals with opportunities that could be seized by a great number of people to disturb public order, such as demonstrations, international conferences, or large-scale events like Euro 2000.

The city mayors now have the authority to detain large groups who are disturbing public order: managed detention. Detention is defined in this case as temporary detention (maximum 12 hours) of the group concerned in a specified location. This detention is possible when there is riotous behaviour, other forms of severe disorder, or even serious suspicion (threat) of the existence thereof.

Managed detention is bound by diverse requirements, such as containment, sufficient space, and the presence of provisions such as toilets, telephones, medical care, food and water, and beds. The locations wherein the groups are detained could be places such as sport centres or school buildings.

---

in The Netherlands. It was noted that the **justice model** best characterizes juvenile law in The Netherlands. And although the emphasis of the law is on trying to address the needs of juvenile delinquents, there has been a slight shift towards more punitive measures since 1995 (i.e., **crime control**). While the Dutch approach to juvenile justice shares many of the characteristics of justice model initiatives by the police, courts, and corrections, it also acknowledges the welfare elements found in the Beijing Rules, the European Convention on Human Rights, and several other major international agreements. However, with the recent shift, Dutch practices may arguably be moving away from the welfare principles.

It was also noted that juvenile justice in The Netherlands is characterized by its protective nature, giving attention to the special needs of young offenders by trying to apply pedagogical sanctions that are congruent with the law.

It was observed that juvenile delinquency has not increased dramatically in recent years. It is felt that this can, in part, be explained by the number of social development initiatives to address the more serious offenders, as well as a continued emphasis on continuing to provide services that embrace the protective forces within the juvenile justice system.

This chapter clarifies that, namely, the nature of juvenile criminality in The Netherlands has changed in recent years. The greatest part of juvenile criminality still consists of age-related offences such as vandalism and petty theft. There is a certain increase in violent crime among youths. The fact that the percentage of serious offenders in recent years has grown from 2% to 4.5% is illustrative.

Finally, we discussed how there are a number of emerging issues. They include: a growing awareness of, and problem with, group/gang activity, the problem of various ethnic and minority groups, youth becoming involved in delinquent activities at a younger age, and an increase in female delinquency.

The challenge in the coming years is whether The Netherlands can create programs that direct themselves toward the early warning signs and interventions by which criminal careers can possibly be avoided. Also, attention to the increasing violence and group-based delinquency will require the attention of politicians and policy makers. To facilitate this process, The Netherlands, as should any country that is experiencing a delinquency problem, should be open to learning from whatever successful initiatives other countries have undertaken. After all, juvenile delinquency is a universal issue.

Henk B. Ferwerda (Ph.D.) is a criminologist and the director of the Advice and Research Group Beke in Arnhem. Prior to establishing the research group, he was employed by the Criminological Institute of the Rijks University of Groningen. Since 1986 he has amassed a diverse list of publications on the following topics: juvenile criminality, street violence, justice in the neighbourhood, group criminality, football vandalism, public criminality, vice delinquency, and early warning signs for problematic behavior among youths.

HELPFUL WEBSITES

Note: A number of these links are in Dutch but they offer a varied overview and facts about juvenile delinquency and the handling of young offenders in The Netherlands.

www.sjn.nl/lyre/index.htm
Links on youth research in Europe
www.politie.nl/home/engels/default.htm
Police in the Netherlands
www.minjust.nl/b_organ/wodc/welkom/WODC_ENG.HTM
The Research and Documentation Centre (WODC) of the Ministry of Justice
www.halt.nl
Halt Nederland (in Dutch)
www.trimbos.nl/indexuk.html
The Trimbos Institute, the Netherlands Institute of Mental Health and Addiction
www.beke.nl
Advice and Research Group Beke (in Dutch)

KEY TERMS AND CONCEPTS

Kick behaviour	Hardcore behavior
Managed detention	Psychopathological behavior
Pedagogical sanctions	Juvenile criminality
HALT	Justice model
Welfare model	Youth judge
Crime control	

STUDY QUESTIONS

1. What do you think of the drug policy in The Netherlands? Do you think that it has an effect on certain types of crimes in The Netherlands?
2. Do you think there is a relation between the development of certain types of crimes and the changes in the juvenile justice system over the past 10 years in The Netherlands?
3. In the chapter you see that the juvenile justice system in The Netherlands changed from a welfare model to a justice model. What are the most important explanations for this change? Are there other countries in Europe where you see the same kind of change in the juvenile justice system?
4. What are the most important reasons for the fact that youngsters with a non-Dutch ethnicity are over-represented in the Dutch juvenile justice system?
5. What do you think of the way the Dutch deal with juvenile delinquents (type and length of sanctions) when you consider the crime-rate among youngsters in The Netherlands? What are the most important differences when you consider the German system?
6. After 1995 there was a change in the discretionary powers of the youth judge in The Netherlands. In what way did it change? What is your opinion about the change? Is the position of the Dutch youth judge unique when you consider the situation in other countries?

NOTES

1 In recent years this group is regarded to be 12-minors or child delinquents.
2 It will later become clear why the word "globally" is used.
3 Source: Central Bureau of Statistics, 1999.
4 Source: Central Bureau of Statistics, 1999.
5 It is an average of around 42,000 criminal minors per year.
6 Source: Central Bureau of Statistics, 1999.
7 (-) means that the offence was absent from the survey taken in that year.
8 In comparison with the police numbers this is 7: 1.
9 With the exception of forensic psychiatry.
10 The public prosecution service in The Netherlands employs more than 2,000 people, including some 450 public prosecutors (Public Prosecution Service, 1999).
11 As a measure of child protection the youth judge may release or remove parental rights or impose a supervision order which includes educational guidance by a social worker.

REFERENCES

Angenent, H.L.W. (1991). *Achtergronden van jeugdcriminaliteit. Bohn Stafleu Van Loghum.* Houten/Antwerpen.

Bartels, J.A.C. (1995). Het nieuwe jeugdstrafrecht. *Trema*, 3:69-75.

Beke, B.M.W.A., and W.W. Kleiman. (1992). *Jongeren en geweldscriminaliteit. Een nadere analyse van de 'harde kern'. Stafafdeling Informatievoorziening, Directie Criminaliteitspreventie.* Ministerie van Justitie, Den Haag.

Beke, B.M.W.A., H.B. Ferwerda, P.H. van der Laan, and A.Ph. van Wijk. (1998). *De dunne draad tussen doorgaan en stoppen. Allochtone jongeren en criminaliteit.* SWP, Utrecht.

Beke, B.M.W.A., A.Ph. van Wijk, and H.B. Ferwerda. (2000). *Juegdcriminaliteit Jeugdcriminaliteit in groepsverband ontrafeld. Tussen rondhangen en bendevorming.* Amsterdam.

Central Bureau of Statistics. (1999). *Policestatistics, statistics of the population and statistics on crime and law.*

Commissie Jeugdcriminaliteit (Commissie Van Montfrans). (1994). *Met de neus op de feiten. Aanpak jeugdcriminaliteit*, Den Haag.

Doreleijers, Th.A.H. (1995). *Diagnostiek tussen jeugdstrafrecht en hulpverlening.* Gouda Quint B.V. Arnhem.

Ferwerda, H.B. (1992). *Watjes en ratjes. Een longitudinaal onderzoek naar het verband tussen maatschappelijke kwetsbaarheid en jeugdcriminaliteit.* Wolters-Noordhof B.V., Groningen.

Ferwerda, H.B., P. Versteegh, and B.M.W.A. Beke. (1995). De harde kern van jeugdige criminelen. In: *Tijdschrift voor criminologie*, Themanummer 'Zin en onzin over jeugdcriminaliteit'. Jaargang, 37(2): 138-153.

Ferwerda, H.B., J.P. Jakobs, and B.M.W.A. Beke. (1996). *Signalen voor toekomstig crimineel gedrag. Een onderzoek naar de signaalwaarde van kinderdelinquentie en probleemgedrag op basis van casestudies van ernstig criminele jongeren. Stafbureau Informatie, Voorlichting en Publiciteit. Dienst Preventie, Jeugdbescherming en Reclassering.* Ministerie van Justitie, Den Haag.

Ferwerda, H.B., and B.M.W.A. Beke. (1998). *Twaalf Stedendebat geweld op straat: hoofdlijnen en suggesties voor beleid.* Ministerie van Binnenlandse Zaken en Koninkrijksrelaties, Den Haag.

Ferwerda, H.B., M. Bottenberg, and B.M.W.A. Beke. (1999). *Jeugdcriminaliteit in de politieregio Zaansteek-Waterland. Een onderzoek naar omvang, aard, spreiding en achtergronden.* Advies- en Onderzoeksgroep Beke, Arnhem.

―――. (1999). *Jeugdcriminaliteit in Zeeland. Een onderzoek naar de omvang, aard, spreiding en achtergronden.* Advies- en Onderzoeksgroep Beke, Arnhem.

Ferwerda, H.B. (2000). Jeugdcriminaliteit en de rol van de groep. De groep als negatieve voedingsbodem. In *Tijdschrift over jongeren*, 1(1): 34-44.

Gorkom, M.C.E. van. (1996). Het nieuwe jeugdstrafrecht. Harmonie of discrepantie tussen juridische en pedagogische opties? In: *TIAZ, Tijdschrift voor adolescentenzorg*, 1: 33-41.

Hakkert, A., A.Ph. van Wijk, H.B. Ferwerda, and T. Eijken. (1998). *Groepscriminaliteit. Een terreinverkenning op basis van literatuuronderzoek en een analyse van bestaand onderzoeksmateriaal, aangevuld met enkele interviews met sleutelinformanten en jongeren die tot groepen behoren.* Stafbureau Informatie, Voorlichting en Publiciteit. Directie Preventie, Jeugd en Sanctiebeleid. Ministerie van Justitie, Den Haag.

Public Prosecution Service. (1999). *Heart of justice. A booklet about the public prosecution service.* The Hague.

Heiden-Attema, N. van der, and M.W. Bol. (2000). *Moeilijke jeugd. Risico- en protectieve factoren en de ontwikkeling van delinquent gedrag in een groep risicojongeren.* WODC, Ministerie van Justitie, Den Haag.

Junger-Tas, J. (1996). *Jeugd en gezin. Preventie vanuit een justitieel perspectief.* Ministerie van Justitie, Den Haag.

―――. (1997). Juvenile delinquency and juvenile justice in The Netherlands. In J.A. Winterdyk (Ed.), *Juvenile justice systems. International perspectives*. Toronto, ON: Canadian Scholars' Press, 55-75.

Keij, I. (2000). *Numbers of foreigners according to various definitions*. Centraal Bureau voor de Statistiek, Den Haag.

Koens, M.J.C. (1995). Het nieuwe jeugdstraf(proces)recht. In: *Familie en Jeugdrecht,* 1: 3-7.

Laan, P.H. van der. (2000). Chances and limits for crime prevention in The Netherlands: developments in recent years. In R. Bendit, W. Erler, S. Nieborg, and H. Schäfer (Eds.), *Child and juvenile delinquency: strategies of prevention and intervention in Germany and The Netherlands*. Utrecht, The Netherlands/Munchen, Germany, pp.: 55-70.

Laan, P.H. van der, A.A.M. Essers, G.L.A.M. Huijbregts, and E.C. Spaans. (1998). *Ontwikkelingen van de jeugdcriminaliteit: periode 1980-1996.* Een tussentijds verslag. WODC, Den Haag.

Leuw, Ed. (1997). *Criminaliteit van etnische minderheden. Een criminologische analyse.* WODC, Den Haag.

Mertens, N.M., M. Grapendaal, and B.J.W. Schamhardt. (1998). *Meisjescriminaliteit in Nederland*. WODC, Den Haag.

Ministerie van Justitie. (1999). *Geweld op straat. Voortgangsnotitie over de maatregelen ter voorkoming en bestrijding*. Den Haag.

Morelli, C., and A. Wolthuis. (2000). The differences between German and Dutch youth criminal law. In R. Bendit, W. Erler, S. Nieborg, and H. Schäfer (Eds.), *Child and juvenile delinquency: strategies of prevention and intervention in Germany and The Netherlands*. Utrecht, The Netherlands/Munchen, Germany, pp.: 143-147.

Pfeiffer, C. (1997). *Juvenile crime and juvenile violence in European countries*. Kriminologisches Forschungsinstitut Niedersachsen, Hannover, Germany.

Schuyt, C.J.M. (1993). Jeugdcriminaliteit in groepsverband. In: *Delikt en Delinkwent*, 23(6): 499-510.

Snel, E., and H.B. Ferwerda. (2000). Youth delinquency in disadvantaged neighbourhoods. In R. Bendit, W. Erler, S. Nieborg, and H. Schäfer (Eds.), *Child and juvenile delinquency: strategies of prevention and intervention in Germany and The Netherlands*. Utrecht, The Netherlands/Munchen, Germany, pp.: 77-90.

Terlouw, G.J., W.J.M. de Haan, and B.M.W.A. Beke. (1999). *Geweld: gemeld en geteld. Een analyse van aard en omvang van geweld op straat tussen onbekenden*. Den Haag, Groningen, Arnhem.

Wijk, A.Ph. van. (2000). *Een verkennend onderzoek naar jeugdige zedendelinquenten*. Advies- en Onderzoeksgroep Beke, Arnhem/Vrije Universiteit, Amsterdam.

Chapter 14

An Overview of Juvenile Justice and Juvenile Crime in Russia

Dmitry A. Shestakov
Professor of Law and Criminology
Member of the Russian Academy of Social Services
Natalia D. Shestakova
Faculty of Law, St. Petersburg State University

FACTS ON RUSSIA

Area: Russia occupies an area of 17,075,400 sq. km. It is the largest country in the world. In accordance with territorial administration there are 21 republics, six territories, 49 provinces, and two cities of federal significance (Moscow, pop. 8.7 million and St. Petersburg, pop. 4.4 million). The country contains ten autonomous former Soviet republics and one autonomous province which are referred to as the Commonwealth of Independent States (CIS). **Population:** At the beginning of 1997 the population was estimated at around 147.2 million—growth rate .21% per year. 73% of the population resides in urban communities while the balance (twenty-seven per cent) are primarily rural dwellers. Representatives of more than one hundred nationalities live in Russia, with the majority (82%) being ethnic Russians. The Tartars account for approx. 3.8%, Ukrainians three per cent, and most others constitute no more than one per cent each. There are many languages spoken throughout Russia, but the state language is Russian. The most popular religion is Russian Orthodox. **Climate:** In recognizing that Russia covers nearly 150° lon-gitude, the weather is as diverse as the cultural climate of the country. The climate varies from continental in the south-western regions to extreme cold in Siberia to monsoon in the Far East. Winter temperatures vary in January from -1° to -50° C, and in July from 1° to 30° C. **Government:** Prior to 1987, when Gorbachev initiated major democratic reforms through openness (glasnost) and restructuring (perestroika), Russia was first ruled under a Tsarist regime and then, after the 1917 Revolution, under a Communist regime until 1985. Today, the democratic federal legal state is made up of a republic form of government. State power in the Russian Federation is realized on the basis of power divided into legislative, executive, and judicial jurisdictions. State power is characterized by a bicameral legislative body consisting of the Federal Assembly, comprised of a Federal Council [178] and the State Duma [450], along with the supreme courts. The head of state and government is a President (Vladimir Putin as of March 2000). Under the constitution, local authorities are recognized and guaranteed autonomy.

*[I]t is obvious that a mere knowledge of the rule of law by no means guaran-
tees that it is observed.*—A.M. Yakovlev (1988)

*Four years have passed since the Russian federation became a state with a
transitional economy. Everyone knows that such countries are characterized
by increased criminal activity across practically the entire spectrum of society.*—G. Lezhikov, 1995—Ninth United Nations Congress on the Prevention
of Crime and the Treatment of Offenders.

THE (TURBULENT) EVOLUTION OF RUSSIAN LAW

Russia, which is one of the oldest states in the world (see Box 14.1), has a
system of legislation that has undergone rapid and dramatic change in recent
years. However, the earliest recordings of Russian law date back to the tenth
century A.D. Its influence and doctrines can be found in the *Russkaya Pravda*
which, among other things, describes the essence of Russian criminal law.
Other major codes of law were formulated in 1497, 1550, 1649, the Military
Rules of Peter I in 1716, and "The Order" of the Empress Catherine II the Great
in 1767.[1]

A characteristic feature of early feudal criminal law was the establishment
of concrete *corpus delicti*. The general concern was not so much about establishing guilt but defining criminal responsibility. Formal responsibility was not
codified until 1864, when the first Russian Penal Code was legislated. The laws
were based on progressive ideas. Desnitski, Kunitsin, and Solntsev were instrumental in formulating the Penal Code. In their works and lectures they
profoundly scientifically elaborated the issues of guilt, subjective characteristics of crime, the meaning of the will, and consciousness of criminals while
they are committing crimes. They also acknowledged the principle of *mens rea*.
Many of their ideas were based on the classical and neo-classical ideas of
justice reform taking place in Western Europe at the time.

The work of G. Solntsev's *Russian Criminal Law* is a consistent system of
the general part of Russian criminal law. Solntsev based his opinions upon the
rules and orders of Catherine II while he criticized the West-European criminal
law literature.

Further legal reform was carried out during the 1860s. The Regulations of
the Criminal Legal Procedure of 1864 were supplemented with Articles 356.1-
356.6. These articles were devoted to the regulation of the execution of minors
from 10 to 17 years of age and the Punishment Regulations of 1864 were adopted.
They reflected the following essential features concerning minors (i.e., juvenile offenders):

- Youth under the age of 10 cannot be charged with misdemeanors.
- Half punishment (the punishment for minors committing the same crimes
  as adults is less strict than for adults) is set for minors from the ages of

---

Box 14.1: Russian History in a Box

Russia's historical and legal roots can be traced back to the Greek and Byzantine Empire. Russia's first important battle towards nationhood was in the thirteenth century when Prince Alexander Yaroslavovich beat back the Swedish army near St. Petersburg, on the banks of the Neva. The prince thereafter was referred to as Alexander Nevsky (meaning "of the Neva"). One of Russia's most honored phrases came from Nevsky, who reportedly said: "That who comes to us with a sword, will die from the sword." The phrase can be found on many WWI and WWII memorials. During the middle ages, territorial Russia grew quickly with hard fought battles against the Turks and Tartars in the southwest and with the Baltic states in the northwest under Peter the Great in early eighteenth century. The spoils in the aftermath of Napoleonic war of 1812 and the abolishment of serfdom in 1861 provided the impetus for change. It was during this period that the peasant movement known as "Narodniki" spawned the uprising of the peasant class. And in spite of rapid growth and industrialization, a Revolution in 1905 attempted to slow down the changes. In the nineteenth century, Russia made a valuable contribution to development of the world's culture (e.g. LevTolstoi and F. Dostoevski), art (e.g. composers Chaikovski and Musorgski), and science (e.g. Mendelee and Lobachevski). WWI brought much hardship and loss of lives to the Russian people. Russia became politically very unstable. It led to an overthrow of the monarchy in February 1917. Finally, on 25 October (or 7 November by the new calendar) the RKP (Russian Communist Party), with the help of German financial backing, dethroned the Tsarist government. This marked the beginning of 70 years of Soviet Russia under Communism. Private property was abolished and all private land was transferred to the State. Under Joseph Stalin's rule, religion was abolished, millions of innocent people were either killed or exiled to Siberia, and all private land was transferred to the State. When Mikhail Gorbachev came to power in 1985, he introduced a number of fundamental reforms known as "glasnost," or openness, which helped Russia move towards democratization and a market economy. Combined with "perestroika," or restructuring, the changes began to stir economic, legal, political, and social reform. Finally, in 1991, the 70-year domination of the Marxist-Leninist-Stalinist totalitarian state collapsed, as did the former Soviet Union, and the Cold War came to an abrupt end and the Warsaw Pact disbanded. Boris Yeltsin's social democracy party became Russia's first popularly elected president in June 1991. His sweeping reforms led to the breakup of the Soviet Union into its constituent republics, and formed the Commonwealth of Independent States. A controversial election in June 1996 between democracy and a return to communism marked another milestone in Russian history. In a second run-off election in July, Yeltsin's party prevailed. In 2000, Vladimir Putin—former Director of a Federal Department of Safety and later Prime Minister of Russia—was elected as a President of Russia.

---

10 to 17. Minors under 14 can be placed in the custody of parents or guardians or in home correctional facilities.

- Minors must be detained separately from adults (see Box 14.2).
- If the age of a minor is important to the charge(s) or to his or her punishment, then the court appoints a search for birth documents to double-check the age of the offender (Article 413 of the Punishment Regulations).

- The parent, tutor, or relative can "hand in a recall" (appeal).
- Juveniles under age 14 are not permitted to testify under oath.
- Corrective shelters instead of imprisonment should be used with minors.

Box 14.2: Corrective Shelters

According to the "Rules on Corrective Shelters" in 1866, the imprisonment of juveniles was to be dealt with in the same manner as that for adults. They were initially operated by the churches, companies, or in private homes. After the Revolution, they were placed under the directorship of the Ministry of Internal Affairs and they have been attached to its department. The purpose of the shelters was to provide (re)education and work projects.

In keeping with the former socialist philosophy, an emphasis is placed on the coordination of home, school, and community. Delinquency was viewed as an indicator of the failure to apply basic precepts in the education of Russian youth. Legal rights, unlike in most Western countries, were clearly spelled out by the state rather than presumed to exist naturally. Therefore, in early times, the juvenile justice system could be best described as having represented a **crime control model** (see Figure 1—Introduction).

The revised Criminal Code of 1903 stipulated the conditions and requirements for sentencing juveniles. Some of the key criteria include:

- Juveniles between the ages of 14 and 17 who committed a serious crime were primarily sent to educational-corrective institutions (see Box 14.2). If there was no such opportunity, then the minor would be sent to specially adapted units attached to the adult prisons or custody houses.
- Female juveniles were sent to nunneries. If it were possible, then they too would be sent to educational-corrective institutions.
- Juvenile offenders could be imprisoned for eight to 12 years. However, youths between the ages of 10 and 14 were usually sent to the educational-corrective institution. This was preferred over the use of fines or other corrective measures. With respect to juveniles between 17 and 21 years of age, capital punishment was replaced by "exile for life." In Russia this meant 15 years imprisonment, which was subject to possible early release after serving one-third of the sentence.

Before the Russian Revolution there were two types of juvenile justice trends: sociological and classical. The classical model is mostly conservative. In the classical criminological tradition, emphasis is placed on the main process of law and not on circumstantial factors. The sociological perspective (a modified, neo-classical interpretation) still follows the criminal codes of law, but at the same time takes the changes of society into consideration. These perspectives have had an enduring impact on how we view juvenile justice and the causes of juvenile crime to this day. Sergievski, Vladimirov, Kistyakovski, Foinitski, and Koni were among the most well known scientists-criminalists of Tsarist Russia.

The question of criminal responsibility of juveniles was raised after the 1917 October Revolution. However, with the dramatic political changes that transpired during the 1920s, criminal legislation underwent repeated revisions— first under the Criminal Code of 1922 and then the General Beginnings of Criminal Legislation of 1924 before the final changes were incorporated in the 1926 Criminal Code. The code placed priority on compulsive education over measures of criminal punishment. This represented a shift from a strict **crime control model** to a **justice model** (see Figure 1—Introduction). This theme was most blatantly expressed in 1935, when Soviet legislation abolished juvenile courts.

Let us now turn to the 1950s and 1960s. This period was marked by the reign of Joseph Stalin (1928 to 1953) and the Khrushev reforms (1956 to 1964).

Along with the many political changes, criminal legislation was also amended. In conjunction with the development of democratic principles of law and an emphasis on lawfulness, the Principles of Criminal Legislation of the Soviet Union (SU) and the Union's republics were adopted. The age of the criminal responsibility was raised from 14 to 16.

While the underlying principles of the legislation focused on legalistic elements, the philosophy of the legislation reflected the neo-classical ideas of justice, with an emphasis on due process and punishment proportionate to the crime. For example, the severity of any punishment was measured against the gravity of the crime. Hence, tolerance for dangerous recidivists was minimal. Judges, however, were required to take into consideration all the extenuating circumstances of the offence. If the court found that correction of the juvenile offender could be obtained without criminal punishment, then it could use compulsory measures of an educational character.

The principles of strict crime control were balanced against the possibility of mitigating circumstances. These elements were incorporated in the Principles of 1958 and Criminal Codes of the SU's republics. The principles were adopted between 1960 and 1961. They include:
- A reduction in the range of punishable deeds by limiting the number of offences which existed earlier.
- A general reduction of punishment for many crimes.

- The possibility of liberation from criminal responsibility and the use of measures of public influence by holding to bail (Article 52 of the Criminal Code) and by transmission of the case to Comrades Court (Article 52 of the Criminal Code). For example, when one commits an offence that is not considered to be criminal (e.g., public drunkenness), he or she would not be taken into custody but placed into the custody of their employer, where they would be subject to embarrassment before workers, students, or colleagues.
- An increased emphasis on educational measures which focused on re-education and resocialization rather than stressing criminal responsibility.
- An amendment on 15 February 1977, now allows for the adjournment of the punishment. (If a person is convicted to not more than three years of imprisonment for the first time, the court may adjourn the decision for one to two years, taking into consideration the character of the committed offence, the personality of the offender, and other circumstances. After the period of adjournment is over, the offender can either be sent to serve the punishment or be declared debt free by the court).

Having presented an overview of the evolution of Russian law, we can now examine juvenile justice within a more contemporary framework.

CONTEMPORARY RUSSIA

During the period when Russia was being declared as a legal state (c. 1917), criminal reforms were also taking place. One of the main shifts in legal reform was an increased emphasis on recognizing individual and human rights.

The principle of embracing humanism through legal reform reflects the intention to provide young people with criminal-legal measures of safety through the use of due process. As first defined by the father of the Classical School of thought, Cesare Beccaria (1738 to 1794), and expressed in the Beijing Rules, the UN Riyadh Guidelines, and the European Convention on Human Rights, the purpose of punishment should not be the infliction of harm or humiliation, but to serve as a deterrent. In the aftermath of the political reforms of the early 1990s, policy makers have moved towards incorporating legal reforms for juvenile offenders that respect a young offender's rights and reflect the guidelines and recommendations of the various international agreements.

The principles constitute a refinement of graded responsibility and propose a two-tier model of juvenile justice. The re-emergence of Russian criminology and a more open dialogue with Western countries have played a significant role in the reforming of criminal legislation (see Box 14.3).

Box 14.3: The (Re)emergence of Criminology in Russia

According to research conducted by Louise Shelly (1980), Soviet legal and criminology scholars, prior to the collapse of the Soviet Union in 1991, were incapable of drawing insightful conclusions on crime "because of a combination of ideological and intellectual constraints" (p. 111). These constraints were in part the result of internal population controls. It was not until recently in law schools, where criminology is taught, that scholars were given more liberal access to crime and delinquency data, thus enabling more insightful discussions and evaluations of juvenile crime in Russia.

In 1994, a new Criminal Code (CC) of Russia was adopted. Today it defines the current aspects of criminal responsibility and other legal matters as they pertain to juvenile offenders. Matters pertaining to legal procedure and the regulation of the order of criminal proceedings can be found in the Criminal Procedure Code of Russian Soviet Federated Socialist Republic (RSFSR [1960]).

The 1994 Criminal Code has a separate chapter devoted to the peculiarities of juvenile criminal responsibility and punishment.

Under the new Code, provisions for both punishment and compulsory measures of (re)education have been incorporated. For example, the Supreme Court of Russia states that the courts cannot apply criminal responsibility for first-time offenders who have committed a serious offence when it is believed that some re-education can be attained through the use of alternative measures as described under Article 90 of the CC. (Acts of the Supreme Court…, 2000).

The Supreme Court also states that it is necessary to decide the possibility of application for a juvenile of a punishment not connected with imprisonment. For this purpose, it is important to take into consideration not only requirements provided for in Article 60 of the CC for any person (not only juvenile), but also circumstances called in Article 89 of the CC, such as life and educational conditions of a juvenile, level of his psychological development, other features of his personality, and the influence of older people.

The CC provides for the peculiarities of punishment appointment for juveniles. In particular, life imprisonment cannot be appointed for a juvenile under 18 years old as well as capital punishment (part 2 Article 57 and part 2 Article 59 CC).

The fact of being a juvenile is called among the first circumstances that soften punishment (art. 61 C.C.). And for those youth who recruit other youth into criminal activity, their punishment is more severe than for the youth being recruited (Article 63 CC).

The Code provides for a rule that was known to pre-Revolutionary legislation, according to which the rules about the peculiarities of juvenile's responsibility and punishment can be directed at young offenders between the ages of 18 to 20.

PECULIARITIES OF CRIMINAL RESPONSIBILITY

Russian juvenile law is clear in identifying who can be considered a youth at risk when establishing criminal responsibility. Under Article 10 of the Criminal Code, criminal responsibility is assigned to youths who were at least 16 years of age before they had committed an offence. The law further notes that upon turning 16, the youths acquired the cognitive and development ability, as a rule, which allows them to be aware of their actions (i.e., forming *mens rea*). However, the law recognizes that youths between the ages of 14 and 16 may be capable of forming intent. Therefore, legislation provides for reduced culpability for youths as young as 14 (the minimum age of criminal responsibility) with diminished responsibility.

In accordance with Article 20 of the Criminal Code, youths between the ages of 14 and 16 are considered criminally responsible for a specific range of offences. They include:

1. homicide (Article 105 of CC),
2. intentional assault and battery, causing health disorder (Article 111, 112),
3. kidnapping (Article 126), rape (Article 131),
4. violence of a sexual character (Article 132),
5. theft (Article 158), robbery (Article 161),
6. burglary (Article 162),
7. swindle (Article 163),
8. illegal possession by means of transport, horse, or another valuable property without a purpose of a repine (Article 166),
9. intentional destruction or damage of property (Article 167),
10. terrorism (Article 205),
11. deliberately false information about an act of terrorism (Article 207),
12. hooliganism (p. 2,3, Article 213),
13. theft or extortion of weapons or explosives (Article 226),
14. theft or extortion of drugs (Article 229), and
15. destroying of means of transportation transport roads (Article 267) .

Upon reaching the age of 16, all youths are subject to criminal responsibility.

The Criminal Code provides for an exclusion when only a person older then 18 years old can be subject to responsibility. It pertains to certain types of criminal offences such as encouraging the involvement of a juvenile into committing a crime.

The gravity of the offence also has a bearing on whether the juvenile will receive corrective punishment or be sent for re-education (Article 90). In accordance with Article 90 of the Criminal Code, the following compulsory measures of educational character can be used:

- giving a warning;
- placing under strict supervision of parent(s) or guardian(s);
- obligation to compensate damages; and
- limitation of leisure and establishing special requirements for the behavior of a juvenile.

If a juvenile is not determined to be criminally responsible, then their file is referred to the Committee on Juvenile Affairs.

Committee on Juvenile Affairs (CJA)

Committees on juvenile affairs operate in accordance with the Principles on the Committees on Juvenile Affairs, which were set forth in 1968. However, some of its propositions are invalid because they contradict the legislation currently in force.

In accordance with Article 17 of the Principles on CJA, the committee has a right to consider the following cases of delinquency:

- youths up to the age of 14, who have committed a dangerous public act, and
- youths between the ages of 14 and 16 who have committed a dangerous public act.

Before 1 January 1997, the CJA had the right to consider cases involving the delinquency of youths who were between the ages of 16 and 18 and who had committed an infraction that contains elements of crime. But there was disagreement within the CJA on how to proceed with such cases. The controversy evolved around the interpretation of Articles 8 and 10 of the Criminal Procedure Code (CPC).

With the enactment of the new Criminal Code of Russian Federation on 1 January 1997, changes were also made to the Criminal Procedure Code, which states that the aforementioned cases are now only considered by the court. The new code replaced the code of 1960. Thus, the legislation has taken into account that the mandate of the CJA is illegal as it contradicts the Constitution of Russian Federation. In particular CJA jurisdiction operations are in contravention with Article 118 of the Constitution of Russia, which states that justice in Russia can only be carried out by a court of law.[2] Furthermore, the CJA violates the UN Convention on the Rights of the Child adopted by the United Nations in 1989. Article 8 of the convention states: a child should not be separated from his or her parents against their will unless deemed necessary by a trained official whose concerns are supported by the court. The court can then deem it to be in the best interests of the youth that such separation is necessary for the well being of the young person.

Until recently, as the analysis of CJA activity showed, the CJA identified a significant number of its cases as being juvenile delinquents. For instance in 1990, 294,978 cases were considered, of which approximately 14% were considered cases involving juvenile delinquents.

During 1991, the CJA handled 30,810 cases that involved offences committed by public gangs. Of this total, 447 cases involved youths under the age of 14. Their average age was nine. 17% of all the cases involved juveniles between the ages of 14 and 16, most of whom had committed criminal acts containing elements of *corpus delicties*. If there is a case where there is not enough evidence to prove the crime, then criminal proceedings are arrested. Approximately 15% (4,627) of the CJA judgments resulted in referring the juvenile offender for special education training (see Box 14.4).

Until recently, the CJA played a major role in the struggle with juvenile crime. Its role is being strengthening while establishing centers of prevention at all administrative levels.

Box 14.4: Discussion on the Fate of the CJA

Legally speaking, the mandate of the CJA is illegal, as it contradicts the Constitution of Russian Federation. In particular, CJA jurisdictional operations are in contravention with Article 118 of the Constitution of Russia that states that justice in Russia can only be carried out only by a court of law. Furthermore, the CJA violates the UN Convention on Children's Rights. Article 8 of the Convention states: "A child should not be separated from his parents against their will unless deemed necessary by a trained official whose concerns are supported by the court." The court can then deem it to be in the best interests of the youth that such separation is necessary for well being of the young person.

TYPES OF CRIMES COMMITTED

Before we discuss the types of crimes being committed, it should be noted that according to the head of the Institute of the Ministry of Internal Affairs of the Russian Federation, Pavel Ponomarev, in 1994 only about one third of the total numbers of crimes committed were officially registered. Therefore, the *dark figure* (i.e., amount of unrecorded crime) of crime for juvenile crime, given the findings in many Western countries, is likely to be quite large. The reader should therefore view the data with some caution (Ponomarev, 1996), as Russia (and this contribution) must reply on official crime/police or other statistics.

Box 14.5: A Special Teaching and Educational Institution

In 1995, a government regulation was introduced which provided for "a special teaching and educational institution for children and juveniles with deviant behavior" (Government of RF 25.04.1995, Collection of Law N 18. 1995). The special teaching and educational institution areas provide psychological, medical, and social rehabilitation, including behavior correction and adaptation into society, and also provision of the conditions for primary general, fundamental general, middle (complete) general, and primary professional education. The establishment of separate institutions for boys and girls or mixed institutions is also possible. The institution may be of an open type and accomplish preventive functions, or of a closed type—for juveniles who have committed dangerous public actions as stipulated by the Criminal Code. They are considered in need of special conditions of education and teaching, and special pedagogical individualized treatment. This represents a major ideological break in Russian practices and is more characteristic of the *parens patriae* philosophy found in most Western juvenile justice systems.

In general, juvenile crime in Russia today consists primarily of thefts of personal property, robberies, burglaries, hooliganism, and thefts of state property. The more serious and violent crimes such as rape, intentional assault, and homicides only make up a small percentage of the crime structure (see Table 14.1). However, between 1985-1995, murder and "heavy bodily injuries" increased threefold, while the number of rapes fell by 43% (Asquith, 1996). These patterns are not unlike those in many Western countries where violence inflicted by juveniles has increased and there has also been a general qualitative change in the type of violence inflicted. This current profile did not always officially exist in Russia. Under the socialist system, youth crime was reported to be low (Borodin, 1980). But throughout the 1980s, as economic, political, and social turmoil within the country spread, Keller (1987:27) reported the "beginning of alienation, disillusionment and rebellion among Soviet youth, including a growing drug problem." Recent public opinion surveys reveal that crime is ranked second behind price increases in terms of public concerns (Lezhikov, 1995). Russia's Interior Ministry drug chief Alexander Sergeyev recently noted that the number of drug users (among youth) has more than doubled in the past 10 years (Ward, 1996). The drug trade is estimated to top $550 million US a year. This trend is also partially related to a number of social problems, such as the increase in AIDS and other related health concerns.

The three main areas of criminal activity are property crimes (more than 60%), hooliganism and vandalism (25%), and crimes against persons (15%). In accordance with social learning perspective based theories, it is interesting to

Table 14.1 Amount of Juveniles Committed Crimes

Proportion of Juveniles Committed Crimes and having been Convicted in Russian Empire (1874-1912)

Years	Number of convicted	Juveniles (in the total amount of convicted), %
1874	54 934	16,5
1875	52 548	16,2
1876	55 241	15,7
1877	55 787	16,8
1878	57 911	17,4
1879	64 139	17,4
1880	69 867	17,1
1881	75 069	17,4
1882	73 509	17,0
1883	72 706	17,1
1884	78 164	16,6
1885	82 277	16,0
1886	91 315	15,5
1887	97 522	15,9
1888	93 045	16,3
1889	94 783	16,1
1890	110 792	16,7
1891	102 933	17,1
1892	112 878	16,9
1893	105 085	17,5
1894	92 927	17,8
1895	101 161	-
1896	99 495	19,8
1897	106 387	18,6
1898	115 257	13,6
1899	126 452	17,4
1900	118 123	18,2
1901	118 754	18,1
1902	119 902	13,0
1903	120 195	18,5
1904	111 389	20,5
1905	101 663	22,1
1906	114 265	21,1
1907	144 143	20,9
1908	150 546	-
1909	175 040	20,2
1910	158 825	-
1911	176 343	20,5
1912	176 898	21,4

Proportion of Juvenile Crimes Committed in Russia (1987-1997)

Years	Total amount of people who committed crimes	Proportion of Juveniles crimes committed, %
1987	969 388	12,1
1988	834 673	15,6
1989	847 577	17,7
1990	897 299	17,1
1991	956 258	16,7
1992	148 962	16,4
1993	1 262 737	16,1
1994	1 441 568	13,9
1995	1 595 501	13,0
1996	1 618 394	11,9
1997	1 372 161	11,8

Characteristics of Criminals in 1999 and 01-02.2000

Period	Total		Dynamics (percent change) %		Proportion in total amount of people committed crimes, %	
	1999	01-02.2000	1999	01-02.2000	1999	01.-02.2000
Number of people committed crimes	1,716,679	265,680	15.9	5.6	100	100
Juveniles (among them)	183,447	27,544	11.3	-1.8	10.7	10.4
Students (among them)	124,407	19,887	19.8	4.7	7.2	7.5

note that more than 75% of all juvenile offences are committed in group or peer settings. For example, among such juveniles, organized begging is widespread. Young children beg in the metro (underground). An elder juvenile who does most of the planning and takes most of the money stolen usually leads them (Minina, 1999).

However, unlike what appears to be the case in many Western countries, the groups tend to be small (i.e., two to three persons) and are considered unstable. The group generally exists for less then three months from the time they begin to commit their crimes. In cities like Moscow, youth gangs, along with Gypsy hustlers, have become a growing concern. In 1994, Curtis Sliwa of the American Guardian Angels organization visited Moscow and suggested that a "criminal mindset" was beginning to emerge among the youth and that perhaps a Guardian Angel Chapter might be established. On the other hand, the more serious offences are generally recognized as being committed by more stable groups who tend to include adults with criminal experience. Nearly one group out of three is mixed (underage with adults). Groups who in recent years have become more organized and sophisticated in nature commit almost half of the group-based crimes.

As indicated in Table 14.1, the proportionate distribution of juvenile crimes varies by the type of crime. Serious crimes only account for around 17% of all youth crime (5% involve murders and 10% assaults), hooliganism accounts for 13% while the majority of juvenile crime involves robberies of personal property. So while the Western media tend to portray crime in Russia as out of control, the profile is not dissimilar from many Western countries. Similar views were expressed at the international conference on juvenile justice in Central and Eastern Europe held in Glasgow in 1996 (Asquith, 1996). It should also be remembered that under the old regime, crime was seldom acknowledged and official statistics essentially did not exist.

The number of persons committing crimes between the ages of 14 and 17 were: in 1989, 490,995; in 1990, 505,211; in 1991, 525,788; in 1992, 626,227; in 1995, 209,777.The proportion of juveniles in the general number of offenders: in 1989, 17.7%; in 1990, 17.1%; in 1991, 16.7%; in 1992, 16.4%; in 1995, 12.0%; and in 1999, 10,7%.[2] These rates, although increasing, tend to be lower than those in most Western countries. However, consistent with many Western countries Russia has been witness to more and more younger juveniles (ages 14 to 15) becoming involved in delinquent behavior.

Since the early 1970s and the collapse of the former Soviet Union, there has been a constant, but not dramatic, increase in juvenile delinquency as well as adult crime in Russia (Asquith, 1996). There has also been a marked increase in recidivism rates (see Table 14.2).

While the concept of juvenile crime in Russia is legally prescribed by law as encompassing youth between the ages of 14 and 18, as is the case in most countries, the nature and extent of delinquency varies by age. Delinquency

Table 14.2 Types of Crimes Committed by Juveniles

Proportion of Crimes committed by Juveniles for 1991

All crimes	16.4 %
Serious crimes	17.0
Robberies and burglaries	29.0
Theft of state property	24.0
Theft of personal property	32.2
Hooliganism	13.0
Stolen vehicles/means of transportation	30.5

patterns and trends differ according to social status, emotional maturity, cognitive development, and level of education (see Box 14.5). In the 1970s and 1980s, youths between the ages of 14 and 15 constituted not more than 20% of juvenile cases, of which only 5% involved females. However, between 1985 and 1995, there has been a 75% increase in offences by young females and their representation in the juvenile justice system. And by 1995, the rate of juvenile delinquent activity among females was growing one and a half to two times that of delinquency rates for young males where the ratio of males to female offenders is approximately 9:1. Such trends have been expressed in other contributions to this text. Based on the available data, it would appear to suggest that the trends observed since 1991 will continue to increase.

EXPLANATIONS OF DELINQUENCY

At the turn of the century, explanations for delinquency were based on writings of Marx and Engels. They were developed in Russia by Vladimir Ilyich Lenin (1870-1924). He wrote that criminality was caused by conflicting forces of socio-economic competition. And, notwithstanding the reliability of official crime statistics of the time, official crime data supported this assertion. Between 1940 and 1975, as Russian Communism became the norm, crime declined 44.1% and 18% between 1958 and 1975 alone (Borodin, 1980).

In Russia, the causes of juvenile delinquency would appear to encompass many of the same social-negative phenomena and processes that determine crime in general. Among Russian scholars it is generally felt that the etiological features of juvenile delinquency are connected to general "criminogenic" processes, phenomena, and situations that are primarily related to socialization factors. It is believed these factors play a direct role in the motivation for youth crime. Some of the specific factors that have been studied include:

1. Negative influences in the family. In 30% to 40% of juvenile cases, problems of alcoholism, abusive family settings, and parents who themselves engaged in illicit activities was present.
2. Difficult financial position and/or break-ups in the family.
3. Negative family and/or educational influences.
4. Adult offenders influence the younger population to commit crime. In approximately 30% of criminal cases juveniles are recruited by adults to commit the crimes. The penalty for a juvenile is less serious than that for an adult. Pickpocketing is a common example in which this takes place.
5. The effects of the rapid social and economic changes, as well as some of the technological changes.

6. Aggressive feelings, feelings of low self-esteem, or suffering from a sense of despair over the uncertainty in their future. These are dangerous symptoms of a deterioration in the moral and psychological state of society.

7. The significant "loss of moral guidance through the former **Young Communist League**, the Young Pioneers and other youth political organizations" (Asquith, 1996: 11).

Collectively, the recent dramatic economic, social, technological, and political changes in Russia have created a sense of **anomie**. Russian society has become marked by a lack of cohesion, cooperation, and consensus as to what is in the best interests of the people and the country. This disparity of goals and means creates strain, as described in Robert Merton's work on strain theory (Einstadter and Henry, 1995). In addition, there has been a general decline in moral standards, and an increasing number of children (juveniles) are growing up without morals. Together, these conditions may create a disenchanted environment. As can be seen in Table 14.3, juvenile crime has increased at a staggering rate. Amongst the adult population, organized crime and black market activity has not only spread throughout Russia, but has also

**Table 14.3 Growth of Juvenile Crime 1971-1990
(increases are in comparison with 1971)**

Rate of juvenile crime per 100,000: Youths 14-17

Year	Rate	Percent Change
1971	549	
1975	628	+14
1976	623	+13
1977	615	+12
1981	787	+43
1985	1017	+85
1986	978	+78
1987	965	+76
1990	1320	+140

**Crimes committed by Juveniles and with their participation in
1999 and 01.-02.2000**

Period	Amount	Dynamics (percent change) %	Proportion of investigated crimes, %
1999	208,813	10.0	9.6
01-02.2000	31,165	-.5.1	9.2

spread to foreign countries like the United States and other countries covered in this collection (generally, see Goodwin, 1995; Raine and Cilluffo, 1994).

Although limited, a number of Russian studies have examined the relationship between juvenile crime and socio-environmental factors related to juvenile crime. Some of these include:

1. neglect and/or absence of proper parental supervision and support;
2. neglect of future victims, which promotes situation for crimes (in 20% to 50% of cases negative behavior, such as drug use, alcohol abuse, and escape from the home, precedes the crime);
3. lack of constructive employment opportunities;
4. lack of organized leisure activities;
5. limited opportunity to educate potential offenders about the law;
6. lack of accountability for criminal behavior; and
7. the proportionate increase in the number of youths demonstrating retarded intellectual and cognitive development as a result of disorganization in the family and in the system of education.

A final explanation that has been put forth, from a North American perspective, is that youth crime in Russia is the unfortunate consequence of the rapid emergence of capitalism and democracy (Erlanger, 1996; Goodwin, 1995). Although crime rates in Russia are still significantly lower than those in the United States, certain types of criminal activity have grown significantly since 1991—in particular mafia-style gangs, racketeering, and organized crime. Goodwin describes the current scene as resembling "gangland America of the 1930s." Erlanger (1996) further notes that the Criminal Code had not kept up with the rapid social changes. The 1960 Code was a much revised and patched together document based on a social system that considered private business criminal, and remained full of contradictory or ambiguous laws. It is hoped that the new code will enable authorities to better respond to the changing social and criminal scene in Russia.

RECIDIVISM

Prior to 1991, the Soviet state claimed that only a small percentage of juveniles became criminals, and depending on the region, recidivism varied between 3% and 10%. This was considerably lower than the rate for many Western countries. Part of the "success" was attributed to the ability to enforce communism and supposedly eliminate misery and the indigence of labourers.

While the juvenile problem has increased dramatically in recent years, official statistics indicate that recidivism rates among juveniles are less than that among adults (their share among the general number of recidivists during the period from 1986 to 1993 fluctuated between 5% to 11.8%). However, it is important to note that since the majority of delinquent acts are committed by older youth, subsequent acts are conducted after the age of 18. Hence, they no longer qualify as juveniles. We believe however that the "true" rate of recidivism is in fact quite high. In addition, a number of legal and judicial practices, such as adjournment of sentence, suspended sentence, sentencing without proper explanation, and providing intensive control for behaviour, influence recidivism. However, informed use of the discretionary options has been shown to have a positive impact on reducing the risk of recidivism.

THE YOUTH JUSTICE PROCESS

In the Ministry of the Internal Affairs, a special service for predicting juvenile infringement of law exists. This service collects information about the minors who are disposed to deviant behaviour and their families. Workers in the service are generally persons with a teaching background or training in psychology. They carry out contacts with registered juveniles and juveniles without a dwelling (i.e., homeless), and then attempt to provide education and housing for them.

As noted earlier, the administrative procedures for handling juvenile offenders are defined by the general rules spelled out in the Criminal Legal Procedure Code (**CLPC**) of Russia; in particular, Chapter 32 of CLPC, which defines the legal rights and responsibilities of minors (i.e., ages 14 to 18). There are also special rules for procedure on crimes committed by persons under 18. These are found in Articles 391 through 402 of the CLPC.

The formal order of procedure is influenced by the age and social-psychological peculiarities of the youth. The procedures are intended to provide due consideration for the rights of a youth and reflect a concern for educative or welfare measures. These peculiarities help to promote a greater sense of fairness and due process when determining criminal responsibility.

Until recently in Russia, the accused did not have a right to legal counsel. Under the old system, defence council only became involved after the preliminary investigation was complete. And while this has changed, neither the police nor the Crown is required to inform the young offender of a right to counsel. Such a practice reflects the accusatorial process of Russian justice, and the model has been subject to abuse and corruption throughout the justice system (see Figure 14.1).

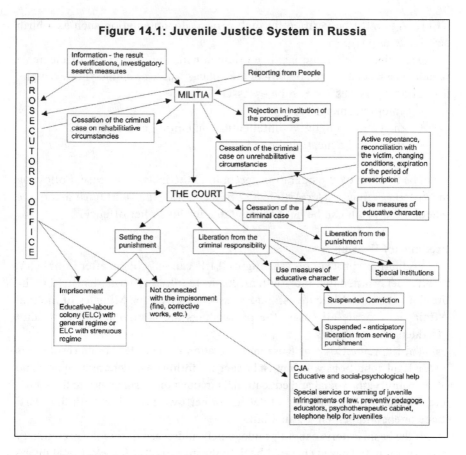

Figure 14.1: Juvenile Justice System in Russia

Initial Contact

As noted earlier, the Russian model of juvenile justice is based on the **justice model**. Once a youth has been referred to court, a preliminary hearing is conducted in order to ascertain jurisdiction and procedural arrangements (see Figure 14.1). These procedures are strictly formal. With changes in 1991, judges are no longer nominated by local Party officials, but may be appointed after serving at least five years in the legal profession and must be at least 25 years of age (Constitution Art. 119). Unlike most Western countries, appointments can be extended for up to 10 years.[4] The objective of the initial contact is to establish the facts about the offender in order to assess whether there is a case for criminal responsibility. In order to do so, three specific procedures must be followed.

First, the exact age of the minor must be established. This is necessary in order to determine which legal procedures can be applied under Article 5 of the

CLPC. Age must be verified through official documentation such as a birth certificate or passport.

After the youth's age has been determined, the second set of elements which must be considered pertain to the youth's "state of being." For example, the following issues have to be assessed:

- emotional maturity;
- the youth's cognitive, intellectual, and moral character; and
- living and educational conditions.

The final set of considerations pertains to the facts of the case. Following the criteria defined under Article 392 of the CLPC, the court must determine whether the youth can be held accountable for his or her offence.

Preliminary Hearing

Preliminary procedures (see Figure 14.1) can only begin after initial contact has determined that the youth meets the required criteria identified in the previous section. While investigators associated with the Ministry of Internal Affairs investigate all cases, the proceedings are similar to those of adult offenders.

The Supreme Court of Russian Federation is very clear in its resolutions on the legal conditions which must be met and followed in determining criminal responsibility: the social and educational circumstances surrounding the youth, and whether the youth acted under his or her own accord or with the assistance or encouragement of an adult.

If the basic criteria cannot be adequately addressed during the preliminary investigation, the case is handed back to the investigator for additional investigation. Only after the court is satisfied that it has sufficient evidence upon which to assess the implications of the alleged crime will the case be allowed to come before the court. In order to ensure that the essential court conditions can be met, inquiry agencies (the local militia office for preventing juvenile infringements of law) are used. The investigators for the agencies are qualified professionals (see Box 14.6). Besides inspectors of the local militia office for preventing juvenile infringements of law, preventive pedagogues (teachers) working in the system of the Ministry of Education, social workers of the Ministry of Social Defence, and volunteers from the CJA may all participate in the preliminary inquiry.

In accordance with Article 393 of the CLPC, the investigator can recommend that the young offender be detained while awaiting trial. This option can only be applied to serious offences. However, if the investigator pronounces such a judgment, the presiding judge or crown prosecutor must question the minor to ensure that the decision to detain the minor is in the best interests of

---

Box 14.6: Delinquency and Social Control in Russia

The share of juvenile delinquency during 1989 to 1995 fluctuated from 17.7% to 12%. Rejuvenation of juvenile delinquency by the increase of the share of the younger group of 14 to 15 years old is to be observed. These changes are connected with the dramatic social changes in Russia that have become apparent with the relaxing of social services normally available to minors and a reduction in the social control mechanisms for their behavior, from the family as well as from society in general. Russia's former well-developed educational system has also experienced a breakdown in standards with the fiscal problems of the state. As reflected in the opening quote from Lezhikov, the social and economic conditions correspond with a number of the sociological-based theories of crime and delinquency often found in American literature.

---

both the youth and society at large. Should the recommendation to detain the youth be supported by the court, the minor is entitled to appeal the decision. The appeal must be done in accordance with Article 220 of CLPC. This can take place at any time during the preliminary inquiry or during the court examination.

Because of the special status of juvenile delinquents, there are special provisions (i.e., Article 394 of the CLPC) that allow the minor to be placed under the guardianship of his or her parent(s), a relative, or suitable guardian(s) as recognized by the court. Article 158 provides for the right to a defence and representation. The guardian must state in writing (in arbitrary form) that they recognize their responsibility to supervise the minor and to bring the youth to court as required. The conditions are formally defined in a subpoena provided by the investigator or a senior administrator where the youth attends work or school. While formal in nature, the process does provide for the least restrictive alternative to be used—hence acknowledging the special status afforded young offenders.

The act will receive special attention during the preliminary investigation if it involves the participation of an adult. In an effort to reduce any further influence by the offending adult, the case is processed as quickly as possible. If there is enough evidence to prove that the minor is guilty, they do not charge the adult and minor separately, but together.

Since most minors attend school, a teacher may be asked by the crown and/or defence to participate in questioning a minor who is still under the age of 16. However, as stipulated under Article 397 of the CLPC, a teacher can also be involved during the preliminary inquiry of youth older than 16, but only if the minor is considered to suffer from a disorder that causes distress or a psychological disability—mentally deficient. The teacher has a right, with the permission of the investigator, to not only question the youth but also to comment on the observations made by the investigator. The process of enabling one of the minors' teachers to be involved in the preliminary examination not only helps to ensure continuity but also ensures that all relevant facts are weighed fairly by the crown and defence. The intent is to recognize the special needs of the youth. In this fashion our system reflects elements of the **participatory model** (see Figure 1—Introduction).

Unlike most Western countries, the Russian juvenile justice system does not look favorably on including the expert testimonies of psychologists or psychiatrists during the preliminary stage. This dates back to the strong classical influences that existed prior to the Revolution. However, the presence of legal representation is necessary if there is sufficient evidence to show that the minor is mentally deficient, but not necessarily mentally ill.

One of the inherent legal rights juveniles are entitled to (Article 399 of the CLPC) is to have their parent(s) involved in their legal representation. In addition, the investigator may either request the involvement of the parent or deny their participation if there are reasonable grounds to believe that it is necessary for the interests of the minor.

In summary, in keeping with the justice model, the preliminary hearing is a critical element of the legal process. In order to fully establish the facts of the cases, it may be necessary to detain the youth while the facts of the case are being determined. The CLPC focuses on the fact that the juvenile's rights are in need of a particular defence. Therefore, there is a special provision in Chapter 32 of the CLPC that regulates procedures on crimes committed by juveniles, and includes an additional guarantee of their rights and interests.

Trial Process

All juvenile cases are heard in a general court of law and require the participation of the youth and his or her lawyer. Unless it is felt that the case could have a negative impact on the youth, all juvenile cases are heard in open court. In addition, the court has a right to remove the minor from court when evidence, which according to the defence or crown could have a negative effect on the minor, is presented. For example, if the question of whether the parents need to be subpoenaed for legal representation or the minor's educational and emotional status is being discussed. Therefore, while resembling a justice model, the trial process allows for mitigating circumstances—somewhat analogous to the *parens patriae* philosophy found in many Western juvenile justice systems.

As of 26 December 1996, the Russia Federation Council approved a constitutional law stipulating that the Russian president will appoint judges and that all courts must be funded entirely by the federal budget.

Trial Provisions

Unlike Western countries but similar to most Central and Eastern European countries, Russia has no special court for juveniles. The law used to make provisions for possible liberation from criminal responsibility and punishment by referring adult and juvenile cases to the **comrade court**. But since 1985, this measure has not been used because it no longer fits the changing social structure. The public has grown apathetic as it tries to find its way under the new mantle of capitalism and democracy. This has not helped the plight of Russian youth.

As a possible alternative, current laws do provide for the possibility of deferring a convicted juvenile to a public educator, who is trained to provide specialized educative support, similar to child-care workers or probation officers found in many other countries. The law also provides the option for juvenile cases to be tried either in common court or by judge and jury. In either case, specific conditions apply.

Before a trial can commence, the court must meet certain criteria. The court must inform the institution or organization where the minor studies or works. They must also inform the CJA regarding the time and place where the case will be tried, and, if not already addressed, ensures that the minor will have representation in court. Once these conditions are in place, then in accordance with the legalistic model of justice, the trial is conducted in an **adversarial** manner (CPC Article 49).

If the minor has no parents, lives alone, or lives with a person who does not qualify as a legal tutor or guardian, the court must appoint a representative from the Guardianship and Trusteeship Agency to legally represent them. Such representation is considered necessary in order to protect the needs and rights of the minor. However, if such representation can be thought to have a negative bearing on the case, Article 399 of the CPC provides conditions that can exclude such participation. And although there are provisions to protect against the violation of the needs and rights of a young offender, in practice, the rights of juveniles are not always protected.

After hearing all the evidence (interrogation of the accused, estimation of written and material evidence, experts' resolutions, pleadings, hearing of the last word of the accused, and withdrawing to the consultative room to pass the sentence), the court can then make its legal decision and pass sentence (see Box 14.7).

In summary, since 1991 Russian law has made provisions to protect the rights of young people within the juvenile justice system and the legal system. Collectively, the new provisions reflect many of the recommendations of the major international agreements, ranging from the Beijing Rules to the Euro-

Box 14.7: The Role of the Investigator

Investigators, who investigate cases of juvenile crimes, have a particular specialization. The investigator holds investigative actions, interrogation, and conformations, brings an accusation, decides whether to send the case to the court or to the CJA, draws up the indictment, which is approved by the prosecutor and, together with the criminal case, is sent to the court.

pean Convention on Human Rights. Unfortunately, when one examines how juvenile cases are in fact dealt with, juvenile delinquents' rights and needs do not always take priority during the trial process.

Selection of Punishment

Law, as having a range of dispositional discretion, defines sentencing practices. The range of dispositions can be found in the relevant sections of the Criminal Code. Before passing sentence, the presiding judge takes into consideration the minor's character and the extent of public danger that resulted from the crime. The judge weighs these facts in determining the severity of punishment deemed necessary to ensure the offender recognizes his or her responsibility. The general procedural guidelines for sentencing are defined under Article 37 of the CC.

The sentencing of minors is further affected by the general provision of Article 38 of the CC, which requires that the youth's personality and character be considered in the sentencing process (see Box 14.6). The actual list of punishments, excluding the conditions and dimensions of its fixing, can be found in Articles 21 through 23 of the CC. The range of punishments include: custody, correctional work without imprisonment (e.g., community service work), fine, absolute discharge, entrusting a duty to redress committed harm (e.g., victim reconciliation), confiscation of personal property thought to interfere with the rehabilitation process, deprivation of the ranks, and—as an exclusive punishment—capital punishment. However, the disposition must fit both the crime and individual's character. Therefore, in some circumstances certain punishments cannot be applied, for example, discharge from office or deprivation of the ranks. Furthermore, in accordance with the principles of "due process" and recognizing the special status of minors, Russian law recognizes that some measures should not be considered justifiable forms of punishment for minors. For example, under Article 23 Part 2 of the Criminal Code, capital punishment cannot be used against persons under the age of 18, and Article 24 stipulates that a minor cannot be incarcerated for more than 10 years. There are no exceptions to this stipulation.

Finally, even though youth custody is still regularly used, Russian officials acknowledge the negative effects of imprisoning juveniles, and this has prompted some initiatives to more custodial based alternatives, such as labour colonies, as well as develop measures that reflect Recommendation No. R(87) 20 from the Council of Europe and other international guidelines (Asquith, 1996).

Labour/Penal Colonies

As noted above, the practice of alternative sanctions is gaining acceptance among Russian judges. The court has the legal right to place the young offender in a correctional institution as an alternative to prison (see Box 14.8), where they are educated and taught about the workforce. Other administrative measures could include community hours or fine payments. Article 63 of the CC provides for the use of such sanctions as long as the minor is not considered a serious public risk, and if it is believed that the youth could be re-educated. These measures are not punishment, they do not involve convictions, and they are sizably milder than conventional measures of punishment. Essentially, these measures are the same as those that are used by the CJA. However, if the court feels that correction through re-education is not viable, then incarceration may be used to protect society. In such cases the youth is not only considered a risk to society, but he or she has not expressed any sense of remorse.

As is the case in many Western countries, juvenile offenders serve their sentences separately from adults. They are sent to educational-labour colonies (also used in the Ukraine) specifically intended for minors under Article 24 of the CC. Males charged for the first time are regularly incarcerated while first-time female offenders are generally sent to re-educational colonies. Repeat male offenders are kept in a higher security prison than are first-time offenders.

For first-time offenders incurring a sentence of less than three years, the court is obliged under Article 401(2) of the CPC to examine the possibility of substituting incarceration with an alternative sanction. In accordance with

---

Box 14.8: Educational-Labour Colonies

Educational-labour colonies represent an alternative to imprisonment for juveniles. There are two basic provisions: 1) educational-labour colonies with a general regime similar to the work camps found in North America and recently introduced in Western Australia, and 2) the educational-labor colonies with their intensive regimes—similar to the boot camps more commonly found in the United States (see Ch. 18). The first is for serving the punishments of juvenile males who are convicted to imprisonment for the offence, that is, not "heavy" for the first-time offenders, and all convicted juvenile females. The second type of labour programs is used only for convicted males who either were imprisoned before or who had been sent to the former type of educational-labor colony and had violated claims (requirements) of the regime.

Article 46(1) of the CC, the court is obliged to consider the minor's personality and ability to benefit from re-education before resorting to incarceration. Should the court decide that imprisonment or correctional work is the appropriate sanction, the court may substitute probation as a form of a suspended sentence under Article 44 of the CC.

Even though the Russian model of juvenile justice is largely based on the justice model, the agents of the court recognize the importance of providing alternative preventative sanctions whenever possible. Considerable emphasis is placed on understanding the causes and conditions that prompted the crime in the first place. Consistent with the various international declarations for the rights of children, formal sanctions are used as a last resort if the range of alternatives can be argued to not be in the best interests of society. Hence, the prosecutorial and sentencing processes are very individualized for minors and, as stated earlier, the primary objective is to focus on crime prevention through re-educative dispositions.

THE FUTURE: A NEED FOR REFORM

Since the dramatic economic, political, and social changes in Russia after 1991, the problem of juvenile delinquency has become more evident. The shift from old Russian traditions is still taking place, as many of the legal and political directions remain undefined. But the toll of the changes has been reflected in a general increase in the delinquency rates. The pattern and trends of delinquency are similar to those being experienced by Hungary (see Ch. 8) and other Central and Eastern European countries (see Asquith, 1996). This is in spite of the fact that there has been an increased acceptance of Western ideas on how to address delinquency both socially and politically.

Over the past few years, Russia has experienced:

- An increase in the rate delinquency. For example, in 1999 there were 208,813 officially recorded juvenile crimes. This represented 9.6% of all known crimes. The numbers represent a 10% increase since 1990.
- An increase in the number of violent crimes committed by minors.
- An increase in the number of minors re-offending.
- An increase in group-related juvenile activity, as well as an increase in juvenile crimes involving so called "mixed" groups (i.e., adults and minors) and organized criminal groups—especially in the area of the drug trade.
- An increase in the number of minor crimes involving the use of alcohol and drugs.
- The establishment of more juvenile courts in a number of states.

Given the recent trends in juvenile crime in Russia, it appears that the previous system of social prevention seen under the former Soviet Union has fallen into decay. It is necessary to address this growing problem. The old punitive prevention policies must be replaced with programs and legislation that can strike a balance between accountability and addressing the needs of the minor and the family. These measures should be based on interdisciplinary and interagency approaches that are able to address the social and economic factors that contribute to the delinquency problem. In accordance with the UN Beijing Rules (see Box 1—Introduction) and other major international related agreements, our juvenile justice system needs to find a balance between a strict legalistic justice model and a welfare model, that recognizes the special needs of young persons and has been recommended as the "universal" model for all countries. In partial response to this need, a special inquiry into the relationship between family problems and delinquency was initiated in 1995.

During the mid-1970s in Russia, the scientific trend of "**Family Criminology**" began to emerge (see D. Shestakov, 1996). The perspective considers in detail the connection between family problems and crime, and beginning in 1995 the State Duma initiated a project known as "On Prevention of Family Violence." This legal reform project also includes a project concerning the so-called "family courts," where cases of juvenile delinquency are supposed to be considered. The purpose of the project is to help identify and address the needs of children at risk, as well as protect their rights and interests. However, in light of the fact that a significant number of delinquent offences are related to negative social conditions within the family, consideration must be given to the establishment of special "family courts." These courts could focus on the greater social issues while balancing legal concerns of criminal, civil, and family matters. It is anticipated that such courts will be established after the final results of the "On Prevention of Family Violence" project.

SUMMARY

The future of juvenile justice in Russia is likely to undergo major changes as the face of Russian society continues to evolve. What may appear to be positive reform policies to outsiders have been met with mixed reactions in the Soviet Union. Newfound freedoms (e.g., speech, assembly, and multi-candidate elections) are in sharp contrast to Russia's long history of authoritarian structures. The transition has not gone smoothly due to long suppressed inter-ethnic fights, labour turmoils, and soaring crime rates. In such a climate it hardly appears likely that progressive social reform for juvenile justice will be quick in coming. However, we are optimistic, and any such changes must be based on a sound examination of the facts and trends.

The changes should also emphasize the importance of prevention, rather than relying on our antiquated punitive practices of crime control. In order to accomplish some of these broad goals, there is a need for more reliable information, such as self-report and victimization data. And now that we are able to exchange information more freely with other countries and collaborate on the development of appropriate measures for addressing delinquency and other juvenile issues, it would be beneficial to examine and compare our needs and goals with those of other countries—especially those whose history may have followed a comparable path to that of Russia. In his concluding remarks, Asquith (1996: 15) states that Russia, along with its neighbours should consider a "centralized information source of all matters relating to juvenile delinquency" that could be used to guide legislative reforms and identify alternative sanctions.

Dmitry A. Shestakov (Doctor of Law, Professor of the Department of Criminal Law and Criminology of the Law Faculty of the St.-Petersburg State University, president of the International Criminology Club by the Law Faculty of the St.-Petersburg State University, actual member of the Academy of social sciences, criminologist, and writer) was born 2 January 1949, in St.-Petersburg. He is known as a founder of the Family School of Criminology, a branch of general Russian Criminology. In addition, he has developed nontraditional views on crime and social control; introduced alternative explanations for abolishing capital punishment in Russia, as well as called for the removal of the principle of retaliation for Russian criminal law; and has raised the issue of political criminology within Russian criminology.

    D. Shestakov has published nearly 180 academic works on criminology, family criminology, and criminal law. In addition, he has written fictional stories that have been published in Russia, England, Germany, Canada, The Netherlands, Poland, and the United States. Some of his works include: *An Introduction into the Criminology of Family Relations* (Leningrad, 1980); *Murder on the Ground of Family Conflict* (Leningrad, 1981), and *Family Criminology* (St.-Petersburg, 1996). D. Shestakov is a responsible editor of collective monographs and an author of the first draft of the Law "On preventing Family Violence."

Natalia D. Shestakova (Master of Law) was born on 11 September 1976, in St.-Petersburg. She graduated from the Law Faculty of the St.-Petersburg State University in 1998. Between January and July of 1999, she conducted research in the University of Leiden (The Netherlands) and during from August to December of 1999, she was involved in research at Indiana University of Pennsylvania in the United States. She is currently completing her doctor dissertation on "Invalidity of transactions" (i.e., fraud) at the Law Faculty of St.-Petersburg State University while working as a lawyer at the Administration of St.-Petersburg. She has several publications in Russia, The Netherlands, and Canada.

HELPFUL WEBSITES
http://eurochild.gla.ac.uk/documents/coe/reports/juvenile_justice//jj&jd%281%29.htm
    Although not specifically oriented to Russia's juvenile justice system, this site was

prepared by Professor Stewart Asquith in 1996 at the University of Glasgow. The document was prepared after a meeting of 13 Central and Eastern European countries (including Russia) who attend a colloquium on juvenile justice. The site offers an excellent overview of juvenile justice and juvenile delinquency from the represented countries.

http://arapaho.nsuok.edu/~dreveskr/rus/html.ssi The Russian Federation site that has numerous links to social, economical, political, and criminal justice information. Although not specific to juvenile justice, this is a rich resource link for students interested in learning more about Russia.

www.mvdinform.ru This site provides some data on crime in Russia, as well as data on juvenile delinquency.

KEY TERMS AND CONCEPTS

Crime control model	Justice model
G. Solntsev	Committee on Juvenile Affairs (CJA)
Young Communist League	CLPC
Comrade court	Adversarial
Labour/Penal colonies	Participatory Model
Family criminology	

STUDY QUESTIONS

1. How has Russia's history influenced the development of juvenile justice? How well have the ideas of socialism been integrated with Western ideas of juvenile justice?
2. Describe the key differences between the former crime control model and the justice model and the recent move towards a participatory model. How well have the transitions been actualized?
3. How do the causes of delinquency in Russia compare with other European countries and other parts of the world?
4. To what extent are the difficulties Russia is experiencing in trying to fulfill its intentions to honor the Beijing Rules and European Convention on Human Rights experienced in other countries? What appear to be primary factors that hinder compliance with the recommendations and standards?
5. What promise does "family criminology" represent for young offenders in Russia? Are there any factors that can be garnered by looking at systems in other countries?

REFERENCES

Russian titles were translated into English for this contribution.

Act of the Supreme Court. (2000). "About the judicial practice on juvenile crime cases." #7.

Asquith, S. (1996). "Juvenile justice and juvenile delinquency in Central and Eastern Europe: A review." (Online—see Web Links, above).

Borodin, S.V. (1980). Soviet Union. In *Justice and troubled children*. V.L. Stewart (Ed.). NY: New York University Press.

Einstadter, W., and S. Henry. (1995). *Criminology theory*. Orlando, FL: Harcourt Brace.

Erlanger, S. (1996). Images of lawlessness distorts Moscow's reality. *CJ Europe,* 6(2): 5-6.

Gaverov, G. (1985). Problems of legislation and judicial practice improving in the field of the application of the measures of educational character to the juveniles. *Problems of Preventive Crimes Improving.* Irkutsk.

Goodwin, T. (1995). Crime in Russia: Bitter fruit of capitalism and democracy. *Synapse,* 34: 1-5.

Hard fortunes of the youth—Who is guilty? (1991). Moscow, Russia.

Juvenile delinquencies and their prevention. (1983). Kazanski University.

Keller, B. (1987). Russia's restless youth. *The New York Times Magazine.* (pp. 14-53).

Lezhikov, G.L. (1995). Russia: Statistical information on crime and its use of crime control. *CJ International* (Online).

Legal problems of preventing delinquency. (1990). Tomsk, Russia.

Miheev, R. (1985). The age: Criminal-law and criminology problems. *Problems of Preventive Crimes Improving*, pp. 3-17.

Minina, S.P. (1999). Juvenile Crime and counteraction. St.-Petersburg.

Peculiarities of the delinquency in different regions and problems of effective preventing of it. (1985). (N/A).

Ponomareu, P.G. (1996). Legal measures against legalization of criminal arrests as means of combating organized crime in Russia. *AJCS Today*, (14)4:1, 3.

Popular Science Journal. *The Youth*, (No. 2. 1992). St. Petersburg.

Primachenok, A. (1990). Improving of the criminal-law system of measures to prevent juvenile delinquency. Minsk, Russia.

Raine, L.P., and F.I. Cilluffo (Eds.). (1994). *Global organized crime: The new empire of evil*. Washington: The Center for Strategic and International Studies.

Russian legislature of 20th century. (1987). Moscow.

Shelly, L. (1980). Policing soviet society: The evolution of state control. *Law and Social Inquiry*, 15(3): 479-520.

Shestakov, D. (1996). *Family criminology*. St. Petersburg.

Sibiryakov, S. (1993). *The children—Delinquency-trouble*. Volgograd, Russia.

Sidorova, V. (1981). Practice of the compulsory measures of an educational character use. *Soviet Justice,* N 7, pp. 9-10.

Some questions of an application of the legislation on juvenile delinquency: An overview of the judicial practice. (1983). *Bulletin of the Supreme Court of the USSR,* N 6, pp. 35-40.

Velchev, A., and G. Moshak. (1990). The minor and delinquency. Kishinev, Russia.

Ward, O. (1996). Use of hard drugs soaring with young rich Russians. *Toronto Star* (Online).

Chapter 15

The Scottish Juvenile Justice System: Policy and Practice

Lesley McAra
Centre for Law and Society
University of Edinburgh

FACTS ON SCOTLAND

Area: 78,470 sq. km. **Major Cities:** Edinburgh (capital city), Glasgow, Dundee, and Aberdeen. **Climate:** Temperate, cool summers and increasingly mild winters. **Economy:** Decline in traditional heavy industry such as mining and steel-making. Main industries currently include electronics, oil, natural gas, chemicals, textiles, clothing, printing, paper, food processing, tourism, banking, and finance. **Population:** At the time of the 1991 census the population stood at 4,962,152 (a census is due to take place in 2001). The number of young people has been declining over the past 20 years: the number of 16 year olds, for example, fell from 95,000 in 1981 to a low of 58,400 in 1993. While there was a slight increase to 66,500 in 1997, numbers are expected to remain between 60,000 to 70,000 over the next decade. **Structure of Government:** Since the Union in 1707 Scotland has been part of the United Kingdom (which also comprises England, Wales, and Northern Ireland). Although governed by the UK Parliament at Westminster between 1707 and 1998, Scotland has always had a separate legal and education system. From 1999 Scotland has had its own Parliament for devolved, domestic matters (including justice, education, and health). For other UK-wide issues it is still subject to the UK Parliament at Westminster. There are currently 32 elected local authorities in Scotland which have responsibility for the administration of *inter alia* education and social work. Unlike many other Parliamentary democracies there is no written constitution. However the European Convention on Human Rights has recently been incorporated into Scots law (*Human Rights Act,* 1998).

"Society is, we believe, seriously concerned to secure a more effective and discriminatory machinery for interventions for the avoidance and reduction of juvenile delinquency."— Kilbrandon, 1964.

A principal aim of comparative criminal justice research is to explore the relationship between the characteristics of different criminal justice systems and the specific cultural contexts within which they are located (see Nelken, 1994, 1997). The Scottish system of juvenile justice provides a useful point of comparison with other Western juvenile justice systems primarily because the distinctive nature of Scottish civic and political culture has enabled the system to resist the trends evident in many other Western systems towards populist punitiveness (see McAra, 1999; McAra and Young, 1997).

The quotation at the beginning of this chapter is particularly apt in the context of the issues which I will be exploring in this chapter. It comes from the report of the **Kilbrandon Committee** set up in the 1960s to review the then existing juvenile justice system. Although written over 30 years ago, it continues to give a flavour of key aspects of Scottish civic culture—in particular the sense of *common-ownership* with regard to the problems posed by youth offending and the continued commitment to the development of effective practice. Aside from a short period during the 1970s and 1980s, the quotation also reflects a recurrent preoccupation of key policy elites that existing structures of juvenile justice are inadequate to the task of reducing offending among children and young people and need to be reformed. Indeed, it is the precise interplay between the concerns of such policy elites and broader political and cultural processes that, I will suggest, determines the precise character of the juvenile justice system at any particular juncture.

This chapter divides into four linked, but quite distinct, sections. The first gives an overview of the development of the Scottish juvenile justice system over the past two centuries and explores the manner in which social, political, and cultural processes have impacted on the evolution of institutions for dealing with troubled and troublesome children. The second section describes the system as it currently operates, the characteristics of cases which go through the system, and the nature of contemporary disposals for child offenders. The third section focuses on empirical data relating to the nature and pattern of offending among young people in Scotland. In addition to data culled from official sources, it draws on the early findings of the Edinburgh Study of Youth Transitions and Crime (The Edinburgh Study) a longitudinal program of research on pathways into and out of offending.[1] The chapter concludes with a review of a number of key issues currently under consideration within the system.

THE DEVELOPMENT OF JUVENILE JUSTICE IN SCOTLAND

While **welfarism** has remained a cornerstone of the Scottish juvenile justice system, debates around the appropriate treatment of child offenders have always been bifurcated between a welfarist perspective (focused on the needs of the individual child) and what may be termed a public interest perspective (focused on what are conceived as broader societal concerns or the concerns of the general public) (see McAra, 1999).

In this section of the chapter it will be suggested that the history of the Scottish juvenile justice system can be divided into three distinct periods, which I have termed the era of punishment, deterrence, and reform; the triumph of welfarism; and the era of protective tutelage. The first of these periods was characterized by a high degree of tension between welfarist and public interest perspectives; during the second period, welfare principles came to dominate institutional responses to offending; by contrast, in the third and most recent period, there has been a resurgence of the public interest perspective and a shift away from a purely child-centred institutional ethos. The system has changed in response both to macro social, economic, and cultural change over the course of the twentieth century and to shifts in the interests of elite groups who have had a key role to play in shaping the policy agenda within Scotland.

Punishment, Deterrence, and Reform: Juvenile Justice in the Nineteenth and Early Twentieth Centuries

Although there is little surviving historical documentation about the emergence of separate institutions for dealing with child offenders in Scotland, that which does exist suggests that developments in the nineteenth and early twentieth centuries paralleled those in England and Wales (see Murphy, 1992; Bruce, 1982; Smout 1972).

As in England and Wales (see Chapter 5), early institutions of juvenile justice emerged in rather a piecemeal way. Key nineteenth-century initiatives were the development of reformatories primarily for offenders, industrial schools for the children of the "perishing classes,"[2] the gradual segregation of children from adults in prison, and the abolishing of transportation for children. Notable Scottish institutions included Dr. Guthrie's Ragged Schools for the poor and destitute in Edinburgh (set up in 1847), William Quarrier's homes for children with special educational and/or behavioral needs (set up in the west of Scotland from 1878), and Canon Jupp's children's homes at Aberlour (instituted in 1875).

These early institutions were characterized by an ambiguity in penal aims between concerns to "rescue" and reform children and also to punish and deter them (see Gelsthorpe and Morris, 1994; Bruce, 1982). This was partly a reflection of the competing and often contradictory sets of interests which underpinned early developments.

Commentators have described these interests as stemming variously from:

1. genuinely philanthropic and often Christian-inspired concerns about the welfare of children;
2. ruling class concerns about the threats posed to social order by the children of the so-called dangerous classes (in particular the urban poor);
3. the requirement to maintain a disciplined and orderly workforce to service the needs of industrial capital;
4. and in the late nineteenth century, social imperialist concerns regarding the physical and moral degeneracy of the children of the urban poor, children who in later years would be expected to form the core of the fighting forces needed to defend and further expand the burgeoning British Empire (see Muncie, 1999; Blanch, 1979; Radzinowicz and Hood, 1986).

These interests themselves have to be understood against a backdrop of broader social, political, and economic change brought about by the full flowering of industrial capitalism and the concomitant process of urbanization. Such processes had a major impact on the nature and function of family life and conceptions of childhood. During the course of the nineteenth century, the family became a more specialized domestic unit, severed from its traditional productive roles under feudalism (see Muncie, 1999). As a direct consequence of the Factory Acts and restrictions on the hours which women and children could work, there was also greater differentiation of roles within the family and the consolidation of childhood as a separate phase requiring special protection and increased parental responsibility (see Aries, 1973; Shorter, 1976; Humphries, 1977; Smelser 1959).

The formal separation of the adult and juvenile justice systems in Scotland and England and Wales occurred in 1908 with the passage of the *Children Act*. As a result of this Act, Sheriff, Burgh, and Justice of the Peace (JP) Courts in Scotland were required to act as juvenile courts on certain days of the week. Although court procedures were modified to try to ensure that children could understand what was happening, no fundamental changes were made to the principles of criminal procedure (see Morris and McIsaac, 1978). It was not until the 1930s that specially constituted juvenile courts staffed by "suitably qualified justices" appeared in Scotland. These courts were enabled by the *Children and Young Persons (Scotland) Act* of 1932 which also imposed a duty on the courts to have regard for the welfare of the child. Only four juvenile courts were ever established[3] and most cases of juvenile offenders continued to be dealt with in Sheriff and Burgh courts.[4] The age of criminal responsibility was set at age eight by the *Children and Young Persons (Scotland) Act* 1937.

These early developments were underpinned by a fundamental ambivalence towards juvenile offenders. On one hand, there was an explicit recognition that the welfare of the child should have a key role to play in decision-making, and many of the disposals available to the courts were reformative in orientation. Both industrial schools and reformatories (renamed Approved Schools in the 1930s), for example, were described in the 1908 *Children Act* as places in which children could be "lodged, *taught*, and fed." The setting up of Borstals in the same year was intended to provide a sentence of between one and three years for young offenders aged between 16 and 21 during which they would be subject to *treatment* and *training*.

On the other hand, many of these disposals were quite punitive in effect. Overcrowding and poor sanitation were common, as were beatings and other severe punishments for relatively minor infractions (see Pinchbeck and Hewitt, 1973; Radzinowicz and Hood, 1986). While the 1908 Act did institute some restrictions on the use of imprisonment for young offenders, this was to ensure that prison did not lose its deterrent effect by being used too soon. Furthermore periods of penal servitude were retained as an incapacitative measure for the "truly depraved and unruly" to minimize their "evil influence" on others. The Act also made provision for the retention of corporal punishment (whipping) as a disposal.

The piecemeal approach to reform continued during the 1930s and in the immediate post World War II era, with only a gradual growth in child-centered services. The 1930s, for example, saw the inauguration of school psychological services and child guidance clinics for children with behavioral difficulties. Additionally, police liaison schemes were instituted in some areas, in which specially trained police officers worked at a community level with young offenders. During the postwar period, the *Children Act* 1948 created local authority children's departments with an "obligation to consider the needs and abilities of children in their care." Legislation was also passed to enable the probation service to supervize juvenile offenders in need of care and control.

Although many of these new initiatives were welfarist in orientation, the juvenile justice system continued to be torn between welfarist and criminal justice imperatives. This was principally because, in the case of offenders, the gatekeeper to many of the new services continued to be criminal justice agencies. The tensions that beset the juvenile court—in particular, between the requirement to look after the needs of the child and to act also as a formal court of law within a predominantly public interest perspective—was one of the precipitating factors for the review of juvenile justice in Scotland conducted by the Kilbrandon committee in the early 1960s. It was this review which laid the ground work for the new **Children's Hearings** System.

The Triumph of Welfarism: 1968 to 1995

The period between 1968 and 1995 can be seen as the high point of welfarism in juvenile justice in Scotland. This is in direct contrast to the system in England and Wales, in which there was a major retreat from welfarist principles (Cavadino and Dignan, 1997).

The primacy of the welfare principle was set in train by the *Social Work (Scotland) Act* 1968. This Act had far reaching consequences for both the adult and juvenile justice systems because it placed social work at the heart of the criminal justice enterprise. The Act abolished the separate probation service in Scotland and handed over to the newly constituted local authority social work departments areas of criminal justice which in other jurisdictions remained the property of criminal justice agencies (see McAra and Young, 1997). Importantly, the Act also abolished the existing juvenile courts and established a new institutional framework for juvenile justice, the Scottish Children's Hearings System, which remains largely in force today.

These structural changes were driven by a coherent vision of criminal justice known as the "Kilbrandon philosophy," named after the chairman of the committee set up to examine the problems of the existing system of juvenile justice in Scotland. It stressed that juvenile offending and other troublesome behaviors should be regarded as manifestations of deeper social and psychological malaise and/or failures in the normal up-bringing process (Kilbrandon Committee, 1964). The overall aim of the new juvenile justice system was to deal with the child's needs, with the best interests of the child to be paramount in decision-making. In order to achieve this, the Kilbrandon Committee recommended that a new tribunal be set up—the Children's Hearing—which was not staffed by experts but by ordinary members of the public. The system (implemented in April 1971) was to be administered by a new official, the Reporter. Procedures were to be informal, with the aim of involving children and their families in the decision-making process (see below for more detailed discussion).

It is important to remember that at the outset, the Crown reserved the right to prosecute children who had committed the most serious offences (such as rape, serious assault, or homicide) in the adult court system. A number of commentators have argued that, although this undermined important aspects of the Kilbrandon ethos, it was a necessary compromise in order to ensure the support of the Crown Office, the judiciary, and the police for the new Hearings System (see Morris and McIsaac, 1978). I would suggest that this compromise is in keeping with the bifurcatory (i.e., between welfare and public interest) tendencies already inherent within the system.

The very different fates of the 1968 *Social Work (Scotland) Act* (fully implemented) and the 1969 *Children and Young Person's Act* (partially implemented) again have to be understood against the backdrop of broader political, social, and penal change. The retreat from welfarism in England and Wales was precipitated by a number of processes including the election of a Conservative government committed to law and order principles, the resistance of key players in the criminal justice system to the main precepts of the Act (in particular magistrates and the police), and finally a growing moral panic about youth crime in the context of a broader penal crisis linked to the decline in faith in rehabilitation and prison overcrowding (see Gelsthorpe and Morris, 1994; Cavadino and Dignan, 1997).

By contrast, in Scotland the new institutions of juvenile justice had the support of key elites within the Scottish Office and the criminal justice system itself. In addition, a concerted media campaign extolling the uniqueness of the new institutions of juvenile justice helped garner public support (see Morris and McIsaac, 1978). However, one of the principal factors marking out Scotland from England and Wales was the distinctive nature of Scottish civic culture which had emerged by the 1960s. This culture stemmed from a strong democratic tradition in key civic institutions, such as the education system and the church, accompanied by a growing dominance of socialist and communitarian principles at the local government level (see McAra, 1999). This civic culture enabled the Scottish justice system to resist the siren voices proclaiming the decline of the rehabilitative and served to shore up and reproduce the predominantly welfare-based penal culture which underpinned both the adult and juvenile justice systems in Scotland during the 1970s and 1980s (see McAra, 1999).

Protective Tutelage: 1995 to 2000

Most of the institutional arrangements set up by the *Social Work (Scotland) Act* remain in force today. However, a number of recent policy developments have arguably laid the groundwork for a third phase of juvenile justice, one that I have termed **protective tutelage**. This new phase of juvenile justice has been characterized by a gradual penetration of public interest discourse into the Hearings System itself. Public interest, however, is now more strongly associated with public protection, individual rights, and risk management than with punishment and deterrence. This phase has also been characterized by a massive increase in the panoply of controls over children and their families, as issues of juvenile justice have become increasingly caught up in the new Labour government's social inclusion and social crime prevention agendas. The effect of this has been a gradual narrowing of the differences between the Scottish and English and Welsh juvenile justice systems.[5]

Penetration of Public Interest Discourse into the Hearings

Signs of change were evident at least as far back as the arrangements for secure accommodation introduced by the *Health and Social Services and Social Security Adjudications Act* (1983). As a result of this Act, the hearings were enabled to require a child to reside in secure accommodation where he or she was unlikely "to injure other persons." There is an implicit acceptance in this section of the Act that issues of public safety can take priority over the best interests of the child, and, as a consequence, secure care can be used as a mechanism for *incapacitation* rather than for addressing need.

The penetration of public interest discourse into the Hearings System was, however, more explicitly marked by a number of the changes introduced by the *Children (Scotland) Act* 1995. The passage of this Act was the culmination of a major review of the Children's Hearings System which occurred in the wake of the Orkney and Fife inquiries (prompted by issues of child protection; see Edwards and Griffiths, 1997) and increased concern about persistent offending (McAra and Young, 1997). This Act enabled the Hearings System to place the principle of public protection above that of the child's best interests in cases where the child presented a significant risk to the public. It also empowered sheriffs to substitute their own decision for that of the panel in disputed (and appealed) cases.

What the first of these developments suggests is that the hearings are being explicitly directed to work within a bifurcated discursive framework: considering public protection questions in high risk (to the public) cases and the welfare needs of the child in low risk and other child protection cases. The second development (the increased powers of the sheriff) indicates a greater concern for the due process rights of children and their families as well as the growing importance accorded to a public interest perspective in the Hearings (see Cleland, 1995).

Social Inclusion and Social Control

The public interest perspective has become even more firmly entrenched within the juvenile justice system as a result of the Labour government's commitment to social inclusion and to social crime prevention strategies. A key aspect of these strategies is to reduce youth crime by promoting safer communities; confronting the causes of crime as they relate to such factors as poor parenting, unemployment, and social isolation; providing support for victims of crime; promoting early intervention prior to the establishment of a pattern of offending; and developing effective programs to assist established offenders to change their behavior. This is exemplified in the policy documents *Partnership for Scotland* (HMSO, 1999) and *Safer Communities in Scotland* (HMSO,

1999) and in the *Invest to Save* pilot projects, in which interventions are to be targeted on at-risk families (see Hogg, 1999 for an overview).

At one level, these policies do display a continued commitment to welfare values, in particular through their emphasis on the promotion of behavioral change and the integration of offenders into the community. However, they are being driven as much by a community and victim-centered ethos as the child-centered ethos which characterized the system between 1968 and the mid 1990s. On the other hand, the effect of these policies may be to increase both formal and informal mechanisms of social control. Within the ambit of these policies, children identified as being at risk of offending are likely to be subject to high levels of scrutiny and surveillance, as will their families and the communities in which they live. It is in these ways that the Scottish system is beginning to reflect the recent changes in the English and Welsh juvenile justice systems wrought by the *Crime and Disorder Act* (1998) and early intervention initiatives such as the *On Track Multiple Interventions* programme (HMSO, 1998) (see Chapter 5 in this volume).

The drive towards protective tutelage and the narrowing of the differences between Scotland and England and Wales has arisen out of a number of complex processes. Firstly, the election of a Labour government in 1997 brought in an administration which was more in tune with Scottish political and civic culture than the previous Conservative administration had been. The emphasis on community safety and community participation, for example, is broadly in keeping with communitarian values. As such, it provides a generally acceptable framework on which to reconstruct key elements of penal policy. Secondly, the process of devolution has facilitated what has been termed "joined up government," more specifically, the development of an integrated policy strategy exemplified by the gradual elision between the social inclusion and the youth justice agendas. Thirdly, changes have been precipitated by a loss of faith among key elites (in particular the judiciary, the police, and central government) in the effectiveness of the Children's Hearings System for dealing with persistent offenders (as indicated in the research findings of Hallet *et al.*, 1998; and McAra, 1998).

The shift towards protective tutelage also has to be understood against the backdrop of more macro social, economic, and cultural change. A number of commentators have argued that western penal systems are undergoing profound change in response to the social and economic processes associated with late modernity, in particular the rise of the risk society, globalization, and the accompanying loss of state sovereignty (see Douglas, 1992; Garland, 1996; O'Malley, 1992). The incursion of the risk discourse into crime control and penal practice has led to more rigorous policing of both socially included and excluded groups, accompanied by a shift away from rehabilitation to the management of potentially dangerous populations (Lianos, 2000; Bauman, 2000; Pratt, 2000). Moreover, commentators such as Garland and Rose, suggest that advanced liberal societies are no longer able to sustain their role as the principal provider of security within their own territorial boundaries and, as a consequence, increasingly devolve responsibility for crime control and community safety onto active individuals and communities themselves (so-called "responsibilization strategies") (see Rose, 1999; Garland, 1996). Some commentators have linked this devolution of responsibility to the incursion of risk into social discourse. Within a risk society, individuals perceived as rational subjects have the ability to become "skilled and knowledgeable about crime prevention and crime risks" and thereby are able to assume responsibility for aspects of crime control which formerly fell firmly within the ambit of the state (see O'Malley, 1992, 1996).

Scotland was initially resistant to some of these penal trends, due to the strength and influence of elite policy networks and to the characteristics of Scottish civic culture, which continued to valorize community integration and mutual support in the face of increased polarization and marginalization (see McAra, 1999). Risk management and responsibilization strategies were reconstructed into core components of effective practice with offenders. At the beginning of the twenty-first century, this appears to be changing, and Scotland is now embracing a more fragmented and self-contradictory penal discourse, in which notions of public protection and individual rights and responsibilities, together with community dynamics, have increasingly come to challenge, rather than complement, the welfare ethos. A key focus of this new discourse has, of course, been youth crime.

To summarize: a consistent feature of juvenile justice policy has been the manner in which debates have been bifurcated between a welfare perspective and public interest perspective. The trend in recent years has been for the public interest perspective to penetrate more deeply into the aspects of the system, which (at least since the instigation of the Hearings System) had been the sole preserve of welfarism. The changing character of the system has been shaped both by broader social, political, and economic changes and by the nature of the key interest groups who at any one juncture have influence or, indeed, control over the policy agenda.

Having set out the history and development of juvenile justice in Scotland, we can now turn to a more detailed description of the system as it operates today.

The Structure and Operation of the Juvenile Justice System

The Children's Hearings System

The types of cases dealt with by the Children's Hearings System and the range of decisions made can be seen from Figure 15.1. This shows the numbers of cases that passed through the system in 1996/97 (the latest year for which published statistics are available) and it also usefully illustrates the various stages of the system.

The Reporter

Under the Children's Hearings System, children who have offended or are in need of care or protection are referred to the Reporter. While anyone can refer a case to the Reporter, in practice most referrals come from the police (72% in 1996/97), with a smaller number of cases being referred by the social work department, the procurator fiscal (prosecution) service, or from schools.

Since the implementation of the *Local Government etc. (Scotland) Act* in 1994, administration relating to the role of the Reporter has been centralized and all Reporters are now employed by the Scottish Children's Reporter Administration. Reporters are not required to be legally qualified and may have a background in such fields as social work or education (see Edwards and Griffiths, 1997).[6]

The task of the Reporter is to investigate referrals and on the basis of the evidence decide whether there is a prima-facie case that at least one of the grounds for referral to a Hearing has been met *and* that the child is in need of compulsory measures of care. As can be seen from Figure 15.1 the majority of referrals result in no further action (59% in 1996/97), although a small proportion may be referred for informal advice or supervision to the social work department or to a police juvenile liaison officer.

Grounds for Referral

There are currently 12 grounds on which a case may be referred to a Hearing as set out in the *Children (Scotland) Act* 1995 (see Box 15.1). These grounds are principally concerned with the child as being at risk of harm from others (through, for example, lack of parental care or living in the same household as a victim or perpetrator of child sexual abuse) and with the child's behavior (through, for example, offending, truanting from school, being beyond control of any relevant person, or the misuse of drugs, alcohol, or volatile substances).

In order for a Hearing to proceed, the child and the parents must accept the grounds for referral. For children referred on offence grounds, this means admitting guilt. Where the grounds are disputed, the case will be referred to

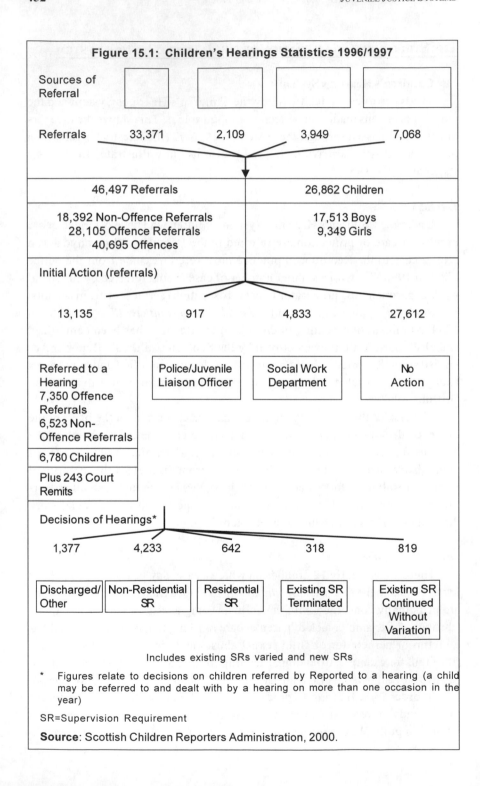

Figure 15.1: Children's Hearings Statistics 1996/1997

Sources of Referral

Referrals   33,371   2,109   3,949   7,068

46,497 Referrals	26,862 Children
18,392 Non-Offence Referrals 28,105 Offence Referrals 40,695 Offences	17,513 Boys 9,349 Girls

Initial Action (referrals)

13,135   917   4,833   27,612

Referred to a Hearing 7,350 Offence Referrals 6,523 Non-Offence Referrals	Police/Juvenile Liaison Officer	Social Work Department	No Action

6,780 Children

Plus 243 Court Remits

Decisions of Hearings*

1,377   4,233   642   318   819

Discharged/Other	Non-Residential SR	Residential SR	Existing SR Terminated	Existing SR Continued Without Variation

Includes existing SRs varied and new SRs

*   Figures relate to decisions on children referred by Reported to a hearing (a child may be referred to and dealt with by a hearing on more than one occasion in the year)

SR=Supervision Requirement

Source: Scottish Children Reporters Administration, 2000.

> ## Box 15.1: Grounds for Referral *Children (Scotland) Act* 1995
>
> The child:
> - is beyond the control of any relevant person;
> - is falling into bad associations or is exposed to moral danger;
> - is likely to suffer unnecessarily or be seriously impaired in his (sic) health or development due to lack of parental care;
> - is a child in respect of whom any of the offences mentioned in Schedule 1 of the *Criminal Procedure (Scotland) Act* 1995 have been committed;
> - is or is likely to become a member of the same household as a child in respect of whom any of the above Schedule 1 offences have been committed;
> - is or is likely to become a member of the same household as a person who has committed any of the above offences;
> - is or is likely to become a member of the same household as a person in respect of whom an offence under Sections 1 to 3 of the *Criminal Law (Consolidation) (Scotland) Act* 1995 (incest and intercourse with a child by a step-parent or person in position of trust) has been committed by a member of that household;
> - has failed to attend school regularly without reasonable excuse;
> - has committed an offence;
> - has misused alcohol or any drug, whether or not a controlled drug within the meaning of the *Misuse of Drugs Act* 1971;
> - has misused a volatile substance by deliberately inhaling its vapour other than for medicinal purposes; and
> - is being provided with accommodation by a local authority under Section 25 or is the subject of a parental responsibilities order obtained under Section 86 of this Act, and in either case his behavior is such that special measures are necessary for his adequate supervision in his interest or the interests of others.

the Sheriff Court for a proof hearing. This follows the Kilbrandon recommendation that adjudication on the facts of case should be separated from the disposal of a case.

The Hearing

The Hearing itself is a tribunal consisting of three members (including at least one woman and one man) drawn from the Children's Panel for the particular local government area. Members of the Children's Panel are volunteers and should be selected from a wide range of occupations, social backgrounds, and neighborhoods. The representativeness of panels has been a matter of concern over many years, the evidence until recently suggesting that women, older people, and the middle class were over-represented (see Reid, 1998; Hallet et al., 1998).

The overall task of the Hearing is to decide whether compulsory measures of care are necessary. The *Children (Scotland) Act* 1995 has identified three main principles on which such decisions should be based:[7]

- the welfare of the child throughout his childhood should be the paramount consideration (s.16(1));
- taking account of the age and maturity of the child, the Hearing should give the child the opportunity to express his views if he wishes and have regard to these views (s.16[2]); and
- no supervision requirement or order shall be made unless the Hearing consider that it would be better for the child that their requirement or order be made than none should be made at all (s.16[3]).

As was noted, the Act also enables the Hearing to make a decision which is not consistent with the welfare principle where it is necessary to protect the public from serious harm (s.16[5]).

Where compulsory measures of care are considered necessary, the Hearing can impose a residential or non-residential supervision requirement, both of which ensure statutory social work involvement. The Hearing may also specify what this supervision should entail (see below). As indicated in Figure 15.1, the most common outcome of a Hearing is the imposition of a non-residential supervision requirement (60% of disposals in 1996/97).

Statistics show that in most years a higher proportion of non-offence referrals receive supervision requirements than offence referrals. In 1996/97, for example, just over 80% of both boys and girls referred on non-offence grounds received a supervision requirement in contrast to just over half of those referred on offence grounds (SCRA 2000). Meanwhile, supervision requirements normally last up to one year, but are subject to review and can be extended. Indeed in 1996/7 most children who were subject to review had their supervision requirement continued.

Age of Children Dealt with by the Hearings System

The majority of children dealt with by the Hearings System are under the age of 16.[8] However, children can be kept in the system until the age of 18 through the extension of supervision requirements. In practice, most offenders between the ages of 16 and 18 are dealt with in the adult criminal justice system, although courts do have the power to remit such cases to the Hearings System for advice and /or disposal. As indicated in Figure 15.1, there were only 243 court remits in 1996/97; this represents less than one-quarter of one percent of court disposals given to young adult offenders. Research evidence suggests that Sheriffs consider the Hearings System as too soft an option for the majority of 16 to 17 year olds and will only remit cases in which the welfare element far outweighs the seriousness of the offence (McAra, 1998). Moreover, the Hearings System itself seems reluctant to retain 16 and 17 year olds, with most supervision requirements being terminated once children reach their sixteenth birthday (Waterhouse et al., 1999).

An evaluation of the Hearings System conducted by Waterhouse et al. (1999) indicates that one of the main reasons for termination of supervision at age 15 is the absence of co-operation by the young persons themselves. However, a further reason may be the lack of financial incentives for local authorities to seek to retain children in the Hearings System beyond the age of 16. While adult social work criminal justice services are currently funded 100% by the central government, local authorities pay for childcare services. While the Hearings System can in theory access these services, local authorities have to bear the additional costs, and this may act as a disincentive. The *Crime and Punishment (Scotland) Act* (1997) does contain a provision which will bring such placements under the scope of the 100% funding initiative, but, as yet, there is no commencement date.

CHILD OFFENDERS AND THE COURTS

While the Children's Hearings System forms the core of the Scottish juvenile justice system, it is important to remember that a number of child offenders under the age of 16 as well as the majority of those aged between 16 and 18 are dealt with by the courts.

Children Under 16

Children aged between eight and 16 will normally only come before the courts when they have been accused of an extremely serious crime such as rape or homicide or (in the case of children aged 15 or over) for certain offences which would involve a penalty of disqualification from driving.[9]

The numbers of children under the age of 16 who are dealt with by the courts are extremely small. In 1998 for example (the latest year for which figures are available) this amounted to only 140 children (135 boys and five girls) with a charge proven. As indicated in Table 15.1, most of these children were remitted to the children's hearings for disposal. Children who are sentenced to a period of custody will normally serve their time in secure care; once they reach the age of 16 they may be transferred to a young offenders institution.

Older Children (Aged 16 to 17)

The majority of offenders aged between 16 and 17 are subject to the same procedures as adult offenders. The police will refer their cases to the procurator fiscal. The fiscal will decide whether there is sufficient evidence to prosecute and whether it is in the public interest to proceed. S/he will then decide

Table 15.1: Persons Aged Under 16 with a Charge Proved, 1998

Disposal	Children Aged Under 16 Percent (n=140)
Custody	15
Community Service	*
Probation	15
Fine	14
Admonition or Caution	15
Other (includes remits to the Children's Hearings)	41

* less than 1%

Source: Scottish Executive (1999).

in which court and under which procedure (solemn or summary) the case should be dealt with.

The published statistics on court disposals group together all young persons aged between 16 and 20, rather than separating out each age. As indicated in Table 15.2, a fine is the most common disposal for both males and females. There are, however, a number of gender differences with regard to other disposals received. Males receive proportionately higher levels of custody and community service than females, and twice as many females receive admonitions and cautions as males. This is likely to be a reflection of the more serious and persistent patterns of offending with which male offenders present, rather than indicative of any leniency towards females.

Table 15.2: Persons Aged 16 to 20 with a Charge Proved, 1998

Court Disposal	Males Aged 16 to 20 (n=29,310)	Females aged 16 to 20 (n=3,361)
Custody	14	7
Community Service	6	3
Probation	9	11
Fine	55	49
Admonition or Caution	12	26
Other (includes remits to the children's hearings for offenders aged 16 or 17)	3	4

Source: Scottish Executive (1999).

THE NATURE OF AVAILABLE DISPOSALS

Having set out the roles of the Children's Hearings System and the courts in juvenile justice, we will now shift our attention to the nature of available disposals.

Supervision Requirements

The main disposals available to the Children's Hearings System are residential or non-residential supervision requirements. The social work department administers these disposals. According to the provisions of the *Children (Scotland) Act* 1995 (s 52[3]), supervision may include protection, guidance, treatment, and control (see Moore and Whyte, 1998). In 1997, guidance on home supervision was issued by the then Scottish Office Social Work Services Group (SWSG). This stated that supervision should aim to reduce offending behavior and specified that offenders should have at least fortnightly contact with their supervising social workers. It also stated that local authorities should provide programs of supervision, which will maintain the confidence of both panel members and the wider public.

Under a non-residential supervision requirement, the child will remain in their own home for the period of supervision. A residential supervision requirement, however, may require the child to reside with a foster family, in some form of local authority residential care, or to be detained in secure care (see below).

Specialist Programs

In recent years a number of specialist programs for child offenders have been developed. Independent sector agencies in the field of criminal justice have taken a lead role in such developments. Examples include two programs targeting persistent young offenders (the Freagarrach project in central Scotland and the Apex CueTen project in Fife) as well as the SACRO[10] (Fife) Young Offenders Mediation Project, as set out in Box 15.2. These programs have generally been based on cognitive behavioral methods and/or principles of restorative justice.

Secure Care

Each year around 250 children are detained in secure care—about 25% of these come via the courts, the rest from the Children's Hearings System. Little detailed research has been undertaken regarding the types of work undertaken with offenders in secure care, nor the long-term effects of such detention on offending behavior. A recent inspection report, however, found a lack of fo-

	Box 15.2: Examples of Specialist Programs	
Project	Target Group	Aims/Nature of Intervention
Freagarrach Funded by Scottish Executive. Administered by Barnardos (children's charity).	12 to 16 year olds diverted from Children's Hearings.	Aims to help offenders confront the consequence of their offending behavior and deal with pressures which might lead them back to offending; intensive program based on cognitive behavioral methods.
Apex Cue Ten Funded by the Scottish Executive and administered by Apex (an independent sector organization) with input from Fife Constabulary and Local Authority.	14 to 16 year olds diverted from Children's Hearings.	To reduce offending by changing young people's attitudes to training and employment, key objectives being to develop employment related skills and to introduce offenders to the world of work and further training. Based on social skills development and practical application of skills acquired.
SACRO (Fife) Young Offenders Mediation project administered by SACRO with input from the local Reporter, the social work department, and the police.	11 to 16 year olds showing signs of developing a pattern of offending behavior, referred by the Reporter.	Three main principles: the need for early intervention, the inclusion of a victim perspective, and voluntary reparation. Offenders may undertake a task for the victim or wider community, meet the victim to discuss their offending behavior; or write a letter of apology or explanation to the victim. Occasionally offenders participate in a non-mediation program which concentrates on addressing offending.

cused interventions and recommended the further development of programs based on social skills training and cognitive behavioral methods (see SWSI, 1996; Hogg, 1999). The report also revealed that there were very few differences between these young people and those in other forms of local authority care. Given also that secure care can now be used as an incapacitative measure, it seems that many young people are being detained in regimes which are not necessarily in their best interests.

Specialist Disposals for Older Children

There are very few specialist schemes developed for offenders aged 16 to 17 who are retained by or remitted to the Children's Hearings System. One notable scheme, however, has been the "CHOSI" program in North Lanarkshire. This is run by the procurator fiscal service in conjunction with social work, and its main aim is to provide individual care plans for offenders. It is targeted at 15 to 18 year olds, thus bridging the transitional years between the Hearings System and the adult criminal justice system.

For offenders aged between 16 to 18 who go through the adult court system there are a range of specialist disposals which have been developed under the 100% funding initiative (implemented in 1991). Such disposals include intensive probation schemes, such as those run by National Children's Homes (NCH), and specialist drug and alcohol programs (see McIvor and Barry, 1998 for further discussion).

Having explored the operation of the system and the nature of disposals, we will now look at patterns of youth crime in Scotland to show in more detail the scope of the problems with which the juvenile justice system has to deal.

EXTENT AND PATTERN OF YOUTH CRIME

Commentators on the juvenile justice system in Scotland are generally in agreement that young people are responsible for a disproportionately large amount of crime. Recent estimates suggest that 37% of all crimes and offences in Scotland are committed by young people aged between eight and 20 (The Prince's Trust, 1997) and that a high proportion of these crimes and offences are committed by a small number of persistent offenders (see Hogg, 1999).

It is, however, notoriously difficult to obtain accurate statistics on levels of offending among children and young people, not least because police-recorded crime statistics do not include information regarding the age and sex of the offender. The most reliable "official" measures available are statistics on referrals to the Children's Hearings System and statistics on criminal proceedings in the Scottish courts. Each of these, however, has major limitations. For example, decisions to refer a case to the Reporter at any given time will be as much a reflection of the level of available resources, patterns of agency activity, and agency priorities, as a reflection of the levels of youth crime. Similarly, statistics on court proceedings are partly a product of the decision-making practices at earlier stages of the criminal justice process, which serve to filter out many cases before they reach the courts. As such, these statistics can only provide a partial account of the levels of youth crime.

In order to supplement the official statistics used in this section, I am going to draw on the early findings of the Edinburgh Study of Youth Transitions and Crime (The Edinburgh Study). This is a major longitudinal program of research exploring pathways into and out of crime for a cohort of 4,300 children who started secondary school in August 1998. The early findings from our self-report questionnaire provide additional information about the nature and pattern of offending among young people, as well as giving some early indication as to the mechanisms and processes which lead to offending among both girls and boys.

1. The Official Picture

Referrals to the Reporter

As will be recalled, children can be referred to the Reporter on offence or non-offence grounds. Offence grounds have comprised the most common ground for referral in almost every year since the inception of the Children's Hearings System in 1971. Nonetheless, offence referrals have significantly decreased as a *proportion* of all referrals over time. In the first year of operation, around 87% of referrals to the Reporter were on offence grounds (Edwards and Griffiths, 1997), however, by 1996/97 this had decreased to 60% (SCRA 2000).[11]

The actual *numbers* of offence referrals have fluctuated between 21,000 and 28,000 per annum. The evidence suggests that variations in the number of referrals from year to year may be occurring in tandem with fluctuations in the under-16 population. For example there was a rise in the number of offence referrals in the mid-1990s from 23,120 in 1993 to 28,105 in 1996/97, and this occurred at the same time as a gradual rise in population among the under-16 age group, from a low point in 1993 (see facts on Scotland above).

When expressed as referrals per 1000 of the under-16 population, the statistics suggest that offending rates among children have been relatively stable over time. Referrals on offence grounds have varied between around 12 to just over 14 per 1000 of the under-16 population during the mid-1980s to mid-1990s. Although there was a slight rise in rates of referral during the 1990s this merely restored referrals to their mid-1980s level.

There are a number of key differences in referrals patterns for boys and girls. As highlighted in Figure 15.2, boys are referred at a much higher rate per 1000 population than girls (around the low to mid-40s for boys in the mid-1990s as compared with around 11 to 13 per 1000 population for girls during the same period). Importantly, there is some evidence that referrals rates for girls have

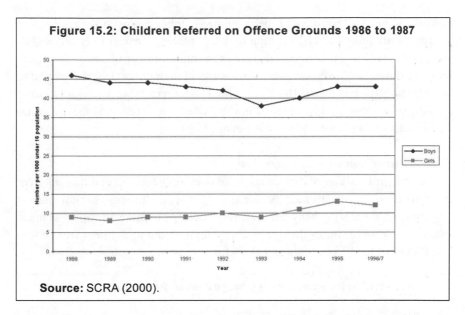

Figure 15.2: Children Referred on Offence Grounds 1986 to 1987

Source: SCRA (2000).

been gradually increasing over time from around 8 to 9 per 1000 population in the mid-1980s to between 12 and 13 per 1000 population in the mid 1990s.

Much has been made of this increase by commentators on the system, as it does seem to confirm trends in other jurisdictions that girls may be increasingly engaging in offending behavior. However, without further research, it is difficult to determine whether the changing pattern of referrals does in fact mark a significant behavioral change on the part of girls in Scotland or whether it merely reflects a change in the readiness of agencies and the general public to report girls for offending behavior.

The peak age of referral on offence grounds is at age 15 for both boys and girls (SCRA, 2000). What this demonstrates is that children are increasingly coming to the attention of the Children's Hearings System for offences at the very point of transition to the adult criminal justice system. A relatively high number of these offenders are likely to have had a history of involvement with the Hearings on non-offence grounds. In research conducted by Waterhouse et al. (1999)[12] many of the children in their cohort referred for offending had prior referrals to the Reporter for non-offence reasons (mostly for truancy, being beyond parental control, or for risk associated with offences against children). Early involvement with the Hearings System was also found to be a warning signal for later intensive involvement (Waterhouse et al., 1999).

Unfortunately, SCRA statistics do not give any information about the types of offences to which referrals to the Hearings relate. The Waterhouse evaluation found, however, that the majority (23%) of offenders within their cohort had been referred for property related offences. Most offences were of a petty nature (e.g., theft by opening lock-fast places, breach of peace, vandalism, and shoplifting), although there were a small number of serious and persistent offenders. Thirty-six (8% of offenders in their cohort) were reported to have committed more than 10 offences, and just over 4% were alleged to have committed around 28% of the total number of offences reported for the group of offenders as a whole (Waterhouse et al., 1999).

Evidence from Court Proceedings Statistics

Court proceedings statistics show an overall decline in convictions over the past 10 years for offenders under the age of 18. Although, as indicated in Figure 15.3, there have been some slight variations in this pattern, most notably with regard to the slight rise in convictions in the mid-1990s from a low point in 1994 for 17 year olds and 1993 for 16 year olds.

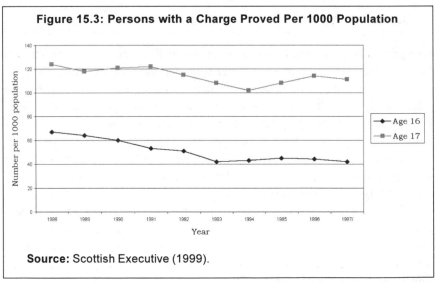

Figure 15.3: Persons with a Charge Proved Per 1000 Population

Source: Scottish Executive (1999).

Any decline in conviction rates is, however, likely to be a reflection of the growth of alternatives to prosecution targeting the young adult offender group, rather than an indication of a major decline in offending (Hogg, 1999). Since the mid-1980s, there has been a huge expansion of diversion from prosecution schemes (in the wake of the recommendations of the Stewart Committee). These schemes have recently come under the ambit of the 100% funding policy initiative.

Not dissimilar from the picture in other contributions covered in this text, there are significant gender differences in patterns of conviction (see Figure 15.4). Males at each age group have a far higher rate of conviction per 1000

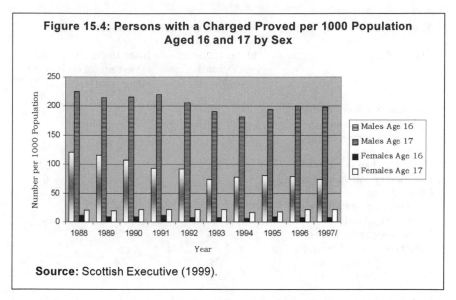

Figure 15.4: Persons with a Charged Proved per 1000 Population Aged 16 and 17 by Sex

Legend:
- ▨ Males Age 16
- ▥ Males Age 17
- ■ Females Age 16
- ☐ Females Age 17

Source: Scottish Executive (1999).

population in comparison with females, with the rate of conviction for both genders increasing dramatically with age. Indeed the peak age for convictions occurs at age 18 for males and at age 22 for females (SWSI, 1998).

Unlike SCRA statistics, court proceedings statistics do give information on the nature of offences for which young people have been convicted. However, the available data group together all young people under the age of 21, rather than breaking the numbers down into separate years. Table 15.3 sets out patterns of conviction for males and females in 1998 (a typical year). As can be seen, convictions for serious violent and sexual crimes are rare, with most offenders being convicted of miscellaneous offences, crimes of dishonesty (mainly shoplifting) and, to a slightly lesser extent, motor vehicle offences.

2. Evidence from The Edinburgh Study of Youth Transitions and Crime

As stated earlier, the overall aim of the Edinburgh Study is to explore pathways into and out of crime for our cohort of 4,300 children who started secondary school in Edinburgh in August 1998.

In the first round of administering the self-report questionnaire, respondents (at age 11½ to 12½) were asked about whether they had ever engaged in any of the 15 types of offending behavior ranging from relatively minor offences such as being noisy or cheeky in public to more serious offences such as fire-raising or theft using force.

In common with other self-report studies undertaken in Scotland (see Jamieson et al., 1999; Anderson et al., 1994), our findings suggest that experience of offending is quite commonplace among the cohort. Just over three-

Table 15.3: Persons with a Charge Proved 1998—Crimes and Offences

Crime/Offence	Males Under 21 Percent (n=29,445)	Females Under 21 Percent (n=3,366)	Total Percent (n=32,811)
Non-sexual Crimes of Violence	5	2	5
Crimes of Indecency (Includes crimes relating to prostitution)	*	2	*
Crimes of Dishonesty	27	34	27
Fire-raising and Vandalism etc	6	4	6
Other Crimes (includes drugs and crimes against justice)	9	9	9
Miscellaneous Offences (includes simple assault, breach of the peace)	33	34	33
Motor Vehicle Offences	20	15	20

* less than 1%

Source: Scottish Executive (1999).

quarters of all boys (78.8%) in the cohort and around two-thirds of the girls (66.4%) had committed one or more of the offending behaviors included in the questionnaire. The mean volume of offences committed was 8.4 for the cohort as a whole. There were, however, significant gender differences, with the mean volume being twice as high for boys (11.02) as for girls (5.74).[13] Boys also tended to be involved in a greater variety of offences than girls.

Again, as with other self-report studies, our findings also suggest that the types of offence in which young people engage tend to be fairly petty in nature (see McVie and Smith, forthcoming). Very few children in the Edinburgh Study cohort admitted involvement in the most serious offences such as fire-raising, breaking into a building, or theft using force. As indicated in Table 15.4 the most common activities were fighting,[14] shoplifting, theft from home, being noisy or cheeky in public, and graffiti. The table also indicates significant gender differences in the prevalence of offending for all offence categories except graffiti and theft from home.

Explanations of Gender Differences

The early findings of the Edinburgh Study suggest that offending risk among both boys and girls may be related to the absence (or relaxation) of a multi-layered set of controls involving the individual characteristics of the

Table 15.4: Prevalence of Offending by Gender		
Offence Type	Males Percent (n=2172)	Females Percent (n=2128)
Fighting ***	64.8	41.6
Shoplifting ***	31.9	22.2
Theft from home	31.0	29.7
Noisy or cheeky in public ***	31.0	19.8
Graffiti	28.0	27.1
Fare dodging ***	27.2	20.0
Truancy ***	21.7	13.4
Vandalism ***	20.7	6.7
Carrying a weapon ***	18.4	5.0
Theft from school **	12.6	10.0
Set fire to property ***	6.3	1.7
Riding in a stolen vehicle ***	4.1	0.8
Theft from a vehicle ***	2.4	0.2
Breaking into a building ***	3.5	1.0
Theft using force ***	2.8	0.5

Asterisks: significant gender differences: ** = p<0.01, *** = p<0.001

Source: Edinburgh Study of Youth Transitions and Crime (Sweep 1 data). The author is involved in this project; this is the first time the data has been published.

child, their family and peer relationships, and (more tentatively) the dynamics of the neighborhoods where they live.[15]

With regard to the individual characteristics of the child, controls relate to personality characteristics such as degree of impulsivity, as well as the cognitive skills associated with moral reasoning processes and perceptions of the seriousness of various forms of delinquent behavior (the latter two of which may inhibit and thereby control impulses to offend; see McVie and Smith, forthcoming). Initial analysis reveals that there is a strong relationship between volume of offending and high levels of impulsivity (.4.67); poor moral reasoning (-.580), and perception of offending behaviors as non-serious (-.413).

In respect to family and peer controls, these relate to both the degree to which families supervise their children, know what time they will be home, and set limits for them and the extent of influence peer groups have over children.

Finally, with regard to controls at the neighborhood level, we measured the child's perception of social cohesion and informal social control mechanisms within his/her neighborhood. A measure of neighborhood problems was also included (for example, not enough street lights, drug needles or syringes lying around, neighbors fighting in the street). The results show that there appears to be a relationship between volume of offending, weak neighborhood cohesion (-.065), weak levels of informal social control (-.107), and high levels of neighborhood problems (.204). While these relationships are not as strong as those between individual, peer, and family controls and offending, they are statistically significant.

Implications of Statistical Patterns: Conclusions

To conclude this section, far from indicating that juvenile crime is rising out of control, the official statistics on referrals and convictions suggest that offending rates may have been relatively stable over time. Much juvenile offending that comes to the attention of official agencies tends to be fairly petty in nature and overwhelmingly committed by boys. Nonetheless, there is some evidence for the existence of a small number of children who are serious and persistent offenders and who may be responsible for a disproportionate amount of the offences which have been attributed to young people. However, the lack of published information makes it difficult to estimate with any degree of accuracy the nature and scale of their offending.

The findings from the Edinburgh study indicate that the roots of offending for both boys and girls may lie in the complex interactions between the individual characteristics of the child, the nature of their peer and family relationships, and the informal mechanisms of social control within their neighborhoods. These findings provide some justification for the development of a multi-level approach for dealing with offending, focused on early interventions with children and their families, and broader social policies aimed at strengthening community bonds. Such an approach accords in many respects with the social inclusion agenda discussed in the first section of this chapter.

CURRENT ISSUES IN JUVENILE JUSTICE

In this final section of the chapter we will examine some of the main issues currently facing the juvenile justice system in Scotland. These relate to the effectiveness of interventions, key transitions and juvenile justice, and the impact of the incorporation of the European Convention on Human Rights into Scots law.

The Effectiveness of Interventions

The effectiveness of supervision for child offenders has come under intense scrutiny in recent years in the light of research evidence that the Children's

Hearings System may be far more effective in dealing with children in need of care and protection than it is in dealing with offenders (see Hallet et al., 1998). Concerns have focused on the lack of resources available to the Hearings as well as the lack of specialist skills and knowledge among supervising social workers (see Whyte, 1996; Hallet et al., 1998). However, even the more specialist programs that have been developed (as described in Box 15.2 above) have had rather mixed results in terms of their impact on offending. While the recent evaluation of the Freagarrach project found that the program led to reductions in offending for around 60% of attendees, these levels of success have not been reproduced elsewhere (see Smith, 1998; Lobley and Smith, 1999; Sawyer, 1998).

During 2000, the Advisory Group on Youth Crime issued a consultation document (*It's a Criminal Waste: Stop Youth Crime Now*, HMSO, 2000). This document argues that the findings of the "what works" literature should be extended to the development of programs for children who offend.[16] Moreover, these programs should be accessible to the Children's Hearings System, as well as the procurator fiscal service and the courts.

The "what works" literature claims that effective programs should be based on five key principles (described in more detail in Box 15.3): the risk principle, the criminogenic need principle, the responsivity principle, the community-based principle, and the principle of program integrity (McGuire, 1995).

It is certainly clear that the Children's Hearings System, as it currently operates, does not fully match up to the principles of effective programs as set out above. In particular, the system fails to measure up to the principle of

---

Box 15.3: Principles on which Effective Programs should be based

(i) The risk principle: the degree of intervention should be tailored to the level of risk presented, with the most intensive supervision targeted only on the highest level of risk. Too much intervention in the case of a low risk offender would be positively damaging.

(ii) The criminogenic need principle: interventions should be focused on the aspects of the child's behavior or social circumstances directly linked to their offending behavior as, for example, peer associations, family difficulties, or issues relating to personal controls.

(iii) The responsivity principle: programs should be tailored to the learning capacities of the individual child and also should be based on cognitive behavioral methods.

(iv) The community-based principle: programs work best when delivered in a community-based setting, as this facilitates real life learning.

(v) The principle of program integrity: programs should be delivered by highly trained and well-motivated staff, they should be adequately resourced and managed, and they should be subject to some form of evaluation.

program integrity given the major resource constraints identified earlier and the fact that the supervision of child offenders is undertaken by childcare teams who are not trained in the requisite skills. Similarly, it is not clear that risk assessments are routinely undertaken with child offenders or that childcare teams would always be capable of making such assessments.

It could be argued that the claims made by the works literature go against the grain of many aspects of the Kilbrandon philosophy itself. As highlighted above, the Kilbrandon philosophy is based on the notion that children who offend should not be distinguished from children who are in need of care and protection, as their problems stem from the same source. The criminogenic need principle, however, suggests that not only are offenders required to be distinguished from non-offenders, but that a careful distinction needs to be made between the child offender's general welfare problems and those problems that have a direct bearing on the offending behavior itself. Targeting interventions on the latter may be to the detriment of the holistic approach advocated by Kilbrandon.

Key Transitions and Juvenile Justice

In addition to concerns about effectiveness, the attention of policy-makers has also been focused on two key transitions within the justice system: child offenders' first contacts with criminal justice agencies and the transition from the juvenile to the adult criminal justice system. Both of these transitions touch on current debates regarding definitions of childhood.

First Contacts with the System: The Age of Criminal Responsibility

The age of criminal responsibility in Scotland is currently set at eight, and this is the first age at which children can be referred to the Children's Hearings System on offence grounds. Scotland has one of the lowest ages of criminal responsibility in Europe.[17] The Advisory Group on Youth Crime has recommended that the age of criminal responsibility in Scotland be now raised to age 12.

The debate about age, stage of maturity, and criminal responsibility is a complex and controversial one. As stated in the Kilbrandon report, whatever age is chosen will inevitably prove to be rather arbitrary. However it is certainly questionable whether the majority of children at age eight could "live up to the moral and psychological components of criminal responsibility" or (if they came before the courts) would be capable of understanding and participating effectively in court proceedings (see T *v. United Kingdom* (2000) 30 EHRR 121). With regard to the latter, Scots law could be vulnerable to a challenge under the European Convention of Human Rights.

The Transition between the Juvenile and Adult Justice Systems

The normal point of transition from the juvenile to adult justice systems occurs at age 16. Again, Scotland is out of kilter with many European countries, which place the transition point at age 18.

There is a consensus among many commentators that the transition between the children's hearings system and the adult courts is too abrupt and that young offenders find it difficult to adjust to the very different ethos of the latter. Those in favor of raising the point of transition argue that the adult criminal justice system is not geared to dealing with the needs of 16 to 17 year old offenders. Many of these offenders present with problems relating to substance misuse, high levels of victimization, or family relationship difficulties, and many are immature and emotionally under-developed. As such, it is considered that they would benefit from the more holistic approach offered by the Children's Hearings System.

There has been little rigorous research undertaken on the long-term outcomes for young offenders who make the transition from the Hearings to the courts. It is difficult to track offenders through the two systems, not least because each has different record-keeping practices, and information systems are not always compatible. The Waterhouse research, however, did follow up offenders in their cohort for a period of two years. Their findings provide some support for the claim that 16 to 17 year olds in the adult criminal justice system are a particularly vulnerable group. Just under one-third of these offenders were sentenced to a period of custody by the courts, confirming the concerns of many commentators that young offenders tend to become "up-tariffed" relatively quickly once they enter the adult system (Waterhouse et al., 1999; Whyte, 1996).

The Incorporation of the European Convention on Human Rights (ECHR)

As noted above, the ECHR was incorporated into Scots law by the *Human Rights Act* 1998. The stated position of central government is that the principles of the ECHR will strengthen rather than weaken the Scottish juvenile justice system. However, it is arguable that the ECHR poses a number of challenges to the juvenile justice system both of substance and of principle. It is likely that these challenges will have greatest effect with regard to the treatment of cases referred on non-offence grounds (and in particular child protection cases), not least because the ECHR may serve to enhance the rights of parents (see Edwards [2000] for further discussion).

The ECHR has already had a major impact on court procedures for dealing with child offenders under the age of 16. In the wake of the ruling on the cases of Thompson and Venables[18] (also see Chapter 5), new arrangements have been introduced to facilitate the child's understanding of, and participation in, court procedures.

At the time of writing, (Autumn 2001) no challenge has been made to the processes and procedures of the Children's Hearings with regard to offenders. However, there are a number of aspects of the Hearings system which may not be compatible with the ECHR. One example is that of legal representation. As mentioned earlier, legal aid is available for children at proof hearings and appeals, but it is not available for the Hearing itself. Consequently, a legal representative accompanies very few children. This is vulnerable to challenge under Article 6, which states that everyone charged with a criminal offence has the right to legal assistance and to be given it free of charge, if he has not sufficient means to pay for it. Moreover, the use of secure care as an incapacitative measure for children who pose a risk to the public may also be vulnerable to challenge under Article 5. This article states that the only lawful detention of a minor is for the purpose of educational supervision (or his lawful detention for the purpose of bringing him before the competent legal authority).

Finally, recent years have seen a gradual incursion of public interest and rights discourse into the Hearings System. It would seem that the incorporation of the ECHR could mark a quantum leap in this process. The formalism of rights talk may indeed rest uneasily with key precepts of the Kilbrandon philosophy, in particular with the consensual non-adversarial character of the Hearings. Nonetheless, it may throw into sharper focus elements of the juvenile justice system which, some commentators argue, have undermined children's rights for many years: the low age of criminal responsibility, the indeterminacy of the supervision requirement, the neglect of due process rights, and the highly discretionary nature of decision-making at both the Reporter and Hearings stage (see Morris and McIsaac, 1978; Lockyer and Stone, 1998).

SUMMARY

Although part of the United Kingdom, Scotland has its own distinctive history and distinctively different juvenile justice system. Within Scotland, policy on juvenile offenders has always been bifurcated between a public interest and welfarist perspective. The precise interplay between the concerns of key policy elites and broader social and cultural processes has determined which of these perspectives has triumphed at any particular juncture. After a period in which welfarism was in ascendance, recent years have seen the public interest perspective increasingly coming to challenge dominant modes of discourse within the system. The elision between the youth justice and social inclusion agenda has contributed to this process, heralding an era of protective tutelage that may serve to undermine rather than strengthen key aspects of the Kilbrandon philosophy. To return to the quotation at the beginning of this chapter, Scottish society still seems concerned with securing a more effective and discriminatory machinery for dealing with children and young people who offend. As seems to be the case in a number of other contributions in this textbook, there is less certainty regarding the principles upon which such a machinery should be based.

Lesley McAra is a lecturer in criminology and member of the Centre for Law and Society, University of Edinburgh. Before taking up her present post she worked as a senior research officer in the Scottish Executive Centre Research Unit, managing and conducting research on social work criminal justice services. Her research interests lie in the general areas of the sociology of punishment and the sociology of law and deviance. Her particular interests include the interface between social work and criminal justice; gender, crime, and criminal justice; and juvenile justice. With David Smith, she is currently leading a team that is studying youth transitions and crime in Edinburgh by charting the development of a cohort of 4,300 young people and mapping the social geography of the city.

KEY TERMS AND CONCEPTS

Children's Hearing System	Kitbrandon Report
Welfarism	Public Interest
European Convention on the Rights of the Child	
Protective Tutelage	

HELPFUL WEBSITES

www.scotland.gov.uk: The Scottish Executive.
www.childrens-hearings.co.uk: The Children's Hearing System.
www.sacro.org.uk: Scottish Association for the Care and Resettlement of Offenders.
www.statsbase.gov.uk: Government Statistical Service.
www.law.ed.ac.uk/cls/esytc/: Edinburgh Study of Youth Transitions and Crime.

STUDY QUESTIONS

1. What were the reasons for the divergence of the Scottish and English systems of juvenile justice during the 1970s and 1980s?
2. What impact is the European Convention of Human Rights likely to have on the nature and operation of the Scottish juvenile justice system? Will it strengthen or undermine the principles of the children's Hearings System?
3. How effective is the Children's Hearings System in dealing with persistent young offenders?
4. What is the appropriate age at which young offenders should make the transition to the adult criminal justice system?

NOTES

1. The Edinburgh Study is funded by the Economic and Social Research Council. The author of this chapter is co-director of the programme with Professor David Smith.
2. One of the first industrial schools in Scotland was set up by Sheriff Watson in 1841 (see Murphy, 1992) Industrial schools were given formal recognition in Scotland by the *Industrial Schools Act* 1854, predating similar legislation in England and Wales by three years.
3. In Aberdeen City and the three counties of Ayr, Fife, and Renfrew.
4. For example in 1962 around 77% of cases were dealt with by Sheriff and Burgh courts as compared to only 16% in the juvenile courts.
5. This is not to say that that the Scottish system is replicating all aspects of the new juvenile justice system in England and Wales, merely that the ethos of the two systems is coming closer together.
6. The Secretary of State (now the First Minister under devolution) has the power to prescribe qualifications for the Reporter but has never done so.
7. It should be noted that these principles should also guide decision-making by the courts.
8. At the time of writing, the age of criminal responsibility in Scotland is eight. This is currently under review (see below). While children between the ages of 0-16 can be referred on non-offence grounds, only children over the age of eight can be referred on offence grounds.
9. In Scotland there are three levels of criminal court: the District Court which deals with summary offences only; the Sheriff Court which deals with both summary and solemn (more serious) cases; and the High Court which deals with solemn cases. Children under the age of 16 can only be dealt with in the Sheriff or High Court.
10. Scottish Association for the Care and Resettlement of Offenders.
11. Indeed, statistical evidence indicates that during the 1980s non-offence referrals rose by a startling 182% in contrast to a mere 5% rise in offence referrals The rise in non-offence referrals has been attributed to increased public awareness of child protection issues, exacerbated by the publicity attached to the events in Cleveland, Rochdale, and Orkney (Lockyer and Stone, 1998). These events each concerned suspected cases of child sexual abuse and highlighted failures in official agency procedures. For further details see Lockyer and Stone, 1998.
12. This research examined the Children's Hearings history and social and personal circumstances of a cohort of 1,155 children dealt with by Reporters at February 1995. The cohort was followed up for two years (see Waterhouse et al., 1999).
13. This is a minimum estimate of the average number of times a respondent had engaged in the listed behaviors. The total volume of offending was based on highly conservative assumptions: 6 to 10 occasions was counted as 6 and 11+ occasions was counted as 11.
14. This included fights with siblings and is likely to be fairly petty in nature.
15. It should be stressed at this point that data analysis is still at an early stage and more complex multi-level analysis will be required to explore the strength and direction of the interactions between each of the three levels of control. The relationship between social control and offending is the subject of a forthcoming paper by McAra and McVie.

16. Using meta-analysis, the works literature claims to have identified features of programs which can impact positively on offending behavior (see McGuire, 1995).
17. In France it is set at age 13; in Germany, Austria, Italy, and many Eastern European countries it is set at age 14; and in Spain, Belgium, and Luxembourg at age 18.
18. Thompson and Venables were convicted of abduction and murder of two-year-old Jamie Bulger. In their applications to the Commission, they alleged *inter alia* that they had been denied a fair trial in breach of Article 6 of the Convention, which indicates that a defendant should be able to understand and participate in criminal proceedings against him. This allegation was upheld by the European Court of Human Rights, the judgment stating that such procedures as had been put in place to facilitate understanding and participation were inadequate (see *T v. United Kingdom* [2000] 30 EHRR 121). Although Thompson and Venables were convicted in the English courts, their case has had a major impact in Scotland.

REFERENCES

Anderson, S., Kinsey, R., Loader, I., & Smith, C. (1994). *Cautionary tales: Young people, crime, and policing in Edinburgh*. Aldershot: Avebury.

Aries, P. (1973). *Centuries of childhood*. Harmondsworth: Penguin.

Bauman, Z. (2000). Social issues of law and order. *British Journal of Criminology* 40.2.

Blanch, M. (1979). Imperialism, nationalism and organised youth. In J. Clarke *et al.* (Eds.), *Working class culture*. St. Martin's Press.

Bruce, N. (1982). "Historical background." In Martin, F. and Murray, K. (Eds.), *The Scottish juvenile justice system*. Edinburgh: Scottish Academic Press.

Cavadino, M., & Dignan, J. (1997). *The penal system: An introduction*. 2nd ed. London: Sage.

Cleland, A. (1995). Legal solutions for children: Comparing Scots law with other jurisdictions. *Scottish Affairs* 10: 6-24.

Douglas, M. (1992). *Risk and blame: Essays in cultural theory*. London: Routledge.

Edwards, L. (2000). Incorporation of the European Convention on Human Rights: What will it mean for Scotland's children? In Loux, A. (Ed.), *Human Rights and Scots Law*. Oxford: Hart.

Edwards, L., & Griffiths, A. (1997). *Family law*. Edinburgh: Green/Sweet and Maxwell.

Garland, D. (1996). The limits of the sovereign state. *British Journal of Criminology* 36.4.

Gelsthorpe, L., & Morris, A. (1994). Juvenile justice 1954-1992. In Maguire, R., Morgan, R., & Reiner, R. *The Oxford Handbook of Criminology*. 1st ed. Oxford: Oxford University Press.

Hallet, C., Murray, C., Jamieson, J., & Veitch, B. (1998). *The evaluation of the Children's Hearings in Scotland, Volume 1: Deciding in children's interests."* Edinburgh: The Scottish Office Central Research Unit.

Hogg, K. (1999). *Youth crime in Scotland. A Scottish executive policy unit review*. http://www.scotland.gov.uk/library3/law/youth.pdf

Humpries, J. (1977). The working class family, women's liberation and class struggles: The case of nineteenth-century British history. *Bulletin of Union of Radical Political Economists* 9.3: 25-1.

Jamieson, J., McIvor, G., & Murray, C. (1999). *Understanding offending among young people*. Edinburgh: The Scottish Executive Central Research Unit.

Kilbrandon Committee. (1964). Report on children and young persons, Scotland. Edinburgh: Her Majesty's Stationery Office.

Lianos, M., & Douglas, M. (2000). Dangerization and the end of deviance: The institutional environment. *British Journal of Criminology* 40.2.

Lobley, D., & Smith, D. (1999). *Working with persistent juvenile offenders: An evaluation of the Apex Cue Ten Project*.Edinburgh:The Scottish Office Central Research Unit.

Lockyer, A., & Stone, F. (Eds). (1998). *Juvenile justice in Scotland: Twenty-five years of the welfare approach*.Edinburgh: T. & T. Clark.

McAra, L. (1998). *Social work and criminal justice. Volume 2: Early arrangements*. Edinburgh: The Stationary Office.

McAra, L. (1999). The politics of penalty: An overview of the development of penal policy in Scotland. In P. Duff & N. Hutton (Eds.), *Criminal justice in Scotland*. Aldershot: Dartmouth.

McAra, L., & Young, P. (1997). Juvenile justice in Scotland. *Criminal Justice* 15.3.

McGuire, J. (1995). *What works: Reducing offending–guidelines from research and practice*. Chichester: Wiley.

McIvor, G., & Barry, M. (1998). *Social work and criminal justice. Volume 6: Probation*. Edinburgh: The Stationery Office.

McIvor, G., & Barry, M. (1999). *Diversion from prosecution to social work and other service agencies: Evaluation of the 100% funding pilot programs*. Edinburgh: The Scottish Executive Central Research Unit.

McVie, S., & Smith, D. (Forthcoming) *Theory and method in the Edinburgh Study of Youth Transitions and Crime*.

Moore, G., & Whyte, B. (1998). *Social work and criminal law in Scotland*. 3rd ed. Edinburgh: Mercat Press.

Morris, A., & McIsaac, M. (1978). *Juvenile justice? The practice of social welfare*. Cambridge Studies in Criminology. Cambridge: Heinemann.

Muncie, J. (1999). *Youth and crime: A critical introduction*. London: Sage.

Murphy, J. (1992). *British social services: The Scottish dimension*. Edinburgh: Scottish Academic Press.

Nelken, D. (1994). Whom can you trust? The future of comparative criminology. In Nelken, D. (Ed.), *The futures of criminology*. London: Sage.

Nelken, D. (1997). Understanding criminal justice comparatively. In Maguire, R. Morgan, R., & Reiner, R. (Eds.), *The Oxford handbook of criminology*. 2nd ed.. Oxford: Oxford University Press.

Newburn, T. (1997). Youth, crime and justice. In Maguire, R. Morgan, R., & Reiner, R. (Eds.), *The Oxford Handbook of Criminology*. 2nd ed.. Oxford: Oxford University Press.

O'Malley, P. (1992). Risk, power, and crime prevention. *Economy and Society* 21.3.

O'Malley, P. (1996). Risk and responsibility. In Barry, A., Osborne, T., & Rose, N. (Eds.), *Foucault and political reason*. London: UCL Press.

Pinchbeck, I., & Hewitt, M. (1973). *Children in English society*. Vol. 2. London: Routledge & Kegan Paul.

Pratt, J. (2000). The return of the wheelbarrow men; or the arrival of postmodern penalty. *British Journal of Criminology* 40.1.

Radzinowicz, L., & Hood, R. (1986). *A history of English criminal law. Volume 5: The emergence of penal policy*. London: Stevens.

Reid, B. (1998). Panels and Hearings. In Lockyer, A., & Stone, F. (Eds.), *Juvenile justice in Scotland: Twenty-five years of the welfare approach*. Edinburgh: T. & T. Clark.

Report of the Committee on Protection and Training (Morton Committee). (1928). Edinburgh: Her Majesty's Stationery Office.

Rose, N. (1999). *Powers of freedom: Reframing political thought*. Cambridge: Cambridge University Press.

Shorter, E. (1976). *The making of the modern family*. London: Collins.

Smelser, N. (1959). *Social change in the industrial revolution*. London: Routledge & Kegan Paul.

Rutter, M., Giller, H., & Hagell, A. (1998). *Antisocial behavior by young people*. Cambridge: Cambridge University Press.

Sawyer, B. (2000). *An evaluation of the SACRO (Fife) Young Offender Mediation Project*. Edinburgh: The Scottish Executive Central Research Unit.

Smith, D. (1998). Programs for Serious and Persistent Offenders. In Scottish Executive, *Children, young people and crime in Britain and Ireland: From exclusion to inclusion*. Edinburgh: Scottish Executive.

Smout, T. (1972). *A history of the Scottish people 1560-1830*. London: Collins/Fontana.

Social Work Services Group. (1991). *National objectives and standards for social work services in the criminal justice system*. Edinburgh: The Scottish Office.

Social Work Services and Prisons Inspectorates for Scotland. (1998). *Women offenders: A safer way: A review of community disposals and the use of custody for women offenders in Scotland*. Edinburgh: The Stationery Office.

Social Work Services Inspectorate. (1996). *A secure remedy: A review of the role, availability and quality of secure accommodation for children in Scotland*. Edinburgh: The Stationery Office.

The Prince's Trust. (1997). *Young people and crime in Scotland*.

Waterhouse, L., McGhee, J., Loucks, N., Whyte, B., & Kay, H. (1999). *The evaluation of the children's hearings in Scotland. Volume 3: Children in focus*. Edinburgh: The Scottish Executive Central Research Unit.

Whtyte, B. (1996). *Re-examining juvenile justice in Scotland*. New Waverley Papers: Social Work Series. University of Edinburgh, Social Work Department.

Whyte, B. (1998). Rediscovering Juvenile Delinquency. In Lockyer, A., & Stone, F. (Eds.), *Juvenile justice in Scotland: Twenty-five years of the welfare approach*. Edinburgh: T. & T. Clark.

Young, P. (1997). *Crime and criminal justice in Scotland*. Edinburgh: The Stationery Office.

Chapter 16

Juvenile Justice in South Africa

Ann Skelton
Department of Justice, Pretoria
Hennie Potgieter
South African Law Commission Consultant

FACTS ON SOUTH AFRICA

Area: 1, 219, 912 sq. km. South Africa is situated on the southern tip of Africa, bounded by the Atlantic Ocean to the west and the Indian Ocean to the East. Its borders meet Namibia, Botswana, Zimbabwe, Swaziland, and Mozambique. Lesotho is a landlocked country within the boundaries of South Africa. **Population**: In excess of 37 million in 1996. Based on the 1996 census, the population breakdown is approximately 76.3% African, 8.5% Coloured, 2.5% Indian, and 12.7% White. Of these, approximately 55.4% of the population live in urban areas. The population discrepancies between provinces are worthy of note because of the vast income and living standard disparities between people living in urban and rural areas. In the Northern Province, 88.1% of the population live in rural areas. In Gauteng, the smallest but economically strongest province, 96.4% live in urban areas (this province includes two major cities, Johannesburg and the capital, Pretoria). Patterns of immigration are complex in South Africa. Destabilization in countries to the north of South Africa (particularly Mozambique) resulted in a large refugee population. Recently, refugees and illegal immigrants began arriving from war-torn areas further north. **Economy**: In 1994 South Africa accounted for 44% of the combined gross national product of all countries in the sub-Saharan African region. The country has considerable mineral wealth, with mining, quarrying, and manufacturing forming major industries. It is one of the largest producers of gold, diamonds, platinum, and chromium in the world. **Climate**: The country's subtropical location, on either side of 30 degrees South, accounts for warm, temperate conditions. **Government**: South Africa is a constitutional democracy. The Constitution provides national, provincial, and local spheres of government. The national government is mainly responsible for policy, while the provincial and local spheres are mainly responsible for implementation. Each of the nine provinces has an elected legislature, and there are almost 850 local government structures in South Africa. The ruling party is the African National Congress, which has a five-year term.

The government will, as a matter of urgency, attend to the tragic and complex question of children and juveniles in detention and prison. The basic principle from which we will proceed from now onwards is that we must rescue the children of the nation and ensure that the system of criminal justice must be the very last resort in the case of juvenile offenders. - Nelson Mandela, in his first address to the democratically elected Parliament, 1994.

Hunter-gatherers known as the San and pastoralists known as the Khoi originally populated South Africa. Farmers from east and central Africa joined them about 1,700 years ago. In 1652 the country was colonized by the Dutch and later by the British. In 1948 the National Party came to power and, during its ensuing reign, initiated the policy of apartheid. The struggle against apartheid took place over decades, a conflict in which children themselves were involved. Formal negotiations began in 1990 when Nelson Mandela and other political leaders were released, and a negotiated settlement was finally reached in 1994, saving South Africa from a violent revolution, which had at times seemed inevitable. In April 1994 South Africa held its first democratic elections, and in 1996 the final South African Constitution was adopted.

Prior to colonization customary law governed people's interactions. **Customary law** differed from tribe to tribe, but it was essentially a system based on restitution and the search for harmonious living. Disputes, whether criminal or civil, were resolved through customary courts led by elder community members or chiefs. The chief's courts were co-opted to some extent by the colonizers, and became part of an imposed control system. Nevertheless many children in South Africa continue to live under customary law today, with customary courts having survived in rural areas (Van Eden, 1995).

The civil and criminal justice systems in South Africa are primarily Roman Dutch law, with some influence from the British and continental systems. In the political system there are nine provinces, but law-making is generally undertaken at a national level, with some subsidiary law-making powers being granted to provinces. All laws are subject to the Bill of Rights in the South African Constitution, and the Constitutional Court is the highest court in the land. Most criminal matters are heard in the magistrates' courts. South African magistrates are professional people, all of whom hold law degrees or diplomas. Very serious crimes such as murder are heard in the High Court, presided over by judges.

THE DEVELOPMENT OF JUVENILE JUSTICE IN SOUTH AFRICA

During the 1970s and 1980s thousands of young people were detained in terms of the emergency regulations for political offences, causing a national and international outcry. At the time, political organizations, human rights lawyers, and detainee support groups rallied to the assistance of many of these children. Their efforts centred on children involved in political activism, but there were equally large numbers of children awaiting trial on crimes which were non-political in nature but which could invariably be traced to the prevailing socio-economic ills caused by apartheid. There was no strategy to ensure that these youngsters were treated humanely and with adherence to just principles. By the end of the 1980s the number of political detentions waned but the country's police cells and prisons continued to be occupied by large numbers of children caught up in the criminal justice system. The 1989 Harare International Children's Conference provided a springboard for the development of the child rights movement in South Africa.

Because of the focus on the struggle to achieve basic human rights in South Africa, the call for a fair and equitable child justice system emerged somewhat later than in many comparable countries. The first intensive calls for such reforms in the early 1990s emanated from a group of non-governmental organizations (NGOs) who went into courts, police cells, and prisons to provide assistance to juveniles awaiting trial.

In 1992 these NGOs initiated a campaign to raise national and international awareness about young people in trouble with the law. They issued a report, which called for the creation of a comprehensive juvenile justice system, for humane treatment of young people in conflict with the law, for diversion of minor offences away from the criminal justice system, and for systems that humanized rather than brutalized young offenders (Juvenile Justice Drafting Consultancy, 1994).

A further initiative, launched in 1992 by the National Institute for Crime Prevention and Rehabilitation of Offenders (**NICRO**),[1] was an important milestone in child justice history. NICRO decided to offer courts alternative diversion and sentencing options that aimed to promote the emerging restorative justice concepts specifically focussed on youth. With no enabling legislation in place, the diversion programs and alternative sentencing options now offered by NICRO are widely accepted, are the subject of various National Director of Public Prosecutions (NDPP)[2] circulars, and have been implemented in practice in most urban areas of the country (see Box 16.1). However, a caution was sounded that in the absence of clear guidelines concerning diversion and

---

Box 16.1: Tragic death of Neville Snyman

In October 1992, 13-year-old Neville Snyman was killed by his cell-mates in a Robertson police cell while awaiting trial on charges of housebreaking. He had allegedly broken into a store to steal sweets, cool drinks, and cigarettes. Neville's tragic death forced the realization that effective and humane methods of dealing with children in the criminal justice system were imperative.

alternative sentencing, there are substantial inconsistencies and contradictions regarding the cases that are considered (Community Law Centre, 1995).

In 1993, at an international seminar on "Children in Trouble with the Law," a paper was presented which called for a comprehensive juvenile justice system (Skelton, 1993). A drafting committee (the Juvenile Justice Drafting Consultancy) set up following the conference published *Juvenile Justice for South Africa: Proposals for Policy and Legislative Change* in 1994. The new vision needed to encompass the charging, arresting, diverting, trying, and sentencing of young offenders in a system that would affirm the child's sense of dignity and worth and clearly define the role and responsibility of the police, prosecutors, probation officers, and judicial officers with due regard to the rights of victims. In short, it needed to be innovative, inexpensive, and creative (Juvenile Justice Drafting Consultancy, 1994).

With the coming to power of the new democratically elected government the stage was set for transformation of the way in which children were dealt with by the criminal justice system. The Minister of Justice requested the South African Law Commission to include an investigation regarding juvenile justice in its program; this led to the appointment of a project committee, which began its work in the beginning of 1997. It produced a discussion paper with draft legislation in 1998, and after a period of consultation with a wide range of role-players (including children themselves), a report accompanied by a proposed draft **Child Justice Bill** was finalized in August 2000. The second part of this chapter describes the provisions of the draft bill.

THE CURRENT LEGAL FRAMEWORK

There is currently no separate statute that deals with child offenders. The draft Child Justice Bill, when passed by Parliament, will be the first statute which contains a set of provisions creating a system for dealing with children accused of crimes. Children are not materially treated differently from adults in the current justice system, but, inasmuch as a separate system for child offenders can be gleaned from various legislative provisions, it could be characterized as a **justice** oriented **model** with a strong emphasis on the protection of procedural rights (see Figure 16.1).

At present a number of special provisions relating to the handling of arrested persons under the age of 18 years are scattered across a variety of statutes.[3] The Constitution of the Republic of *South Africa Act*, No. 108, 1996, introduced a Bill of Rights that sets out a number of children's rights at section 28. The rights specific to children accused of crimes are to be found at section 28(1)(g): "Every child has the right not to be detained except as a measure of last resort, in which case, in addition to the rights the child enjoys under

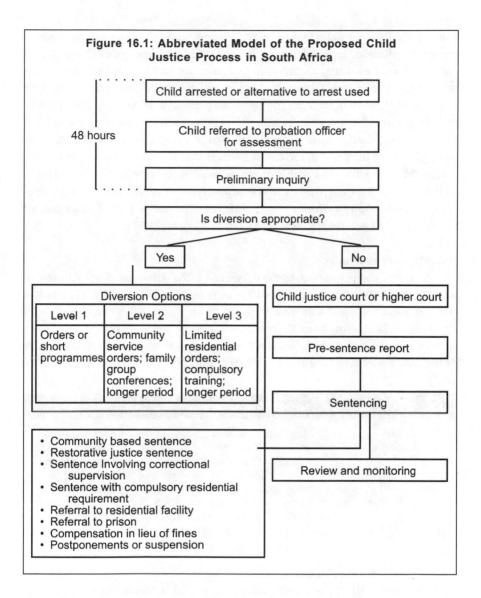

Figure 16.1: Abbreviated Model of the Proposed Child Justice Process in South Africa

sections 12 and 35, the child may be detained only for the shortest appropriate period of time and has the right to be (a) kept separately from detained persons over the age of 18 years, and (b) treated in a manner, and kept in conditions, that take account of the child's age."

Minimum age of criminal capacity

Common law governs certain aspects of the law, the most relevant of these being the rules relating to the minimum age at which children may be held responsible for criminal acts. South African common law in this regard is based on the two Roman Law rules of *doli capax* and *doli incapax* (Burchell and Hunt, 1983). According to the *doli incapax* rule children below the age of seven years are irrebuttably presumed to lack criminal capacity and cannot be prosecuted. Children between the ages of seven and 14 years are rebuttably presumed not to have criminal capacity. This presumption can be rebutted if it can be established by the prosecution that a child knew that the act was wrongful at the time and in the circumstances that the offence was committed, and further that s/he was capable of acting in accordance with that knowledge. The courts in South Africa have not properly applied the test, and the presumption relating to children between the ages of seven and 14 years has all too frequently been rebutted (Van Oosten and Louw, 1997).

Police powers and duties

Arrest is the primary method of securing the attendance of children in court. Other options in the *Criminal Procedure Act*, No. 51 of 1977, include a written notice to appear in court issued by the police, or the issuing of a summons. The use of these alternatives has been hindered by the fact that a written notice can only be issued for very minor offences and by the necessity of locating a parent or guardian prior to the handing over of the notice (see Box 16.2).

Box 16.2: Diversion

Diversion is practiced in South Africa. Although the current law does not specifically provide for diversion, experiments with diversion of young offenders were pioneered by NICRO in 1992 with the co-operation of the Department of Justice. The organization is currently providing diversion services to approximately 8,000 children annually, and plans are underway to increase this number. The programs offered are: the Youth Empowerment Scheme, Pre-trial Community Service, Victim-Offender mediation, Family Group Conferences, and "The Journey" (an outdoor adventure program). NICRO has also recently started a program for young sexual offenders.

Probation services to children accused of crimes

Probation officers in South Africa are social workers employed by the Department of Social Development. The department has made a concerted effort to provide additional probation officers and to ensure ongoing up-to-date training on child justice issues for all probation officers. Traditionally, the main role of probation officers has been to compile pre-sentence reports after the conviction of a child. In recent years the focus has shifted, with probation services playing a role immediately after arrest. Probation officers have increased their services to children in detention during the awaiting trial period, and one of their tasks is to establish and maintain contact between children and their families. In some cities "family finders" have been employed on an *ad hoc* basis by probation services. These are community volunteers who assist in tracing the families of children who have been arrested.

The courts

There is currently no official specialization of courts for children accused of crimes. In some major urban areas there are sufficient numbers of children being charged with crimes to warrant the setting aside of a court or courts to deal with such matters. These are called "juvenile courts," and they are held *in camera*. However, the personnel in such courts are not specially selected or trained, although some personnel members have gained considerable experience and expertise through practice.

Legal representation

Children have a right to legal assistance where a substantial injustice would otherwise occur and where a child or his or her family cannot afford to pay for the services of a lawyer. State-funded legal representation can be obtained through the Legal Aid Board. Although the percentage of children being legally represented has increased in recent years (Skelton and Makhathini, 1992, and Ehlers, 1999), representation still occurs in less than 50% of court cases involving child offenders. A large number of children who are offered state-funded legal aid decline these services, which indicates a need for education of children who have come into contact with the criminal justice system. There is currently no specialization among lawyers regarding legal representation of children (Zaal and Skelton, 1998).

Pre-trial detention

After arrest, children may by law be detained in a police cell before the first court appearance. After appearing in court, the child may not be remanded back to police cells. If the child cannot be released into the care of a parent or guardian, the child should be accommodated in a place of safety or (in limited circumstances) in a prison.

Detention in a police cell following arrest is limited to 24 hours according to law (section 29 of *Correctional Services Act*, the result of an amendment in 1996) although this period is frequently extended to 48 hours. As a general rule all children do appear before a court within 48 hours of arrest. Although the law does not allow children to be remanded back to police cells after having appeared in court, this is sometimes done on the order of a magistrate. These incidents tend to occur in rural areas where there is a lack of alternative facilities within a reasonable distance from the court (Sloth-Nielsen, 1996).

Children of 14 years or older can be detained in prisons during the awaiting trial period if there is no secure place of safety within a reasonable distance
from the court, and if they are charged with one of the following offences:
murder, rape, armed robbery, kidnapping, illicit conveyance or supply of drugs,
and any conspiracy, incitement, or attempt to commit any of these crimes. In
addition to these categories, the magistrate has the discretion to order a child
of 14 years or older to be detained in a prison if s/he is of the view that the
circumstances are so serious as to warrant such detention.

Approximately half of the children currently awaiting trial are placed in
prisons through the operation of this "serious circumstances" clause. In April
2000 the number of children awaiting trial peaked at 2,716. The number had
been steadily rising since 1996 (see Figure 16.2). The April figure caused the
government to undertake an inter-sectoral investigation into the causes of the
rising number. This involved visits to the four prisons housing the largest
number of children awaiting trial. The investigating team also met with magistrates, prosecutors, police, and probation officers in order to identify the problems and discuss possible solutions. The team identified delays in the criminal
justice process as the major factor leading to the rise in numbers. Although the

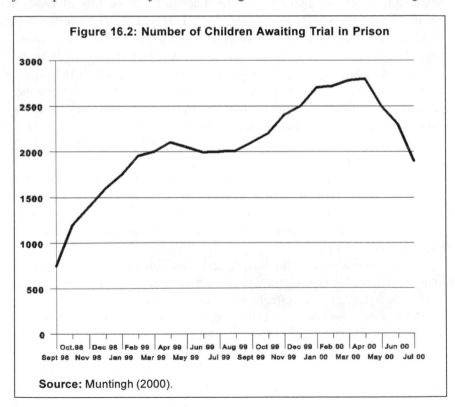

Figure 16.2: Number of Children Awaiting Trial in Prison

Source: Muntingh (2000).

team's recommendations for solving the problems have not at the time of writing been fully acted upon, the prison figures for May, June, and July have dropped, with the July figure being back below the 2,000 mark. It would appear that the discussions with the relevant role-players have borne fruit.

The concept of secure care is new in South Africa. The Inter-Ministerial Committee on Young People at Risk spearheaded the establishment of secure care facilities as an alternative to imprisonment by the Department of Social Development. This process began in 1996 and the end of 2000 will see the establishment of one secure care facility in each of South Africa's nine provinces. An amendment to the *Child Care Act* in 1999 allows for the formal registration of secure care facilities.[4]

Sentenced children

Children may be sentenced to reform schools (managed by the Department of Education)—compulsory residential facilities offering academic and technical education. The advantage of reform schools is that the sentences are relatively short, and children are permitted to have regular contact with their families. They may even go home during school holidays. The problem, however, is that, owing to the uneven geographical distribution of the facilities, they are not equally accessible to all children in the country, and sometimes children are placed far away from their homes. Questions have also been raised about the quality of care in these facilities (Inter-Ministerial Committee on Young People at Risk, 1996).

Children can be sentenced to imprisonment (see Box 16.3). Under the current law there is no limit regarding a minimum age linked to a sentence of imprisonment. The number of children imprisoned is highest among 16- and 17-year-olds, although Correctional Services statistics showed a head count of 14 children in the seven- to 13-year age-group serving sentences on 11 October 1999.

Sentencing

Corporal punishment as a sentence for offenders under the age of 18 years was struck down as unconstitutional by the Constitutional Court in 1996 and is therefore no longer used as a sentence. A range of non-custodial sentences is available to the courts for the sentencing of convicted children. It is possible to postpone the passing of sentence conditionally. In the case of unconditional postponement, the court does not pass sentence but warns that the offender may have to appear again before the court if called upon to do so. The postponement may be made conditionally for compensation, such as rendering of a benefit or service to the victim; community service; instruction or treatment; and supervision or attendance at a centre for a specified purpose.

Box 16.3: Deaths of children in detention

Despite the described legal protections for children in detention, a number of deaths in detention have occurred in recent years:

- Lubabalo Maweni (13) was beaten to death by an adult cellmate in Butterworth police cells in May 1997.
- Stephen Dube (11) died in the Waterval police cells of injuries sustained prior to or during arrest in February 1999.
- Andre Van Zyl (17) committed suicide in a lock-up room in Porter Reform School in March 1999.
- Werner Coetzee (17) allegedly committed suicide by hanging himself using a bed sheet in Odendaalsrus Prison in May 1999.
- Monica Mkansi (17 year-old girl) allegedly committed suicide while being detained in a police cell in Phalaborwa in December 1999.
- James Mofokeng (17) who was placed in a police cell with adults, was found dead, naked below the waist, in August 2000.

Enquiries have been launched into these deaths by the government departments concerned, and the deaths in police cells are being investigated by the Independents Complaints Directorate, a semi-independent body which investigates complaints against police. These deaths indicate an urgent need for dramatic improvement regarding the protection of children deprived of their liberty in South Africa.

Postponement of sentence is used regularly by the courts, particularly for non-violent offences (Skelton, 1997).

Case law has established age to be a mitigating factor upon sentencing, and a probation officer's report is required in all cases involving child offenders who are sentenced to imprisonment. In practice, children under the age of 14 are not often sentenced to imprisonment—from the period October 1998 to September 1999, a total of 66 children under 14 were sentenced to terms of imprisonment, compared with 4,564 children aged from 14 to 17 years.

The majority of children under the age of 18 serve prison sentences of less than five years. According to the Department of Correctional Services' statistics on 11 September 1999, there were 1,375 children serving prison sentences. Of these, 239 or 17% were serving terms of longer than five years. As is possible with all prisoners in South Africa, a parole board may proffer early release to children serving sentences.

The Department of Correctional Services' statistics show that the number of children sentenced to imprisonment is steadily dropping, which may indicate a softening in judicial attitudes, but could also be partially the result of a lower conviction rate owing to problems in the criminal justice system. The credibility of this latter possibility is strengthened by the fact that the number of children being detained while awaiting trial has generally been on the increase during the same period.

Review of sentences

The South African legal system has an effective and reasonably prompt review system. All children sentenced to terms of imprisonment of more than six months have their sentences taken on automatic review by a judge of the High Court, and sentences are regularly set aside or altered through this process. During 1999, two High Court cases arising from the review process have highlighted problems in the system regarding children in detention.

NUMBER OF CHILDREN ENTERING THE CRIMINAL JUSTICE SYSTEM PER YEAR IN SOUTH AFRICA

A study undertaken by the Applied Fiscal Research Centre (AFReC) at the University of Cape Town in 1999 provided estimated figures of the number of children arrested each year. The estimation was done by starting with the total number of children reflected in the 1996 census figure, and then calculating the likely percentage of cases attributable to children (based on percentages in other comparable countries) (see Figures 16.3a and 3b). These figures do hold up against the prison statistics (after the standard attrition of cases has been taken into consideration), which are the only reliable statistics available.

Although it is often reported that crimes committed by children are on the increase, this is not borne out by statistics. Data compiled by Central Statistical Services shows a steady drop in the number of children convicted per year since 1977 (Muntingh, 1999).

Recidivism

There has been little research into the patterns of recidivism (the tendency to commit further crimes) regarding juvenile crime in South Africa. The only longitudinal study in this regard was carried out by NICRO in October 1998 (Muntingh, 1998). This is a study of seven years of diversion of child offenders in South Africa. It was found that of the 468 children covered by the research, only 32 (or 6.6%) proceeded to re-offend after attending a NICRO diversion program. The average time lapse from completing the program to re-offence was 7.2 months. This research shows that, when children are given the opportunity of being diverted away from the courts to properly designed programs, the incidence of recidivism is very low. Unfortunately there are no comparable figures regarding the recidivism rates of children going through the criminal justice system, although international research indicates that recidivism is likely to be considerably higher among children who have gone though the criminal justice system.

Figure 16.3a: Calculating Process

Calculation Process	Total
Number of children between seven and 18 years of age ('96 Census)	9,943,097
Average % of children coming into conflict with the law nationally	12%
Total number of cases allegedly involving children reported to police	330,372
Average % of cases unfounded or perpetrator untraced	60%
Number of cases unfounded or perpetrator untraced	198,223
Number of cases proceeding beyond police action	132,149

Figure 16.3b: Breakdown of cases into categories

Crime	Offences Included in Crime Categories	Cases as % of Total Cases Reported in 1998
Economic	Burglary, stock theft, shoplifting, vehicle theft, theft out of car, other theft, arson, malicious damage to property, fraud	62.38%
Aggressive	Murder, attempted murder, culpable homicide, robbery, public violence, crimen iniuria, kidnapping, assault with intent to do grievous bodily harm, common assault	31.56%
Sexual	Rape, attempted rape, indecent assault	2.46%
Narcotics	All drug-related crimes	1.79%
Other	Illegal firearms, drunk driving	1.80%

(The two tables above are adaptations by Ann Skelton from tables which appear in the AFReC Report (Barberton with Stuart, 1999)).

THE LAW COMMISSION'S PROPOSED CHILD JUSTICE BILL

The framework

In translating its recommendations for a new child justice system into a legislative draft known as the "Child Justice Bill," the South African Law Commission had to take account of a variety of sometimes competing factors. First, the South African Constitution, defining "child" as a person under the age of 18 years, *inter alia* stipulates that every child has the right not to be detained as a measure of last resort, to be kept separately from persons over the age of 18, and to be treated in a manner and kept in conditions that keeps account of the child's age. In addition to echoing the international instruments' principle that a child's best interests are of paramount importance, the Constitution also guarantees the procedural rights of all arrested, detained, and accused persons, which would include those of children. The second factor that influenced the drafting was the modern trend towards restorative justice, which resonates with African concepts of justice such as reconciliation, restoration, and harmony (Allot, 1977). The central purpose of a customary law court is to acknowledge that a wrong has been done and to determine what amends should be made (Dlamini, 1988). These considerations provided a springboard for conceptualizing a child justice model. Third, an escalation of crime and media reports of young persons committing heinous crimes have led to a public expectation that the law should be tough on crime in general, irrespective of whether an offence is committed by an adult or a child. Calls for "zero tolerance" are frequently heard. Within these determinants, a comprehensive, legislative child justice structure had to be found and developed.

The blending of the first two influences, namely children's rights and restorative justice, results in a healthy balance between rights and responsibilities, with victims' rights being considered alongside those of the child offender. The draft bill recommended by the Law Commission bears evidence of this balance. It is imbued with the language of the international instruments, and while the Commission has not considered it necessary to restate the articles contained in the South African Constitution, the draft bill gives effect to the constitutional guarantees for children accused of crimes. The draft bill contains both an objectives and a principles clause. The objectives clause emphasizes the procedural rights of children and links the central theme of Article 40 of the UN Convention on the Rights of the Child to the indigenous concept of *ubuntu*,[5] thus Africanizing the international principles by emphasizing family and community. The third influence, namely public concern about crime, has been addressed by provisions in the draft bill which allow for children charged with serious, violent offences to be tried in a criminal court at a higher jurisdictional level, to be imprisoned both during the awaiting trial-period and as a sentence option (see Box 16.4). These measures are, however, framed as a last resort. It also contains a provision that criminal records for serious and violent offences should not be expunged (see Figure 16.3b above).

Age and criminal capacity

Cognizant of the fact that the Committee on the Rights of the Child has consistently criticized countries that have established a minimum age of criminal capacity of 10 years or younger, the Commission has recommended that the minimum age should be raised from seven to 10 years, implying that children below the age of 10 years cannot be prosecuted.[6] In order to protect the category of children aged between 10 and 14, it was further recommended that a rebuttable presumption should apply that such children do not have the capacity to appreciate the difference between right and wrong and to act in

Box 16.4: Defining the proposed Juvenile Justice System in South Africa

In deciding where to place the proposed South African model within the welfare/justice divide, regard was had to the debates on the welfare versus justice models that have unfolded during the twentieth century. The danger of sacrificing due process rights in favour of a **welfarist** approach became clear with the US Supreme Court case *In re Gault*. The Law Commission, mindful of this danger, has opted for an inter-sectoral model which follows a primarily justice approach with welfare support mechanisms. The model focuses on diversion options that promote accountability, coupled with a vigilant approach to the protection of the due process rights of children. There is a strong influence of restorative justice, as evidenced by the provisions for family group conferences, restitution, and compensation. It simulates what has been described in Canada as a **modified justice model** and, like the Canadian model, envisages a dual handling process that distinguishes between less serious and serious offenders.

accordance with that appreciation. The presumption may be rebutted if it is subsequently proved beyond a reasonable doubt that a child did have the capacity at the time of the commission of an offence. An additional protection afforded to this category of children is that the Director of Public Prosecutions[7] has issued a certificate confirming an intention to proceed with prosecution. This approach is intended to encourage the diversion of children in this age group in the majority of cases, while still preserving the discretion of the prosecutor with regard to the prosecution of such children.

Regarding the rebuttal of the presumption that will apply in respect of accused children between the ages of 10 and 14, the draft bill provides that either the prosecution or the defence may request an evaluation, at state expense, of the child by a suitably qualified person regarding the child's cognitive, emotional, psychological, and social development. It is envisaged that this provision will mainly be utilized by the defence, as it can hardly be conceived that the prosecutor, who is burdened with rebutting the presumption, will endanger his or her case by leading evidence which may prove that the child concerned did not have the capacity to distinguish the difference between right and wrong at the time of the commission of the offence. It is further recommended that all children, in the mentioned category, who have not been diverted and who end up in court must be represented by a legal practitioner.

In consonance with the South African Constitution, the draft bill establishes the upper age limit at 18, meaning that it will apply to all children who have not yet turned 18. In respect of the category of children aged between 14 and 18, it is presumed that such children do have the capacity to appreciate the difference between right and wrong and to act in accordance with that appreciation.

As many children accused of crimes in South Africa do not know their exact ages, the draft bill proposes certain measures to overcome the problem when a child's age is uncertain or in dispute. (For a comparison see Chapter 12, Namibia). For instance, a list of documents and other forms of relevant information that may enable a probation officer to estimate a child's age, on the basis of which a magistrate may determine the age of a child, is prescribed. This age is then considered to be the correct age of the child until evidence to the contrary is brought to light.

Police powers and duties

The draft bill encourages the use of alternatives to arrest. Such alternatives include requesting a child to accompany the police official to attend an assessment or issuing a written notice to attend a preliminary inquiry (discussed below). The alternatives may be used with regard to any offence, but must be used with regard to minor offences (which are listed in a schedule to the bill) unless there are compelling reasons not to do so. The National Commissioner of the South African Police Service is also empowered to issue a national instruction setting out the circumstances in which a police official may issue an informal warning instead of arresting a child or using an alternative to arrest.

If a child has been arrested, or an alternative to arrest has been effected, the police official is required to notify, apart from the child's parent, a probation officer of the arrest or the use of an alternative within 24 hours. An assessment of the child then has to be conducted by the probation officer for consideration at the preliminary inquiry, which must take place within 48 hours of the arrest.

Detention of children and release from detention

The draft bill provides for a number of principles that are to be considered by any person who makes a decision regarding the detention or release of a child. The principles are set out hierarchically, stating that preference should be given to releasing a child unconditionally to his or her parent, but that conditions linked to the release must be considered if the child would otherwise be detained. Bail should likewise be considered if detention is the only alternative, and, finally, detention should be a measure of last resort. If detention cannot be avoided, the least restrictive form of detention appropriate to the child and the circumstances must be selected.

Importantly, a child can only be remanded to a prison to await trial if the child is 14 years of age or older; if charged with a serious or violent offence (listed in a schedule to the bill); or if detention in a place of safety or secure care facility is not possible. In an attempt to reflect broad consensus that detention of children in police cells pending trial should be avoided, the bill prohibits such detention if after conclusion of the preliminary inquiry it is found that the matter cannot be diverted.

Diversion

Since diversion has been growing rapidly in South African juvenile justice practice, especially through the efforts of NICRO, a statutory framework for diversion was needed. It was considered that future development could be encouraged with enabling legislative provisions. As most children in South Africa charged with crime have committed non-violent offences, diversion forms a central feature of the proposed legislation. The purposes of diversion include concepts such as:

- encouraging the child to be accountable for their actions;
- providing an opportunity for victims to express their views, encouraging restitution, and promoting reconciliation; and
- reintegrating the child into their family and community, preventing stigmatization, and preventing the child from acquiring a criminal record.

A range of innovative diversion options is set out in three varying levels of intensity. A series of orders for new diversion options have been designed, such as a compulsory school attendance order, a family time order, a positive peer association order, a good behavior order, and so forth. These orders allow children to remain in their homes while providing a back-up to parents and families having difficulty in guiding their children through adolescence.

Probation officers, tasked with the compulsory assessment of each child who has been arrested or in respect of whom an alternative to arrest was used, may make recommendations regarding diversion to be recorded on an assessment report. This report has to be referred to the relevant prosecutor. Upon consideration of the recommendations, the prosecutor may exercise power to withdraw the charges or must arrange for the opening of a preliminary inquiry to consider diversion.

The preliminary inquiry

A dramatic departure from conventional South African criminal procedure is contemplated in the proposal for a preliminary inquiry. Contrary to the mainly adversarial nature of criminal trials, the preliminary inquiry envisages a compulsory pre-trial round-table discussion presided over by a magistrate and involving the child, the parents, the prosecutor, the probation officer, and the police. The objectives of the preliminary inquiry, *inter alia*, are to:

- establish whether a child can be diverted and, if so, to which diversion option;
- provide the prosecutor with an opportunity to assess whether there are sufficient grounds for the case to proceed to trial; and

- determine the release or placement of a child.

The capacity of the prosecutor as *dominus litis* is retained in the draft Bill in that it gives the prosecutor the final say as to whether the matter can be diverted after consideration of all relevant information. Where the prosecutor decides to proceed with the prosecution, the matter may be set down for plea and trial in an appropriate court. A magistrate who has presided over a preliminary inquiry and has heard any information prejudicial to the impartial determination of the matter is precluded from presiding over any subsequent trial.

The child justice court

Since there is no separate criminal court for children in South Africa, the Commission has recommended the establishment of a child justice court with a particular identity. The draft bill requires chief magistrates to designate such a court in each district, and that court must, as far as possible, be staffed by specially selected and trained personnel. The courtroom, where practicable, should be located and designed in a way that is conducive to the dignity and well being of children, the informality of the proceedings, and the participation of all persons involved. The sentencing jurisdiction of a district magistrate's court would apply to the child justice court. Although the possibility of hearing cases involving a child accused in higher courts is retained, the draft bill encourages the preferential use of the child justice court.

Provisions have also been included in the draft bill to promote the establishment of One-Stop Child Justice Centres. Such centers provide offices to be utilized by police and probation officers, facilities to accommodate children temporarily pending the finalization of the preliminary inquiry, and a child justice court.

In order to facilitate the speedy finalization of trials involving accused children, it is further proposed that where a child remains in detention pending trial and the trial is not concluded within six months from the date upon which the child has pleaded to the charge, such child must be released from custody unless the charge is one of murder, rape, aggravated robbery, or robbery involving the taking of a motor vehicle.

Sentencing

The draft bill provides for a wide range of sentencing options. These include:

- community-based sentences, which do not involve a residential requirement and which allow a child to remain in his or her community;

- restorative justice sentences, such as referral of the child to a family group conference or victim-offender mediation;
- correctional supervision, which may be suspended or postponed on the condition that a child be placed under the supervision of a proba- tion officer or correctional official and that the child performs a service for the benefit of the community;
- referral of the child to a program with a periodic and limited residence requirement, a residential facility,[8] or a prison;
- the postponement or suspension of any sentence, with or without conditions; and
- fines, which may not be payable to the state but may, in prescribed circumstances, be paid as compensation to persons or to a community organization, charity, or welfare organization.

The draft bill prohibits the imposition of life imprisonment on a child who was under the age of 18 years at the time of committing the offence and pro- vides that a child who has been sentenced to attend a residential facility may not be detained in a prison or in police cells while awaiting designation of the place where the sentence will be served. The current procedure for review of sentences has been largely retained.

Legal representation

The draft bill entitles a child to legal representation during any procedures under the proposed legislation and provides for legal representation at state expense when the child is remanded in detention pending plea and trial, when there is a likelihood that a sentence involving a residential requirement will be imposed upon conviction, and when the child is at least 10 but not yet 14 years of age and the matter will be tried in court. A child who is entitled to legal representation at state expense may not waive this right. If not satisfied with the appointed legal representative, the child may make a fresh application for the appointment of another person. If the child indicates that no legal repre- sentative is desired, the court must appoint a legal representative to assist (as opposed to representing) the child.

Monitoring structures

The draft bill establishes a number of structures to monitor and enhance the effective implementation of the proposed legislation. The idea is to ensure that the legislation will be workable in practice and that future difficulties, inconsistencies, and loopholes that might emerge are addressed in a respon- sible way, based on sound research, with appropriate consultation. Hence the draft bill establishes monitoring structures at district, provincial, and national levels.

Expungement of records

The draft bill prohibits the expungement of the record of the conviction of and sentence imposed upon a child who has committed certain serious offences (listed in a schedule to the bill). In respect of other offences, the presiding officer, at the time of sentencing the child, must also make an order regarding the expungement of the record of the child's conviction and sentence. In making a decision regarding expungement, the presiding officer must consider the nature and circumstances of the offence as well as the child's personal circumstances or any other relevant factor. A date must be set upon which the expungement must take place, which date may not be less than three months nor more than five years from the date of the sentence. The presiding officer must also impose, as a condition of expungement, a requirement that the child must not be convicted of a similar or more serious offence between the date of imposition of the sentence and the date of expungement.

CURRENT ISSUES RELATING TO SOUTH AFRICAN JUVENILE JUSTICE TODAY

Increasing crime control approaches

In recent years the South African Parliament has to some extent been influenced by **crime control** ideas emanating largely from the U.S.A. This creates an increasingly difficult environment for juvenile justice law reform. At the end of 1997 the Parliamentary Justice Portfolio Committee cast a vote in favour of a bill on minimum sentences. Although the minimum sentences in the proposed legislation were not mandatory, in deference to the South African Constitution, the similarity of this bill to the American approach of "three strikes and you're out"[9] alerted criminal law reformists to the fact that the government was moving away from a balanced human rights approach to an approach in which fighting crime was the overwhelming consideration (Sloth-Nielsen, 1999).

The initial draft of the legislation included offenders under the age of 18 years within its ambit. Non-governmental organizations rallied and made both written and oral submissions on the draft bill to the Portfolio Committee on Justice, arguing that the idea of minimum sentences for children would go against the UN Convention on the Rights of the Child and the South African Constitution which both state that detention of children should be a measure of last resort, and that minimum sentences for children would in fact make imprisonment a first resort notwithstanding the "escape clause" which would allow the court, in its discretion, to deviate from the minimum sentence. Perhaps as a result of these submissions, the bill was changed so that children under the age of 16 years are now completely excluded from the ambit of the *Criminal Law Amendment Act*, and 16- and 17-year-olds, while included in its ambit, are treated differently in that the onus is on the state to show that there are substantial and compelling reasons why the minimum sentence should be imposed.

The efforts to exclude children from the effects of new bail legislation did not yield the same positive result. In 1997 the law relating to bail was changed to make it more difficult for accused persons charged with certain serious violent crimes to be released on bail. Submissions to the Justice Portfolio Committee, requesting that the bill should not include children within its ambit, were not favourably considered. The final Act made no differentiation based on age—this legislation, like the legislation on minimum sentences, is based on lists of offences and under-plays the individual circumstances of the offender.

A further example of how American crime control concepts are gaining ground in South Africa is the development of the *Prevention of Organized Crime Act,* which draws heavily on Californian legislation dealing with street gangs. The Act provides factors to guide the courts in determining whether a particular individual is a gang member. One of the factors to be considered is whether the person "resides in or frequents a particular criminal gang's area and adopts their style of dress, use of hand signs, language or tattoos." This is evidently very broad and may spell danger for many teenagers who enjoy wearing clothing and bearing tattoos that make them look similar to the members of a local gang (Skelton, 1999).

Involvement of children in criminal gangs

During the apartheid years, young people were involved in political structures. This gave them identity and a sense of belonging. It has been observed that the end of apartheid led to the breakdown of structures which had actually provided a focussed life for young people and that the gap which was left has been filled by criminal gangs (Simpson, 1997). Pinnock (1997) has observed that prior to colonization and apartheid there were rituals that clearly marked the passage from childhood to adulthood and that these have disappeared. He suggests that programs should provide what young people are searching for and should include a "rites of passage" element.

Gender issues

Females account for only a small portion of child offenders. Figures obtained from the Durban Magistrate's Court showed that only 300 out of 2,712 children charged in the period June 1996 to June 1997 were girls—approximately 11% of the total—and that the majority of them were charged with theft. The three reform schools for girls in South Africa have been receiving fewer and fewer girls from the criminal justice system in recent years, with the result that two have closed. Although these are positive factors in many ways, they do lead to a situation that, when a girl is accused of a serious or violent crime, there are fewer options, and she is more likely to be placed far away from home than is the case with boys (SA Law Commission, 1998).

Socio-economic circumstances

The socio-economic circumstances in which the majority of South Africans live are conducive to crime. There are currently few effective crime prevention programs and virtually no reintegrative programs. Thus, children who have completed a diversion program or a sentence return with little or no preparation to the same circumstances that led them into crime in the first place. The South African government has made a commitment to poverty alleviation, community development, and job creation for young people. These broad-ranging programs may take some years to come to fruition, and in the meanwhile it falls mainly to cash-strapped community-based and non-governmental organizations to provide appropriate assistance to young people (Financial and Fiscal Commission, 1998).

SUMMARY

In this chapter an attempt was made to distinguish between the juvenile justice system in South Africa as it is currently operating and the proposed new child justice system, which has been the subject of research for the past three years. The present system does not take into account South Africa's commitments as a country which has ratified the UN Convention on the Rights of the Child, does not incorporate the principles and values underlying the newly adopted Constitution, and fails to a large extent to establish an identifiable system geared towards the special needs of child offenders.

It is well-known that South Africa's crime rate features among the worst. Gangsterism, poverty, and illiteracy are but a few factors underpinning the present negative socio-economic trends. Public anger in the face of the current climate of escalating crime has to some extent caused the government to implement measures, including legislation, not only to address societal problems but also to be seen as having adopted a "tough-on-crime" stance. Notwithstanding the fact that research has indicated that the number of serious crimes committed by young people is not on the increase, the drafters of the proposed Child Justice Bill had to take the public attitude towards crime into account. A balance had to be struck between societal demands and the growing international trend towards **restorative justice** and the positive reintegration of young offenders into their families and communities through diversionary measures. The realization that diversion of minor offences away from the formal criminal justice system does not necessarily mean that young offenders who have committed such crimes will be treated softly may still need to dawn on members of the public. It is hoped that the proposed legislation will be dealt with in Parliament in such a way that it becomes clear that the main objective is to treat children differently from adults, according to their individual needs, backgrounds, and the seriousness of their actions.

A restorative justice approach in the field of child justice has to some extent been phased in through efforts of NICRO in recent years, but there is currently no substantial legal framework for a welfarist approach. The child justice system proposed by the Law Commission is essentially an **inter-sectoral model** which follows a primary justice approach with welfare support mechanisms and can be described as a **modified justice model**.

The Law Commission's report and the draft Child Justice Bill summarized in this chapter were handed to the South African Minister for Justice and Constitutional Development, Dr. Penuell Maduna, on 8 August 2000. In light of Parliament's busy legislative program for the remainder of 2000 and 2001, it is envisaged that the draft bill will be debated and considered by the Parliamentary Portfolio Committees during the course of 2002. The United Nations Development Program (UNDP) and the S.A. Ministry for Justice and Constitutional Development have, during the course of 1999, entered into an agreement for UN technical assistance in the field of child justice, giving rise to the UN Child Justice Project. Located in the Department of Justice as part of the Directorate on Children and Youth Affairs, the main objective of the project is to assist the government in the implementation of the new legislation proposed by the Law Commission. The project will assist with the development of the new system for dealing with children accused of crimes in a number of ways:

- enhancing the capacity and use of programs for diversion and appropriate sentencing of children;
- finding ways to protect children in detention;
- supporting the implementation of the new legislation;
- raising awareness and training of personnel; and
- helping to establish a monitoring structure.

Finally, unlike most other contributions in this reader, the South African juvenile justice system is in the process of being transformed. As was evident throughout the chapter, we have been able to consider the experiences of other countries as well as the approaches of various international instruments and initiatives adopted in the field of child/youth justice. Although the details of the proposed new system are yet to be approved and finalized by Parliament, the foundation of a system built on internationally recognized standards has already been laid.

Ann Skelton obtained her B.A. LL.B. degree in 1985 and was admitted as an advocate of the High Court of South Africa in 1988. She was appointed by the minister of justice in 1997 to lead a project of the South African Law Commission to develop a comprehensive new juvenile justice statute. She is currently the national co-ordinator of the Child Justice Project, a UN technical assistance project based in the Department of Justice in Pretoria.

Hennie Potgieter obtained his B.Iuris LL.B. degree in 1984 and was admitted as an advocate of the High Court of South Africa in 1987. He was appointed assistant master of the High Court in 1985, working in the field of deceased and insolvent estates, and was later seconded to the South African Law Commission as a researcher involved in law reform and the drafting of remedial legislation. He is currently a consultant at the Commission and assisted the project committee on juvenile justice in the development of the draft Child Justice Bill.

HELPFUL WEBSITES

www.sn.apc.org/users/clc/children/index.htm. This is the website of the Children's Rights Project by the Community Law Centre (an NGO) at the University of the Western Cape. It provides information about the project, contains South African cases and judgments involving children and also has a number of valuable links to child related sites.

www.law.wits.ac.za/salc/salc.html This is the SA Law Commission website. It contains the report on juvenile justice submitted to the Minister of Justice and Constitutional Development, which reports on and reflects the proposed draft Child Justice Bill. (approx. 320 pages).

www.childrenfirst.org.za A sited committed to presenting African perspectives on the situation of children in Africa and South Africa. It strives to promote and protect the rights and well-being of children, and to stimulate debate on models of good practice for working with children.

www.cjcj.org The American Centre on Juvenile and Criminal Justice's site whose mission it is to reduce society's reliance on the use of incarceration as a solution to social problems.

KEY TERMS AND CONCEPTS

NICRO	Child Justice Bill
Inter-sectoral model	Modified justice model
Doli capax	Crime Control
Restorative justice	Customary Law
welfarist	In re Gault
Inter-sectorial Model	

STUDY QUESTIONS

1. The South African criminal justice system is adversarial in nature. In terms of new proposals, a procedure called the preliminary inquiry, which will mainly be

inquisitorial and will take place prior to trial (which will be less formal but still adversarial), is envisaged. To what extent is a hybrid of adversarial and inquisitorial procedures found in other countries?

2. In order to fortify the notion that child offenders should be treated individually, an assessment of each child offender by a probation officer will be made compulsory in the new proposals for child justice in South Africa. The assessment will have to be concluded prior to the proposed preliminary inquiry in order to furnish those present at the inquiry with sufficient background information to make an informed decision as to what should happen to the child. Are similar assessments done in other countries, and, if so, by whom?

3. How does the proposed procedure for the expungement of criminal records of child offenders in South Africa compare to those of other countries? Which countries have legislative provisions for expungement of records?

4. Diversion of less serious offences away from the formal criminal justice system will form a central feature of the proposed South African child justice system. The proposed diversion (and sentencing) mechanisms emphasize restorative justice principles, compensation of victims, supervision of offenders, community service, and the ultimate reintegration of offenders in their families and communities. Do diversion and sentencing mechanisms in other countries have a different emphasis?

NOTES

1   The National Institute for Crime Prevention and Rehabilitation of Offenders, a non-governmental organization partially subsidized by the government.

2   The National Director of Public Prosecutions, the highest prosecuting authority in the country.

3   The *Criminal Procedure Act*, No. 51 of 1977, the *Child Care Act*, No. 74 of 1983, the *Probation Services Act*, No. 116 of 1991 and the *Correctional Services Act*, No. 8 of 1959.

4   *Child Care Amendment Act*, No. 13 of 1999.

5   An African philosophy of humanity and humanitarian co-existence.

6   This recommendation incidentally corresponds with recent recommendations of the Hong Kong Law Reform Commission, as evident from its *Report on the age of criminal responsibility in Hong Kong,* May 2000 (see Chapter 6).

7   The head of State Prosecutors in each province in South Africa.

8   The South African child and youth care system is currently undergoing transformation. The current reform schools and schools of industry, relics of a colonial era, are being rationalized and renamed. The term "residential facility" is therefore used to cover all forms of residential care, excluding prisons.

9   The US Federal *Violent Crime Control and Law Enforcement Act* of 1994 contains a three-strikes provision.

REFERENCES

Allot, AN. (1977). The people as law makers: Custom, practice and public opinion as sources of law in Africa and England. *Journal of African Law*: 21.

Burchell, J., & Hunt, P. (1983). *South African Criminal Law and Procedure*. 2nd ed. Cape Town: Juta.

Barberton, C., with Stuart J. (1999). *Costing the implementation of the Child Justice Bill: A scenario analysis*. Research Monograph No. 14, AFReC. Cape Town: University of Cape Town.

Community Law Centre. (1995). *Law, Practice, and Policy: South African Juvenile Justice Today*. Cape Town: University of the Western Cape.

Dlamini, C. (1988). *The Role of Chiefs in the Administration of Justice*. Unpublished LL.M thesis, University of Pretoria.

Ehlers, L. (1999). Children's views on a new juvenile justice system. *Article 40*, 1(2): 6-8.

Financial and Fiscal Commission. (1998). *Report for UNICEF and UNDP*. Pretoria.

Inter-Ministerial Committee on Young People at Risk. (1996). *In Whose Best Interests? Report on Places of Safety, Schools of Industry and Reform Schools*. Pretoria: Ministry of Welfare and Population Development.

Juvenile Justice Drafting Consultancy. (1994). *Juvenile Justice for South Africa: Proposals for Policy and Legislative Change*. Cape Town: Allies Printers.

Muntingh, L. (1998). *The Effectiveness of Diversion Programmes—a Longitudinal Evaluation of Cases*. Cape Town: NICRO.

Muntingh, L. (2000). Statistics: Children awaiting trial. *Article 40*, 2(3): 12.

Pinnock, D. (1997). *Gangs, Rituals, and Rites of Passage*. Cape Town: African Sun Press.

Simpson, G. (1997, 5-6 Feb). Youth crime in South Africa. Conference paper presented at a conference entitled "Appropriate justice for young people: Exploring alternatives to retribution." Cape Town: Institute of Criminology (University of Cape Town) and NICRO.

Skelton, A. (1997). Children, young persons, and the criminal procedure. In J.A. Robinson (Ed.), *The Law of Children and Young Persons in South Africa*. Durban: Butterworths.

Skelton, A. (1993, 15-17 Oct). Raising ideas for a juvenile justice system. Conference paper presented at an international seminar entitled "Children in trouble with the law." Cape Town: Community Law Centre (University of the Western Cape).

Skelton, A. (1999). Juvenile justice reform: Children's rights and responsibility versus crime control. In C.J. Davel (Ed.), *Children's Rights in a Transitional Society*. Pretoria: Protea Book House.

Skelton, A., & Makhatini, O. (1993). Report on the juvenile justice project. Unpublished paper. Lawyers for Human Rights, South Africa.

Sloth-Nielsen, J. (1996). Pre-trial detention of juveniles revisited: Amending section 29 of the Correctional Services Act. *SACJ*: 61.

Sloth-Nielsen, J. (1999). The juvenile justice law reform process in South Africa: Can a children's rights approach carry the day? *Quinnipiac Law Review*: 469.

South African Law Commission. (1998). *Discussion Paper 79: Juvenile Justice*. Pretoria.

Van Eden, J. (1995). What can indigenous African customs teach contemporary juvenile justice? Unpublished paper, Institute of Criminology (University of Cape Town).

Van Oosten, F.F.W., and Louw, A.S. (1997). Children, young persons, and the criminal law. In J.A. Robinson (Ed.), *The Law of Children and Young Persons in South Africa*. Durban: Butterworths.

Zaal, F.N., & Skelton, A. (1998). Providing effective representation for children in a new constitutional era: Lawyers in the criminal and children's courts. *SAJHR*: 519

Chapter 17

Juvenile Justice and Youth Crime: An Overview of South Korea

Hyun-Hee Lee
Samsung S1 Crime Prevention Institute
Kun Lee
Department of Urban Sociology,
University of Seoul

FACTS ON SOUTH KOREA

Area: Approximately 99,373 sq. km. South Korea occupies the southern part of the Korean Peninsula, which extends for approximately 1,000 km southward from northeast China. South Korea is bordered by the Democratic People's Republic (North Korea) to the north; East China Sea to the south; the East Sea (Sea of Japan) to the east; and the Yellow Sea to the west. It covers one time zone. The climate is moderate with heavier rainfall during the winter months. Seventy per cent of the land is mountainous. **Population**: Approximately 47.3 million in 2000. Ethnic group is homogeneous. Language is Korean. Korea's population characteristics have changed very rapidly in the last 30 years. The proportion of the population in urban areas has risen from 30% in the 1960s to 80% in 2000. For example, 45% of the entire population lives in Seoul and its contiguous area, the metropolitan city of Incheon, and Kyonggi province. The average life span has increased from 62.3 years in 1971 to 74.4 in 1997. The growth rate is approximately 10.7% annually. The education level has increased rapidly as well. The proportion of those who go beyond high school education has increased from 15% in the 1970s to 60% in 1999. **Economy**: Korea has rapidly developed over the past 30 years. The GDP per capita has risen from US$249 in 1970 to US$11,380 in 1996, but dropped to US $8,581 in 1999 due to the Asian financial crisis in 1997 and 1998. Because of the steady growth up until 1997, the unemployment rate had been around 2% to 4%, which rose to 6.8%, and has now settled around 4%. The industrial sector has experienced the most dramatic growth since the 1970s. The proportion of workers in the manufacturing sector has increased from 15% to 22%, and in the service sector has increased from 35% to 70%. **Government**: Korea has a long history, established in 2000 B.C. as Kochosun. Since then, five dynasties—Kyguryo, Paekjae, Shilla, Koryo, Chosun—rose and fell until 1910, when Korea was colonized by Japan. At the end of World War II, in 1945, Korea was liberated from Japan and formally recognized as the Republic of Korea in 1948. In 1950, the Korean War broke out, and

Korea was divided into two nations, North Korea and South Korea. The government structure of South Korea is patterned mainly on the presidential system of the United States and is based on separation of powers among the legislature, the executive, and the judiciary. The President is the chief of state, head of the executive branch and commander of the armed forces, and is elected for a single five-year term by direct popular vote. Legislative authority rests with the unicameral National Assembly. Most of the National Assembly members are elected by direct popular vote for a four-year term, and the rest are appointed by political parties.

At 15 I set my heart on learning; at 30 I firmly took my stand; at 40 I had no delusions: at 50 I knew the Mandate of Heaven; at 60 my ear was attuned; at 70 I followed my heart's desire without overstepping the boundaries of right.
– Confucius, Analects 2:4.

This chapter will present an overview of the characteristics of juvenile delinquency and the juvenile justice system in Korea. Beginning with the historical development of juvenile justice, we will present the background, basic ideas, concepts, and overall images of the Korean juvenile justice system. We will then describe the trends and patterns of youth crime over the past 30 years. This will be followed by an overview of the structure of the juvenile justice system and the judicial procedures. The chapter will conclude with a discussion of some important legislative and social issues in the Korean juvenile justice system.

HISTORICAL DEVELOPMENT OF JUVENILE JUSTICE

Our modern legal system emerged at the end of the Chosun dynasty era (1392 to 1910). In the late nineteenth century, the Korean peninsula was the place where the Great Powers[1] of the time competed to gain control over East Asian territories. Under the competitive influences of the Great Powers, Korea began to change its entire system, including the legal system. Traditional institutions established on the basis of Confucian values had to be changed to adopt Western values. The Korean government steadily assimilated the codes of Western civil laws.

Ironically, not the Western Powers, but rather the Japanese pushed forward the first movement towards modernization in Korea. It began with the Political Reform in 1894, called the **Kabo Reform**, under the strong influence of Japan. New Korean law was modeled after the Japanese reform policies of the Meiji Restoration (1868). Although the Kabo political reform ended in 1895, the influence of the Great Powers persisted.

Direct and massive changes in the Korean legal system took place after Korea was occupied and colonized by Japan in 1910. Therefore, as with the Japanese legal system, the Korean legal system can trace its origins in Roman and Germanic laws. Western influences on the Korean legal system evolved in the aftermath of World War II. The Korean legal system began to have features from both the continental and Anglo-American legal systems. After World War II, the U.S. military governed Korea until the Korean government was established in 1948.

Korea revised its codification and began to establish a modern legal system. The new laws, however, were not properly implemented because of the Korean War (1950 to 1953). After the war, Korea formally adopted the Criminal Code in 1953, the Code of Criminal Procedure in 1954, the Civil Code in 1958, and the Civil Procedure Law in 1960. In 1958 the Juvenile Law, the core of the Korean juvenile justice, was established.

Although Korean elites tried to get rid of the Japanese influences in the legal system, traces still lingered (see Miyazawa, 1991; Yokoyama, 1997; Research and Training Institute of the Ministry of Justice, 1999). As originally received through Japan, Korean law including the juvenile law retained the most fundamental principles and procedures of continental jurisprudence.

Below is a chronological overview of the major developmental steps of juvenile justice and the preventive institutions in Korea.

- Chosun dynasty—Great Law of Kyungguk (Governance for the Nation). Defining the prohibition of incarceration for those who are below 15 years old, except for cases of rebellion, murder, or robbery.
- 1923—Chosun Juvenile Welfare Facilities Law proclamation. Building some accommodation houses in Hamheung, Mokpo, and Incheon by the Japanese colonial government.
- 1942—Chosun Juvenile Law and Chosun Correction Law proclamation. Establishment of the Kyungsung Juvenile Court (former Seoul Family Court) and Kyungsung Correction Center (former Seoul Juvenile Training School) by the Japanese colonial government.
- 1945—Establishment of juvenile training schools in Daegu, Pusan, and Gwangju.
- 1957—Establishment of the children's counseling center in each province.
- 1958—Modern Korean Juvenile Law proclamation. Definition of discretionary power of public prosecutor and referring of a juvenile case to family court and juvenile division of district court with various disposition options.
- 1977—Establishment of Juvenile Detention and Classification Office.
- 1981—Adoption of Suspension of Prosecution of Juvenile Offender on the Fatherly Guidance Condition of Public Prosecutor (diversion program).
- 1988—First introduction of probation with suspension in the community for juveniles.

IDEAS AND WORKINGS OF JUVENILE JUSTICE

The Korean juvenile justice system is established on the philosophical concept of *parens patriae*. Section 1 of the Korean Juvenile Law demonstrates the essence of this idea: "the goal of the Juvenile Law is for the delinquent juvenile to be raised socially, healthily, and safely by taking special measures of punishment and putting him/her under probation for the correction of delinquent behaviour." This law embodies the **welfare model** of the justice system.

The mission of the justice system is to provide care and protection for delinquent youth. Although juvenile offenders must be punished, the punishment procedure takes into account the personality and the needs of the child irrespective of the criminal act (with the exception of the most serious of crimes; see below). The reasons for treating juvenile delinquents differently from adult offenders are as follows: 1) young persons are not yet fully grown-up; 2) they are readily influenced by their immediate environment; and 3) offences tend to happen accidentally rather than intentionally. To this end, the role of the juvenile justice system is not limited to just treatment, but extended to pedagogical aspects of rehabilitation (Lee, L., 1991; Lee, J., and Ahn, 1995; Won, 1997; Gatti, 1991).

However well-established the legislative procedures might be, the ideal of the welfare model has been difficult to achieve. In actual workings of the juvenile justice system, all elements of corrective measures such as pedagogical treatments, psychological assistances, and provisions for the better environment have rarely been executed. Furthermore, it has been financially and socially difficult for the Korean government to put the welfare model into practice. Even after the introduction of probation with community supervision in 1988, the pedagogical and welfare aspects of the juvenile justice system have not been properly implemented. As a result, the Korean juvenile justice system, though established on the basis of the welfare model, works more-or-less like a **justice model**; that is, it is more punishment oriented than welfare oriented (see Figure 1—Introduction).

SUMMARY OF THE KOREAN JUVENILE LAW

1. Definitions of Juvenile Crime and Delinquency (Section 4, Juvenile Law). Juveniles are legally defined as those youth between the ages of 14 to 20. Juvenile court has the jurisdiction over three kinds of juveniles: juvenile offender, law-breaking youth, and pre-delinquents.
    *   **Juvenile offender** is one who is suspected of violating the laws when between the ages of 14 to 19. Offenders of 20-years-old, or older, are referred to the adult justice system.

- **Law-breaking youth** is one who violates laws at the age of 12 or 13. This age group does not have responsibility for their criminal acts nor the punitive responsibility as well. Juveniles under the age of 12 do not appear in police or judicial statistics.
- **Pre-delinquent** is one (i.e., ages 12 to 19) who is prone to commit some criminal offences. This category reflects the broad range of prohibited behaviors such as immoral and indecent conduct, association with vicious persons, habitual truancy from school, using intoxicating liquor, and disappearing from home without parental consent.

2. All juvenile criminal cases must first be referred to the public prosecutor's office. Referring a case back to the juvenile court is within the discretion of the public prosecutor. Although it is contradictory to the principle of paternalism of juvenile justice, prosecutors have a large discretionary power. France, Austria, Italy, and Germany utilize a similar position whereas in Japan (see Chapter 11) and almost all states of the United States (see Chapter 18) the judge has the discretionary power.

3. A hearing must be held to understand the general condition and characteristics of the juvenile offender so as to determine the nature of the delinquency.

4. Information about the family and social environment of the delinquent juvenile as well as the criminal motivation and the possibility of recidivism must be included in the juvenile court. Such information is used to reach a disposition.

5. Juvenile Law specifies the procedure and punishment levels for all juvenile offences. The procedure is more protective toward young offenders and punishment is less severe than for adult cases.

TRENDS AND CHARACTERISTICS OF YOUTH CRIME

> *Ok, Ok, Ok, Ok, No more education*
> *Enough, enough, enough, enough*
> *In the dark classroom that has eaten us,*
> *My youth is too good to be wasted.*
> *I will make you more expensive*
> *More than the one next to you.*
> *Step on other's head*
> *One by one*
> *You can.*
> – Class Room IDEA, Very famous Korean Rap song written by Seo Taiji

CRIME STATISTICS AND DATA

In Korea, three sources of formal crime statistics are available: 1) the National Police Agency compiles crime statistics which are published annually in the *White Paper on Police*; 2) the Supreme Prosecutor's Office produces data on crime, prosecution, and correction; they publish their annual data in *Crime Analysis*; and 3) the Judicial Research and Training Institute analyze crime data, focusing on the trend analysis; their findings are published annually in *White Paper on Crime*. These three reports include data on juvenile delinquency and the justice system in general. For youth, the Ministry of Culture and Tourism also publishes the *White Paper on Juvenile*. It contains comprehensive data on the life of Korean juveniles.

Among these sources, *Crime Analysis* has been the primary source of juvenile crime data. The Supreme Prosecutor's Office, which has the responsibility for handling all the criminal records gathered by the police, has a discretionary power to release the data. Because of its monopoly, researchers have difficulty in accessing the data and have not been able to address data problems properly. For this reason, a certain level of skepticism exists about the official crime statistics (see Kim and Lee, 1991; Park, 2000). However, because of its unique nature, *Crime Analysis* has been the most reliable data source for crime analysis in Korea.

Other types of crime data, such as victim survey and self-report survey data, have only been recently gathered. The Korean Institute of Criminology conducted the first juvenile victim survey in 1990 and a second one in 1998 (see Kim et al., 1991; Noh, et al., 1998). A valid and reliable self-report survey has not been conducted in Korea. Recently, however, some scholars began to argue the necessity for conducting victim surveys and self-report surveys in order to better understand crime and delinquency in causal terms (Shim and Cho, 1991; Park, 2000).

LONG TERM ASPECTS OF YOUTH CRIME

Overall Trends
Over the past 30 years, crime has been a growing concern in Korean society. Figure 17.1 shows the changes in the number of penal code offenders per 100,000 adults and that of 100,000 youth between 1966 and 1998. Korean official statistics define youth as those between the ages of 12 to 20 and adults as those who are 20 years or older. Both age groups display a very similar trend. Their crime rates began to increase in the mid-1970s and continued until the early 1980s when there was a slight decrease. The delinquency rate increased again in the 1990s.

Crime increase in the 1970s is attributed to the baby-boom after the Korean War (1950 to 1953) and the ensuing rapid industrialization period (Choi and Park, 1993; Samsung Economic Research Institute, 1996).

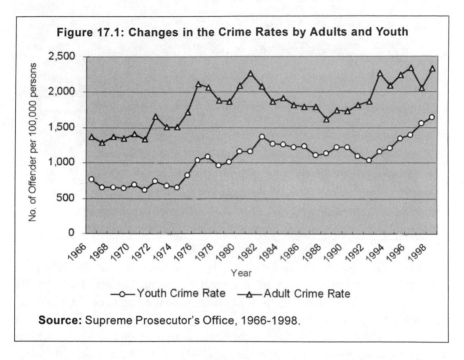

Figure 17.1: Changes in the Crime Rates by Adults and Youth

Source: Supreme Prosecutor's Office, 1966-1998.

The urban population grew rapidly—33.5% in 1966, 48.4% in 1975, 65.4% in 1985, and 78.5% in 1995. Koreans were forced to change their traditional life style and value systems based on rural village life. Economic growth and personal success emerged as important social values. Korean society experienced *psychological anomie* (Lee, J., and Han, 1995; Cho and Han, 1995). Furthermore, the urbanization process that increased the geographical mobility, population density, and anonymity is closely related to the crime increase (Messner, 1986; Lee, 1994; Chung, 1998). However, when the urbanization and industrialization was stabilized and the effect of the baby boom lessened in the 1980s, the crime rates decreased slightly (Samsung Economic Research Institute, 1996).

The proportion of youth in the total of penal code crime offenders has been relatively low. Figure 17.2 shows the changes in the percent of youth in the whole population and that in the total crime offenders. Even when the youth population began to increase in the early 1970s, youth crime remained at the same level. Furthermore, the rate at which youth crime has grown has never exceeded the rate at which the youth population has grown.

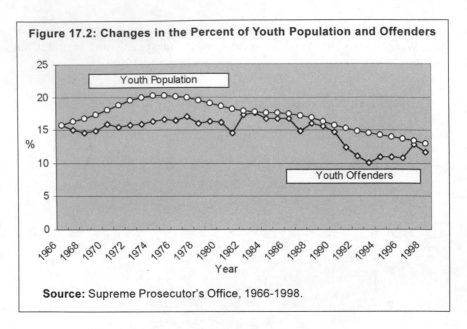

Figure 17.2: Changes in the Percent of Youth Population and Offenders

Source: Supreme Prosecutor's Office, 1966-1998.

One possible explanation for relatively low youth crime involvement is the Korean's high level of devotion to educational achievement. Traditionally, Koreans have had a strong desire for college education and continue to do so. In high schools, most students respect those students who perform well in school work. Other kinds of extra-curricular activities tend to be discouraged (Samsung Institute of Social Psychiatry, 1997). Under the pressure of college entrance examination and the uniform value for school achievement, adolescents seem to be less likely to be involved in crimes.

Trends by Crime Types

Although the incidence of youth crime has been relatively low, the fact that the youth crime rate has increased over the past 30 years cannot be ignored. Figure 17.3 shows the changes in the youth crime rates for both violent and property crimes.

Changes in the violent youth crime rates and youth crime property rates show somewhat different trends. Violent crime rates that had been relatively stable until the mid-1970s increased rapidly for the next 10 years, fluctuated from the middle of 1980s until the early 1990s, and then increased again in the 1990s. On the other hand, property crime rates among youth declined in the 1960s, increased in the early 1970s, declined in the late 1970s, increased in the early 1980s, declined until 1990, and then increased throughout the 1990s.

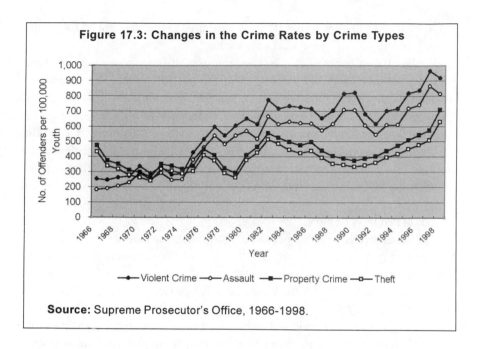

Figure 17.3: Changes in the Crime Rates by Crime Types

Source: Supreme Prosecutor's Office, 1966-1998.

One distinctive difference comes from the surge of violent crimes in the middle of the 1970s along with the decline of property crimes in the late 1970s. In the 1960s, adolescents committed more property crimes than violent crimes, but this tendency began to change. The number of violent crime offenders among youth increased from 20,000 in 1974 to 40,000 in 1977. Since then, adolescents have committed more violent crimes than property offences.

Trends of Violent Crimes

In Korea violent crimes consist of murder, rape, assault, and robbery. Assaults account for more than 80% of all violent crimes. However, these statistics should be regarded with caution because of the Korean criminal law and counting system. Assault in violent crimes in Figure 17.3 includes the violators of the "Special Law for Assault and Related Criminal Conducts" enacted in 1962 mainly to control potential offenders who might commit assault. However, the law also includes such offences as illegal detention, trespassing, and threat. As a result, official statistics for violent crimes in Korea is vague. Therefore, it is necessary to look at the trends of other types of violent crimes separately. The number of murders per 100,000 youth has been stable at less than two throughout the 30-year period. There were approximately 60 cases per year in the late 1990s. The rape rate has ranged from 10 per 100,000 in the 1960s to a high of 51.6 in 1982. The rates began to decline in the early 1990s to

9.3 in 1998. The decline in the 1990s is attributed to the special law for sexual assault and spread of sex education in schools.

Unlike the offences of murder and rape, assault and robbery among young persons has increased significantly over the past 30 years. The number of assault offenders per 100,000 youth increased from 184.8 in 1966 to a peak at 865.9 in 1997. The number of robbery offenders per 100,000 increased from around 10 in the 1960s and 1970s, around 30 in the 1980s, around 40 in the 1990s, and to the highest point of 60.5 in 1998. This increasing tendency has become a source of general concern about the violence and seriousness of youth crime in Korean society (Won, 1997; Kim and Noh, 1999).

Trends of Property Crimes

In Korea property crimes consist of theft, fraud and embezzlement, dereliction, stolen goods, and damage. Theft is the most common type of property crime, accounting for approximately 90% of all property offences.

The crime rate for theft fluctuated between 200 and 500 per 100,000 youth until 1990, but increased throughout the 1990s, and reached a peak of 629.6 in 1998. The crime rate for fraud and embezzlement increased more than three-fold in the 30-year period, from around 20 offenders per 100,000 youth in the 1960s to 66.9 in 1998.

Seriousness of Youth Crimes

Figure 17.4 shows the changes in the percent of youth offenders by crimes types. In this figure, the percentage of the general youth population is presented as a baseline to illustrate the relative size of youth crime. For some violent crimes youth have represented a disproportionately high number of offenders, which has produced a violent image of youth crimes. For robbery and theft, the proportion of young offenders has been much larger than that of the general youth population throughout the 30-year period. Moreover, the proportion of young offenders has steadily increased. For example, the proportion of those committing robbery has increased from the 30% level in the 1960s to the 50% level in the 1990s. Also, the proportion of youth among all theft offenders increased from around 30% in the 1960s to more than 60% by the late 1990s.

For rape, youth have comprised a large proportion of crime offenders, ranging from 25% to 50% until 1990. But in the 1990s, the youth proportion of rape offenders declined significantly. For assault, the proportion of youth has fluctuated around that of the general youth population. Only for murder and fraud have the relative proportions of offenders remained below the baseline for youth.

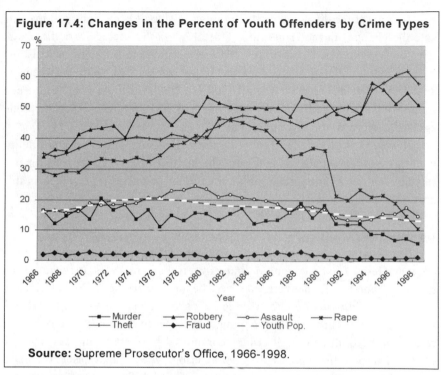

Figure 17.4: Changes in the Percent of Youth Offenders by Crime Types

Legend: —■— Murder   —▲— Robbery   —○— Assault   —✱— Rape   —+— Theft   —◆— Fraud   — — Youth Pop.

Source: Supreme Prosecutor's Office, 1966-1998.

As illustrated in Figure 17.4, the most serious crimes involve robbery, while rape has seen the most dramatic decline—again attributed to new legislation and educational programs in schools. For robbery, seriousness is based on its recent increase, level of violence, and, above all, its relative frequency. For theft, seriousness is based on the volume of theft incidents as well as its continued growth. Rape used to be a serious crime for youth in the amount and relative size, but much less so now. Assault is serious in terms of the amount of it committed by youth, but not so much so in terms of its relative frequency and violence level. Murder is the most seriously violent crime, but its relative frequency is not at the serious level and fortunately has been decreasing recently. Fraud is serious in terms of its increasing trend, but not so serious in terms of the amount and relative frequency.

PROFILE OF JUVENILE OFFENDERS

Age

The average age of juvenile delinquents in Korea used to be around 17 but it fell below the age of 17 in the early 1990s. As the average offence age declined youth crime became a significant social issue.

To control for the age-specific population size, it is necessary to investigate the changes in the crime rate. Table 17.1 shows the age-specific crime rates by crime types. Up until the 1990s, the crime rate for youth had always been positively related to age. This seemingly stable relationship between age and crime rate shifted in the early 1990s. By 1995, the most crime prone age group were youth aged 17, followed by age 16. In 1998, the most crime prone age group were youth 18 years of age.

However, as reflected in Table 17.1 the relationship between age and delinquency involvement also depends on whether the crime is violent or property related—an observation common to most other countries represented in this text.

Gender

Sex differences in criminal behaviour are universal. Traditionally, females are much less likely to commit delinquent acts than are males. In recent years, however, female offender activities have begun to increase in Korea (Kim and Kim, 1993). Columns 1 and 2 in Table 17.2 show the proportion of female offenders among youth and adult populations respectively. They reveal that the rate of both youth and adult crimes committed by females increased in the 1990s. However, the increase differed by crime types: for adolescent females violent crimes increased substantially, while for adult females property crimes increased substantially.

Such a difference results in the contrasting trends in the proportion of youth among female offenders by crime types, shown in column 3. The proportion of young female property crime offenders decreased in the 1990s, while the proportion of youth among female violent crime offenders increased.

The decreasing proportion of female offenders does not imply decreasing criminal offenders. Columns 4 and 5 show the crime rates for 10,000 female youth and female adults, respectively. Overall, the youth and adult crime rates increased considerably in the 1990s. Of these changes, the most distinctive portion is the sharp increase in the youth crime rate for violent crimes in 1995 and 1998. This recent change may be an early signal for an emerging social problem—namely, female violence.

Juvenile Justice System in Korea

Process of Juvenile Justice

In the sense that juvenile offenders and delinquents enter the juvenile justice system through the police, prosecutor, and the court, the judicial pro-

Table 17.1: Number of Offenders per 10,000 Youth of the Same Age							
	Under 14	14	15	16	17	18	19
Penal Code Crime							
1980	15.2	50.9	91.8	125.1	174.5	213.9	282.7
1985	8.6	59.8	112.5	168.5	216.6	266.8	326.4
1990	12.9	74.2	125.9	173.9	203.9	263.3	319.8
1995	15.9	145.7	248.2	295.5	299.7	283.7	280.3
1998	13.3	171.1	268.9	321.1	344.2	374.0	365.1
Property Crime							
1980	11.3	36.9	52.0	52.5	55.0	51.4	55.4
1985	5.8	41.8	62.1	67.6	66.3	66.1	69.1
1990	8.1	44.3	55.3	51.8	47.3	42.0	37.6
1995	6.7	71.8	91.7	83.8	65.1	44.6	38.4
1998	5.2	95.7	117.4	109.5	87.0	69.5	55.0
Violent Crime							
1980	2.5	12.6	36.8	66.9	110.2	143.2	185.0
1985	2.3	17.4	49.5	99.2	147.6	194.8	246.4
1990	4.2	29.4	70.2	120.8	154.8	216.7	274.2
1995	8.5	73.0	155.4	210.1	232.3	235.8	237.2
1998	7.6	74.8	150.5	209.4	254.1	300.1	304.2

Source: Supreme Prosecutor Office, 1980, 1985, 1990, 1995, and 1998.

cedure for juveniles is not different from that for adults. However, unlike the adult system, the juvenile justice system has two separate courts with two independent procedures. Selection of the courts and procedures for a juvenile case is based on the juvenile delinquent's age and the seriousness of offence. The juvenile court handles all cases of law-breaking juveniles and pre-delinquents, whereas the criminal court handles all cases of juvenile offenders.

Figure 17.5 shows the judicial procedure for each case. For the criminal court case, the public prosecutor must be involved in the process, although such a procedure is absent for the juvenile court case. The public prosecutor has discretionary power to decide whether to refer cases to criminal court or to juvenile court. For a juvenile protective case however, police must directly refer the case to juvenile court. Whereas criminal court is the same as adult court, juvenile court is actually either the juvenile division in the family court or juvenile division in district court.

Protective Activities of the Police

In most cases, the police are the offender's first contact point with the justice system. The police arrest juvenile delinquents and refer them to the court or a prosecutor. In some cases, parents, neighbors, schoolteachers, or welfare agents refer delinquent juveniles to the juvenile court. Section 4(2) of

Table 17.2: Some Crime Related Indexes of Female Youth

| | Proportions (%) | | | Number of Offenders per 10,000 females | |
	(1) Female Youth	(2) Female Adult	(3) Youth Female	(5) Adult	
Penal Code Crime					
1980	5.4	12.0	6.0	14.1	72.8
1985	4.6	10.0	5.0	13.6	74.2
1990	4.1	10.4	3.1	13.2	98.3
1995	7.2	14.9	3.6	29.2	155.2
1998	10.1	16.4	4.9	51.7	180.7
Property Crime					
1980	7.6	18.6	8.9	6.5	21.8
1985	6.2	16.0	7.7	6.1	21.0
1990	5.0	15.1	6.1	3.9	14.2
1995	7.8	25.3	3.3	8.3	48.5
1998	9.5	26.9	4.5	13.9	52.9
Violent Crime					
1980	2.2	11.2	2.8	3.4	38.8
1985	3.1	7.1	4.1	5.9	39.8
1990	3.6	9.0	2.7	8.6	71.8
1995	6.8	11.6	4.2	20.1	91.4
1998	10.2	13.5	5.4	36.6	114.1

Source: Supreme Prosecutor Office, 1980, 1985, 1990, 1995, and 1998.

Figure 17.5: Juvenile Justice System in Korea

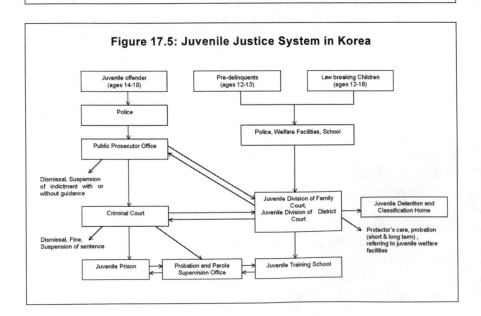

the Juvenile Law stipulates that the chief of the police station must directly transfer the delinquent youth to the juvenile court when the police find him/her to be a pre-delinquent or law-breaking youth. When the police arrest a juvenile criminal offender, the police chief must transfer the delinquent youth to the public prosecutor. Although the police investigate criminal conduct, they do not have the authority to handle the case, except for violations of traffic law and minor offences. In these minor cases, the police can issue a fine and request a summary trial proceeding.

Patrol and supervision over places harmful to juveniles are one of the main activities of the police. Police patrol around entertainment quarters in an effort to abate delinquent behaviors, such as consuming alcohol, smoking, keeping a knife, and fighting. For instance, in 1999, police arrested some 250,000 juveniles for misdemeanors. Most of the offenders were either sent home and/or notices were sent to their respective schools.

Guidance programs represent another initiative police use to prevent juveniles from engaging in delinquent activities (see Box 17.1). Usually along with communities and schools, each police station runs a "Crime Prevention Class," in which they visit schools and give a lecture to the students about how to avoid engaging in criminal activities. In 1999, 14,000 schools participated in the program. Another guidance program is the "Class of Love" program for pre-delinquents. Thirteen district police headquarters run it in collaboration with voluntary youth organizations (National Police Agency, 2000).

Notwithstanding the above initiatives, whether these programs are working is questionable. Because of the lack of resources, Korean police are unable to effectively implement them. Moreover, community support is generally lacking because of cultural barriers. Until recently, the centralized police system of community-based policing did not receive much attention. Therefore, it will take time before the police are able to implement working programs of protective activities for youth.

Criminal Procedure for Juvenile Offenders

Once a young person is determined to be a juvenile offender, the public prosecutor becomes involved in the legal procedure. The public prosecutor has to decide whether to prosecute the juvenile offender or to suspend the indictment. If the case is to be prosecuted, the public prosecutor has to decide whether to refer the youth to criminal or juvenile court. Under Juvenile Law, section 49(1) stipulates that if the case can not be resolved using a disposition not more severe than a fine, then it must be referred to juvenile court.

> ### Box 17.1: The "Initiative for Safe Schools" campaign launched by the Supreme Public Prosecutor's Office
>
> School violence increased more than seven fold between 1993 and 1997. This gave rise to considerable public concern. School violence became more violent and group-oriented. The age of offenders and victims became younger, and the proportions of female offenders and victims increased. Many young students have been plagued by school violence, and some even took their own lives to escape from the fear of it.
>
> In order to cope with school violence, the Supreme Public Prosecutor's Office launched the "Initiative for Safe Schools" campaign in September 1997. This campaign tries to mobilize parents, schools and related government sectors, and citizens' groups in cooperative activities for safe schools. The program consists of 1) the implementation of a hotline at the public prosecutor's offices across the country, 2) reinforcement of regulations at school and in their vicinities, 3) organizing civil surveillance forces by parents and volunteers, 4) preventive activities such as using counseling and education programs, 5) guidance activities for delinquent juveniles such as counseling and training programs, 6) traffic safety programs, 7) provision of spaces and facilities for youth cultural activities, and 8) medical assistance for offenders and victims.

The public prosecutor can also place a juvenile offender under probation or in the **conditional probation program** which is referred to as *Suspension of Prosecution of Juvenile Offender on the Fatherly Guidance Condition*. The conditional probation program was enacted in 1978 to reduce the negative effect of imprisonment. In this program, a young offender is placed on tentative probation, and volunteers guide the youth to a normal social life throughout the probation period. Volunteers are usually influential persons in the community where the delinquent juvenile lives.

In 1998, the prosecutor's office handled 148,558 cases, of which 36.3% (53,972 cases) were sent to criminal court; 14.2% (21,037 cases) were sent to juvenile court; 41.6% (61,864 cases) were suspended, including 6.2% (9,182 cases) of those who were placed on the conditional probation; and 7.9% (11,669 cases) were dismissed (Judicial Research and Training Institute, 1999). Compared to adult cases in which 54.5% of 2,196,565 cases were sent to the criminal court, and only 10.9% cases were suspended, punishments for juveniles tend to be milder, reflecting the **welfare** aspects of Korean juvenile justice.

However, the policy of milder punishments for young offenders has not worked well at the operational level in recent years. For example, the suspension of prosecution began to reveal certain aspects of inefficacy. The proportion of those who were placed into the program decreased from 9.2% in 1994 to 6.2% in 1998, whereas the proportion of those who committed a crime again after having been released from the program increased from 3.7% in 1994 to 5.4% in 1998. Although some scholars (Lee, Y., 1991, 1993; Oh, 1995) attribute problems to the lack of professional training of volunteers, the program seems to be in need of revision on a number of different levels. Furthermore, the welfare ideal for the juvenile justice system may not hold without improving community relations in Korea.

Exceptional Provisions for Juvenile Offenders

Although the criminal trial for young offenders is similar to that for adults, again, punishments for juveniles are milder than for adults. For instance, 11.6% of juvenile offenders were sentenced to imprisonment and 22.9% were sentenced to probation in 1998, whereas 27.1% of adult offenders were imprisoned (Judicial Research and Training Institute, 1999). Moreover, our Juvenile Law stipulates some exceptional provisions for the protection of juvenile criminal offenders. In determining the sentence, the court relies heavily on the clinical and social reports prepared by probation officers and specialists. Other important provisions are as follows:

- neither capital punishment nor life imprisonment for youth under 18 years old;
- alleviation of the parole conditions for juvenile (in comparison with adult);
- restricting the issue of a warrant of arrest for juvenile offenders,
- sentencing within the minimum and maximum range;
- pre-trial investigation performed to decide on terms and possibility of probation; the probation officer must collect and present data—the offender's motivation, social environment, psychological state, etc.— to the court;
- separate and specialized youth courts and correctional programs; and
- court appointment of the public defender in case of the absence of a private attorney.

Disposition of Juvenile Offenders by the Criminal Court

Of the 21,288 indicted juveniles in 1998, 13% (2,777) were sentenced to imprisonment and 22.9% (4,900) were given a suspended sentence. Our Juvenile Law stipulates that there be separate custody of juvenile offenders from adults. There are two male juvenile prisons in Korea. One is for first-time offenders, and the other is for recidivists. In 1998, 1,888 youths were incarcerated in juvenile prisons. The number of incarcerated juveniles has decreased slightly since the mid-1990s, yet it is interesting to point out that the number of juvenile offenders increased during the same period. This contrast seems to be related to the fact that the Korean juvenile justice system is moving towards less extreme, more intermediate, and more diversified sanctions.

Disposition of Juvenile Court

There are five juvenile courts in Korea: one Juvenile Division of the Family Court in Seoul, and four Juvenile Divisions of the District Court in other provinces. Juvenile courts handle juvenile protective cases referred by the police, public prosecutors, and back from the criminal court. In 1998, for example, of 39,910 protective cases, 16.4% (6,552 cases) came directly from the police, 55.9% (22,322 cases) came from the public prosecutor's office, and 27.6% (11,035 cases) came from the criminal courts (Judicial Research and Training Institute, 1999).

When a juvenile protective case is referred to juvenile court, the judge has discretionary power to determine whether the case should be dismissed or whether young offenders should receive some type of correction. The judge takes into account various information related to the delinquent juvenile, such as family background, psychological character, criminal history, and other related matters.

The judge obtains this information from the investigation performed by the special investigator in the juvenile court and the juvenile detention and classification office. The court investigation includes interviews with the delinquent juvenile, parents, and friends. Psychiatrists, psychologists, social workers, and other specialists participate in the investigation process. However, most information about the juvenile comes from the classification office. There are five classification offices for juvenile cases, located in the larger cities: Seoul, Daegu, Daejeon, Busan, and Gwangju. These offices detain delinquent juveniles for investigation. The investigator conducts an interview, observes behavior, assesses personality and psychiatric state, and investigates the living environment of the delinquent juvenile.

Based on the information taken in the investigation, the judge determines the level of sentence. As in most Western countries the sentencing procedure places emphasis on diverting juveniles from the formal adjudication process. There are seven types of sentences available to the court. They include:

- placement at home in the custody of parents or guardians,
- short-term probation for six months, and
- long-term probation for two years.

Other alternative sanctions include community services and learning sanction, possibly with probation and sanctions with maximum 50 hours for short-term probation and 200 hours for long-term probation. There is also:

- placement in child welfare facilities under the Child Welfare Law and the Social Welfare Law, which can involve a six-month period with a possible extension of one term;

- placement in a hospital or nursing home;
- sentence to the Juvenile Training School, short-term; and
- sentence to the Juvenile Training School, long-term.

In 1998, of all 39,300 juvenile court cases, only 5.5% (2,194 cases) were dismissed and 94.4% (37,081 cases) were sentenced (Judiciary Research and Training Institute, 1999). Most sentences, however, were not so severe in that only 7.8% (3,081 cases) were referred to training schools and others were referred to a certain kind of open custody: 34.9% (13,712 cases) were long-term probation, 32.4% (12,719 cases) were short-term probation, 17.1% (6,708 cases) were in the custody of parents or guardians. Compared to other types of sentences, placement in welfare facilities accounted for only 2.2% (851 cases), and there were only 10 cases where placement in a hospital was used as a correctional measure.

Given that the Korean juvenile justice system is welfare orientated, limited use of welfare and health facilities is not desirable. As a way of compensating for the lack of resources, juvenile justice shares responsibility for hospital expenses. Hence, such placements are used sparingly. It would appear that Korean juvenile justice has to put more effort, time, and resources forth to further the welfare and health institutions in respect to the correction of juvenile delinquency.

CORRECTIONS

Probation with Supervision in the Community

The idea of community-based sanctions is a comparatively new concept for juvenile justice in Korea. The Korean justice system adopted **probation with supervision** in the community for juveniles in 1989 and for adults in 1997 (see Box 17.2). Introduction of probation with supervision is a turning point in the Korean judicial system. As a type of **intermediate sanction**, probation with supervision changes the concept of sanctions from a punitive and formal process to an informal and rehabilitative orientation.

Despite its recent inception, the supervised probation program is already being widely used for both juveniles and adults. For example, 67% of all cases in youth court (26,431 juveniles) were directed to supervised probation programs in 1998, and 132,639 adults were put into the program in 1998—a 35% increase over 1997.

The outcome of the program has been evaluated and deemed successful, especially for juvenile delinquents. Participation in the program seems to reduce the chance of committing a crime even after the youth is released from the program. For example, the recidivism rate of the supervised juvenile has stayed

Box 17.2: Volunteers in the Probation with Supervision Program

This program started in July 1989. Before then, it existed only in the regulation but was not actually implemented. In 1989, the Prosecutor's Office launched the program within the community. Probation offices were formally established to support the program, probation officers were hired, and voluntary guardians were selected. In 1998, 334 probation officers were on duty, and 5,129 volunteers were working for the program across the country.

Given the heavy caseloads per probation officers at present, the volunteer's role in the program is important. Before 1994, volunteer selection was little more than status-oriented, as most of the volunteers were big shop owners or officials of the local government and local schools. In 1994, volunteer selection procedure was changed to improve the operation of the program. Since then, volunteers have been selected among teachers, counselors, welfare workers, and other juvenile related workers.

Although this change has been very positive to the program, there remain several problems in the use of volunteers. The first problem is the low participation rate among the volunteers. It can be improved by combining the program with local welfare organizations and colleges. Particularly, considering only 172 college students were working for the program in 1999, recruiting more college students would benefit the program significantly. Secondly, volunteers need to be trained to deal with delinquent juveniles more professionally. The probation office provides 24 hours of training over a three-month period. But one survey conducted in 1994 showed that less than 20% of the volunteers had completed the training program. For training to work properly, a more intensive training program has to be developed as a requirement (Lee, D.W., 1999).

around 10%, much lower than the recidivism rate for all juvenile offenders—22% to 24% (Kim, 1988; Choi et al. 1993; Oh, 1999).

Despite the success of the supervised probation program, it has operational problems. First, because it is in its inception period, the program lacks trained experts and professionals, especially among probation officers, welfare workers, and voluntary guardians (Linder and Savarese, 1984; Kim and Lee, 1995; Oh, 1999). Secondly, the caseloads for the probation officers are too heavy. For instance, one Seoul probation officer took care of 294 cases in 1998 (lee, Y.H., 1999). Thirdly, various intermediate sanctions need to be utilized to accommodate specific cases. To date, the Korean justice system has implemented only a few types of intermediate sanctions such as probation with community services and learning sanctions. Other possible intermediate sanctions include split sentence, boot camps, intensive supervision programs, and electronic monitoring (Lee, 1999).

Juveniles under Detention

Referring to the juvenile training school is the severest sentence in the juvenile court. Since the first juvenile training school was established in 1942,

11 more training schools were built across the country. The role of the training school is not to punish, but to rehabilitate and to educate delinquent juveniles. There are various types of juvenile training schools, mostly distinguished by their training goals. Training can be vocational, educational, and psychotherapeutic. Of the schools, five focus on education, three focus on vocational training, two on vocation and education, one on habitual delinquents, and one is for young female offenders.

In 1998, 7.8% juvenile court cases were referred to the training school, of which 1,884 cases were short-term sentences, and 1,197 cases were long-tem sentences (see Box 17.3). There has been a decreasing tendency to detain juvenile delinquents in training schools, as sanctioning methods diversified. For example, the proportion of referral to training schools among the juvenile court cases has decreased from 17% in the mid-1970s to below 10% in the 1990s. Moreover, even the length of detention has been shortened in the 1990s. The proportion of long-term sentences among all detention cases decreased from 66% in 1989 to 40% in 1998 (Judicial Research and Training Institute, 1999).

Box 17.3: Chunan Juvenile Correctional Institution[2]

Located about a one hour drive from Seoul, the juvenile prison first opened on 31 March 1938 and was known as the Inchun Juvenile Prison. It was renamed Chunan Juvenile Correctional Institution in November 1990. The facility accommodates only males who are under the age of 20. However, if they are involved in an education program they can be accommodated until age 23. The institution emphasizes academic and vocational education. Students are tested upon entry as to which form of education they are best suited for. The facility can accommodate some 115 juveniles. Courses can also be taken via correspondence as well as on site. There are also special moral education programs, work release systems, special activities (Boy Scouts, boxing, musical bands, farmers' dancing, and a host of other special arts programs). The institution is run in a para-military fashion with the students displaying impeccable manners and the grounds being kept exceptionally well.

While the number of inmates in training schools is declining, criticism against the efficacy of the school has begun to appear. In the survey, 68.9% of former long-term inmates had returned to the school for the other crimes (Lee, B., and Noh, 1993: 76). Such an undesirable outcome is a result of overpopulation, shortage of staff, and poor facilities. In another survey (Lee and Kim, 1995: 21), training staff in the juvenile training schools identified quality of staffing as a problem and that, contrary to the schools' stated objectives, discipline and punishment were the main forms of dealing with students.

These problems seem to reveal that training schools are not functioning properly as a rehabilitation or correctional measure. Rather, they work like a punishment institution and generate a labeling effect. Again, it seems that Korean juvenile justice may have to put much more effort, time, and resources into improving the educational function and correction capabilities in juvenile training schools, as well as changing the basis of the system from the ideological welfare model to a more realistic one.

SUMMARY

This chapter presented an overview of the Korean juvenile justice system and the trends of youth crime since the 1970s. A modern legal system appeared in the late nineteenth century under the influence of the Great Powers of the time. Full-fledged change in the Korean legal system came during the Japanese colonization period, 1910 to 1945. After the liberation from Japan and the Korean War of 1950 to 1953, Korea enacted the modern Juvenile Law in 1958.

The second section described the trends and patterns of juvenile crimes. It was observed that since the 1970s Korean society has experienced rapid industrialization and urbanization. These changes parallel increases in both youth and adult crime. Even so, the relative proportion of youth crimes remains comparatively low at around 10%. However, recent trends in youth violence and increasing female delinquency rates have prompted a new level of concern.

The third section presented the structure and procedures of the Korean juvenile justice system. Korean juvenile justice was built on the concept of *parens patriae*, and thus embodies the welfare model in essence. Under the guise of the welfare model, juvenile justice operates not to punish, but to improve the rehabilitation of delinquent juveniles.

The Korean juvenile justice system has two courts with two separate procedures. The juvenile court handles law-breaking juveniles and pre-delinquents, whereas the criminal court handles juvenile offenders. Juvenile offenders are those who are between 14 and 19, and have violated a law; law-breaking juveniles are those who are 12 and 13, and have violated a law; and pre-delinquents are those who are between 12 and 19, and are prone to commit some criminal offences.

The public prosecutors play a decisive role in criminal court cases. They have discretionary powers to determine where the case should be sent. There are three options: to prosecute in the criminal court, to prosecute in the juvenile court, or to dismiss. They also can suspend the prosecution and put a juvenile offender under tentative probation on conditional basis. Once the case is referred to the criminal court, the judge imposes a sentence ranging from dismissal to long-term imprisonment in juvenile prison.

In juvenile court cases, judicial procedures are rather simple. The judge determines the type of sentence based on the information gathered by the investigation and the juvenile detention and classification office. The least severe sentence is placement at home in the custody of parent(s) or guardian, and the most severe sentence is the long-term placement in a training school. Most offenders are sentenced to probation and placed in the custody of parents.

Introduction of probation with supervision in the community is a significant step towards a diversion of justice program. As an intermediate sanction, supervised probation has been widely used in the juvenile court in recent years and has produced seemingly successful outcomes.

However, this program does not seem to provide an educational and correctional function. Moreover, juvenile training schools are identified as institutions of punishment rather than as correctional and educational settings. Thus, the ideal of the welfare model does not seem to be well-supported at the operational level. Until this can be properly addressed, the Korean juvenile justice system needs to be more realistic about its goals if it hopes to make them work effectively.

Hyun-Hee Lee (Ph.D) is a chief researcher at Samsung S1 Crime Prevention Institute in Seoul, Korea. Since 1994, she has focused most of her research interests on crime and delinquency in Korea. She has published papers on alcohol and deviance, community structure and crime, imprisonment and recidivism, crime analysis using GIS, and crime in cyberspace. Her recent interest in juvenile justice is deviance on the Internet and cyberspace.

Kun Lee (Ph.D.) is a sociologist and an associate professor at the University of Seoul, Korea. Since 1994, he has focused most of his academic efforts on the sociology of the labor market in Korea, information technology and society, and cyberspace and the community. Most recently, his interests also include the study of juvenile delinquency in Korea.

HELPFUL WEBSITES

http//www.sppo.go.kr The Supreme Public Prosecutor's Office
http://www.kic.re.kr Korean Institute of Criminology
http://www.police.go.kr National Police Agency
http://www.nanet.go.kr The National Assembly Library
http://www.nso.go.kr National Statistical Office
http://www.moj.go.kr Ministry of Justice

KEY TERMS AND CONCEPTS

Welfare Model	Juvenile Law
Criminal Court	Juvenile Court
Discretionary Power	Female Offender
Suspension of Prosecution	Probation with Supervision

Kabo Reform   Justice Model
Juvenile Offender   Law-breaking Youth
Pre-delinquent   Conditional Probation Program

STUDY QUESTIONS

1. What are the distinctive features of Korean youth crime? Are these features unique to Korea? If there is a distinctive feature in Korea, what would be the reason for the uniqueness?
2. Discuss the differences between the criminal court and the juvenile court in Korea.
3. Discuss the role of the public prosecutor in the juvenile justice system and the level of prosecutor's power and responsibility in comparison with the judge's in Korea and other countries.
4. Korea began to implement diversion programs and community-based corrections in recent years. What has been the obstacle in implementing these programs?
5. Does the juvenile justice system in Korea move toward the welfare model? Review the principles of the welfare model and justice model (see Figure 1—Introduction), and compare the strength and weakness of these models as they relate to Korea.
6. Discuss the similarities and differences between the juvenile justice system of Korea and Japan.

NOTES

1   The Great Powers were England, France, Germany, Russia, Japan, United States, and China. These countries were competing for control and power in eastern Asia.
2   Information on the institution is based on a personal observations by John Winterdyk who visited the facility in 1998 and who was given additional information by the administration of the institution.

REFERENCES

Cho, S.Y., & Han, S.J. (1995). The Changes of Population and Cities in Korea after the Liberation, in *The Structural Transformation and Social Development after the Liberation* (written in Korean). Ed. Korean Association of Sociology and Korean Association of Social History.

Choi, I.S., Jin, S.M., & Kim, Y.J. (1993). *A Study on the Current Practices and the Effectiveness of Probation Program for Juvenile Offenders* (written in Korean). Korean Institute of Criminology.

Choi, I.S., & Park, S.J. (1993). *Social Structure and Crime* (written in Korean). Korean Institute of Criminology.

Chung, G.S. (1998). Urbanization and urban crime (written in Korean). *Korean Association of Public Safety and Criminal Justice Review* 7.

Gatti, U. (1991). The future of juvenile justice. Paper Presented at the 1st International Conference of the Korean Institute of Criminology.

Judicial Research and Training Institute. (1999). *White Paper on Crime* (written in Korean).

Kim, J.H., & Kim, E.K. (1995). *A Study on Female Delinquency* (written in Korean). Korean Institute of Criminology.

Kim, J.H., Noh, S.H., Oh, S.J., & Jang, E.S. (1991). *A Study on Juvenile Victimization* (written in Korean). Korean Institute of Criminology.

Kim, J.H., & Lee, D.W. (1991). *A Study on Improvement of National Crime Statistics* (written in Korean). Korean Institute of Criminology.

Kim, J.H., & Lee, D.W. (1995). Practices and remedies of juvenile probation (written in Korean). *Korean Criminological Review* 6(4).

Kim, S.E., & Noh, S.H. (1999*). The Trends of Juvenile Crime in Korea, 1966-1998* (written in Korean). Korean Institute of Criminology.

Kim, S.H. (1988). Situation and analysis on the supervised probation program (written in Korean). *Juvenile Crime Study* 6.

Lee, B.G., & Noh, S.H. (1994). *A Study of Prediction of Juvenile Recidivism* (written in Korean*).* Korean Institute of Criminology.

Lee, B.G., and Kim, S.U. (1995). *A Study on the Living Conditions and Education at Juvenile Reformatory* (written in Korean*).* Korean Institute of Criminology.

Lee, D.W. (1999). Probation and crime prevention committee (written in Korean). Paper presented at the 24ᵗʰ Seminar on Criminal Justice Policy. Korean Institute of Criminology, Seoul.

Lee, H.H. (1994). *Residential Area Characteristics and Crime* (written in Korean). Ph.D. Dissertation. Ewha Womans University, Daehynn-dong.

Lee, H.H. (1999). Intensive Supervision Programs in U.S. (written in Korean). Paper Presented at the 24ᵗʰ Seminar on Criminal Justice Policy. Korean Institute of Criminology.

Lee, J.O., & Han, Y.H. (1995). The changes of Korean family after the liberation, in *The Structural Transformation and Social Development after the Liberation* (written in Korean). Ed. Korean Association of Sociology and Korean Association of Social History.

Lee, Y.H. (1993). Correction and rehabilitation of juvenile delinquency (written in Korean) in *Juvenile Problem.* Ed. Korean Youth Development Institute.

Lee, Y.H. (1991). An empirical study on the effectiveness of protective disposition for juvenile delinquents (written in Korean). *Korean Criminological Review* 2(3).

Lee, Y.H. (1999). Duties and roles of the probation officer (written in Korean). Paper presented at the 24ᵗʰ Seminar on Criminal Justice Policy. Korean Institute of Criminology, Seoul.

Linder, C., & Savarese, M.R. (1984). The evolution of probation: The historical contribution of the volunteer. *Federal Probation* 48(2).

Messner, S.F. (1986). Modernization, structural characteristics, and social rates of crime: An application of Blau's macrosociological theory. *Sociological Quarterly* 27(1).

Ministry of Culture and Tourism. (1999). *White Paper on Juveniles* (written in Korean).

Miyazawa, K. (1991). Juvenile delinquency and juvenile justice in Japan. Paper Presented at the 1ˢᵗ International Conference of the Korean Institute of Criminology.

National Police Agency. (2000). *White Paper on Police (written in Korean).*

Noh, S.H., Kim, S.E., Lee, D.W., & Kim, J.S. (1999). *A Study on Juvenile Victimization* (written in Korean). Korean Institute of Criminology.

Oh, Y.K. (1995). Suspended prosecution with supervision for juvenile offenders: Its practices and direction for improvement (written in Korean). *Korean Criminological Review* 6(4).

Oh, Y.K. (1999). Retrospect and prospect of supervised probation program (written in Korean). Paper Presented at the 24ᵗʰ Seminar on Criminal Justice Policy. Korean Institute of Criminology.

Park, S.J. (2000). Result comparison of official data and victim survey (written in Korean). Paper Presented at the Annual Meeting of Korean Sociological Association.

Research and Training Institute of the Ministry of Justice, Japan. 1999. *White Paper on Crime* (written in Japanese).

Samsung Economic Research Institute. (1996*). Transformation of Korean Society and Response: Social Development and Crime* (written in Korean). Policy Report No. 96-15-052.

Samsung Institute of Social Psychiatry. (1997). *Research Report on the Psychiatry of Examinee for College Entrance*. Report No. 97-1.

Shim, Y.H., & Cho, J.H. (1991). *Introduction to Victimization Survey* (written in Korean). Korean Institute of Criminology.

Supreme Prosecutor's Office. (1966-1998) *Crime Analysis* (written in Korean).

Won, H.W. (1997). Ein Vergleich der Deuschen mit der Koreanschen Jugendkriminalitat (written in Korean). *Korean Criminological Review* 8(2).

Yokoyama, M. (1997). Juvenile justice: An overview of Japan. In *Juvenile Justice Systems-International Perspectives*. Ed. J.A. Winterdyk. Toronto: Canadian Scholars' Press.

Chapter 18

Delinquency and Juvenile Justice in the United States[1]

Mark Christopher Stafford
Tracey L. Kyckelhahn
Department of Sociology
University of Texas at Austin

FACTS ABOUT THE UNITED STATES

Area and Density: Almost 4 million square miles, with 73 people per square mile. There are 50 states in the United States (U.S.), including the island of Hawaii in the Pacific Ocean and Alaska in northwest North America, which is separated from the rest of the continental states by Canada. **Population:** Over 270 million people in 1999. Males make up 49% and females 51% of the population. The 1999 median age was 36. Approximately 83% of the population is white; 13% is black; and 4% is either American Indian, Alaskan Native, or Asian/Pacific Islander. About 76% of the U.S. population ages five and over speak only English; of those who speak another language, most speak Spanish. Washington, D.C. is the nation's capital. **Climate:** Varies considerably by region and state. The midwestern city of Chicago, Illinois, has an average daily temperature of 49 F (17 C), and the southwestern city of Dallas, Texas, has an average daily tem-perature of 65 F (33 C). Juneau, Alaska, which is in the most northern state, has an average daily temperature of 41 F (9 C); and the average is 77 F (35 C) in Honolulu, Hawaii, the most southern state. **Economy:** The U.S. economy involves agriculture, forestry, and manufacturing (e.g., manufacture of industrial machinery and electronic equipment). Finance, insurance, and real estate also constitute a substantial part of the economy. Wheat and other grains were major agricultural exports in 1998. The leading trade partners are Canada, Western Europe, and Japan. **Government:** A federalism (federal republic) comprised of a national government, 50 state governments, and many local governments, including those for counties, cities and towns, school districts, and special districts. There are two major political parties: Republican (conservative) and Democrat (liberal).

The law that created the juvenile court in the U.S. was to "be liberally construed to the end that ... the care, custody, and discipline of a child shall approximate ... that which should be given by its parents" (Revised Statutes of the State of Illinois, 1899, Sec. 21 in Bremner, II, 1970:511).

BRIEF HISTORY OF U.S. AND U.S. JUVENILE JUSTICE

Vikings discovered America as early as 1000; however, European expansion did not begin until the late 1400s and early 1500s (Degler, 1973). The earliest European settlers were Spaniards who encountered native Indians. The English settled in the early 1600s by establishing colonies; the colonies declared independence from England in 1776 and achieved it by means of the American Revolution.

Colonial law at the time of the Declaration of Independence "was English law and the system of courts and justice thoroughly British" (Degler, 1973:124). Although independence did not end English legal influence, the American legal system was organized differently than the English system. For example, "American courts tended to simplify the complexities of British legal machinery, which was largely uncodified, and to organize constitutional and statute law into written codes" (Degler, 1973:124).

Eighteenth-century American criminal law did not distinguish between juvenile delinquency and adult crime. Instead, Americans relied on **common law**, which specified that children under the age of seven could not be guilty of a serious crime (Bremner, *I*, 1970:307). Children under age 14 also could not be guilty unless it was shown that they could distinguish right from wrong. If so, they were to be judged as adults, along with anyone age 14 or older, although some colonies made exceptions by establishing older age limits. If found guilty, juveniles could receive the same punishments as adults, including the death penalty (Streib, 1987). However, judges and juries usually were more lenient toward juveniles (Platt, 1969).

Nineteenth-century reformers believed that increasing industrialization, urbanization, and immigration in the U.S. had caused moral decline, and they feared that any child "not carefully and diligently trained to cope with the open, free-wheeling, and disordered life of the community would fall victim to vice and crime" (Rothman, 1971:210). Those fears were especially strong for orphaned, poor, and vagrant children whose families may have been unable to protect and nurture them. Reformers reasoned that if families were not up to such tasks, child-saving institutions should intervene. Houses of refuge and, later, reformatories were institutions created as substitute families to be used when necessary for raising children.[2]

Reformers did not worry that they might be violating the rights of children; on the contrary, they believed that "a good dose of institutionalization could only work to the child's benefit" (Rothman, 1971:209). State courts affirmed that belief by rejecting complaints by parents whose children had been institutionalized. An important case involved **Mary Ann Crouse** whose father objected that her institutionalization was unconstitutional because there had been no jury trial. In a landmark decision in 1838, the Pennsylvania Supreme Court supported the state's power to institutionalize children. "May not the natural parents, when unequal to the task of education, or unworthy of it, be superseded by the *parens patriae*, or common guardian of the community?" (*Ex parte Crouse* 4 Wharton [Pa.] 9 [1838] in Bremner, *I*, 1970:692). The court concluded that houses of refuge were more like schools than prisons; thus, children did not need the same procedural safeguards accorded adults in criminal trials.

In contrast to the court's conclusion in the Crouse case, there was increasing evidence that houses of refuge "had become prisonlike warehouses for large numbers of children from the margins of society" (Empey, Stafford, and Hay, 1999:40), and these houses had failed in rehabilitating problem children regardless of whether they were located in urban or rural settings (Bremner, *I*, 1970:696-697).

By the end of the 1800s, reformatories were criticized for being little more than prisons that did not rehabilitate (Bremner, *II*, 1970:439-440). Reformers could have abandoned the rehabilitative ideal entirely, but instead they created juvenile courts as another possible means for rehabilitating problem children. In 1899 Illinois created the first statewide juvenile court system to handle such problems as child abuse, neglect, dependency, and juvenile delinquency. To maintain the state's *parens patriae* power, the juvenile court was "designated a ... non-criminal court ... which ... assumed that disposition of juvenile cases would be in the best interests of the child and need not be overly concerned with the child's rights" (Bremner, *II*, 1970:440). Court sessions were informal with few procedural safeguards to protect juveniles, and the law that created the court was to "be liberally construed to the end that ... the care, custody, and discipline of a child shall approximate ... that which should be given by its parents" (Revised Statutes of the State of Illinois, 1899, Sec. 21 in Bremner, *II*, 1970:511). By the mid-1900s, all states had established juvenile courts, as had many other nations (Caldwell, 1961).

REFORMS IN U.S. JUVENILE JUSTICE

In the 1960s, the juvenile court and its rehabilitative ideal were seriously challenged, stemming from a series of U.S. Supreme Court decisions. In the 1966 *Kent* case (383 U.S. 541 [1966]), the Court pointed to a gap between the rehabilitative ideal and the reality of juvenile-court processing: "The child receives the worst of both worlds: ... he gets neither the protections accorded to adults nor the solicitous care and regenerative treatment postulated for children." The next year in the *Gault* case (387 U.S. 1 [1967]) the Court continued to point to that gap and, contrary to the conclusion in the 1838 Crouse case, ruled that several procedural safeguards should be provided to juveniles facing the possibility of institutional confinement: notice of charges, assistance of counsel, opportunity to confront and cross-examine witnesses, and a privilege against self-incrimination.

The Supreme Court's assessment of the juvenile court in the 1960s was accompanied by increasing arrest rates of young people. Moreover, substantial increases in the number of 16- to 24-year olds (the age group most likely to violate the law) led to increased fears of juveniles and calls for control of their behavior.

At about the same time, evidence began to accumulate about the ineffectiveness of rehabilitation programs. The most influential evidence was provided by Robert Martinson and his colleagues (Martinson, 1974:25; Lipton, Martinson, and Wilks, 1975) who concluded from an extensive review of rehabilitation programs that "with few and isolated exceptions, the rehabilitative efforts that have been reported so far have had no appreciable effect on recidivism." That conclusion was a shocking blow to supporters of the rehabilitative ideal, and it was only made worse by subsequent reviews that reached similar conclusions (e.g., Sechrest, White, and Brown, 1979).

All of these factors—the Supreme Court's assessment of the juvenile court, increasing arrest rates of young people, and evidence about the ineffectiveness of rehabilitation programs—led to calls to rethink the juvenile justice system and even to abolish it (Dawson, 1990). Throughout the 1980s and 1990s, there was increasing public pressure in the U.S. to "crack down" on juvenile offenders—to "get tough on kids."

Many states changed their juvenile codes to deemphasize rehabilitation (i.e., welfare model) and more strongly emphasize public protection, punishment, justice, deterrence, and accountability (i.e., **crime control model**) (Feld, 1993:245-246; Snyder and Sickmund, 1999:Chapter 4). For example, the purpose of the 1996 Texas Juvenile Justice Code (Chapter 51.01) was mainly to "provide for the protection of the public and public safety." Consistent with that purpose, the Code was first to "promote the concept of punishment for criminal acts" and then, second, to rehabilitate. Although identifying rehabilitation as a purpose (albeit a secondary one), the Code revealed only a partial commitment to the rehabilitative ideal by linking it to accountability: "to provide treatment, training, and rehabilitation that emphasizes the accountability and responsibility of both the parent and the child for the child's conduct." That partial commitment was at odds with judicial interpretations of earlier (pre-1960) Texas Juvenile Justice Codes, which said that the purpose of the juvenile justice system was "not one of punishment, but ... protection of the child for its own good, ... not ... to convict and punish juveniles but to guide and direct them."

Related legislative changes in various states in the 1980s and 1990s included a shift from indeterminate to determinate and mandatory sentencing such that fixed and specified sentences were given to juvenile offenders, with the terms set by legislators (Feld, 1993:219). Moreover, juveniles could be tried more easily in adult criminal courts than in juvenile courts (Snyder, Sickmund, and Poe-Yamagata, 2000).

Other evidence of a "crackdown" on juvenile offenders in the U.S. is the increase in the institutionalization or other out-of-home placement of juvenile offenders (e.g., placement in foster homes) since the 1980s (MacKenzie, 1999). Moreover, some states are permitting the execution of persons who were teenagers at the time they committed their offences (*Thompson v. Oklahoma* 487 U.S. 815 [1988]; *Stanford v. Kentucky* 109 S.Ct. 2969 [1989]).

PUBLIC BELIEFS ABOUT CRIME/DELINQUENCY

Many Americans are concerned about crime and violence. A 1999 Gallup Poll estimated that 17% thought that crime/violence was the most important problem facing the country (Pastore and Maguire, 2000:94). Although that percentage is high, it is lower than earlier in the 1990s. In 1994, more than twice as many respondents to a Gallup Poll (37%) said that crime/violence was the most important problem.

Thirteen percent of a nationwide sample of teenagers in 1999 said that crime/violence in school was the most important problem facing young people (Pastore and Maguire, 2000:96). In contrast, 23% said that drug use was the most important problem.

The U.S. has relatively high crime and delinquency rates, so it is scarcely surprising that many Americans fear crime. Forty-one percent of respondents in a 1998 National Opinion Research Center survey indicated that they were afraid to walk alone at night in their own neighborhoods, with those most likely to express fear being females, blacks and other minorities, and lower-income people (Pastore and Maguire, 2000:120-121).

In a 1996 National Opinion Survey on Crime and Justice, almost half of the respondents (48%) identified rehabilitation as the most important goal of imprisonment (Pastore and Maguire, 1999:131). In contrast, 15% identified punishment and 33% identified crime prevention/deterrence. While blacks were more likely than whites (56% vs. 48%) to identify rehabilitation as the most important goal of imprisonment, Hispanics were more likely than either blacks or whites (42% vs. 32% and 31%) to say that crime prevention/deterrence is the most important goal.

Despite considerable support for rehabilitation, support for the death penalty is very high among Americans. In a 1999 Harris Poll, 71% of respondents said they believed in capital punishment (Pastore and Maguire, 2000:133). Moreover, that percentage has been increasing over the past few decades; as late as 1965, only 38% of Americans supported the death penalty.

DELINQUENCY IN THE U.S. AND TRENDS

Are juveniles more likely than adults in the U.S. to violate the law? Has the amount of delinquency been increasing? Different sources of information can be used to answer such questions. First, there are official data compiled by the police and other legal officials. Second, there are unofficial data: self-report surveys that ask juveniles about their commission of delinquent offences; and victimization surveys that ask about experiences as victims of crime and delinquency. Third, there are homicide victimization data compiled by the National Center for Health Statistics.

Official Arrest Data

The most widely used source of official data on U.S. delinquency are the *Uniform Crime Reports* (*UCR*), which provide data on arrests of juveniles (defined in *UCR* as persons under age 18) for many offences. Juveniles accounted for approximately 16% of all the 1999 arrests for serious violent offences—murder, rape, robbery, and aggravated assault—and they accounted for 32% of arrests for serious property offences—burglary, larceny/theft, motor vehicle theft, and arson (F.B.I., 2000:222-223). Juveniles comprised about 26% of the U.S. population in 1999; hence, proportionately speaking, juveniles were less likely than adults to be arrested for violent offences, and they were more likely than adults to be arrested for property offences.

The same pattern holds when particular types of serious violent and property offences are considered. Juveniles were involved in less than 20% of the 1999 arrests for murder, rape, and aggravated assault; hence, they were under-represented in arrests for those offences. Among arrests for serious violent offences, juveniles were represented proportionately only for robbery, with 25% of the arrests involving them. In contrast, juveniles were over-represented in arrests for all serious property offences. They accounted for approximately 34% of the arrests for burglary, 31% of the arrests for larceny/theft, 35% of the arrests for motor vehicle theft, and a whopping 54% for arson.

The *UCR* also provides data on arrests for less serious offences. Juveniles were over-represented in arrests (accounted for more than 26% of arrests) for vandalism, disorderly conduct, curfew/loitering, and running away. The last two offences are "status offenses," which are illegal only for juveniles (i.e., they are unique to the status of being a juvenile) (F.B.I., 2000:222-223).

Proportionately speaking, juveniles were much less likely than adults to be arrested for prostitution, fraud, forgery, vagrancy, embezzlement, and gambling. Alcohol and drug abuse are commonly portrayed in U.S. media accounts as juvenile rather than adult problems. However, contrary to those reports, juveniles were under-represented in arrests for driving under the influence, drunkenness, drug abuse, and liquor law violations.

What have been the recent trends in U.S. juvenile arrests? Figure 18.1 plots the number of juvenile arrests per 100,000 juveniles ages 10 to 17 for murder, rape, robbery, aggravated assault, burglary, larceny/theft, and motor vehicle theft for 1975 to 1999 (arson is not plotted because *UCR* did not report arson arrests over the entire period). Arrest rates are plotted rather than the number of arrests because the number of juveniles in the U.S. (and their percent of the total population) has varied over time.

For each of the offences except burglary, the arrest rate for juveniles increased from 1975 to 1994. For example, the rate at which juveniles were arrested for murder increased 132% (from 5.7 juvenile arrests per 100,000 population ages 10 to 17 in 1975 to 13.2 in 1994). However, the juvenile arrest rate has decreased for each offence, including burglary, since 1994; all of the decreases have been substantial. For example, the juvenile arrest rate for murder decreased 64% from 1994 to 1999—from 13.2 to 4.7—with the 1999 rate being the second lowest in the 25-year period. The 1999 juvenile arrest rates for robbery, burglary, and larceny/theft were the lowest in the period.

Problems With Official Arrest Data

As is the case in most other countries, most juvenile offenders are never arrested; hence, arrest data tend to underestimate the actual amount of delinquency (this is often referred to as the **dark figure** of crime). Moreover, arrest data may reflect biases of law enforcement officials. For example, there may be racial/ethnic and gender biases. Law enforcement officials also may change their behavior over time, "cracking down" at some points by arresting more offenders and "letting up" at other points by arresting fewer offenders. Thus, there could be increases or decreases in arrests over time without changes in actual delinquent behavior.

Unofficial Data: Self-Report Data

Because of problems with arrest data, researchers have turned to unofficial (i.e., not collected by legal officials) data on delinquency, most commonly to self-report data. They conduct surveys, either by interviews or self-administered questionnaires, asking questions such as: "During the last 12 months [or some other designated period, such as the last 6 months], how often have you ... [a description of some offence, such as 'used marijuana']?" Survey

Figure 18.1: Juvenile Arrest Rates per 100,000 Population, Ages 10-17

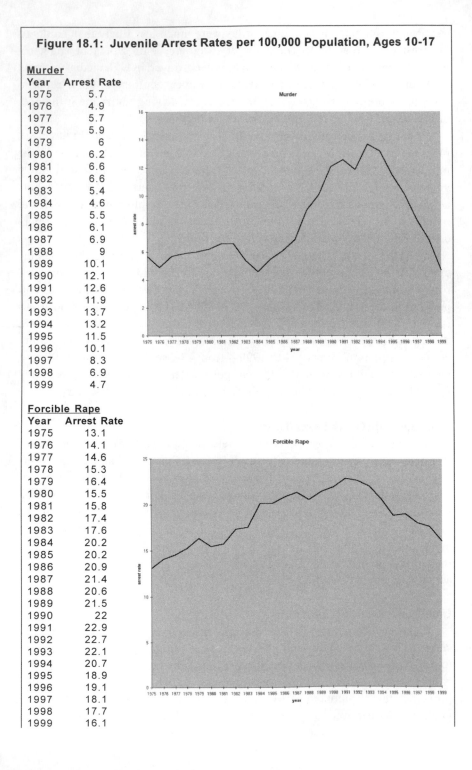

Murder

Year	Arrest Rate
1975	5.7
1976	4.9
1977	5.7
1978	5.9
1979	6
1980	6.2
1981	6.6
1982	6.6
1983	5.4
1984	4.6
1985	5.5
1986	6.1
1987	6.9
1988	9
1989	10.1
1990	12.1
1991	12.6
1992	11.9
1993	13.7
1994	13.2
1995	11.5
1996	10.1
1997	8.3
1998	6.9
1999	4.7

Forcible Rape

Year	Arrest Rate
1975	13.1
1976	14.1
1977	14.6
1978	15.3
1979	16.4
1980	15.5
1981	15.8
1982	17.4
1983	17.6
1984	20.2
1985	20.2
1986	20.9
1987	21.4
1988	20.6
1989	21.5
1990	22
1991	22.9
1992	22.7
1993	22.1
1994	20.7
1995	18.9
1996	19.1
1997	18.1
1998	17.7
1999	16.1

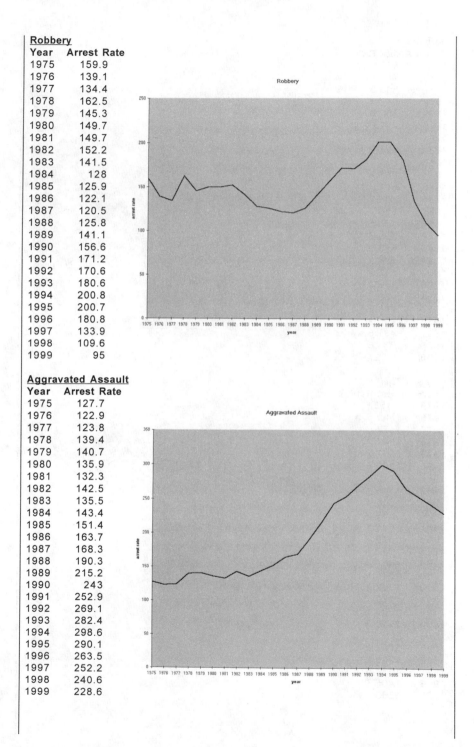

Robbery

Year	Arrest Rate
1975	159.9
1976	139.1
1977	134.4
1978	162.5
1979	145.3
1980	149.7
1981	149.7
1982	152.2
1983	141.5
1984	128
1985	125.9
1986	122.1
1987	120.5
1988	125.8
1989	141.1
1990	156.6
1991	171.2
1992	170.6
1993	180.6
1994	200.8
1995	200.7
1996	180.8
1997	133.9
1998	109.6
1999	95

Aggravated Assault

Year	Arrest Rate
1975	127.7
1976	122.9
1977	123.8
1978	139.4
1979	140.7
1980	135.9
1981	132.3
1982	142.5
1983	135.5
1984	143.4
1985	151.4
1986	163.7
1987	168.3
1988	190.3
1989	215.2
1990	243
1991	252.9
1992	269.1
1993	282.4
1994	298.6
1995	290.1
1996	263.5
1997	252.2
1998	240.6
1999	228.6

Burglary

Year	Arrest Rate
1975	849.1
1976	787.5
1977	800.5
1978	847.1
1979	803.6
1980	767.6
1981	739.7
1982	721.1
1983	639.7
1984	587.9
1985	606.7
1986	588
1987	575.4
1988	535
1989	520.8
1990	533.9
1991	528.3
1992	517.2
1993	483.6
1994	493.2
1995	463.2
1996	452.9
1997	431.5
1998	383.6
1999	327

Larceny-Theft

Year	Arrest Rate
1975	1553
1976	1501.5
1977	1477.5
1978	1537.7
1979	1567.2
1980	1500.6
1981	1479.5
1982	1549.1
1983	1516.7
1984	1559.5
1985	1613.1
1986	1649.8
1987	1692.8
1988	1690.4
1989	1646.9
1990	1767.1
1991	1773.7
1992	1696.5
1993	1633.7
1994	1758
1995	1752.2
1996	1716.2
1997	1654.1
1998	1405.5
1999	1263.3

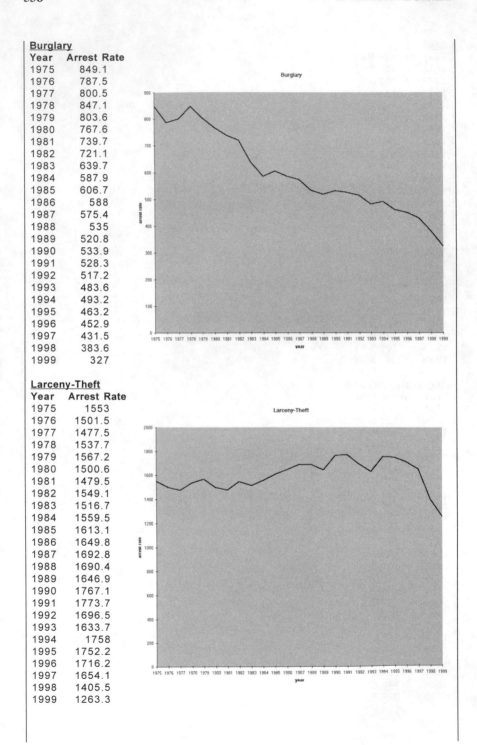

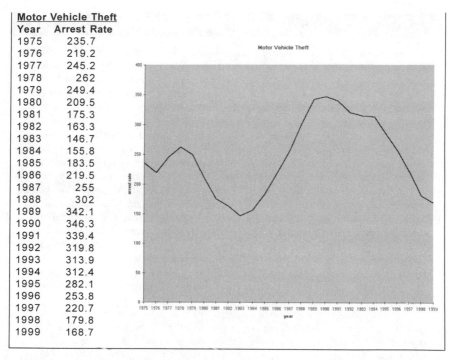

Motor Vehicle Theft	
Year	Arrest Rate
1975	235.7
1976	219.2
1977	245.2
1978	262
1979	249.4
1980	209.5
1981	175.3
1982	163.3
1983	146.7
1984	155.8
1985	183.5
1986	219.5
1987	255
1988	302
1989	342.1
1990	346.3
1991	339.4
1992	319.8
1993	313.9
1994	312.4
1995	282.1
1996	253.8
1997	220.7
1998	179.8
1999	168.7

respondents may be national samples of youths, or they may be more limited samples, such as high school students in a particular city or state. Regardless, the principal advantage of self-report over arrest data is that they are not limited to offenders who have been caught by law enforcement officials (see Box 18.1).

Column 1 of Table 18.1 shows the results of a self-report survey of a sample of U.S. high school seniors conducted by researchers at the University of Michigan. Whereas a low percentage of juveniles are arrested in a particular year, a high percentage report committing delinquent offences. For example, 91% of 1999 high school seniors reported arguing with one or both parents (a status offence) at least once during the last 12 months; 31% reported theft under $50; 28% reported taking something from a store; 24% reported unlawful entry of a house or other building; and 19% reported taking part in a group fight (including, but not limited to, a gang fight).

The University of Michigan survey has been conducted annually since 1975; hence, it is possible to examine changes in self-reported delinquency over time. The last column of Table 18.1 reveals substantial increases from 1975 to 1999 in the percentage of high school seniors who reportedly committed theft over $50 (89% increase), auto theft (77% increase), arson (47% increase), hurt someone badly (41% increase), used a weapon to rob someone (41% increase), and damaged work property on purpose (39% percent increase).

Box 18.1: Accuracy of Self-Report Surveys

Self-report surveys are one of the main tools used by social science researchers to study everything from political beliefs to crime and delinquency. However, questions on such sensitive topics as crime and delinquency can be threatening, so methods have been developed to increase the accuracy of responses to self-report surveys. Researchers have compared the responses from anonymous surveys in which the researcher does not know the names of the respondents with responses from confidential surveys in which the researcher knows the names of the respondents but guarantees that their identities will not be revealed. If one type of survey produces more reports of crime and delinquency, then it is believed that type produces more accurate responses, since few people should admit to something potentially stigmatizing, like crime and delinquency, if they had not done it. Although it might be thought that anonymous surveys would reveal more crime and delinquency (and thus be more accurate than confidential surveys), researchers have not found this to be consistently true. For example, O'Malley *et al.* (2000) analyzed the results from a U.S. survey of eighth and tenth grade students' drug use. Some students took the survey confidentially, while others did so anonymously. O'Malley *et al.* (2000) found no difference in reported drug use between the types of surveys at the tenth grade level. However, eighth grade students who completed anonymous surveys reported slightly more drug use than those who completed confidential surveys.

Social science researchers increasingly have looked to computers to increase the accuracy of responses to self-report surveys. Computer technology is believed to have at least two benefits. Survey questions can be answered in complete privacy, which should reduce the chances that a person would give false responses out of fear of stigmatization. In addition, literacy is not required for survey completion because respondents can be given an audio recording of the questions. Turner *et al.* (1998) examined the benefits of computer technology in the 1995 National Survey of Adolescent Males (NSAM), which asked about HIV-risk behaviors, drug use, and interpersonal violence. Some respondents were given a paper version, and some were given an audio-CASI (computer-assisted self-interviewing) version. Turner *et al.* (1998) found that the audio-CASI greatly increased reporting of some behaviors, especially those thought to be most stigmatizing, such as male-male sexual contact and crack and cocaine use. Use of computer technology might, therefore, increase the accuracy of self-report surveys.

However, the increases pertain to offences with relatively low percentages of students who committed them. For example, only 10.6% of the 1999 high school seniors (column 1) reportedly committed theft over $50 during the 12 months preceding the survey. In 1975 only 5.6% of the high school seniors reportedly committed that offence, so an 89% increase from 1975 to 1999 corresponds to an absolute increase of only 5%. The absolute increase for auto theft was 3%, .8% for arson, 3.9% for hurting someone badly, 1.1% for using a weapon to rob someone, 2% for damaging work property on purpose. The small base rate for these offences (i.e., the small percent that committed the offence at the beginning of the period) means that any increase at all resulted in very large percentage increases.

Table 18.1: Percentage of High School Seniors Reporting Involvement in Delinquent Offenses During the Last 12 Months

Offenses	1999*	% Change 1975-85	% Change 1985-95	1995-99	1975-99
Argue with parents	90.8	1.1	1.5	0.7	3.3
Theft under $50	31.0	-7.1	4.3	-1.3	-4.3
Take something from a store	27.7	-24.5	12.8	-7.4	-21.1
Unlawful entry of a house/building	23.6	-6.8	-10.3	0.4	-16.0
Take part in a group fight	19.2	18.4	-9.7	3.2	10.3
Fight at school/work	14.7	24.7	-18.7	-0.7	0.7
Hurt someone badly	13.4	21.1	7.0	8.9	41.1
Damaged school property on purpose	13.4	7.8	1.4	-4.3	4.7
Theft over $50	10.6	25.0	32.9	14.0	89.3
Damaged work property on purpose	7.1	7.8	12.7	14.5	39.2
Auto theft	6.9	43.6	-14.3	43.8	76.9
Theft of car part	4.8	19.6	-23.9	-5.9	-14.3
Use of weapon to rob someone	3.8	29.6	0	8.6	40.7
Hit teacher	3.1	0	0	0	0
Arson	2.5	11.8	31.6	0	47.1

* Not a percentage change but the actual percentage of 1999 high school seniors reporting involvement in delinquent offenses at least once during the last year.

Except for the offences with small base rates, there were no large increases from 1975 to 1999 in the percentage of high school seniors who committed property offences, and there actually were percentage decreases for some offences (see, for example, figures for taking something from a store and unlawful entry of a house or other building in the last column of Table 18.1). For many violent offences—hitting teachers, fighting at school or work, and group fighting—the percentage changes, if any, were small.

In addition to property and violent offences, the University of Michigan survey also asks questions about drug use (results not shown here). The illegal drugs most widely used by U.S. high school seniors are alcohol and marijuana (reportedly used by 74% and 38% of 1999 high school seniors during the last 12 months) and cigarettes (used by 35% of 1999 high school seniors during the last month) (Pastore and Maguire, 2000:236-237).

There have been decreases in reported drug use for many types of drugs since peaks in the late 1970s (Johnston, O'Malley, and Bachman, 1994:78-79; Pastore and Maguire, 2000:236-37). Between 1975 and 1979, alcohol use during the last 12 months increased, but has decreased since then. Similarly, reported marijuana use during the last 12 months peaked in 1979, but there were decreases from 1980 to 1992. Since then, reported marijuana use generally has increased, but reported use in 1999 was still far below the peak in the late 1970s. Cigarette use during the last month peaked in 1976, decreased until the early 1980s, and then leveled off. In the 1990s, cigarette use increased, but it was still lower in 1999 than in 1976 (Johnston, O'Malley, and Bachman, 2000:32). The peak year for cocaine use during the last 12 months was 1985, but it decreased from then until 1993 when it started to increase. Again, however, the level of reported use in 1999 was still far below the level reported in 1985 (Johnston, O'Malley, and Bachman, 2000:14).

Newer drugs also have been included in the University of Michigan survey. "Ice," a crystal form of methamphetamine, reportedly was used by about 1% of high school seniors from 1989 to 1993. There was a slight increase from 1993 to 1998, but there was a decrease in 1999 (Johnston, O'Malley, and Bachman, 2000:20). Rohypnol, the "date-rape drug," was added to the survey in 1996, and since then it has been used by about 1% of U.S. high school seniors (Johnston, O'Malley, and Bachman, 2000:28). Steroids, usually taken for increasing muscle mass and strength, are used primarily by males and were added to the survey in 1989. Steroid use among U.S. high school seniors decreased from 1989 to 1992, but since then has gradually increased, reportedly used by about 2% of 1999 U.S. high school seniors (Johnston, O'Malley, and Bachman, 2000:34).

Victimization Data

Victimization surveys provide another kind of unofficial data on crime and delinquency. The most comprehensive victimization survey in the U.S. is the **National Crime Victimization Survey**, which has been conducted since the early 1970s. Every person age 12 or over in a selected household (approximately 45,000 households in 1999) is interviewed and reinterviewed at six-month intervals for three years (Pastore and Maguire, 2000; Rennison, 2000). The questions are worded something like this: "During the last six months, has anyone raped you or attempted to rape you?"

Victimization rates for both violent crimes (rape, robbery, and assault) and theft are higher for juveniles (ages 12 to 19) than adults (age 20 and over) (Rennison, 2000). Moreover, the violent victimization rate is higher for older juveniles (ages 16 to 19) than younger juveniles (ages 12 to 15), while the opposite is true for the theft victimization rate (Rennison, 2000). The violent victimization rate for juveniles ages 12 to 17 increased from the mid-1980s to the early 1990s and then decreased substantially (Snyder and Sickmund, 1999).

The National Crime Victimization Survey gathers information on victims' perceptions of the age, sex, and race of the person(s) who victimized them in violent crimes. Offenders are perceived as disproportionately young, black, and male, which is important because those populations have the highest victimization rates (Rennison, 2000). There are two explanations for the similarity between victims of violence and violent offenders. First, people are more likely to be victimized when they associate frequently in groups disproportionately made up of offenders. Hence, "younger persons are more likely to be victims of violent crime than older persons because the former are more likely to associate with other youth who are, themselves, disproportionately involved in violence" (Sampson and Lauritsen, 1990:111). Second, it may be that violence victims and offenders are the same people. In this connection, one of the best predictors of victimization is self-reported offending (Sampson and Lauritsen, 1990).

Homicide Victimization Data

The National Crime Victimization Survey does not include questions about homicide. However, data on homicide victims are compiled each year by the National Center for Health Statistics (NCHS) from records of all deaths occurring in the U.S. Information on cause of death is collected by each state and provided to NCHS or is coded by NCHS from copies of original death statistics.

According to NCHS, in the mid-1990s homicide was one of the leading causes of death for young people below age 25 (Snyder and Sickmund, 1999). Unlike many other offences, homicide victimization rates tend to be higher among young adults than teenagers (Empey, Stafford, and Hay, 1999). In every age group, black males have the highest homicide victimization rate and white females have the lowest (with black females usually ranking second and white males ranking third).

Figure 18.2 shows juvenile homicide victimization rates per 100,000 population ages 10 to 19 for the years 1975 to 1997 (National Center for Health Statistics, annual). The risk of being murdered increased for both juvenile white males and juvenile black males from 1975 to the mid-1990s, but black males experienced the largest increase. The black male homicide victimization rate remained relatively stable (actually decreased slightly) from 1975 to 1984, but it more than tripled from 1984 to 1993, followed by a decrease since then. By contrast, the white female victimization rate remained virtually unchanged

Figure 18.2: Juvenile Homicide Victimization Rates per 100,000 Population
Ages 10-19, U.s., 1975-1990

White Males

Year	Homicide Rate
1975	4.5
1976	4.3
1977	4.7
1978	5.1
1979	6.1
1980	6.3
1981	5.7
1982	5.2
1983	4.4
1984	4.4
1985	4.4
1986	5.1
1987	4.3
1988	4.8
1989	5.5
1990	7.1
1991	8
1992	8.3
1993	8.3
1994	8.4
1995	8.2
1996	6.9
1997	6.2

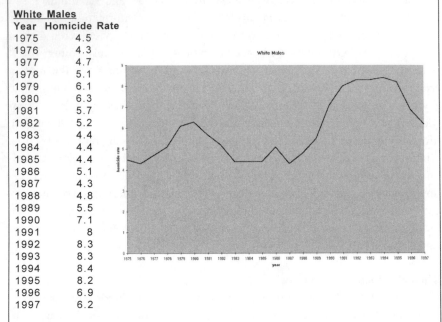

Black Males

Year	Homicide Rate
1975	27.2
1976	24.7
1977	23.4
1978	21.8
1979	26.3
1980	26.9
1981	27.5
1982	25.9
1983	23.5
1984	21.6
1985	25.2
1986	28.4
1987	34.1
1988	42.3
1989	50
1990	63.4
1991	70.5
1992	67
1993	73.5
1994	70.9
1995	58.8
1996	53.5
1997	45.6

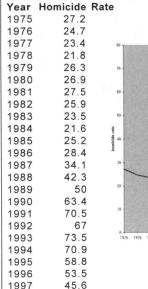
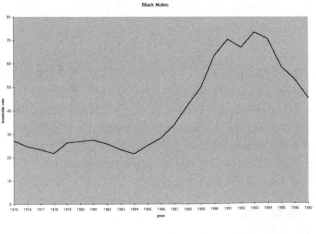

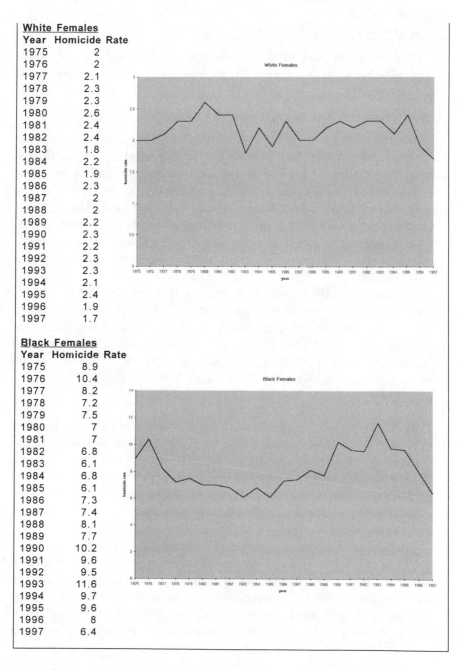

White Females

Year	Homicide Rate
1975	2
1976	2
1977	2.1
1978	2.3
1979	2.3
1980	2.6
1981	2.4
1982	2.4
1983	1.8
1984	2.2
1985	1.9
1986	2.3
1987	2
1988	2
1989	2.2
1990	2.3
1991	2.2
1992	2.3
1993	2.3
1994	2.1
1995	2.4
1996	1.9
1997	1.7

Black Females

Year	Homicide Rate
1975	8.9
1976	10.4
1977	8.2
1978	7.2
1979	7.5
1980	7
1981	7
1982	6.8
1983	6.1
1984	6.8
1985	6.1
1986	7.3
1987	7.4
1988	8.1
1989	7.7
1990	10.2
1991	9.6
1992	9.5
1993	11.6
1994	9.7
1995	9.6
1996	8
1997	6.4

from 1975 to 1997; and while black females experienced an increasing risk of murder from 1985 to 1993, the increase (a 90% increase from 6.1 to 11.6) was much smaller than the increase for black males.

CAUSES OF JUVENILE DELINQUENCY

What causes delinquency? Many theories and studies have addressed that question by emphasizing peers, family, school, and juveniles' demographic characteristics.

Peers

One of the strongest correlates of delinquency is association with delinquent peers. According to Sutherland's (1947) **differential association theory**, delinquent behaviour is learned through intimate social relations, including peer relations. Juveniles who associate with delinquent peers are likely to violate the law because they learn attitudes that condone it. Akers' (1985) **social learning theory** extends differential association theory by claiming that delinquency results not only from learned attitudes but also from reinforcements (rewards and punishments) for delinquency and modeling (or imitation) of others' behavior.

Consistent with the logic of both theories, Warr and Stafford (1991:857) found that "the behavior of friends affects adolescents' [delinquent] behaviour through their attitudes about delinquency." However, more consistent with social learning theory than differential association theory, is the fact that regardless of "their own attitudes toward delinquency ... adolescents are strongly influenced by the behavior of friends."

Family

Weak attachment to parents also is strongly correlated with delinquency (Loeber and Stouthamer-Loeber, 1986). According to Hirschi (1969), **attachment** involves affectional ties between juveniles and parents. If juveniles are strongly attached to parents, they will be less likely to commit delinquency. If attachment to parents is weak, juveniles will not internalize conventional norms, nor develop respect for authority, and, consequently, will be more likely to commit delinquency.

Can parents do anything to reduce the effects of delinquent peer associations? Warr (1993:251) reported that among juveniles who spend "a great deal of time" or "quite a bit of time" with their parents, especially on weekends, there is little or no effect of association with delinquent peers or delinquency. Time spent with parents may restrict juveniles' opportunities to commit delinquency; for example, it may prevent attendance at weekend parties involving alcohol and drug use.

School

Cohen (1955) has argued that lower-class boys are evaluated against a **"middle-class measuring rod"** in schools, but that they are destined to fail because they lack ambition, thrift, and courtesy. School failure is said to lead to a collective frustration among lower-class boys, which leads to delinquency. Many studies have found that students who do the worst in school are the most likely to commit delinquent offences (e.g., Rankin, 1980; Wiatrowski, Griswold, and Roberts, 1981). However, this is not limited to lower-class boys; school failure is related to delinquency among juveniles in all social classes, and among girls as well as boys.

Age, Gender, Social Class, and Race

Many researchers have examined the extent to which delinquency is correlated with demographic variables, such as age, gender, social class, and race. U.S. arrest rates increase rapidly during the teenage years, peak at about age 18, and then decrease (Empey, Stafford, and Hay, 1999), although the peak age is higher for violent offences than property offences (Jensen and Rojek, 1998). The age pattern in self-reported data is similar to that in arrest data, with self-reported delinquency tending to increase through the teenage years and the peak age varying by offence (Elliott et al., 1983).

Males accounted for approximately 78% of all arrests of juveniles in 1999 (F.B.I., 2000); indeed, females accounted for a majority of juvenile arrests only for running away and prostitution. However, the ratio of the male to female arrest rate has been decreasing since 1960 (Jensen and Rojek, 1998). Like arrest data, self-reported delinquency is higher for males than females, and the ratio of male to female self-reported delinquency has been decreasing over time, albeit only for serious offences (Jensen and Rojek, 1998:139-141).

Public conceptions and media accounts in the U.S. often depict delinquency as committed mainly by economically disadvantaged (lower-class) juveniles. The **Uniform Crime Reports** do not include data on the social class of arrested juveniles, but there are many studies that examine the relationship between social class and officially recorded delinquency (Tittle and Meier, 1990). The evidence is mixed, with some studies showing that lower-class juveniles are over-represented in official data and others indicating little or no over-representation. The best conclusion to be drawn from these studies is that there is a slight tendency for lower-class juveniles to be overrepresented in official data, but the differences by social class are not nearly as large as differences by age and gender. The same conclusion can be drawn from studies of the relationship between social class and self-reported delinquency, although there is some evidence of more serious, repetitive delinquency among lower-class juveniles (Tittle and Meier, 1990; Farnworth et al., 1994).

As for race, black juveniles tend to have higher arrest rates than white juveniles, particularly for violent offences (Empey, Stafford, and Hay, 1998:58-61). However, self-reported data paint a different picture; there are much smaller black/white differences in self-reported delinquency than in arrest data (Hindelang, Hirschi, and Weis, 1981:35, 169-170; Elliott, 1994).

U.S. JUVENILE JUSTICE PROCEDURES

As Feld (1993:209) has observed: "Juvenile courts' procedures are structured by an amalgam of United States Supreme Court constitutional decisions such as *Gault*, state statutes, judicial opinions, and court rules of procedure." One consequence is that there is considerable variation in juvenile court procedures from one jurisdiction to the next. Thus, the following description of juvenile court procedures represents only a very broad outline (see Figure 18.3).

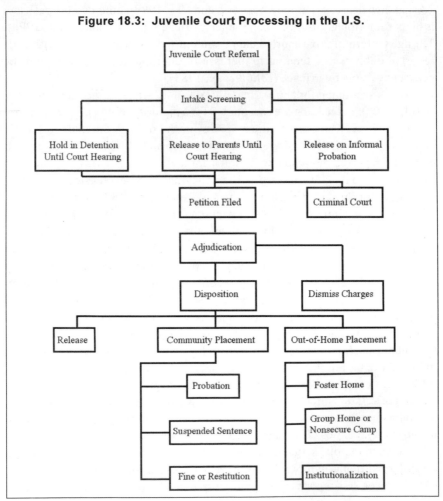

Figure 18.3: Juvenile Court Processing in the U.S.

The typical delinquency or status offence case begins with a referral to juvenile court by police, parents, school officials, probation officers, social service agencies, or victims (Snyder and Sickmund, 1999:97).[3] Although there was variation by type of offence, about 85% of all 1997 delinquency cases were referred to juvenile courts by the police. In contrast, other referral sources accounted for almost half of the formally processed status offence cases in 1997 (Sickmund, 2000).

Soon after a case is referred to juvenile court, a decision is made by an intake officer, judge, or prosecutor to either process the case formally or informally. In 1997, 43% of all delinquency cases were processed informally. Almost half of these were dismissed, with many of the others resulting in voluntary probation, restitution, or community service. Even a higher percentage of status offence cases were processed informally (roughly 80% that came to the attention of juvenile courts or child welfare agencies, according to Sickmund, 2000).

Compared to informally processed cases, formally processed cases tend to involve more serious offences (Puzzanchera et al., 2000). Moreover, both the number of formally processed delinquency cases and the case rate (cases per 1,000 juveniles) increased in the 1990s (Puzzanchera et al., 2000:7).

Juveniles may be held in secure detention while their cases are being processed formally. Detention is used when there is reason to believe that a juvenile is a threat to the community or is at risk of physical harm if returned to the community. Moreover, many of our juveniles are detained to ensure their appearance at formal hearings or to allow for diagnostic evaluations (Puzzanchera et al., 2000).

The decision to hold a juvenile in secure detention typically is made by probation officers or detention workers (Snyder and Sickmund, 1999). In 1997, juveniles were detained in about 25% of all formally processed delinquency cases; this was true of 6% of all formally processed status offence cases, with most involving liquor law violations, running away, and ungovernability (Sickmund, 2000).

One of the first decisions that must be made during intake screening is whether a case will be processed in adult criminal court instead of in juvenile court (Feld, 1993). In some states, a juvenile court judge must authorize all transfers to criminal court by waiving the juvenile court's jurisdiction to the case ("judicial waiver"). In other states, prosecutors have the discretion to file certain types of cases in either juvenile or criminal court ("prosecutorial waiver" involving "concurrent jurisdiction between juvenile and criminal courts over certain offenses"—Feld, 1993:233). In still other states, prosecutors are required to file certain serious cases involving juvenile offenders in criminal court ("legislative offense exclusion"). While judicial waivers focus on the offender and "individualized clinical assessments of the offender's amenability to treatment" (Feld, 1993:234), prosecutorial waivers and legislative exclusions focus on the offence and the appropriate punishment. Increasingly, juvenile cases are being transferred into criminal courts by prosecutorial or legislative actions rather than by judicial waivers (Snyder and Sickmund, 1999), which reflects the general shift away from the rehabilitative ideal in U.S. juvenile justice.

Transfers to criminal court by judicial waiver accounted for about 1% of all formally processed delinquency cases in 1996 (Snyder and Sickmund, 1999). The highest percentage of transfer cases involved offences against persons (43% of all cases transferred by judicial waiver in 1996), followed by property offences (37% of all cases), drug offences (14%), and public order offences (6%) (Snyder and Sickmund, 1999).

If a case is handled in juvenile court, a delinquency petition is filed, which states the charges and requests the court to adjudicate the juvenile as a delinquent. Petitions for adjudicatory hearings almost always are granted. At the adjudicatory hearing (trial), the facts of the case are presented and witnesses are called (Snyder and Sickmund, 1995). "A youth referred to juvenile court for a delinquency offence may be adjudicated ... a delinquent after admitting to the charges in the case, or after the court finds sufficient evidence to prove ... that the youth committed the facts alleged in the petition" (Snyder and Sickmund, 1995:133).

In 1997, about 60% of all petitioned delinquency cases were adjudicated as were about 50% of all petitioned status offence cases (Puzzanchera et al., 2000). After a juvenile is adjudicated as delinquent, a disposition plan is developed by the probation staff, sometimes along with the prosecutor, recommending to the judge what should done to the juvenile. There are many options, including fines, restitution, probation, institutionalization, community service, and referral to a community-based treatment program, such as a drug-counseling program.

More than half (about 60%) of all adjudicated cases (both delinquency and status offence cases) resulted in probation in 1997 (Puzzanchera et al., 2000). Juveniles on probation remain in their communities and continue their normal activities, such as school and work. However, probation usually entails certain conditions, such as meeting regularly with a probation officer, adhering to a curfew, and refraining from further delinquency. There also may be provisions for the revocation of probation if the conditions are violated; when probation is revoked, the court may impose a more severe disposition, including institutionalization (Snyder and Sickmund, 1999).

About 30% of adjudicated delinquency cases and 14% of adjudicated status offence cases resulted in out-of-home placement of juveniles in 1997, including placement in a training school, camp, ranch, privately-operated facility, foster home, and group home (Puzzanchera et al., 2000:15). Delinquency cases involving public-order offences and offences against persons were most likely to result in out-of-home placement in 1997 (Puzzanchera et al., 2000). The relatively high likelihood of out-of-home placement for public-order offences is at least partially because escapes from institutions and probation violations are counted in this offence category. As for adjudicated status offence cases, running away and ungovernability were most likely to result in out-of-home placement (Snyder and Sickmund, 1999).

Many cases that are processed formally do not result in adjudication of a juvenile as a delinquent or status offender (41% of all petitioned delinquency cases and 48% of petitioned status offence cases in 1997—Puzzanchera et al., 2000). However, many such "nonadjudicated" cases still result in juveniles agreeing to voluntary (informal) dispositions, including probation and out-of home placement. About 60% of all nonadjudicated delinquency cases in 1997 were dismissed by the court, and this was true of 67% of nonadjudicated status offence cases (Puzzanchera, 2000). However, in 21% of nonadjudicated delinquency cases, juveniles agreed to informal probation; in 2%, they agreed voluntarily to out-of-home placement. In 10% of nonadjudicated status offence cases, juveniles agreed to informal probation; in 1%, they agreed to out-of-home placement.

DISCUSSION AND CONCLUSIONS

Many recent juvenile justice reforms in the U.S. are linked to a shift in the legal rights of juveniles (Stafford, 1995). The *parens patriae* doctrine, which justified the creation of the juvenile court in the late 1800s and guided U.S. juvenile justice policies through the mid-1960s, gave legal officials the power to protect juveniles. Hence, juveniles were granted **protective rights** out of a belief that they lacked the capacity to care for themselves and make effective choices. "Protection and rehabilitation [were] the keystone [of the juvenile court through mid-1960s], giving judges almost unlimited discretion" (Horowitz, 1984:4). However, during the past several decades, juveniles have been granted fewer protective rights and more **liberating rights**. The shift has stemmed from a growing belief that juveniles can make choices that are just as effective as those made by adults. Increasingly, it has been believed that juveniles need such liberating rights as due process in juvenile court, free expression in school, and abortion choice. However, the extension of liberating rights to juveniles has led to an expectation of greater responsibility among them and a demand that they be held accountable for their actions, hence, a crime control approach.

The shift from protective to liberating rights has not been complete. Some U.S. juvenile justice policies continue to grant protective rights to juveniles. For example, reliance on probation as the most common disposition for adjudicated juvenile court cases continues to reflect a longstanding belief that juveniles deserve a second chance when they violate the law and that they can be rehabilitated or, as reflected in the Gault case, that although juveniles do not need not all the protections accorded to adults in criminal trials, they should at least have "the essentials of due process and fair treatment" (quoting from *Kent*, p. 562).

There is inevitable tension from granting both protective and liberating rights to juveniles, which is illustrated by a problem faced by the American Civil Liberties Union (A.C.L.U.) (Rosenbaum, 1989). In a draft of a brief for the Supreme Court in the late 1980s, A.C.L.U. attorneys argued that teenagers are ineligible for the death penalty because they lack the capacity to make effective choices about committing capital offences. However, at that same time, other A.C.L.U. lawyers were arguing before the Court in abortion cases that teenage girls *do* have the capacity to make effective choices about having abortions. The tension centered on whether to argue for a protective right or a liberating right for juveniles. Recognizing the impossibility of arguing before the same Court that *both* types of rights should be granted to juveniles, the A.C.L.U. resolved the problem by declining to file a brief in the death penalty case.

The shift in U.S. juvenile justice during the past several decades away from the rehabilitative ideal toward a crime control model has created similar tensions. Indeed, the juvenile justice system can be characterized as "schizophrenic" as a consequence of its older (albeit continuing) focus on the need to protect juveniles and its newer focus on the need to hold them accountable for their wrongdoings and punish them. However, an important question has been ignored with the order maintenance shift: has there been improvement in the physical, psychological, and social well-being of juveniles because of the shift from protective rights and the rehabilitative ideal to liberating rights and an emphasis on punishment and accountablity? There is considerable need for more research on the impact of recent juvenile justice reforms in the U.S. For example, there is little systematic evidence on the impact of transferring juvenile offenders to the adult criminal justice system (Snyder, Sikmund, and Poe-Yamagata, 2000:6-7). Until such issues are carefully considered, officials will be operating in the dark about the consequences of many U.S. juvenile justice policies.

Mark Stafford received a B.A. degree in sociology from Southern Methodist University and M.A. and Ph.D. degrees in sociology from the University of Arizona. He is a professor in the department of sociology at the University of Texas at Austin where he has been associate chair and graduate adviser. He is an author of *American Delinquency: Its Meaning and Construction*, and currently he is finishing a co-authored book on the causes of homicide. He is a former fellow at the Center for Advanced Study in the Behavioral Sciences and an associate editor of *Criminology*. His research interests include the deterrent effects of punishment and the relation between family structure and delinquency.

Tracey Kyckelhahn received B.A. and M.A. degrees in sociology from the University of Texas at Austin and is now pursuing a Ph.D. degree there. Her research interests include the relation between family structure and delinquency.

HELPFUL WEBSITES

www.ojjdp.ncjrs.org/facts/facts Office of Juvenile Justice and Delinquency Prevention

www.ncjj.org/ National Center for Juvenile Justice

www.ojp.usdoj.gov/bjs/abstract/scjs99 The Sourcebook of Criminal Justice Statistics, 1999

www.ncjrs.org/ National Criminal Justice Reference Service

www.la.utexas.edu/research/cccjr/index The Center for Criminology and Criminal Justice Research—The University of Texas at Austin

KEY TERMS AND CONCEPTS

Common Law

Parens Patriae

Gault

Dark Figure

Differential Association Theory

Attachment

Uniform Crime Reports

Liberating Rights

Mary Ann Crouse

Kent

Crime Control Model

National Crime Victimization Survey

Social Learning Theory

Middle-class Measuring Rod

Protective Rights

STUDY QUESTIONS

1. What events led to the creation of juvenile courts in the U.S.?
2. How did the U.S. juvenile justice system change during the 1980s and 1990s? How do the changes reflect international standards and guidelines?
3. According to arrest data, has the amount of delinquency in the U.S. been increasing? What is the answer according to self-reported data?
4. What are some of the most important causes of delinquency? How do they compare to other countries covered in this text?
5. What are the major steps in juvenile justice processing in the U.S.?

NOTES

1 With much gratitude to Elena Christopher.
2 The first houses of refuge were built in the 1820s in large cities, such as New York, Boston, and Philadelphia; their goal was to rehabilitate (reform) not just young law-violators but all children with problems (Bremner, *I*, 1970:671).

3   In this section, "delinquency" is distinguished from "status offenses." While status
    offenses typically are considered "delinquency" in the U.S. (in the sense that all
    law-violating behavior by juveniles is "delinquency"), reports of U.S. juvenile
    court data use special terminology; that terminology is adopted here. Whereas
    "delinquency" in this section refers to an act that would be a "crime" if committed
    by an adult, a "status offense" denotes an act that is illegal *only* for juveniles.

REFERENCES

Akers, R.L. (1985). *Deviant Behavior: A Social Learning Approach*, 3rd ed. Belmont,
    CA: Wadsworth.

Bremner, R.H. (Ed). (1970). *Children and Youth in America: A Documentary
    History.* 3 Vols. Cambridge, MA: Harvard University Press.

Caldwell, R.G. (1961). "The Juvenile Court: Its Development and Some Major
    Problems." *Journal of Criminal Law, Criminology and Police Science,* 51:493-511.

Cohen, A.K. (1955). *Delinquent Boys: The Culture of the Gang.* New York: Free Press.

Dawson, R.O. (1990). The Future of Juvenile Justice: Is It Time to Abolish the
    System? *Journal of Criminal Law and Criminology* 81:136-155.

Degler, C.N. (1973). *The Democratic Experience: A Short American History*, 3rd ed.
    Glenview, IL.: Scott, Foresman and Company.

Elliott, D.S. (1994). Serious Violent Offenders: Onset, Developmental Course, and
    Termination. *Criminology* 32:1-21.

Elliott, D.S., Ageton, S.S., Huizinga, D., Knowles, B.A., & Canter, R.J. (1983). *The
    Prevalence and Incidence of Delinquent Behavior: 1976-1980. National Estimates
    of Delinquent Behavior by Sex, Race, Social Class and Other Selected Variables. A
    Report of the National Youth Survey (Project Report No. 26)*. Boulder, CO: C/A
    Publications.

Empey, L.T., Stafford, M.C., & Hay, C.H.. (1999). *American Delinquency: Its Meaning
    and Construction*, 4th ed. Belmont, CA: Wadsworth.

Farnworth, M., Thornberry, T.P., Krohn, M.D., & A.J. Lizotte. (1994). Measurement
    in the Study of Class and Delinquency: Integrating Theory and Research. *Journal
    of Research in Crime and Delinquency* 31:32-61.

Federal Bureau of Investigation. (2000). *Crime in the United States: Uniform Crime
    Reports, 1999.* Washington DC: U.S. Government Printing Office.

Feld, B.C. (1993). Criminalizing the American Juvenile Court. In *Crime and Justice:
    An Annual Review of Research*, Vol. 17. Ed. Michael Tonry. Chicago: University of
    Chicago Press. 197-280.

Griffin, P., Torbet, P., & Szymanski, L. (1998). *Trying Juveniles as Adults in Criminal
    Court: An Analysis of State Transfer Provisions*. Washington, DC: Office of Juvenile
    Justice and Delinquency Prevention.

Hindelang, M.J., Hirschi, T., & Weis, J.G. (1981). *Measuring Delinquency*. Beverly
    Hills, CA: Sage.

Hirschi, T. (1969). *Causes of Delinquency.* Berkeley, CA: University of California
    Press.

Horowitz, R.M. (1984). Children's Rights: A Look Backward and a Glance Ahead. In
    Legal Rights of Children, ed. Robert M. Horowitz & Howard A. Davidson. New
    York: McGraw-Hill. 1-9.

Jensen, G.F., & Rojek, D.G. (1998). *Delinquency and Youth Crime*, 3rd ed. Prospect
    Heights, IL: Waveland Press.

Johnston, L D., O'Malley, P.M., & Bachman, J.G. (1994). *National Survey Results on Drug Use from the Monitoring the Future Study, 1975-1993. Vol. I: Secondary School Students.* Rockville, MD: National Institute on Drug Abuse.

Johnston, L D., O'Malley, P.M., & Bachman, J.G. (2000). *Monitoring the Future: National Results on Adolescent Drug Use, Overview of Key Findings, 1999.* Bethesda, MD: National Institute on Drug Abuse.

Krisberg, B., Schwartz, I.M., Litsky, P., & Austin, J. (1986). The Watershed of Juvenile Justice Reform. *Crime and Delinquency,* 32:5-38.

Lipton, D., Martinson, R., & Wilks, J. (1975). *The Effectiveness of Correctional Treatment: A Survey of Treatment Evaluation Studies.* New York: Praeger Publishers.

Loeber, R., & Stouthamer-Loeber, M. (1986). Family Factors as Correlates and Predictors of Juvenile Conduct Problems and Delinquency. In *Crime and Justice: An Annual Review of Research,* Vol. 7. Ed. Michael Tonry & Norval Morris. Chicago: University of Chicago Press. 29-149.

MacKenzie, L.R. (1999). Residential Placement of Adjudicated Youth, 1987-96. Fact Sheet #117. Washington, DC: Office of Juvenile Justice and Delinquency Prevention.

Maguire, K., & Pastore, A.L. (Eds). (1995). *Sourcebook of Criminal Justice Statistics, 1994.* Washington DC: U.S. Government Printing Office.

Martinson, R. (1974). What Works? Questions and Answers About Prison Reform. *The Public Interest,* 35:22-54.

McGarrell, E.F., & Flanagan, T.J. (Eds.). (1985). *Sourcebook of Criminal Justice Statistics, 1984.* Washington, DC: U.S. Government Printing Office.

National Center for Health Statistics. Annual. *Vital Statistics of the United States.* Vol. II, Part A. Hyattsville, MD: Public Health Service.

O'Malley, P.M., Johnston, L.D., Bachman, J.G., & Schulenberg, J. (2000). A Comparison of Confidential Versus Anonymous Survey Procedures: Effects on Reporting of Drug Use and Related Attitudes and Beliefs in a National Study of Students. *Journal of Drug Issues* 30:35-54.

Pastore, A.L., & Maguire, K. (Eds.). (2000). *Sourcebook of Criminal Justice Statistics, 1999.* Washington, DC: U.S. Government Printing Office.

Platt, A.M. (1969). *The Child Savers: The Invention of Delinquency.* Chicago: University of Chicago Press.

Puzzanchera, C., Stahl, A.L., Finnegan, T.A., Snyder, H.N., Poole, R.S., & Tierney, N. (2000). *Juvenile Court Statistics, 1997.* Washington, DC: Office of Juvenile Justice and Delinquency Prevention.

Rankin, J.H. (1980). School Factors and Delinquency: Interactions by Age and Sex. *Sociology and Social Research* 64:420-434.

Rennison, C. M. (2000). Criminal Victimization 1999: Changes 1998-99 with Trends 1993-99. Washington, DC: Bureau of Justice Statistics.

Rosenbaum, R. (1989). A Tangled Web for the Supreme Court. *The New York Times Magazine,* March 12: 60.

Rothman, D.J. (1971). *The Discovery of the Asylum.* Boston: Little, Brown.

Sampson, R.J., & Lauritsen, J.L. (1990). Deviant Lifestyles, Proximity to Crime, and the Offender-Victim Link in Personal Violence. *Journal of Research in Crime and Delinquency,* 27:110-139.

Sechrest, L., White, S.O., & Brown, E.D. (Eds.). (1979). *The Rehabilitation of Criminal Offenders: Problems and Prospects.* Washington, DC: National Academy of Sciences.

Sickmund, M. (2000). Offenders in Juvenile Court, 1997. Juvenile Justice Bulletin. Washington, DC: Office of Juvenile Justice and Delinquency Prevention.

Snyder, H.N., & Sickmund, M. (1995). *Juvenile Offenders and Victims: A National Report*. Washington, DC: Office of Juvenile Justice and Delinquency Prevention.

Snyder, H.N., & Sickmund, M. (1999). *Juvenile Offenders and Victims: 1999 National Report*. Washington, DC: Office of Juvenile Justice and Delinquency Prevention.

Snyder, H.N., Sickmund, M., & Poe-Yamagata, E. (2000). *Juvenile Transfers to Criminal Court in the 1990s: Lessons Learned from Four States*. Washington, DC: Office of Juvenile Justice and Delinquency Prevention.

Stafford, M.C. (1995). Children's Legal Rights in the U.S. *Marriage and Family Review* 21:121-139.

Streib, V.L. (1987). *Death Penalty for Juveniles*. Bloomington, IN: Indiana University Press.

Sutherland, E.H. (1947). *Principles of Criminology*, 4th ed. Philadelphia: J.B. Lippincott Co.

Tittle, C.R., & Meier, R.F. (1990). Specifying the SES/Delinquency Relationship. *Criminology*, 28:271-299.

Tittle, C.R., Villemez, W.J., & Smith, D.A. (1978). The Myth of Social Class and Criminality: An Empirical Assessment of the Empirical Evidence. *American Sociological Review* 43:643-656.

Torbet, P., Griffin, P., Hurst, Jr., H., & MacKenzie, L.R. (2000). *Juveniles Facing Criminal Sanctions: Three States That Changed the Rules*. Washington, DC: Office of Juvenile Justice and Delinquency Prevention.

Turner, C.F., Ku, L., Rogers, S.M., Lindberg, L.D., Pleck, J.H., & Sonenstein, F.L. (2000).Adolescent Sexual Behavior, Drug Use and Violence: Increased Reporting with Computer Survey Technology. *Science,* 28:867-873.

Warr, M. (1993). Parents, Peers, and Delinquency. *Social Forces,* 72:247-264.

Warr, M., & Stafford, M. (1991). The Influence of Delinquent Peers: What They Think or What They Do? *Criminology,* 29:851-866.

Wiatrowski, M.D., Griswold, D.B., & Roberts, M.K. (1981). Social Control Theory and Delinquency. *American Sociological Review* 46:525-541.

CASES

In re Gault, 387 U.S. 1 (1967)
Kent v. United States, 383 U.S. 541 (1966)
Stanford v. Kentucky, 109 S. Ct. 2969 (1989)
Thompson v. Oklahoma, 487 U.S. 815 (1988)

MEMBER OF SCABRINI MEDIA

Quebec, Canada
2002